EMERGING ISSUES IN FOREST POLICY

Throughout history, forests have played a central role in the development of human civilization – providing fuel that heats our homes and fires our industries, structural materials that transport and shelter us, and paper that lends permanence to our transitory thoughts and endeavours.

Within the last few decades, it has become increasingly apparent that forests and their wealth of resources bear directly upon many of the most pressing social, economic, and environmental concerns of our time.

This volume draws together forty of the foremost experts in forest policy to address the diverse range of issues which characterize the intimate interrelationship between forests and humankind. These issues include the regional and global environment, timber supply, competitiveness and international trade, social impacts, multiple and competing resource use, and the Third World.

This is a comprehensive and timely book that sheds light on some of the fundamental issues concerning forestry and forestry policy.

PETER N. NEMETZ is an associate professor in the Faculty of Commerce and Business Administration at the University of British Columbia.

EDITED BY
PETER N. NEMETZ

HONORARY ASSOCIATE EDITORS:
WILLIAM F. HYDE
ROGER A. SEDJO

Emerging Issues
in Forest Policy

UBCPress

Vancouver

ISBN 0-7748-0401-7 (hardcover) ✓
ISBN 0-7748-0419-X (paperback)

Canadian Cataloguing in Publication Data

Main entry under title:
Emerging issues in forest policy

Includes bibliographical references and index.
ISBN 0-7748-0401-7 (bound). — ISBN 0-7748-0419-X (pbk.)

1. Forest policy. I. Nemetz, Peter N., 1944–

SD561.E44 1992   333.75'15   C92-091100-5

UBC Press
University of British Columbia
6344 Memorial Rd
Vancouver, BC V6T 1Z2
(604) 822-3259
Fax: (604) 822-6083

What a magnificent passage, BN;
with the rising sun,
a river of gold
floated on cloudtops
from the horizon to our feet —
you will inspire us
for as long as we live.

Contents

FORESTRY AND THE THIRD WORLD

Tables and Figures

Chapter 1

Chapter 4

Chapter 5

Chapter 16

Foreword

Those who make policy for forest products companies, timber investment organizations, environmental nongovernmental organizations or governments face a daunting array of uncertainties. The interactions between ecologic and economic systems, each of which by itself merits careful attention, define this complex policy setting. The biophysical facts matter, but so too do human values.

Rapid changes in the environment external to the forest sector accompany the already complex endogenous dynamics of this coupled system. Changes in atmospheric concentrations of carbon dioxide directly and indirectly affect the development of forest ecosystems. Increased incomes, derived in part from the exploitation of natural systems, drive greater concern for nonexploitative relationships with these same natural systems. Emerging political structures denigrate the desirability of collective action while celebrating the potency of the individual.

The world is in the final stages of the transition between old growth forests and those created by human stewardship. The transition began perhaps three millennia ago in the Mediterranean cradle of human civilization and has been completed in many regions such as the U.S. South. The transition is at a sharp point of inflection in others such as the U.S. Pacific Northwest, and the end is in sight, although only still distant in others, such as British Columbia. Massive forest areas remain unlogged – in Canada, in the Soviet Union, and in tropical regions of the world – but the ultimate disposition of these lands is perhaps less certain now than ever before.

Impacts of policy decisions taken in one locality are increasingly global and are increasingly understood to be so. International trade links economies of disparate parts of the globe. Actions taken to develop communities in one region may destabilize those in another. Actions taken to protect the nonpecuniary values of forest in one region may inadvertently destroy those of another. Barry Commoner's 'First Law of Ecology' – that everything is connected to everything else – not surprisingly turns out to hold true for human societies.

This collection of readings spans the core elements of these policy dilemmas. Pick and choose from the topics or read the entire volume with care. Policymaker, policy scientist, or scientist interested in policy will find much of value here.

DEAN CLARK S. BINKLEY
FACULTY OF FORESTRY, UBC

EMERGING ISSUES IN FOREST POLICY

Introduction

Peter N. Nemetz

Throughout history, forests have played a central role in the development and, indeed, survival of humankind. Despite the profound differences between the world of the twentieth century and early history, forests continue to nurture human beings – with fuels that heat our homes and fire our industry, with structural materials that transport and shelter us, and with paper that lends permanence to our transitory thoughts and endeavours. While it is difficult, if not impossible, to imagine the evolution of our modern world without the tree and its prodigious harvest, it has become increasingly apparent in the last few decades that forests serve an indispensable function in a complex ecological system which sustains not only the human species but all life on our fragile planet.

The principal goal of this volume is to address the diverse range of policy issues which characterize the intimate inter-relationship of forests and humankind. The focus of this work can be summarized by five critical questions.

First, to what extent are the detrimental byproducts of human activity, in addition to our direct utilization of forests, contributing to the decline of this vital resource; and how does the loss of global forests impact on other essential components of our ecosystem? Second, how can we formulate and implement policies which will guarantee the continued supply of adequate forest resources for this and future generations; and, in particular, how critical are societal concepts of ownership and tenure to the achievement of this goal? Third, how crucial are technological change and international trade in sustaining a healthy forest sector and dependent economy? Fourth, how can we remedy or ameliorate the negative social impacts of our industrial forest development; and how can we integrate intelligently the management of our forests with other resources

TABLE 1
World production of forest products by major commodity group, 1961-88

Year	Roundwood (1,000 cu m)	Lumber and railway ties		Panel products (1,000 cu m)	Wood pulp (1,000 t)	Paper and paperboard	
		Softwood lumber (1,000 cu m)	Total (1,000 cu m)			Newsprint (1,000 t)	Total (1,000 t)
1961	2,050,551	263,251	344,219	26,281	61,531	14,362	77,493
1965	2,223,128	293,171	382,476	41,893	77,806	17,017	97,615
1970	2,463,422	312,099	414,553	69,560	101,936	21,492	126,481
1975	2,582,994	304,740	405,096	84,437	102,103	20,442	130,472
1980	2,933,730	333,738	450,031	101,115	125,820	25,415	170,220
1981	2,939,363	315,592	430,039	100,376	125,180	26,513	170,954
1982	2,935,395	311,509	422,852	96,255	119,576	24,961	167,267
1983	3,049,196	327,308	441,463	105,530	128,216	25,999	177,224
1984	3,163,214	343,226	460,831	108,571	135,618	27,777	189,948
1985	3,195,050	348,836	467,465	111,847	135,488	28,246	192,678
1986	3,298,860	361,388	483,029	117,494	140,802	29,347	201,994
1987	3,384,208	377,364	504,678	123,662	146,258	30,593	212,509
1988	3,431,072	378,582	506,431	125,877	151,183	32,108	224,329

SOURCE: Forestry Canada (1990), 195-203, 211
General categories:
Roundwood = logs and bolts, pulpwood, other industrial roundwood, fuelwood, and charcoal
Lumber = softwoods and hardwoods
Panel products = plywood, particle board, veneer sheets, hardboard and building board, and rigid insulating board
Wood pulp = chemical, semi-chemical, mechanical, and dissolving
Paper and paperboard = newsprint, printing and writing paper, wrapping and packaging paper and board, tissue and sanitary paper, and other

TABLE 2
World exports of forest products by major commodity group, 1961-88

Year	Roundwood (1,000 cu m)	Lumber and railway ties		Panel products (1,000 cu m)	Wood pulp (1,000 t)	Paper and paperboard	
		Softwood lumber (1,000 cu m)	Total (1,000 cu m)			Newsprint (1,000 t)	Total (1,000 t)
1961	38,351	36,352	40,981	3,084	9,773	7,732	12,772
1965	49,768	43,950	49,434	5,292	12,480	8,985	16,489
1970	96,382	49,348	57,424	9,728	16,921	10,641	23,387
1975	100,942	43,250	52,410	12,436	15,078	9,369	23,074
1980	116,957	65,938	79,625	16,323	21,188	12,321	35,041
1981	100,190	60,646	72,534	16,758	20,197	12,922	35,364
1982	99,035	61,439	73,094	15,442	18,533	11,508	33,667
1983	101,076	79,576	83,780	17,387	21,080	12,143	36,812
1984	103,400	72,755	86,112	18,232	21,529	13,127	39,902
1985	106,499	73,473	85,981	19,284	21,777	13,807	40,907
1986	107,004	73,656	87,041	20,605	23,291	14,170	43,500
1987	118,456	78,825	94,320	23,450	24,628	14,565	47,207
1988	125,583	81,355	99,558	25,471	25,510	14,469	51,119

SOURCE: Forestry Canada (1990), 195-203, 212

General categories:

Roundwood = logs and bolts, pulpwood, other industrial roundwood, fuelwood, and charcoal

Lumber = softwoods and hardwoods

Panel products = plywood, particle board, veneer sheets, hardboard and building board, and rigid insulating board

Wood pulp = chemical, semi-chemical, mechanical, and dissolving

Paper and paperboard = newsprint, printing and writing paper, wrapping and packaging paper and board, tissue and sanitary paper, and other deemed essential to human welfare? And, finally, what are the central issues which bear upon forest practice and utilization in the Third World – where most of the human population resides, where many forest-related problems appear most critical, and where the paucity of robust economic, political, and ecological systems threatens the process of human development and survival?

FORESTRY AND THE ENVIRONMENT

As human population has increased and the pace of industrialization has accelerated, our traditional demand for global forest resources has not only grown but has also been supplemented by new direct and indirect uses of trees and their products. Tables 1 and 2 summarize world production and trade of major forest products over the period 1961-88. The combination of domestic and international demand for timber, fuel, and agricultural and ranch land has led in many parts of the globe to non-sustainable levels of forest removal and associated deforestation. As outlined in Table 3, these rates are particularly high in many developing countries of Africa, Latin America, and Asia.

Pressure on global forest stocks and their land base from felling and burning is increased by the externalities of human activity. As *Judith Clarkson and Jurgen Schmandt* note in their chapter on the role of air pollution in forest decline, 'three forms of pollution that were hardly recognized or, at least, did not create large scale problems only a few decades ago, now cause harm to forests – acid rain, ozone, and global warming.'

Through the process of industrialization, the role of humankind has been transformed from that of a minor player in the ecological drama to one that can profoundly change but, ironically, cannot control, the course of our global environmental future. Anthropogenic emissions of many industrial byproducts have reached enormous proportions and, in many cases, dwarf their natural counterparts. For example, an American study states that 'on an annual basis, natural sources of NOx are estimated to contribute about 11 per cent (within a range of 4-28 per cent) of total NOx emissions. Natural biogenic sources (marine and terrestrial) are estimated to contribute 1-5 per cent of total sulphur compound emissions' (National Acid Precipitation Asssessment Program (NAPAP) 1990: F-41; see also Table 4). While Clarkson and Schmandt observe that forest damage from anthropogenic pollution has 'not yet had a measurable impact on the world production and consumption of forest products,' the longer-

TABLE 3
Selected national rates of deforestation in the 1980s

Country	Deforestation (1,000 ha/yr)	Country	Deforestation (%/yr)
Brazil	3,650	Côte d'Ivoire	5.2
India	1,500	Nepal	4.0
Indonesia	920	Haiti	3.8
Colombia	890	Madagascar	3.5
Myanmar	677	Sri Lanka	3.5
Mexico	615	Mauritius	3.3
Zaire	588	El Salvador	3.2
Cote d'Ivoire	510	Comoros	3.1
Sudan	504	Canada	3.1
Nigeria	400	Jamaica	3.0
Thailand	397	Burundi	2.7
Ecuador	340	Guinea-Bissau	2.7
Malaysia	310	Nigeria	2.7
Peru	300	Nicaragua	2.7
Venezuela	245	Niger	2.6
Paraguay	212	Thailand	2.5
Cameroon	190	Gambia	2.4
Viet Nam	173	Mali	2.4
USA	159	Algeria	2.3
Libya	156	Liberia	2.3
Madagascar	150	Rwanda	2.3
Philippines	143	Honduras	2.3
Tanzania	130	Ecuador	2.3
Laos	130	India	2.3
Nicaragua	121	Myanmar	2.1
Mozambique	120	Guatemala	2.0
Bolivia	117	Benin	1.7
Canada	55	USA	0.1
World total	15,517	World total	0.4

SOURCE: UNEP (1991), 180-4

TABLE 4

Anthropogenic versus natural sources of sulphur and nitrogen compounds in Canada and the u.s.

	Units	Area	Canada	u.s.	Data year
Total sulphur compound emissions (as S) per year					
Anthropogenic	million metric tonnes	east	1.2	8.4	1985-7
Natural [a]	million metric tonnes	east	<0.1	0.1-0.4	1985-7
Total anthropogenic emissions of SO_2 per year	million metric tonnes	national	3.7	21.0	1985
Total emissions of NO_x per year					
Anthropogenic	million metric tonnes	national	1.9	18.6	1985
Natural [b]	million metric tonnes	national	2.0-3.0	0.7-5.2	1985

SOURCES: Federal/provincial RMCC (1990), 3-102; NAPAP (1990), F-41-F-43; Environment Canada (1980, 1981a)

[a] Principal sources are: soil biogenic 48.4%, marine biogenic 10.1%, lakes biogenic 2.3%, vegetation 1.7%, sea salt 37.1%, soil dust 0.1%, forest fires 0.2%

[b] Principal sources are: microbes, vegetation, oceans, volcanoes, geothermal steam, lightning

term consequences of this process can have profound economic and ecological effects.

The inextricable linkage of forests and climate is the subject of the chapter by *Barbara Kronberg and William Fyfe*. The authors focus their study on the key role of forests in global water, energy, and carbon cycles. Reproduced here is the now famous graph of sinusoidal changes in atmospheric carbon dioxide as measured at Moana Loa in the Hawaiian Islands. A detailed description is provided of the complex chain of ecological events set in motion by deforestation, including impacts on solar radiation, precipitation, evapotranspiration, surface runoff and erosion, and carbon balances. The authors compare the effects of deforestation in both Canada and Brazil and arrive at the remarkable conclusion that

> international attention that has been given to the condition of Amazonian forests may be a factor in the present slowing of the exponential rate of deforestation (Climate Alert 1990). Thus, the future of Amazonian forests may not be as bleak as that of the Canadian forests, which the international community, in general, believes to be unendangered. Furthermore, the Amazonian forest does not directly underpin the Brazilian economy.

While this conclusion may seem overly pessimistic, it does underscore the necessity for extraordinary attention to matters of forest policy in a country such as Canada, where the forest industry's direct contribution to Gross Provincial Product ranges as high as 9.3 per cent (Table 5), and exports of forest products at $22.779 billion represent 16.9 per cent of total Canadian exports (Forestry Canada 1990:66).

In this volume's third chapter, which is devoted to forestry and the environment, *Frederick Cubbage, James Regens, and Donald Hodges* also focus on the nexus between forestry and climate change. They summarize the potential impact of deforestation on the process of global warming, the effects of such massive climatological change, and the singular difficulties which face the formation and implementation of public policy in this meta-policy domain.

Statistics compiled by the United National Environment Programme (UNEP 1991:16) and the World Resources Institute (WRI 1990:346) suggest that global land-use change (principally from deforestation) accounts for approximately one-quarter to one-third of anthropogenic emissions of carbon dioxide. And, as Table 6 illustrates, in many Third World countries, deforestation is the leading cause of such emissions.

TABLE 5

Forest industry direct contribution to Canadian GDP by province, 1986

Province	GDP at factor cost	Logging industry	Wood industries	Paper & allied industries	Forestry services	Total forest industries	
	(million $)	(million $)	(million $)	(million $)	(million $)	(million $)	%
Newfoundland	6,076	46	6.0	[a]	13.0	[a]	[a]
Prince Edward Island	1,404	2	6.4	0.0	1.3	10.0	0.7
Nova Scotia	11,573	79	56.9	213.2	13.9	363.0	3.1
New Brunswick	8,863	190	131.6	383.2	27.0	731.4	8.3
Quebec	103,118	584	1,073.8	2,675.0	66.6	4,399.7	4.3
Ontario	175,057	509	928.1	2,349.3	84.3	3,870.9	2.2
Manitoba	16,773	27	72.6	100.2	5.4	204.8	1.2
Saskatchewan	16,928	33	49.9	[a]	6.7	[a]	[a]
Alberta	56,083	83	262.8	159.4	56.3	561.2	1.0
British Columbia	51,041	1,132	2,040.7	1,494.7	75.5	4,742.4	9.3
Total	449,224	2,686	4,629.3	7,558.4	350.1	15,223.8	3.4

SOURCE: Forestry Canada (1990), 166
[a] Withheld for reasons of confidentiality

TABLE 6
Selected data on carbon dioxide production by country and source, 1980

(1,000 t of carbon/year)	Fossil fuel combustion and cement	Land use changes
USA	1,259,281	
USSR	895,504	35,000
China	406,440	69,000
Brazil	48,178	336,100
Japan	254,881	
Indonesia	25,825	191,900
Germany, FR	208,021	
United Kingdom	160,551	
Colombia	10,724	123,300
France	132,129	
India	95,547	33,000
Poland	125,436	
Canada	115,820	
Thailand	10,922	94,500
Mexico	71,001	33,400
Côte d'Ivoire	1,403	100,500
Italy	101,564	
Laos	50	84,700
German Democratic Republic	83,678	
Nigeria	18,588	59,500
Philippines	9,970	56,700
Czechoslovakia	66,094	
South Africa	58,230	
Malaysia	7,636	49,900
Australia	55,348	
Spain	54,546	
Romania	54,489	
Myanmar	1,308	51,200
Peru	6,423	45,000
Ecuador	3,666	39,900
Venezuela	24,456	17,900
Netherlands	41,364	
Viet Nam	4,593	36,100
Zaire	941	35,000
World totals	5,037,102	1,782,600

SOURCE: UNEP (1991), 16-20

Studies on the potential effects of global warming have predicted a broad range of consequences, including marked shifts in temperature and rainfall patterns, with potentially detrimental impacts on food-producing regions; sea-level changes which could threaten large, densely populated coastal areas; and the increased intensity and prevalence of 'super' storms.

It is one of history's unfortunate ironies that many of the countries of the Third World, least endowed with resources to prevent continued deforestation, may be the most vulnerable to its local and global effects. Cubbage et al. note that

> successful retention of tropical forests and afforestation of plantations will require substantial cultural change and economic progress in developing countries. The industrialized countries also went through a period of forest exploitation and destruction for centuries, so we should not be overly ethnocentric in condemning such actions by developing countries.

The cogency of this observation is illustrated by J.V. Thirgood's remarkable study (1981:2-3) on the history of forest depletion in the southern and eastern parts of the Mediterranean basin. As Thirgood states:

> No other part of the world so strikingly drives home the story of man's failure to maintain his environment ... Once the focal point of western civilization, the region is now economically depressed ... Southern Italy, where the Hellenes settled Graecia Magna nearly three thousand years ago and developed a centre of Grecian culture – where Herodotus, the historian, lived, where Pythagoras advanced the science of Geometry, and where Aecshylus wrote his plays – was a land of forests ... It was ... in the scorched heart of Sicily at Piazza Armerina, that a mosaic extending over a quarter of an acre was discovered – the floor of a fourth century Roman villa, depicting woodland hunting and wildlife scenes – at a site now surrounded by a landscape of barren grey hills ... Even the most cursory reading of the history of the nations of the region shows the part played by forests and forest products in the lives of nations, of kings and nobles, and of the common man; how the political, social and military history of these countries, their rise and fall, their geographical and social nature has been inextricably bound up with the deforestation of the land.

Thirgood's observations are striking and lend powerful support to the necessity of weighing historical precedent, even when formulating policies to address problems quantitatively and qualitatively different from the past.

The complex interaction of forests and our environment as depicted in the first three chapters in this volume provides an archetypal example of the extraordinary challenges which can characterize the confluence of science and economics in public policy. In the scientific realm, the study of human-forest-environment interactions has been characterized by limited information, scientific uncertainty, an inadequate theoretical approach to the systemic effects of policy intervention, and a sparsely articulated description of the nature and magnitude of global ecological risks. Several illustrations of these deficiencies are provided in the first three chapters, including the belated recognition of the existence and impact of the long-distance transport of pollutants – a problem created in part by a narrowly focused effort to control local pollution exposure; the lack of information on the recovery of deforested ecosystems; a research focus on single rather than multiple forest and environmental stress factors; and the lack of rigorous scientific proof of causal relationships between pollutants and forest damage, and forest loss and climate change.

Yet, given the potential magnitude of the risks in the involuntary global experiment induced by humankind's industrial activity, one can legitimately ask whether the elusive goal of scientific certainty can, or should, be a precursor to policy response. The conventional calculus of risk analysis is inappropriate in the presence of 'zero-infinity' outcomes; that is, those with low probability but potentially enormous consequences. A risk-averse strategy may be most appropriate despite the extra costs of that subset of preventative strategies which may ultimately prove to be non-productive.

The process of formulating effective policy is constrained not only by the limits of scientific knowledge but also by several critical economic factors which characterize the interaction of forestry and the environment. As with many other environmental issues, the identification and measurement of benefits associated with specific courses of environmental control present unusual difficulties. A not insignificant part of the problem in the policymaking process stems from what is characterized in the discipline of economics as 'market failure.' Included under this rubric are: imperfect information; environmental externalities (i.e., those negative effects which lie outside the market system); issues of intergenerational equity stemming from the long-term effects of our current action or inaction; and public or collective goods, such as protection from global climate change, preservation of species diversity, and maintenance of soil productivity. In each of these cases, market responses lead to an under-provision of the optimal level of socially desirable commodities or actions.

From the perspective of social decisionmaking, two additional impediments hamper the achievement of effective policies: first, is the imbalance between financially tangible benefits from forest exploitation that can accrue to a relatively small sector of society and the potentially larger but less tangible ecological and attendant economic and social benefits from optimal forest use which will accrue to all global citizens both present and future. The specific result of this imbalance in the distribution of costs and benefits is a distortion away from optimality in the decisionmaking process. Second, is the fact that the global nature of some of the forest/environment issues requires international co-operative action. Here the economic problem of free-riding as well as the uneven distribution of costs and benefits can hamper effective action. The completion of three major international environmental conventions within the last few decades provides some hope that effective progress can be made on the control of CO_2 emissions.[1] Nevertheless, the absolutely central role of fossil fuel combustion and forestry products to both the process of industrialization and basic human survival within many parts of the Third World casts serious doubts on the ability to reach an easy solution to this problem. Any salutary response to this issue in the Third World would be a necessary but not sufficient condition for problem resolution because of the existence of other greenhouse gases[2] and the as yet unproven ability of the industrialized nations to significantly alter their production of CO_2.

In sum, the complex linkages between forestry and the environment pose one of the greatest challenges to humankind: failure to overcome the scientific and economic impediments to the resolution of this problem will imperil the continued amelioration of the human condition on this planet. One vital component of this endeavour is the maintenance of our current forest inventory and the formation of viable and inter-related strategies for forest removal and regeneration.

TIMBER SUPPLY

The resolution and, indeed, definition of a major policy problem linked to the supply of a natural resource such as forests requires an adequate assessment of the resource base itself. This poses an important challenge within both the Third World and developed countries. In Thailand and the Philippines, for example, it was not until the advent of satellite-based remote sensing that the magnitude of deforestation was appreciated (Thailand Development Research Institute 1987; Bee 1987). In the face of economic pressure, the forest cover in Thailand shrank by 18.9 per cent from 1961 to 1973 and a further 26.5 per cent by 1985.

Within North America, there have been periodic critiques of the inadequate information and/or deficient assessment of accessible timber stocks (U.S. GAO 1991; House of Commons Canada 1990; BC Forest Resources Commission 1991). In a manner analogous to mineral resource assessment, it is essential to differentiate between the total physical stock and economically recoverable stock of timber. The economic value of any given forested area is dictated by a broad range of factors, including accessibility as determined by terrain and distance to mills and markets; stand age and associated tree size; wood quality; the volume of merchantable timber per hectare; and species mix.

A report of the BC Ministry of Forests (1984:4) provides a particularly cogent example (Table 7) of the multitude of factors that bear upon the measurement of 'net presently productive available and suitable' forest land – a value equal to only 24 per cent of total provincial forested areas.

A major focus of recent forest policy debate in Canada has been what is called 'not satisfactorily restocked' (NSR) or 'nonstocked' land. Table 8 summarizes estimates by Forestry Canada (1990:2) of these areas by province. Values range from a low of 0.3 per cent of total productive land in New Brunswick to a high of 16.5 per cent in the Yukon. Caution must be exercised in the interpretation of these data, however, as both numerator and denominator require qualification. The denominator of 'productive' land does not, in and of itself, imply availability for harvest, as land within this category may be removed because it is in parkland, is too steep to harvest, or is in an environmentally sensitive zone or deferral area. In addition, for accuracy, the numerator must be limited to the subcomponent 'backlog NSR,' which excludes deforested land where an acceptable three- to seven-year regeneration period has not yet elapsed. For example, the BC Ministry of Forests' (1988:25) estimates of total backlog NSR on good, medium, poor, and low sites in BC totalled 845,582 hectares in 1988. This represents 3.2 per cent of the total productive and available forest land of 26,148,257 hectares in the same year.

The creation of an adequate resource inventory, which considers both quantity and quality, is only the first step in the policy process centred on the forest resource base. As *William Thompson et al.* demonstrate in their contribution on rehabilitating backlog NSR land in

TABLE 7
Calculation of net presently productive available and suitable forest land in BC

Summary of forest land area: TSA's and TFL's		Area in hectares
Total area - excluding major parks		88,907,918
Alienations		
Crown grants		
Parks		
Total alienations	6,938,022	
Unalienated area		81,969,896
Non-forest		
Alpine forest		
Water		
Open range		
Total not productive	38,705,293	
Forest land		43,264,603
Land losses accounted for in TSA reports		
ESA's and land withdrawals		
Total not available	2,383,746	
Available forest land		40,880,857
Not suitable		
Inoperable		
Problem forest types		
Total not suitable	14,713,917	
Potentially productive available and suitable		26,166,940
Not stocked		
NSR/DSD		
NC		
Total not stocked	3,560,368	
Presently productive available and suitable		22,606,572
Land losses not accounted for in TSA reports		
Total additional not available	1,316,226	
Net presently productive available and suitable		21,290,346

SOURCE: BC Ministry of Forests (1984), 4
DSD = Disturbed Stocking Doubtful
ESA = Environmentally Sensitive Area
NC = Non-commercial
NSR = Not Satisfactorily Restocked
TFL = Tree Farm Licence
TSA = Timber Supply Area

TABLE 8
Non-stocked forest land by province, 1986
(million hectares)

Province	Productive forest land	Non-stocked land	Non-stocked as % of total
Newfoundland	11.18	0.71	6.4
Prince Edward Island	0.28	0.01	3.6
Nova Scotia	3.85	0.16	4.2
New Brunswick	6.09	0.02	0.3
Quebec	54.79	2.54	4.6
Ontario	38.29	4.08	10.7
Manitoba	14.92	1.57	10.5
Saskatchewan	15.89	1.50	9.4
Alberta	25.44	0.82	3.2
British Columbia	51.10	4.04	7.9
Yukon	7.56	1.25	16.5
Northwest Territories	14.32	0.01	0.1
Canada	243.71	16.71	6.9

SOURCE: Forestry Canada (1990), 2

BC, computer-assisted economic analysis can provide an exceedingly useful methodology to assist the formation of public policy. The complexity of the analysis required to fully inform the decisionmaking process is acknowledged by the authors, who state that the 'expectation of future price increases and choice of discount rate can profoundly affect the expected returns from silvicultural investments. For many natural resources, real prices have declined over the past century or more (Barnett and Morse 1963). Such has not, however, been the case for timber.' While the authors find 'rather modest financial returns to investments in the rehabilitation of backlog NSR lands,' they acknowledge the necessity for a more comprehensive study, which includes considerations of other forest 'outputs,' such as wildlife, recreation and aesthetic values, land and water conservation, employment, community stability, regional development, and general option values. Some of these broader issues are addressed in later chapters in this volume.

Uncertainty in the long-term supply of timber in the United States is the subject of the chapter by *Darius Adams*, who focuses on two central characteristics of North American, and especially United

States, forestry: first, the declining supply of natural old-growth stands and the transition to more managed forestry practices; and, second, the growing importance of non-timber values. While some of the recent popular debate over multiple demands on the forest resource base has focused on the northern spotted owl, the issues are in fact much broader and encompass not only environmental and non-commodity issues but also competing sectors such as agriculture, energy, mining, and urban development. Adams concludes that:

> Private inventories will not be able to sustain past harvest trends, necessitating some absolute decline in industrial harvest in the West and in non-industrial cut in the South. After 2010, the maturation of large areas of young-growth in both the West and South will bring the prospect of rising harvests and stability to declining prices ... Adjustments to a permanently reduced timber supply in the u.s. would be complete by about 2010.

Adams documents the pressure on the u.s. Forest Service, as one arm of government, to make reasoned and balanced policy decisions on forest harvest and use in light of the increasing role of competing resource demands.

The difficulty of governments making such decisions is illustrated in a different national context by *J. Hansing and Soren Wibe* in their discussion of Swedish timber policy over the last two decades. The authors describe a remarkable series of misconceived and counterproductive policy decisions which have 'actively contributed to increased imports to a country where there was a physical abundance of wood.' This chapter provides a compelling example of the dangers of ignoring or casually over-riding market mechanisms. Yet the authors present a balanced prescription for the appropriate role of the market by concluding that

> more confidence should be placed in market forces and their capability to create equilibrium in the timber market. Of course, this is not the same as saying that all forestry regulations are unnecessary. But administrative regulations should aim primarily at protecting the non-priced goods and services in forestry (e.g., scenery values, recreation values, the role of forests in preserving wildlife, and so on). Except for regulations on mandatory replanting, timber production could, and should, be handled by the market.

The three chapters in this section provide insights into the complex issues inherent in timber supply forecasts and policy decisions within the public realm. Governments have, for years, grappled with the difficult issue of how to induce behaviour among private sector actors, such as forest companies, which will allow their use of forest resources to achieve broad social goals – paramount among which is the continuation of an adequate resource supply.

COMPETITIVENESS AND INTERNATIONAL TRADE IN FORESTRY

While the maintenance of adequate supply is clearly necessary for the continued health of the forest industry, it is not always sufficient. As Table 9 indicates, many of Canada's forest products are traded internationally and, thus, are vulnerable to continuing changes in the global marketplace. Fundamental and rapid changes within the international market have brought a new urgency to the assessment of product competitiveness. Traditional considerations of static comparative advantage among basic factors of production, such as capital, labour, and land, have been superseded by more sophisticated economic models of dynamic changes in a broader range of factor inputs (Porter 1990; UNIDO 1986).

Drawing on the results of their global Timber Supply Model, *Kenneth Lyon and Roger Sedjo* track evolving patterns of comparative advantage in timber supply. The authors note that 'comparative advantage in timber production and harvests shifted as several factors changed. These include the world's inventory of timber, the world population and its location, natural and human-aided regeneration of forests, technological change, and development of plantation forests.' They conclude:

> For most of this history, comparative advantage depended almost exclusively upon harvesting and transporting costs because the harvests were from old-growth forests and any regeneration that occurred was natural. The world now, however, is experiencing a transition to the intensive cropping of trees for a large fraction of the commercial timber harvest. Comparative advantage in this shift is critically concerned with the biology and the costs of planting and growing, in addition to harvesting and transporting ... [W]e predict that the traditional producers of the northern temperate climate regions, such as Canada, the Pacific Northwest, and the Nordic countries, will continue to be major producers but at somewhat reduced production levels after their old-growth forests have been harvested.

Profound changes in international comparative advantage are not limited to forest harvesting or to forestry itself. Within the last few

TABLE 9

Value of Canada's export of forest products
($ million)

Year	Lumber		Woodpulp	Newsprint	Other paper, paper board	Other forest products	Total
	Softwoods	Total					
1970	638	664	785	1,110	166	230	2,955
1971	799	830	798	1,084	173	227	3,112
1972	1,128	1,174	830	1,158	222	262	3,646
1973	1,559	1,599	1,082	1,288	286	323	4,578
1974	1,254	1,290	1,889	1,726	424	297	5,626
1975	949	973	1,834	1,746	304	270	5,127
1976	1,611	1,649	2,186	2,003	375	362	6,575
1977	2,339	2,387	2,158	2,382	468	532	7,927
1978	3,158	3,229	2,181	2,886	616	717	9,629
1979	3,821	3,901	3,083	3,222	824	860	11,890
1980	3,263	3,352	3,873	3,684	1,012	898	12,819
1981	2,913	2,989	3,819	4,326	983	858	12,975
1982	2,847	2,913	3,221	4,086	1,028	853	12,101
1983	3,896	3,965	3,049	3,956	1,142	1,106	13,218
1984	4,182	4,257	3,906	4,784	1,417	1,370	15,734
1985	4,523	4,595	3,405	5,412	1,472	1,359	16,243
1986	4,893	4,980	4,072	5,661	1,794	1,431	17,938
1987	5,745	5,859	5,473	6,029	2,237	1,643	21,241
1988	5,234	5,415	6,496	6,201	2,431	2,038	22,581
1989	5,379	5,509	6,939	5,665	2,553	2,113	22,779

SOURCE: Forestry Canada (1990), 66

years, several major research studies within both Canada and the United States have attempted to provide prescriptions for perceived external threats to major domestic industries (Dertouzos et al. 1989; Rugman and D'Cruz 1990, 1991; Council on Competitiveness 1991; Porter 1991). The issue of competitiveness is intimately related to productivity, and this variable is, in turn, closely linked to the availability of technology and its application. As illustrated in Tables 9-11, Canada's trade in forest products is heavily dominated by lower valued commodity goods such as pulp, newsprint, and sawn wood. While these exports have traditionally represented a major component of our trade balance (Table 10), the international market is changing in a manner which no longer guarantees the continuation of this massive source of external revenue. Two developments in particular signal a major challenge to Canada's future success with its traditional production, marketing, and trade strategies within the forest sector: first, the emergence of low cost competitors within the Third World (such as Brazil in pulp and paper); and, second, the increasing importance and economic benefits associated with higher value added (i.e., more processed) forest products (Table 11). An early warning of the latter threat appeared in a report on BC's forest products industry prepared by Woodbridge, Reed, and Associates (1984) for the federal Ministry of State for Economic and Regional Development. To quote:

> An increasing number of higher valued end products is being introduced by the international forest products industry ... The BC forest products industry has not responded to the majority of these market changes ... BC is facing a changing market, where growth for its traditional lower valued commodity forest products is much more limited than it was in the past. To remove this market constraint to growth, a shift in product profile is required ... The strategy choices for existing companies to achieve higher value added in processing and improved profitability include: upgrading of an existing product, secondary manufacturing, [and] a partial or complete change of technology.

The most recent and comprehensive analysis of the new and potentially threatening competitive environment facing all Canadian industry has just been produced under the sponsorship of the federal government and the Business Council on National Issues (Porter 1991). Prepared by Professor Michael Porter of the Harvard Business School, this study both diagnoses and prescribes. Several passages from this report bear directly on the forest products sector:

TABLE 10
Canada's trade by major commodity group, 1989
(million $)

Commodity	Exports*	Imports	Net flow
Forest products	22,886	3,397	19,489
Lumber - total	5,583	483	5,100
Softwoods	5,382	221	5,162
Plywood, veneer	296	151	145
Particleboard and wood building board	236	32	204
Wood pulp	6,940	174	6,766
Newsprint	5,665	6	5,659
Other paper and paperboard	2,564	1,266	1,298
Pulpwood	21	38	-17
Wood chips	165	8	157
Other crude wood materials	262	184	78
Other wood products	1,154	1,055	99
Farm products	7,550	6,812	738
Live animals	589	140	449
Food, feed, beverages, and tobacco	6,961	6,672	289
Fish products	2,439	739	1,700
Energy	13,431	5,721	7,710
Coal and other crude bituminous	2,082	711	1,371
Crude petroleum	4,462	3,607	855
Petroleum and coal products	2,385	982	1,403
Natural gas	3,023	0	3,023
Uranium and radioactive elements and isotopes	818	0	818
Electricity and parts	662	420	242
Metals and minerals	21,150	12,515	8,640
Metal ores, concentrates, and scrap	4,872	1,659	3,213
Iron and steel	2,723	2,586	137
Nonferrous metals	9,988	2,970	7,018
Other metals and minerals	3,566	5,300	-1,729

Commodity	Exports*	Imports	Net flow
Other products	70,130	103,000	-32,875
Chemicals and fertilizers	7,259	8,131	-872
Textiles	568	2,240	-1,672
Machinery	5,003	12,202	-7,199
Transportation and			
automotive products	40,789	38,710	2,079
Other products	16,512	41,717	-25,210
Special trade transactions	757	2,850	-2,096
Total	138,340	135,033	3,306

SOURCE: Forestry Canada (1990), 65
* includes re-exports

In the forest products cluster, three industries: sawn wood, news-print and market pulp, account for 75 per cent of total exports. There is almost no export position in more sophisticated segments such as fine paper (16).

Market pulp [and] newsprint ... are examples of Canadian industries that have relied on basic factor endowments for their international competitiveness success (38).

Pulp and paper companies in Canada have not considered technology to be an important source of advantage (40).

Although pulp and paper ... has long been one of the country's most important industries, there are very few specialized educational programs devoted to meeting the industry's needs for highly skilled employees (41).

One of the significant weaknesses in the Canadian forest sector identified by the Porter report is the low level of research and development: 'The Canadian pulp and paper industry spent the equivalent of 0.3 per cent of sales on R&D in 1988, while the industry in Sweden, Japan and Finland spent between 0.8 and 1.0 per cent of sales' (50). Inadequacies in R&D funding are not limited to the forest sector nor are they limited to Canada. While the United States, for example, leads in total R&D expenditures, a more accurate assessment of the potential usefulness of such funding should consider the levels of R&D as a percentage of national income, the percentage of R&D devoted to non-defence industries, and the area of research

TABLE 11
Profile of forest export composition, 1988

Commodity	World ($000)	World % of own total	Canada ($000)	Canada % of own total	USA ($000)	USA % of own total	Europe ($000)	Europe % of own total
Fuelwood	16,821	0.0	0	0.0	0	0.0	16,658	0.0
Charcoal	66,782	0.1	0	0.0	3,989	0.0	37,681	0.1
Sawlogs and veneer logs (c)	3,211,945	3.7	248,800	1.4	2,089,613	19.0	256,170	0.6
Sawlogs and veneer logs (NC)	2,913,481	3.4	12,000	0.1	159,989	1.5	440,053	1.1
Pulpwood	2,041,972	2.4	113,095	0.6	287,085	2.6	836,426	2.1
Chips + particles	859,268	1.0	76,717	0.4	286,191	2.6	92,076	0.2
Wood residues	110,028	0.1	18,890	0.1	0	0.0	81,645	0.2
Other industrial roundwood	172,220	0.2	11,691	0.1	8,567	0.1	99,492	0.3
Sawn wood (c)	10,648,072	12.4	4,435,829	25.3	1,134,009	10.3	3,688,628	9.3
Sawn wood (NC)	4,124,231	4.8	171,871	1.0	679,689	6.2	957,605	2.4
Veneer sheets	1,033,878	1.2	117,821	0.7	160,325	1.5	489,737	1.2
Plywood	4,845,956	5.6	121,054	0.7	253,901	2.3	954,326	2.4
Particle board	1,596,587	1.9	162,545	0.9	81,106	0.7	1,274,971	3.2
Fibreboard, compr	543,133	0.6	32,324	0.2	49,013	0.4	299,690	0.8
Fibreboard, n. compr	142,847	0.2	6,802	0.0	42,795	0.4	80,309	0.2
Mechanical wood pulp	427,162	0.5	115,813	0.7	3,439	0.0	228,627	0.6
Semi-chemical wood pulp	46,797	0.1	0	0.0	0	0.0	46,797	0.1
Chemical wood pulp	13,189,461	15.4	4,834,859	27.6	2,390,077	21.7	4,211,754	10.6

Dissolving wood pulp	1,067,057	1.2	148,720	0.8	503,610	4.6	302,568	0.8
Newsprint	8,469,516	9.9	5,037,221	28.7	295,474	2.7	2,706,515	6.8
Printing + writing paper	13,511,924	15.7	1,252,713	7.1	271,736	2.5	10,901,195	27.5
Other paper + paperboard	16,839,232	19.6	613,039	3.5	2,297,134	20.9	11,652,553	29.4
Column sums	85,878,370	100.0	17,531,804	100.0	10,997,742	100.0	39,655,476	100.0
Actual reported totals	85,008,544		17,440,576		10,723,247		39,535,536	
% discrepancy	1.0		0.5		2.5		0.3	

SOURCE: FAO, (1990)

c = coniferous

NC = non-coniferous

compr = compressed

n. compr = not compressed

to which such funds are devoted (e.g., basic, applied, product, or process). Tables 12 and 13 present some salient data in this respect.

Two contributions to this volume specifically address the inter-related issues of technical change, productivity, and competitiveness within the forest sectors of both Canada and the United States. As *David Bengston and Hans Gregerson* remark:

> Study of technical change and recognition of its importance in the forest-based sector has been relatively slow in coming, despite the fact that new technologies have had a tremendous influence on the value and patterns of utilization of forest resources in this century ...
> An important characteristic of both public and private R&D in the forest industries is a low level of research intensity relative to other industries and sectors.

The authors conclude that 'other countries and regions are clearly increasing their investment in forestry and forest products research (and research in other fields) more rapidly than are the U.S. and Canada,' despite the fact that 'economic rates of return to research investments [in the forest sector] ... are generally in the range of 20 to 80 per cent – comparable to estimated returns to investment in agricultural research.'

The authors conclude, on a somber note, that

> relatively low private research intensity (research expenditures as a per cent of sales) in the forest industries is a cause for concern, as is the low public research intensity (research expenditures as a per cent of value of total industry production) relative to agriculture. Concern over the long-run implications of under-investing in research is motivated, in part, by an extensive body of literature linking investment in research to productivity growth in forestry (Jakes and Risbrudt 1988), agriculture (Ruttan 1982), and various industrial sectors. Low research intensity may, therefore, represent a threat to the future productivity and competitiveness of the forest-based sector.

As major a problem as this may pose for the United States, the situation facing Canada is potentially more severe, given the significantly greater role of forest products in Canada's balance of payments. In this volume, *Tae Oum and Michael Tretheway* specifically address the comparative productivity performance of the pulp and paper sector in Canada with its American counterpart. Their conclusions are not encouraging:

TABLE 12

Research and development data by selected countries

Country	R&D ($U.S. million)	% of national income	% funded by public funds	% of govt. R&D to defence	% of govt. R&D to industrial development	Year of data
U.S.	126,115	2.89	48.0	65.6	0.2	1988
Japan	76,249	3.35	18.4	4.8	4.8	1988
USSR	61,481	5.47	46.8			1987
Germany, FR	35,690	3.21	37.7	12.5	14.5	1987
France	21,896	2.64	50.9			1988
UK	16,926	2.70	38.5			1986
Canada	8,000	1.58	58.0	3.1		1990

SOURCES: Keizai Koho Centre (1991), 26; Statistics Canada (1990), 16; Council on Competitiveness (1991), 14; Statistics Canada (1991), 306, 312.

TABLE 13
Canadian research and development by industry, 1988

Industry	R&D ($ million)	R&D as % of company sales
Mining and oil wells	79	0.5
Mining	46	0.5
Crude petroleum and natural gas	33	0.6
Manufacturing	3,228	1.5
Food, beverages, and tobacco	87	0.3
Rubber and plastic products	22	0.5
Textiles	43	1.1
Wood	33	0.3
Pulp and paper	145	0.3
Primary metals (ferrous)	31	0.3
Primary metals (non-ferrous)	130	0.9
Metal fabricating	38	1.1
Machinery	82	2.6
Aircraft and parts	423	16.1
Other transportation equipment	199	0.5
Telecommunication equipment	715	17.0
Electronic parts and components	34	5.1
Other electronic equipment	298	11.3
Business machines	294	3.4
Other electrical products	64	1.4
Non-metallic mineral products	20	0.6
Refined petroleum and coal products	149	0.5
Drugs and medicines	133	4.0
Other chemical products	200	1.3
Scientific and professional equipment	51	2.5
Other manufacturing industries	36	2.0
Services	1,185	1.4
Transportation and other utilities	121	0.4
Electrical power	231	1.1
Computer services	212	12.3
Engineering and scientific services	356	16.5
Other non-manufacturing industries	265	1.1
Total all industries	4,492	1.4

SOURCE: Statistics Canada (1990), 65, 76

Productivity improvement becomes the key element in strengthening [the Canadian pulp and paper industry's] position in the world market relative to its major competing nations ... The empirical results on total factor productivity indicate that during our study period (1963-84), overall productivity (TFP) of the u.s. industry improved significantly faster than that of its Canadian counterpart. This is especially so since 1980 ... Since the Canadian industry exports over 70 per cent of its outputs to the u.s., this TFP result poses a serious question for the long-run viability of the Canadian industry. The industry must take steps to improve its overall productivity for its survival.

While the dynamics of the international marketplace mandate a commitment to increased competitiveness, the achievement of greater productivity does not guarantee the continued health or survival of an industry so profoundly dependent on export markets. The crucial variable is access to such markets. Within the last two decades, the world trading community has witnessed the evolution of two mutually inconsistent phenomena – on the one hand, an increased emphasis by many national governments and international agencies on the extraordinary gains from unconstrained international trade; and, on the other hand, the perpetuation, and in some cases acceleration, of protectionist activity in the form of non-tariff barriers and other trade constraining activities. One potential manifestation of this dichotomous phenomenon is the threatened emergence of regional trading blocs, characterized by low or non-existent intra-bloc tariffs but significant inter-bloc trade barriers.

To Canada, in particular, these issues are of the utmost importance, as they may ultimately threaten the vitality of the national economy. Canada's forest products trade is extraordinary in many respects. As indicated by Table 14, these products comprise the largest export of such goods among all the world's nations. The bulk of this trade is conducted with the United States (Tables 15-17) and, as a consequence, lends particular urgency to Canada's bilateral trade relations. The next two contributions in this section specifically address this issue – one from the American perspective, the other from the Canadian perspective.

The historic step taken by Canada on 1 January 1989 with the implementation of a free trade agreement with the United States represented the recognition and acceptance by Canada of two emerging geo-economic realities: first, in an environment of increasing globalization and competitiveness of markets, the necessity for Canada to promote the efficiency of its domestic industry and to reap the gains associated with the free flow of goods and services; but, sec-

TABLE 14
Forest product exports by major exporting countries, 1988

Country	($u.s. million)
World	85,008,544
Canada	17,440,576
USA	10,723,247
Finland	8,184,396
Sweden	7,405,495
Germany, FR	5,860,696
France	3,217,218
USSR	3,040,900
Indonesia	2,872,868
Malaysia	2,571,735
Austria	2,491,811
Netherlands	2,009,473
Brazil	1,759,888
Belgium-Lux.	1,649,380
United Kingdom	1,506,580
Norway	1,387,492
Italy	1,184,369
Japan	1,031,281
Portugal	933,011
China	771,535
Switzerland	758,493
Singapore	742,380
Spain	736,139
Chile	634,963
Yugoslavia	598,775
New Zealand	439,444
Korea	396,047
Hong Kong	380,711
Czechoslovakia	352,938
Australia	352,011
South Africa	324,550
Romania	313,550
Denmark	287,682
Philippines	278,931
Cote d'Ivoire	236,147
Poland	233,496
German Democratic Republic	182,200

Country	($u.s. million)
Hungary	135,289
Gabon	131,497
Thailand	130,448
Congo	117,533
Cameroon	112,673
Papua New Guinea	108,932
Ghana	100,073

SOURCE: FAO (1990), 295-6

ond, the necessity to protect Canada's position with its largest trading partner, whose own complex and potentially vulnerable economic condition has engendered increasing protectionist sentiment within some of the nation's most powerful economic lobbies. In this volume, *Roy Boyd and Kerry Krutilla* use general equilibrium analysis to measure the impact of the Free Trade Agreement (FTA) on the u.s. forestry products and timber industries. In a sense, their econometric results represent the ideal and best state, that is, the maximum gains which can be achieved by both parties with a full and unencumbered application of the Free Trade Agreement. The authors conclude that 'the results of the general equilibrium model indicate that the FTA should have a modestly positive impact on the u.s. domestic forest industries and timber producers. Market-driven demand increases and lower production costs tend to offset the producer price impacts of increased competition caused by trade liberalization.'

The authors make a significant additional observation to the effect that 'the model, because of the degree of sectoral aggregation, does not pick up short-term losses or gains for specific forest industries above or below the industry average; as a consequence, it is conceivable that some specific forest industries, for example, softwood lumber, could actually experience short-term losses which are not reflected in the results.' In this observation lies one of the difficulties which has continued to impede the smooth transition to a total free trade system between Canada and the United States. It is the nature of comparative advantage that, in a process of change toward free trade, some industries will gain and others will lose. The realization of the inherent net economic gains to both nations in a free trade agreement depends upon an acceptance and facilitation of the necessary industrial restructuring. The process of adjustment is impeded by industries and their lobby groups who are unwilling to accept shifts in economic activity. Symptomatic of this resistance are the

TABLE 15
Canadian forest products exports by country, 1989

Country	Value ($000)
U.S.	14,733,293
Central America	211,625
Mexico	37,523
South America	194,965
Brazil	60,047
Chile	1,328
Venezuela	71,824
Africa	144,730
Algeria	94,873
Morocco	5,830
Middle East - Africa	20,551
Europe	3,626,523
Western Europe	3,614,622
Economic Community	3,467,320
Belgium-Luxembourg	324,155
Denmark	2,533
France	334,264
Germany, FR	792,482
Greece	22,139
Ireland	46,829
Italy	492,053
Netherlands	164,181
Portugal	7,899
Spain	58,663
UK	1,222,123
Scandinavia	39,080
Finland	12,257
Norway	1,894
Sweden	24,929
Other Western Europe	108,223
Eastern Europe	11,900
USSR	29,593

Country	Value ($000)
Asia	3,505,365
PRC	146,758
Hong Kong	65,967
India	60,438
Japan	2,540,966
Korea, South	242,854
Middle East - Asia	80,377
Southeast Asia	203,740
Taiwan	157,989
Oceania	329,754
Australia	307,960
New Zealand	19,410
World	22,778,800

SOURCE: Forestry Canada (1990), 97

TABLE 16

Canada-United States trade in forest products, 1989
($000)

Commodity	Exports to USA	Imports from USA	Balance (net exports)
Primary wood products			
Wood chips	37,847	7,966	30,152
Total	150,909	227,724	-76,443
Wood-fabricated materials			
Softwood lumber	3,358,941	219,640	3,140,638
Total	4,484,522	886,768	3,606,127
Wood pulp	3,097,426	166,276	2,931,609
Paper products			
Newsprint	4,795,778	5,841	4,789,937
Total	7,000,435	1,516,397	5,499,697
Total forest products	14,733,293	2,797,165	11,960,990

SOURCE: Forestry Canada (1990), 97, 101, 105

TABLE 17

Canada's exports of forest products to the U.S. and Japan, 1989
(by commodity group)

Commodity		U.S. ($000)	Japan ($000)
Primary wood products		150,909	262,366
Logs, bolts	total	29,177	135,057
	softwood logs	24,472	132,463
Pulpwood	total	13,034	208
	softwoods	11,000	205
Wood chips		37,847	126,851
Other primary products		70,851	251
Wood-fabricated materials		4,484,522	1,093,268
Lumber	softwoods	3,358,941	1,051,666
	hardwoods	53,380	13,093
Shingles and shakes		208,659	414
Veneer	softwoods	25,248	1,121
	hardwoods	93,353	3,085
Plywood	softwoods	11,251	12,917
	hardwoods	43,011	0
Waferboard		193,204	1,284
Particleboard		36,608	149
Fibreboard		28,403	2,899
Other wood products		199,393	1,841
Other n.e.c.		233,071	4,800
Wood pulp and paper products		10,097,861	1,185,332
Wood pulp	total	3,097,426	1,032,189
	chemical	3,043,720	952,864
Paper products		7,000,435	153,143
	newsprint	4,795,778	43,663
	other paper and paperboard	1,899,558	102,838
	book and writing paper	948,910	76,516
	fine paper	397,851	1,227
	tissue and sanitary	62,108	0
	wrapping and packaging	131,233	9,413
	paperboard	151,423	15,601
	building paper and paperboard	23,228	23
	converted paper	184,805	58
	other paper products	305,098	6,643
Total forest products		14,733,293	2,540,966

SOURCE: Forestry Canada (1991), 83

this resistance are the continuing petitions for trade remedies on a broad range of commodities. Such petitions are accompanied by economic arguments concerning unfair trading practices, which vary in the extent of their legitimacy. The issue of de facto government subsidies has been the subject of intense debate with respect to international trading practices, yet the broad and complex network of both explicit and implicit subsidization in all major global trading nations defies simple resolution. (For informative discussions of the role of subsidies and other market barriers to international trade, see Hufbauer and Erb 1984; and Emerson et al. 1988.)

It is the broader economic and political issues and their bearing on prospects for Canada-u.s. trade in forest products which are the focus of the chapter by *Irving Fox*. As the author observes, 'the importance of the policy issues associated with forest product trade between the two countries transcends the trade's economic significance.' Fox focuses, in particular, on the dynamics of the American political system and its potential influence on the flow of goods between Canada and the u.s.:

> If there is a significant downturn [in the u.s. economy], an effort to limit imports of Canadian forest products is very likely. In spite of u.s. obligations under GATT and the existence of the FTA, there remain a number of ways in which the u.s. can limit imports of Canadian forest products. In considering these possibilities it should be kept in mind that the FTA made little change in the ability of each country to impose non-tariff barriers.
>
> The structure of political relationships within which the u.s. federal government operates is such that a well organized, regionally concentrated industry adversely affected by imports can usually muster the strong support of senators and congressmen from the affected region. These delegations are in a position to bargain with other senators and congressmen for their support ... In the absence of significant concern in other regions of the country, a minority of the Congress representing a minority of the population can succeed in determining congressional policy.

The frequent result of such political influence on the formation of public policy is a diminution in total economic welfare. The nature and magnitude of such losses are illustrated in a case study, by *Michael Margolick and Russell Uhler*, of restrictions on the export of raw logs from British Columbia. This policy is not restricted to BC, of course, and is duplicated in such disparate jurisdictions as the National Forests of the western United States (u.s. GAO 1985) and Indonesia (Simatupang et al. 1988). The inherent socio-economic complexity of such policies is illustrated in Indonesia by the fact that restrictions on roundwood exports coupled with favourable tax policies may have contributed to the emergence of that country as the world's leading exporter of plywood (FAO 1988) with 49.8 per cent of the world market in 1988 – up from 0.3 per cent in 1977.

In their study, Margolick and Uhler model the impact on the BC economy of totally removing log export restrictions. The authors observe that

> these restrictions impose a cost on the logging sector of the British Columbia forest products industry in that logs must be sold at a price below what it would otherwise receive. On the other hand, the processing sector of the industry derives a benefit since it can buy logs at prices below what it would otherwise have to pay. It is the recognition of these costs and benefits in the forest industry as a whole that has sparked interest in examining whether British Columbia would be better off if log export restrictions were removed or, at least, modified.

The results of the authors' analysis suggest that 'the removal of log export restrictions results in higher short-run net benefits to the British Columbia economy and always results in a gain in long-run net benefits.' In demonstrating the magnitude of the net benefits accruing from this gain in allocative efficiency following removal of a barrier to free market operation, the authors caution that 'the benefits and costs to the different sectors of the forest industry are measured in financial terms and do not take account of the other costs of reallocation of economic activity. Whole communities may be adversely affected, and the personal and psychological costs of such upheaval are not taken into account in this analysis.' Some of the broader, yet relevant, issues of adjustment costs, non-market values, and distributional criteria which bear upon public policy decisions in this area are addressed in the following section of this volume, which discusses the social impacts of forestry.

THE SOCIAL IMPACTS OF FORESTRY

As *David Wear and William Hyde* state in their chapter concerning distributional issues in forest policy:

> Resource allocations can be evaluated on both efficiency and equity grounds. While those in the private sector may focus exclusively on the former, equity or distributional questions have come to dominate

the field of [u.s.] public forest management and policy. The profession's current approach to forestry policy issues focuses, however, on efficiency issues and generally fails to sufficiently address distributional consequences.

The authors focus on two types of concerns: (1) 'community stability' issues regarding the influence of public forestry on local economies and employment (chiefly in the National Forests of the western United States); and (2) special tax treatments for timber growing as well as programs designed to promote timber supply through subsidies for the planting of trees in the private sector (principally in the u.s. South).

In this insightful analysis, Wear and Hyde describe the pathologies of well-intentioned but inadequately conceived policies and detail the need for

> clear statements of distributional or rural development roles for forestry programs. A part of defining these roles is an understanding and acceptance of the real limitations these policies may have in influencing rural development and income ... [Another part] is removing the vague normative focus of community stability and rural development policies and focusing instead on measuring the distributional consequences of management actions at the level of regional labour markets in terms of specific goals.

Certainly one explanation for the not infrequent counterproductive or ineffective results of such public policies is the conjoint existence of erroneous preconceptions and inadequate research about complex and diverse policy impacts. The study of program implementation and post-implementation monitoring has traditionally been the impoverished stepchild of policy analysis.

In their contribution to this volume, *Peter Berck et al.* critically re-examine the issue of community stability – one of the central distributional considerations in forest policy. The authors use a social accounting matrix (SAM)

> to make estimates of how variable output would be in Humboldt County, California (a very timber dependent community) if it were dependent upon auto production or a diversified basket of the gross national product rather than upon timber. The model allows us to separate the effects of being a small, isolated county with an open economy from the effects of being dependent upon timber per se.

The conclusions flowing from this research provide important insights into the limits to the effectiveness of public policy remedies. The authors conclude that

> although forestry does not have a different cv [coefficient of variation] from much of the rest of manufacturing, forestry is usually practised in a far more isolated locale than is manufacturing ... Clearly, the lack of diversification costs Humboldt a higher cv of employment. That does not mean that there are any feasible policies to reduce the cv ... Two types of policies could reduce the employment cv in forest-dependent communities. The national government could intentionally stabilize housing starts. While this would certainly be appreciated in Humboldt county, the same argument could be made with greater force for those Midwest communities dependent upon agriculture and for just about any community dependent upon a single manufacturing industry. This lack of truly special status, combined with a desire to use monetary policy to meet other macro goals, makes this type of national policy very unlikely. The second type of policies are those that diversify industry locally. The remote nature of the Humboldt economy and its small size both argue for a rather limited amount of possible diversification. Without changing the nature of the economy by turning it into a major metropolitan area, the limit to diversification seems to be a 16 per cent reduction in employment cv.

The final chapter devoted to social issues broadens considerably the scope of this discussion by comparing the impact of the increasing globalization of forest products markets on two disparate groups of communities – Kyoto Prefecture in Japan and the Interior of British Columbia. Despite the profound differences in social and economic organization of these two regions, *Patricia Marchak* finds a direct linkage between community decline in both areas. This is a comprehensive analysis which transcends economic considerations and draws upon the author's considerable expertise in sociology and anthropology. As Marchak observes,

> I note developments that undermine the economic and social viability of rural communities and contribute to the depletion of softwood forests. It is not, however, my objective to argue that international markets are, in some absolute sense, 'bad.' Rather, my intention is to show cause for taking such social and environmental impacts into account and for including them in our evaluations of economic transactions ... The issues raised here are global. Industrial societies and

free market forces do not protect, and in BC's case, have not given rise to cohesive, family-oriented communities; neither do they protect forests and aesthetic values.

The broader context of multiple resource use of the forested land base is the subject of the next section in this volume.

FORESTRY AND MULTIPLE RESOURCE USE

In their contribution, *Michael Bowes, John Krutilla, and Thomas Stockton* provide an example of the type of comprehensive multidisciplinary research required to formulate public policy for multiple resource use. While focusing on water yield augmentation issues in one particular watershed in northern California, this research effort has much broader utility and significance. As the authors state, 'the [U.S.] Forest Service is now facing rising pressures to provide high levels of both timber and non-timber services,' but

> the relative lack of attention to the valuation of water flows from the National Forests is, unfortunately, typical of the manner in which the non-timber services of the forests were dealt with in the recent multiple-use planning effort mandated by the National Forest Management Act of 1976 (NFMA). Few people, for example, spent much effort in estimating the value of the recreational services of their forest lands in this recent round of forest plans ... This paper represents an effort on our part to incorporate the value of these non-priced services of water flow into a more complete economic treatment of multiple-use public land management.

This type of work forces policymakers to reconsider the critical process of valuing multiple outputs from forested land and the utility of appropriate multidisciplinary research methodologies with respect to achieving socially acceptable and productive policy alternatives.

In his historical comparison of the management of temperate mountain forests in the Swiss Alps and Colorado Rocky Mountains, *Martin Price* traces the increasing recognition in twentieth century forest policy of the importance of multiple resource use. Such uses are extremely diverse and include water supply, air pollution mitigation, recreation, landscape protection and aesthetic values, livestock grazing, protection of wildlife and fish stocks, ecosystem and genetic diversity, and option and existence values as well as timber production. It is the author's contention that early forest policies in the U.S. and Switzerland, based on a sustained-yield concept of wood output, have hampered the attainment of these broader social goals. He concludes that

> many of the conditions assumed for forestry based on the production of sustained yields of wood no longer exist in the two regions – if they ever existed. Thus, the policies based on this traditional sustained-yield concept, which have officially guided the management of the forests of these regions for most of this century, have been and continue to be inappropriate ... A primary consequence is that the current structure of the forests is neither what was intended by the policies nor is it particularly suitable for fulfilling their objectives.
>
> Recent policies for both regions realize, to a greater or lesser extent, that a new concept of sustained-yield forestry is necessary for managing mountain forests where the provision of public goods, such as recreation and protection (from natural hazards and of watersheds), is a primary objective. This philosophical change has been proposed by Wiebecke and Peters (1984), who suggest that the concept should be redefined as having the objective of ensuring the provision of all outputs desired by present and future generations. Thus, it should explicitly consider long-term, often unquantifiable values of the forests as well as economic criteria and need not necessarily be based on wood extraction as the primary means of producing these outputs ... Conclusions drawn from the study of these two sub-regions may well be relevant to other mountain regions ... In a period of rapid change in economic and political systems, and with the prospect of anthropogenic climate change within the next few decades, it seems appropriate to consider that flexibility should be a key characteristic of all forest management policies and their means of implementation.

To this point, this volume has been devoted largely, although not exclusively, to forestry issues characteristic of the developed world. In many respects, however, the most pressing issues in forestry today find their sharpest focus in the Third World – the subject of the final section of this book.

FORESTRY AND THE THIRD WORLD

With expected growth in population, industrialization and accompanying pressure on the land base, forests of Africa, Asia, and Latin America increasingly bear the ultimate burden of feeding the population, assisting in the creation of national wealth, and safeguarding the global climate. That these diverse yet vital goals may not be mutually consistent illustrates the absolute importance of developing coherent and effective forest policy within these diverse geopolitical regions.

Central to the successful resolution of many of the critical forest challenges faced by the nations of the Third World is an appreciation of the linkages between resource use and institutional structures – broadly defined to include the economic, political, and legal frameworks of social decisionmaking at the national, regional, and local levels of governance. In much of the Third World, especially those regions most impoverished, forestry is characterized less by Western-style timber and fibre extraction than by subsistence recovery of fuelwood, fodder, and forage. This 'social forestry,' so central to the lifestyle of millions of global inhabitants, has only recently begun to attract rigorous analysis. Table 18 demonstrates the exceedingly high reliance of many African nations on fuelwood as a source of energy.

In his contribution to this volume, *William Hyde* develops some of the formal hypotheses necessary for the intellectual development of this topic. As defined by Hyde,

> forestry for local use in rural community development, which we abbreviate as 'social forestry,' is any forestry (except large-scale commercial plantation and industrial forestry) so long as it emphasizes the responses of local consumers to forest-produced goods and services: usually fuelwood, fodder, and forage, sometimes water, soil protection, and other tree and interplanted non-wood crops ... [T]his definition permits ... domestic consumption of household-produced forest products, and it permits market exchange. It incorporates the original concept of social forestry as well as the concepts of community forestry and agroforestry.

With this comprehensive statement of the concept of social forestry, the author proceeds to formulate critical hypotheses concerning its broad objectives, issues of efficiency and distributional equity, cultural constraints to decisionmaking, the evaluative criteria of sustainability and public participation frequently used by international donor or lending agencies in their support of social forestry projects, and the central issue of resource tenure and property rights.

Considered by many economists as central to issues of forest policy, tenure and the nature of its associated property rights remains a controversial and inadequately understood concept even within the forest-based industrialized economies of the North. In an insightful study undertaken in Canada, Haley and Luckert (1990) identify at least twelve characteristics of property rights which may be used to

TABLE 18
Selected data on fuelwood dependency, 1987
(thousand metric tons of coal equivalent)

Country	Fuelwood	Total commercial energy consumption	Fuelwood as % of (fuelwood + commercial)
World	569,809	9,614,855	5.6
Bhutan	982	3	99.7
Equatorial Guinea	149	2	98.7
Guinea-Bissau	141	2	98.6
Malawi	4,338	280	93.9
Burundi	1,270	92	93.2
Nepal	5,346	425	92.6
Burkina Faso	2,570	220	92.1
Chad	1,070	99	91.5
Ethiopia	12,110	1,150	91.3
Mozambique	5,007	477	91.3
Tanzania	9,642	935	91.2
Uganda	3,885	399	90.7
Rwanda	1,867	196	90.5
Central African Republic	1,150	134	89.6
Laos	1,162	138	89.4
Mali	1,624	198	89.1
Cambodia	1,661	211	88.7
Benin	1,481	205	87.8
Ghana	8,683	1,394	86.2
Haiti	1,762	317	84.8
Somalia	2,146	417	83.7
Zaire	10,178	2,139	82.6
Kenya	10,521	2,267	82.3
Sudan	6,332	1,481	81.0
Liberia	1,558	372	80.7
Niger	1,301	343	79.1
Madagascar	2,204	620	78.0
Gambia	294	87	77.2
Sierra Leone	910	298	75.3
Guinea	1,276	474	72.9
Myanmar	5,565	2,595	68.2
Zambia	3,714	1,874	66.5

Country	Fuelwood	Total commercial energy consumption	Fuelwood as % of (fuelwood + commercial)
Nigeria	31,240	16,891	64.9
Honduras	1,620	890	64.5
Paraguay	1,699	939	64.4
Guatemala	2,356	1,409	62.6
Angola	1,367	826	62.3
Papua New Guinea	1,844	1,154	61.5
El Salvador	1,383	899	60.6
Sri Lanka	2,710	2,066	56.7
Senegal	1,203	946	56.0
Togo	214	193	52.6
Cameroon	3,210	2,913	52.4
Côte d'Ivoire	3,017	2,764	52.2
Viet Nam	7,578	7,400	50.6

SOURCES: UN (1990, 1991)

describe forest tenure: comprehensiveness, duration, transferability, right of tenure holder to economic benefits, exclusiveness, security, use restrictions, allotment types, size specifications, operational stipulations, and operational controls. The authors conclude that little theoretical justification for, or empirical testing of, the inter-relationship of such tenure characteristics and the behaviour of forest tenure holders has been provided. The paucity of such analysis within an advanced forest economy such as Canada gives at least one indication of the problem of discerning such relationships in developing nations. Not infrequently, Western guidance and funding of Third World forestry projects are burdened by inadequate understanding of the local institutional context and misinformed about the theoretical constructs of social system behaviour and response.

In his contribution to this volume, *Daniel Bromley* provides a cogent reconceptualization of property rights as authority systems and establishes a strong linkage between such concepts and potentially disastrous forest policies being implemented in many parts of the Third World. The author concludes that

the nominal property structure (where by 'nominal' I mean whether something is held as private property, as state property, or as common property) is less important for managerial performance than is the effectiveness of the authority system (the rights and duties) that accompanies a particular property regime. These institutional arrangements represent the 'real structure.'

Much effort is expended arguing over which particular property regime is most conducive to improved forest management in the developing countries. If some small fraction of that effort were, instead, devoted to a careful consideration of the institutional arrangements that give meaning to each property regime, forest management would be much improved.

Bromley tracks the loss of local control over natural resource management as newly independent nations have taken de jure control over forestry. In the presence of inadequate administrative resources, such policies have inevitably led to the degradation of forests. The author makes a compelling case for reconsideration of the value of local common property regimes which permit communities to exercise effective control over their own resource base. In so doing, Bromley identifies a pervasive misconception which impedes the intellectually rigorous analysis of common property regimes – the confusion of common property with open access. Garrett Hardin's (1968) much cited work, 'The Tragedy of the Commons,' has entrenched in economic literature a serious and destructive confusion of these disparate concepts. As Bromley states:

> Common property represents private property for the group (since all others are excluded from use and decisionmaking) and . . . individuals have rights (and duties) in a common property regime (Ciriacy-Wantrup and Bishop 1975). This capacity to exclude – a trait shared with private property regimes and with state property regimes – stands as the sine qua non of common property as distinguished from open access. This fundamental point is missed by all of those who confuse open access resources with common property resources.

In a companion piece devoted to the complex issue of property rights and forestry, *John Bruce and Louise Fortmann* provide a reflective re-examination of three conventional wisdoms which can impair the formation and implementation of effective policy:

(1) People only plant trees on land with secure property rights.
(2) Forests and trees held in common will inevitably be degraded/deforested.
(3) The best way to protect forests is exclusion, managed and enforced by the state.

In this article we explore in detail the relationship between afforesta-
tion/deforestation and property rights in the three tenurial situations
paralleling the three conventional wisdoms: the agricultural holding,
the commons, and the state forest reservation.

The picture of forestry tenure in the Third World presented by Bruce
and Fortmann is significantly more complex and culturally rich than
that implied by simpler models of Western forest systems. At least
four strong conclusions emerge from their analysis. First, trees can
be an object of property rights separable from the land on which they
are located and may, in fact, secure tenure in land. Second, in a
theme echoed in other chapters on Third World forestry in this volume, too little attention has been paid to the role of women in forestry in developing countries – a potentially critical group whose
participation, or lack thereof, in forestry decisionmaking can profoundly influence the success or failure of any decisions which may
be made. Third, in concert with the analysis provided by Bromley,
the authors conclude that 'the inability or unwillingness of the state
to perceive or acknowledge local property claims and management
practices lies at the root of [deforestation].' And, fourth, 'American
forestry professionals (and presumably those whom they train)
bring to their work in the Third World a strong predilection for large-
scale comprehensive government resource management – a progressive era tenet which perpetuates colonial forest policy legacy
and is not necessarily appropriate to the conditions of some developing countries.'

The importance of understanding local institutions and traditions
in formulating successful forest policy in the Third World is further
illustrated by *Rutger Engelhard's* case study of wood for energy development in Kenya. Once again, the importance of intricate socio-
cultural factors in Third World forest policy and, in particular, the
critical but unappreciated role of women is highlighted as Engelhard
describes the initially unsuccessful attempts of the Kenya Woodfuel
Development Programme (KWDP) to solve serious local woodfuel
problems. The author describes the eventual resolution of this problem, where, 'by transcending technical considerations and encompassing traditional value systems in its intervention strategy, the
KWDP created an ambience in which change could take place and the
domestic fuelwood problems could be solved.'

The final chapter on Third World forestry issues is equally
iconoclastic, challenging the conventional wisdom among foresters
and many development economists that plantation forestry in developing nations is economically preferable to natural forest manage-

ment. Using a case study from Indonesia, *Roger Sedjo* finds that 'the financial returns to natural forest management systems can be much more favourable than is commonly believed, and ... financial returns to natural forest management are comparable to those likely to accrue to plantation forests in many situations that are common in the Asia-Pacific region.' In light of these findings, Sedjo asks the central question, 'why isn't natural forestry practised more often?,' and offers three answers:

> Governments frequently undertake inappropriate policies related to their natural resources, often, in effect, promoting economically and ecologically inferior projects (Repetto and Gillis 1988). These policies fail to properly value the timber resource as well as the environmental and other non-timber benefits provided by the forest ... Furthermore ... concession agreements typically are provided for too short a period of time to provide the firms with incentives to take a long-term view toward the management and sustainability of the resource ... A final speculation as to the apparent preference of non-economic plantation forestry over natural tropical forest management is the well-known preference of the large international development banks for large over smaller projects.

The picture which these five chapters paint of Third World forest policy is disturbing. Governments of many developing countries struggle with an inadequate information base, understaffed, undertrained, and underfunded administrative agencies, and a lack of appreciation of the subtle linkages between social, economic, and political structures and the implementation of effective forest policy. In many cases, such governments have turned to the developed nations for policy guidance and external funding. Western ignorance of local institutional variables coupled with overly simple and preconceived models of effective decisionmaking structures have led to well-documented and frequently disastrous results.

In conclusion, many of the lessons one can draw from the Third World experience with forest policy can, in fact, inform our own resource decisionmaking. These lessons include: a need to rethink some of our most entrenched preconceptions, to adopt a more eclectic and multidisciplinary approach to forest policy, and to recognize the complexities and subtleties of the issues which characterize the interaction of human-made and natural systems.

ACKNOWLEDGMENTS

I would like to express my gratitude to the following individuals for their generous advice in the preparation of this book: Vivian Banca, Richard Barichello, Clark Binkley, James Brander, Adrian Cooper, Christopher Dodd, Adam Femech, Robert Guy, Rick Harris, Werner Kurz, Les Lavku-lich, Cindy Pearce, Everett Peterson, James Shelford, Kirk Smith, Barbara Spencer, William Stanbury, and Don Wilson. Special thanks are owing to my colleague Ilan Vertinsky for his continued support and encouragement of this project. Finally, I am most grateful to both Bill Hyde and Roger Sedjo for lending their names to this undertaking. With their participation, we have been able to attract as contributors many of the leading experts in the field of forestry and forest policy. I absolve any and all of these colleagues for any errors of commission or omission, which remain the sole responsibility of the editor.

NOTES

1 These are: the November 1979 UN-ECE Convention on Long-Range Transboundary Air Pollution (with thirty-five signatures and thirty-two ratifications as of 1990); the 16 September 1987 Montreal Protocol on the Substances that Deplete the Ozone Layer (with forty-six signatures and sixty-five ratifications as of 1990); and the 22 March 1989 Basel Convention on the Control of Transboundary Movements of Hazardous Waste and Their Disposal (with 106 signatures and five ratifications as of 1990). (Source: UNEP 1991:383-93.)

2 These include water vapour, carbon dioxide (CO_2), methane (CH_4), chlorofluorocarbons (CFCs), nitrous oxide (N_2O), and tropospheric ozone (O_3). Their estimated contribution to global warming is as follows: CO_2: 50 per cent, CH_4: 16 per cent, O_3: 8 per cent, N_2O: 6 per cent, CFCs and others: 20 per cent. The contribution from forestry is estimated at CO_2: 10 per cent and methane: 4 per cent. (Source: WRI 1991:24.)

CHAPTER ONE

The Role of Air Pollution in Forest Decline

Judith Clarkson and Jurgen Schmandt

Many factors can affect the health of forests. Most notably, climatic changes can result in reduced viability of trees and, in the long run, migration of species and entire vegetation zones. Another factor, also frequently related to climatic conditions, is the death or decline of trees associated with disease. In the last twenty years it has become apparent that forest decline has accelerated and, in many cases, human-made pollutants appear to play a significant role.

Three forms of pollution that were hardly recognized or, at least, did not create large scale problems only a few decades ago, now cause harm to forests – acid rain, ozone, and global warming. Extensive research on acid rain and ozone has been undertaken in North America and Europe during the 1980s. The largest effort – the National Acid Precipitation Assessment Program – was funded by the U.S. government for over ten years and, except for publication of the final report, is now·complete. The program cost $570 million and involved some 2,000 scientists (National Acid Precipitation Assessment Program 1990b). So far we know little about the impacts of global warming on different ecosystems, including forests. But the body of available knowledge is growing rapidly (International Panel on Climate Change 1990). Pollution that is damaging to forests is caused by industrialization, particularly the combustion of fossil fuels. Complex atmospheric processes are involved. The specific causes, pathways, and effects of acid rain, ozone, and global warming are entirely different. We discuss acid rain in detail, include references to ozone, and conclude with a section on the potential effects of global warming.

FOREST DAMAGE FROM ACID DEPOSITION AND OZONE

Acid rain occurs both naturally and as a byproduct of industrialization. Since the late 1960s its increasing intensity in industrialized areas of the world has been observed. In eastern North America, for example, industrial emissions of sulphur exceed natural emissions by a factor of ten or more (National Acid Precipitation Assessment Program 1990a). As a result, human-made acid rain has become an important research area as well as an urgent policy concern. The starting point for acid rain – or, more accurately, acid deposition (because it occurs in wet and dry forms) – is the combustion of sulphur rich fuels, mostly coal or oil. Sulphur dioxide is released into the atmosphere and, after undergoing photochemical transformations, can return to the earth as sulphuric acid, either in a wet form, as rain, fog, or snow, or in a dry form, as gases or particles. Power-generating plants and industrial boilers and smelters are the main sources of sulphur dioxide emissions. Nitrogen oxides also contribute to the formation of acid deposition. In this case, nitric acid is produced. Oxides of nitrogen also react with volatile organic compounds in the atmosphere, resulting in the formation of ozone. Mobile sources – cars and trucks – are the principal sources of nitrogen oxide pollution.

Acid deposits occur either in proximity to emission sources or, particularly if tall smoke stacks are used by plants, hundreds of miles downwind. The very existence of long distance pollution was disputed well into the 1970s. Governments of several countries, among them the United States, Great Britain, and West Germany, only reluctantly and slowly accepted scientific findings about long-distance transport of air pollutants (National Research Council 1981, 1986). Severe confrontations between 'polluters' and 'victims' resulted, pitting against each other coal-rich regions and downwind states, provinces and countries. Controversies have been particularly intense between England and Scandinavia, eastern and central Europe, the American Midwest and New England, upstate New York and southeastern Canada. While damage from acid deposition in proximity to industrial facilities has been documented for over a century, the long-distance variety was only discovered when energy production reached high levels in the decades following the Second World War.

The end result of acid deposition is damage to lakes and rivers, deterioration of human health, corrosion of materials, damage to

cultural resources, reduced visibility, and increased stress to forests
(Crowling 1989). The potential for ecosystem degradation by acid
deposition from long-range transport of air pollutants across national boundaries was first described by Oden in 1968. At that time,
acid precipitation was still little understood. For most of the 1970s it
was viewed as a serious but regional problem. Now a larger view is
emerging, placing acid deposition in the broader context of multiple
human-induced changes to the atmosphere, including conventional
pollution, depletion of the ozone layer, and increased concentration
of greenhouse gases (Gorham 1989). These are different but related
consequences of increased industrialization and, in the last analysis, of population growth. These various forms of pollution interact
with each other, but we do not yet fully understand how. Singly and
as a group they are likely to have wide-reaching impacts on the condition of ecological, social, and economic systems worldwide. A
new and demanding research and policy agenda is beginning to address global change *as a human-made phenomenon* (Office of Science
and Technology Policy 1989). Global change is likely to receive increasing attention in research and policy development as a key issue
of the next century.

On a global scale, acidification problems and the potential for related forest damage are serious in highly industrialized regions. So
far, effects are greatest in Europe and the eastern parts of North
America, though effects in the two continents seem to be markedly
different. Factors explaining these differences include higher population density, more intensive forest management, and reluctant
control of automobile emissions in western Europe. Almost total environmental neglect in eastern Europe may explain the larger forest
damage experienced there. In general, forest damage in Europe is
higher than it is in North America. A third region of acidification is
emerging in the southern part of China and may cause significant
damage to forests. At present anthropogenic emissions of sulphur
and nitrogen oxides are still low in most tropical countries, but they
are increasing rapidly. Considering current levels of industrialization, as well as the sensitivity of soils and surface waters, additional
potential problem areas are likely to emerge in northern and eastern
regions of Latin America, Western Equatorial Africa, large parts of
the Indian subcontinent, and Southeast Asia (Rodhe 1989).

Projected emissions of air pollutants also suggest that impacts
will reach the global scale. Over the next several decades, Europe
and North America are not expected to experience major increases in
the emissions of sulphur and nitrogen oxides. The major countries,

at least in the West, have adopted control measures against sulphur dioxide and, less consistently, nitrogen oxides. As a result, emission reductions will materialize. Between 1975 and 1990, sulphur dioxide emissions from utilities in the United States have decreased by 30 per cent, primarily because more low-sulphur coal was burned and cleaner combustion technologies were used (National Acid Precipitation Assessment Program 1990a:1). Yet even in regions with environmental controls in place, acidification and its effects, including forest damage, will continue and, possibly, worsen in some regions. This is due to the delayed acidification of aquatic and terrestrial ecosystems from emissions in the past. But the main problem areas will be in the developing world. Asia, Africa, and South America are likely to experience major increases in acidifying atmospheric emissions (Galloway 1989). Therefore, forest damage in these regions is to be expected.

In contrast to predictions made several years ago, forest damage has not yet had a measurable impact on the world production and consumption of forest products. Although demand for wood-based products continues to be high, supplies of wood appear to be adequate at least to the year 2000. Lower rates of production are forecast for Europe than for the world as a whole, and major shortages of firewood are predicted in many developing countries (Kuusela 1987). Thus, from a purely economic point of view, forest damage resulting from air pollution is still small enough to be made up for by nonaffected areas.

Because the economic impacts have, so far, not been large, and because the exact relationship between specific air pollutants and ecological damage has not been established, the United States waited for almost twenty years before including special acid rain provisions in the 1990 amendments to the Clean Air Act. The policy debate within the United States was drawn-out. One difficulty was caused by the fact that areas affected by the pollution (mostly the northeastern states) are often geographically and politically removed from the source of the problem – mostly industry and electric utilities in the Midwest. Under these conditions it was unclear who should bear the cost of the controls; those that produce the pollution or those that stand to benefit most from control strategies. The same reasons complicated the international conflicts over acid rain that erupted between the United States and Canada and within the European Community (see Schmandt et al. 1989 for further discussion of this issue). Long after the international controversy had calmed down, the United States moved in 1990 to reduce sulphur emissions. The motivation, at this point, was less to improve relations with Canada than to resolve the dispute between the Midwest and New England. Domestic rather than international goals dominated.

HISTORICAL EVIDENCE

Evidence of accelerated forest decline during the last twenty-five years has been accumulating both in Europe and in North America. The most publicized instance of decline attributed directly or indirectly to human-made pollution occurs in the Black Forest in Germany. In this case, it is the rate of decline that has alerted the public to the seriousness of the situation. In the late 1970s silver fir first began to show signs of damage. This was followed by Norway spruce and, in 1982, by hardwoods such as beech and oak. Damage is greatest on west-facing slopes, with older trees at higher elevations suffering most. However, depending on how damage is defined, and this has been an area of controversy, as many as 50 per cent of the trees were at one point considered in danger. In the case of fir trees more than 80 per cent were reported as being affected (Mackenzie and El-Ashry 1988:5-6).

More recently, estimates of damage have been revised downwards. For several years now, the German federal government has conducted detailed statistical surveys of forests. In the 1988 report, only half of all tree stands were reported as healthy, with the remainder classified as having experienced weak or medium damage. An emergency program instituted by the German Research Council found that conifers produce more needles than are needed early in the growing period. Therefore, up to 25 per cent needle shedding later in the year is normal. Because needle shedding had been used as the key indicator for light damage, the forest survey categories are being revised. Based on better understanding of tree biology, experts now agree that the 'light damage' category should be omitted from damage estimates. If this correction is made, only fifteen per cent of the trees are considered damaged. The most recent assessment also shows differences between species. Conifers are improving slightly, while oak and beech are suffering more. In this case, severe pest infestations play a major role. The most serious damage is observed in high elevations, particularly among older trees. Particularly heavy damage is reported in parts of East Germany. Prior to reunification, damage reports had been kept secret. Severe damage is also reported in some areas of Czechoslovakia (Krause et al. 1983; Prinz 1987; authors' clipping file).

Unlike the United States, forest damage in Europe, particularly in Germany, has been an issue that received enormous attention from the public, the media, and policy makers. By now the dust has cleared and a more balanced assessment is possible. It seems that virtually all commercially important tree species in Central Europe show signs of novel forest damage. Symptoms include chlorosis, visible thinning of tree crowns, decrease in growth and root bio-mass, and changes in the size and shape of leaves. Trees over sixty years old are most affected, and only a small portion of trees have died. Airborne chemicals are implicated because no single force or combination of natural forces can explain the observed changes in forest condition. Crowling (1989:169-71) categorizes the observed changes as 'circumstantial evidence of causality.'

Damage in Europe was not always associated with industrial ac-tivities, except along the Czechoslovakian border. Two major theo-ries evolved. First, industrial pollution is only one source of stress. Bad forest management practices may have had much to do with ob-served damage in Germany. Other contributing factors include drought, pests, and winter damage. Even so, the principal policy re-sponse in Germany was against industrial pollution. In 1983 a law was passed requiring all power plants that will operate beyond 1993 to install high efficiency flue-gas desulphurization systems by 1988 for sulphur dioxide and by 1990 for nitrogen oxides. The goal was to half the level of sulphur dioxide emissions, which in 1982 amounted to 3.9 million tons (Office of Technology Assessment 1984:310).

A second pollution pathway implicates the internal combustion engine. Car exhaust fumes, which contribute both ozone and nitro-gen oxides, were identified as the source of forest damage outside industrial regions along the autobahns. An easy reduction of nitro-gen oxide emissions could be achieved by imposing speed limits on freeways, but the automobile lobby has been successful in opposing such a move. Catalytic converters, which have been mandatory in the United States for twenty years, are only now being installed in large numbers of cars in countries belonging to the European Eco-nomic Community.

In North America forest damage is more limited. The first example in the United States that established a causal relationship between air pollution and forest injury was documented in the San Bernadino National Forest, seventy-five miles east of Los Angeles. Damage was first noted in the early 1950s and, by the late 1960s, had affected more than 100,000 acres of Ponderosa and Jeffrey pines. The symp-toms (specifically, chlorosis of older needles) did not exactly fit those caused by drought, insect infestations, or disease. Although drought may have been a contributing factor, more drought-sensitive tree species were healthier than were other species, despite several very dry years. Between 1980 and 1985 the number of affected pine trees increased from 48 to 87 per cent. Recent data indicate that these two species are particularly sensitive to ozone, and controlled exposure experiments, in which polyethylene bags containing ozone were placed on branchlets, established a causal relationship (Mackenzie and El-Ashry 1988:5). For ozone, therefore, rigorous scientific proof of a causal connection between an air pollutant and forest decline has been established (Crowling 1989:169).

All other cases of damage in North America fall in the categories of circumstantial or limited evidence (Crowling 1989:170-1). Red spruce in the Appalachians, particularly at high altitudes, suffer from dieback of tree tops and branch tips, decrease in radial growth, and increased mortality in New York, New Hampshire, and Vermont. In addition to acid deposition, which is particularly acute in areas covered for prolonged periods by cloud cover, significantly increased levels of lead, copper, and zinc were found in the forest floor. Other factors, such as nutrient-deficient soils, frost damage, insect pests, and root pathogens, have contributed to the decline but do not correlate with the widespread nature of the dieback. Although climatic factors, in particular harsh winters, could explain some of the effects, air pollution is most likely a significant predisposing factor (McLaughlin et al. 1987). The damage resembles that described for European spruce-fir trees exposed to nutrient leaching on poor soils in a similar ozone/acid rain environment (National Acid Precipitation Assessment Program 1987:7-18).

In the United States and Canada, six specific instances of forest decline that can be attributed to air pollution have been reported:

(1) San Bernadino National Forest, California. Deterioration associated with high ozone levels, having the greatest effect on Ponderosa and Jeffrey pine, two species known to be particularly sensitive.

(2) White pine in the eastern United States. Reductions in growth rate associated with sensitivity of different genotypes to ozone.

(3) Red spruce in the eastern United States. Greatest effect in above-cloud forests where tree foliage may be exposed to mist with an average pH of 3.6 and high concentrations of hydrogen peroxide.

(4) Yellow pine in the southeastern United States. Decreased growth rate may be due to natural factors compounded by air pollution.

(5) Pine Barrens, southeastern New Jersey. Abnormally low growth rates may be due to acid deposition on nutrient-deficient soils with poor buffering capacity.

(6) Sugar maple, northeastern United States and southeastern Canada. Maple decline is often associated with pests or disease. However, air pollution appears to be a predisposing factor, with greatest effects evident in areas with high ozone levels (National Acid Precipitation Assessment Program 1987:7-21).

The summary statement of the National Acid Precipitation Assessment Program, issued in 1990, summarized research on forest damage as follows: 'There is no evidence of a general or unusual decline of forests in the United States or Canada due to acid rain.' A more qualified conclusion was inserted in the *Assessment Highlight:*

There is currently no widespread forest or crop damage in the United States related to [acidic deposition]. However, cloud acidity, together with a complex combination of other factors (ozone, soil acidification, climate) contribute to reduced cold tolerance in high-elevation spruce in the eastern United States. This can contribute to damage to trees above cloud level during winters with particularly low temperatures. Adverse effects on forests in other regions of the country are associated with ozone. (National Acid Precipitation Program 1990a:7).

A number of experts, including Crowling, Loucks, and Oppenheimer, took exception to this statement, pointing out that the summary statement was correct only to the extent that observed forest damage is not widespread at this time. But this was not the same as saying that there was no problem. These critics are particularly concerned with the longer-term effects of acid rain on forest soils. Potential changes, which are reported at length in a number of National Acid Precipitation Assessment reports, can lead to long-term deficiencies in soil nutrients (Roberts 1991:1,302-4).

The research results now available suggest four broad conclusions: (1) acid deposition contributes to stress on forests, (2) ozone causes forest damage, (3) the interaction between different stress factors – some natural, some human – is extraordinarily difficult to disentangle, and (4) reductions in emissions of sulphur dioxide and nitrogen oxides will result in multiple benefits, including reduced stress on forest systems. The following section elaborates on these points.

CAUSAL AGENTS

The extent to which air pollution can be held directly responsible for the deteriorating health of affected forests is to some extent a semantic argument. Often tree death can be directly attributed to the infestation of a pest or the spread of disease. However, such widespread devastation is often associated with the increase in industrialization and automobile use. Four types of injurious substances are involved in forest decline:

(1) Toxic gases (ozone, SO_2, and fluoride) which can penetrate stomata and damage foliage as a result of brief periods (hours, days, or weeks) of exposure.
(2) Toxic metals (aluminum, lead, mercury, cadmium, zinc) which accumulate over years (or decades) and are gradually released from the soil in amounts that inhibit growth.
(3) Excess nutrients (particularly nitrogen) that alter normal patterns of growth and development. These impacts extend over weeks, months, years, or decades.
(4) Growth-altering organic chemicals (such as ethylene, aniline, or dinitrophenol) that change growth patterns over an unknown time frame (Crowling 1989).

Forest decline is defined as a situation in which deterioration and death of trees is caused by a combination of biological and non-biological stress factors (Mackenzie and El-Ashry 1988:4). The result is a progressive weakening of trees, leading to the death of portions of the foliated canopy. The gradual loss of vigour ultimately results in a reduction in growth rate and increased susceptibility of the trees to secondary factors such as disease. Stress factors have been classified by Manion into three categories, as shown in Table 1. There is widespread agreement among experts that natural as well as human factors contribute to forest decline. Air pollution is a predisposing factor, with different pollutants acting independently or synergistically. Both geographical evidence and laboratory experiments have been used to establish causal relationships between specific pollutants and forest damage.

Early in the twentieth century the death of trees in the immediate

TABLE 1

Factors influencing decline of forest trees

| | Types of influencing factors | | |
	Predisposing	Inciting	Contributing
Functional role	Chronic weakening	Triggering episodes	Accelerators
Stressing agents	Climate	Insect defoliation	Bark beetles
	Soil moisture	Frost	Canker fungi
	Genotype of host	Drought	Viruses
	Soil nutrients	Salt	Root-decay fungi
	Air pollutants	Air pollutants	Competition
	Competition	Mechanical injury	

SOURCE: S.B. McLauglin (1985), 'Effects of Air Pollution on Forests: A Critical Review,' *Journal of the Air Pollution Control Association* 35(5):512-34

vicinity of industrial plants could be attributed to specific pollutants. A metal smelter in British Columbia emitting more 10,000 tons of sulphur dioxide was responsible for the death of trees more than fifty miles away. In Spokane, Washington, fluoride emissions from an aluminum ore reduction plant killed all of the trees within a three square mile area (Mackenzie and El-Ashry 1988:4). However, as early as 1907, Wislicenus distinguished between the chronic effects of low level pollutants, most prevalent in coniferous trees, and the acute effects associated with short-term high exposure. In both cases, sulphur dioxide was the primary suspect (Prinz 1987).

During these early days of the industrial revolution, forest damage (and damage to other crops or even human health) was accepted as unavoidable close to metal smelters and combustion facilities. In time, emissions were controlled in order to reduce these effects. As yet, we have only limited experience and even less scientific evidence with which to identify regions where rates of continuing change in the chemical climate exceed the elastic limits of ecosystem resiliency and adaptability. 'Nowhere are these uncertainties more evident than in the forests of Central Europe and parts of eastern North America' (Crowling 1989).

Acute exposure to locally dispersed primary pollutants is well documented. Chronic exposure to regionally dispersed secondary pollutants is more difficult to study for several reasons:

(1) The symptoms may be subtle, variable, and difficult to distinguish from the effects of other stress factors.
(2) The concentration of pollutants may vary.
(3) Two or more pollutants may act additively, synergistically, or antagonistically.
(4) Pollution-induced changes may not affect the productivity of whole forests unless the total number of affected trees becomes so large that the ecosystem becomes under-stocked.
(5) The effects of airborne pollutants may be difficult to distinguish, using rigorous scientific methods, from those of natural stress factors (Crowling 1989).

With the passage of the 1970 Clean Air Act, the u.s. Congress recognized that high levels of air pollution, particularly in urban areas, were unacceptable and had to be controlled. Sulphur dioxide, produced primarily by industrial plants and coal-fired electric utilities, was known to be a lung irritant, and other pollutants, including particulate matter, were known to cause reduced visibility. By concentrating on ambient air quality, the Act encouraged the use of tall stacks to dispose of pollution so that local air quality standards could be met. This technique resulted in the dispersion of air pollutants, which travel over long distances and undergo various chemical transformations, including the production of acidic compounds. Unwittingly, early control measures exacerbated acid deposition far away from emitting sources.

As a result of this and subsequent legislation, it has been more difficult to establish exact causal relationships between specific pollutants and ecological damage. However, it has been shown that prevailing winds bring industrial pollutants from the Midwest to New England and southern Canada, where they have resulted in acidification of lakes and damage to forests. Pollution control measures mandated by the 1975 revisions of the Clean Air Act have resulted in reductions in the concentration of airborne sulphur compounds, and the rate of lake acidification in the Northeast has slowed (Mohnen 1988). But these measures were taken to improve visibility and health. Acid rain was not addressed in the legislation.

In Canada and several European countries, acid rain legislation was passed in the 1980s. For many countries the target of reducing emissions by 50 per cent was defined as a goal that could be obtained within ten to twenty years. In the United States, it was not until the Clear Air Act Amendments of 1990 that pollution reduction became mandatory and was specifically targeted on reduction of acid deposition. The Act calls for cuts in sulphur dioxide emissions

TABLE 2

Chemical transformation of air pollutants

Pollutant	Contributing factors	End product
NO_x	OH (in air)	HNO_3 (nitric acid)
NO_x + VOC		O_3 (ozone)
VOC	HO_2 (in air)	H_2O_2 (hydrogen peroxide)
SO_2	H_2O_2 and O_3	H_2SO_4 (sulfuric acid)
	OH + O_2 (in air)	
	Oxidants (wet surfaces)	

SOURCE: The National Acid Precipitation Assessment Program (1987), *Interim Assessment: The Causes and Effects of Acidic Deposition, Vol. 1, Executive Summary.* (Washington, DC: U.S. Government Printing Office), 1-3

by up to 10 million tons annually. Current emissions from utilities are estimated to be 17 million tons. Reductions are to occur in two phases. Phase I takes effect 1 January 1995 and mandates reductions by the dirtiest 111 power plants. Phase II takes effect five years later and sets a general emissions limit for utilities of 1.2 pounds of sulphur dioxide per million Btu (Lee 1991).

PHYSIOLOGICAL MECHANISMS

The acidity of rainfall is defined in terms of pH units, a measure of the concentration of hydrogen (H) ions. Rainfall is almost always more acid than is pure water, and variations exist from region to region. However, it is generally agreed that a pH of less than 5.6 is abnormally acidic (pH 7 is neutral and a reduction of one pH unit represents a tenfold increase in the concentration of H ions). A variety of pollutants contribute to this acidification: sulphur dioxide (SO_2) from coal-fired power plants, nitrogen oxides (NO_x) from power plants and automobiles, and volatile organic compounds (VOC) from automobiles and natural sources are the primary components. In the presence of sunlight, the reactions responsible for the production of sulphuric and nitric acid are shown in Table 2.

An added complication is the fact that acid rain is only part of the problem. Acid rain, or wet deposition, only constitutes about one half of the acid deposition resulting from air pollution. Dry deposition, either as particulate matter or as undissolved gases, is much harder to measure and tends to be deposited closer to the emission source. Because it is deposited directly onto the leaves of plants, dry deposition may be particularly important for heavily vegetated (particularly forested) areas. There may also be chemical interactions with soil constituents. The increased solubility of metals at lowered pH levels is one example of a toxicity problem that could arise.

A summary of the major known effects of air pollution is shown in Table 3. In general, these effects act either through direct contact with the leaves or as a result of changes in soil nutrient balance. However, it must be recognized that rigorous scientific proof of a causal relationship between air pollutants and forest decline has only been established for ozone; the causality for other pollutants is still circumstantial or limited (Crowling 1989).

For instance, a variety of pine species are particularly sensitive to ozone. The death of Ponderosa and Jeffrey pine in the San Bernadino National Forest occurs where twenty-four-hour ozone levels exceed 0.05 parts per million from May to September. Ozone enters the stomata of leaves and needles, particularly when the trees are enveloped in mist. Damage to wall membranes of mesophyll cells, which contain chlorophyll, results in an inhibition of photosynthesis, reduced carbohydrate production, and stunted growth. Seedling experiments suggest that ozone is reducing the growth of most conifer and hardwood forests in the eastern United States (Mackenzie and El-Ashry 1988:14-17).

Two other effects have also been attributed to ozone. McLaughlin (1987) has suggested that the reduction in carbohydrate storage experienced in high ozone concentrations is exacerbated by an associated increase in plant respiration during night hours. In addition, ozone accelerates the normal leaching of nutrients from leaves. This is particularly severe where light intensity is high and nutrients scarce (Mackenzie and El-Ashry 1988:17). Thus, ozone damage is likely to be greatest in exposed (high elevation) areas on nutrient-poor soils.

In contrast, acid deposition appears to have its greatest effect after contact with soils. However, at very low pH, sulphuric acid is known to cause significant foliar damage, especially as it dries onto the leaves. In red spruce, acid deposition can damage the stomatal wax plugs that regulate water loss and facilitate gas exchange. There is also evidence of nutrient leaching from needles as hydrogen from rainfall is exchanged for magnesium, calcium, potassium, and sodium in the needles (Mackenzie and El-Ashry 1988:18). Again, these effects will be exacerbated on nutrient-poor soils where the roots cannot take up nutrients fast enough to compensate for the foliar loss.

On contact with soils, acid deposition depletes nutrients by replacing calcium, magnesium, and potassium with hydrogen ions.

TABLE 3

Hypotheses for forest decline

Effect	Causative factor	Mechanism
Depression of photosynthesis	Ozone Hydrogen peroxide in clouds	Diffusion into leaves and oxidation of cell wall membranes, causing destruction of chlorophyll-containing foliar cells
Leaching of foliar nutrients	Acid deposition	Hydrogen ions replace cations of calcium, potassium and magnesium faster than compensatory uptake through roots
Reduced frost hardiness	Nitrogen oxides	Excessive foliar nitrogen uptake in high elevation conifers may extend growing season and delay cold hardening
Leaching of soil nutrients	Acid deposition	Replacement of base cations from the root zone by hydrogen and aluminum ions
Aluminum toxicity to roots	Acid deposition	Where calcium to aluminum ratios are low, death of fine roots may lead to water and nutrient stress
Reduced microbiological action	Acid deposition	Reduction of litter breakdown, soil structure formation and conversion of plant nutrients to available forms

SOURCE: The National Acid Precipitation Assessment Program (1987), *Interim Assessment: The Causes and Effects of Acidic Deposition, Vol. IV, Effects of Acidic Deposition* (Washington DC: Government Printing Office), 7-23 to 7-25

This effect is particularly severe in soils that are already acid and therefore have little buffering capacity. A deficiency in any one of these minerals will have specific impacts on a tree's health. Magnesium is required for photosynthesis. Under conditions of deficiency in conifers, it moves from the older to the newer outer needles and the older needles turn yellow and eventually die. Potassium is needed for both root and shoot growth and limited availability results in a similar yellowing of older needles. In contrast, calcium, which is needed for cell wall development, is not mobile and the growth of new shoots and roots is reduced under limiting conditions; foliage is lost from the ends of the branches (Mackenzie and El-Ashry 1988:24).

These conditions of nutrient deficiency are exacerbated where concentrations of aluminum are high. Mobilization of aluminum under acid conditions inhibits root uptake of calcium and magnesium and impairs water transport within the tree. This has the added effect of increasing sensitivity to drought. In red spruce seedlings exposed to high concentrations of aluminum, foliar nutrients were depressed and root growth was stunted, making the trees more susceptible to soil-borne pathogens (Mackenzie and El-Ashry 1988:20). Toxic levels of aluminum and iron are thought to account for a 90 per cent reduction in fine root biomass in a German beech forest during a dry summer (McLaughlin 1987).

In small quantities, addition of nitrogen to soils may be beneficial in exerting a fertilizing effect. However, excess nitrogen can be harmful if vigorous growth leads to a deficiency of other nutrients. In addition, there is evidence that there is an increase in shoot to root ratios, especially with rapid absorption of nitrogen through the leaves. This would be expected to increase susceptibility of the trees to moisture stress. Another consequence of this fertilizing effect appears to be increased sensitivity to cold damage as a result of delayed winter hardening (McLaughlin 1987).

McLaughlin suggests that the effects of air pollutants fall into three general categories:

(1) direct effects on carbon assimilation by changing the rate of photosynthesis, respiration, and translocation and by altering the pattern of storage, mobilization, and utilization of energy reserves;

(2) altered plant-water relations as a result of reduced uptake through roots and changes in transportation patterns and disruption of foliar water control mechanisms;

(3) nutrient disturbances as a result of altered availability of nutrients and increased foliar leaching.

Of course, all of these factors are inter-related. A reduction in carbon assimilation will affect the rate of growth and, therefore, the development of a healthy root system. This, in turn, will depress water and nutrient uptake independent of any direct effects attributable to soil conditions.

EMERGING CONSENSUS ON FOREST DAMAGE FROM ACID RAIN AND OZONE

Scientists now generally agree that there is no single causal factor that is responsible for forest damage. Instead, there are a variety of human-made causes interacting with natural events and processes. Together, they induce stresses in forests that culminate in the decline of both individual species and whole ecosystems. The multitude of long-term changes in affected areas result in a formidable web of interactions, all of which makes the research task very complex and time consuming (Klein and Perkins 1987).

The above discussion suggests that the problems associated with upsetting the physiological balance within the tree when, for example, root growth is not adequate to support the amount of foliage produced are linked to many factors that can produce forest decline. Thus, as summarized in Table 1, many factors can contribute to forest decline, and it is usually impossible to establish a direct cause of tree death. It is clear, however, that air pollution is a contributing factor.

Some specific examples have been given of tree damage as a result of exposure to a specific pollutant. Many such examples exist where laboratory experiments have established, under controlled conditions, the effects of individual pollutants on a specific species under specific conditions. Unfortunately, it is not always easy to extrapolate to a mixed forest growing under different conditions of climate and soil. Invariably, it is a combination of atmospheric conditions combined with specific climatic or nutrient conditions that damage the trees. A good case in point is the situation as it is thought to have unfolded in West Germany.

Exposure to high concentrations of ozone may have damaged cellular membranes in leaves, resulting in increased water loss, nutrient leaching by acid rain, and photosensitization. The latter, under poor soil conditions and high light intensities, leads to a reduction in chlorophyll content and needle yellowing. The resulting depression in photosynthetic activity results in reduced carbohydrate production and loss of root growth. The latter, together with soil acidification, results in reduced nutrient uptake. This, in turn, causes migration of magnesium and potassium from the older to the newer needles, with death of the needles progressing from the inner to the outer parts of the branches. The trees also appear to have an increased incidence of fungal disease (Krause et al. 1983).

As with other environmental problems, it is difficult to compare the costs of controlling pollution levels with the benefits accrued. This is especially true when the specific effects of pollutants cannot be quantified, and the pollution is being dispersed over a wide area a considerable distance from its source. There is no doubt that acid deposition and ozone from both industrial plants and mobile sources are harming many of our ecosystems. Even if the value of lost timber could be estimated, this would still be only a fraction of the total loss when the importance of forests for wildlife, recreation, and watershed management are considered.

The fact that most forest damage assessments to date have evaluated only the effects of single stress factors on forest health means that realistic management information is not available. This approach must be replaced by studies that examine the 'sum of the stresses and their interactions and feedbacks within the complex functioning of natural ecosystems' (Likens 1985). Likens himself, in his study of the forest ecology of the Hubbard Brook Valley, has demonstrated this methodology. But his study also illustrates how complex and resource intensive such an approach is. The same integrative strategy is called for at the policy level.

If there is a single policy lesson to be drawn from the issue of forest damage in Europe and North America, it is the need to change strategy from one focused on control of single pollutants, individual effects, and small political subdivisions (states, provinces, or Lander) to a more comprehensive approach. A strategy encompassing various pollutants is needed, and control measures are best implemented on a large regional scale. The United States, Canada, and Europe need to move from single-pollutant controls to 'an integrated (multiple pollutant and regional) program for management of air quality' (Crowling 1989). Such an approach to policy makes sense not only for forests but also for human health, historical buildings, and the ecosystem as a whole. Yet, while logic dictates comprehensiveness, practical considerations will prevent us from going very far and very fast in this direction. The experience from Europe and North America shows that multi-media, multi-jurisdictional policies are difficult, because legal, social, and economic differences between political jurisdictions stand in the way.

EFFECTS OF GLOBAL WARMING ON FORESTS

As we reach the end of the twentieth century, the scale and diversity of human interventions in natural systems has reached levels that cause global change. Thirty years ago, when environmental risks became a concern, the key industrial countries started by regulating pollution in proximity to industrial installations and in large urban concentrations. Acid rain moved environmental policy from the local to the regional level. Global warming forces us to expand our understanding of pollution and of policy measures to deal with it to the global scale.

So far, global warming has not occurred. Yet its precursor – increased concentration of greenhouse gases in the atmosphere – is in place and has been measured. Studies of climate changes in the past have shown precise correlations between temperature and carbon dioxide concentrations in the atmosphere. Above all, the theory underlying global warming is solid and accepted by the majority of atmospheric scientists (International Panel for Climate Change (IPCC) 1990). Therefore, the probability of human-made global warming is high.

Warming of the earth is predicted to result from steadily increasing emissions of carbon dioxide (and several other so-called greenhouse gases). In contrast to the other forms of pollution discussed above, carbon dioxide is a life-supporting substance and an essential raw material for photosynthesis in green plants. It only becomes a pollutant when its concentration in the atmosphere increases so that it can trap radiant heat from the sun near the earth's surface and thus cause the temperature to rise. Measurements taken since 1958 show a steady increase of carbon dioxide in the atmosphere. Compared to pre-industrial times, almost 30 per cent higher concentrations have been reached, and scientists predict that the concentration of carbon dioxide will have doubled by 2030 or 2050. For the next hundred years an increase in average global temperature of 0.3 degrees C per decade is expected (International Panel for Climate Change, 1990b).

Should these predictions materialize, the temperature of the earth will reach higher levels than those experienced in previous human history. And perhaps even more importantly, the rate of change may be too fast for allowing ecosystems, in particular forests, to adapt.

The predicted temperature increase will not be evenly distributed.

Temperatures will increase less close to the equator and more close
to the poles. Global climate models project that global warming will
be up to 2.5 times higher than the global average in high latitudes (60
- 90 degrees) and up to 1.4 times higher in the middle latitudes (30 -
60 degrees). The departure from the global norm will be most pronounced during winters and somewhat less during summers (WMO-
UNEP 1988). Forests in middle and high latitudes are likely to be severely and adversely affected. Highly specialized species – those
with very specific habitat and food requirements – are likely to be
most vulnerable. As a result of global warming, species are likely to
become extinct at an accelerating rate. (The summary of forest impacts in this and the following paragraphs is based on the work of an
expert group at the 1991 Woodlands Conference, HARC 1991.)

Tree species are likely to be especially sensitive in the warmer and
drier parts of their ranges, particularly in soils that are thin, coarse,
and in upland areas. Where soil water is depleted by an increase in
evaporative demand, trees will be under stress and rapid changes
can be expected. Ecotones – transitions between ecosystems – are
likely to be especially sensitive.

Increased temperatures, sustained over a period of years, could
produce a widespread, catastrophic, drought-induced decline in the
world's temperate and boreal forests. Widespread drought would
likely result in increased incidences of disease and large catastrophic fires in the world's forests. The subsequent release of
methane and carbon dioxide from the decaying vegetation into the
atmosphere would add significantly to the atmosphere's burden of
greenhouse gases. The natural migration of species may be impaired by the rapidity of climate change. Extensive development
(freeways, cities, agriculture) may act as barriers for migrating species.

As a forested region dries out, other regional resources will be affected. Forests using up moisture in the soil will reduce volume in
nearby streams, thus killing fish and causing water quality to decline. Upland soil erosion and nutrient loss would increase sediments and nutrient loadings downstream, and suspended particulates from forest fires would increase air pollution.

Climatic alterations beyond mere changes in temperature may be
particularly strong in the tropics. But our ability to assess the possible effects of global warming on tropical forests is much poorer
than is our ability to make these assessments for temperate, more
northern forests. Droughts or lengthy dry seasons are likely to dras-
tically alter tropical regions. A recent simulation of climate change

indicated that the Amazon rain forest is likely to suffer significant decline as a result of the lengthening of its dry seasons. Historically, natural ecosystems have responded to long-term climatic change with migration of individual species at differential rates. This implies dispersal and establishment on the leading edge of the forest and decline on the retreating edge that is induced by competitive displacement or drought. But current, human-induced climatic changes appear likely to occur over a time period too short to allow trees and other plants to migrate. Plant migration is also limited by human-made barriers to migration. Today, natural habitats are often islands among agricultural and urban landscapes that impede the natural dispersal of vegetation, thus blocking migration.

Declines in tropical rain forests have ecological implications for other regions. The number of migrating birds that summer in temperate and boreal regions and winter in the tropics could decline precipitously, thereby affecting predation on insects and transport of seeds as well as pollination in both parts of their range. The deforestation of tropical rain forests can directly alter regional climates, because the loss of vegetation cover can significantly reduce regional rainfall. For example, 50 per cent of the rainfall in the Amazon region has been reported to come from the evapotranspiration of the forest itself. Decline of forests in tropical highlands (mountains) will not only influence the whole hydrological cycle but will add to massive soil erosion, flooding, and silting of natural and human-made water channels in downstream areas.

As with other effects of global warming, forest decline will pose the biggest problems for developing countries. Rich countries, where managed forests have long been maintained, can afford to replant forests with species that are more adjusted to new climatic conditions. Poor countries, where natural forests dominate, will not have the resources to undertake massive reforestation projects. On a worldwide scale, the importance of forests will increase, because they act as a sink for carbon dioxide. If large areas were reverted to forests, at least a partial offset of the greenhouse effect would become possible. The International Panel on Climate Change working group on response strategies sees value in this approach but warns that 'currently available policies, technologies, and practices in forestry ... are likely to be only partially effective in reducing the predicted growth emissions' (IPCC 1991:78). Wide-ranging changes in management and policy would be called for. Botkin, in his winning Mitchell Prize paper, suggests that global warming may force us to revise our approach to forests, forest management, and nature by better appreciating the constantly changing nature of ecosystems and the need to take into account natural as well as human change factors:

> [Recent studies on forests in the Great Lakes region] reveal a very different forest from that of nineteenth century writings [by the scholars who framed our approach to forest management]: a forest that is continually changing at many temporal scales ... Our management of [forest] resources has been predicated on a constancy and simple kind of stability of nature. Today, as we realize that we may have set in motion, through global warming, environmental changes that will dwarf those of nineteenth century human activities, we still pretend that the environment, unless directly altered by our hands, will maintain a constant condition, or if disturbed from that constant condition, will return to its former state of equilibrium. A new approach is needed. (Botkin forthcoming)

CONCLUSION

Both acid deposition and global warming pose difficult policy challenges. Part of the difficulty results from the technical complexity of the issues. It takes time and resources to understand the causes, pathways, and effects of pollution. This process is well underway. It is doubtful, however, that the scientific effort provides the guidance needed by policy makers. The u.s. National Acid Precipitation Assessment Program provides a sobering illustration of this point. The program had been started with the explicit aim of preparing a solid scientific foundation for policy design. Critics charged at the time that the Reagan administration supported the program primarily in order to buy time and delay action. But when Congress and the Bush administration were finally ready to act, a different problem emerged. NAPAP had become so exhaustive and rigorous that results were not yet available. In particular, the economic analysis of different control options had been postponed because the scientists in control of the program decided to analyze facts rather than options. One of the key questions for policy makers was the relationship between emissions and acid deposition – was it linear or not? NAPAP had developed a large Regional Acid Deposition Model to answer the policy makers' question. There would be a much stronger justification for new controls if it could be shown that a reduction in sulphur dioxide emission would lead to a similar reduction in acid precipitation. The model has been described as a modeller's dream and a beautiful piece of science, but it turned out to be much too complex to help the process of policy development. As a result, the control options finally endorsed into legislation were developed without much benefit from NAPAP research (Roberts 1991).

Hopefully, this lesson will be remembered in the case of global warming. At present, the major policy effort in response to the threat of global warming is focused on negotiating an international convention aimed at stabilizing and, eventually, reducing greenhouse gas emission. This would be accomplished by setting emission quotas for each nation, allowing for some increase in emissions for developing countries whose energy use lags behind industrialized nations. Capping or reducing emissions would be a way to get to the root of the global warming problem – the rapidly increasing use of fossil fuels.

An alternative way to deal with the problem of global warming would be to rebuild the world's energy system around non-fossil fuels. Eventually, because of the limited availability of conventional fuels, new energy sources will have to take the place of coal, gas, and oil. Nuclear energy, had it not been so badly managed in several countries, should by now have been ready to supply a steadily increasing part of the world's energy needs. Other sources of alternative energy are still far from technical or economic feasibility. But there is also the more general question underlying global change: If global warming is the prototype of other global problems, can we afford not to act on the most fundamental cause threatening the future of the planet? World population now numbers 5.8 billion. Another doubling of the world's population is projected for 2050. At present, this perspective remains entirely outside the discussion of the global warming convention.

There are still other problems with a world convention. The complexity of negotiating, implementing, and enforcing binding national quotas is mind boggling and probably beyond the capacity of existing political institutions. It is already clear, after two years of intensive negotiations, that the draft convention prepared for adoption at the 1992 World Environment and Development Conference in Brazil will be little more than a declaration of intent. Other measures are clearly needed. A grassroots strategy, built around the most critical risks different regions are likely to experience, can appeal to the self-interest of individual regions in preparing for the future.

A number of arguments support action on global warming short of and in addition to a full-fledged international convention. In many places the results of climate change are likely to exacerbate existing environmental and resource problems. The report of the second Villach Conference urged, therefore, that climate change be controlled in the context of other environmental problems in a particular area. 'Climatic change will not occur in isolation. Increasing amounts of atmospheric and aquatic pollutants can be expected from urban-industrial growth. The response to climatic changes will be affected by these increased pollutants. The importance of these interactions and the need to investigate them further cannot be overemphasized' (UNEP-WMO 1988).

Regions may be in a good position to deal with climate change in a broader context. Regional actions to prepare for and adjust to climate change may be less traumatic than international agreements involving radical changes in economic activities such as energy production and utilization. Over time, a useful division of labour can emerge between international and regional actions. Policies aimed at slowing, or eventually stopping, global warming will require concerted international action. At the other extreme, most adaptive policies will be regional in nature, because they respond to particular regional vulnerabilities and opportunities (Schmandt 1991).

The specific concerns of forestry would be an important component of regional greenhouse policies. With respect to agriculture and forestry, the 1991 Woodlands Conference recommended maintaining and increasing the diversity of ecosystems, crop varieties, technologies, and farming systems and strengthening the regenerative process as keys to reducing vulnerability to global warming. These recommendations may be broken down as follows:

(1) Policies should emphasize the protection of biodiversity through species and ecosystem conservation programs. Special conservation programs for habitats in which the microclimate is cooler than the regional macroclimate are needed.

(2) Crop genetic diversity and respect for traditional agricultural knowledge and technology can be enhanced by developing flexible agricultural systems and options for new food supplies as well as by recycling and local resource regeneration.

(3) Each region should monitor its forests, streams, and soils for early drought warning signs. Should drought occur, policy measures to reduce water use should be implemented.

(4) Changes in forests and agricultural systems must be linked when assessing the impacts of climate change. These linkages can be studied by examining the impacts of climate change on agroforestry. Agroforestry can utilize a traditional system that combines aspects of agriculture with forest management procedures.

(5) To overcome the barriers to natural ecosystem migration, poli-

cies should be aimed at introducing into these systems new species that can expand buffer zones in preserved or managed areas. Transplanting or assisting in the migration of species might be useful in commercial fishing and agriculture and might save some endangered species (HARC 1991).

CHAPTER TWO

Forest-Climate Interactions: Implications for Tropical and Boreal Forests

B.I. Kronberg and W.S. Fyfe

INTRODUCTION

Forests and climate are inextricably linked. Forests continually communicate with the atmosphere and, in so doing, regulate exchanges of energy and materials between forest ecosystems and the atmosphere. Vast amounts of solar energy are dispersed by forests via physical processes (absorption, reflection, and evapotranspiration) and biogeochemical processes (carbon fixation, decomposition of biotic materials, and evapotranspiration). Forests are the major components of the continental biosphere, and forest habitats support the most diverse reservoir of land plants and animals.

Since the middle of this century exploitation of forests for commercial purposes has disrupted forest ecosystems at rates which greatly exceed those for ecosystem construction by natural processes. In some tropical and boreal forest regions, removal of original forest exceeds 50 per cent. This level of deforestation already may be affecting processes by which energy and materials are exchanged between the atmosphere and the land surface, thereby influencing climate. The concomitant losses to the diversity of the biosphere are incalculable.

In this article we wish to review the state of knowledge of interactions between the atmosphere and the tropical and boreal forests. We underscore the need for realistic forest policies which ensure that rates of forest disruption are balanced against rates of ecosystem recovery. Given the present meagre knowledge of how tropical and boreal forests function, this is a most challenging and urgent task for all nations, especially those economically dependent on forest resources.

COMPARING TROPICAL AND BOREAL BIOMES

Forests are the most extensive continental biomes (life zones). The tropical and boreal regions contain ~35 per cent of the world's forests, and, together, they cover at least 10 million square kilometres (1 billion hectares) of closed high forests and an equal amount of open woodland and modified forests (Bruenig 1987). Boreal and tropical forests evolved on geological timescales of hundreds to thousands of years under very different conditions. The boreal forests were repeatedly devastated during the past 2 million years by glacial advances and retreats. The impact of these geologically recent climate changes on tropical forests is less certain. Palynological and geochemical evidence indicates that during the last ice age savannahs extensively replaced forests in Amazonia (Prance 1978), and in some amazonian regions aridity obtained (Kronberg et al. 1991). However, tropical climate changes were not uniform, as illustrated in the Malesian Archipelago where humid climates prevailed (Bruenig 1987).

Both forest ecosystems sustain themselves by positive feedback between their components. For example, large areas of tropical forests, such as in Amazonia, overlie highly weathered terrains which have not been geologically renewed for millions of years and, therefore, which have very low soil nutrient reserves. This limitation on biomass productivity is compensated for by the capacity of these tropical forests to store and recycle nutrients within the biomass. Boreal forests, for very different reasons, also have limited access to nutrients due to frozen ground in some places and to very thin soils or coarse grained glacial sediments in other places. Further limitations on biomass productivity in the boreal biome include low temperatures, long periods of moisture stress, wind, fire, and insects. It is this array of inter-related limiting factors and the higher degree of small scale variation in the under, middle, and overstorey vegetation mosaic that make boreal systems difficult to model. For example, northern tree species are found in almost any mixture in a range of habitats, mainly by being wind pollinated and not depending on other species, such as insects or birds, for pollination (Woodwell 1989).

With respect to biogeochemical cycles, boreal forests store significantly more carbon in their soils and associated peatlands than do tropical forests. This makes the boreal biome much more important as a global carbon sink. If the current climate warming continues (Folland et al. 1990), release of volatile carbon compounds from boreal regions could have a significant impact on the atmospheric carbon budget. Tropical forests have key roles in global water and energy cycles.

ROLE OF FORESTS IN REGULATING FLOWS OF ENERGY AND WATER

The boreal forests and, especially, the tropical forests are important in regulating regional and global water and energy cycles. In forested tropical regions (latitudes between 12° N and 10° S), large quantities of latent heat are produced as water is vaporized mainly from leaf surfaces. This heat is subsequently released to the atmosphere during cloud formation. At these latitudes, latent heat is the largest source of atmospheric heat and is derived largely from air masses rising over South America, Africa, and the major islands in the Far East (Newell 1971). Furthermore, tropical regions provide most of the sensible heat (i.e., heat exchanged as air passes over the Earth's surface) that is transported poleward and balances negative radiation losses at higher latitudes (Molion and Betancurt 1981; Molion 1990).

In their semi-quantitative comparison of energy fluxes from different ground covers, Molion and Betancurt show that exchanging forest for other land covers (such as cultivated plants, pasture, or bare soil) perturbs both sensible and latent heat fluxes to the atmosphere. Forest removal results in more direct solar radiation being reflected (i.e., the albedo is increased) and, therefore, less energy available for transpiration and evaporation of intercepted rain. It is estimated that latent heat fluxes from bare soils are typically less than half those from forest. In Amazonia, for example, forests may evapotranspire ~50 per cent of rain reaching the forest canopy (Salati and Vose 1984). Evapotranspiration, typically, has three components: transpiration by plants, soil moisture evaporation, and evaporation of rainfáll intercepted by forest cover. (The last component refers to rain which returns to the atmosphere as water vapour, without reaching the forest floor.) Forest floors also have high capacities for water retention, which may be profoundly altered by forest removal.

Widespread deforestation sets in motion a chain of events. Forest clearing immediately increases surface runoff. Excess waters are diverted to rivers and (eventually) oceans and permanently lost to the system. Concomitantly, there are reduced rates of evapotranspiration and soil moisture recharge and precipitation. This results in diminishing water fluxes to the atmosphere and less cloud formation.

The overall effect is an increase in solar radiation and less total water in the system. Measurements by Schubart (1977) in Central Amazonia demonstrate a tenfold decrease in soil permeability five years after converting forested land to pasture. Furthermore, in the deforested areas, the upper soil layer had been eroded by 10 cm. (The natural rate of soil formation is ~3 cm per century.)

The forest canopy protects the soil surface from the mechanical impact of raindrops. In its absence, particle aggregates are more easily broken down and smaller particles seal soil pores resulting in lower infiltration rates, which may already have been diminished by intensive agricultural practices. Increases in overland flows are accompanied by substantial increases in soil erosion. In forests, interception of raindrops by the canopy diminishes their kinetic energy, thereby reducing surface water flow rates and increasing residence times of water molecules in contact with plant components (roots, stems, leaves, etc.). In their studies of erosion rates (sediment yields) as a function of rainfall and ground cover, Langbein and Schumm (1958) report sediment yields as much as three times higher from land under grass cover than those from forest-covered lands, which received four times the amount of rainfall as did the grasslands. In Amazonia the extensive forest removal over the past fifteen years in the Madeira River watershed is reflected in the threefold increase in its sediment load, measured by Meade and his colleagues in 1979, over that reported by Gibbs in 1967.

In boreal ecosystems, energy and hydrologic processes are further complicated by snow and frost dynamics (Persson 1980). The contribution of evapotranspiration to rain inputs will be less important than it is in tropical forests, and precipitation will be derived mainly from moisture advected into the system (Molion and Betancurt 1981). The coupling of atmospheric processes to those operating in the boreal forest-lake ecosystem mosaic is emphasized in a rare twenty-year record of climatic, hydrologic, and ecological observations (Schindler et al. 1990). The data show increases of 2°C, over the past two decades, in air and water temperatures and an increase of the ice-free season by three weeks. Higher than normal evaporation and lower than normal precipitation were accompanied by decreased rates of water renewal in lakes and increased areas of forest destroyed by fires. (The area of forest that burned in 1989, 6.4 million hectares, exceeded by approximately twenty times that which burned, in the same region, between 1950 and 1978.) In catchments affected by fire, increases in wind velocities, water surface transparency, and exposure to wind of lakes caused changes in lake thermal structure and in numbers of certain aquatic organisms. (Increases in transparency of lake waters, due to lower inputs from forests of dissolved, coloured organic matter, resulted in increased penetration of solar energy.) Lake chemistry was affected by a decline in water renewal and increased inputs from burned forested watersheds as well as from wetlands with lower water tables. These perturbations to boreal-lake ecosystem complexes are anticipated from large scale forest losses by clear-cutting and could reinforce regional climate changes already underway.

FOREST-ATMOSPHERE INTERACTIONS AND THE GLOBAL CARBON CYCLE

Forests cover one-third of the global land surfaces and their associated ecosystems comprise two-thirds of the total terrestrial carbon pool (Reichle 1975). The amount of carbon stored in global trees (~750 billion tons) is complemented by about twice as much carbon stored in forest soils (Houghton and Woodwell 1989). The atmosphere contains roughly the same amount of carbon as does the Earth's forests, which they sequester by using atmospheric carbon dioxide in the photosynthetic production of plant material. Through this process and the concomitant process of respiration ~100 billion tons of carbon, or ~14 per cent of the total atmospheric carbon content, is exchanged each year between forests and the atmosphere.

The most direct evidence for the influence of forests on the global carbon cycle is the observed annual sinusoidal oscillation in the concentration curve of atmospheric carbon dioxide, which is more pronounced in northern hemisphere measurements than in those from southern hemisphere stations (Ember et al. 1986; and Figure 1). These oscillations are attributed to the annual cycle of metabolism in seasonal forests. In spring and summer the dominance of photosynthesis is reflected in the downward swing of the oscillation. The atmospheric carbon dioxide concentration increases again in fall and winter when respiration dominates. The influence of seasonal dynamics of northern forests on atmospheric carbon dioxide concentrations is underscored by the rapid (<1 month) response in atmospheric levels of carbon dioxide (Moore and Bolin 1987). The influence of boreal forests is evident from the much greater amplitude (8 ppm) observed at Point Barrow, Alaska (71° N) over that (3 ppm) observed at Mauna Loa, Hawaii (20° N) (D'Arrigo et al. 1987). These researchers' results also indicate that the combined boreal forests of North America and Eurasia account for 50 per cent of the mean seasonal carbon dioxide amplitude at Point Barrow. Throughout the present decade a consistent year by year increase in amplitude has

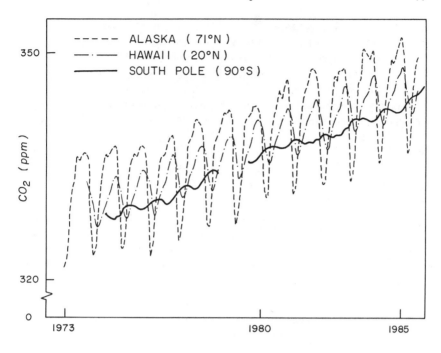

FIGURE 1
Atmospheric concentration of CO_2

been measured (Woodwell 1987) and, presumably, is caused by changes in rates of photosynthesis and respiration in the seasonal northern temperate and boreal forests. Understanding the factors affecting these recent changes in the seasonal signal, apparently due to forest-atmosphere interaction, requires more detailed knowledge than we now have of the response of forests to changes in their external environment.

Another uncertainty is the size of the soil carbon pools in tropical and boreal forests as well as the flux rates of carbon into and out of these major terrestrial carbon pools. Soil carbon content appears to decrease significantly with increases in the ratio of temperature to precipitation (Brown and Lugo 1982). These factors would account for the smaller amounts of carbon stored in tropical forest soils than in those of boreal forests. In boreal regions, the high ratio of precipitation to evapotranspiration has contributed to the creation of vast areas of peatlands. The effects of climate on wetland dynamics and peat accumulation are not well understood. Northern wetland terrains, between 50-70° N, contribute ~63 million tons per year, or ~60 per cent, of global methane wetland emissions to the atmosphere

(Matthew and Fung 1987). Permafrost depth may be a key factor in future trends in northern wetland emissions of carbon compounds to the atmosphere. During the past forty years, there is evidence from peatlands, in the discontinuous permafrost zone, for increased thawing (Ovendene 1989).

It is not known exactly how much carbon is stored in forests. Some models suggest that the boreal forest biomass may be expanding (Tans et al. 1990). However, there is no indication of the mechanisms involved. The further uncertainty of deforestation rates makes it impossible to know how current changes in these ecosystems are affecting atmospheric carbon dioxide levels (Hileman 1989). From a global perspective there is no doubt that terrestrial biomass is being reduced and that the greatest reductions are those involving forests (Whittaker and Likens 1975). The chief reduction process is replacement of older forests with younger growth. Forest carbon contents are further reduced by decay of soil organic matter following clearing.

GLOBAL CARBON CYCLE LINKAGES TO OTHER BIOGEOCHEMICAL CYCLES

Biotic processes are mediated by reactions involving at least twenty-five macro, micro, and trace nutrient elements (Mertz 1981). The source of most of these elements (except C, N, O, H) are the rocks at the earth's surface. Nutrient elements are released as rock-forming minerals (mainly feldspars) are changed, by chemical weathering reactions, to clay minerals, and soil waters are concomitantly enriched in nutrients. The biosphere's intertwining of several cycles of elements links biomass productivity to soil fertility, which is controlled by regional geologic history – in particular, the time elapsed since the last regional renewal of land surfaces with volcanic, glacial, or alluvial debris (Kronberg and Fyfe 1989). Plant roots retain nutrients from soil waters, which continue to be charged with nutrients until weathering advances sufficiently for soil waters to lose contact with primary rock and nutrient-rich clay minerals. Intensely weathered soils are infertile and are characterized by high proportions of iron, aluminum, and silicon oxides (Kronberg and Melfi 1987).

Most tropical forests, such as those of the lower Amazon Basin, overlie highly infertile soils (Kronberg et al. 1979). To accommodate the scarcity of nutrients, these forests have evolved mechanisms for nutrient retention and recycling, by which nutrient flows are closed within the biomass (Jordan 1985). Small losses to ground waters are replenished by nutrient additions from rain and aerosols. Fragile rainforest nutrient reserves have profound consequences for the use of these terrains for large scale agroforestry. Small scale agroforestry has sustained inhabitants of lowland tropical regions for centuries (Nye and Greenland 1960). The difference in scales is crucial. In small clearings used for 'shifting' cultivation, nutrients supplied by biological debris remaining after forest burning and clearing are sufficient for a few harvests. These small disruptions to local ecosystems are repaired naturally after several years of fallow. However, in large scale agroforestry, ecosystem disruptions are irreparable. Sustainable agroforestry is also practised successfully in Amazonia on extensive river floodplains, covering ~10 per cent of the basin, where soils are renewed each year by the deposition of nutrient-rich sediments from andean regions.

In boreal forests, nutrient dynamics are also complex (Bruenig 1987). Colder soil temperatures depress microbial activity and nutrient flow rates relative to those in tropical forest ecosystems. The main feature of boreal forest soils is their large reserves of nutrients, particularly nitrogen, held in litter and other organic material (Wein and MacLean 1983). The accumulation of humus in northern forests removes nutrients from circulation, and nutrient supply may become limiting to plant growth. In northern forests, spontaneous fires are important in nutrient cycling. Post-fire effects include changes in plant growth and species composition, which may be dramatic due to increased availability of soil nutrients and light. In areas affected by permafrost, fire is especially important for increasing nutrient availability. There is little information on how post-fire conditions affect nitrogen fixation and other processes associated with the 'plant-microbiological-litter-soil-organic matter' interface. While volatilization losses may be large, increases in soil temperature and availability of metal nutrients may result in higher rates of decomposition and nitrogen fixation (Wein and MacLean 1983).

RESPONSE OF TROPICAL AND BOREAL FORESTS TO GLOBAL CHANGE

Over the past century, human activities have caused imbalances in natural biochemical cycles and have set in motion a global experiment. The principal activities involved are fossil fuel combustion, dispersal of synthetic chemicals into the open environment, biomass burning, forest destruction, and soil degradation. That this experiment is underway is evident from the progressive changes in composition of the global atmosphere, specifically in the constantly increasing levels of approximately thirty radiatively-active (greenhouse) gases such as carbon dioxide, methane, carbon monoxide, oxides of nitrogen and sulphur, and chlorofluorocarbons. These modifications to the atmosphere have the potential for changing Earth's climate by affecting atmospheric processes which control Earth surface temperatures (Bach 1988).

Climate change predictions for the middle to high latitudes of the northern hemisphere agree on a warming of ~5° Celsius over the next one to three decades (Manabe and Wetherald 1986). These temperature changes coupled with increases in atmospheric carbon dioxide could, at first glance, be assumed to enhance tree growth rates in the northern temperate and boreal forests. Further analysis illustrates the complexity of the interactions of factors affecting biotic processes in forests. Rates of photosynthesis and respiration are affected by the availability of energy, water, inorganic nutrients, and changes in temperature. The effect of atmospheric carbon dioxide concentration is difficult to assess (Mooney et al. 1991). A major uncertainty concerns changes in net carbon storage in forests – that is, how will changes in atmospheric temperatures and chemistry affect the ratio of carbon inputs via photosynthesis to carbon exports via respiration and decomposition processes? Reconnaissance studies of ecosystem response indicate that respiration is more sensitive to temperature increases than is photosynthesis (Woodwell 1987). There is also tentative evidence that enhanced respiration rates may be releasing more carbon than is being photosynthetically fixed from northern ecosystems (T.A. Stone personal communication). The questions regarding changes in carbon balance in forests is an urgent one, as forests may account for as much as two-thirds of global photosynthesis (Kramer 1981).

Current climate models indicate that the response of major ecosystems will not be uniform in either space or time. Our ability to predict responses of forests to global change is limited by our fragmentary knowledge of natural biogeodynamical interactions in forests as well as of quantitative information on the rate and extent of deforestation. Boreal forests are more dependent on climate than are most other ecosystems. The tentative information available indicates a northward shift in the northern boundary of the boreal forest by 100 to 700 km, and by 250 to 900 km in the southern boundary. Predicted biomass productivity changes include decreases from normal by 2-12 per cent for southern locations and increases from normal of ~50 per cent in the northern zone (Environment Canada 1989). One model of the impact on bioproductivity in boreal forests of induced climate warming, resulting from a doubling in atmospheric carbon dioxide concentrations, shows the largest increase in growth in maritime boreal regions, such as Labrador, southern Greenland, Iceland, northern Fennoscandia, and around Bering Strait (Kauppi and Posch 1988). Growth in mid-continental northern forests is forecast to be affected by moisture stress. The general scenario, for northern mid-latitude land surfaces, of the effects of increases in atmospheric carbon dioxide and other trace gases would be reduced soil moisture (Mitchell and Warrilow 1987). Snowmelt, which replenishes soil moisture, would occur earlier and drying would occur in late spring when the land surface absorbs a large amount of solar energy because of strong insolation and the disappearance of snowcover with high albedo. It is unlikely that increased precipitation would offset moisture losses by higher evapotranspiration rates due to increased land surface temperatures.

The initial response of boreal forest ecosystems to carbon dioxide-induced climate change is likely to be greatest along ecosystems boundaries. At the southern boreal boundary, with cool temperate forests, models suggest that tree growth will be enhanced on soils which retain adequate water and will decline on moisture deficient soils (Pastor and Post 1988). Woodwell (1987) also draws attention to the sensitivity of the deciduous/conifer forest transition zone. The prediction is that the rate of northward migration of coniferous forests in response to climate warming would not be matched by the much slower rate of northward migration of deciduous forests.

A key question regards the rate of forest migration. One scenario is that weakened trees would fall prey to insects or disease and would be felled by storms or fires, which are expected to increase in frequency as climate changes (Roberts 1989). There is genetic evidence from the cool temperate/boreal transition that some species of trees are adapting to climate change by increasing their northern range, and their progeny no longer prefer conditions at their former southern boundaries (R. Farmer personal communication). Palaeo-ecological data from northern Scotland show that forests ~4,000 years ago migrated at a rate of 0.4 to 0.8 kilometres per year, which is considered to represent maximum values for forest migration rates (Gear and Huntley 1990). Pollen studies also indicate forest tree migration rates after the last ice age of 25 to 200 kilometres per century, depending on species. These rates are up to an order of magnitude lower than those predicted over the next few decades for the displacement of the southern boreal boundary by 250 to 900 kilometres (Melillo et al. 1990). Thus, it is possible that northward migrating deciduous forests will not keep pace with the northward retreat of boreal forest trees (Woodwell 1987).

Tropical deforestation could affect regional and global climate.

Forest clearing diminishes evapotranspiration and, hence, the return of moisture to the atmosphere. Models predict a lengthening of the dry season, which would make it difficult to replace tropical forests after large scale deforestation (Shukla et al. 1990). Biomass burning, especially in tropical regions, produces large amounts of trace gases and aerosols which play important roles in atmospheric chemistry and climate. These activities affect biogeochemical cycles and may be perturbing global nitrogen balances (Crutzen and Andreae 1990).

IMPLICATIONS FOR FOREST POLICY

Boreal Forests (Canada)

Forest policy for the 1990s and beyond should recognize that an estimated 65 per cent of original Canadian boreal forest has been logged over at least once, and that under current government-industry agreements a further 25 per cent of original forest has been made commercially available (McLaren 1990). Thus, it is possible that by 2010, only about 10 per cent of original Canadian boreal forest will be intact. The widespread degradation of boreal forests within less than two centuries raises questions regarding the commercial viability of these impoverished ecosystems. There is little information on regeneration of Canadian forests. It is estimated that almost half of the 1 million hectares of forest cleared each year fails to regenerate sufficiently to be considered economically viable (McLaren 1990). Part of the problem concerns monoculture tree-planting, which ignores the natural succession of under, middle, and overstorey vegetation, which distinguishes a forest from a tree plantation. It should be emphasized that the adequate assessment of ecosystem recovery and tree seedling survival rates requires decades of quantitative measurements.

A major obstacle to forest regrowth after clearing is the disruption of nutrient cycles and the loss of nutrient reserves by biomass removal, chemical and physical erosion, and losses to the atmosphere of volatile carbon and nitrogen compounds. There is little documented information on the recovery of deforested ecosystems. One study of northern hardwood forest regeneration indicates that six to eight decades may be needed to replace biomass and nutrients lost in harvesting (Likens et al. 1978). Another study from a North Carolina pine plantation showed that nitrogen losses during clearcutting may be diminished substantially by microbial immobilization if the forest floor is left intact (Vitousek and Matson 1984). Field studies by Perry and colleagues (1989) also show that disruption of plant-soil microbiosphere associations is a major factor in forest ecosystem degradation.

An important issue to be addressed by forest policy is the difference between stumpage fees levied on industry and the market price paid for forest products. This, combined with government subsidies to industry for pulp and paper plants, road building, and so on, indicates to society that virgin trees are cheap and discourages the efficient use of materials derived from trees. Stumpage fees should be increased and subsidies revised to reflect the real cost of raw materials, including forest regeneration times. Until this is achieved, the forest product recycling industry is unlikely to be profitable (Young 1991).

Appropriate forest management strategies are difficult to formulate in the absence of fundamental knowledge of how boreal forests function. For example, no long-term studies have been undertaken from which to establish suitable sizes for clearcuts, which will vary between sites and depend on factors such as slope, soil depth, and soil chemical and physical properties. There is an immediate need for the initiation of long-term field experiments in both virgin and perturbed boreal ecosystems. The failure to invest in long-term forest research experiments increases the likelihood that the forests of the twenty-first century will not be of sufficient quality to sustain the Canadian economy as they do presently. Contingency plans should be put in place to cover the possible rapid demise of northern forest ecosystems. If current climate warming trends continue into the next century, climate-induced ecosystem degradation will reinforce landscape changes caused by commercial forest clearing. These plans should address a range of initiatives from understanding patterns and processes in degraded ecosystems (for example, at what level can impoverished ecosystems be used commercially?) to restructuring the Canadian economy for the eventuality that, in the next century, forest ecosystems may no longer be a cornerstone of the economy.

The need for action is immediate because the demise of the forests could happen in as short a period as one to two decades (Kronberg 1991). Short-term action should include protection of old-growth forests. The suggestion that replacement of slow growing old-growth forest by faster growing younger, intensively managed forest would reduce atmospheric carbon dioxide levels has been addressed by Harmon and his colleagues (1990). The critical factor is the amount of carbon stored within a forest – not the annual uptake of carbon. Studies by Harmon's research group have shown that the conversion of 5 million hectares of old growth American west coast forests to younger plantations in the past century added ~2 billion tons of carbon to the atmosphere.

The most appropriate immediate action may be to review the ways in which provincial governments licence forested lands, in particular, the long-term costs to the taxpayer of existing agreements. Canadian forests belong to the public, and ensuring governments' accountability to the electorate may lead to greater protection of Canadian forests. The implication for future generations of Canadians of continuing current forest management styles should be the subject of public debate. There will be no quick fixes. The failure to adopt forest policy based on long-term ecological research has left Canadians with the likely prospect of a decline in their standard of living until the national economy is restructured.

Tropical Forests (Brazil)

The international attention that has been given to the condition of amazonian forests may be a factor in the present slowing of the exponential rate of deforestation (Climate Alert 1990). Thus, the future of amazonian forests may not be as bleak as that of the Canadian forests, which the international community, in general, believes to be unendangered. Furthermore, the amazonian forest does not directly underpin the Brazilian economy.

Clearing of the Brazilian portion of the amazonian forests accelerated in the 1960s and 1970s (Hecht and Cockburn 1990). At that time Amazonia was viewed as a vast untapped agroforestry and mineral resource region. Megaprojects were initiated, such as the 'Jari' agroforestry project. At Jari the forest component was based on replacing virgin forest with fast-growing gmelina trees to produce pulp and paper for the international market. An innovative floating pulp mill was built in Japan and 'parked' on the banks of the Jari River, and the idea was born that one could bring the pulpmill to the forests. The fate of this project was documented by Kinkead (1981). Financial problems could be traced to the failure to recognize the infertility of amazonian soils, combined with replacing a forest characterized by over 100 tree species per hectare with a monoculture plantations of trees not indigenous to the region. (Henry Ford's amazonian rubber plantations had failed under similar circumstances a few decades before.) The failure to establish a project based on knowledge, which was available at that time, of ecosystem fragility and soil infertility paved the way for ecological and economic disaster (Fearnside 1988; Kronberg and Fyfe 1984).

A major factor in the large-scale degradation of western amazonian forests was the colonization of that area by poor farmers displaced from southern Brazilian lands, which were greatly enhanced in value by the initiation of the 'alcohol fuel' program. In this strategy, sugar cane would be cultivated for the production of alcohol. Roads accessing Amazonia from the south and built with loans from international agencies, accelerated the migration. Again, planners failed to recognize the infertility of amazonian soils. Migrants, compelled to move after every few seasons, clear more and more forest in order to survive (Flavin and Pollock 1985). Throughout Amazonia, vast areas have also been converted to pasture. In this way, landowners claim subsidies and participate in real estate speculation. However, the profits realized by these activities are in no way linked to agricultural production (Fearnside 1990).

The control of forest clearing in Brazil, as in Canada, is in the hands of the government. Environmental regulations exist in both countries but many are not enforced. To change this situation, the problem of deforestation must be given higher priority in national agendas. A major obstacle to achieving the reversal of rates of deforestation is that the financial benefits of forest removal are large and go to a small group. The far greater, long-term environmental, social, and economic costs of forest degradation are being borne by growing numbers of planetary citizens, as human perturbations to forest-climate interactions continue.

CHAPTER THREE

Climate Change and the Role of Forest Policy

Frederick W. Cubbage, James L. Regens,

and Donald G. Hodges

THE ISSUE

Global climate change has become an increasingly important public policy and international issue in the last few years. Scientific evidence suggests that accelerated climate change may be occurring, primarily because the burning of fossil and biomass fuels releases carbon dioxide (CO_2) and other trace gases into the atmosphere at a rate greater than that experienced in the past (Blake and Rowland 1988; Harrington 1987; MacDonald 1988; Ramanathan 1988). This accumulation of CO_2 and other small-molecule gases, which account for about as much atmospheric build-up as does carbon dioxide, is believed to trap long-wave infrared radiation in the atmosphere, thereby warming the earth and raising mean global temperatures (Dowd 1986; Houghton and Woodwell 1989). Release of excess carbon and other gases through fossil and biomass fuel combustion is the major component of the problem, emitting 57 per cent of the greenhouse gases. Massive clearing of forests also has contributed to the build-up of atmospheric carbon dioxide by eliminating a means of converting CO_2 to other forms of carbon (Marshall 1989).

The CO_2 build-up and resulting increased retention of long-wave radiation, commonly called the greenhouse effect, could cause the earth's average temperature to rise as much as two to five degrees Celsius within the next fifty to 100 years (Schneider and Rosenburg 1989). If they are realized, such dramatic changes in temperature could have significant impacts on natural resources as well as on our social and political institutions. Uncertainty surrounding the rate and magnitude of climate change, or even whether climate change will occur (Michaels 1989), creates substantial obstacles to design-

ing and implementing effective policy responses. The seeming re-
moteness of the threat and the necessity for international co-opera-
tion also constrain policy action. Thus, the challenge confronting
policymakers is one of piecing together reasonable scientific analyses and appropriate policy responses into a coherent course of public action. This paper examines the role that forest policy can play in
reducing adverse carbon balances which may accelerate global
warming.

The earth's total carbon pool is distributed between organic and
inorganic forms. Fossil fuel reserves account for 20.5 per cent of the
total pool. The oceans contain about 74 per cent of the world's carbon, mostly in the form of carbonate and bicarbonate ions. An additional 3 per cent is held by world soils; 1 per cent by world vegetation. The remaining carbon, approximately 1.5 per cent, is held in
the atmosphere, circulated, and used in photosynthesis (Houghton
and Woodwell 1989; Joyce et al. 1990).

Since the middle of the nineteenth century, fossil fuel combustion
has emitted about 135 to 170 billion metric tons of carbon into the air.
Forest clearing for cropland and fuelwood has contributed an additional 80 to 160 billion metric tons. Although the oceans have func-
tioned as a sink to absorb some of this excess carbon, atmospheric
concentrations have increased measurably since the industrial revolution. For example, atmospheric CO_2 levels were estimated to be 280
parts per million in 1860. By 1987 they were measured at 348 parts
per million. Since 1958, when scientists began to routinely monitor
CO_2 levels, they have risen 10 per cent (Postel 1988b).

Fears that such rapid changes will have drastic effects on the
Earth's ecosystems and society's physical and political infrastructure form the underlying basis for concerns over climate change.
Global warming would shift temperature and rainfall patterns. Some
key food-producing regions would become more vulnerable to heat
waves, drought, and the loss of irrigation water. Cooler regions
could benefit from extended growing seasons, while some Asian
countries may benefit from wetter weather (Allen et al. 1989; Easterling et al. 1989). Warmer temperatures would reduce the polar ice-
caps, thus raising sea levels. Depending on the topography of
specific sites, this potential rise could cause great damage in coastal
areas or necessitate expensive preventive measures. Such shifts
also may have immense effects on agriculture, forestry, and wildlife
(Hodges et al. 1988). To the degree that these impacts are realized,
the economies of industrial and developing countries alike would be
strained severely.

FOREST IMPACTS

Proposals to reduce the rate of global warming must focus on two principal components of the carbon cycle: (1) burning less fossil and biomass fuels, and (2) recapturing more carbon compounds in forests. Both of these activities can be modified. The relevant question for policymaking purposes is how effective these efforts can be in reducing the rate and magnitude of climate change. Reducing fossil fuel emissions certainly is crucial to decreasing the rate of CO_2 and trace gas build-up. But reducing biomass fuel emissions and sequestering carbon in forests also may play an important role. The Earth's trees, shrubs, and soils hold about 2.3 trillion metric tons of carbon, about triple that stored in the atmosphere (Joyce et al. 1990; Woodwell 1983). When vegetation is cleared or burned, or just left to decay, the carbon and nitrogen it contains, along with some in the underlying soil, is released into the atmosphere. Methane is also created during combustion. Each year, about 11 million hectares (28 million acres) of tropical forests are destroyed through the combined actions of land clearing for crop production, fuelwood gathering, and cattle ranching (Postel 1988a). Commercial timber harvesting occurs on an additional 4.3 million hectares, but these areas remain in forests. Houghton et al. (1987) estimated that the net release of carbon to the atmosphere from tropical deforestation is about 1.5 to 2.0 billion metric tons per year. Since about 4.5 to 5.0 billion metric tons are emitted each year by fossil fuel burning, about one-quarter of the total annual incremental atmospheric carbon build-up could be attributed to deforestation (Postel 1988b).

Improved retention of tropical forests and better growth of existing forests could reduce much of this net carbon loss from forest lands. Trees both use and produce CO_2. When photosynthesis is occurring at a rapid rate, trees will use much more CO_2 than they emit, storing the carbon in other forms, such as wood in the tree and tissue in the leaves. When photosynthesis is not occurring at moderate rates, trees will emit more CO_2 through respiration into the atmosphere than they use in photosynthesis.

How much carbon do forests retain? A productive southern pine or Douglas-fir forest could produce approximately fifteen cubic metres per hectare per year. Assuming that fifteen cubic metres are associated with twenty-four cubic metres of biomass, and that one cubic metre of biomass contains 0.26 tons of carbon, one hectare of forest could sequester 5.67 metric tons of carbon each year (Sedjo and Solomon 1989).

Reduced carbon emissions and increased carbon storage in trees could help ameliorate global warming substantially. Postel (1988a) estimates that successfully planting and maintaining an additional 121 million hectares in trees by the year 2000 would create forests that would absorb roughly 710 million metric tons of carbon every year until the trees reach maturity. That would cut net carbon releases from tropical forests almost in half. The American Forestry Association (AFA) also supports planting trees on a total of 9.3 million hectares of marginal cropland in the South. Given the productivity of these lands and the density with which trees could be planted, this would provide a net annual reduction of about 54 million metric tons of carbon. This represents about 3 per cent of the estimated losses to tropical deforestation, which would be a small but significant improvement in global CO_2 balances.

The AFA also proposes planting trees in urban U.S. environments to absorb carbon and provide shade-cooling effects as well. The association estimates that 100 million trees could be planted in cities. This could yield a net reduction of 5,900 metric tons of carbon per year in the United States. Globally, this is insignificant for carbon storage. But locally, the cooling effects of the shade could be important in reducing energy consumption. Reforestation programs offer other advantages. In urban environments, trees would help reduce ambient temperatures and provide more pleasant surroundings. Wood fibre provides the raw material for many industrial lumber and paper products, which may also offer long-term carbon storage benefits when used as lumber or when buried in landfills.

Reforestation would help reverse the loss of valuable forest ecosystems, resulting in improved habitat for wildlife and better water quality. Forests are a renewable resource, and tree plantations could provide fuelwood for vast regions of the world that depend almost exclusively on forest fuels. Excessive reliance on this option as an energy resource would, however, cause local air pollution and increase methane emissions, which would contribute to warming.

Slowing the destruction of existing forests also would be critical for reducing CO_2 build-up. Reducing the destruction due to tropical deforestation by one-quarter per year would reduce their net carbon releases by about the same amount – 350 million metric tons per year. This would amount to a 6 per cent net reduction in incremental atmospheric carbon emissions annually.

Climate change also has implications for forest distribution and productivity. If regional mean temperatures increase significantly, then the range of many important commercial timber species could change significantly. The loblolly pine range could move further north, onto less productive highland and mountain sites. The

Douglas-fir range might contract slightly but move upslope to higher elevations. These resource changes could have substantial impacts on timber yields and the wood processing industries (Hodges et al. 1988).

FOREST POLICY OPTIONS

What policies might be pursued in order to reduce the rate of increase in atmospheric carbon? What role can forests and forest policy play? What are the relative merits of market processes and government programs in developing forest policies that could help sequester carbon in forest lands?

Market Processes

Can markets help reduce deforestation? Will they help firms adapt adequately to changing resource bases? Perhaps. For instance, some of the rapid deforestation in developing countries can be attributed to their unwise timber pricing policies. Timber is often priced cheaply, much below prevailing world market prices, in order to encourage development and to open new areas for settlement. These incentives encourage more forest destruction to occur than would be the case without favourable government concessions. One market solution that would help encourage forest retention would simply be extracting higher prices for timber concessions, thus encouraging greater utilization of existing harvests and less pervasive destruction and waste (Repetto 1988a,b).

Markets also may be extremely efficient at fostering technological changes that will help countries adapt to changing resource bases. High product prices will attract producers; high input costs (e.g., timber prices) will force marginal firms out of business. For example, in the 1930s, the cutover southern u.s. forests were gradually being reforested naturally with southern pines. These pines were used mostly for lumber, but various technological developments allowed them to be used for the manufacture of kraft pulp and newsprint. The South is now the world's leading producer of pulp and paper due to these research development and adoption efforts fostered by market processes. Since many forest products firms in the South now worry about adequate future pine timber supplies at reasonable prices, they are shifting to a greater use of hardwoods in their pulp making or are switching to products that use predominantly hardwoods, which are more plentiful. These market responses have occurred over a period of time no longer than that proposed for substantial climate changes.

Another advantage of market mechanisms is their relative efficiency in reallocating production between countries, based on their comparative advantages. Most predictions of global climate change are very general in nature, and confidence in predictions of weather patterns decreases greatly at regional levels. It may be unwise to implement large-scale government reforestation programs based on limited knowledge of localized biophysical impacts. Perhaps it would be much better to let these changes occur naturally and to let the market sort out the winners and losers from climate change effects.

Markets have been effective in prompting forest regeneration and timber growing. Massive areas of softwoods have been established via planting or natural regeneration in the U.S. South for pulpwood and in the Pacific Northwest for sawtimber (Mangold et al. 1991). Similarly, large eucalyptus and softwood plantations have been established in Brazil in response to local demands for pulpwood. Scandinavian forests have been managed for decades to promote continued reforestation and contributions to the countries' forest-based economies. These substantial forestation programs are only partially attributable to market demand for wood, however; public policies also have been instrumental in their development (Royer 1987).

Markets may also prompt increased tree-planting in urban environments, rural regions, and developing countries in order to help sequester carbon. Trees may reduce heat so much that they will pay for themselves in cities. Perhaps timber prices will increase enough to make wide-scale planting programs economically attractive. And maybe environmental protection, agroforestry, or other conservation rationales will become compelling in the Third World. Increased afforestation due to these market-based signals could reduce atmospheric carbon build-up – but we doubt it.

Public Programs

Despite the merits of timber markets, many of the benefits of protecting or planting forests, such as improvement of global climate, preservation of biological diversity and endangered species, and protection of soil productivity and water quality, are common-pool or collective goods that are not exchanged in market processes. These goods are non-rival and non-exclusive, so markets fail to provide socially desirable levels of production or protection for such goods. As a result, current market prices fail to capture their full value. Thus, public policies must be employed to protect these non-market goods.

Consideration of policy options to encourage forests needs to address both domestic and international programs. Policies must also include components that address forest preservation in a natural condition, forest management (scientific growth, harvest, and regeneration of forests), and afforestation (planting of currently barren or agricultural lands).

Government policies should be used to encourage conservation of tropical forests. Unplanned or subsidized timber cutting should be eliminated to the extent possible. Settlement programs often fail to yield long-lasting, desirable outcomes. Land is often cleared, burned, and farmed until it is degraded and abandoned, often being left in an unproductive state. Government funds spent on short-term development programs would be better invested in long-term solutions, such as agroforestry, or focused on the most productive agricultural lands. This could leave more forests in their natural state or ensure that they be extensively managed. Plantation forestry in the tropics is also a viable option. The very fast growth of native and exotic species in the tropics can provide substantial carbon storage. These forests can be used for fuelwood or forest products, lessening pressures on native forests.

Successful retention of tropical forests and afforestation of plantations will require substantial cultural change and economic progress in developing countries. The industrialized countries also went through a period of forest exploitation and destruction for centuries, so we should not be overly ethnocentric in condemning such actions by developing countries. Instead, we should encourage policy options that may meet goals of individual countries and help meet broader global objectives as well. Additionally, we should pursue domestic policies that will help mitigate effects of climate change and environmental degradation.

Government ownership is one means of protecting and managing forests. The first progressive conservation movement in the United States resulted in the reservation of about 61 million hectares of forested lands in the western United States. Subsequent laws authorized the purchase of another 14 million hectares that had been disposed of and cut over, mostly in the East. These lands are now managed for a variety of outputs, ranging from timber to wilderness.

The u.s. model of government ownership of forest lands may be applicable to developing countries. Other countries may reserve forest lands themselves, or they may use creative new funding mechanisms, such as debt for equity exchanges, to protect forest lands. In these swaps, a debtor nation agrees to protect some critical forest or wildlife habitat in exchange for partial payment or release from its foreign debt. Agencies such as the World Bank and the Agency for International Development also can contribute to forest retention by incorporating incentives to safeguard native forests in their loans and programs.

Reforestation and Afforestation Financial Incentives

Large-scale reforestation or afforestation efforts require major government programs and funding. South Korea has invested vast sums in fuelwood plantations for local community use. The Philippines has provided loans and subsidies to local landowners to plant and develop tree plantations to furnish a domestic pulp mill. New Zealand reforested much of its native forests (that were cut over in the 1930s and 1960s) with radiata pine plantations. These programs were funded by the public sector, usually occurring on government-owned lands. All of these projects have planted trees for subsequent local fuelwood or industrial timber harvests.

The United States is currently underwriting the massive Conservation Reserve Program, which pays landowners to remove highly erodible lands from crop production and place them in a permanent cover of grass or trees. The total program is intended to reserve 16 million hectares (40 million acres) of land in the u.s. Two million hectares (5 million acres) was planned for conversion to tree plantations, but the program will fall short of this goal. Under the program, the federal government pays one-half the total cost of planting the seedlings (about $170 per hectare) and then makes annual rental payments for ten years. To date, these payments have averaged about $120 per hectare ($45 per acre) (Conservation Reserve Program Work Group 1989). Given these costs, the government program expenses for tree-planting alone would amount to $87 million per million hectares planted; rental payments for all ten years would be $1.2 billion per million hectares planted. These, obviously, are substantial expenses but may actually be cheaper than making crop payments for the same land. They also prevent environmentally harmful u.s. agricultural practices on sensitive lands – practices akin to the destructive farming practices criticized in developing countries.

Establishing plantations on former u.s. croplands is likely to be relatively inexpensive. Sedjo (1989) estimates that average costs for plantations in different parts of the world would typically range from $230 to $1,000 per hectare, with a mean of about $400 per hectare.

Planting trees on old u.s. cropland would fall at the bottom of the range. At the above rates, Postel's (1988a) proposal to plant 120 million hectares in trees could cost from $30 billion to $120 billion. This would exclude any costs for land procurement. These costs would amount to about 3 to 12 per cent of the annual u.s. government budget and are obviously immense. This indicates that tree-planting efforts to sequester carbon must clearly involve international cooperation and funding.

Moulton and Richards (1990) estimated that an extensive tree-planting program on marginal agricultural land in the u.s. alone could sequester 732 million metric tons (more than one-half of the annual u.s. CO_2 emissions) at a cost of $19.5 billion annually. A 20 per cent reduction in u.s. CO_2 emissions would cost $4.5 billion per year and involve 56 million hectares.

The United States also has ongoing tree-planting programs called the Forestry Incentives Program and the Agricultural Conservation Program. Both of these federal programs pay part of the costs of planting for farmers but are funded at levels of less than $20 million per year, which has led to less than 125,000 hectares of forest land being planted in both programs each year. It also provides federal income tax credits and deductions for tree-planting for owners of small tracts and, until the 1986 tax reform law took effect, provided preferential capital gains tax treatment for timber income for all owners.

Management Advice and Education

For most of the twentieth century, federal and state foresters in the United States have developed educational programs promoting forest management and have provided advice to private forest landowners. The u.s. Forest Service tirelessly promoted forest protection, management, and use at the turn of the century. The landmark Clarke-McNary Act of 1924 promoted co-operative federal and state efforts to protect privately owned forests from fire, to grow seedlings for forest planting, and to advise private landowners. A number of programs since then have been designed to promote forestry and conservation on private lands.

These models of providing education and information may help to create favourable public attitudes for retention of forest lands in less developed countries as well. Protection, however, will not come easily. Pressures for destruction and development of native forests are intense. The recent murder of Francisco Mendes Filho of the rubber-tappers union in Brazil, who helped lead public campaigns for native forest protection, suggests that public education and information campaigns alone will be inadequate given such virulent opposition.

SPECIAL CONSIDERATIONS

Forest policies designed to reduce the build-up of atmospheric CO_2 and trace gases ultimately must seek a balance between forest harvest and forest growth. Forest harvesting and clearing are greatly outpacing planting and reforestation. Reversing this trend by encouraging forest retention and reforestation could lead to forests storing more carbon than they emit or, at least, sustaining a dynamic equilibrium. However, achieving an equilibrium or net carbon storage involves addressing several unique policy issues.

First, trees will usually capture and store the most carbon when they are growing fast, that is, when they are producing the most wood. Relatively young stands will tend to store the most wood in trees. Mature trees, however, will grow little and decay much. This is ameliorated somewhat because there will be continued carbon storage and build-up in the forest floor and soils of old-growth stands. Exposing forest soils in old-growth stands, such as in tropical forests and the u.s. West, may cause carbon volatilization and loss from the forest floor alone, for which it will take many years for faster growth of young stands to compensate.

These biological characteristics of tree growth and forest ecology suggest that a mix of forest management techniques would be appropriate to improve net carbon storage in forests. Fast growing intensive-culture plantations, with five to ten year rotations, might seem attractive at first because of the very high growth rates. But their rapid harvest and use for fuelwood would probably do little to help store carbon for long periods of time. Also, they would store little carbon in the forest floor. A recent study of forests in the Pacific Northwest revealed the different carbon storage capacities of young and old forests. Harmon et al. (1990) concluded that 60-year-old Douglas-fir forests store 259 to 274 mg of carbon per hectare, while a 450-year-old forest could hold more than 600 mg of carbon per hectare. Old-growth temperate or tropical forests might best store carbon by retention or by selective cutting in order to prevent loss of carbon in the forest floor. If clear-cutting is used, the land should be reforested quickly to recapture the benefits of carbon storage.

A second concern is related to the first. If developed or developing countries try to preserve as many forests as possible in their natural state without allowing any timber harvests, the net effect may be perverse. They may be able to set aside some forests, but they will probably prompt accelerated liquidation of remaining forests by people who fear that they will be regulated or prohibited from cutting trees. Even control of harvests in reserved forests will be extremely difficult, given population pressures, low standards of living, and enforcement difficulties. Thus, successful forest policies must carefully mix preservation, protection, and management lest they accelerate existing destructive forest clearing practices.

Finally, it is worth noting that stands will not store carbon indefinitely. They will inevitably grow old and die or be harvested. If they are used to make lumber or paper, carbon may be retained in those products much longer before degradation. Lumber products with a long storage life will help most in long-term carbon storage. If trees are burned for fuel or to clear land, they will release carbon and methane quickly during combustion. Harmon et al. (1990) estimated that of the 325 mg of carbon per hectare harvested in the Pacific Northwest, 138 mg is converted into long-term storage. The key to long-term improvement in carbon balances via forests will be to retain the carbon in forest products, increase forest land retention, and improve forest management to minimize carbon losses from forest floors during harvest and regeneration.

One other advantage of timber growth and harvest that is often noted by foresters is that wood products require less energy to manufacture than do alternative building or wrapping materials. Steel, concrete, and plastics all require more energy, which would, of course, exacerbate any carbon imbalances. They are also less biodegradable (USDA Forest Service 1982).

CONCLUSIONS

While the prospect of increasing global temperature caused by elevated atmospheric CO_2 concentrations is accepted by much of the scientific community, uncertainty remains about the impact of climate change on terrestrial ecosystems. We know, nonetheless, that forests are important in absorbing carbon dioxide in wood and in the forest floor. In fact, besides reducing fossil fuel use, forests are the most important mechanism for limiting atmospheric concentrations of CO_2 and other trace gases. These unique characteristics of forests make them crucial in developing public policies to mitigate the effects of global climate change.

What policy options are likely to be desirable? Several key points seem apparent. Pricing timber at levels at least equal to world market price should be used to reduce tropical deforestation to the extent possible. Vigorous pursuit of this policy alone would prevent waste, destruction, and needless burning of valuable growing stock. Even market prices for timber, however, are unlikely to reflect the total value of protecting forest land. Values such as protection from global climate change, preservation of species diversity, and maintenance of soil productivity are collective in nature and distant in time. Markets have difficulty in efficiently allocating use of such resources. Thus, timber market signals should be supplemented by public policy interventions designed to protect these values.

Public programs should be authorized and funds appropriated to prevent deforestation and to encourage reforestation and afforestation. This is only prudent, because deforestation has been estimated to cause up to one-quarter of the incremental CO_2 generated annually in the world. Forestry programs may already have environmental and industrial benefits. The significant benefits of ameliorating climate change may provide further linkages that enhance the attractiveness of public forestry programs. On the other hand, forest and environmental interest groups may have ulterior motives for supporting new programs based on their prior production or preservation agendas rather than on the global climate benefits alone. Decisionmakers need to be sensitive to these linkages and hidden agendas in policymaking.

Economists, legislators, and budget examiners may well look askance upon forestry programs. The programs will promote forestry, at substantial expense to present generations, for the principal benefit of future generations, based on somewhat less than overwhelming evidence of need. This does not sound like a prescription for legislative success – nor should it be were it merely a forestry program. But the possible immense consequences of coping with climate change should prompt the prudent implementation of economically efficient action now. To delay is likely to be economically and socially unwise.

All reasonable policies to encourage forest retention, expansion, and productivity should be considered. Feasible efforts should be made to protect tropical forests from destruction and degradation. Harvesting, regenerating, and managing of most tropical and temperate forests should continue, however, in order to keep stands growing at rapid rates and to prevent needless liquidation of non-preserved stands. Afforesting barren lands can also contribute to improved carbon storage. Developed countries can contribute substantially by afforesting marginal farm lands, maintaining existing lands in productive condition, and funding efforts in less developed countries.

Clearly, the costs of forest planting, care, and reforestation are great. When coupled with the problems of identifying regional impacts of climate change, initiating policy responses becomes difficult. The challenge for public policy will be to begin to take appropriate action soon, despite the difficulties. Otherwise, the potential economic and social costs attributable to climate change may be immense. Forest policy can play an important role in limiting greenhouse gas levels, thus slowing the rate of global warming and reducing the associated costs to society.

CHAPTER FOUR

Rehabilitating the Backlog of Unstocked Forest Lands in British Columbia: A Preliminary Simulation Analysis of Alternative Strategies

W.A. Thompson, P.H. Pearse,

G.C. van Kooten, and I. Vertinsky

INTRODUCTION

Among the most controversial forest management issues in British Columbia is reforestation and, in particular, the adequacy of reforestation programs to restore forests denuded by logging, fire, insects, and disease. A measure of the inadequacy of past reforestation efforts is the accumulated backlog of land that remains unstocked – the so-called Not Satisfactorily Restocked (NSR) lands. The adequacy of current reforestation programs is reflected in the changes in this category.

The NSR lands attract a great deal of attention from foresters, who see them as a threat to future timber supplies, and from environmentalists, who regard them as evidence of faulty resource management. As a result, rehabilitation of the NSR lands has been given high priority in recent governmental forestry programs. The objective is to ensure that the reforestation effort on lands logged or otherwise denuded is sufficient to ensure that there will be no increase in the NSR backlog and to eliminate the backlog through specially directed rehabilitation efforts over the forthcoming decade (Ministry of Forests 1988a, 1989, 1990).

This paper examines the magnitude and character of the NSR backlog problem and presents a preliminary economic analysis of the task of restoring these lands to a productive condition. One purpose of this study is to examine the effects of alternative ways of allocating the available funds among NSR sites. Another purpose is to illustrate how computer-based analytical models can be used to investigate economic problems of forest management and to assist in the design of silvicultural programs.

The last few years have witnessed rapid developments in computer-based analytical systems and their applications to forestry problems (Brumelle et al. 1990). Because of their capacity to accommodate large quantities of data and to analyze them quickly and flexibly, these new techniques are particularly helpful in projecting long-term timber supplies for whole forests or regions, and in revealing the impact of harvesting and silvicultural programs. Moreover, these new tools have greatly facilitated economic analysis of alternative courses of action faced by forest managers, thereby providing important guidance for decisionmaking.

All this has come at a time when forestry in Canada is confronted with major policy questions calling for economic analysis: the best allocation of forest land between competing and compatible uses, the most advantageous allocation of harvest over time, and the optimum allocations of silvicultural funds between forest treatments and regions.

In the next two sections, we briefly examine the rehabilitation problem and alternative criteria for establishing priorities among NSR lands of different types and qualities and in different locations. Next, a simulation model used in the current study is described. This is followed by the simulation results and discussion. Finally, we draw some conclusions relevant to forest policy in British Columbia.

REHABILITATION PROBLEM

Information about the magnitude of the NSR backlog in British Columbia is summarized by forest region and site class in Table 1. These numbers, which summarize the more detailed data used in the analysis below, were extracted in 1987 from the forest history records of the British Columbia Ministry of Forests (hereafter, the ministry). For present purposes we have excluded the unstocked lands that the ministry refers to as 'Current NSR.' These are lands that have been deforested by logging or natural causes, but the period of three to five years normally allowed for establishment of a new crop has not yet elapsed. These are properly regarded as lands in normal transition from one crop to another. Also excluded is the ministry's 'Disturbed, Stocking Doubtful' (DSD) category, which are lands that have been disturbed and at least partially deforested, but for which no information is available concerning their state of reforestation. The areas in Table 1 show only 'Backlog NSR' lands which have been denuded, the accepted regeneration period has elapsed, and the land remains inadequately reforested, presenting a special problem for rehabilitation.

TABLE 1

Backlog of not satisfactorily restocked forest land in
British Columbia

	Backlog NSR area (thousand hectares)			
Site quality	Coast	Southern Interior	Northern Interior	Total province
Good	2.3	58.8	106.7	167.8
Medium	26.4	204.7	216.5	447.6
Poor	15.4	82.9	160.1	258.4
All sites	44.1	346.4	483.3	873.8

SOURCE: Ministry of Forests (1988b)
NOTE: Sites best suited for deciduous species are excluded. These numbers do
        not reflect recent FRDA accomplishments.

Though not distinguished in Table 1, some backlog NSR lands are classified separately as 'non-commercial brush' (NCB) lands, which, as the name implies, have become overgrown with brush or non-commercial species of trees. This categorization is important for two reasons: one is that rehabilitation of these lands requires removal of the existing cover, adding significantly to the cost; the other is that some of these lands are occupied by deciduous trees which, though not now merchantable, may become so in the future through changes in technology or economic conditions.

The NSR backlog is further subdivided into three categories of site quality – good, medium, and poor (the latter including the ministry's 'low' site class) as shown in Table 1. These categories indicate relative land productivity, an important consideration in determining priorities for rehabilitation. Finally, the ministry disaggregates these into land types categorized by the species to which the forest land is considered to be best suited. We draw on these sub-classifications below.

Different sources and assessments made at different times report wide variations in the magnitude of the NSR backlog (Pearse, Lang, and Todd 1986a). Many of these variations can be attributed to: differences in classification criteria, such as the stocking level, considered to be 'satisfactory'; revisions of data resulting from more recent or more thorough surveys; changes in the available forest land base; real increases over time in the NSR area as a result of fires, pests, and logging; and decreases due to natural and artificial regeneration.

More recently, changes have resulted from the extensive surveys and vigorous reforestation programs under the federal-provincial, cost-shared Forest Resources Development Agreement (FRDA). This is particularly true for good and medium sites, where FRDA reforest-ation efforts were concentrated. For example, the data base we used for the analysis below had 168, 448, and 258 thousand hectares of backlog NSR land on good, medium, and poor sites, respectively, whereas the latest ministry figures are 91, 345, and 250 thousand hectares (Ministry of Forests 1990).

The 874 thousand hectares of backlog NSR lands in British Colum-bia indicated in Table 1 provide the starting point for our analysis. This is a little less than 4 per cent of the 22.1 million hectares of non-deciduous forest land in the province. Much of this backlog – over 55 per cent – is in the remote northern interior forests of the vast Prince George and Prince Rupert forest regions. A large proportion of these lands is of poor site quality.

ANALYSIS OF ECONOMIC PRIORITIES

Our analysis is designed to yield answers to several questions of in-terest to forest policy makers contemplating backlog NSR rehabilita-tion programs such as:

(1) How much would it cost to rehabilitate all the backlog NSR lands?
(2) Given a limited budget, sufficient to rehabilitate only some of these lands, how should priorities be established in order to maximize:
  (a) the area rehabilitated?
  (b) the additional growth of timber?
  (c) the economic gain?
(3) Which of the NSR backlog lands can be expected to yield bene-fits in excess of the cost of rehabilitation, and how much would it cost to rehabilitate them?
(4) What are the regional impacts of NSR backlog land rehabilita-tion?

Each of these questions is relevant at a different level of decision-making in forest management planning. As we shall see, they are listed here in order of sharply increasing requirements of data and assumptions to be made by the analyst. Correspondingly, precision in the numerical forecasts declines.

In approaching these issues, we assume that the ultimate objec-tive of investing in the restoration of unstocked forest lands is to generate benefits that flow from increased timber growth. The funds

available for this purpose are limited, however. The task is, therefore, to allocate the available funds between the whole array of NSR
lands of different characteristics and in different localities in such a
way as to generate the maximum possible benefits.

A few observations about this economic objective must be made
at the outset. First, to generate the maximum gain from investments
in silviculture we must take account not only of the benefits generated but also of the costs of generating them. The net gain is the difference between the two. Thus, the economic objective is, more specifically, to distribute the available funds in such a way that the *net
benefit* is maximized.

Second, while we consider mainly the *financial benefits* that accrue
in the form of commercial timber, we recognize that reforestation
can affect, positively or negatively, other economic goods, such as
wildlife, aesthetics, or water supplies. The occurrence and importance of these other effects vary widely from one site to another and
must be considered in the context of particular situations, supplementary to a strategic financial analysis of the type developed here.
Policymakers may want to respond to other concerns as well in de-
ciding how and where to allocate funds, including concerns about
employment, community stability, and regional development.
Again, these must be considered in light of particular circumstances, as suggested below.

Third, time is an important element in any investment decision,
and expected costs and benefits spread or scattered through future
years must be reduced to their equivalent present values so that they
can be compared in consistent terms. This calls for discounting future values at an appropriate discount rate. Thus, our objective is to
identify all the categories of NSR lands that should be selected for rehabilitation in order to generate the maximum possible present
value of timber benefits with the limited funds available.

With sufficient information we could assess, for each NSR site, the
cost of rehabilitating it and the present value of the additional timber
that would result from the treatment. We could then show, for each,
the ratio of the benefits to the costs. This indicates the expected benefits per dollar of cost or, in other words, the economic efficiency of
the investment in each case. If we ranked all the NSR sites in the
province according to their benefit/cost ratio and selected from
those with the highest ratio as many as the available budget allows,
we would be assured of achieving our objective: the maximum possible expected benefit would be realized by allocating the funds to
the selected projects.

Inevitably, the available data about the forest inventory are too

uncertain and incomplete to permit a precise analysis. The cost of rehabilitating a parcel of backlog NSR land depends on its location, accessibility, terrain, vegetative cover, and a host of other variables,
most of which are not recorded. For present purposes, we must resort to available statistics on average costs in each region for the major components of rehabilitation, mainly the cost of seedlings, planting, and, in some cases, site preparation and brush removal.

Correspondingly, the data required for estimating the benefits of
rehabilitation are weak. A fundamental question is the present
value of the crop that would result if the site were not treated; clearly,
only the value of the rehabilitated crop *in excess of the value that would
accrue anyway* can be counted as a benefit of the rehabilitation. Future values of timber, the age at which crops will be harvested, the
risks of losses in the meantime, the appropriate rate of discount, and
other uncertainties limit the reliability of benefit estimates. Nevertheless, modern analytical systems enable the best available information to be brought to bear on such problems, and, as long as the
limits to the precision of the results are recognized, they can provide
decisionmakers with valuable guidance about the implications of alternative choices as well as with much more consistent indications
of priorities than are otherwise possible.

ANALYTICAL MODEL

The analytical model used in the present study was developed by a
team of researchers at the Forest Economics and Policy Analysis Research Unit of the University of British Columbia and a private consulting group, both sponsored by British Columbia's Ministry of
Forests (Phelps et al. 1990). This computer simulation model projects the forest inventory and timber harvest for a forest area, given
specifications of forest protection, silviculture, economics and harvest targets, priorities, and constraints. These management specifications can be varied, and the effects of different combinations of
practices on the inventory and timber yield can be examined. The
projected outcomes can then be used to evaluate alternative programs of silvicultural investments. The model structure is depicted
in Figure 1. Only its basic elements are described here; a detailed
technical discussion of the model is available elsewhere (Phelps et
al. 1990).

The forest inventory used in the model is that for the forest lands
of British Columbia regulated and administered by the ministry as
tree farm licenses (TFL's) and timber supply areas (TSA's). The ministry has 'netted down' these data. That is, areas have been excluded

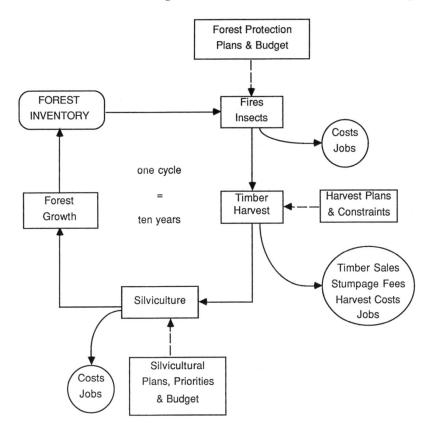

FIGURE 1
Flowchart of the British Columbia silviculture planning model

from the productive and available forest land base which are 'not commercially viable. These include inaccessible (inoperable) areas, noncommercial tree species and non-merchantable forest cover (Problem Forest Types)' (Ministry of Forests 1984a:B2). The 'netted down' or 'potentially productive, available and suitable' area is 64 per cent of the available forest land (Ministry of Forests 1984a). This forest inventory covers 22.1 million hectares (excluding deciduous sites) classified by region, predominant tree species (known as 'growth type'), site quality, past silvicultural treatment, distance to mills, and age class.

For present purposes, the province has been divided into three forest regions, which are aggregations of the ministry's administrative regions (Figure 2). These are: *Coast*, which combines the Vancouver region and the coastal part of the Prince Rupert region; *North-*

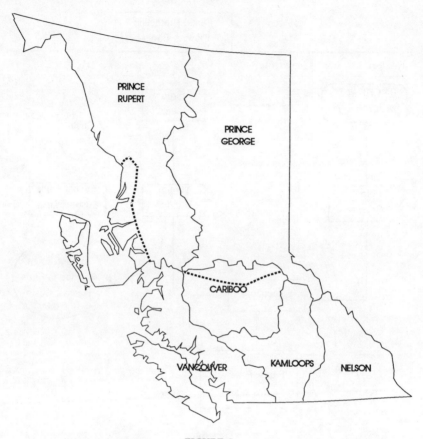

FIGURE 2

Map of British Columbia showing the six Ministry of Forests administrative
regions and the amalgamation of these into the three regions analysed in
this study (see dotted lines)

ern Interior, which includes the Prince George region, the interior
part of the Prince Rupert region, and the northern part of the Cariboo
region; and *Southern Interior*, corresponding to the Kamloops, Nelson, and the remainder of the Cariboo regions. This aggregation
best accommodated our data on tree species and growing conditions
as well as limitations of computer space.

Within each region, forest types were aggregated into six *growth
types*, designated by the dominant species, as indicated in Table 2.
For the purposes of this study, the 'deciduous' type was excluded.
This is because, in British Columbia, deciduous species have, historically, commanded little or no value and little is known about
their silviculture.

TABLE 2
Growth types by forest region

Region	Growth type	Classification*
Coast	1. fir	1-8, 27, 32-34
	2. cedar	9-11
	3. hemlock	12-17, 28-31
	4. balsam	18-20
	5. spruce	21-26
Southern Interior	1. fir	1-8, 27, 32-34
	2. cedar/hemlock	9-17
	3. pine	28-31
	4. balsam	18-20
	5. spruce	21-26
Northern Interior	1. fir	1-8, 27, 32-34
	2. cedar/hemlock	9-17
	3. pine	28-31
	4. balsam	18-20
	5. spruce	21-26

NOTES: * Numerical designations refer to the Ministry's classification of forest types. Data on growth types are classified according to good, medium, and poor site uality, except for Northern Interior type 1, where sites are not distinguished (these are included with 'medium' sites in subsequent tables).

Growth types were subdivided into three *site qualities*: good, medium, and poor. On better sites, volume growth is faster, and the timber sells for a higher price because of the larger dimensions of the trees. Differences in *distance* from forest lands to mills were accounted for by further dividing lands into 'near' and 'far' classes, with lower operating costs for near lands.

The forest inventory is divided into sixteen *age classes*. Twelve represent ten-year age classes, from 0-9 years to 110-19 years. All stands 120 years and older are included in a single 'old-growth' class and are assumed to have ceased growing. Two other classes represent land on which forest regeneration has been delayed for such causes as insufficient seed, destruction by wildlife, or competition from weeds. One of these categories is assumed to progress into the first real age class in one decade, the other category in two decades.

The final age class consists of the lands classified as backlog NSR, described earlier. These lands have been denuded and have remained unsatisfactorily restocked for longer than the acceptable regeneration period; in most cases they are expected to remain unsatisfactorily restocked for many years unless they are artificially rehabilitated. Nevertheless, many of these lands support trees, albeit of low-valued species or at low density or both. This illustrates the economic sensitivity of NSR rehabilitation programs, because change in timber prices, costs, or utilization technology can significantly alter the commercial value of such stands and the advantage of rehabilitating them (Pearse, Lang, and Todd 1986a).

The model projects the inventory by decades, calculating the changes due to timber harvests, natural losses, regeneration, and stand improvement. In addition, age classes are advanced. Forest growth is accounted for by volume-age relationships which are specific to each combination of region, growth type, site class, and treatment category. The model dynamics and outputs are determined by five program modules: protection, harvest, silviculture, economics, and growth. Each of these is briefly described below.

Forest Protection

The protection submodel calculates losses of forest area caused by fire and insect pests. A fraction of the losses is available for salvage; the remainder is divided between the age-zero, regeneration delay, and NSR backlog classes.

Fire losses depend upon age, region, and growth type. These are determined by baseline parameters, which were calculated from aggregated historic data for the province's forest regions (Table 3). These prospective baseline loss rates are modified by regional budget allocations for fire fighting pre-organization (monitoring and preparation) and control (for details see Phelps et al. 1990).

Effects of two major pests are simulated in the model: western budworm and bark beetles. Effects of 'slow' pest and disease problems (e.g., root rot) are treated implicitly in the volume-age relationships and in the silviculture calculations through frequency of successful regeneration and stand enhancement. Each insect pest attacks trees of one or two growth types which are above some minimum age of vulnerability. Budworm attacks interior Douglas-fir aged eighty years and over; bark beetles attack interior pines and spruces aged sixty years and over. The fraction of vulnerable stands attacked depends upon the base attack rate for each region and regional expenditures on pest monitoring and pest control. Stands attacked by budworm are unavailable for harvest during the decade of attack and do not grow during that decade (i.e., do not advance in age class). Stands attacked by bark beetle die. A fraction of the area is

TABLE 3
Fire losses: per cent of forest area burned per decade

Growth type	Coast	Southern Interior	Northern Interior
Immature forest (1-80 years)			
Fir	1.23	3.05	0.43
Cedar	1.27	—	—
Cedar/hemlock	—	2.23	1.67
Hemlock	0.16	—	—
Pine	—	3.65	5.82
Balsam	0.10	0.62	2.39
Spruce	0.04	3.55	9.90
Mature forest (80 + years)			
Fir	1.33	1.06	0.15
Cedar	0.16	—	—
Cedar/hemlock	—	1.67	1.92
Hemlock	0.17	—	—
Pine	—	0.52	2.77
Balsam	0.42	1.04	1.94
Spruce	0.09	2.25	6.16

SOURCE: Calculated from historical data collected by the Ministry of Forests over the past fifty years

available for salvage; the remainder re-enters the pool of land available for regeneration.

Annual losses from fire and insects are quite variable. For example, while the average area of mature and immature timber burned over the past ten years was 64 thousand hectares (Ministry of Forests 1988a), the areas burned in 1985-6, 1986-7, and 1987-8 were 35, 10, and 22 thousand hectares, respectively (Ministry of Forests 1986, 1987, 1988a). Likewise, during those three years, the areas of forest killed by bark beetles were 346, 205, and 73 thousand hectares, and the areas attacked by defoliators were 266, 624, and 969 thousand hectares, respectively (Ministry of Forests 1986, 1987, 1988a). Finally, these losses were not distributed evenly over the province; over 90 per cent were in the Interior.

Timber Harvest

The harvest submodel determines the classes of forest to be cut based on the current state of the forest land base, a target volume to be harvested (annual allowable cut, henceforth called AAC), and a user-specified set of cutting priorities and constraints. Both clear-cuts and selective cuts are available options. The latter is applied only to Douglas-fir in the Southern Interior. Harvest priorities and constraints include: maximum fraction of cut to be taken from salvage (25 per cent); minimum volume per hectare (150 m^3/ha for Coast and Northern Interior; 100 m^3/ha for Southern Interior); minimum age and cutting cycle for selective cut (age 100 every 20 years); and priority of cut within growth type (lowest cost first). The AAC target annual harvest was set to 70 million m^3, which approximates the current annual harvest from provincially regulated lands.

Silviculture

The silviculture submodel provides the framework for exploring the implications of alternative silvicultural programs. Four silvicultural options are distinguished in the model: (1) 'no treatment' – harvested land is allowed to regenerate naturally without any intervention; (2) 'basic' – appropriate treatment to ensure successful regeneration of commercial species on the site; (3) 'incremental' – spacing and fertilization of young stands (age twenty to thirty years); and (4) 'backlog' (also called 'intensive') – clearing, site preparing, and planting of backlog NSR lands. Option (1) is unacceptable under current ministry regulations and is only included for comparison with 'basic' silviculture. Option (2) is defined by ministry standards and must be implemented on all clear-cut forest land regulated by the ministry. The treatments which comprise 'basic' silviculture vary with individual site conditions but include site preparation, natural regeneration, and planting. A mix of these treatments, distinct for each land class, is incorporated in the model. 'Incremental' silviculture (3) is not considered in this study, where the focus is on the results of 'backlog' NSR rehabilitation (4).

Each silvicultural option is comprised of a number of specific practices, such as site preparation, planting, and fertilization, employed to achieve the given objective. The combination of practices varies according to land and forest characteristics. We assume an average mix in terms of their frequency, costs, effects on stand age-volume relationship, and effects on timber age-value relationship (Smith 1989a). Costs were accounted in terms of both money and labour. Constraints were imposed by a limited silvicultural budget.

Priorities for treatment of land classes were based upon silvicultural objectives (see Silvicultural Strategies, below). Consequences of silvicultural activities are changes in frequency of successful

TABLE 4

Average silvicultural treatment costs for backlog NSR rehabilitation
(dollars per hectare)

Growth type	Site quality	Coast	Southern Interior	Northern Interior
Fir	Poor	1,460	290	—
	Medium	2,011	555	1,242
	Good	1,859	320	—
Cedar	Poor	1,163	—	—
	Medium	1,694	—	—
	Good	1,696	—	—
Cedar/Hemlock	Poor	—	2,422	832
	Medium	—	1,362	533
	Good	—	1,084	371
Hemlock	Poor	1,242	—	—
	Medium	1,058	—	—
	Good	1,352	—	—
Pine	Poor	—	455	997
	Medium	—	558	889
	Good	—	533	561
Balsam	Poor	1,400	1,685	4,693
	Medium	1,168	1,007	1,221
	Good	1,352	483	561
Spruce	Poor	1,715	3,493	2,030
	Medium	1,784	1,241	807
	Good	3,058	1,898	994

SOURCE: Smith (1989a)

stand establishment, in growth rate (i.e., volume-age curve), in timber value (i.e., value-age relationship), and in recovery of backlog NSR land to productive status.

Average backlog NSR rehabilitation costs (Table 4) were estimated for each land type (region, growth type, and site quality) from the ministry's 1987 Steady State Plan (Smith 1989a). Treatment costs included surveying, site preparation, planting, brushing and weeding, conifer release, and spacing of stagnated stands as needed. Distance to mill was not included as a cost factor. Finally, all treatment costs were scaled upward to reflect current costs by making average rehabilitation cost for each region match those reported in the ministry's Annual Report (1987-8:76-7, Tables L-1 and L-2, assuming 18.2 ¢/seedling) – 1,340, 968, and 1,170 $/ha for Coast, Southern In-

terior and Northern Interior, respectively. Several factors contribute
to the high variation in treatment costs between different land types.
Low costs for some land types arise where only modest treatment is
required to bring stands of existing trees up to ministry standards,
while high costs occur in remote areas with high access costs. It
should be noted that surveys may show that forest land considered
to be NSR is now adequately stocked. This has been common in the
Southern Interior, lowering the average cost of NSR reduction. While
surveying does not rehabilitate forest land in any biological or physical sense, it does have a similar effect by correcting its designation
in the forest inventory.

Economics

The economics submodel calculates the financial costs of and returns from the simulated management activities. It also calculates
employment levels. The results of these calculations are used both to
implement cost, net return, and labour constraints on forest protection, harvest, and silviculture, and to provide primary outputs of
forest management performance.

Gross revenue from harvest for each land class is calculated as the
volume of timber harvested times the specific price for that class of
timber. Timber prices depend upon species and mix of log grades.
Log mix is modelled implicitly as a function of region, growth type,
stand age, site quality, and past silvicultural treatment.

Average log prices for each timber growth type, age, and region
were estimated from current Vancouver log market prices and data
on net logging profits, stumpage rates, and operating costs
(Nawitka 1987; Ministry of Forests 1988a; Sterling Wood 1988; Statistics Canada 1989). These data were used to estimate average log
prices for old-growth timber. From these average log prices and the
Vancouver log market data, the average mix of log grades for old-
growth timber was estimated. Since there are few open sales of logs
in the BC interior, the data for the BC coast were used for the whole
province. Average log prices for younger age classes of timber were
estimated by expert judgment of the shift in log mix from the age at
which each growth type yields economically usable logs to age class
110 years and greater. Representative examples of age-price relationships are given in Table 5A.

Operating cost of harvesting and delivering wood to the mill was
split into two components: delivered wood cost (*dwc*), which varied
directly with harvest volume, and road cost (*rc*), which varied directly with the area cut. Average *rc* for each of the three simulated re-

TABLE 5A
Assumed relationships between stand age and value (dollars per m³) for naturally regenerated spruce stands on good sites

| | | | | | Stand age class | | | | Old |
Region	40	50	60	70	80	90	100	110	growth
Coast	0	36	41	46	51	56	61	66	71
Southern Interior	0	0	18	24	31	38	45	48	49
Northern Interior	0	15	20	26	31	38	45	48	49

TABLE 5B
Assumed relationships between stand age and volume (m³ per hectare) for naturally regenerated spruce stands on good sites

| | | | | | Stand age class | | | | Old |
Region	40	50	60	70	80	90	100	110	growth
Coast	439	610	748	854	928	982	1,028	1,061	1,163
Southern Interior	116	164	210	254	294	331	365	396	501
Northern Interior	110	168	224	276	321	359	391	418	456

SOURCE: Ministry of Forests (1988b)

gions was estimated from ministry annual reports (1986-7, 1987-8) as 135, 116, and 181 \$/ha for the Coast, Southern Interior, and Northern Interior, respectively. Average operating cost for the BC coast was estimated as \$47.71 per m^3 (Williams and Gasson 1986; Williams 1987; but see also Sterling Wood 1989), and average road cost on the coast was estimated as \$0.19 per m^3 (Ministry of Forests 1987, 1988a). The difference was taken as average delivered wood cost (\$47.54 per m^3). Based on a similar analysis for the BC interior (Williams and Gasson 1987), we estimated an average *dwc* of \$39.86 per m^3 (but see also Sterling Wood 1989). To reflect the variation in operating cost, the wood supply was divided into two distance categories, 'near' and 'far.' For the near category, average *dwc* and *rc* were taken as 10 per cent lower than the regional average, while, in the far category, *dwc* and *rc* were taken as 10 per cent higher than the regional average. This representation of variation in operating cost limits our analysis of the impact of small changes in price or cost on the extensive margin.

The public return from timber harvested is the stumpage value; the private return is the gross return minus harvesting, delivery, basic silviculture, and stumpage costs. Stumpage values are calculated according to the ministry's current practice. The value of each separately authorized cutting permit is appraised using a complicated procedure intended to account for the widely varying circumstances and conditions in different areas and at different times. The resulting appraised values are then scaled so that they will generate, on average, a target revenue which the ministry fixes separately for the Coast and the Interior regions. The appraisal process thus determines the stumpage price for a particular tract relative to the average for each region (subject to a minimum price of 25¢/per m^3). Regional average stumpage values of \$10.59 and \$8.59 per m^3 for the Coast and Interior regions, respectively, were used.

Regional 'permanent' employment is directly proportional to volume harvested: 956 and 222 human-years per million m^3 of wood harvested for the Coast and Interior regions, respectively (Statistics Canada 1989). The different constants of proportionality reflect differences in labour productivity between regions. Indirect and induced employment within British Columbia is calculated as 1.1 human-years per human-year of direct employment (Jacques and Fraser 1989). Inter-regional indirect or induced employment effects are ignored. Regional 'temporary' employment is direct employment in forest protection and silviculture during the period (e.g., fire fighting, tree-planting).

Forest Growth

For each forest land class (region, growth type, site quality, and silvicultural treatment class) the model has an age-volume relationship (see Table 5B for an example). These give the average volume of merchantable timber per hectare for each age category of the given forest land class. The relationships for naturally regenerated stands were developed by aggregating provincial data for all the TSA's in British Columbia. Mean annual increments ranged from 1.2 m^3 per year for Douglas-fir on poor sites in the Southern Interior to 12.5 m^3 per year for Sitka spruce on good Coastal sites. These mean growth rates are realized if stands are harvested when annual increment equals mean annual increment. Volume-age relationships for planted and silviculturally enhanced stands are hypothetical, based upon the judgment of professional silviculturists and very limited data. For the examples in this paper, we have assumed no increase in volume or value for planted stands compared with natural stands ('enhanced' stands are not considered in this study). Implicit in these value assumptions is that any decline in wood quality of planted second-growth timber compared to old-growth would be compensated for by improvement in other log attributes.

SILVICULTURAL STRATEGIES

The analytical model described above was used to examine the implications of alternative strategies for rehabilitating the province's backlog NSR lands using existing policies of forest protection and basic and incremental silviculture. Four separate analyses were conducted, each aimed at a distinct objective. Thus, each calls for a different criterion for choosing between the regions and land categories to be treated.

The first of these strategies is to *rehabilitate all the backlog NSR lands*. The resulting costs and benefits provide a base case with which more discriminating policies can be compared. In this case, the total cost is unconstrained and is determined by the computations. For the purpose of the analysis it was assumed, however, that the total program of rehabilitation would be carried out under a five-year program, with an equal expenditure in each year.

The remaining three strategies are relevant in the more realistic circumstances of a limited program budget. Accordingly, in each case a budget of $150 million was assumed, with $30 million to be expended in each year (which is roughly the current level of expendi-

TABLE 6

Backlog NSR lands selected for treatment under a $150 million reha-
bilitation program using alternative criteria for establishing
priorities[1]

Region	Growth type	Maximize area rehabilitated[2]	Maximize wood production[2]
Coast	Fir		g
	Cedar		g
	Hemlock		g, m
	Balsam		g, m
	Spruce		g, m
Southern Interior	Fir	g, m, p	g, m, p
	Cedar/Hemlock		g
	Pine	g, m, p	g, m
	Balsam	g	g
	Spruce		
Northern Interior	Fir		
	Cedar/Hemlock	g, m	g, m
	Pine	g	g
	Balsam	g	g
	Spruce	m[3]	g[3]

NOTES: [1] Program assumed to be funded at $30 million per year for 5 years (see
text)

[2] Letters g, m, and p refer to quality classes as good, medium, and poor.

[3] Only part of Northern Interior spruce could be treated, due to budget constraint.

ture). The strategies specify different criteria for selecting the limited range of sites that can be treated within this budget constraint.

The most straightforward of these selective strategies is to *maximize the area rehabilitated* with the available budget. This involves
choosing the sites that can be treated at *lowest cost* per hectare. The
result is indicated in Table 6, which shows those classes of backlog
NSR lands, among all the combinations of site qualities, growth
types, and regions, that can be accommodated within the $150 mil-
lion budget using this criterion.

Another strategy is to *maximize the additional wood production*
given the limited budget. This requires choosing those sites which
will yield the maximum mean annual increment in timber *volume* per

dollar of expenditure on rehabilitation. Analysis of this strategy requires, in addition to the data needed for the preceding cases, estimates of expected growth rates in the form of volume-age relationships for the range of land categories. It also requires assumptions about harvesting ages; for present purposes the ministry's procedure of selecting the age at which the mean annual increment reaches its maximum (which is also consistent with this strategy) was adopted. The sites selected under this criterion are indicated in Table 7. In contrast to the results under the maximum area strategy, these results include the full range of growth types in the Coast region and the highest site quality classes in all regions.

The fourth strategy is to *maximize the financial return* on the $150 million to be expended. This involves choosing, from the backlog NSR sites, those that will generate the greatest *value* in additional timber per dollar of rehabilitation cost. The ranking was determined by calculating benefit-cost ratios for backlog NSR land rehabilitation. The benefits were the discounted gross returns from future harvest; these were equal to discounted price times volume of future harvest. Costs were the silvicultural treatment costs plus discounted future harvest costs. For ranking the backlog NSR sites, costs associated with forest protection and maintenance were ignored, and losses of timber to fire or insect pests were assumed to be zero. All costs and prices were assumed constant (net of inflation), and timber harvest was assumed to be scheduled to maximize the benefit-cost ratio.

Past government investments in silviculture in BC, reflect that the government has employed a low discount rate for such investments (presumably because forests yield values other than commercial timber value, as noted above). In this study, we employed a discount rate of 1.5 per cent, which was imputed from revealed preferences as embodied in recent governmental silvicultural investments, assuming an expectation of constant real timber prices. It is important to recognize that these benefit-cost ratios were used only to *rank* land classes for rehabilitation. The land classes selected by this procedure, indicated in Table 7, correspond more closely to those based on maximizing wood produced than to those based on maximizing area rehabilitated. Since the backlog NSR lands with benefit-cost ratios greater than 1.0 can be rehabilitated for $60 million, the remaining $90 million of the $150 million budget is allocated to the highest ranking lands with a benefit-cost ratio less than one. Investment in these lower value lands may still be economically justified if one includes non-timber values or posits a lower discount rate.

)

TABLE 7

Benefit-cost ratios for NSR land rehabilitation at 1.5 per cent discount rate[1]

Growth type	Site quality	Coast		Southern Interior		Northern Interior	
		Near	Far	Near	Far	Near	Far
Fir	Poor	0.47	0.41	0.58	0.49	—	—
	Medium	0.71	0.61	**0.87**	0.75	**0.94**	0.80
	Good	**1.07**	**0.90**	**1.32**	**1.10**	—	—
Cedar	Poor	0.49	0.43	—	—	—	—
	Medium	0.79	0.68	—	—	—	—
	Good	**1.17**	**0.98**	—	—	—	—
Cedar/Hemlock	Poor	—	—	0.32	0.29	0.51	0.44
	Medium	—	—	0.75	0.65	**0.87**	0.73
	Good	—	—	**1.08**	**0.92**	**1.23**	**1.02**
Hemlock	Poor	0.62	0.53	—	—	—	—
	Medium	**0.88**	0.73	—	—	—	—
	Good	**1.07**	**0.90**	—	—	—	—
Pine	Poor	—	—	0.66	0.57	0.46	0.41
	Medium	—	—	0.78	0.66	0.64	0.56
	Good	—	—	**1.12**	**0.94**	**1.12**	**0.94**

Balsam	Poor	0.60	0.52	0.48	0.44	0.24	0.23
	Medium	**0.86**	0.72	**0.82**	0.72	0.78	0.69
	Good	**1.08**	**0.90**	**1.16**	**0.97**	**1.16**	**0.97**
Spruce	Poor	**0.94**	0.80	0.35	0.33	0.40	0.37
	Medium	**1.12**	**0.95**	0.80	0.70	**0.81**[2]	0.73
	Good	**1.16**	**0.99**	**0.82**	0.71	**1.01**	**0.86**

NOTES: [1] Under a $150 million rehabilitation program to maximize financial return from timber harvest, backlog NSR lands with benefit-cost ratio equal to or greater than 0.81 were selected (highlighted above).
[2] Only a fraction of this land class would be treated due to budget constraint.

Evaluation of Alternative Strategies

Timber Value

The implications of choosing the sites to be treated according to the various criteria outlined above are compared in Table 8. The assumed budget of $150 million is shown to be less than one-sixth of the amount that would be needed to rehabilitate all of the NSR backlog, but it would be enough to treat almost one-third of the total area.

Given the budget of $150 million, selection of sites for rehabilitation on the basis of maximizing the area treated would result in 11 per cent more backlog land being rehabilitated than would be the case if the choice were made on the basis of maximizing wood production. However, the latter strategy would result in nearly 10 per cent more wood production than would the former. The strategy of selecting sites to maximize financial returns would result in significantly less area rehabilitated and less volume of wood production than could be achieved by other strategies, but the net financial benefit generated by the silvicultural program would be substantially greater.

In terms of cost effectiveness, or the accomplishment per dollar of expenditure, all three of the selective strategies show results superior to the rehabilitation of all NSR lands. Table 8 shows that they would achieve roughly double the area and volume of wood per dollar expended.

The alternative strategies are compared in terms of financial criteria in the bottom half of Table 8. Regardless of discount rate, the strategy based on financial maximization yields the highest benefit-cost ratio and the highest net financial benefit. However, its relative merit is closely linked to the discount rate. At the highest discount rate examined (4 per cent), none of these strategies for investment in backlog NSR land rehabilitation yields significant financial returns to timber production.

A sensitivity analysis was conducted to assess the impact of a reduced silvicultural budget and of higher or lower timber prices on the results. Since each silvicultural strategy ranks projects on the basis of a maximization criterion and funds the best projects first, the marginal return per dollar cost will be a decreasing function of the budget. As shown in Table 9, a 50 per cent budget reduction reduces the benefit which is maximized by less than 50 per cent. The reduction in other benefits is often greater than 50 per cent but *can* be smaller. However, the net discounted return at 1.5 per cent is now

TABLE 8
Benefits and costs of alternative NSR backlog rehabilitation strategies, net of those expected in the absence of rehabilitation[1]

Evaluation criterion	Rehabilitate all backlog NSR	Maximize area rehabilitated	Maximize wood production	Maximize financial return[2]
Cost (million $)	**960**	150	150	150
Area rehabilitated				
Total (1,000 ha)	874	**276**	249	188
ha per $1,000 cost	0.9	1.8	1.7	1.3
Increment in annual yield				
Total (1,000 m³/y)	2,342	754	**823**	682
m³/y per $1,000 cost	2.4	5.0	5.5	4.5
Financial return[2]				
(discount rate 0.0%)				
Gross total[3] (million $)	231	129	231	**700**
Gross benefit/cost ($/$)	0.24	0.86	1.54	4.67
Net total[4] (million $)	-729	-21	98	550

(continued on next page)

TABLE 8 (*continued*)

Evaluation criterion	Rehabilitate all backlog NSR	Maximize area rehabilitated	Maximize wood production	Maximize financial return[2]
Financial return[2] (discount rate 1.5%)				
Gross total[3] (million $)	45	25	45	**136**
Gross benefit/cost ($/$)	0.05	0.17	0.30	0.91
Net total[4] (million $)	-915	-125	-105	-14
Financial return[2] (discount rate 4.0%)				
Gross total[3] (million $)	3	2	3	**9**
Gross benefit/cost ($/$)	0.00	0.01	0.02	0.06
Net total[4] (million $)	-957	-148	-147	-141

NOTES: [1] The forecasts were calculated using optimization methods: potential losses due to fire and pests were ignored, and optimal timber management was assumed.
[2] Restricted to commercial timber value for a single timber rotation
[3] Volume x (discounted price − discounted harvest cost)
[4] Gross return (discounted) − rehabilitation cost

TABLE 9

Effect of a 50 per cent budget cut (from $150 to $75 million) on backlog
NSR rehabilitation

Evaluation criterion	Maximize area rehabilitated	Maximize wood production	Maximize financial return
Area (1,000 ha)	**160**	118	103
Change from higher budget	-42%	-53%	-45%
Annual increment (1,000 m³/y)	409	**498**	439
Change from higher budget	-46%	-39%	-36%
Gross financial return[1]	7	45	**98**
Change from higher budget	-72%	-0%	-28%

NOTES: [1] Commercial timber benefits for one timber rotation, in million dollars, at 1.5
              per cent discount rate

positive ($23 million), whereas it was negative (- $14 million) under
the larger budget.

As financial return is very sensitive to timber prices, the effect of a
± 20 per cent change in timber prices over 100 years was projected for
the aggregate discounted (at 1.5 per cent) financial return for each of
the three maximization strategies. The resulting changes were ± 503
per cent for area maximization, ± 327 per cent for volume maximization, and ± 95 per cent for financial return maximization. Although
the financial returns for all three strategies are highly sensitive to
timber prices, the strategy which maximizes expected financial return proves to be, financially, the most risk averse.

The analysis was extended using the model described above to
consider impacts of NSR backlog land treatments upon: (1) future
timber yields; (2) regional distribution of benefits; (3) employment;
and (4) the environment.

Future Yields

The simulation model showed, for each of the silvicultural strategies, that harvests would begin increasing after eighty years. The
additional timber flow would continue for about fifty years, with the
greatest impact between 100 and 120 years from the present (Table
10). These increases would be from 2 to 3 per cent above the 'no treatment' alternative for the strategies based on a $150 million budget to

TABLE 10

Incremental benefits in future timber harvest (million m^3 per year) and in future financial returns (million dollars per year) due to rehabilitation of NSR land in 1990-5

Forecast timber harvest (million m^3/year)				
Decade from present	Rehabilitation of all backlog NSR	Maximize area rehabilitated	Maximize wood production	Maximize financial return
8	0.1	0.0	0.1	0.1
9	0.5	0.2	0.4	0.4
10	2.5	0.8	1.4	1.9
11	3.9	1.2	0.9	1.5
12	2.9	1.3	0.6	−0.3
Forecast returns from timber harvest (million $)				
Decade from present	Rehabilitation of all backlog NSR	Maximize area rehabilitated	Maximize wood production	Maximize financial return
8	−0.3	−0.1	0.2	0.3
9	2.7	1.0	1.8	2.0
10	15.7	4.5	8.0	11.6
11	26.4	7.9	5.6	8.4
12	20.1	5.9	1.9	−2.3

nearly 7 per cent for the total rehabilitation strategy. A corresponding increase in timber revenue would be realized (Table 10).

Regional Distribution

Regional distribution of silvicultural expenditures and land rehabilitation varies considerably according to the strategy implemented (Table 11). The area maximization strategy concentrates backlog NSR land rehabilitation in the Southern Interior (70 per cent), with the remainder in the Northern Interior (30 per cent). The NSR backlog interregional budget allocation for this strategy is similarly divided: 75 per cent to the Southern Interior, 25 per cent to the Northern Interior and none to the Coast. This division reflects the occurrence of low-cost NSR backlog recovery opportunities in the Southern Interior in contrast to the high costs often required on the Coast. In the Southern Interior, surveys reveal that many sites classified as NSR are, in fact, satisfactorily stocked, and that sites with understocked forests

TABLE 11

Regional distribution of NSR rehabilitation effort for the four rehabilitation strategies investigated

| | Budget allocation | | | |
Region	Rehabilitation of all backlog NSR	Maximize area rehabilitated	Maximize wood production	Maximize financial return
Coast	6.2%	0.0%	16.4%	8.6%
Southern Interior	34.1%	74.6%	54.3%	27.6%
Northern Interior	58.9%	25.4%	29.3%	63.8%
Total (in million $)	960	150	150	150

| | Area rehabilitated | | | |
Region	Rehabilitation of all backlog NSR	Maximize area rehabilitated	Maximize wood production	Maximize financial return
Coast	5.0%	0.0%	8.3%	5.1%
Southern Interior	39.6%	69.6%	67.7%	38.8%
Northern Interior	55.3%	30.4%	24.0%	56.1%
Total (in 1,000 ha)	874	276	249	188

NOTE: Columns of percentages sum to 100

can often be rehabilitated by modest planting programs to make them satisfactorily stocked. On the Coast, brushing is commonly required prior to planting.

In contrast to area maximization, the volume maximization strategy allocates 16 per cent of the backlog NSR rehabilitation budget to the Coast. This allocation, the highest percentage of any of the strategies examined, reflects the higher growth rates for many commercial tree species on good and medium coastal sites compared with Interior sites. While the budget allocated to the Southern Interior under this strategy (54 per cent) is smaller than that allocated for the area maximization strategy (75 per cent), about two-thirds of the rehabilitated NSR land area would be in that region under either strategy. However, the actual area rehabilitated under volume maximization (169 thousand ha) would be lower than that under area maximization (192 thousand ha).

The strategy which maximizes financial return leads to a very different regional distribution of backlog NSR land rehabilitation and budget allocation than do the other two maximization strategies, with much more investment in the Northern Interior than in the Southern Interior. In fact, the inter-regional distribution of NSR land area rehabilitated would be nearly identical to that of the strategy which treats all NSR backlog. That is, regional NSR land rehabilitation would be proportional to regional backlog NSR area. Inter-regional budget allocation under financial return maximization would also be very close to that of the 'all backlog NSR' treatment strategy. But as shown earlier, the benefits per dollar cost of the two strategies differ significantly (Tables 8 and 10), with maximization of financial return outperforming the 'all backlog NSR' treatment strategy on all measures of cost effectiveness.

Employment

The direct impacts of the alternative silvicultural strategies on employment can be divided into two parts: an effect on 'permanent' employment (timber harvesting and processing), which is directly proportional to the volume of wood harvested; and an effect on 'temporary' employment (predominantly silviculture work), which varies directly with expenditures on silviculture. Thus, the major direct impacts of NSR land rehabilitation on employment are proportional to the effects on timber harvest (Table 10) and NSR rehabilitation expenditures (Tables 8, 11).

The biggest increase in employment is in temporary employment of tree planters and other silvicultural workers to implement the rehabilitation. Program spending of $30 million per year for five years would create a 30 per cent increase in temporary silvicultural employment, while rehabilitation of all NSR backlog lands over five years would create a 130 per cent increase. Permanent forest employment would not be affected during this period. Following the rehabilitation period, neither temporary nor permanent employment would be significantly affected until the rehabilitated timber lands are harvested and basic silviculture is carried out. At that time, extending from about 80 to 130 years from now, permanent employment would be increased 1 to 4 per cent and temporary employment would be increased 3 to 7 per cent above the levels forecast in absence of NSR land rehabilitation.

Environment

Environmental benefits of rehabilitating backlog NSR lands occur in several ways. Despite their importance, however, the limitations of the available data base makes their assessment difficult. A possible indicator of environmental benefit is the area of backlog NSR lands returned to forest production. By definition, the area maximization strategy returns the greatest area to timber production. But in addition to planting denuded land, backlog NSR rehabilitation includes conversion from non-commercial to commercial tree species and supplementation of the stocking of understocked commercial species. These latter activities do not increase the 'greening' of former forestlands. A better indicator would be the area of denuded land which is returned to forested condition, but inadequacies in the available data base preclude such a measure.

Another conceivable indication of environmental benefit is the increment in timber growth, which could be regarded by environmentalists as timber available to 'exchange' for timber on lands from which they wish to exclude logging. However, the effect of backlog NSR rehabilitation on the AAC is not as simple, with issues of forest age structure and even flow of timber complicating the relationship. It should be further noted that the simulation model forecasts that *at current costs and prices* and the current AAC, the economically accessible timber will be severely depleted within two to three decades. Thereafter, and possibly sooner, the timber harvest will be limited de facto by economic considerations rather than by the AAC. While the timing of the anticipated 'falldown' in harvest levels varies with assumptions about economic behaviour of firms and the potential impact of technology on prices and costs, the extensive margin will dominate commercial timber management in British Columbia in the near future. Thus, the suggestions that restocking the NSR backlog will allow the current harvest rate to be increased, or that this extra wood can be 'traded' for mature forest tracts, are simplistic.

DISCUSSION AND CONCLUSIONS

In this study we found rather modest financial returns to investments in the rehabilitation of backlog NSR lands. Two recent studies which evaluated silvicultural investments in British Columbia estimated higher financial returns than were found here. In the first, Pearse, Lang, and Todd (1986b) considered reforestation of backlog NSR lands. They estimated that if rehabilitation was restricted to good and medium sites and was distributed over different land classes in proportion to their areas of backlog NSR land, then 150 thousand hectares could be rehabilitated for $142.5 million, yielding a mean annual growth of 944 thousand m^3. They also estimated that if rehabilitation was directed towards the most cost-effective 152 thousand hectares of backlog NSR land, the same budget would suffice, and it would yield a mean annual growth of 1,206 thousand m^3 of wood. This implies an average cost of $938 per hectare and a mean annual yield of 7.9 m^3 per hectare.

The present study reveals a cost of $602 per hectare and an annual yield of 3.3 m^3 per hectare for the rehabilitation strategy designed to maximize wood production (see Table 8). While our annual yield estimate may be conservative, mean annual yields greater than 7.0 m^3 per hectare (without silvicultural investment beyond stand establishment) are found only on good coastal sites in BC (c.f. Smith 1989b). Thus, Pearse, Lang, and Todd's estimate of potential wood production per dollar invested may be optimistic.

A recent study by a consulting group evaluated incremental silvicultural opportunities in BC, such as spacing, and identified many attractive investments (Nawitka 1987). Comparing their optimistic conclusions with our more cautious ones, we note two crucial differences in economic assumptions. The first is their lower estimate of average delivered wood cost; the second is their assumption that log prices (but not harvesting costs) will increase at 1 per cent per annum in real terms (net of inflation). To illustrate the combined effect of these different economic assumptions, consider a 100-year old stand of coastal Douglas-fir on a good site with average delivered wood cost. Nawitka's (1987) study estimates 7 per cent greater merchantable volume, 4 per cent greater current log price, and 48 per cent lower delivered wood cost as compared to this study. These differences combine to produce an 895 per cent higher net value of timber in Nawitka's study. But when we compare the net present value of Douglas-fir now being planted on a 100-year rotation, the different assumptions about future prices make an even greater difference between the values assigned by the two studies. The forecast price for Douglas-fir logs 100 years in the future is 180 per cent higher in Nawitka's study than in ours. Thus, their study estimates the value of the example stand used 100 years from now to be 4,093 per cent more than the value estimated in our study.

As noted above, expectations about future price increases and the choice of discount rate can profoundly affect the expected returns from silvicultural investments. For most natural resource products, real prices have declined over the past century (Barnett and Morse 1963). Such has not, however, been the case for timber. Manthy (1978) found that the real price of lumber in the U.S. increased 1.7 per cent per annum from 1871 to 1973. More recently, Sedjo and Lyon (1989) reviewed the literature on long-term timber prices and concluded that the real price of industrial roundwood in North America had increased by about 1 per cent per annum from 1900 to 1950 but that the rate of increase had dropped to about 1/3 per cent since 1950. For British Columbia, Ghebremichael, Roberts, and Tretheway (1989) estimated real log price increases of 0.9 per cent and 0.1 per cent for the Coast and Interior, respectively, over the period 1950 to 1985.

The choice of discount rate for public investments has long been a subject of debate. Government guidelines in British Columbia and Canada recommend that a real discount rate of 8 to 10 per cent be used (Loose 1977). These guidelines were based upon calculations by Jenkins (1973, 1977) who applied methods developed by Harberger (1972) to Canadian data. Subsequently, however, Jenkins' work was strongly criticized (Summer 1980a,b; Burgess 1981; Spiro 1987). In a detailed re-examination of the choice of social discount rate for public forest investments, Heaps and Pratt (1989) concluded that the appropriate rate was equal to the real yield on government bonds, that is, 3 to 5 per cent in Canada. Additional analysis presented in Heaps and White (1991) supports this range of rates.

To contrast with the conservative expectation of log prices and low discount rate used in our analysis above, we recomputed the benefit-cost ratios of rehabilitating NSR lands using a 4 per cent discount rate and a 1 per cent per annum increase in real log prices. Although the estimated net present values changed for most land classes, the *ranking* of backlog silvicultural investments across land classes changed very little. Good sites of most growth types in all three regions were forecast to provide positive returns, the exceptions being spruce in both Interior regions and Douglas-fir in the Northern Interior.

In our study we do not account for non-timber values and other benefits which can be derived from reforestation. Thus, investment in projects for which the study shows financial benefit-cost ratios less than 1.0 may be appropriate. Environmental benefits can be significant even in the short term in particular locations; for example, recreation and land and water conservation. Among the timber values which are derived from reforestation but ignored in our analysis are the benefits of improved quality of wood produced, improved geographical distribution, and reduced costs of harvesting. Appropriate silvicultural investment strategies might also reduce the extent of fire, insect, and disease problems, thus reducing forest management costs. Our study is also conservative in assuming constant real costs. Technological changes and industry restructuring which reduce the cost of wood harvesting and processing, and those which increase the utilization of immature timber, are likely to make reforestation economical. This may be true even if environmental benefits, option values, and other non-timber values are excluded from the assessment.

Another immediate significant economic benefit of reforestation which has considerable value but is difficult to assess is the preservation and opening of options for future industrial development. The prospect of future access to resources is an important stimulant to industrial investment. Firms are more likely to invest in a region if the investment not only provides access to the resource at present but also ensures the access to an enhanced resource base in the future.

Investments in reforestation have costs in terms of lost opportunities for other types of forestry investments, including, for example, incremental silviculture. These must be considered when the level of investment in reforestation is decided. Given the limited budget for reforestation, it is important to improve efficiency through better targeting of investments. This study demonstrates the effects of different choice criteria for reforestation and their impacts upon performance in different benefit dimensions. Clearly, efficiency must be defined in terms of the trade-offs one is willing to make between different benefit dimensions. At the minimum, one should not accept investments which are inferior, in comparison to others, on every benefit dimension. Furthermore, choices between reforestation options should not be made without considering the future protection and maintenance of the resources. More thought and planning should be devoted to the integration of decisions concerning planting, stand tending, forest protection, industrial restructuring, and technological development.

ACKNOWLEDGMENTS

This study was funded by the British Columbia Ministry of Forests. The report has been reviewed and approved for distribution. However, this approval does not necessarily signify that the contents reflect the views or policies of the ministry. The authors are grateful to the ministry for providing support and data for this project. The ministry is not responsible for the analysis or the findings in this paper, however; the authors take full responsibility for any weaknesses, mistakes or misinterpretations.

CHAPTER FIVE

Long-Term Timber Supply Prospects in the United States: An Analysis of Resources and Policies in Transition

Darius M. Adams

Over the next two decades, timber supplies in the United States will be affected by major changes in the private resource base and public timber harvest policies. On private lands, the concentration of both inventory and harvest will shift from older stands of natural origin towards younger, managed stands of smaller average size. On public lands, the management focus will shift away from timber and towards greater emphasis on natural system preservation and non-commodity outputs. If recent trends in harvest are continued, stocks of merchantable timber on industrial lands in the West and both industrial and non-industrial lands in the South will fall sharply relative to harvest.[1] The transition to managed young-growth on these lands may involve some form of supply hiatus as a result. At the same time, prospective trends in public management policies may act to amplify supply developments in the private sector. With the growing importance of non-timber values, harvest levels on federal and some state lands seem likely to fall in the near term, though the extent is not yet clear.

In the long term, public harvest policies remain a key factor in the supply outlook together with prospective rates of private investment in forest management. As a result of past harvest and investment decisions, industrial lands presently contain large areas of immature and more intensively managed timber. Given this inventory structure and the continuation of investment at roughly historical rates, growth and inventory should expand substantially and the stage should be set for some resurgence in harvest. Prospects for non-industrial lands, where past rates of investment have been much lower but more volatile, seem far less certain. Because these lands comprise such a large portion of the u.s. timberland base, even small changes in investment patterns can have major effects on long-term supply.

This paper examines timber supply prospects in the U.S. over the next five decades. The impacts of potential variations in public timber harvest and rates of private management investment are given detailed attention as two major sources of uncertainty in both the near- and long-term outlook. The next two sections provide background on the current status of private timber resources in the U.S. West and South and some of the considerations that may influence public timber harvest. The fourth section presents the results of computer simulations of three 'alternative futures' involving different assumptions on private investment and public harvest.[2] A final section summarizes results and comments on timber supply policies.

RESOURCE DEVELOPMENTS ON PRIVATE LANDS

This discussion focuses on private timber resources in the West and South.[3] These are the primary timber supply regions in the U.S., providing the bulk of processed products. Timber production in the North comprised about 16 per cent of the U.S. total in recent years and is consumed in a roughly equal mix in both solidwood and fibre products. Forest resources in this region will undergo important changes over the next five decades, but the trends are expected to be less constrained by resource quality and quantity considerations here than elsewhere.

Western States

Timber harvest from private lands in the West has shown considerable historical variation across subregions and between industrial and non-industrial ownerships. After a sharp rise and peak in the late 1920s and a further peak in the early 1950s, industrial cut has been stable to declining with much cyclical variation. Non-industrial harvest shared the same early behaviour but by the 1980s had declined to less than half of its level in the 1950s. Harvest detail by region and owner group is shown in the left portion of Figure 1 for the period since 1950.

Past harvest behaviour is clearly reflected in the age class structure of both private inventories and harvests in the early 1980s. This is illustrated in the first column of data in Table 1 for the Douglas-fir and California regions.[4] In the Douglas-fir region, industrial harvest has remained at relatively high levels since the mid-1960s. Old-

TABLE 1

Per cent of timberland base and harvest by age group for private owners in the Douglas-fir and California regions

Region / Owner Age group	1980		2000		2030	
	Area	Harvest	Area	Harvest	Area	Harvest
Douglas-fir / Industry						
< 50 Years	76.2	1.7	88.7	32.1	93.5	76.5
50 - 100	17.1	62.9	11.2	67.7	6.5	23.5
> 100	6.7	35.4	0.1	0.2	0.0	0.0
Douglas-fir / Non-industrial						
< 50 Years	61.5	7.0	50.7	3.1	55.4	1.3
50 - 100	31.4	42.6	48.0	91.0	44.1	95.9
> 100	7.0	50.5	1.3	5.9	0.5	2.8
California / Industry						
< 50 Years	27.4	0.0	74.4	2.6	99.4	99.1
50 - 100	45.6	41.3	22.6	82.0	0.6	0.9
> 100	27.0	58.7	2.9	15.4	0.0	0.0
California / Non-industrial						
< 50 Years	24.5	3.2	23.3	1.1	35.6	1.1
50 - 100	53.8	47.2	39.3	40.9	18.0	27.5
> 100	21.7	49.5	37.4	58.0	46.4	71.4

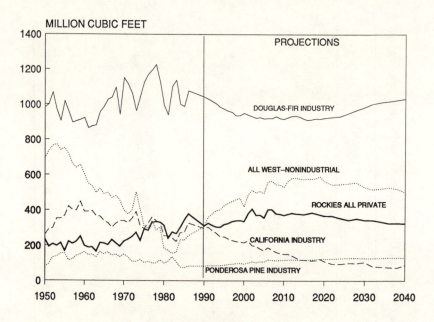

FIGURE 1
Private sawtimber harvest in the western United States with base case
projections to 2040

growth stands have been almost entirely harvested, more than
three-quarters of the inventory is less than fifty years of age, and
natural origin second-growth provides the bulk of current harvest.
Non-industrial lands also have little remaining old-growth, but declining cut since the 1950s has left a larger portion of the land base in
second-growth and a smaller portion in stands less than fifty years
old. Cut is about evenly split between the two oldest classes. In contrast, California industrial harvest has trended gradually downward
since the mid-1950s (see Figure 1), while non-industrial cut has fallen sharply. For both owner groups, nearly three-quarters of the
1980 inventory was merchantable young-growth, and harvest was
somewhat heavier in the old-growth classes.

As harvest has proceeded on western private lands, aggregate
timber growth has expanded. The trend in net stock or inventory position depends on the growth/drain balance of the specific region-
owner group and has generally, though not uniformly, fallen. This is
illustrated by the uneven changes in the inventory data in the left
portion of Table 2. For industrial inventories in Washington, Oregon, and California, growth is nearing or has surpassed cut in the
last decade, leading to a slower decline or actual increase in inven-

TABLE 2

Softwood growing stock inventories by region and private owner group in the West and South with base case assumption to 2040 (million cubic feet)

Region / Owner	1952	1962	1970	1977	1987	2000	2010	2040
Douglas-fir / Industry	32.7	27.4	23.8	22.0	20.1	17.8	18.3	23.6
Ponderosa pine / Industry	4.0	4.0	4.0	3.8	4.3	5.3	5.4	5.4
California / Industry	11.3	9.6	8.2	7.5	7.9	5.2	4.3	4.1
Rockies / All private	19.4	19.9	20.0	19.3	17.9	18.7	17.4	13.7
All West / Non-industrial[1]	29.3	26.7	24.6	22.4	24.0	30.0	30.9	29.9
Southcentral / Industry	9.7	13.1	13.5	14.4	13.5	14.5	20.4	24.9
Southcentral / Non-industrial	11.3	16.1	23.6	28.8	31.6	26.7	27.0	33.0
Southeast / Industry	6.5	7.5	8.3	8.7	10.3	11.0	12.5	13.2
Southeast / Non-industrial	23.9	26.7	30.7	34.5	34.4	33.9	32.8	27.3

NOTE: [1] Excludes non-industrial lands in the Rockies

tory. On non-industrial lands, inventory trends are strongly influenced by changes in the land base itself. The bulk of western private forest lands shifting to agricultural, urban, or other non-forest uses comes from the non-industrial category, and losses have occurred steadily from this ownership since the early 1950s. On a per unit area basis, non-industrial inventories have actually increased slowly over the historical time span shown in Table 2.

These observations suggest a conservative view of future supply prospects for private lands in some parts of the West, at least in the near-term. With rapidly dwindling old-growth and a highly imbalanced distribution of timberland area between sub-merchantable and young-growth age groups, industrial ownerships in the Douglas-fir and California regions may be unable to sustain recent rates of harvest. At the same time, non-industrial lands may provide only a limited substitute source. The sharp historical decline in non-industrial harvest depicted in Figure 1 occurred despite rising real timber prices and growing per acre inventories. Though the exact causes are not known, it is suspected that the growing diversity of objectives for holding forest land among non-industrial owners and their declining dependence on timber harvest as an income source have contributed to this trend.

In the long term, the large areas of immature timber on industrial lands will provide some basis for increased harvest as they grow towards merchantable sizes. Harvest potential will also depend on changes in the forest land base and the rate and form of investment in timber management. Table 3 gives timberland areas for western softwood types together with a detailed breakdown of the management status of private softwood stands in the Douglas-fir region. Figures for 1980 are actual, for 1990 are estimates, and for later years are assumptions used in the base case projection. It is estimated that the aggregate private timberland base in the West will fall by some .35 million acres during the decade of the 1980s. More than two-thirds of the loss in non-industrial holdings will have been acquired by industrial owners. Rates of net loss over the next five decades are projected to be somewhat slower but with only limited inter-owner transfer.

In the critical Douglas-fir region, it is estimated that a substantial portion of natural origin stands on industrial lands has been converted to some form of intensive management prior to 1990. This trend is assumed to continue in the future, with nearly three-quarters of the softwood land base under intensive management by 2040. The impact of these changes on harvestable volumes can be substantial. For example, the cumulative yield difference at age fifty

TABLE 3

Western private timberland base in softwood forest types and distribution of softwood base by management intensity classes in the Douglas-fir region (land base in millions of acres)

Region/Owner		1980	1990	2010	2040
Douglas-fir / Industrial					
Softwood land base		6.068	6.165	7.003	6.968
Management distribution					
	Natural	60.9%	46.4%	25.1%	13.5%
	Plant	4.7%	7.1%	10.8%	14.2%
	Intensive	34.4%	46.5%	64.1%	72.3%
Douglas-fir / Non-industrial					
Softwood land base		2.627	2.570	2.246	2.061
Management distribution					
	Natural	87.1%	82.0%	70.1%	52.4%
Base case	Plant	1.8%	4.2%	8.1%	15.9%
	Intensive	11.1%	13.8%	21.8%	31.7%
Softwood land base				2.567	2.383
Management distribution					
Intensive	Natural			59.0%	43.3%
mngmnt	Plant			9.3%	15.0%
case	Intensive			31.7%	41.8%
California / Industrial					
Softwood land base		2.307	2.305	2.269	1.877
California / Non-industrial					
Softwood land base		3.259	3.146	2.722	2.257
Other West / Industrial					
Softwood land base		4.357	5.021	4.998	5.008
Other West / Non-industrial					
Softwood land base		13.581	12.643	12.482	12.263
Total industrial		12.732	13.491	14.271	13.853
Total non-industrial		19.467	18.359	17.451	16.581
Total softwood land base		32.199	31.850	31.720	30.434

between mid-site Douglas-fir stands receiving the most intensive form of management and those which are planted but not subsequently treated is nearly 25 per cent.[5] Of equal importance in the near-term supply picture, the intensively managed stand contains trees of sufficient size to be eligible for harvest at age forty-five in contrast to age fifty-five for the planted stand. On non-industrial lands, the management shift in the last decade has been less dramatic. Projections for the base case call for a continuation of past rates of conversion.

Southern States

Long-term historical harvest trends on private lands in the South are roughly similar to those in the West, although, with earlier access and settlement, cut rose faster and peaked somewhat sooner in the early portion of this century. Following The Second World War, merchantable timber stocks were low and stumpage prices were high relative to the West. As a consequence, harvest fell on most private ownerships until the early 1960s. Since that period, with accelerating growth in the fibre products industry, technical changes in the solidwood sector, and continued expansion of timber inventories through plantation establishment, harvest has grown steadily. The left portion of Figure 2 shows region and ownership detail for total softwood removals since 1950. Unlike the West, non-industrial ownerships have consistently been the dominant timber source in the South.

As illustrated in Table 4, inventory in softwood types on southern industrial land during the early 1980s was heavily concentrated in immature age classes, while on non-industrial ownerships mature classes comprised a relatively larger proportion.[6] These differences reflect both higher harvest rates (both on a per unit area and per unit inventory basis) and higher rates of new plantation establishment on industrial lands. Despite high rates of harvest, growth has generally exceeded harvest on industrial lands since the early 1950s. With the exception of the most recent decade in the South-central region, inventory has grown steadily as a result (see the lower part of Table 2). Growth has also outpaced harvest on non-industrial lands. As in the West, however, lands alienated from the forest base come primarily from this owner group, with considerable variation across regions. Thus, in Table 2, we see a steady increase in South-central non-industrial inventory, while a reduction of more than 6 per cent in the Southeastern non-industrial land base between 1977 and 1987 effectively stabilized the softwood stock in that region.

Timberland area plays a particularly critical role in long-term pro-

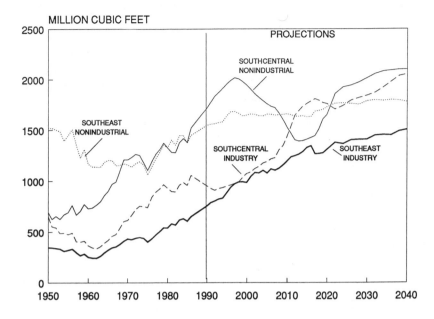

FIGURE 2
Private timber removals in the southern United States with base case
projections to 2040

jections for the South. Over the period for which reliable data are available, private timberland area in the South has been more volatile than in any other u.s. region. This reflects the relatively labile economic margin between agricultural and forest uses and, in more recent years, between rapid urban and infrastructural expansion in the South. As noted above, non-industrial ownerships are the source of greatest variation. Recent historical data on southern timberland areas and assumptions developed for the base case projection are shown in the upper portion of Table 5.

The most important aspect of timber management investment as it relates to long-term supply in the South is the acreage converted to new pine plantations. Areas for conversion come from non-plantation forest types (natural pine, mixed oak-pine, and various hardwood types) and from non-forest (primarily agricultural) lands. Over the past two decades, the area planted to pine in the South has more than doubled. The lower portion of Table 5 gives estimates of the net effects of these planting rates in terms of pine plantations as a per cent of the total private timberland base during the 1980s. Between 1980 and 1990, it is estimated that the pine plantation area on industrial ownerships rose by more than 70 per cent, with the larg-

TABLE 4

Per cent of timberland base and harvest by age group for private owners in the South

| Region / Owner | 1980 | | 2010 | | 2035 | |
Age group	Area	Harvest	Area	Harvest	Area	Harvest
Southeast / Industry						
20 Years	60.0	5.7	94.0	81.9	89.0	59.2
> 20	40.0	94.3	6.0	18.1	11.0	40.8
Southeast / Non-industrial						
20 Years	34.9	8.5	56.3	9.7	51.7	6.5
> 20	65.1	91.5	43.7	90.3	48.3	93.5
Southcentral / Industry						
20 Years	73.7	12.8	97.5	90.0	91.3	49.7
> 20	26.3	87.2	2.5	10.0	8.7	50.2
Southcentral / Non-industrial						
20 Years	50.7	6.4	91.5	67.1	59.8	5.5
> 20	49.3	93.6	8.5	32.9	40.2	94.5

TABLE 5

Southern timberland area and per cent in pine plantations (including base case and intensified management scenario assumptions to 2040)

Total timberland base (million acres)				
Region / Owner	1980	1990	2010	2040
Southcentral / Industry	21.6	21.3	20.9	22.2
Southcentral / Non-industrial	78.6	77.9	75.0	72.7
Southeast / Industry	16.0	16.8	17.0	17.0
Southeast / Non-industrial	62.8	58.4	55.9	54.4
Total	179.1	174.4	168.7	166.3

Plantations as per cent of total timberland base				
Region / Owner	1980	1990	2010	2040
Base case				
Southcentral / Industry	12.2	28.4	57.6	63.3
Southcentral / Non-industrial	3.8	5.4	11.7	13.5
Southeast / Industry	33.4	45.7	62.5	65.5
Southeast / Non-industrial	6.4	9.5	17.0	18.8
Total	8.4	13.4	24.3	27.2
Intensified management				
Southcentral / Non-industrial			12.8	16.0
Southeast / Non-industrial			21.1	27.9

est gains in the South-central area. Increments on non-industrial lands were less dramatic but still substantial at some 2.7 million additional plantation acres (roughly 2 per cent of the non-industrial land base).

Base case projections in the right portion of Table 5 assume that industrial owners continue to undertake conversion opportunities at rates comparable to those of the recent past. At these relatively rapid rates of investment, most financially attractive opportunities are exhausted by 2010. In the past decade, rates of management investment (mostly planting) on non-industrial lands have increased sharply. This has been due in part to the establishment of a variety of publicly funded planting subsidies, including those under the

Conservation Reserve Program (CRP) of the 1985 Food Security Act. A significant portion of these new investments have also taken place without subsidy. In the base case, the CRP program is assumed to continue through 2010, and investments follow the higher rates observed in the recent past. After 2010, most of the eligible area for CRP will have been treated and investment rates will fall roughly to their long-term historical average levels.

The implications of these observations (and the base case assumptions) for sustaining *current* levels of private timber supply in the South are reasonably favourable. But harvests in the South have grown steadily for the past two decades, and even a fairly conservative demand forecast would suggest some likelihood of continued expansion in the near-term future, at least in the fibre products sector. In this context, the resource prospects seem more limited. To support a rising harvest, non-industrial lands would require an age class distribution somewhat more like those on industrial lands and far more rapid rates of plantation establishment than were observed in the past. At present rates of planting, non-industrial owners could harvest their mature material and then face an 'age class gap' with insufficient immature stands moving into harvestable sizes. With sufficiently rapid growth in harvest, as might be occasioned by the need to substitute for reduced non-industrial harvest, industrial owners could cut through their mature stock to minimum harvest age material fairly quickly. It is not clear if past rates of plantation establishment have been sufficient to then sustain cut with such an inventory structure (i.e., one with little or no timber above the minimum harvest age).

TIMBER HARVEST FROM PUBLIC LANDS

Public timber harvest in the U.S. originates from lands managed by the U.S. Forest Service (the national forests), Bureau of Land Management, an array of other federal agencies, and several state and other non-federal owners. The National Forests provide nearly two-thirds of total public harvest. The bulk of these lands, and 80 per cent of national forest cut, is located in the West. Some two-thirds of 'other government' lands are located in the East, but about two-thirds of other government harvest is concentrated in the West: the Bureau of Land Management (mostly in Oregon) and certain state forests (predominantly those in Washington and Oregon) being the most important suppliers. The left portion of Figure 3 shows historical data for national forest harvest, with regional detail, and the aggregate of all other government cut.

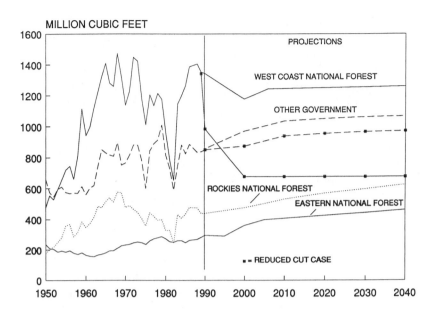

FIGURE 3
u.s. public softwood harvest with base and reduced cut cases

Following the Second World War, strong demand for forest products and declining private harvests brought expanded markets for national forest timber. The Forest Service shifted from its custodial management policy of the inter-war years towards a more active program of timber sales. Harvest in the western states grew rapidly as a result, roughly tripling in two decades. By the late 1960s, cut was approaching sustainable levels under existing management plans in the West, and an array of new management priorities brought significant changes in Forest Service supply policies. Old methods of harvest scheduling were supplanted by a new even-flow doctrine. Substantial areas of land were redesignated as wilderness or undeveloped reserves and removed from the timber harvest base. In unreserved areas, harvest planning and practices were modified to reduce adverse environmental impacts and deleterious effects on non-commodity uses of the forest. As a consequence, harvest has gradually declined over the past twenty years.

National Forest harvest patterns in the East are dominated by the southern states, where private timber supply and output of the solidwood products industry underwent a major contraction during the 1950s and early 1960s. The reduction in timber demand was sufficient to stabilize National Forest harvest as well. With the revival of the industry in the mid-1960s, eastern National Forest harvest has increased in line with expanding resource growth and inventory.

Timber management policies of the most important 'other government' ownerships are similar to those of the Forest Service as is the history of their harvest programs over the past four decades. Harvest changes since the end of the Second World War have come largely through shifts in the western regions. For example, the large harvest increment seen in Figure 3 during the 1960s is almost entirely the result of increases in Bureau of Land Management harvest in western Oregon.

The allowable cut levels on national forest lands are determined, to a first approximation, through a periodic planning process authorized by the Renewable Resources Planning Act (as amended by the National Forest Management Act). After nearly a decade in preparation, plans for all national forests are complete. In the aggregate, they call for harvest increases in the Rockies and in the East, based on expanding resource inventories and increasing growth. As a result of land withdrawals and changes in management practices, plans for national forests in the western coastal states call for a significant reduction in harvests relative to average levels observed during the 1970s and 1980s.

But even with the plans complete, the future course of national forest cut remains highly uncertain. The Forest Service has faced increasing pressure over the past three decades to increase its recognition of environmental and non-commodity benefits in its planning and management activities. The agency would certainly argue that the new plans do so to a far greater extent than they did in the past. But environmental and recreation advocates clearly do not agree. Many of the management changes proposed by these groups would act to further reduce national forest harvest. Three current issues merit specific attention:

(1) As a result of recent litigation, the u.s. Fish and Wildlife Service reclassified the northern spotted owl as a threatened species in forests of Washington, Oregon, and California under the 1978 Endangered Species Act.[7] In subsequent court rulings, the Forest Service was enjoined from selling or harvesting timber in these states in areas which might contain suitable habitat for the owl until it develops an acceptable plan for mitigating management impacts on the latter. A joint agency task group of wildlife biologists (the Interagency Scientific Committee or ISC) was established to determine steps neces-

sary to ensure the survival of the owl. The isc returned its report in 1990.[8] Under the isc recommendations, modifications of existing management plans would involve additional reservation of appropriate habitat (primarily in old-growth stands) and changes in harvesting activities in adjacent areas, further reducing the harvest potential of affected forests below the levels of the plans. In addition to these developments, efforts may also be made to reserve large areas of old-growth ecosystems in the West through direct legislation establishing reserves.

(2) Pressure will almost certainly continue for the establishment of many of the remaining roadless areas on national forests in the West and East as wilderness under the 1964 Wilderness Act, their disposition in the new plans notwithstanding.

(3) The Forest Service has been criticized by both governmental (e.g., the General Accounting Office) and environmental groups for offering 'below cost' sales – sales which do not yield a positive appraised price under customary pre-sale appraisal procedures. Again, direct legislation or provisions linked to annual budget appropriations could be used to limit such sales, thereby reducing cut and providing time for legislative or other actions to permanently reserve the affected areas.

While the greatest controversy surrounding such actions has been centred in the West, lands and harvest would be affected throughout the national forest system. Obviously, the degree and timing of any harvest reductions will vary with the mix of actions taken. At an extreme, some groups have called for a reduction of national forest harvest by nearly one-half to meet the above concerns (Wilderness Society 1989). The actual outcome of these efforts in terms of harvest changes, and the potential for gaining further reductions through legislative means, are highly uncertain. It does seem clear, however, that pressures on the Forest Service to reduce harvest will continue in the future.

Some of the largest other government agencies face prospects similar to those confronting the Forest Service. The outcome of the current spotted owl issue, for example, will have important impacts on harvest from Bureau of Land Management lands in western Oregon. Even at the state level, agencies such as the Washington Department of Natural Resources are reassessing their old-growth harvesting and wildlife habitat policies.

ALTERNATIVE FUTURES

Over the next two decades, there is evidence that the structure of private inventories in the u.s. will constrain the trajectory of private harvest and responses to any changes in price. In this context, variations in public harvest become a key source of uncertainty in the overall supply potential. As the projection period lengthens, timber management investment decisions will alter the private inventory base and emerge as a further major source of long-term supply uncertainty. To provide a quantitative appraisal of future timber supply prospects and to explore the impacts of changes in public supply and private investment, a large scale simulation model of the u.s. forest sector was employed to generate five-decade projections of sector behaviour.[9] Three scenarios were examined.

The base case employs the private investment assumptions described in the preceding sections. National Forest harvest follows the levels of the recently completed plans in the Rockies and in the East but continues at recent average historical levels in the Pacific coastal states (see Figure 3). Since the National Forest plans have yet to be implemented in these states (and in their current form may never be activated), historical levels provide a more appropriate basis for contrast. A reduced public harvest case (reduced cut) assumes that the Forest Service and Bureau of Land Management in Oregon, Washington, and California take extensive steps to preserve old-growth ecosystems and habitat for a variety of species. Management plans are assumed to be modified to the full extent recommended by the isc. Public harvest levels under this scenario are shown in the right portion of Figure 3. Aggregate u.s. levels of national forest and other government harvest are 25 per cent and 10 per cent, respectively, below base case levels by 2000 and are assumed to remain at these lower levels for the remainder of the simulation.[10] All of this adjustment occurs in the western coastal states, where national forest harvest falls by roughly 42 per cent.

An increased private investment scenario (intensified management) assumes that non-industrial owners adopt somewhat more intensive management practices than they do in the base case. This scenario is of interest both to illustrate the importance of management investment assumptions in the projection and to suggest the potential for future supply augmentation from policies influencing non-industrial management. The specific increments in investment were derived from an analysis of treatment opportunities conducted by the Forest Service (usfs 1990). This study identifies those areas and treatments promising to yield positive present net values at real discount rates ranging from 4 to 10 per cent. The set of investments employed here are those yielding at least a 10 per cent real rate. They represent some 30 per cent of the total acreage with positive present values at a 4 per cent discount rate. This latter area, in turn, is but a small fraction of all acres which might feasibly be converted to timber production or be treated to expand output.

In this simulation, only changes in the Douglas-fir region and the South were considered. Management levels are summarized in Tables 3 and 5. In the Douglas-fir region, the effect of this shift is to raise the proportion of non-industrial lands in some form of intensive management by 10 per cent by 2040. Planted pine acreage on non-industrial lands in the South-Central region rises by 2.5 per cent and by 9.1 per cent in the Southeast. The Forest Service estimates the cost of such investment in 1989 dollars at roughly $1.6 billion. The simulation assumes these investments to be made in equal annual increments over the 1990 to 2040 period.

All three scenarios employ the same assumptions regarding macroeconomic developments in the U.S. (as these influence demand for wood and fibre products) and trends in non-wood costs, technology, and trade in all products except lumber.[11] Softwood lumber imports from Canada are endogenous to the projection model. In brief, the macroeconomic assumptions portray a gradually declining rate of aggregate economic growth in the U.S. as the population ages and growth in the work force slows. Real gross national product (GNP) growth rates fall from the 3 per cent to 4 per cent range, characteristic of the last three decades, to the 2 per cent to 3 per cent range. With the exception of a modest rise due to the 'baby boom echo' in the period 2010 to 2020, housing activity declines steadily over the projection. This, too, reflects the aging population and the assumption that the U.S. housing stock will be maintained through increased upkeep and alteration expenditures rather than directly replaced through demolitions and addition of new units. In the solidwood sector, growth in demand under this outlook is limited and comes almost entirely from upkeep and repair, nonresidential, and manufacturing uses. In the fibre products sector, consumption growth slows in line with GNP and as a result of assumed increases in the use of recycled fibers.

Costs of logging and hauling sawtimber are projected to rise at a somewhat faster rate than in the past in all U.S. regions and Canada, due primarily to projected reductions in the average diameter of timber harvested. Over the 1990 to 2040 period, cost increases range from 45 per cent in the Douglas-fir Region to 55 per cent in the South. Non-wood processing costs in softwood lumber, in contrast, decline in the simulations (ranging from -16 per cent to -24 per cent across all regions for the fifty year projection period) due to continued improvement in milling efficiency. Wood utilization in all solid-wood processing also increases, with the largest gains in the South, where the reduction in log diameters is expected to be most limited. In trade, the u.s. is projected to remain a large net importer of paper and board products. Exports of lumber and plywood rise only modestly from current levels. In the base case, log exports from the Douglas-fir region are projected to fall by roughly 20 per cent between 1990 and 2000 in response to rising stumpage and log prices in the region. Under the reduced cut scenario, with much larger increases in timber prices, Douglas-fir log exports fall by nearly 50 per cent. These reductions reflect increasing availability of softwood logs in other parts of the Pacific Rim, the substitution of softwood lumber from non-u.s. sources, and the substitution of non-wood for wood products by major Pacific Rim importers.

Base Case Results

Projected levels of private harvest for the West and South are shown in the right portions of Figures 1 and 2. Details of inventory and harvest by age group are shown in the right portions of Tables 1 and 4. Regional sawtimber stumpage prices are shown in Table 6, together with projected domestic softwood lumber production and imports. The stumpage price tabulation gives the clearest summary picture of timber supply events, with sustained growth in real prices through 2010 and rough stability thereafter.

Price growth during the 1990s is driven by the step-down in West Coast public harvest and declining cut on industrial lands in the Douglas-fir and California regions. By 2000, industrial inventory in these two regions is heavily concentrated in the youngest age groups, and an increasing portion of cut comes from timber just reaching the merchantability limit. Under these conditions, recent harvest levels cannot be sustained. While non-industrial ownerships nearly double their cut in response to rising prices, the increment is not sufficient to maintain the aggregate harvest level. By 2000, however, with no further reductions in public harvest and industrial cut more nearly in line with growth, upward price pressure from the West diminishes sharply.

Stumpage prices continue to rise during the period from 2000 to 2010 due to private timber supply limitations in the South. By the end of this period, the age class structure of private inventories has shifted sharply towards the youngest classes, and cut on most own-

TABLE 6

Projected sawtimber harvest, stumpage prices, u.s. softwood lumber output and imports under base case, reduced cut, and intensified management scenario assumptions

Concept / Simulation	Average 1986-8	2000	2010	2020	2040
Sawtimber harvest					
(billion cubic feet)					
West					
Base	4.32	4.18	4.30	4.28	4.28
Reduced cut		3.66	3.69	3.72	3.72
Intens. mngmnt.		4.18	4.29	4.31	4.28
South					
Base	2.79	2.88	2.74	3.27	3.88
Reduced cut		2.80	2.64	3.18	3.84
Intens. mngmnt.		2.87	2.83	3.50	4.22
Sawtimber prices					
($ 1967 per MBF)					
West					
Base	35	49	66	76	77
Reduced cut		69	85	95	95
Intens. mngmnt.		48	62	72	67
South					
Base	43	57	73	81	76
Reduced cut		57	76	89	87
Intens. mngmnt.		55	68	78	60
u.s. softwood lumber output					
(billion board feet)					
Base	36.8	39.1	40.0	43.9	49.0
Reduced cut		36.2	36.4	40.4	45.9
Intens. mngmnt.		39.1	40.2	45.6	52.0
u.s. softwood lumber imports					
(billion board feet)					
Base	14.2	11.0	12.3	12.5	9.3
Reduced cut		13.8	15.4	15.4	12.3
Intens. mngmnt.		11.0	12.0	11.2	7.4

(continued on next page)

TABLE 6 (*continued*)

Concept / Simulation	Average 1986-8	2000	2010	2020	2040
Real U.S. softwood lumber price index (1967 = 100.0)					
Base	119.4	157.6	167.2	176.2	170.4
Reduced cut		168.7	179.9	188.2	181.2
Intens. mngmnt.		157.1	164.9	172.8	162.1

erships comes predominantly from material of minimum merchantable size (Table 4). Patterns of harvest and substitution between owners are reversed from those in the West in the previous decade. Non-industrial ownerships face the most severe problems and their cut remains stable or declines, while substantial price increases are required to secure expanded industrial harvest. By the end of the decade, growth once again exceeds harvest and cut resumes its rising trend on all ownerships.

Beyond 2020, stumpage prices stabilize or fall in all regions. Adjustments to a predominantly young-growth private inventory are complete. With only a few exceptions, private timber stocks and harvest in both the West and South are either stable or expanding. By 2040, private forest lands are approaching something like the forester's classic regulated state, with a rotation at roughly the minimum merchantable age. On industrial lands, at least 90 per cent of the timberland area is in the youngest age groups in all regions. The age class shift is much less dramatic on non-industrial lands.

In product markets, the base case assumptions yield a gradual expansion in total U.S. consumption over the projection period but with decreasing dependence on imports. Completion of the private inventory transition at about 2010 forms the watershed for behaviour in both the solidwood and fibre sectors. Growth in domestic output of pulp, paper, and board accelerates after this point, particularly in the South. Panel products are characterized by a major shift from softwood plywood to OSB/waferboard, with substitution particularly rapid during the period of rising sawtimber prices in the first two decades of the projection. Domestic softwood lumber production expands fast enough after 2010 to meet growing consumption and to capture a rising portion of the U.S. market (Table 6).

TABLE 7

Simulated changes in sawtimber harvest for the West

Year	Total	Public
	(million cubic feet)	
2000	-520	-540
2010	-610	-575
2040	-560	-520

Results of the Reduced Cut Case

The initial effects of a reduction in public harvest should be to raise stumpage prices in U.S. regions, which should, in turn, stimulate additional harvest on private lands and raise product prices and imports. These are the results shown in Table 6. In the softwood lumber market, domestic production falls relative to the base case, while imports rise. The difference between these two adjustments, about -0.6 billion board feet at its largest point in 2020, is roughly the net reduction in U.S. demand due to higher product prices.

Developments in the stumpage market are also illustrated in Table 6 and in Table 7 which presents a tabulation of simulated changes in total and public sawtimber harvest for the West.

Increased stumpage prices do expand private harvest through the year 2000 in the West, and total sawtimber harvest falls by less than the reduction in public cut. Accelerated harvest exacerbates private inventory problems, however, and by 2010 (and for the rest of the simulation) the total harvest reduction exceeds the decline in public cut alone. The structure of private inventories is sufficiently limiting to constrain both inter-owner substitution in regional stumpage markets and inter-regional substitution in product markets. The only significant supply increase comes from imports.

Results of the Intensified Management Case

Most of the additional investments implemented in this scenario involve some form of plantation activity. As a result, yield increments are delayed by roughly one rotation. The response lag is evident from Table 6. The near-term supply limitations and stumpage price inflation of the base case are essentially unaltered. Increases in harvest and reductions in stumpage prices develop in a cumulative fashion in the third through fifth decades. Prices in the South fall steadily from 2020 onward. The bulk of the area treated is concentrated in the South, in forest types with minimum harvest ages nearly half those in the West. With only limited expansion in merchantable inventory and falling stumpage prices due to early harvest expansion in the South, there is little response from the West over the course of the simulation. In product markets, wood cost reductions passed through to softwood lumber producers lead to expanded domestic production, primarily in the South, and to reduced imports.

To explore the potential range of timber supply effects from large-scale adoption of intensified management practices on non-industrial lands, a further simulation was conducted, using the full set of treatment opportunities and yielding at least 4 per cent. This involves some 42 million additional acres of plantations in all regions (75 per cent in the South), more than three times the level in the intensified management case. Results in terms of timing and relative regional impacts were qualitatively similar to the intensified management scenario. Harvest and price impacts were, of course, far larger, with stumpage prices in all regions falling to 1986-8 average levels by 2040.

SUMMARY AND POLICY IMPLICATIONS

Given the conditions and assumptions underlying the simulations in the preceding section, some resurgence in stumpage price inflation in the u.s. seems likely over the next two decades. Private inventories will not be able to sustain past harvest trends, necessitating some absolute decline in industrial harvest in the West and in non-industrial cut in the South. After 2010, the maturation of large areas of young-growth in both the West and South will bring the prospect of rising harvests and stability to declining prices. Beyond these general prospects for trends in future timber markets, the simulation results also have implications for three broad areas of forest policy in the u.s.: (1) the welfare impacts of changing management policies on public lands, (2) materials policies designed to control the long-term cost of wood products, and (3) options for offsetting near-term reductions in private harvest.

Results of the reduced cut scenario give an indication of the extent, distribution, and timing of impacts in the forest products sector due to revised public land policies emphasizing non-timber values and preservation of natural systems. In general, private resource owners would benefit, product consumers would lose, and the effects on mill owners would be mixed, depending on region. The benefits of natural system preservation must be weighed against these market-induced shifts.

At the producer level, impacts are heavily concentrated in the West, where the bulk of federal and state-owned lands are located, with sharply reduced effects on other domestic regions. Limited stocks of merchantable timber on private lands leave little room for private-public harvest substitution in the West or for South-West substitution in product markets. As a result, reductions in total harvest would be at least as large as reductions in public cut. The near-term run-up in both stumpage and wood products prices would be accelerated. Private landowners in all regions would benefit from higher stumpage prices. Mill owners in the West would lose as stumpage supply shrinks, while those in the East and Canada would gain from higher prices and increased demand for their products. Users of wood products as a group would also lose with rising prices and declining consumption. Adjustments to a permanently reduced timber supply in the u.s. would be complete by about 2010. As in the base case, both product and stumpage prices would be roughly stable in subsequent years, though at higher levels.[12]

Growing economic scarcity of timber and its potential impact on the use of wood products and nonrenewable substitutes has been a continuing concern in the u.s. throughout the post-Second World War period. Unlike most other industrial raw materials, real prices of wood products have risen steadily over the past 150 years. Past long-range studies by the u.s. Forest Service and others have projected continued real price growth in the long-term future.[13] Though the u.s. has never adopted a unified timber supply policy in response to these concerns, a significant number of forest policy measures, at both state and federal levels, have been enacted to ensure or enhance long-term timber supply and to stabilize timber prices.[14] The most widely employed approaches have been state-level forest practice regulations, various forms of subsidization of non-industrial private management, and programs which divert marginal agricultural land to forest cover.

Results of the foregoing simulations that show stabilizing prices after 2020, even with reduced public harvest, might be interpreted as implying that further efforts to augment timber supply are unwarranted. A closer view, however, suggests the opposite conclusion. Price stability in both the base and reduced cut scenarios derives from the maturation of large areas of private young-growth timber in the West and South. To a significant extent these future 'waves' of new timber were created by the restocking requirements mandated in forest practice laws in the West and by an array of regeneration subsidy programs heavily concentrated in the South, which encouraged replanting of cutovers or afforestation of agricultural lands. Reduced efforts to sustain private supply would set in motion a cycle of reduced regeneration activity that would stimulate price growth in the next thirty to fifty years, depending on the regional mix of changes. Alternatively, policies to support higher levels of private management, as illustrated in the intensified management case, could sustain the projected period of price stability beyond 2040 and potentially offset prospective supply reductions on public lands.

Appropriate policy responses to the near-term *private* harvest reductions projected in the scenarios have been widely debated in the West and are of growing concern in the South (see, for example, Bruner and Hagenstein 1981; Le Master, Baumgartner, and Adams 1983; USFS 1988; Le Master and Beuter 1989). Available policy options dealing directly with timber supply appear to fall into three broad categories. None appear to hold much promise as a means of forestalling or offsetting a near-term private harvest decline.

At an early stage in the development of the Forest Service's land management planning process, accelerated harvests from old-growth stocks on the national forests (so-called 'departures from even flow') were seen as a potential vehicle for spanning gaps in private cut of the sort shown in the simulations (Adams and Haynes 1983). National Forest cut could be temporarily expanded to substitute for private harvest, then reduced to even-flow levels. A related alternative would involve increased investment in intensified management or reduction of statutory rotation ages on public lands. Both changes, acting through the even-flow constraint and assuming sufficient existing stocks of harvestable timber, could raise current cut. With the National Forest planning process now complete, and given trends towards natural system preservation, withdrawals of land from the timber base would seem to make harvest reductions the near certain outcome and departures effectively impossible. In this context, management intensification or manipulation of rotation ages would likely act only to partially sustain, but not to expand, current harvest. Thus public timber policy now seems destined to exacerbate rather than to limit the impacts of declining private cut.

Private supply might be augmented by extending in various ways the array of traditional forest policy tools: timber and land taxation, forest practice regulation, timber investment subsidies, and landowner information programs. Unfortunately, these approaches are also of limited value because of their focus on the long term. Like the intensified management case, most are heavily directed at the regeneration decision with impacts, albeit potentially sizable, at least three to four decades away.

Timber available for domestic processing into products might be expanded through various trade restrictions, including limitations on the export of logs. This latter form of restriction presently applies to the largest part of federal timber harvested throughout the West and was recently extended to state-owned timber. In practice, log export restrictions would be of major significance only in the Douglas-fir region. While such restrictions have received much attention in recent debate, it is evident that they do nothing to augment timber supply but simply redirect it to domestic processors. Impacts of declining private supply on mill owners would be reduced, to be sure, but at the cost of losses to log exporters and private land owners.

NOTES

1 Industrial private landowners are defined to include firms that also operate processing facilities such as lumber mills, pulpmills, log export facilities, and so on. Non-industrial owners are not integrated to processing.

2 A base case is employed as a comparator for other scenarios which differ only in assumptions about resource developments. Some of the key resource assumptions in the base case are described in the following sections.

3 The geographic regions employed in this paper include: Douglas-fir region (western Oregon and Washington); Ponderosa pine region (eastern Oregon and Washington); California; Rocky Mountains (Arizona, New Mexico, Montana, Utah, Nevada, Wyoming, Idaho, Colorado, and South Dakota); Southeast (Virginia, North and South Carolina, Georgia, Florida); South-Central (Mississippi, Alabama, Louisiana, Arkansas, Texas, Oklahoma, Tennessee, and Kentucky), and North (the remaining contiguous states). The West includes the Douglas-fir, Ponderosa pine, California, and Rockies regions. Alaska and Hawaii are not included.

4 In this tabulation for the western regions, fifty years is the rough age boundary of timber merchantability. Stands as young as forty-five years (on average) can be commercially harvested if they occur on high sites or are intensively managed with attendant increases in growth. Stands between 50 and 100 years are presently termed second-growth, being mostly of natural origin after earlier logging. Stands over 100 years are, roughly speaking, old-growth.

5 These stands are planted with genetically improved stock, precommercially thinned, fertilized, and commercially thinned at age thirty.

6 Minimum merchantable harvest ages are approximately twenty years in the Southeast and twenty-five years in the South-Central region, reflecting broad differences in site quality and growth rates.

7 This ruling may also impact timber harvesting and management on private lands, but the extent is not yet clear.

8 This report is sometimes referred to as the 'Thomas Report,' after its principal author (Thomas 1990).

9 Simulations were conducted with the Timber Assessment Market Model (TAMM) developed by the U.S. Forest Service for use in its decennial Renewable Resource Assessment studies. The model is an updated version of the work described in Adams and Haynes (1980) and Haynes and Adams (1985). The base case presented here is a modified form of the 'equilibrium price' projection contained in USFS (1990).

10 Estimates of harvest reductions were developed by the author based on published information from public agencies and environmental groups regarding the harvest impacts of actions on reserve old-growth systems and critical habitat for rare or threatened species. The scenario is intended to be indicative of the types of harvest reductions which might occur and is not an accurate estimate of the reductions needed to achieve these broad environmental protection objectives.

11 Conditions underlying the simulations are discussed in detail in USFS (1990), 104-30.

12 Adams and Haynes (1989) offer a more detailed regional accounting of the impacts of potential reductions in public harvest.

13 For examples of projections see USFS (1958, 1974, 1988). Discussion of the policy implications of rising real timber prices can be found in the Report of the President's Advisory Panel on Timber and the Environment (1973) and in USFS (1982). In the latter report, see, especially, Chapter 8, which concludes: 'Restraining future rises in timber prices through increases in supply presents an opportunity to satisfy future demand for industrial materials at minimal cost to the individual citizen and to society.'

14 Despite several executive-level reviews, the U.S. has never adopted a broad materials policy to guide future industrial development and weigh environmental and economic trade-offs (see, for example, Cliff (1973).

CHAPTER SIX

Rationing the Supply of Timber: The Swedish Experience

J. Hansing and S. Wibe

INTRODUCTION

Economic laws and regulations often have a life of their own. They are introduced easily in periods of imbalance in the market – when there is a surplus or shortage situation, when prices are unusually high or low, or when there is a disturbance of any other kind. When the market does not function, politicians feel the pressure to act, and a new law is the easiest way to restore balance, equilibrium, or 'fairness.'

A law is, almost by definition, easily justified at the time of its introduction. But time goes by and things change. Economic conditions change continually; high prices become low prices and surplus is transformed into shortage. And people change their behaviour in the market in order to take account of such a new law. Thus, the situation which created and motivated the original law is soon transformed into something totally different.

But the law remains and often gives the impression that authorities can control the situation. A commission may have been formed, for example, to control price development, and it is natural to fear that the abolition of such a commission would be a step towards galloping inflation. Therefore, it is safest to keep the law and the commission. Of course, people working with the law – in our case the members of the price commission – are the strongest supporters of the law. They naturally feel that they are doing an important job, and every attack on the law is refuted as irresponsible and ignorant.

In this paper we will tell the story of such a law. This law is now called the Wood Fibre Law, earlier known as Paragraph 136a in the general Building Law, which was introduced in the middle of the 1970s, in a time when there was much public concern over the coming crisis in the supply of timber in Sweden. This law requires governmental permission for capacity expansions in the forest industry. To require this permission, firms normally have to show how and where they plan get the raw material. The intent of the law was the best possible – to ensure enough supply of timber to the industry. In this paper we try to show that the real outcome was not, perhaps, as good as was the intention.

The paper is organized as follows. In the first section we present the most important features of Swedish forestry; in the next section, we present the Wood Fibre Law, its birth, and its development; we then present an evaluation of the effects of the law; and in the final section, we present a concluding discussion.

INSTITUTIONAL SETTING

The Swedish forests have four main ownership categories. The state owns about 20 per cent, the forest industries own 25 per cent, local communities and the state church own approximately 10 per cent, and private persons own about 45 per cent. This distribution has been stable over a long period, as shown in Table 1.

The demand for wood fibre comes from four sources: the pulp and paper industry, sawmills, the board industry, and the fuel sector. This last sector has increased considerably since the oil crisis and the announcement of the discontinuation of Swedish nuclear power. Use of fuelwood presently has strong political support, and the sector enjoys generous tax reductions.

By far the largest user of wood fibre is the pulp and paper industry, which accounts for about 70 per cent of total demand. The industry uses mainly pulpwood, but over 20 per cent of consumption consists of residues from sawmills. The industry competes with other sectors on the market for wood. The board industry can also use residues from sawmills, and the fuel sector can use both sawmill residues and pulpwood. Competition from sawmills is limited to roundwood of smaller dimensions.

Sawmills initially account for about 45 per cent of total demand, but only half of this is transformed to sawnwood. The remaining amount is sold as different kinds of residues to other sectors. The board and the fuel sectors each account for approximately 5 per cent of total demand. The board industry is suffering from low profitability and a declining market. The reverse is true for the fuel sector, which has almost doubled (in terms of wood demand) since the early 1970s.

TABLE 1
Different ownership categories 1932-81 in terms of per cent of total forest area

Year	1932	1951	1981
Private	50.1	50.3	46.8
Forest industry	25.7	24.8	25.8
The state	18.3	18.5	20.3
Other juridical persons (local communities, the state, church, etc.)	5.9	6.4	7.5

BIRTH AND DEVELOPMENT OF REGULATION

The stem volume of forests in Sweden was 2.74 billion m^3 in 1985. Contrary to what a majority of Swedish citizens believe, this figure has risen considerably during the last sixty years. In 1925, when the first national inventory was completed, the standing volume was estimated at 1.76 billion m^3. The average rate of increase between 1925 and 1985 was thus 0.75 per cent per year.

The net growth of forests is not due to decreased cutting. Since the 1920s, felling has had a weak, long run tendency to increase, but growth has always been greater than felling. Presently, Swedish forests grow at a rate of approximately 100 million m^3 per year (ob or 'overbark'), whereas total cutting amounts to 65-70 million m^3. The time paths of growth and felling are displayed in Figure 1.

During the 1960s, the Swedish economy grew unusually quickly. This also affected the wood demanding sectors, and a result of this increase was a sharp increase in overall felling (see Figure 1). At the same time, growth stagnated and even began to decline somewhat, probably as a result of the high level of cutting in the beginning of the century. The result of these two trends was that the net growth of stock stagnated in the beginning of the 1970s. As a result of the international boom situation in 1974, demand (and felling) increased further, and this particular annual forest growth was – for the first and, so far, only time – lower than felling. For that year, and that year only, the stock of forests declined.

The situation might not have given birth to a new law if it had not

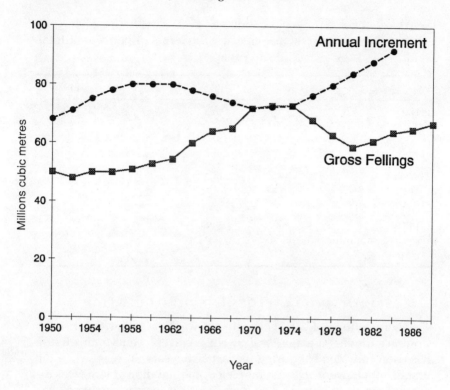

FIGURE 1
Growth and fellings in Sweden, 1930-85 (annual data each fifth year)

coincided with the great debate on the 'limits to growth.' In the beginning of the 1970s, reports like those of the Club of Rome began to
appear, and the forest situation in Sweden was then naturally seen
as a perfect illustration of the Club's thesis on the exhaustion of the
world's resources. Politicians wanted to act, and a governmental
committee was called upon to investigate the matter.

The committee tried to forecast growth and felling separately to
see if any gap would appear before the year 2000. Forecasting growth
was a rather easy task, since well documented biological growth
functions existed and the forest distribution on different age classes
was well known. Fellings clearly depended on demand, but how
could demand be forecasted? The commission chose the easiest
method and simply asked the industry about its expansion plans.
This method had some severe shortcomings, which turned out to be
fatal for the forecast. First of all, the investigation was carried out in a

year with an exceptionally high price and demand situation. Naturally, the firms were very optimistic about future development. Second, firms were asked about their expansion plans but not about their shutdown plans. Third, no assumptions about prices were included in the questionnaire.

The 'forecast' resulted in a severe shortage of wood. Growth of demand, as measured by the expansion plans, was much greater than was growth of the forests. An economic analysis of the situation would have led to the conclusion that wood prices would increase, thereby eliminating the shortage. But prices were absent, and the committee's conclusion was that the country needed a law that could help to distribute the limited resource to the many potential users.

The law was initially introduced, in 1976, as an additional paragraph (136a) to the general Building Law. Disregarding special cases, the content of the law was that permission was needed for every expansion demanding more than 10,000 m^3 of domestic wood resources. This law applied to economic units (i.e., firms) and implied that a firm was allowed to increase capacity in one plant if, at the same time, the use of wood decreased in another unit.

The permission was given by the government, but the application was sent to many different organizations (local communities, other firms, branch organizations, and so on.) – often as many as fifteen to twenty – for consideration. Local communities had the right to a veto. The permission was not limited to a simple 'yes' or 'no.' The firm could obtain permission for a certain percentage of the applied amount, and special conditions could be added. The handling time for one application was normally six to twelve months. The fuel sector was not included at the beginning, but its growth led to fear of 'excess use' of wood as fuel. From 1983 onward, fuel plants were treated equally with other forest industry operations.

From the development of growth and felling (Figure 1), it was soon obvious that the forecast from 1975 was wrong. Growth was much higher than was originally estimated (possibly due, in part, to the fertilization effect of nitrogen in the air) while demand was much lower. In the beginning of 1976, the world economy entered a period of recession and production fell in all sectors. As in all recessions, this led to a fall in demand, cancelling of expansion plans, and an increased shutdown of older plants.

The result for the forest is clearly visible in Figure 1. Since the mid-seventies, growth has far exceeded demand, and the stock of forests has grown considerably. In 1989, fellings were about 70 per cent of growth, and the increase in standing volume was greater than ever.

In addition to this, the import of wood to Sweden increased and became a matter of great concern to the government in the mid-eighties.

Thus, ten years after the introduction of the law, the situation was thus completely different. There was no shortage of wood, imports were high and increasing, and the overall problem was to find a way to increase felling in Sweden. The raison d'etre for the law had disappeared. Probably as a result of the changed situation, the Ministry of Industry formed an internal committee in 1986 to analyze the law. But this analysis did not conclude that the law was unnecessary – the committee suggested that it should be modified, and a new version, the Wood Fibre Law, was approved by Parliament in 1987. The purpose of the law was no longer to secure the long run supply of wood to the industry but to 'counteract shortages in the supply of raw material to industry.'

The committee feared that a free market would create problems, at least in certain regions. Two kind of threats were viewed as particularly important. First, they feared that the pulp and paper industry would expand 'too much,' thereby creating problems for sawmills and board-making plants, especially inland. Second, there was a fear that the increased use of fuelwood would lead to problems for the industry as a whole and that this, in turn, would create employment problems.

The new law is very similar to the old but there are some minor changes. With the new law, only large plants need permission to expand. On the other hand, all expansions must be examined, even small ones and those based on imported wood. According to the Wood Fibre Law, every capacity change in the fuel sector now requires permission.

EFFECTS OF THE REGULATION

The most important aspect of the Wood Fibre Law (or, in fact, laws) is the rationing of timber. This rationing is denied by the authorities who point to the fact that most applications are approved. But this is only partly true. During the period 1976-84, applications from the pulp and paper industry were approved in 87 per cent of the cases (measured in terms of volume). The corresponding figure for sawmills was 66 per cent, and the figure is probably still lower for the fuel sector. From these figures only, the rationing aspect cannot be ignored. In addition, the figures are only the visible part of the effect. It is more than likely that some firms (on some occasions) refrained from applications, since they knew (or suspected) that either they would not obtain permission or would meet with difficulty.

Adding all these effects, it is obvious that the Wood Fibre Law can be viewed as a form of rationing. One effect of the law is to decrease capacity expansion in industry and another is to decrease the price of timber. But it is likely that the price and quantity effects are not the only (and perhaps not even the most important) effects of the law. Since domestic wood is rationed, we would expect a switch to raw material not covered by the law, notably, to imported wood. It can also be observed that the industry can pay more than the domestic price for imported wood. One of the effects of this situation is a de facto redistribution of rent between productive agents (as some are allowed to expand and others are not) and to non-productive agents (such as local communities). The existence of this rent will induce all sorts of behaviour. First, firms will try to protect their situation by trying to prevent others from getting permission. Second, firms are willing to pay for permission (e.g., to the authorities granting permission). Both are typical examples of normal rent-seeking behaviour.

In our empirical analysis, we will focus on some of the effects of the Wood Fibre Law. The effects on capacity expansions are analyzed using standard econometric methods, whereas other effects are discussed without quantitative measurements.

Effects on Capacity

Capacity developments in the Swedish pulp industry are illustrated in Figure 2, which shows that capacity increased steadily from 1955 to the mid-seventies, when it began to stagnate and even to decline. The stagnation coincides with the introduction of paragraph 136a of the Building Law, but also with the international recession in the mid-seventies.

In order to handle the trend in capacity development statistically, we worked with yearly changes in capacity (YCC) as the dependent variable. The explanatory variables chosen were (1) changes in forest inventory, (2) level of profit in the pulp and paper industry, (3) changes in export prices for pulp, (4) cost of capital, and (5) a dummy variable for 1976 and onward. The logic behind the choice of variables is the following. Long run capacity is proportional to forest inventory and export prices. Change of capacity is, accordingly, proportional to changes in these variables. A high level of profit (one year) or a low cost of capital are, on the other hand, proportional to changes in capacity since, for instance, a high level of profit leads to high investments (i.e., large changes in capacity). As the most prob-

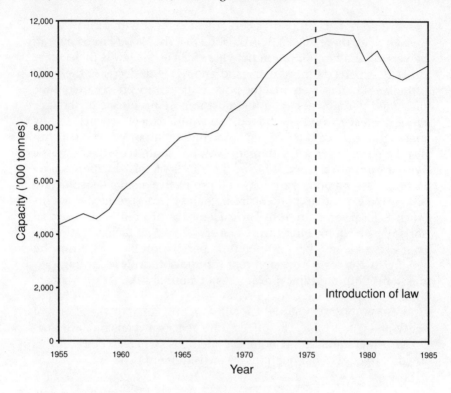

FIGURE 2
Capacity of the Swedish pulp industry, 1955-85

able theoretical effect of the law is a decrease in normal annual expansions, which decreases relative capacity expansions, a dummy variable, taking the value 1 for each year after 1976, was chosen to take these effects of the law into account. If we denote the independent variables by X_1 - X_5, and parameters by a_0 - a_5, the resulting equation is:

$$YCC = a_0 + a_1X_1 + a_2X_2 + a_3X_3 + a_4X_4 + a_5X_5$$

The results of the estimations are provided in Table 2.

Table 2 shows that the explanatory power of the equation is good. (It should be remembered that models working with yearly changes normally obtain very low coefficients of determination.) The Durbin-Watson statistic is low, which indicates that auto-correlation is a problem, and the results should, therefore, be interpreted

TABLE 2

Results of OLS regression. Dependent variable changes yearly in capacity in the pulp industry

Constant	a_0	249	234	304
		(2.15)	(2.41)	(5.26)
Annual change in stock	a_1	3.34	3.7	2.65
		(1.39)	(1.97)	(1.81)
Level of profit	a_2	11.4	13.6	13.3
		(1.07)	(2.45)	(2.42)
Change in pulp prices	a_3	0.57		
		(0.25)		
Cost of capital	a_4	−33.4	−33.1	
		(−0.88)	(−0.89)	
Dummy for law	a_5	−345	−331	−453
		(−2.09)	(−2.16)	(−6.51)
	R^{-2}	0.67	0.68	0.68
	DW	1.15	1.16	1.24

NOTE: All variables are five-year moving averges. Independent variables, except the dummy, are lagged two years. T-values are listed in brackets

with some caution. The explanatory variables have the expected sign in all cases, and the statistical significance is acceptable, except perhaps for a_3 and a_4. The value of the dummy variable is between −331 and −453. In this context, this should be interpreted to indicate that the yearly changes in capacity would have been more than 300,000 tons greater if the law had not been introduced. If correct, this implies that the production capacity for the pulp industry would have been about 3 million tons greater today if the law had not been introduced. This is most probably an exaggeration, since it would imply a 15 per cent increase in annual felling in Sweden. However, it can be regarded as an estimation of the upper limit of the effects on capacity.

An alternative way of estimating the effects of the law is to make comparisons with a country with similar conditions but without a corresponding law. The natural choice here is Finland, since the Swedish and Finnish industry operate on the same market and under similar conditions. The development of the Swedish and Finnish share of world production of pulp is displayed in Figure 3, which shows that both countries' share of total world production decreased during the 1970s. However, the share for Finland rose again

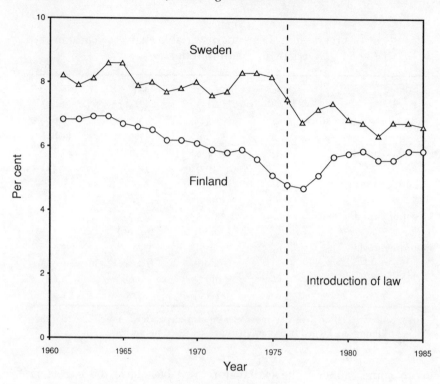

FIGURE 3
Swedish and Finnish pulp industry's share of world production 1961-85

after 1977, whereas the share for Sweden continued to fall. This simple comparison is also an indication that the Swedish law effectively prevented an expansion of the pulp sector.

The collected results, accordingly, indicate that the effect on capacity was negative. It is, of course, difficult to be precise for the quantitative effect, but the important thing is the sign. A negative effect on capacity is supported by the empirical evidence at hand.

Substitution Effect

Our theoretical analysis predicted a switch from domestic to foreign supply as an effect of the law. In Figure 4, we have illustrated foreign trade in wood fibre (mainly pulpwood). The import of wood fibre increased sharply after the mid-seventies and has since continued to increase. Presently, almost 15 per cent of total wood supply in Sweden is imported. The development illustrated in Figure 4 clearly sup-

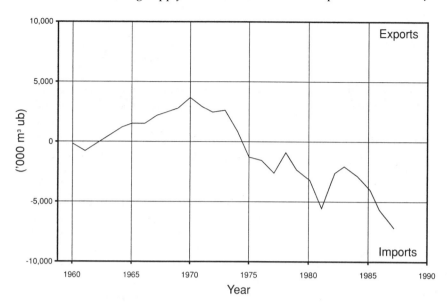

FIGURE 4
Swedish foreign trade in wood fibre (saw timber, pulpwood, and chips),
1960-87

ports the hypothesis that the law has contributed to an increase in imports. Again, however, the evidence is not without objections. Figure 4 shows that the decline in foreign trade began before the law was implemented. It can be argued that the development is simply a reflection of long-term trends not considered here, and that the law is without effect.

But there is other non-quantitative evidence to support the substitution hypothesis. This can be found in the formulation of permission given by the government. When a sample of expansion permission (licences from the government to the industry) was collected, it was discovered that the decisions often contained at least an indirect recommendation to import wood. A typical formulation is the following: Company AA has applied to expand production thereby using a total of xx m^3 raw material. The government allows a total consumption of YY m^3 (normally about 90 per cent of xx). Of this, domestic raw material may be maximum zz m^3 (normally about 90 per cent of YY). These kinds of formulations were also used after the introduction of the new Wood Fibre Law in 1987. For instance, the company Korsnas AB applied to use 2,931,000 m^3 of raw material in a plant. It obtained permission to use 2,900,000 m^3. At most,

2,623,000 m^3 of coniferous trees was allowed to be used, and anything in excess of 2,753,000 m^3 was to be imported. (This particular decision was taken 4 April 1988, and decisions of this type were the rule rather than the exception.)

It is clear both from the decisions and from the statistics that the Wood Fibre Law has contributed to an increase in imports to Sweden. This is a remarkable fact since the government, at the same time, launched a campaign against imports. Thus, during the time that responsible ministers expressed their concern over the rapidly increasing import of wood, governmental decisions directly encouraging imports were taken. There was also some confusion as to whether or not there was a real shortage of wood in the country. Decisions under the Wood Fibre Law, of course, maintained that there was a shortage. For instance, in a decision in 1986, the government maintained that 'the limited availability of raw material must lead to restrictive measures to expansions in the industry.' (Felling in 1986 was about 70 per cent of total growth.) However, in the same year, the minister responsible for forestry claimed that cuttings must increase in order to decrease wood imports. The conclusion is, thus, that the Wood Fibre Law actively contributed to increased imports to a country where there was a physical abundance of wood.

Rent-Seeking Behaviour

The existence of a rent often leads to rent-seeking behaviour. An example of this occurs when 'insiders' try to protect their privileges by preventing entrance to the market. This behaviour was typical for the branch organizations representing the different users. These organizations could (and should) express their view on every single case when the application was sent to organizations for consideration before governmental decision.

The pulp and paper industry, normally a strong voice for a free competitive economy, was a strong opponent of the law in the 1970s. However, at the end of the decade, the fuel sector appeared as a strong potential buyer. The attitude of the pulp industry then changed, and it became a strong advocate of the law, especially, as expected, regarding expansions in the fuel sector. The core of the 'argument' was that it was economically wrong (from society's point of view) to use wood as fuel, since more export value (per m^3) could be obtained if the wood was processed into paper. A more convincing argument (at least for economists) is that the fuel sector obtained all sorts of state subsidies and that competition, accordingly, was 'unfair.'

The sawmill industry, which sold raw material to the fuel sector (in the form of residues), was of the opinion that the Wood Fibre Law should not be applied to the fuel sector. (The price of chips also increased sharply in the beginning of the 1980s when demand from the fuel sector grew.) But the same sawmill industry was against free competition from the giants in the pulp industry and argued that expansions in the latter industry should therefore be controlled according to the law.

The fuel sector was finally, for obvious reasons, a strong opponent of all regulations. Since this sector started from zero, the only possible change was expansion, which, of course, threatened the pulp industry. The fuel sector had the most problems in obtaining permission and many times was only allowed to buy particularly expensive forms of wood.

Not only the branch organizations but regional authorities, local communities, trade unions, and others were watching their particular interests. The distribution of raw material was, accordingly, not based solely on willingness-to-pay but also on relative strength of organizations and their ability to influence decisionmakers. Even the decisionmakers themselves – representatives of the political apparatus – were interested in obtaining a share of the rent. What they could do was to force the firms to undertake politically popular projects as a sort of payment for permission to expand. In one case, a firm promised to undertake an investigation of fishing conditions in a nearby river. Other projects could be the building of forest roads or other investments aimed at stimulating timber supply.

The behaviour of the different firms and organizations with respect to the Wood Fibre Law proved to be a good illustration of the Marxist thesis that 'the vested interests never lie.' The common denominator was that they were all seeking rent. The law contributed to a (small) step away from the market and towards a negotiation economy.

CONCLUSION

The Wood Fibre Law, earlier known as Paragraph 136a of the Building Law, was introduced in response to what many believed was a coming crisis in the supply of timber in Sweden. However, the forecast underlying this scenario was wrong. Soon after the introduction of the Wood Fibre Law it was obvious that there was no shortage of wood in the country. The standing volume of forests, which has been increasing ever since the first national inventory in the 1920s, continued to increase after the law was approved, and felling presently accounts for only 70 per cent of annual growth.

The law was not withdrawn, even though its raison d'etre had disappeared. An official investigation in 1986 acknowledged that there was plenty of timber in the country, but, nevertheless, a law was needed 'to counteract shortcomings in the supply of timber to industry.' The rationing continued, more or less, in the same way as before.

The analysis shows that the effects of the Wood Fibre Law have been negative: capacity expansion of the pulp industry has been hampered and imports of wood into Sweden have been stimulated. All this has happened when the overall government policy was aimed at stimulating cuttings and lowering the import of wood. In addition, the Wood Fibre Law has stimulated all sorts of rent-seeking behaviour and a (small) transition has taken place from a market to a negotiation economy. It is hard to avoid the conclusion that the law has been a failure.

There are several lessons to be learned from this. The basic failure of the lawmakers was to ignore economic factors and to forecast supply and demand without reference to prices and cost. If they had used economic analysis, the conclusion would have been that the high prices of 1974 would lead to a decline in demand rather than to an exhaustion of the wood resource.

Economic analysis was not used when the Wood Fibre Law was written. Unfortunately, this is not unusual for analyses of the forestry sector. It is often believed that forestry – being a natural resource sector – is unsuitable for economic analysis and that, for example, supply and demand are determined by factors other than price and cost. But the existence of non-economic supply and demand factors (such as biological growth conditions) does not, in itself, make economic analysis unnecessary. The essence of economic analysis is not that price is the only determinant of demand and supply, but that price is the endogenous variable common to all markets. Biological growth conditions are exogenous and are similar to a given institutional setting. Prices are controllable, normally flexible, and constitute the decisive factor in creating market equilibrium. This is true for goods in general and timber production is no exception.

One lesson is, obviously, that more confidence should be placed in market forces and their capability to create equilibrium in the timber market. Of course, this is not the same as saying that all forestry regulations are unnecessary. But administrative regulations should aim primarily at protecting the non-priced goods and services in forestry (e.g., scenery values, recreation values, the role of forests in preserving wildlife, and so on.) Except for regulations on mandatory replanting, timber production could, and should, be handled by the market.

CHAPTER SEVEN

Comparative Advantage in Timber Supply: Lessons from History and the Timber Supply Model

Kenneth S. Lyon and Roger A. Sedjo

The discussion of comparative advantage is a discussion of the costs of production relative to market price. The countries, firms, or individuals with a comparative advantage are those with the production costs less than or equal to the market price at the given exchange rate. In addition, to use resources where they have a comparative advantage is to utilize them at their most highly valued use. The study of past timber harvests, which is a study of past comparative advantage in timber production, is useful because it provides insight into the future and it identifies the economic principles involved. The process of generating forecasts of future timber harvests uses these principles and generates predictions of future comparative advantage. In addition, this study of anticipated comparative advantage contains information about the role of the various regions in this supply process.

The paper is divided into three sections and a final summary. We first state some episodes from history that display the characteristics of comparative advantage in timber supply. In the second section we interpret these episodes to identify the economic principles involved. The third section contains our predictions for future comparative advantage. These are derived using our Timber Supply Model (Sedjo and Lyon 1990).

EPISODES FROM HISTORY

Historically, forest resources have been largely obtained by drawing down the naturally generated old-growth forest. The Mediterranean basin was once occupied by large forests. The cedars of Lebanon were renowned in the ancient world for their size and utility for construction. Over the millennia the forest resource of the Mediterranean region was gradually mined as, first, the accessible low-lying forests were removed and, later, those less accessible forests were removed (Thirgood 1981). Simultaneously, many of these forest-lands were converted to other land uses, such as pasture and crop-ping. The experience of other regions is similar in the sense that cut-ting progressed from more to less accessible sites and many forest-lands were converted to other uses. For example, in the u.s., first the accessible forests of New England and the mid-Atlantic states were cut, then the Lake States and the pineries of the South, and, finally, the Pacific Coast forests were the target of logging to meet the indus-trial wood needs of the nation (Clawson 1979). These historical ex-amples demonstrate the process of utilizing existing accessible stands and then obtaining additional wood by moving to new, typi-cally less accessible forests, which may be in a more remote location or in more difficult terrain. In recent years, Canada has experienced a similar shift, as the focus of logging shifted from the maritime provinces in the east to the accessible parts of the coastal forest of British Columbia and then to the less accessible forests of the inte-rior of British Columbia and Alberta.

Some of these logged-over areas were converted to agricultural or urban uses. However, at most times and places forests will regener-ate naturally if the process is left undisturbed. Examples of massive natural regeneration abound. The denuded forests of New England and the Lake States have gradually been largely replaced by naturally regenerated second-growth forests. New England, which was less than 25 per cent forested at the time of the Civil War, is now over 80 per cent forested. In the u.s. South, vigorous forests now grow where cotton and tobacco fields flourished for decades. A similar process of return to forest has occurred in many places in Europe and the Nordic countries, and the total forest area of Europe has ex-panded over the past several decades as forests reclaim lands no longer useful in agriculture.

Associated with this natural regeneration of forests is the resur-rection of industrial wood production in previously depleted re-gions. In the u.s., for example, the centre of the industrial wood pro-duction is shifting from the West back to the South. Similarly, the forests of the Lake States region are once again providing industrial wood, this time for various types of composite panelboards. Thus, while society continues to shift its harvests to more inaccessible re-gions, it is also returning to areas which were previously harvested and have been regenerated into new forests that are now reaching maturity.

In the world context, massive additional stores of old-growth forests remain in various places, including Siberia and the far east regions of the Soviet Union, northern Canada, and Alaska as well as in tropical regions, especially the Amazon Basin and the central African forests. However, some of these regions, for example, Siberia, are highly inaccessible. Thus, economic logging and the associated transportation to major markets are costly and not justified by current and past market prices. In other of these regions, and, especially, the Amazon and parts of the tropics, the lack of merchantability of the timber resource and/or extreme species heterogeneity preclude current economic exploitation. While the area of tropical forest is clearly declining, this is largely the result of pressures for land use changes rather than pressures from commercial logging.

Not only have forests regenerated themselves naturally, but humans can and do intervene in the process to make investments in reforestation. The process of forest management has long been engaged in by the Chinese and the Europeans. Most European forests today are the product of forest management as well as of natural processes. A similar statement is applicable for many of the forests of East Asia, including Japan, Korea, and parts of China. While the South's earlier second forest was largely due to natural regeneration, its current third forest is, importantly, the product of very substantial investments in artificial regeneration. In the Pacific Northwest and California, the old-growth forests that are being logged are being replaced largely by artificially regenerated forests. While relatively new to the western hemisphere, artificial regeneration is now being actively practised. In 1987 in the u.s., 1.2 million hectares of forests were planted, with about 1 million hectares in the South and hundreds of thousands of hectares in other regions.

In addition, massive investments in the establishment of industrial forest plantations are occurring in tropical and semitropical regions that have not previously been important industrial wood producers. The plantations, typically, utilize a non-indigenous (exotic) species. The largest of the 'emerging' producers is Brazil, where hundreds of thousands of hectares of new industrial plantations have been established annually for the past fifteen or twenty years. Other significant establishments of industrial forest plantations are occurring in Chile, Argentina, Venezuela, New Zealand, Australia, South Africa, Spain, and Portugal.

Commonly, the plantations of the temperate northern hemisphere are established on land which has recently been logged. Often the same species is planted as was harvested; for example, Douglas-fir in the Pacific Northwest, Southern pine in the u.s. South, and Scots pine in the Nordic countries. Many of the plantation lands, however, are in the subtropics and often are established on lands that have not been forested in recent years. In some cases the lands have never been in forest; for example, the Orinoco River basin in Venezuela. Most species being planted are exotics, predominantly tropical pines, North American pines, and eucalyptus. Brazil alone established an average of over 250,000 ha. per year of exotic forest plantations during the decade of the 1970s, and Spain and Portugal are becoming important forest resource producers through recently established eucalyptus plantations.

During these later years technological change has played an important role in timber harvests. To a large degree, the state of technology defines the resource, its boundaries in economic use, and its value. The history of the development of technology in the wood products industry is the study of innovations which adapt the variable wood resource to the needs of the industry. Small logs have gradually replaced large logs as the feedstock for lumber and veneer mills as the milling techniques improve. Structural panel boards, such as waferboard and oriented strand board made from hardwood chips of previously under-utilized species, are displacing plywood in many of its traditional markets. In pulp and paper production, techniques have gradually developed which allow the utilization of wood fibres that were previously unusable. Southern pine fibre has become usable for newsprint whereas, earlier, spruce was required. Gradually, innovations have allowed the substitution of short fibre for long fibre in the pulpmaking process. In the 1980s short fibre made up about 30 per cent of the wood utilized in u.s. pulpmaking, whereas in the 1950s it made up only about 10 per cent. Eucalyptus pulp, most of it from plantations in semitropical regions established since the 1960s, is now becoming the preferred pulp for many uses in Europe. Genetically superior seedlings give promise of even more rapidly growing trees, perhaps with other desirable characteristics. The above innovations can be characterized as 'wood-extending' in that they expand or extend the economic wood basket from which the economic supply is drawn.

In addition to allowing for the utilization of a wider variety of species, sizes, and qualities of wood, much technology in forest product processing has been of a 'wood-saving' variety. Thus, while the demand for the final products may expand at one rate, the demand for the underlying wood resource will be expanding at a lesser rate, with the difference being due to the introduction of wood-saving technology.

ECONOMIC LESSONS FROM THE EPISODES

From these episodes we see that the comparative advantage in timber production and harvests shifted as several factors changed. These include the world's inventory of timber, the world population and its location, natural and human-aided regeneration of forests, technological change, and development of plantation forests. Our discussion of these shifts is aided by the definition of three categories of forest: (1) old-growth forest; (2) secondary and managed forest; and, finally, (3) planted intensively managed forest plantations. The old-growth forest refers to timber stands that are essentially virgin, having been relatively undisturbed by human activity for a long period of time. These, typically, have large wood volumes because of the age of the trees. Secondary and managed forests refer to major timber-producing regions where the forest is either second-growth forest (which has been logged at an earlier time but has not attained the characteristics of an old-growth forest) or a managed forest (which has replaced an earlier indigenous forest). Forest plantations are the result of conscious management, which includes planting, fertilizing, and other intensive management practices.

Gradually, the world is experiencing a global transition from old-growth forests to managed secondary and plantation stands. Early in human prehistory, the pressures on the world's forests from wood needs were small compared to the large, naturally generated inventories and the forests' own ability to naturally regenerate. Human forest resource needs were met simply through collecting wood within the forest in a manner akin to the hunting and gathering mode utilized by early humans to meet their food needs. Just as hunting and gathering gradually experienced a transition to livestock raising and cropping, so, too, forestry today is experiencing a transition from the harvesting of naturally generated old-growth stands to harvests from forests that are actively managed and that are often the product of large investments in tree-planting and tree growing.

This transition is the result of a number of economic principles. The economics of old-growth forests is concerned primarily with the costs of harvest and transport. Those hectares of forest with a comparative advantage were those that were most accessible and had terrain that was highly suitable for harvest. The economic principles involved were basically those identified by Hotelling (1931) for exhaustible resources with increasing costs of extraction. Through time, as the mining of the forests progressed, the extraction costs in the form of harvesting and transporting costs increased. Throughout this there were always hectares of forest that lay beyond the extensive margin, that is, those that did not have a comparative advantage at current prices. However, as the mining progressed, the hectares immediately beyond the extensive margin gained a comparative advantage as the market price of timber rose. These hectares were, therefore, drawn into the harvest. This geographical shifting of the extensive margin played an important role in the episodic history given above.

During the time period when these old-growth harvests were the predominant source of timber, vast amounts of land were converted to other uses. These conversions also indicate comparative advantage, as the hectares of land thus converted had a higher valued use. Their comparative advantage lies in producing something other than forests. History indicates that in this switch to the most highly valued use the timber may or may not be commercially harvested. This depends upon the value of the stumpage, which, in turn, depends upon the timber's characteristics, the market price of timber, harvesting, and transporting costs. Associated with some of the conversions were 'slash and burn' harvests, which signalled that the stumpage value was negative.

Associated with this mining of the old-growth forests was a long-term upward trend in the real price of timber. As this price rose it became profitable to artificially regenerate the forest after a harvest and to apply other inputs and management practices to the land. The economic principle is that the inputs will be used up to the quantity where the expected value of the marginal product of these inputs discounted from the anticipated harvest time to the application time is equal to the price of the input. We have seen this in the secondary and managed forests. These hectares lie within the extensive margin, that is, they have positive forest land values. Those hectares on and beyond the extensive margin will be naturally regenerated, because the land value of these hectares is zero. Associated with the management of secondary and managed forests is the selection of the optimal rotation age. The concepts involved in this selection date back to Faustmann (1849). The aging decision for a hectare of trees hinges on whether the expected net value of the timber, if harvested today, plus the present value of the future rotations that could be started now are greater than the discounted net value of the timber if harvested next year plus the present value of the future harvests that could then be initiated. The important elements in this decision are the expected price of timber today, next year, and in future rotations; the expected growth of the trees during the coming year; and the interest rate to be used in discounting future money values. The higher the growth rate of the trees, the more attractive the deferring of the harvest; also, the higher the future price of timber relative to the current price, the more attractive the future harvests. A low interest rate favours future harvests in the sense that the lower the interest rate, the longer the optimal rotation period with other things held constant.

The increase in real timber prices caused by the draw-down of old-growth forests has resulted in a change in the comparative advantage of some hectares of land. The expected net present value of the income stream generated by intensively managed forests on these hectares has risen to the point where the land's most highly valued use is plantation forests. This conversion to plantation forest may or may not follow a commercial harvest. The conversion may be from other agriculture or from forests with zero or negative stumpage value. A brief account of these conversions was given above in the historical episodes.

These conversions to industrial forest plantations must be critically concerned with the biology and the costs of planting and growing, in addition to harvesting and transporting. At current timber prices, plantation forest investments are often made in regions and areas that were not previously important industrial wood producers. The location of these investments is not predetermined by the existence or lack thereof of an earlier forest. The cropping mode in forestry and the introduction of a broad array of tree-growing technologies, ranging from fertilizers to genetic improvements in the growing stock, have been complementary. Finally, the establishment of forest plantations at new geographic locations, which were not previously important wood producers, suggests a new structure of international trading patterns in forest resources and, also, in processed wood products. That is, the cropping mode of timber production is being adopted because comparative advantage in industrial timber production is shifting.

PREDICTIONS OF FUTURE COMPARATIVE ADVANTAGE

The same fundamentals that determined comparative advantage in the past will determine it in the future. The trend towards cropping of trees and the use of exotic and biotechnologically improved stock is well entrenched; hence, it is reasonable to anticipate that an increasing portion of world timber supply will come from this source. One way to form predictions about the future shifts of comparative advantage is to organize the relevant information within an aggregate world model. We do this in our Timber Supply Model.

This Timber Supply Model (TSM) is an optimization model that is designed to examine theoretical and practical issues in world timber supply (Sedjo and Lyon 1990). The dynamic characteristics of timber supply, such as aging of trees, harvesting of timber, and regenerating the forest, have been modelled using discrete time optimal control theory. An algorithm for solving this optimization problem has been selected, the computer code written, and the resulting computer program has been implemented on real world forest inventory data, yield functions, cost functions, projected future demand conditions, and so on. The model recognizes that timber harvests come from a capital stock (timber inventory) and that the growth of trees results in additions to that capital stock. This view is particularly important in an environment where a significant portion of the timber harvest is from the inventory of old-growth timber. The TSM allows for the estimation and projections of economic rates of harvest from existing forests – old-growth, naturally regenerated second growth, and human-made forest plantation. The model is particularly well suited for tracing out the system-wide time profile of harvests and wood prices for the period of transition from old-growth forests to a stationary state. The model simultaneously analyzes a number of sites which are at different stages in the transition. It traces out the system-wide time profile of harvests in the aggregate and by site class and also generates the system-wide intertemporal market price.

The time path it generates is optimal in the sense that the model maximizes the discounted present value of the sum of producers' and consumers' surpluses, that is, it provides for the economically efficient solution. As the model traces out the system-wide optimal time profile of harvest volumes and wood prices for the period of transition and beyond, the TSM optimizes regional and site class intertemporal harvest levels while determining the economically efficient levels of silviculture (regeneration input) by time period and site class.

In the application of TSM, we place all of the world's forest resources into two major categories, 'responsive' and 'non-responsive.' Those regions in the 'responsive' set are viewed as responding to economic profit-maximizing incentives and, therefore, generally behave in a manner roughly approximating what we have termed economic optimization. The regions in the 'non-responsive' set are those from planned economies or those where there are data deficiencies.

In TSM, harvest levels are affected by adjustments of seven types: (1) rotation lengths, (2) the rate of draw-down of old-growth inventories, (3) the number of forested land classes that are utilized in the harvest, (4) the level of regeneration input applied to the various land classes, (5) the rate at which new industrial plantations are added to the world's forest producing regions, (6) the rate of technical change – wood-extending, wood-growing, and wood-saving, and (7) changes in production from the non-modelled (non-responsive) regions of the world. The first three of these pertain to the rate at which the existing timber inventory is harvested. These three means of affecting the harvest level might be viewed as short- or medium-term effects. The second three can be viewed as long-term effects within the modelled (responsive) timber producing regions, and they relate to the rate at which new sources of industrial wood are made available or at which the existing timber is used more efficiently. The first four adjustments are determined within the model (endogenously) and are affected by the current and future price as well as by the interest rate. The last three are determined outside the model (exogenously), and are anticipated levels estimated from past and current trends.

Numbers (2) and (3) above bear upon the comparative advantage of a geographic region. A particular land class may or may not enter into the solution to the necessary conditions for an optimal time path. For example, an inaccessible region with high harvest costs may have no harvests if the scenario being examined has a weak demand which generates low prices, but it may be an important supply source if the scenario has a strong demand which generates high prices.

For the application of the model we grouped the timber-supplying regions of the world into ten regions. Seven of these we classify as responsive and three we classify as non-responsive to market forces. The u.s. South, u.s. Pacific Northwest, Canada West, Canada East, Nordic Europe, Asia/Pacific, and the Emerging Region form the responsive set, where the Emerging Region is an aggregate of tropical and semitropical regions which have established forest plantations of non-indigenous species. This region includes Brazil, Chile, New Zealand, Australia, South Africa, Spain, and Portugal. The ussr, the rest of Europe, and all other regions are in the non-responsive set.

The seven responsive regions collectively produce about one half of the total industrial wood produced worldwide. These regions are subdivided into twenty-two site classes. For each site class the following data are incorporated into the model: land area, existing timber inventory, yield function, silvicultural response, harvesting, transport, and roading costs. Both domestic and international transporting costs are included. The international transportation costs link each of the twenty-two site classes to its major market, which is one of the following: (1) Japan, East Asia; (2) north central, northeast U.S.; (3) central Europe.

The world demand for industrial wood, its growth rate, and the growth rate of technological change are imposed on the system. Historical data were analyzed to identify predictions of these items. The growth of industrial wood demand facing the responsive regions is driven by the growth of the demand for wood and paper products and the supply growth of the non-responsive regions.

The optimal time paths have been generated for several scenarios. These have been analyzed and reported elsewhere (Sedjo and Lyon 1990). Here, however, we will discuss primarily our base scenario and its implications for comparative advantage. We also briefly mention some results of our low- and high-demand scenarios.

The outside conditions of the base case are: (1) world demand for industrial wood increases at 1 per cent per year, gradually declining to zero at fifty years; (2) the harvests of the non-responsive regions of the world increase at 0.5 per cent per year, declining to zero at fifty years ((1) and (2) translate into an initial increase of the demand facing the responsive region of the model of about 1.5 per cent per year); (3) new forest plantations are established in the emerging region at a rate of 200 thousand hectares per year for thirty years; (4) the dollar exchange rate is assumed to be at an intermediate level throughout the period of analysis; (5) biotechnological change is occurring at a rate of 0.5 per cent per annum, declining linearly to zero at fifty years and entering into harvest levels through the yield functions which reflect the improved technology in proportion to the investment in regeneration. The 1 per cent growth rate of world demand for industrial wood is less than the growth rate of the 1970s but greater than the rate of the 1970-85 period. Above, we let several growth rates gradually taper to zero over the first fifty years. For demand growth this is consistent with the experience since 1970, because world demand growth has been decreasing. Supply growth from the non-responsive region is projected to taper off because of declining old-growth supplies. We used the same time frame for biotechnology both to be uniform and because we felt that the actual time frame was not critical. We desired, for number crunching purposes, that the system evolve to a stationary state, and we felt that the selection of fifty years would not influence the results for the immediate future.

These conditions are our best guess concerning the future exogenous conditions required for the implementation of TSM, and we feel that they are the set most likely to occur. In addition, we maintain that TSM does an excellent job of integrating all of the regions into a unified worldwide system; hence, we claim that the projections of our base case are the best available at this time. We do not claim to have the best model or projections for any single region; therefore, we view the regional projections as indicative rather than as definitive.

The projections of the base case forecast are interesting but not startling. First, over the fifty-year period 1985 to 2035, harvests of the entire system are forecast to increase about 30 per cent or about 0.54 per cent per year (see Figure 1). Second, as portrayed in Figure 2, over that same period prices are forecast to rise a modest 12 per cent, or an almost negligible 0.2 per cent per year. Third, as indicated in Figure 1, the u.s. South and the Emerging Region are the only regions to experience appreciable long-term increases in harvests over that period. These two regions account for essentially all of the aggregate output increases experienced by the responsive region. The harvest projections are within the range of the experience of the last one and one half decades, and the price projections are within the growth rates experienced since 1950.

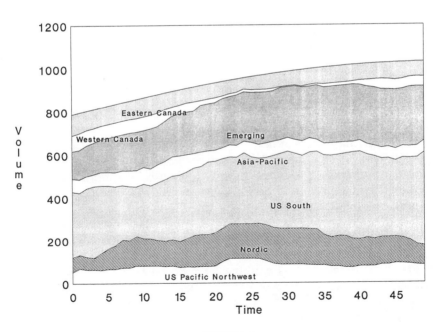

FIGURE 1
Harvest volume over time, base case scenario (millions cubic metres)

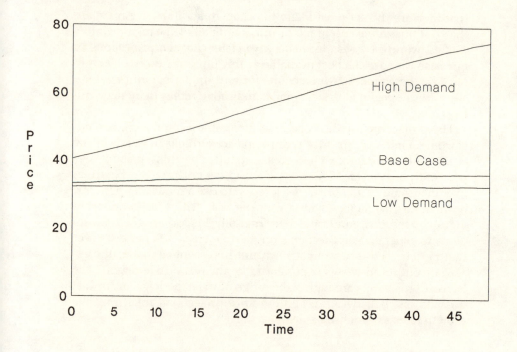

FIGURE 2
World market real price of industrial wood, three scenarios (dollars per cubic metre)

The Pacific-Asian region continues as a modest (by global standards) producer, and the traditional producers of the northern temperate climate regions, such as Canada, the Pacific Northwest, and the Nordic countries, continue to be major producers albeit at somewhat reduced production levels for eastern and western Canada; thus, we predict an erosion of their competitive position. The less accessible land classes of British Columbia and Eastern Canada are not harvested during the next fifty years. The more accessible land classes of these regions, and all land classes of the u.s. Pacific Northwest, enter the harvest, and their old-growth forests are harvested during the first fifty years. After the harvest of the old-growth forests, their harvest levels continue at reduced levels coming forth from natural regeneration. The forecast for the Nordic land classes is similar. The Emerging Region and the more productive and more accessible site classes in the u.s. South are the only site classes to receive high investments in regeneration. This investment is nil for all other site classes. Our forecast, therefore, is that unless a site class is accessible and has a climate conducive to rapid growth, it will not have a comparative advantage in silvicultural investments.

Worldwide there is increasing production from second-growth forests and the forestry plantations of the u.s. South and the Emerging Region, which offset both the declines in old-growth harvests and which accommodate the increases required by increasing demand.

To provide some sense of the overall sensitivity of the system, we describe some results of our scenarios for both higher and lower levels of demand growth. Under the high-demand scenario, which posited that initial demand growth was 2.0 per cent annually, gradually falling in successive years to zero after fifty years, harvest volumes and price are projected to rise at a much more rapid yearly rate, 0.9 per cent and 1.3 per cent, respectively. The differences between the base- and high-demand scenarios reflects both the ability of the system to expand production of harvested wood in response to the higher prices and the necessity of higher prices to generate output increases. The higher current prices allowed additional old-growth land classes to enter the economic timber base, and higher anticipated future prices resulted in higher levels of investment in regeneration and, ultimately, in higher levels of harvest.

Structurally, the u.s. South and the Emerging Region continue to be the largest producers over the first fifty years. However, some of the old-growth regions make substantially higher contributions to harvest levels, since timber stands previously viewed as submarginal by virtue of their location and accessibility are drawn into the economic timber base by the higher real price. These points and others are depicted in Figure 3. All twenty-two land classes entered the harvest by the fortieth year. In addition, the sources of increased harvests included substantially greater investments in regeneration as the result of the incentives created by the higher prices. The comparative advantage of the less accessible parts of the u.s. Pacific Northwest, British Columbia, eastern Canada, and Nordic Europe increased as a result of the higher prices.

The low-demand scenario assumed worldwide demand growing initially at only 0.5 per cent per year, declining to zero in fifty years. For this scenario, timber prices showed no increase (see Figure 2) while, as shown in Figure 4, the worldwide harvest volume annual growth rate was only about 0.25 per cent. Investments in regeneration were quite modest, with most regions justifying only negligible economic investment levels. Furthermore, more land classes were projected as economically inaccessible for harvesting purposes, with eight of the twenty-two land classes falling into this group.

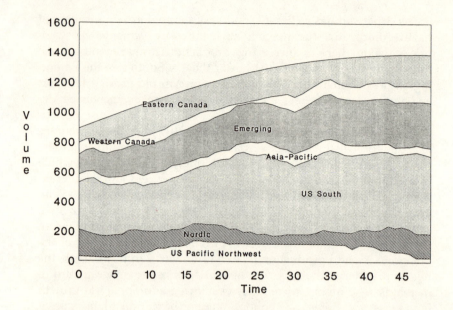

FIGURE 3
Harvest volume over time, high-demand scenario (millions cubic metres)

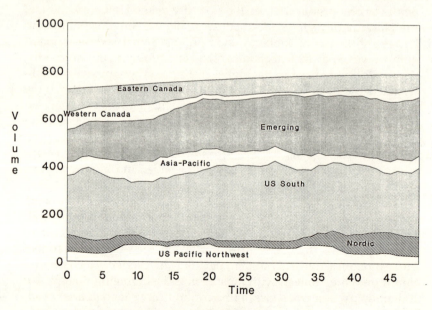

FIGURE 4
Harvest volume over time, low-demand scenario (millions cubic metres)

The regions found to be most responsive to posited changes in demand growth – both increases and decreases – and prices were Canada, both East and West, the Nordic region, and the Pacific Northwest. This was due largely to the fact that these regions had marginal timber lands that became supramarginal at high prices and submarginal at low prices. In addition, regeneration investment levels in some regions, for example the Pacific Northwest, are particularly sensitive to future prices, and the high-demand scenario generates substantial increases in future harvests due to investments. These same regions, not surprisingly, also tended to be susceptible to weak prices. Western Canada, in particular, was projected to experience relatively low levels of future harvest in the event of low demand growth and relatively weak prices.

These results are not surprising. The comparative advantage of the u.s. South and the plantations of the Emerging Region is well established. This comparative advantage is with respect to both the land and silvicultural investments. The comparative advantage of the land classes of the other regions depends upon the level of prices which, in part, depends upon the level of demand and the rate of biotechnological change. At the high prices of the high-demand scenario, all land of the traditional suppliers produces commercial timber, and the more accessible land classes also have a comparative advantage in silvicultural practices. On the other hand, at the low prices of the low-demand scenario, all of the less accessible land classes in the traditional regions were submarginal. At these prices, only the more productive and more accessible land classes of the u.s. South and the Emerging Region had a comparative advantage in silvicultural practices.

SUMMARY

We have examined the economic principles of comparative advantage by surveying timber supply through history. For most of this history, comparative advantage depended almost exclusively upon harvesting and transporting costs because the harvests were from old-growth forests and any regeneration that occurred was natural. The world now, however, is experiencing a transition to the intensive cropping of trees for a large fraction of the commercial timber harvest. Comparative advantage in this shift is critically concerned with the biology and the costs of planting and growing, in addition to harvesting and transporting. Some lands have a comparative advantage in supplying intensively cropped timber, while other lands are on the extensive margin where stumpage price is equal to the harvesting and transporting costs so that the forest land value is

zero. These lands have a comparative advantage in supplying naturally regenerated timber.

We also made predictions about future comparative advantage
through the use of a Timber Supply Model. We found the u.s. South
and the plantations of the Emerging Region to have a comparative
advantage with respect to both land and silvicultural investments.
The comparative advantage of the land classes of the other regions
depends upon the level of prices which, in part, depends upon the
level of demand and the rate of biotechnological change. Under the
most likely set of events, we predict that the traditional producers of
the northern temperate climate regions, such as Canada, the Pacific
Northwest, and the Nordic countries, will continue to be major producers but at somewhat reduced production levels after their old-
growth forests have been harvested.

CHAPTER EIGHT

Technical Change in the Forest-Based Sector

David N. Bengston and Hans M. Gregersen

INTRODUCTION

New technologies can create entire new industries, cause old products to be replaced by new ones, create new inputs or increase the productivity of old ones, and otherwise affect the processes by which goods and services are produced, distributed, and consumed. The role of technical change in the process of economic growth and development has long been recognized. Economists have formally studied the development, diffusion, and impacts of technical change since the 1950s. This body of research has clearly shown that economic forces significantly affect the development and diffusion of new technologies and that the economic impacts of technical change have been substantial. The importance of technical change for the vitality of firms, industries, and national economies has been accepted as almost self-evident. D. Bruce Merrifield, Assistant Secretary of Commerce for Productivity, Technology, and Innovation, strikingly brought home the importance of technical change at the firm level as follows: 'Any company that is not either developing new technology or adapting advanced technology to their present business has made a decision to be out of business in five to ten years' (1987:4).

Study of technical change and recognition of its importance in the forest-based sector has been relatively slow in coming, despite the fact that new technologies have had a tremendous influence on the value and patterns of utilization of forest resources in this century. In the forest products industries, new technologies have offset changes in species availability and growing stock, averting severe dislocations and significant price increases. Technological progress has thus helped keep the 'Malthusian' limit on forest resources at bay: 'As preferred species, sizes, and qualities of wood have become depleted due to increased demand, processing technologies have been adjusted to work with more abundant species and materials previously thought to be unusable' (U.S. Office of Technology Assessment (OTA) 1983:130). This statement exemplifies the definition of technical change often used by economists: Technical change is the substitution of less expensive or relatively abundant resources for more expensive or scarce resources.[1] Hayter (1988) has argued that the rate of technical change in the forest products industries has increased over the past twenty years. The prospects for future technical change seem propitious, with continued application of microelectronics, biotechnologies, and other advanced technologies.

The purposes of this paper are to review the economic and related literature on technical change in the forest-based sector and to discuss major implications for policy. It is not intended to be a comprehensive review but, rather, an overview of key issues and findings. A comprehensive review with detailed discussion of individual studies would be unwieldy – the literature on technical change in the forest industries has grown considerably since Bentley's problem analysis and literature review, in which he states: 'Technological change in the forest industries is a relatively unexplored subject despite its importance' (1970:3).

The paper is organized as follows: The first section provides a brief discussion of several important technical characteristics of the forest-based industries; the second section examines the development of new technology in forestry, focusing on the sources of technical change; the third section surveys research on the diffusion of new technology in forestry; and the fourth section considers the efficiency and distributional impacts of technical change. A final section draws out key conclusions and policy implications.

THREE KEY TECHNICAL CHARACTERISTICS OF FOREST-BASED INDUSTRIES

As a preliminary step in examining technical change in the forest-based sector, this section considers several important technological and economic characteristics: technical rigidity, capital intensity, and heterogeneity of inputs. The purpose is to explore some of the distinctive characteristics of the forest industries that are relevant to a discussion of technical change.

Technical rigidity refers to possibilities for factor substitution and the ease of scale adjustments. An exhaustive study of 181 industries

TABLE 1
Technical rigidity of forest industries

ITR[1]	Forest industries	Total number of industries	Forest industries as a per cent of total
7	None	2	0
6	Paperboard Fibre building paper Paper Fibreboard	11	36
5	Particleboard Hardboard	12	17
4	None	9	0
3	Plywood Wood veneers	26	8
2	Pulp (mechanical) Matches Printed paper	31	10
1	Sawn & planed wood Wooden barrels, drums, boxes & crates	56	3
0	Wooden sashes, doors, door frames & windows Containers & boxes, paper Wooden furniture Houses (wood)	30	13

SOURCE: Adapted from Forsyth et al. (1980)
NOTE: [1]Index of technical rigidity, with a possible range of values from seven
(most technically rigid) to zero (least technically rigid)

throws light on the technical rigidity of forest-based industries relative to other industries (Forsyth et al. 1980). An index of technical rigidity (ITR) was constructed for each industry and summarizes an engineering-based assessment of the opportunities for substituting labour for capital in manufacturing subprocesses. Table 1 shows the ITR's for forest-based industries, together with the per cent of all industries with a particular ITR ranking for which they account. The most rigid industries are those with rankings of seven, of which there are two in total and none in the forest-based category. However, 36 per cent, or slightly more than one-third of those with a ranking of 6, are forest products related industries. A further 17 per cent of industries with a ranking of 5 are forest-based. At the other end of the scale, 13 per cent of the thirty industries with the lowest level of technical rigidity are also forest-based. Note that there is a direct relationship between technical rigidity and the degree of breakdown of the wood raw material. Industries that use whole trees or sawn trees are the least rigid (lumber, boxes, etc.), going on to particles (particleboard), to fibre bundles (fibreboard), and to individual fibres (paper and paperboard). This study concludes that subsectors within the forest-based sector range from very high degrees of technical rigidity to those with hardly any rigidity.

As in the case of technical rigidity, the industries that make up the forest industry sector range across the board in terms of capital intensity (capital per worker). In a study of some 184 industries, Balassa (1977) found that wood pulp ranked second behind petroleum in terms of capital intensity in the U.S., while production of wooden boxes and crates ranked near the bottom. Wood pulp was fifteen times as capital intensive as were wooden boxes and crates. Technical rigidity and capital intensity generally have a direct relationship. Thus, some of the most technically rigid industries, such as pulp and paper, also are some of the most capital intensive industries, while some of the industries with the greatest technical flexibility are among the least capital intensive.

Finally, Rosenberg (1988:25) has discussed the high degree of heterogeneity of inputs in the forest-based industries: 'This heterogeneity is based, of course, upon the fact that the primary input of the industry is an organic material of a remarkable degree of diversity.' The diversity of wood as an input is reflected in differences based on species of tree, age, location, climate, moisture, size of log, and so on. Because the characteristics of wood are so diverse – varying even from one location on the log to another – Rosenberg has argued that research findings are much less generalizable in forest products than they are in industries with more homogeneous primary inputs such as aluminum, iron and steel, pharmaceuticals, or electronics. Knowledge in forest products is often particular and specific rather than overall and theoretical. Thus, according to this argument, the extreme heterogeneity of the wood input complicates and slows down the process of knowledge accumulation and diffusion within the industry.

It is evident that the forest industry sector is not homogeneous in terms of the three technical characteristics discussed here. In fact, it is a highly heterogeneous sector: differences between subsectors within it are as great as any differences one might observe between completely unrelated industries. These differences do have implications for the development, diffusion, and impact of technical change in the forest-based sector and are important to bear in mind in the review that follows.

SOURCES OF NEW TECHNOLOGY IN FORESTRY[2]

New technology in the forest industries originates from many sources, both inside and outside of the forest-based sector, including (1) public and private forestry research and development (R&D), (2) 'informal' research and development, (3) technology imports from other countries, and (4) technology 'imports' from other sectors of the economy. This section briefly examines the potential importance of each of these sources of new technology in forestry.

Public and Private Forestry Research

Public and private research as a source of technical change has been analyzed extensively by economists in recent decades. Numerous case studies of specific technological innovations resulting from research have been carried out as well as aggregate studies investigating the link between investment in research and the resulting technical change in agriculture and other sectors (Ruttan 1982). Recent studies have examined the economic impact of forestry research and have confirmed its importance as a source of technical change. These studies will be discussed later under the heading of the economic efficiency impacts of technical change.

The public and private forestry research system includes a diversity of organizations. In an extensive review and assessment of forestry R&D in Canada, Hayter (1988) identifies the following types of research performers: forest-product manufacturing firms, co-operative (association) R&D laboratories sponsored by firms and by governments, equipment manufacturers, chemical suppliers, small specialized firms (e.g., independent inventors, R&D service companies), federal and provincial governments, and universities. Each of these research performers possess unique strengths and characteristics that define their particular niche in the research system. For example, Hayter notes that universities typically have a comparative advantage in basic research, applied research is best carried out by co-operative laboratories and universities, process and new product development is often in the domain of equipment suppliers and forest-product firms, respectively, and so on. Because of the special-ization of research functions, successful major technological inno-vations in forestry typically involve communication and co-opera-tion between the various performers of R&D. This was found to be the case in the development of structural particleboard technology,[3] which originated with two individual inventors but required the in-volvement of the full gamut of forestry research performers to com-plete the innovation process (Bengston et al. 1988).

An important characteristic of both public and private R&D in the forest industries is a low level of research intensity relative to other industries and sectors. For private R&D, the National Science Foun-dation (1989) reports that R&D expenditures as a proportion of net sales by u.s. lumber, wood products, and furniture firms (standard industrial clarification (SIC) twenty-four and SIC twenty-five) was 0.5 per cent in 1986. u.s. paper and allied products firms (SIC twenty-six) spent about 1.3 per cent of net sales on R&D. This compares to a na-tional average for all u.s. industries of 3.2 per cent in 1986. Hayter (1988) reports that Canadian forest-based industries are also charac-terized by low research intensity.

For public R&D, Mergen et al. (1988) calculated research intensity by region in forestry and agriculture in two ways: (1) research ex-penditures as a percentage of the value of production, and (2) scien-tist years per $10 million of production. In 1980, the first measure of research intensity was estimated to be 0.269 in forestry and 1.234 in agriculture for North America/Oceania. The second measure was calculated as 0.263 in forestry and 0.969 in agriculture for the same year and region. The conclusion that expenditures on forestry re-search are low relative to other industries and sectors of the econ-omy is difficult to escape.

Informal R&D

An often overlooked source of technical change is informal R&D, sometimes called blue-collar R&D or learning by doing. Informal R&D consists of small-scale knowledge-gaining or problem-solving activities carried out by non-scientists outside of formal research departments or organizations. Informal research may be carried out by engineers, entrepreneurs, managers, production workers, non-industrial private landowners, and so on. In some cases, informal R&D is related to what has been termed 're-invention' or the extent to which an innovation is modified by users in the process of its adop-tion and implementation. Rogers (1983) reports that re-invention is very common for certain types of innovations, so the tinkering and informal R&D of users may contribute substantially to technical change. Informal R&D has been studied in agriculture and other sectors, but the importance of this source of technical change in forestry has received almost no attention. The potential importance of informal R&D is suggested by the estimated 4 per cent annual growth in labour productivity in the U.S. pulp and paper industry between 1919 and 1940, despite the lack of major new technologies (Cohen 1984). Historians of technical change have found that individually minor improvements in technology often have a major cumulative effect.

Technology Imports from Other Countries

An increasingly important source of new technologies in forestry is imports from other countries. Data presented by Mergen et al. (1988) indicate that the North American share of global forestry research expenditures dropped from an estimated 42.5 per cent in 1970 to 32.2 per cent in 1981 (Table 2). Other countries and regions are clearly increasing their investment in forestry and forest products research (and research in other fields) more rapidly than are the U.S. and Canada. Technologies generated by foreign research may have a growing impact on the forest-based sector in North America as other countries take the lead in certain areas of technology: 'It is no accident that the leader in mechanical pulping technology is Scandinavia, and the leader in papermaking technology is Japan. This technology will be transferred to North America at an accelerated rate' (Styan 1980:28).

The dominance of European equipment manufacturers in many areas of wood panel technology is another case in point (Anon. 1986). U.S. and Canadian wood products firms have begun to import a substantial amount of European manufacturing technology for structural particleboard in recent years, especially from Germany. In some cases, European firms are supplying whole mills to U.S. firms. Structural particleboard technology has thus come full circle: originally developed in North America, U.S. and Canadian firms now rely on imported technology. Gregersen et al. (1988) quantified the economic benefits of foreign research to the U.S. for structural particleboard and containerized forest tree seedlings. They found significant benefits associated with foreign research and concluded that the foreign influence on U.S. forestry research is increasing.

Technology 'Imports' from Other Sectors

Finally, new technologies developed in other sectors of the economy are an important source of technical change in forestry. The U.S.

TABLE 2

Forestry research expenditures as a per cent of world total by major geographical region

Region	Year	
	1970	1981
North America	42.5	32.2
Western Europe	22.8	24.4
Eastern Europe / USSR	15.8	20.1
Asia	8.4	11.0
Oceania	6.4	5.2
Africa	2.0	3.8
Latin America	2.0	3.4

SOURCE: Adapted from Mergen et al. (1988)

wood-based sector has been shown to be a net importer of R&D investments and technology. An estimated $275 million of R&D was carried out within the sector, and $337 million was used by the sector in 1974 (Scherer 1982). The U.S. lumber and wood products industry used an estimated $131.1 million of R&D in 1974, with only 49 per cent of the total used ($64.2 million) originating within the industry itself (Figure 1). Major industries supplying lumber and wood products with new technology include the following: motor vehicles and equipment; other machinery; and paints, explosives, and other chemical products. The paper and allied products industry used $206 million in research expenditures in 1974, with only 42 per cent (86.4 million) originating within the industry. Other machinery; paints, explosives, and other chemicals; and synthetic resins, fibre, and rubber industries were major suppliers of technology to the paper and allied products industry. An analysis of inter-industry technology flows in the United Kingdom that included the forest industries found that five core industries (chemicals, machinery, mechanical engineering, instruments, and electronics) are of major importance in generating technologies used in a wide range of industries (Robson et al. 1988). A trend towards greater interdependence between industries was also found.

In addition to inter-industry technology flows in the private sector, new technologies developed in non-forestry public research labs sometimes find their way into the forest-based sector. Moore and Fink (1984) analyzed the research programs at six non-forestry federal laboratories in the U.S.: Idaho National Engineering Labo-

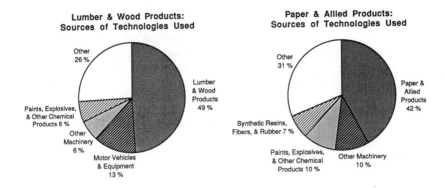

FIGURE 1
Sources of company-financed Research & Development used by the U.S. lumber and wood products and paper and allied products industries in 1974 (adapted from Scherer 1982)

ratory, Jet Propulsion Laboratory, Lawrence Livermore National Laboratory, NASA Lewis Research Center, Oak Ridge National Laboratory, and Sandia National Laboratory, Livermore. They identified thirty-eight areas of on-going research considered to be of potential significant benefit to the pulp and paper industry.

Figure 2 illustrates the wide range of technologies originating outside of the forest-based sector affecting each stage of the production process in forestry. The left-hand side of Figure 2 shows successive stages of production in the timber-based sector, from timber production through end use of the wood-based product. Primary processing uses roundwood or residues as raw material (e.g., pulping, sawmilling), and secondary processing industries use the output of primary processing as raw material (e.g., paper and furniture manufacture). Examples of current and emerging technologies developed in other sectors, but with significant application in the forest-based sector that are (or likely will be) affecting various stages of the production process, are shown on the right-hand side of the figure. This list is by no means exhaustive but is intended to illustrate the range of externally developed technologies that affect the production of forest products.

A number of other topics related to the development of new technology in forestry could be discussed if space allowed, such as the determinants of company R&D spending (Bullard and Straka 1986), patenting activity as a research output measure (Margl and Ellefson 1987), the role of public versus private sector forestry research (Runge 1983), and issues relating to the planning and management

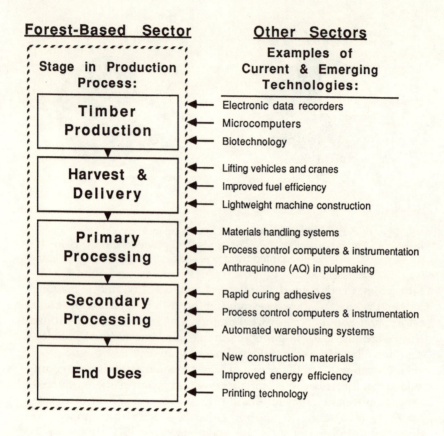

FIGURE 2

Examples of technologies originating outside the forest-based sector affecting successive stages of the production process in forestry (from BLS 1984, 1985, 1986; Tombaugh and Macdonald 1984)

of R&D (Gregersen et al. 1990). A particularly interesting issue that has received almost no attention in the forest-based sector concerns whether technical change has been consistent with relative factor scarcities, that is, the induced innovation hypothesis (see Thirtle and Ruttan 1987).[4] An exception is Rosenberg's (1973) historical analysis of woodworking technology in the United States and Great Britain, which found support for induced innovation. Technologies developed in the U.S. during the eighteenth and nineteenth centuries substituted relatively abundant, cheap wood for relatively scarce and expensive labour. These technologies were considered extremely wasteful in England because a relatively large portion of the log was converted into sawdust. In contrast to the u.s. technologies – but consistent with relative factor scarcities in England – woodworking technologies in England substituted relatively cheap labour for relatively expensive wood. Another historical analysis supporting the induced innovation hypothesis in forestry (for pulping innovations in North America) was carried out by Cohen (1987).

DIFFUSION OF NEW TECHNOLOGY IN FORESTRY

The processes by which innovations – including technological innovations – spread throughout social systems have been studied extensively by scholars in many fields. Thousands of empirical and theoretical investigations into diffusion processes have been carried out over the past several decades (Rogers 1983). The findings of diffusion research may be useful in designing technology transfer programs intended to speed up the adoption of new technologies. Also, an understanding of diffusion is required to assess the impacts of new technologies – economic efficiency impacts depend in part on the speed and extent of diffusion, and distributional impacts depend on the differential pattern of diffusion between groups within society, geographic regions, and so on. Several investigations into the diffusion of technological innovations in forest products have been carried out by economists.[5] Case studies have examined innovations in pulp and paper, wood-based panels, and residential construction.

Pulp and Paper

The earliest and most comprehensive economic study of diffusion in the forest-based industries was Hakanson's (1974) analysis of the international diffusion of special presses used in paper manufacture. Using a simple econometric model, Hakanson studied the inter-firm diffusion of four different types of special presses in six countries (Austria, Italy, Sweden, United Kingdom, United States, and West Germany). He hypothesized that the profitability of adoption, date of first information about special presses, firm size, and an index of innovation would be positively related to early adoption by a firm. Hakanson found that profitability of adoption and firm size explained a significant amount of the variability in adoption rates between firms.

Globerman (1976) studied the diffusion of special presses in the Canadian paper industry. Two econometric models were developed to determine which factors were most important in explaining the diffusion of special presses in Canada. First, a model of inter-firm diffusion was specified and tested. It was found that higher profitability of special press adoption was positively related to early adoption, firm size was not related to time of adoption, and domestically owned firms were slower to adopt than were foreign subsidiaries. Globerman also tested a model of intra-firm diffusion to identify factors associated with the spread of innovations within a firm after initial adoption. It was found that larger firm size contributed to slower adoption within a firm, and that domestic versus foreign ownership was not an important factor in explaining the spread of special presses within a firm.

Another economic study of the diffusion of innovations in the Canadian paper industry was carried out by Martin et al. (1979b). Four technological innovations in the newsprint industry were examined – including special presses – with the emphasis on explaining regional differences in adoption. The authors qualitatively analyzed the impacts of several factors that might explain differences in observed regional differences. Although little supporting data were given, it was concluded that regional differences in the quantity and quality of forest resources and different provincial government policies regarding cutting rights, pollution, and so on, explain the observed regional diffusion patterns.

Stier (1983) examined the diffusion of the sulphate pulping process in the u.s. pulp and paper industry. An econometric diffusion model based on the Gompertz function was developed. An innovative feature of this model was the inclusion of a dynamic diffusion ceiling, in which the ceiling level of adoption was assumed to be a log-linear function of real product price and real gross national product. This study concluded that most of the growth in sulphate pulp production over time can be attributed to upward shifts in the ceiling level of demand rather than to the 'natural rate of diffusion.' Projections indicated that the sulphate process will continue to capture a market share and could account for more than 90 per cent of total u.s. pulp production by the year 2000.

Wood-Based Panels

Several studies have modelled the diffusion of innovations in wood-based panels by using various growth functions (e.g., Leefers 1981; Spelter 1984). One example is an analysis of the diffusion of (nonstructural) particleboard in twenty-five industrialized countries carried out by Buongiorno and Oliveira (1977). Particleboard can be considered both a product innovation in wood panels and a process innovation based on new production technology. Growth of the particleboard share of total wood-based panels in each country was modelled with logistic functions, and the estimated parameters were further analyzed econometrically. It was found that eastern European countries had significantly lower ceiling levels of adoption than did market countries, distance from Germany (where particleboard was first produced) and the availability of large supplies of roundwood were the most important factors in delaying the date of initial adoption of particleboard in a country, and countries with higher economic growth and lower wood availability tended to have more rapid rates of adoption.

The development and diffusion of structural particleboard technology were examined in a historical case study by Bengston et al. (1988), with an emphasis on the contribution of research and development to the diffusion process. Technical, economic, and institutional factors delayed the diffusion of this technology. The substantial impacts of structural particleboard technology include shifting the demand for species (decreased demand for relatively scarce softwoods and increased demand for relatively abundant low-density hardwoods) and a regional shift in structural panel production. This case illustrates the need for technical change strategies that co-ordinate research related to the wood raw material with processing research.

Residential Construction

Several studies have examined the diffusion of wood products innovations in residential construction, a neglected sector in the study of technical change (Strassman 1978). Martin et al. (1979a) examined the diffusion of wood roof trusses in Canada. They concluded that the diffusion of roof trusses has been closely related to cycles in residential construction. This is hardly surprising, but it reinforces Stier's (1983) finding that increases in overall demand can induce more rapid rates of diffusion. It was also concluded that institutional constraints – such as zoning laws – do not impede the diffusion of roof trusses, and that proximity to large local markets is an important factor due to high transportation costs.

In a study of innovation in residential construction in the u.s. (Spall 1971), roof trusses, finger-jointed wood, and six other innovations were studied. Spall's analysis was based on interviews of the managers of twenty firms building single-family housing in Michigan. He concluded that the entrepreneur's extent of adoption of the innovations studied was not correlated with years of formal education, experience in the industry, a rating of receptiveness to innovations, size of firm, or the possibility of increased competition. Adoption or non-adoption was found to depend only on estimates of the profitability of adoption.

Ventre (1979) econometrically analyzed the diffusion of fourteen innovations in residential construction, including, once again, wood roof trusses, several other wood-related innovations, and a variety of non-wood innovations. He considered an innovation to be 'adopted' in an area when local building codes were modified to permit its use. The main finding of this study refuted the common perception of the house-building industry as technologically backward: 'The major significant result of this analysis is to deny the technological lethargy of the building industry and the agencies that regulate it: innovations diffuse throughout the industry – despite the special characteristics cited at the beginning of this paper – in much the same way and at the same speed as in other industries' (Ventre 1979:55).

Finally, Bowyer et al. (1987) developed a model to predict the rate of diffusion for new forest products technologies. They examined a diverse group of technologies, including innovations in construction, softwood lumber, softwood plywood, treated wood products, paper, and composite wood panels. The ex ante approach and the relatively large number of innovations included make this an instructive study, particularly for those interested in forecasting the diffusion of forest products technologies in the early stages of market development.

ECONOMIC IMPACTS OF TECHNICAL CHANGE IN FORESTRY

The potential consequences of technical change are diverse and include economic, environmental, social, cultural, institutional, political, and legal impacts. This section focuses on macro-level economic impacts, reviewing efficiency and distributional impacts in turn. Much research has been carried out on the firm-level impacts of technical change (e.g., Gold et al. 1980 and studies cited therein), but very little has been done at this level of analysis in forestry.

Economic Efficiency Impacts

The impact of technical change that has been most widely studied is, in economic terms, an upward shift in a production function or, equivalently, a downward shift in a supply function.[6] Simply stated, more efficient techniques of production make it possible to produce greater output from a given set of inputs. Several studies have examined the contribution of technical change to productivity growth in the forest industries. The first generation of these studies consists of works such as Manning and Thornburn's (1971) analysis of the rate of technical change in the Canadian pulp and paper industry. This and other first generation studies used Solow's (1957) method to estimate the rate of technical change based on a value-added Cobb-Douglas production function and the assumption of neutral technical change. Manning and Thornburn found a rise in the calculated index of technical change for the pulp and paper industry of 50 per cent between 1940 and 1960, and derivation of the capital production function revealed that all increases in productivity during this period were due to change in technology. Other examples of first generation studies include Robinson's (1975) analysis of the U.S. lumber and wood products industry and Risbrudt's (1979) study of several four-digit U.S. industries.

A shortcoming of these studies and others (e.g., Stier 1980a, 1982; Greber and White 1982) is the assumption of an industry production function in which output is measured as value-added.[7] In the value-added framework, intermediate inputs – such as stumpage and energy – are not treated symmetrically with capital and labour inputs. The value-added model places unnecessary restrictions on the production process and producer behaviour, and, most importantly for analysis of the forest-based sector, rules out change in the forest resource and other intermediate inputs as a type of technical change (Bengston and Strees 1986).

The second generation of forestry studies of the efficiency impacts of technical change used a more sophisticated approach that avoided the value-added model of production and the assumption of neutral technical change. This approach is based on economic duality principles and uses a translog cost function. An early example is Stier's (1980b) analysis of the U.S. lumber industry (SIC 242). Stier estimated an industry cost function with capital, labour, and sawlog inputs and used the parameters to determine the impacts of substitution and technical change on factor demand and unit production costs. The results indicate capital-using (labour-saving) technical change for the period 1950-74, which reduced the labour force by about 50 per cent while output remained almost constant. Technical change was found to be slightly sawlog-saving, but the estimated bias was very small and Stier concluded that technical change has had a negligible effect on wood requirements.

Other studies of biased technical change in the forest industries are summarized in Table 3. As would be expected, all studies report a strong labour-saving bias. The impact of technical change on the

TABLE 3

Summary of empirical studies of non-neutral technical change in North American forest industries

Study	Country	Time period	Method	Industry	Factor-saving Bias[1]
Pulp and Paper					
Sherif (1983)	Canada	1956-77	Translog cost function	Pulp & paper mills (sic 271)	K+, L-, E+, W-
De Borger & Buongiorno (1985)	u.s.	1958-81	Translog variable cost function[2]	Paper (sic 2621)	L-, E+, M-
				Paperboard (sic 2631)	L-, E+, M-
Martinello (1985)	Canada	1963-82	Translog cost function	Pulp & paper mills (sic 271)	K+, L-, E-, W-
Stier (1985)	u.s.	1948-76	Translog cost function	Pulp & paper (sic 26)	K+, L-, W+
Wood Products					
Stier (1980b)	u.s.	1950-74	Translog cost function	Lumber industry (sic 242)	K+, L-, W+
Martinello (1985)	Canada	1963-82	Translog cost function	Sawmills & shingle mills (sic 251)	K+, L-, E+, W-
Martinello (1987)	Canada-bc	1963-79	Translog cost function	Coast sawmills & planing mills (sic 2513)	K+, L-, W.
				Interior sawmills & planing mills (sic 2513)	K+, L-, W-
				Shingle & shake mills (sic 2511)	K+, L-, W-
				Veneer & plywood mills (sic 252)	K+, L-, W.
Meil & Nautiyal (1988)	Canada	1968-84	Translog variable cost function	Softwood lumber	L-, E+, W+

Meil et al. (1988)	Canada- BC Interior	1948-83	Translog variable cost function	Interior softwood lumber	L-, E+, W+
Constantino & Haley (1988)	Canada- BC Coast	1957-82	Translog normalized variable profit function	Sawmills, planing mills & shingle mills (SIC 2511)	L+, W+
	U.S. - PNW	1957-82	Translog normalized variable profit function	Sawmills & planing mills (SIC 2511)	L+, W+

Logging

Martinello (1985)	Canada	1963-82	Translog cost function	Logging (SIC 031)	K+, L-, E+, W+

[1] K, L, E, M, and W represent capital, labour, energy, materials, and wood inputs, respectively. The symbols (-), (+), and (.) indicate factor-saving, factor-using, and factor-neutral technical change, respectively.

[2] Capital is treated as a quasi-fixed input in the short run in the restricted translog variable cost function

wood input is inconclusive. Some studies have found technical change to be slightly wood-saving, others have found a slight wood-using bias, and still others report technical change that is essentially wood-neutral. These discrepancies are not surprising in light of the different time periods covered, industries analyzed, approaches to defining and measuring inputs, and the heterogeneity of wood inputs. The basically negligible impact of technical change on wood requirements is surprising, however. This may be due in part to the changing mix of wood and fibre inputs over time that is not adequately captured in the broad specifications of factor inputs in these studies. It would be highly desirable to expand the set of factor inputs, but, as noted by Smith (1980), failure to include additional factors is almost always due to data limitations.

Several recent studies have examined the economic efficiency impacts of forestry research, that is, they have calculated economic rates of return (ERRS) to research investments (see Jakes and Risbrudt 1988 and studies cited therein). The u.s. Forest Service established a research unit in 1980 to develop methods to evaluate the impacts of forestry research (Lundgren 1986). Other efforts to evaluate the impacts of forestry research include work at Duke University (Hyde 1983; Hyde et al. 1989) and the University of Minnesota (Gregersen 1985). Jakes and Risbrudt (1988) summarize the results of these research impact evaluations. Average annual ERR's reported in these studies differ widely, as would be expected – research impact evaluations employ different methods and assumptions and evaluate a variety of innovations or areas of research in different time periods. But the estimated ERR's are generally in the range of 20 per cent to 80 per cent, comparable to estimated returns to investment in agricultural research. These relatively high rates of return confirm that at least some types of forestry research do have significant economic impacts.

An ambitious effort to evaluate and project the impacts of new technologies in the u.s. forest products sector is reported in the 1989 Resources Planning Act Timber Assessment (USDA Forest Service 1988). This effort considered the impact of new technologies on increasing the efficiency of wood use, reducing the cost of wood products and the cost of using wood in applications, and creating new or improved wood products or wood use applications. A shortcoming of this work is an emphasis on the wood-saving impacts of technical change, that is, measuring technical change as change in product recovery factors (the volume of wood product consumed per unit volume of logs consumed or, in the case of pulp and paper, the volume of pulpwood or fibre consumed per ton of product produced). The studies summarized in Table 3 indicate that wood-saving impacts have been overshadowed by labour-saving impacts. Even if the studies in Table 3 have underestimated the wood-saving impacts because of data limitations, the impacts of labour-saving technical change on the demand for timber have been substantial and need to be explicitly considered.

Distributional Impacts[8]

The preceding paragraphs have discussed the efficiency impacts of technical change. But technical change also entails distributional consequences – some groups within society will be better off as a result of the introduction of a particular technological innovation, while others could be worse off. Contrary to John F. Kennedy's metaphor that 'a rising tide lifts all boats,' a rising technological tide lifts some boats and may sink others. Figure 3 illustrates six key distributional issues and the relationships between issues, that is, the flow of benefits from technical change between various groups within society.

First, distribution of the gains from technical change between time periods is an important issue in forestry. Extremely long production periods compared to many other types of economic activity imply that future generations will benefit from biological research that increases the productivity of tree species with long growing periods. For example, research to produce genetically superior trees may substantially increase forest productivity in the long run, but the benefits from this technical change will not be realized until the end of the first rotation of the more productive trees. The present generation will benefit from new wood utilization technologies with a shorter payoff period.

The regional or geographic distribution of the gains from technical change is a second issue shown in Figure 3. Many technological innovations in forestry may be suited to a limited range of environmental conditions. As a result, geographic regions do not always share equally in the gains from technical change. Consider the simplest case of two regions that supply some forest-based commodity to a single national market. If a major cost-saving technology is developed that is applicable to one region but not to the other, production costs will decline in the first region and remain the same in the second. Given an inelastic demand for the commodity, some of the lower production costs will translate into lower prices in the marketplace. The innovating region will capture a larger share of the national market, and the other region will experience a real loss as a re-

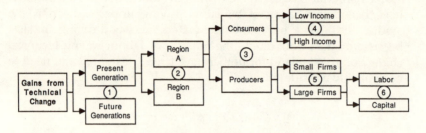

FIGURE 3
Distributional impacts of technical change: six key distributional issues
and relationships between issues

sult of the technical change. If scale economies are present, the loss of market share in the non-innovating region may result in an increase in production costs, further eroding its competitive position. Many examples of forestry innovations having unequal regional impacts could be cited.

Third, part of the gains from technical change affecting a given good or service may be captured by consumers in the form of lower prices and increased quantities marketed. Producers will also share in the gains if they are not entirely passed on to consumers. Two studies have examined the distribution of gains from research and the resulting technical change between consumers and producers in the forestry sector in the United States. Seldon (1985) found that plywood consumers captured about 47 per cent of the benefits of public research on softwood plywood technology between 1950 and 1980. Plywood producers received the remaining share. Newman (1986) examined the distribution of economic benefits of technical change in softwood forestry in the southern United States and attained quite different results. Because softwood timber is an intermediate good, the consumers of softwood were defined as forest products firms that purchase softwood as an input, and producers were defined as the growers of softwood timber. Newman found that softwood producers capture very low or even negative benefits as a result of technical change. In contrast, consumers gained considerably from the lower prices they paid to producers due to a strongly inelastic demand in softwood timber markets.

Fourth, consumers are unlikely to share equally in the gains from technical change. Clearly, the distributional impacts of technical change affecting goods purchased predominantly by wealthy people will be quite different from technical change affecting goods that account for a large portion of the budgets of relatively poor people.

Low income consumers will gain most as a result of technical change affecting goods with income elasticities of demand less than unity, or necessities – the proportion of the consumer's budget spent on such goods falls as income rises.

Fifth, like consumers, producers seldom share equally in the gains from technical change. Large firms are often early adopters of new technologies because they have greater financial resources and incentives to innovate. Early adopters will earn 'innovator's rents' or quasi-rents – short-run profits due to temporarily lower production costs relative to late adopters. Classical economist David Ricardo discussed innovator's rents in his writings dating from the early nineteenth century: 'He ... who made the discovery of the machine, or who first usefully applied it, would enjoy an additional advantage, by making great profits for a time; but in proportion as the machine came into general use, the price of the commodity produced would, from the effects of competition, sink to its cost of production' (Ricardo 1971:378). Based on the meagre evidence supplied by the diffusion studies discussed earlier, it is unclear if large forest products firms are, in fact, early adopters of new technologies. Globerman (1976) found that large Canadian paper firms did not adopt more rapidly than did smaller firms, but Hakanson (1974) found that large paper firms in six countries were earlier adopters of new paper-making technology than were small firms. Certain characteristics of new technologies – such as the capital investment required to adopt – will clearly have a significant effect on whether or not large firms are early adopters.

A final distributional issue depicted in Figure 3 is the division of producer benefits between the factors of production. A key determinant of the distribution of gains between capital and labour is the factor-saving bias of technical change. If technology is labour-saving, the demand for labour and total payments to labour will be lower than would be the case for capital-saving technical change.[9] Similarly, capital-saving technology will reduce total payments to capital relative to what these payments would have been with labour-saving technology. As discussed earlier, technical change in u.s. and Canadian forest products industries has been found to be strongly labour-saving.

CONCLUSIONS AND POLICY IMPLICATIONS

This paper has summarized the relatively large and growing literature on the economics of technical change in the forest industries. Policy implications and implications for future research emerging

from this review are outlined in this section. The distinction between the sources, diffusion, and impacts of new technologies is not
maintained in this section. This distinction was useful in reviewing
the literature, but in terms of policy to move ahead in the various forest industries, it makes sense to consider the sources, diffusion,
and impacts of technology in an integrated fashion. We do need to
make a clear distinction between subsectors and the appropriate
strategies and policies related to them, keeping in mind the integrating factor – the forest resource in all its heterogeneity.

Technologies originating outside of the forestry sector have had a
significant impact on forestry. Scherer (1982) has shown that the u.s.
forest products industries are net importers of technology from
other sectors. It is unlikely that forest products firms have sufficiently adjusted their strategies for technical change to fully take advantage of increased inter-industry technology flows. Firms and
government agencies need to become more proficient about inter-
industry technology diffusion and to develop methods for systematically searching out technological opportunities and threats outside
of the traditional sources. Cost-effective strategies for technical
change will require a greater emphasis on technology search activities and an adaptation of external technologies to the needs of the
forest-based industries. More research is needed to shed light on
inter-industry relationships and the ways in which other industries
have supported or have the potential to support technical change in
the various subsectors of the forest-based sector.

Taken together, the studies by Gregersen et al. (1988) and Mergen
et al. (1988) make a strong case for increased international technology search activities in North American forest products firms to take
advantage of the significant rise in forestry research activity in other
parts of the world. In the coming decades, an increasing percentage
of new technology will be developed abroad, and we must learn how
to tap these resources. u.s. firms in general have performed poorly
in the area of international technology search. Mansfield (1988) analyzed the speed and cost of industrial innovation in Japanese and
u.s. firms and found that u.s. firms are unable to match the Japanese
as quick and effective users of external technology. We need to expand technology search activities and make them fully international
in scope. The Japanese model is one to look at (Montrey and Johnson
1988).

The need to search for and adapt technologies developed in other
sectors and other countries in no way diminishes the need for R&D
carried out within the forest-based sector. Relatively low private research intensity (research expenditures as a per cent of sales) in the

forest industries is a cause for concern, as is the low public research intensity (research expenditures as a per cent of value of total industry production) relative to agriculture. Concern over the long run implications of under-investing in research is motivated, in part, by an extensive body of literature linking investment in research to productivity growth in forestry (Jakes and Risbrudt 1988), agriculture (Ruttan 1982), and various industrial sectors. Low research intensity may, therefore, represent a threat to the future productivity and competitiveness of the forest-based sector. Increased investment in forestry research is needed.

The economic efficiency impacts or potential impacts of technical change directly determine the incentive for companies to create, search for, and adopt new technologies and, thus, relate to the question of diffusion. A better understanding of efficiency impacts is vital if we want to develop policies or strategies to improve the development and diffusion of new technologies.

One economic impact that has received fairly extensive coverage from economists relates to the factor-saving bias of technical change. As shown in Table 3, technical change has been strongly labour-saving, capital-using, and has had a basically negligible effect on wood requirements. This last finding is at odds with evidence of major wood-saving technologies in forest products (e.g., USDA Forest Service 1988; Haygreen et al. 1986) and underscores the need to expand the set of factor inputs and to specify inputs more narrowly in econometric studies of production technologies. The broad specification of inputs in econometric studies strongly suggests that the changing mix of wood and wood fibre inputs over time has not been adequately captured in past econometric studies. Constantino and Haley's (1988) analysis – which includes adjustments for changing wood quality – is a step in the right direction for future research.

We also need to examine distributional impacts in order to identify gainers and losers and to address the question of who should pay for technology development and diffusion. The brief review of the distributional impacts of technical change in forestry was light on empirical studies, mainly because such studies are almost non-existent. The heavy involvement and influence of the public sector in forestry and the relatively large role played by public research suggest that assessment of the distributional impacts of technical change may have important implications for public research policy. For example, large forest products firms are much more likely to employ scientific and technical personnel capable of developing new technologies and keeping abreast of new technologies developed through public sector research and other sources. Small firms typically lack the scientific, technical, and financial resources required to innovate rapidly. If, as a result, large firms reap innovator's rents, this is an argument for publicly supported research and technology transfer programs to speed up the adoption of innovations among small producers and to increase the level of competition in the industry. Another distributional issue with important public policy implications is the question of whether labour-saving technologies in forestry have been stimulated by labour being 'pulled out' of forestry by higher wages in other sectors as opposed to labour being 'pushed out' or displaced by new technologies. The question of whether labour has been displaced or replaced by labour-saving technologies in forestry has not been examined.

Research policymakers, managers, and researchers themselves need to become more aware of the income redistribution effects of technical change. Knowledge of these impacts will better equip decisionmakers to make informed choices about the types of research to carry out and will help managers select new technologies that will have the intended social and economic consequences. More evaluations of the distributional impacts of technical change in forestry are needed to generate this knowledge.

In conclusion, much has been learned about the economics of technical change in the forest-based industries in recent decades. The challenge now is to fill in the many gaps in existing knowledge and to translate research findings in this area into effective private and public strategies for technical change. The differences between segments of the forest-based sector in terms of key technical characteristics, such as technical rigidity and capital intensity, are great and need to be considered in developing strategies for technical change. An industry wide strategy is not realistic, except perhaps in terms of strategies related to the extremely heterogeneous forest resource. Technical change strategies must co-ordinate research related to the wood resource with research related to processing and conversion. The two go hand in hand because the forest-based industries are resource driven.

NOTES

1 Ruttan gives this and two other definitions: Technical change is 'the substitution of knowledge for resources,' and technical change 'releases the constraints on growth imposed by inelastic resource supplies' (1982:237).

2 This section is adapted from Bengston and Jakes (1988).

3 Structural particleboard is a reconstituted wood panel with properties suitable for structural and exterior applications.

4 Several empirical studies have examined the factor-saving bias of technical change in the forest industries, but they have not tested the induced innovation hypothesis. These studies will be discussed in a later section.

5 Studies of the diffusion and adoption of forestry innovations have also been carried out by sociologists and other social scientists (Bengston 1985). In these studies, the diffusion of innovations is viewed as a process that can be explained primarily by social, cultural, and psychological variables. The attitudes and socio-cultural characteristics of individual adopters are often stressed as the most important factors in determining adoption behaviour.

6 Technical change can also cause an outward shift in a demand function through increased product usefulness or quality, but this impact has been largely ignored by economists. Indeed, product innovation in general has been neglected by economists, although it has been studied extensively by marketing researchers.

7 Much of the early empirical analysis of productivity growth and technical change was conducted at the economy-wide level (e.g., Solow 1957). At this level of analysis, working with a value-added model of production is appropriate. When the production accounts of all industries are aggregated, inter-industry flows of intermediate inputs cancel out. The intermediate input of one industry is the output of some other industry, and, therefore, the final output of the entire economy may be represented as being produced only by capital and labour, as in the value-added framework. But application of the value-added model to individual industries or sectors is suspect and has come under increasing attack in recent years.

8 This section is adapted from Bengston and Gregersen (1988).

9 Labour-saving technical change is not equivalent to job-reducing technical change, however. If demand for the final product is highly elastic, cost and price reductions associated with labour-saving technical change may result in large increases in various types of employment within the industry or sector. In other words, labour per unit of output declines, but expansion of the industry or sector results in a net increase in total employment. If product demand is inelastic, however, labour-saving technical change will reduce the demand for labour within the sector.

CHAPTER NINE

A Comparison of the Productivity Performance of the U.S. and Canadian Pulp and Paper Industries

Tae Hoon Oum and Michael W. Tretheway

INTRODUCTION

The forest products industry is one of Canada's major industrial sectors. This industry consists of several subsectors, with pulp and paper production being the most important. In 1986, the gross production of pulp and paper mills was $13.86 billion, accounting for about 3 per cent of the Canadian Gross National Product (GNP). About $11.2 billion of this, or over 80 per cent of the gross production, was exported to international markets. This amounts to approximately 8.8 per cent of total Canadian merchandise exports.

In this export-driven industry, the single most important foreign market is the United States. Traditionally, the Canadian pulp and paper industry derives over 70 per cent of its gross export revenues from U.S. markets. As a result, it is very important for the Canadian industry to keep and enhance its competitive strength relative to its U.S. competitors.

In the long run, competitive success is largely determined by the industry's productivity, input prices, and exchange rates. Since input prices (e.g., wages, interest rates, and energy prices) and exchange rates are often inflexible or difficult for an industry to control, productivity improvement becomes the key element in strengthening its position in the world market relative to its major competing nations. Therefore, it is important for the Canadian industry to know its productivity performance relative to its major competitors, particularly the U.S. industry.

This paper compares trends in productivity between the U.S. and Canadian pulp and paper industries. Productivity growth is measured for labour as well as for other inputs: capital, energy, and materials. In addition, total factor productivity is measured and compared between the two countries. In undertaking this comparison, similar methods of data construction and analysis are employed so that the comparison will be valid.

A few previous studies have separately assessed the total and partial factor productivities of the Canadian and the u.s. pulp and paper industries. Ghebremichael, Oum, and Tretheway (1988) measured the productivity of the Canadian industry using a non-parametric method. Other researchers, such as Muller (1979), Sherif (1983), Martinello (1985), Nautiyal and Singh (1986), and Constantino and Townsend (1986), have focused their research on the structure of production technology of the Canadian pulp and paper industry by estimating production or cost functions. In the process, some of these previous studies have measured average annual rates of change in total factor productivity parametrically. Stier (1985) and de Borger and Buongiorno (1985) have conducted similar studies for the u.s. pulp and paper industry.

Few studies have attempted to compare the productive efficiency of the industry across major competing countries. A joint study by the United Nations Economic Commission for Europe (Geneva), and the Food and Agriculture Organization of the United Nations (Rome) (1988) attempted to measure the productivities of various forest product industries, including pulp and paper, for major producing countries around the world. However, there are some serious methodological problems in the study, particularly in the methods of computing the capital input costs and quantities and output quantity indices.[1] This study corrects for those methodological problems embedded in the UN-FAO joint study.

THE CONCEPT OF PRODUCTIVITY

Economists have argued that economic growth is strongly related to productivity. The word 'productivity,' however, is often misused or misunderstood. In a broad definition, productivity is the amount of output produced per unit of input. There are many specific indicators of productivity. Analysts typically place emphasis on the productivity of labour. However, the use of such a partial factor productivity is dangerous in that its level and growth rate depend on the levels of other inputs employed (e.g., capital). In a world where costs of capital, energy, and materials have soared and competition has become fiercer, the need for more effective management of all resources is critical. Therefore, it is necessary to analyze total factor productivity (TFP) as well as to examine the partial factor productivity of each input.

A partial factor productivity (PFP) is the ratio of total (i.e., aggregate) output produced to the quantity employed of the appropriate input factor (e.g., labour or capital):

$$PFP_t = O_t/X_{jt} \qquad (1)$$

where the subscript t denotes the time period, O is the measure of aggregate output, and X_j is the measure of input of type j. This input 'j' might be labour or, alternatively, energy, capital, or materials. Aggregate output refers to the types of output which are aggregated in order to get a single unit of measurement of the total output of the industry. In the aggregation, outputs with higher prices are given more weight. An example of a PFP would be output per labour-hour. There may, however, be different types and quality of labour in the production process. In this study, labour is broken into two components: production and administration/management. These two components had to be combined, or aggregated, into a single index of labour input employed.

TFP is described as the amount of aggregate output per unit of aggregate input (i.e. an aggregate quantity of all the inputs).

$$TFP_t = O_t/I_t \qquad (2)$$

where the subscript t denotes the time period, O is the aggregate output index, and I is the aggregate input index. TFP differs from the simpler concept of PFP in that the combined impact of all the input factors on the efficiency of a given industry is reflected correctly. High labour productivity, for example, may be due to an excessive use of capital. Such a situation may not be viewed as cost efficient. As demonstrated by Gillen, Oum, and Tretheway (1985), TFP corrects for multi-input problems by recognizing and appropriately weighting the various components of input factors.

In this study, the outputs and inputs for each country are aggregated independently from those of the other country. This is accomplished using the Tornqvist discrete time approximation to the Divisia index procedure. In this procedure, the average of each output's revenue shares (or each input's cost shares) for two adjacent time periods are used as the aggregation weight for creating the output (or input) index. The Tornqvist discrete time approximation to the Divisia index of TFP can be written as:

$$TFP_t/TFP_{t-1} = \exp\left\{ \sum_{i=1}^{n} 0.5(R_{i,t} + R_{i,t-1}) \ln(Y_{i,t}/Y_{i,t-1}) \right. \tag{3}$$

$$\left. - \sum_{j=1}^{m} 0.5(S_{j,t} + S_{j,t-1}) \ln(X_{j,t}/X_{j,t-1}) \right\}$$

where R_i is the share of output type i in total revenue, Y_i is the quantity of output i, S_j is the share of input j in total cost, and X_j is the quantity of that input employed in production. The first term on the right hand side of equation (3) is the aggregate output index. The second term is the aggregate input index. If an input, such as labour, consists of two or more components, then the components are aggregated using a similar procedure to produce a labour quantity index.

The approach used in this paper is sometimes termed a 'nonparametric' approach, as it does not require statistical estimation of the productivity growth rate. A problem with the nonparametric approach is that the resulting TFP measure will include productivity growth due not only to technical change but also to sources such as exploitation of economies of scale and utilization of capital stocks. If (a) firms are input price takers; (b) firms engage in marginal cost pricing; (c) the industry is subject to constant returns to scale; and (d) firms are successful in optimizing their production choices, then (3) will represent the shift in technical efficiency of a neoclassical cost function of the following form:

$$C = (Y_1, \ldots, Y_n, W_1, \ldots, W_m, t) \tag{4}$$

where Y_i represents the quantity of output type i, W_j represents the price of input type j, C is total cost, and t denotes the state of technology. If one or more of these assumptions is violated, then (3) will include not only the technology shift in (4) but also changes in the ratio of output to input due to other reasons such as exploitation of returns to scale, utilization of capital stocks, and so on.

Some of these assumptions are likely to be violated in the pulp and paper industry. Accordingly, our results must be taken for what they are – changes in productivity regardless of source. Decomposition of productivity growth into sources requires application of parametric techniques. However, such results will vary depending on the statistical technique used, specification of the economic model, or specification of the particular form of equation (4). In contrast, the nonparametric approach of (3) avoids these issues and produces a noncontroversial measure, although one that must be used carefully because it is an 'all sources' productivity measure. In spite of its limitations, a measure of TFP will shed light on some important policy issues over and above what partial factor productivities can accomplish.

A comparison of productivity levels across countries requires construction of 'multilateral' input and output indices, which are comparable across different countries as well as being transitive over time within a specific country. Although the methodology for computing multilateral indices of output, input, and productivity is well established (Caves, Christensen, and Diewert 1982), in most cases the data do not allow computation of such indices that are comparable across countries. Computation of a multilateral output index would require either absolute quantity or absolute price series (expressed in a common currency per unit of output) for each of the outputs produced by the industry in addition to the revenue generated from each output. An output quantity series computed by deflating revenues by a country-specific price index is not sufficient for computing a multilateral output index. Similarly, computation of a multilateral input index requires either absolute quantity or absolute price series for each input for each country. Like most other international comparisons, the data available for this research do not allow us to compute a consistent multilateral output or input index. Therefore, in this study the country-specific partial and total factor productivities are computed, and only their growth rates over time are compared.

DATA

The basic data consist of annual industry observations, over the period 1963 to 1984, on quantities and prices of the inputs used and outputs produced by the pulp and paper industry.[2] The u.s. and Canadian industries are treated separately. For Canada, seven types of output were identified, the most important of which were newsprint (representing 41 per cent of industry revenue in 1984), pulp (32 per cent), printing paper (14 per cent), and paperboard (9 per cent). The major input factors of the industry are labour (22 per cent of industry total costs in 1984), capital (25 per cent),[3] energy (14 per cent), and materials and supplies – hereafter referred to as materials (39 per cent). These productive factors were classified into various sub-

components. Labour and materials were each divided into two components, while capital and energy were classified into four and
seven components, respectively.[4] With the exception of energy, the
subcomponents were aggregated using the Divisia index procedure
described above. Energy types were converted into Btu equivalents
and summed.[5] More details on Canadian data are discussed in
Frank, Ghebremichael, Oum, and Tretheway (1990).[6]

Labour quantity was measured by labour-hours, and the price
was measured by compensation per hour. Energy input was measured in Btu's. Pulpwood quantity was measured in tons, and price
was measured as price per ton. Other materials were measured by
deflating their cost by an appropriate national price index. Capital
input was measured by the technique proposed by Christensen and
Jorgenson (1969). The capital price reflects real depreciation, cost of
funds, capital gains or losses, and property tax, all adjusted for corporate income taxation effects (including accelerated depreciation,
where and when appropriate, and investment tax credits). Capital
quantity was obtained from constructing a perpetual inventory from
real investment expenditures and geometric rates of decay.

For the u.s., less detail was available, although similar procedures
were used.[7] Four types of output were available: paper (with a 61 per
cent revenue share in 1984), paperboard (29 per cent), pulp (9 per
cent), and building paper (1 per cent). Four categories of labour were
analyzed. These consist of number of employees in (a) pulp mills,
(b) paper mills, (c) paper board mills, and (d) building and paper
board mills. Total energy use in Btu was reported in the Census of
Manufacturers, so it was not necessary to disaggregate. Two types
of capital were available: equipment and structures. Materials were
available only in aggregate. The input cost shares in the u.s. are
roughly similar to those in Canada:

TABLE 1
Input shares in the pulp and paper industry, 1984

	U.S.	Canada
Materials	48%	39%
Capital	23%	25%
Labour	16%	22%
Energy	13%	14%

TABLE 2

Input quantity indices, Canadian pulp and paper industry,
1963-84

Year	Labour	Capital	Energy	Materials
1963	1.000	1.000	1.000	1.000
1964	1.049	1.100	1.093	1.126
1965	1.077	1.228	1.181	1.272
1966	1.139	1.409	1.260	1.314
1967	1.136	1.531	1.303	1.354
1968	1.126	1.546	1.361	1.393
1969	1.163	1.599	1.398	1.220
1970	1.237	1.721	1.412	1.215
1971	1.206	1.819	1.358	1.206
1972	1.207	1.850	1.416	1.309
1973	1.219	1.855	1.387	1.398
1974	1.318	1.902	1.518	1.479
1975	1.146	1.917	1.226	1.065
1976	1.303	1.955	1.374	1.251
1977	1.266	1.987	1.350	1.287
1978	1.291	1.983	1.396	1.425
1979	1.304	2.010	1.393	1.500
1980	1.301	2.105	1.327	1.484
1981	1.313	2.302	1.283	1.484
1982	1.242	2.382	1.174	1.380
1983	1.190	2.321	1.179	1.552
1984	1.189	2.299	1.267	1.601
Average annual growth rate	0.83%	4.04%	1.13%	2.27%

TRENDS IN THE DATA

Canada

Table 2 shows that from 1963 to 1980, the quantity of labour input increased by 30 per cent, then declined somewhat in the early 1980s, so that the net growth from 1963 to 1984 was 19 per cent. Energy consumption rose by 52 per cent from 1963 to 1974 then fell off dramatically as a result of the run-up of fuel prices, with a net growth of 17 per cent from 1963 to 1982. Energy consumption increased again after 1982, recording a net growth of 27 per cent from 1963 to 1984. Materials consumption cycled a number of times (closely tied to

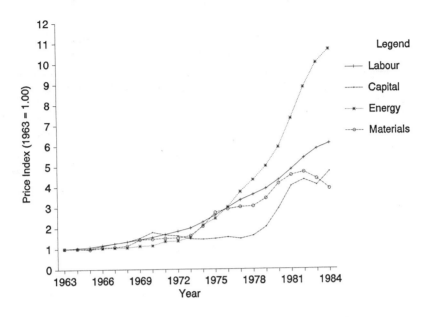

FIGURE 1

Price indices of inputs in the Canadian pulp and paper industry, 1963-84

changes in industry real output), to end up 60 per cent higher by 1984. The most dramatic trend was with respect to capital, with a growth of 130 per cent in the 1963-84 period. During this period industry output rose 102 per cent. Clearly, there was a rapid investment in capital, but a large part of this increase occurred in the 1960s. The average growth rate of capital was 5.6 per cent per year in the 1960-70 period, while it was reduced to 2 per cent per year in the 1970-80 period. It is this capital investment which allowed the industry to keep the growth of other inputs lower than industry output. Figure 1 depicts the changes in the prices of the four inputs.

It is possible to form a weighted average of the four input quantity indices to get an index of the 'aggregate' input quantity.[8] This reflects the total amount of resources (i.e., total factors) employed to produce each year's output. Similarly, the seven outputs can be aggregated to form the aggregate output quantity. Price indices for inputs and outputs can also be constructed. Table 3 displays the aggregate price and quantity indices of both inputs and outputs in Canada. This table reveals that during the 1963-84 period, the aggregate price of output grew at a rate of 6.9 per cent per year, while the quantity index grew at a rate of 3.4 per cent. The aggregate price and quantity of inputs, on the other hand, increased at 8.0 per cent and 2.2 per cent per

TABLE 3

Aggregate output and input indices, Canadian pulp and paper industry, 1963-84

Year	Output indices		Input indices	
	Price	Quantity	Price	Quantity
1963	1.000	1.000	1.000	1.000
1964	1.010	1.087	1.009	1.100
1965	1.004	1.156	1.005	1.208
1966	1.012	1.259	1.097	1.284
1967	1.026	1.258	1.149	1.329
1968	1.012	1.290	1.214	1.352
1969	1.042	1.442	1.425	1.292
1970	1.069	1.438	1.529	1.333
1971	1.079	1.444	1.566	1.338
1972	1.077	1.541	1.587	1.397
1973	1.230	1.812	1.651	1.441
1974	1.772	1.801	1.975	1.528
1975	2.273	1.375	2.380	1.233
1976	2.284	1.641	2.601	1.397
1977	2.423	1.692	2.767	1.407
1978	2.468	1.875	2.923	1.492
1979	2.955	1.946	3.311	1.537
1980	3.478	1.953	4.032	1.531
1981	3.797	1.926	4.711	1.556
1982	3.843	1.765	5.086	1.487
1983	3.561	1.887	5.023	1.541
1984	4.046	2.024	5.048	1.573
Average annual growth rate	6.88%	3.41%	8.01%	2.18%

year, respectively. As can be seen, output quantity grew at a faster rate than did input, suggesting an increase in productivity of some sort. Similarly, output price increases were less than input price increases, suggesting a productivity gain, although a decline in profit rates is an alternative explanation.

United States

Table 4 shows that labour input rose by 8 per cent from 1963 to 1969, then declined to end up 6 per cent lower in 1984 than it was in 1963.

TABLE 4

Input quantity indices, u.s. pulp and paper industry, 1963-84

Year	Labour	Capital	Energy	Materials
1963	1.000	1.000	1.000	1.000
1964	1.002	0.990	1.077	1.063
1965	1.016	1.004	1.130	1.106
1966	1.036	1.033	1.165	1.187
1967	1.062	1.074	1.178	1.186
1968	1.067	1.067	1.294	1.284
1969	1.081	1.071	1.341	1.419
1970	1.060	1.071	1.414	1.427
1971	1.019	1.056	1.538	1.465
1972	1.001	1.058	1.660	1.553
1973	1.012	1.063	1.711	1.682
1974	1.023	1.099	1.597	1.962
1975	0.948	1.142	1.468	1.769
1976	0.983	1.197	1.578	1.989
1977	0.994	1.244	1.587	1.968
1978	0.982	1.294	1.574	1.898
1979	0.997	1.379	1.571	1.855
1980	0.990	1.415	1.545	1.983
1981	0.979	1.436	1.534	1.768
1982	0.938	1.458	1.611	1.457
1983	0.929	1.469	1.632	1.486
1984	0.941	1.488	1.723	1.425
Average annual growth rate	-0.29%	1.91%	2.62%	1.70%

In contrast, the Canadian industry employed 19 per cent more labour in 1984 than it did in 1963. u.s. energy consumption rose by 71 per cent from 1963 to 1973. It fell off over the next two years due to the increase in fuel prices in 1974 and then rose again in 1982. Over the 1963-84 period, u.s. energy consumption rose by 72 per cent as compared to the 27 per cent increase in Canada. Materials consumption rose steadily until 1977 (with a drop in 1975), plateaued until 1980, and then declined. The materials input in 1984 was 43 per cent higher than it was in 1963 (compared to a 60 per cent increase in Canada). Capital stock increased steadily during the sample period. While Canada recorded an increase of 130 per cent in capital over the period, the u.s. increased capital by only 49 per cent. However, contrary to the Canadian case, most of the increase in capital stock in the

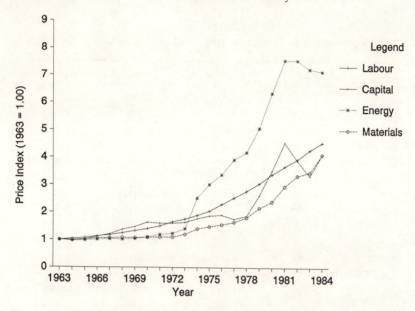

FIGURE 2
Price indices of inputs in the u.s. pulp and paper industry, 1963-84

u.s. occurred since 1970. Not surprisingly, use of labour input decreased as capital investment picked up. For example, the average
growth rate of capital in the 1970-80 period was 2.8 per cent in the
u.s., while this figure was 2.0 per cent per year for Canada. Still, the
capital cost share was lower in the u.s. (23 per cent) than in Canada
(25 per cent).

Figure 2 shows the prices of the individual inputs for the United
States. A comparison of Figures 1 and 2 show that during the 1963-84
period, the prices of energy, labour, and capital inputs rose faster in
Canada than in the u.s., while the materials price rose faster in the
u.s. Table 5 shows that during the 1963 to 1984 period, aggregate input in the u.s. increased at a rate of 1.4 per cent per year (Canada's
aggregate input increased 2.2 per cent). u.s. output increased 3.2 per
cent per year (Canada's output increased 3.4 per cent). The u.s. output price index increased 5.4 per cent per year (a cumulative increase
of 204 per cent), while Canada's output price index increased 6.9 per
cent (a cumulative increase of 305 per cent).

Comparison between Canada and the u.s.

From the tables and figures presented so far, the following
observations can be made:

TABLE 5
Aggregate output and input indices, U.S. pulp and paper industry,
1963-84

Year	Output indices, Price	Quantity	Input indices Price	Quantity
1963	1.000	1.000	1.000	1.000
1964	0.991	1.070	1.007	1.033
1965	1.005	1.124	1.030	1.064
1966	1.032	1.204	1.086	1.116
1967	1.050	1.195	1.122	1.132
1968	1.053	1.284	1.176	1.183
1969	1.091	1.346	1.212	1.249
1970	1.068	1.392	1.267	1.252
1971	1.080	1.406	1.296	1.259
1972	1.068	1.515	1.324	1.298
1973	1.215	1.575	1.424	1.359
1974	1.578	1.575	1.674	1.476
1975	1.816	1.358	1.801	1.376
1976	1.894	1.545	1.914	1.497
1977	1.992	1.592	2.022	1.502
1978	1.990	1.646	2.199	1.479
1979	2.308	1.725	2.663	1.483
1980	2.594	1.741	3.125	1.535
1981	2.834	1.762	3.796	1.456
1982	2.877	1.681	3.902	1.339
1983	2.784	1.842	3.862	1.354
1984	3.040	1.936	4.429	1.344
Average annual growth rate	5.44%	3.20%	7.34%	1.42%

(1) There is a high degree of similarity in the output growth patterns of the two countries, implying a dependence on economic conditions. Output of the Canadian industry grew slightly faster (at 3.4 per cent per year) than did the U.S. output (at 3.2 per cent). In the late 1970's, the Canadian industry's output grew considerably faster than that of its U.S. counterpart.
(2) Canadian output prices grew much faster (at 6.9 per cent per year versus 5.4 per cent).
(3) The U.S. decreased its use of labour by 6 per cent during the

TABLE 6
Partial and total factor productivity, Canadian pulp and paper industry, 1963-84

Year	Partial productivity of				Total factor productivity (TFP)
	Labour	Capital	Energy	Materials	
1963	1.000	1.000	1.000	1.000	1.000
1964	1.036	0.988	0.994	0.965	0.988
1965	1.073	0.941	0.978	0.908	0.957
1966	1.106	0.893	1.000	0.958	0.980
1967	1.107	0.821	0.966	0.929	0.946
1968	1.146	0.835	0.948	0.926	0.954
1969	1.239	0.902	1.031	1.182	1.116
1970	1.163	0.836	1.018	1.184	1.078
1971	1.197	0.794	1.063	1.197	1.079
1972	1.277	0.833	1.089	1.178	1.104
1973	1.487	0.977	1.306	1.296	1.257
1974	1.366	0.947	1.187	1.218	1.179
1975	1.200	0.717	1.121	1.290	1.115
1976	1.259	0.839	1.194	1.312	1.175
1977	1.337	0.852	1.253	1.315	1.203
1978	1.453	0.946	1.343	1.316	1.257
1979	1.492	0.968	1.397	1.298	1.267
1980	1.501	0.928	1.472	1.316	1.276
1981	1.467	0.836	1.501	1.298	1.237
1982	1.421	0.741	1.504	1.279	1.187
1983	1.586	0.813	1.600	1.216	1.225
1984	1.703	0.880	1.598	1.265	1.287
Average annual growth rate	2.57%	-0.61%	2.26%	1.13%	1.21%

TABLE 7
Partial and total factor productivity, U.S. pulp and paper industry, 1963-84

Year	Partial productivity of				Total factor productivity (TFP)
	Labour	Capital	Energy	Materials	
1963	1.000	1.000	1.000	1.000	1.000
1964	1.068	1.081	0.993	1.007	1.035
1965	1.107	1.120	0.995	1.017	1.057
1966	1.162	1.166	1.033	1.015	1.079
1967	1.125	1.113	1.014	1.008	1.056
1968	1.204	1.204	0.993	1.000	1.086
1969	1.245	1.257	1.004	0.949	1.077
1970	1.313	1.300	0.984	0.976	1.112
1971	1.380	1.331	0.914	0.959	1.116
1972	1.513	1.432	0.913	0.976	1.167
1973	1.558	1.482	0.921	0.937	1.160
1974	1.540	1.433	0.987	0.803	1.067
1975	1.432	1.189	0.924	0.768	0.987
1976	1.572	1.291	0.979	0.776	1.032
1977	1.602	1.280	1.003	0.809	1.060
1978	1.676	1.272	1.046	0.867	1.113
1979	1.730	1.250	1.098	0.929	1.163
1980	1.759	1.231	1.127	0.878	1.134
1981	1.800	1.227	1.149	0.997	1.210
1982	1.792	1.153	1.043	1.154	1.255
1983	1.984	1.254	1.129	1.239	1.360
1984	2.057	1.302	1.124	1.359	1.441
Average annual growth rate	3.49%	1.26%	0.56%	2.76%	1.75%

study period (1963-84) while Canada increased its labour input by 19 per cent.

(4) The U.S. increased its use of energy far more than did Canada (a 72 per cent increase versus a 27 per cent increase). Both countries economized in the use of energy following the first fuel crisis.

(5) The growth of Canadian materials input was higher than that of the U.S. (a 2.3 per cent increase per year versus a 1.7 per cent increase). This is expected given the slightly higher output growth for Canada.

(6) The capital input increased substantially faster in Canada than in the U.S. (4 per cent per year versus 1.9 per cent per year). Most of the U.S. increase occurred since the mid-1970s, while the increase in Canada occurred more in the pre-1975 period.

EMPIRICAL RESULTS ON PRODUCTIVITY

Using the methodology described previously, the partial factor productivities (PFP) of the four inputs and the total factor productivity (TFP) were computed, and the results are reported in Tables 6 and 7 for Canada and the U.S., respectively. All of these productivity indices have been scaled by setting 1963 to unity. The partial factor productivities for the Canadian and the U.S. industries are plotted in Figures 3 and 4, respectively. The average annual growth rates for the 1963 to 1984 period are summarized in Table 8:

TABLE 8
Average annual growth rate of productivity

	Canada	U.S.
Labour productivity	2.6%	3.5%
Energy productivity	2.3%	0.6%
Materials productivity	1.1%	2.8%
Capital productivity	-0.6%	1.3%
Total factor productivity	**1.2%**	**1.8%**

Labour, energy, and materials recorded positive productivity growth in both Canada and in the U.S. Both countries enjoyed high growth in labour productivity, although the U.S. growth record is significantly higher than that of Canada. The U.S. industry enjoyed a growth of capital productivity (1.3 per cent per year or 30 per cent cumulative growth), while Canada suffered a reduction in capital pro-

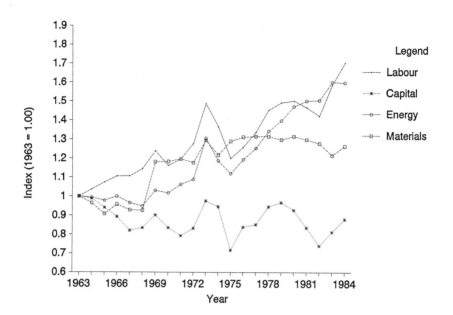

FIGURE 3
Partial factor productivity indices in the Canadian pulp and paper industry,
1963-84

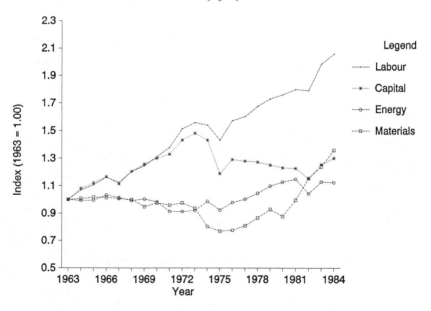

FIGURE 4
Partial factor productivity indices in the U.S. pulp and paper industry,
1963-84

ductivity (-0.6 per cent per year or 12 per cent cumulative reduction) during the 1963-84 period.

A careful examination of Tables 6 and 7 and Figures 3 and 4 allows one to detect a clear historical trend of substituting capital for the other three inputs. For example, Table 2 and Figure 3 together show that as Canada invested heavily in capital inputs (throughout the entire period but especially in the pre-1974 period), productivities of other inputs improved while capital productivity fell. Table 3 and Figure 4 together show that capital productivity of the u.s. industry increased substantially during the pre-1974 period, when the industry's capital input did not increase very much. On the other hand, when the u.s. industry was investing heavily in capital in the later period, its capital productivity started to fall. The Canadian industry appears to have invested heavily in energy saving machinery and equipment due to the high energy prices relative to the u.s. Canada's energy price increased more than tenfold between 1963 and 1984, while the u.s. energy price increased sevenfold. This led to a high growth in energy productivity at the expense of reduced capital productivity.

Figures 5 and 6 compare the growth of labour and capital productivity in the two countries. As can be seen, the u.s. enjoys higher

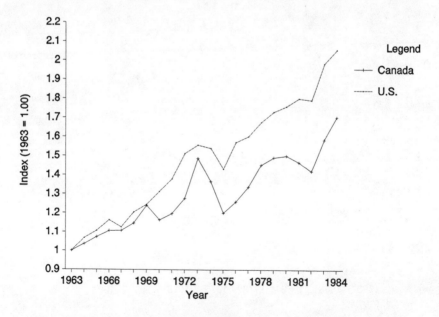

FIGURE 5
Labour productivity in the Canadian and the u.s. pulp and paper industry, 1963-84

growth in both labour and capital productivities. The labour and capital productivities in both countries appear to depend greatly on economic booms and busts. This suggests that the industry has difficulty adjusting these inputs freely as the market demand for their products changes. Therefore, it is important for the industry to make its input employment decisions within a long-term perspective.

The changes in inputs and their productivities have not been constant. In Canada, for example, energy productivity fell in the 1960s. It started to rise in the early 1970s and jumped in 1973, presumably due to the energy crisis. It fell back to the early levels following the crisis, then rose continuously, at a rather rapid rate, until 1982. Indeed, from 1975 to 1981 energy productivity rose an average of 5.0 per cent per year. Figure 6 indicates that capital investment programs in Canada may have been less effective in improving productivity of the industry than were u.s. investment programs. The changes in input and output quantities (Tables 2 through 5) show that the u.s. industry was better able to deal with economic contractions than was the Canadian industry. For example, when the u.s. industry's output decreased by 4.6 per cent between 1981 and 1982, their labour input was adjusted down by 4 per cent while capital input was increased by a small percentage (1.5 per cent). In contrast,

FIGURE 6
Capital productivity in the Canadian and the u.s. pulp and paper industry,
1963-84

when output of the Canadian industry decreased by 10 per cent between 1980 and 1981, they were able to reduce labour input by only
4.5 per cent but had to expand capital input by 13 per cent.

TFP growth is basically a weighted average of the rates of growth
in the four individual PFP's. TFP growth is strongly influenced by
materials, as this accounts for roughly 40 per cent to 50 per cent of industry costs, as well as by capital and labour, which together account for 40 per cent to 45 per cent of costs. The TFP growth rate for
the Canadian industry averaged 1.2 per cent per year (a cumulative
growth of 29 per cent during the 1963-84 period), while that for the
U.S. industry averaged 1.75 per cent per year (a cumulative growth of
43 per cent). It is interesting to note that most of the TFP growth had
occurred during the period in which the industry was heavily investing; that is, the pre-1974 period for Canada and the post-1974
period for the U.S. The relatively high rate of capital investment in
Canada during the pre-1974 period did not result in as much of a div-
idend in terms of TFP growth as did the modest increase in capital
investment by the U.S. industry during the post-1974 period.

Figures 7 and 8 show that TFP growth is strongly influenced by
output growth. Output, input, and TFP all declined precipitously in
1975 with the economic contraction, reaction to the fuel crisis, and
response to the rapid price run-up and corresponding shortage of
U.S. pulpwood. Figure 9 compares the TFP performance of the two
countries. Canada's TFP growth exceeded that of the U.S. for the
1963-80 period (28 per cent growth for Canada versus 13 per cent for
the U.S.). However, during the 1980-4 period, the U.S. industry improved TFP by a whopping 27 per cent while the TFP level of the Canadian industry remained virtually unchanged during the same period. In sum, overall productivity of the industry improved in Canada mostly during the pre-1974 period, while in the U.S. it improved
mostly in the post-1980 period.

Gollop and Jorgenson's study of the productivity of fifty-one U.S.
industrial sectors reported TFP growth of 1.08 per cent per year for
the 'paper and allied products' sector during the 1960-73 period. For
the 1963-73 period, this study's results are somewhat higher at 1.5
per cent growth per year.[9] A nonparametric study of the Canadian
pulp and paper industry conducted by the United Nations (1988)
found an 11 per cent reduction in productivity between 1974 and
1983. Our study finds a 4 per cent gain in TFP during the same period. The difference in empirical results between our study and that
of the UN is at least partially attributable to the major difference in
methodologies employed for constructing capital input and output
quantity indices. There are a number of problems with the UN study,

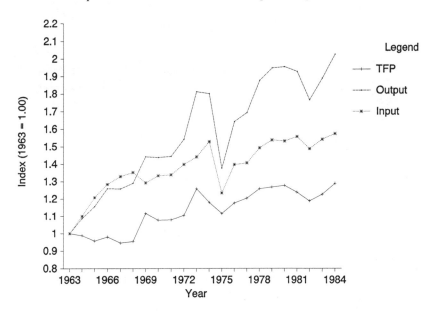

FIGURE 7
Indices of total factor productivity, and output and input quantities in the
Canadian pulp and paper industry, 1963-84

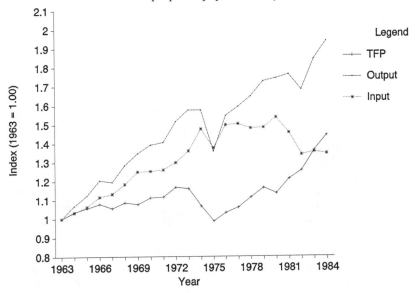

FIGURE 8
Indices of total factor productivity, and output and input quantities in the
u.s. pulp and paper industry, 1963-84

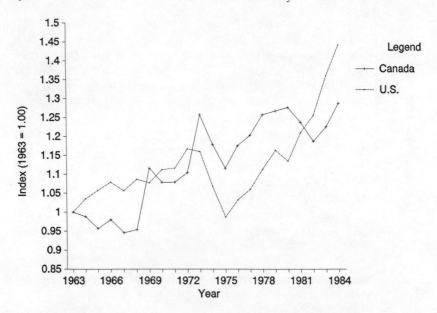

FIGURE 9
Total factor productivity in the Canadian and the u.s. pulp and paper
industry, 1963-84

including its measurement of capital inputs and outputs, and the index number technique used for data aggregation (see note 1).

SUMMARY OF RESULTS AND CONCLUDING REMARKS

Partial and total factor productivities were measured for the u.s. and
Canadian pulp and paper industries using the annual industry aggregate data for the 1963-84 period. The main empirical results may
be summarized as follows:

(1) The u.s. industry achieved a higher average growth rate of
    labour productivity (3.5 per cent per year versus Canada's 2.6
    per cent), materials productivity (2.8 per cent per year versus
    Canada's 1.1 per cent), and capital productivity (1.3 per cent
    per year versus Canada's reduction of 0.6 per cent per year).
(2) Canada achieved significantly higher growth of energy pro-
    ductivity than did the u.s. (2.6 per cent per year versus 0.6 per
    cent), as the Canadian industry appears to have responded to
    a more than tenfold increase in energy price during the 1963-84
    period by heavily investing in energy-saving facilities. Since

energy input accounts for a relatively small portion of the total cost (5 per cent to 10 per cent), this did not contribute a great deal to improving the overall productivity of the Canadian industry.

(3) The u.s. industry achieved a significantly higher TFP growth rate than did Canada during the 1963-84 period (cumulative growth of 44 per cent as compared to Canada's 29 per cent growth). Close to two-thirds of the u.s. TFP growth occurred during the 1980 to 1984 period (27 per cent TFP growth), while most of the TFP growth for the Canadian industry occurred during the pre-1974 period (26 per cent TFP growth).

(4) The high TFP growth period in Canada (pre-1974) coincides with the Canadian industry's heavy capital investment period (with a 90 per cent increase in capital input). This has led to a significant reduction in capital productivity.

(5) The labour, capital, and total factor productivities are clearly affected by the condition of the economy as it influences demands for the industry's outputs. This indicates the industry's difficulty in adjusting levels of labour and capital inputs to changing market conditions.

The empirical results concerning total factor productivity indicate that during our study period (1963-84), overall productivity (TFP) of the u.s. industry improved significantly faster than that of its Canadian counterpart. This is especially so since 1980. This implies that no matter what caused the differential TFP growth rates, the Canadian industry became less cost efficient than did its u.s. competitors. Since the Canadian industry exports over 70 per cent of its outputs to the u.s., this TFP result poses a serious question for the long-run viability of the Canadian industry. The industry must take steps to improve its overall productivity in order to ensure its survival.

Our data on changes in outputs and inputs in both countries reveal that the Canadian industry has been less able to adjust its capital and labour inputs to changing market demands for its outputs than has its u.s. counterparts. This inflexibility in input adjustment, particularly during economic slowdowns, poses an important policy question for the industry. In order to compete effectively with the u.s. competitors, either Canada must adopt management strategies to increase flexibility in labour and capital input quantities and/or management must make an effort to base their labour employment and capital investment decisions on a long-term perspective rather than being unduly influenced by short-term demand fluctuations. For example, if employment terms with labour unions cannot be made more flexible to a changing market and to the competitive conditions of the industry, firms in the industry must take that inflexibility into account in making investment and labour employment decisions. Also, more accurate forecasting of future market situations and output demand is likely to help prevent a drastic reduction in productivity during economic recessions.

During the 1963-84 period, the Canadian industry expanded its capital inputs far faster than did the u.s. industry (130 per cent increase for Canada versus 49 per cent increase for the u.s.). However, the improvements in labour, capital, materials, and total factor productivities by the u.s. industry have been significantly higher than those that the Canadian industry was able to accomplish. The heavier capital expansion by the Canadian industry appears to have improved its energy productivity significantly more than has been the case in the u.s. However, energy accounts for less than 10 per cent of the industry's total cost. These data appear to indicate that Canadian capital investment programs may not have been as effective as were those in the u.s. What is needed in Canada is more rational and economically efficient input employment decisions rather than a grand national policy of conserving energy at any cost.

ACKNOWLEDGMENTS

We would like to thank referees and the editor for helpful comments, and Asghedom Ghebremichael, Sonia Granzer, Joe Tam, and Eva Lau for research assistance. Financial assistance is gratefully acknowledged from ubc's Forest Economics and Policy Analysis Research Unit, the Social Sciences and Humanities Research Council of Canada, and ubc's Centre for International Business Studies.

NOTES

1 There are two major problems associated with the capital input cost calculation in the United Nations study. First, it added financial working capital to the capital cost and quantity computation. This constitutes a double counting because working capital is used for purchases of other factors, such as labour inputs, energy, wood and other purchased materials, and genuine capital assets. Second, it ignored the effects of corporate income tax, tax provisions for capital cost allowances, capital gains or losses, and property taxes when computing the user cost of capital. This would clearly bias the empirical results of the productivity mea-

surement if those factors changed over time or varied between countries. The output volume index was derived by multiplying current year volumes by the respective base-period (1974) prices. This means that the outputs were not aggregated properly. For such an aggregation procedure to be correct, the relative prices of the multiple outputs produced by the industry would have to remain constant. This was not the case when we examined the output prices for the Canadian and u.s. industries.

2 1984 was the most recent year for which data for both countries were available when our research began.

3 Four types of capital were measured: building construction, engineering construction, machinery and equipment, and capital items charged to operating expense. The last was capitalized, and the four categories were aggregated via the Divisia procedure.

4 Labour categories are production and administration/management; materials are pulpwood and others; and fuel types are coal and coke, natural gas, gasoline, oils, lpg, electricity, and others. Capital categories are given in the previous footnote.

5 It is only Btu content of energy types which is relevant for production.

6 The main data source are various Statistics Canada publications: catalogues 36-204, 57-506, 57-208, 62-002, 62-011, 13-568, 13-211. Also used were data from the Canadian Pulp and Paper Association: *1985 Reference Tables*.

7 Primary sources of data were the *U.S. Census of Manufacturers, Economic Indicators*, and 'The Statistics of Paper and Paperboard.' A more detailed discussion of the data construction can be requested from the authors.

8 Shares of each input in total cost are used as weights. The formula for aggregate input is the second term on the right-hand side of equation (3). This formula represents a discrete time approximation to the Divisia index procedure. Aggregate output is the first term.

9 Overall, paper and allied products was at the border between the middle and bottom thirds of industry performers in the 1947 to 1973 time period of their u.s. study.

CHAPTER TEN

The Impact of the Free Trade Agreement on the U.S. Forestry Sector: A General Equilibrium Analysis

Roy Boyd and Kerry Krutilla

INTRODUCTION

On 1 January 1989, a U.S./Canadian bilateral 'free trade' agreement (FTA) became effective. This historic pact will phase out most of the tariff barriers between the United States and Canada over the next ten years and will liberalize quantitative restrictions in a number of specific cases. Although the trade in forest products accounts for a relatively small component of total U.S.-Canadian trade and, on average, receives relatively low levels of tariff protection, the FTA will nonetheless have a measurable impact on the forest products industry and timber producers in the United States. The impact of the FTA on the forestry sector will be manifest directly through lower tariff protection and corollary product demand responses as well as indirectly through general equilibrium linkages that the forestry sector has with other segments of the general economy.

This paper specifically assesses the impact of the FTA on the forest products and timber industries in the United States. The paper employs a computable general equilibrium model of the U.S. economy, which captures both direct, sector-specific and indirect impacts of the FTA on the forestry sector.[1]

BACKGROUND

The U.S./Canadian FTA was negotiated against the backdrop of a rapid expansion in the bilateral trade between the United States and Canada. The value of U.S./Canadian trade increased by close to 50 per cent between 1980 and 1986. The trade in forest products increased by some 40 per cent over the same period but remained a relatively small component of the total value of trade, between 4 per

TABLE 1

U.S. trade with Canada (millions of U.S. dollars)

Year	Total trade	Forest products	(% total)
1980:			
U.S. exports	41,581	431	(1.0)
U.S. imports	40,874	2,282	(5.6)
1981:			
U.S. exports	45,469	492	(1.1)
U.S. imports	45,776	2,218	(4.8)
1982:			
U.S. exports	38,833	333	(0.9)
U.S. imports	46,329	2,050	(4.4)
1983:			
U.S. exports	43,897	481	(1.1)
U.S. imports	51,982	3,118	(5.9)
1984:			
U.S. exports	52,903	497	(0.9)
U.S. imports	66,343	3,374	(5.1)
1985:			
U.S. exports	54,505	496	(0.9)
U.S. imports	68,884	3,544	(5.1)
1986:			
U.S. exports	55,633	557	(1.0)
U.S. imports	68,163	3,351	(4.9)

SOURCE: Normile and Goodloe (1988)

cent and 6 per cent of the total (Table 1). The growth in trade between the United States and Canada has coincided with a worsening overall trade balance for the United States and a depreciation in the Canadian exchange rate relative to the U.S. dollar. The U.S. trade deficit in forest products in 1986 was $2.8 billion out of a total forest products trade of approximately $3.9 billion.

Due at least in part to the trade imbalance, the bilateral trade relationship between Canada and the United States has suffered a number of recent conflicts. In the forest products sector, Section 201 of the U.S. Trade Act was invoked in 1986 to impose a U.S. tariff of 35 per cent on red cedar shingles and shakes imported from Canada. Softwood lumber, as is well known, has also been the subject of controversy. After simmering as a political issue for a number of years, the U.S. initiated a countervail action against Canadian lumber of 15 per cent in October of 1986.[2] This was followed by a retaliatory trade action by the Canadians in the form of a 67 per cent ad valorem tax on corn imported from the United States. This sequence of actions, in turn, stimulated negotiations between the two countries which led to a Memorandum of Understanding (MOU), in which the Canadians agreed to a 15 per cent markup on the price of exported lumber, in the form of an export tax, as a substitute for the u.s. imposed countervailing duty.[3] In addition to these disputes, plywood grading standards have been a chronic irritant in the trade relationship between the United States and Canada. The u.s. industry maintains that Canadian plywood standards constitute a de facto barrier to trade.

Successive rounds of the General Agreement on Tarriffs and Trade (GATT) negotiations have lowered the tariffs levied on forest products traded between the United States and Canada. Current tariff levels on forest products are listed in Table 2. The tariff levels are relatively low, with the exception of more processed products, reflecting the impact of Tokyo round tariff reductions. The most restricted part of the forest products trade clearly is softwood plywood.[4] More than 75 per cent of the forest products trade (by value) now passes between the United States and Canada duty free.

In addition to the import tariffs, both countries maintain partial log export bans. Logs cannot be exported from federal timber lands in the United States, for example.[5] Technical standards are another potential barrier to trade. With the exception of plywood grading rules, however, these standards for forest products are not considered to be a significant barrier to the u.s./Canadian forest products trade.

Free trade negotiations were begun in 1986 by the Mulroney government and Reagan administration, coincident with some of the trade problems between the two countries alluded to above. The agreement was concluded over the course of several years and ratified by Congress under a 'fast-track' approval process. The resulting FTA has two key provisions of direct relevance to the forestry sector: (1) the phase out of most tariffs over a five- or ten-year period (See Table 2) – tariff elimination on most forest products will be phased in equal annual increments over a five-year period;[6] and (2) the establishment of a binding dispute resolution mechanism. Disputes over the interpretation and application of countervailing or antidumping statutes can be referred to the established binational panel for binding arbitration.

The FTA does not pre-empt the right of either country to take safeguard protective actions under GATT rules. It further grandfathers the MOU on softwood lumber and does not alter the log export bans maintained by both countries. The phased tariff reductions for plywood are made contingent on developing an agreement on technical

TABLE 2
Selected import duties: wood and paper products, 1 January 1989

	Canada (%)	United States (%)
Wood products		
Lumber	Free	Free
Softwood plywood	15^1	20^1
Wasteboard/osb	4	4
Particleboard	5	4
Fibreboard	6.5^1	3^1
Shingles & shakes	Free	Free[2]
Flooring	5.5	3.2
Kitchen cabinets	1.5	2.5
Doors	11.3	7.5
Windows	$9.2/12.5^1$	5.1^1
Manufactured houses	5.1^1	9.2^1
Pallets, containers	9.2^1	16.6^1
Pulp & paper products		
Woodpulp	Free	Free
Newsprint	Free	Free
Uncoated groundwood specialty papers	Free	Free
Uncoated wood free papers	6.5	Free
Coated groundwood & specialty papers (LWC)	2.5	2.5
Coated wood free papers	6.5	2.5
Writing papers	6.5	2.4
Kraft linerboard	6.5	Free
Corrugating medium	4.0	4.0
Sack kraft (unbleached)	Free	Free
Kraft papers (bleached)	9.2	2.4
Solid bleached boxboard	6.5	Free
Other boxboard	9.2	Free
Sanitary papers (jumbo rolls)	6.5	Free
Sanitary tissues	10.2	5.3
Paper boxes/cartons	9.2	2.8
Paper sacks/bags	9.2	5.3
Wallpaper	7.5	Free
Paper products (trays, dishes, plates & cups)	10.2	4.3

SOURCE: Canadian Government (1988)

NOTES: [1] Elimination over ten year period – all others will be removed over a five year period

[2] 35 per cent at present (imposed June 1986) – reduced to zero when current safeguard action terminates

standards.[7] The FTA also contains an allowance for a temporary emergency halt of the scheduled tariff reductions during the phase-in period and the reimposition of Most Favored Nation (MFN) rates if imports are demonstrated to cause significant injury to domestic industries.

The impetus behind the FTA was the belief by the political leadership of both countries that widespread economic benefits would accrue from bilateral trade liberalization. The Canadians also were particularly interested in the establishment of the bilateral dispute resolution mechanism, believing that this mechanism would lower the probability of successful U.S. protectionist measures, making markets in the United States more secure for Canadian products.

THE MODEL

The impact of a broad-based trade liberalization on the forestry sector will be significantly influenced by sectoral responses in the rest of the economy. For this reason, a general equilibrium approach is an appropriate modelling methodology for the analysis. The model presented below follows in the tradition of the Shoven and Whalley (1984) tax analysis research and incorporates some of the methodological enhancements of Jorgenson (1984). For example, it recognizes the differences in preferences of consumers as a function of their incomes and specifies a distinct demand system for each group of households. Additionally, a neoclassical microeconomic model of producer behaviour is employed. The model of consumer behaviour is integrated with the model of producer behaviour (which contains a price-responsive input-output component) to provide a comprehensive framework for policy simulations.

The general equilibrium nature of the model is characterized by the determination of a vector of prices for consumer goods and services and producer goods and services that clears all markets. The equilibrium prices determine the optimal allocation of resources, given the endowments of labour, capital, and natural resources (land).

On the production side, technologies are represented by production functions that exhibit constant elasticities of substitution. Technological progress is not assumed to occur over the period of investigation. On the demand side, the model captures the behaviour of consumers (who can also serve as investors), the government, and foreigners. Consumers are grouped according to income and a demand system is specified for each group. Each income group has an endowment of labour and capital and, given the vector of prices,

TABLE 3

Classification of producing sectors and consumer goods and services

Industries	Consumer goods
1 Manufacturing	1 Food
2 Mining	2 Alcohol and tobacco
3 Service	3 Utilities
4 Chemicals and plastics	4 Furnishings and appliances
5 Food and tobacco products	5 Housing
6 Petroleum refining	6 Clothing
7 Financial	7 Transportation
8 Forestry (timber production)	8 Motor vehicles
9 Crude oil and natural gas	9 Financial and other services
10 Agriculture 1: program crops	10 Recreation
11 Agriculture 2: livestock	11 Non-durable household items
12 Agriculture 3: all other agriculture	12 Gasoline and other fuels
	13 Savings

decides the amount to save and invest and the amount of each good and service to consume (purchase). Investment, consequently, is determined by saving. The government levies taxes on factors of production, on output, on income, and on consumption. Revenues are used to distribute income back to consumers and to purchase goods and services as well as capital and labour.

The foreign sector, that is, Canada and the rest of the world, produces imports and consumes exports. The foreign sector can be regarded as consumers who purchase U.S. exports with income from the sale of imports to the U.S. Table 3 details the specific production sectors and types of consumer goods and services considered in the general equilibrium model. The forest products industries are incorporated within the manufacturing sector. (Forest industries account for approximately 8 per cent of the earnings returned to the manufacturing sector.) The analysis which follows assumes that the share of manufacturing represented by forest industries remains stable under the free trade implementation.[8] We now describe the scheme of the model in somewhat greater detail.

Production

The production sector is composed of an input-output model with some flexibility with regard to the substitution of the factor inputs (capital, labour, and land). The degree of flexibility depends, in general, on the choice of functional form for the production function. In the current model, each sector is assumed to have a constant elasticity of substitution (CES) production function where the value added by the specific sector is a function of labour and capital.

For four sectors (the three agriculture sectors and the forestry sector) a third factor of production – land – is included because of its special importance to these sectors. The incorporation of land into the production function is accomplished by nesting the CES production function. In particular, an input is defined which is solely a function (in CES form) of land and capital which, in turn, takes the place of capital in the original production function specification. While it would be possible to simply add land as an explicit input in the production function, this would implicitly assume that the elasticity of substitution between all pairs of inputs are the same. By nesting, however, the substitution elasticities are allowed to differ for different inputs.

Demand

The output of the twelve producing sectors accrues to the owners of the factors of production (i.e., land, labour, and capital) which they sell. With the receipts from these sales, individuals can consume domestic or foreign goods and services, save, or pay taxes to the government. The savings are used for investment, and the taxes are ultimately returned to these individuals.

A review of Table 3 shows that the consumer goods sectors do not match the producing sectors. Final goods and services produced by the producing sectors must go through various channels (i.e., transportation and distribution) before they can be consumed. To address this issue, a transformation matrix is introduced which defines the contribution of each producing sector to the composition of each of the final (consumer) goods and services.

For each category of household, utility is assumed to be a weighted constant elasticity of substitution function of the thirteen consumer goods and services plus leisure. The weights on these goods and services (which are household category specific) are computed as the share of total purchases going to a specific consumer good or service. The nature of the CES utility function implies that the elasticity of substitution is the same between any pair of goods and/or services. Because reliable estimates of the respective substitution elasticities across pairs of goods and/or services are difficult to obtain, they are assumed to equal one for all of the combinations.

Finally, consumers derive utility not only from the consumption of goods and services (which comes about through owning the factors of production) but from leisure as well. There is an explicit treatment of the labour-leisure trade-off in the model.[9] Hence, it is necessary to determine a weight for this factor in the utility function. For the purpose of the current analysis, this value is assumed to be 0.5 times labour income. Boyd (1988) provides a discussion of the choice of this value. Thus, an increase in leisure can lead to an enhancement of individual well-being in the model.

A household's budget constraint is defined such that expenditures on goods and services must be less than or equal to its income, which is the sum of returns to labour, capital, and land. That is, expenditures by a household must be less than or equal to the total factor payments it receives. Maximizing utility subject to this expenditure constraint gives the demand for the various goods and services by consumers (Mixon and Uri 1985). Observe that since savings are considered as one of the items in an individual's utility function, the choice between consumption and savings is made explicit. That is, intertemporal tradeoffs are an integral part of the model.

A second component of the demand for goods and services is investment. Like the final demand by individuals, total investment is disaggregated (through a transformation matrix) by the sector of the economy that produces it. For the purpose of calibrating the general equilibrium model, investment is taken directly from the national income and product accounts (as compiled by the Bureau of Economic Analysis of the U.S. Department of Commerce) and, since savings are assumed to exactly equal investment, personal savings are scaled to equal the gross investment measured for each of the twelve producing sectors.

The final component of demand for goods and services is the demand by Canadian customers and the rest of the world. In the model, exports (i.e., foreign demand) are delineated by the producing sector. A similar delineation is employed for imports (i.e., foreign supply). By employing elasticity estimates found in the literature, export and import demand relationships are constructed for each producing sector.

Taxes

Government tax receipts enter the general equilibrium model specification and affect the model results with regard to factor use, factor prices, and output. The government sector is treated in the model as a separate sector with a constant elasticity of substitution utility function. That is, it is treated in a fashion analogous to one of the household sectors. The elasticity of substitution is assumed to be 1.0. This means that the production function collapses to a Cobb-Douglas type function. The government collects tax revenue in various forms. The explicitly considered taxes include the personal income tax, labour taxes (e.g., social security tax), capital taxes (e.g., corporate income tax), property taxes, and sales and excise taxes. All of the taxes are treated as ad valorem taxes and a marginal rate is identified for each household category, consumer good or service, producing sector, and factor input. In this respect, the model is a distinct improvement over earlier general equilibrium models, which simply employed lump sum transfer schemes or average tax rates. Note that in this model, labour is treated as a variable commodity that is subject to taxation.

With the tax revenues, the government produces public goods and redistributes income. Hence, all such revenue is eventually returned to consumers in the form of transfer payments or subsidies or in the form of payments for capital or labour services (the two factors of production used by the government).

Mathematical Statement of the Model

There are several conditions that the model must satisfy for a general equilibrium to exist. First, there cannot be positive excess quantities demanded, that is

$$\sum_{j=1}^{m} a_{ij}M_j - E_i(\mathbf{P}, \mathbf{Y}) \geq 0 \text{ for c.s. } p_i \geq 0. \tag{1}$$

Here i $(i = 1,2, \ldots , n)$ denotes consumer goods and services, M_j $(j = 1,2 \ldots ,m)$ activity levels, a_{ij} the ijth element in the activity analysis matrix, $\mathbf{Y}$ a vector of incomes for k consumers, $\mathbf{P}$ a vector of prices for n consumer goods and services, and E_i the excess demand for good or service i. The notation c.s. implies that complementary slackness holds for each consumer good or service, that is, if the expression (for a specific good or service i) is multiplied by p_i, then the relationship will hold with equality.

The second requirement for general equilibrium is that the profits associated with a given activity are not positive. That is,

$$\sum_{i=1}^{n} a_{ij}p_i \leq 0 \text{ for c.s., } M_j \geq 0. \tag{2}$$

Finally, all prices and activity levels must be non-negative, that is,

$$p_i \geq 0, 1, 2, \ldots, n, \tag{3a}$$

and

$$M_i \geq_\partial 0, j = 1, 2, \ldots, m. \tag{3b}$$

The actual general equilibrium model is solved using the iterative algorithm nominally referred to as the Sequence of Linear Complementary Problems (SLCP) developed by Mathiesen (1985).

Data

The general equilibrium model is calibrated for the year 1984. For the twelve producing sectors enumerated in Table 3, capital receipts and taxes are computed from data obtained from the Bureau of Economic Analysis of the U.S. Department of Commerce, the U.S. Department of Agriculture, the U.S. Department of Energy, and from Hertel and Tsigas (1987). The various elasticities of substitution used in the analysis were obtained from a variety of sources in the literature on production function estimation (Boyd 1988).

Capital and labour income were obtained from the Bureau of Economic Analysis of the U.S. Department of Commerce. Land income was estimated using factor shares obtained from the Economic Research Service of the U.S. Department of Agriculture and applied to the capital income component noted above.

Data on expenditures on each of the thirteen goods and services by each of the six household categories were obtained from the Bureau of Labor Statistics. By combining this information with the number of households in each household (income) category (these data came from the Bureau of Economic Analysis), the aggregate expenditures on each category of consumer goods and services by each household category can be computed.

The various tax rates used in the analysis were obtained from a variety of sources, including the Internal Revenue Service and the Economic Research Service of the Department of Agriculture (Hertel and Tsigas 1987; Ballard et al. 1985). As noted previously, these are marginal rates. The value of exports and imports were taken from the *Survey of Current Business* (various issues), with the exception of energy data, which were obtained from the U.S. Department of Energy, and the agriculture data, which were obtained from the Economic Research Service of the USDA.

Benchmark tariff rates in the model are MFN rates which reflect the implementation of Tokyo round tariff reductions.[10] Because the number of product lines for which tariff classifications exist greatly exceeds the number of commodity sectors, it was necessary to derive weighted average tariff rates for the sector aggregates in the model. Rates for the United States and Canada were obtained from the Canadian Department of Finance (Lester and Morehen 1988a,b). These numbers reflect actual tariff levels plus ad valorem tariff equivalents of the protective impact of quantitative restrictions and federal procurements. Because the sector classification in the present model did not coincide identically with the sectors in the Canadian model, it was necessary to re-derive tariff for several sectors, using production figures as weighting factors in the manner suggested by Lester and Morehen (1988a,b).

SIMULATIONS

To simulate the impact of trade liberalization, the benchmark tariffs are removed from the United States and Canada. As mentioned, the scheduled tariff elimination under the free trade agreement will be gradual. The policy simulation here reflects the impact of the FTA after complete implementation. Since the primary concern is with the forest products markets and the timber sector, our discussion will deal primarily with results relevant to forestry. However, to sound out the analysis we will briefly consider the more general economic impact of the FTA.

Forest Products Markets

Following trade liberalization, U.S. production, export, and importation of forest products increase (Table 4). The value of imports of forest products increases by $153 million, or by approximately 4.5 per cent, while the value of exports increases by $142 million, approximately 28.6 per cent.[11] Although the percentage change for exports is larger than it is for imports (reflecting the smaller base from which the export change occurs), the absolute increase in the value of exports is smaller than that of imports by $11 million – the amount by which the trade imbalance for forest products worsens as a consequence of the trade liberalization. The $11 million deterioration in the forest products trade account represents considerably less than 1 per cent of the original forest products trade deficit, however (See Table 1), so the trade balance effect of the FTA implementation on forest products is essentially inconsequential.

Earnings returned to forest products producers remain relatively

TABLE 4
Impact of FTA on U.S. forest products markets

	Revenue change (Millions of 1984 U.S. dollars)	Per cent
Domestic earnings	+2.4	<1%
Imports	+153.1	4.5%
Exports	+142.2	28%
Trade balance	-10.9	<1%

stable, increasing inconsequentially by $2 million, less than 1 per cent (Table 4). This fact is of interest because it is often believed that the earnings of domestic industries of import-competing products, such as forest products, will decline with trade liberalization. The earnings impact on producers of the FTA is driven by a number of countervailing factors. Increased competition from higher Canadian imports reduces the relative price of manufactured goods, including forest products, by a small amount (less than 1 per cent), which, all else constant, tends to lower earnings returned to forest industries. Additionally, however, there is the important fact that the relative price of some major production inputs (manufactured goods, refined petroleum, chemicals, and plastics) drop as a result of the trade liberalization. This latter effect, while lowering equilibrium price levels and earnings from production, also tends to increase producer profitability (by lowering production costs) – a benefit from trade liberalization which has not always been perceived by concerned industry trade groups.

General demand increases stimulated by the trade liberalization are the factors which offset the price effects on producer earnings just noted. Part of the demand increase is generated by Canadian customers; as mentioned above, exports of forest products increase by close to 29 per cent. Additionally, however, the domestic production and consumption of some consumer goods which drive the demand for forest products also increase as a result of the trade liberalization. Wood products, such as mouldings and furniture, are used in the consumer good category modelled, in the present case, as 'furnishings and appliances.' Sales of furnishings and appliances increase by some $5 million as a result of the trade liberalization. Pulp and paper are used extensively as 'nondurable household items.' Total sales revenues to retailers in this sector increase by about $2 million. The equilibrium revenue impact in these sectors is driven by a supply-side effect (the beneficial impact of the FTA on production costs) and demand-side effect (the increase in the relative price of some substitute products). The final major use of forest products is for housing. It turns out that the demand for housing unambiguously increases as a consequence of the FTA. The FTA increases consumer income through lower product prices, which has indirect and direct effects on housing demand. The indirect effect is through the savings channel; with a positive propensity to save, increased consumer income causes the supply curve of savings to shift out. This adjustment in the loanable funds market lowers interest rates and stimulates housing demand. Further, increased disposable income of consumers stimulates the demand for housing through a direct consumption effect. The impact of the FTA on the housing market will, consequently, increase earnings received by producers of softwood lumber and plywood.

In summary, the FTA appears to have a very modestly beneficial impact on U.S. forest product markets in the aggregate. While increased Canadian competition will place downward pressure on product prices, two important offsetting benefits accrue: (1) lower production costs from relative price declines of some important production inputs and (2) increased product demands from Canadian and U.S. customers.

Forestry and Land Use

As noted before, there is a small roundwood trade between Canada and the United States, even though both countries impose various log export restrictions. Although the log export restrictions are not affected by the free trade agreement, the trade in logs increases as a consequence of the trade liberalization. The value of log imports to the U.S. increases by about $1.7 million, or by approximately 8 per cent, while the value of log exports increases by about $.5 million. The impact of the FTA in the roundwood market is due to increased demands in final wood-using and intermediate product markets referred to above, which leads to greater derived demands for sawtimber and pulpwood from forested lands.

The most significant impact of the FTA on timber producers is to increase the price and profitability of timber and the value of forested land. The relative price of stumpage increases by 2.1 per cent. This price increase is driven by increases in the derived demand for timber and pulpwood. The relative value of forested land appreciates from the value appreciation of forestry output as well as from demands for land from other economic sectors which result from the trade liberalization. Agricultural crops are one of the most heavily protected sectors in the U.S./Canadian bilateral trade. When trade barriers are eliminated from this sector, the demand for U.S. exports of both program crops (e.g., wheat, barley, corn, etc.) and other crops (e.g., fruits and vegetables) shifts out. This economic adjustment increases the demand for land, which raises its relative price (giving present land owners a capital gain). The general increase in land value will also lead to less land-intensive forestry practices. Thus, viewed in a general equilibrium context, it appears that the FTA has a decidedly positive impact on the timber producing sector.

General Economic Impact

To place the results of the preceding analysis in context, we deal briefly with the general economic impact of the trade liberalization. Table 5 indicates the impact on six consumer groups differentiated by income level. The term 'consumer welfare' in Table 5 refers to a proxy measure, which is based on an index of expenditures on thirteen consumer goods plus the value of leisure for each of the six income groups. Several facts deserve comment. First, the economic impact of the FTA is positive, since no income group is harmed and five out of the six groups exhibit welfare increases. (This fact is consistent with the earlier explanation of the market demand changes for wood-derived consumption products.) Second, the welfare gains to consumers are less than 1 per cent in all cases, so the net impact of the agreement is modest. This reflects the fact that U.S./Canadian trade is a small portion of the United States' total economic product.[12] And third, as might be expected, the economic benefits of trade liberalization are not distributed equally across all income groups – the largest gains are experienced by the highest income groups.[13] This result occurs from the fact that the price of capital relative to labour rises as a consequence of the FTA, and the holdings of capital are largest in the higher income brackets. Somewhat more interesting are the relatively large gains experienced by the lowest income group. This result is explained primarily by the fact that many small farmers are relatively land rich, and landowners experience a capital gain for the reason mentioned before. Included in this income category would be the lowest income owners of private non-industrial forests.

We now consider the exchange rate and trade balance effects. The real exchange rate is often defined as the ratio of tradeable goods to non-tradeable goods (see, for example, Helpman and Razin 1981; and Edwards 1986). Calculating the real exchange rate for both the benchmark and free trade runs of the model reveals that the FTA

TABLE 5
Change in consumer welfare by income classes
(millions of 1984 U.S. dollars)

Income group	Welfare change
0 - $10,000	+13
$10,000 - $15,000	0
$15,000 - $20,000	+9
$20,000 - $30,000	+19
$30,000 - $40,000	+11
$40,000 +	+21

causes the real exchange rate of the U.S. dollar on the world market to appreciate inconsequentially (by about .00087 from a normalized benchmark of 1). The appreciation in the purchasing price of the dollar reflects the fact that high Canadian trade barriers have been removed from sectors, such as agriculture, where the U.S. producers have a relative advantage. Its small absolute value, however, suggests that the FTA implementation will have essentially no impact on the global foreign exchange market for U.S. currency or on the United States' overall balance of payments position.

Sensitivity Analysis

We now consider the robustness of the results to the parameter values in the model. In terms of the results on forest products industries, the most important parameter is the elasticity of substitution between labour and capital in the manufacturing sector. In subsequent runs, this elasticity is raised from its initial value of 0.7 to 1.0 and lowered to 0.4. Raising the elasticity to 1.0 causes relatively more low-cost labour to go into manufacturing but does not appreciably increase manufacturing output. Furthermore, there is little change in the production of consumption goods which create the derived demand for forest-related industries. The production and consumption of housing, non-durable household items, and furnishings and appliances remain virtually unchanged compared with the original calibration, as does the price of timber on forested lands. Lowering the substitution elasticity in manufacturing from 0.7 to 0.4 has no effect on any forest products industry and hardly any effect on any aspect of the economy as a whole. Thus, the stated results are robust with respect to this important parameter.

CONCLUSION

A general equilibrium model was used to model the impact of the free trade agreement on the U.S. forest product industries and timber producers. The general equilibrium approach has several distinct advantages for modelling the impacts of general economic policies such as the U.S./Canadian bilateral free trade implementation. Chief among them is the capability to capture between-sector economic linkages which indirectly affect specific industrial sectors such as forest industries. Indirect effects, such as changes in manufactured input prices or changes in the real rate of interest, can exert as powerful an economic influence on specific sectors as can the more direct effects reflected in final product markets. The general equilibrium approach also captures the impact of policies on production factors (e.g., land) which are largely ignored in partial equilibrium analyses. Finally, a general equilibrium analysis allows for a full and consistent set of sectoral accounts.

The results of the general equilibrium model indicate that the FTA should have a modestly positive impact on the U.S. domestic forest industries and timber producers. Market-driven demand increases and lower production costs tend to offset the producer price impacts of increased competition caused by trade liberalization. The model, because of the degree of sectoral aggregation, does not pick up short-term losses or gains for specific forest industries above or below the industry average; as a consequence, it is conceivable that some specific forest industries, for example, softwood lumber, could actually experience short-term losses which are not reflected in the results. A detailed specification of the forest industries within the general equilibrium context would yield more precise estimates for specific forest products industries and constitutes the logical extension of the present line of research.

NOTES

1 The impact of the FTA on the Canadian economy has been assessed in detail by the Canadian Department of Finance. See Harris (1988) for a description of the model and Canadian Government (1988) for a sectoral assessment of the FTA on the Canadian forest products sector.

2 The International Trade Administration (ITA) made a negative ruling on a similar appeal in 1982. The new ruling was based on a reinterpretation of the 'specificity' criterion in the statute to allow for action against final commodities derived from subsidized inputs.

3 The politics and economic consequences of the lumber dispute have been analyzed by Boyd and Krutilla (1988). The impact of the Canadian export tax, however, has been significantly reduced since the initial implementation as a consequence of amendments to the original MOU. The amendments have allowed British Columbia to substitute provincial stumpage price increases for the export tax and Quebec, through the same process, to reduce the tax to 8 per cent. According to Canadian sources, 90 per cent of the softwood lumber trade from Canada is now exported to the United States duty free (Canadian Government 1988).

4 According to data from the National Forest Products Association, the value of plywood imports into the United States accounts for less than 1 per cent of the total value of U.S. wood products imports (and significantly less that 1 per cent of total U.S. plywood consumption).

5 Notwithstanding log export bans, there is a small trade in logs between Canada and the United States. Data from the National Forest Products Association indicates that the U.S. imported logs valued at $16.2 million from Canada in 1988.

6 For a complete schedule of tariff reductions under the FTA, see the Federal Register, 16 December 1988:50679-910.

7 At the current time, the plywood grading standards issue has not been resolved, so the plywood part of the free trade agreement is not presently being implemented.

8 A comprehensive description of the general equilibrium model together with its parameterization can be found in Boyd (1988).

9 See Deaton and Muelbauer (1980) for more on the labour-leisure trade-off.

10 The Tokyo round tariff reductions were phased in between 1979 and 1987.

11 Model results are based on data for the calibration year 1984. More recent data sets should produce results which are qualitatively similar but may differ somewhat in quantitative magnitudes.

12 It is possible that our estimate of the FTA's impact may be biased downward to some degree. The model does not capture the impact of dynamic factors which would tend to increase welfare. Chief among them are the technical change or scale economies which could be stimulated by a larger and better integrated U.S./Canadian market. (In a 1984 study by Harris, scale economies increased the welfare benefit of the FTA on the Canadian economy relative to the no scale economy benchmark by about 8 per cent.) Also, the present model does not allow for international capital flows and, as a consequence, will not capture any benefits which might accrue from the liberalization of investment under the FTA. The impact of the FTA on investment and capital flows, however, may not be very large, since the Mulroney government had already significantly lib-

eralized investment regulations before the agreement was enacted.
13 This result is consistent with other computable general equilibrium CGE
   runs by Wigle (1986) and Harris (1984).

CHAPTER ELEVEN

Canada-United States Trade in Forest Products: Issues and Uncertainties

Irving K. Fox

Over the last few years, trade between Canada and the United States has received a great deal of attention from political leaders in both countries, and in Canada the public has been deeply involved as well. The primary reason for the prominence of Canada-u.s. trade was the negotiation of the Free Trade Agreement (FTA) and its ratification by both countries. The FTA became the central issue in the Canadian parliamentary election held in the autumn of 1988, which can be attributed, in part at least, to the perceived economic importance of Canadian trade with the United States.

Canadian trade in forest products with the United States constitutes a significant fraction of the total flow of goods between Canada and the u.s. However, the importance of the policy issues associated with forest product trade between the two countries transcends the trade's economic significance. Two controversial actions by the United States government in 1986 cast in sharp relief major issues in the management of trade relations between the two countries. The first of these was the imposition by the United States of a 35 per cent duty on shakes and shingles imported from Canada (referred to as the Shakes and Shingles Case). The second was a major controversy over the proposed imposition of a countervailing duty on softwood lumber imported from Canada on the grounds that timber harvesting was subsidized by four Canadian provinces (referred to as the Softwood Lumber Dispute). This dispute culminated in a negotiated settlement which provided that Canada would impose a 15 per cent export tax on softwood lumber destined for the u.s.

The Free Trade Agreement ratified in 1988 (Government of Canada, External Affairs 1988) neither altered these two actions nor materially changed the laws on which they were based. In addition to forest trade policy issues associated with theses two cases, a number of uncertainties about factors that affect the pattern of trade in forest products between the two countries are evident. It is the purpose of this paper to identify and illuminate the policy issues and uncertainties that will be associated with trade in forest products between Canada and the United States during the coming decade.

GENERAL CONTEXT

Forest products may be classified into two broad categories: wood products and pulp and paper. Wood products that are traded include pulpwood and chips (that are used in paper manufacturing), logs, lumber, plywood, particle board, and a variety of veneers. There are certain features of the forest industries and the pattern of trade in forest products that have implications for the issues and uncertainties considered in this paper. First, the flow of forest products from the United States to Canada is generally only about 10 per cent of the flow from Canada to the United States (Statistics Canada 1986a,b). Second, in both countries the forest product industries are regionally concentrated. In Canada, the forest industry is concentrated in British Columbia, Ontario, and Quebec, which account for about 85 per cent of the employment in the forest industries (Canadian Forest Industries Council 1986). In the United States, the South and West account for about 90 per cent of the wood pulp production (Jegr 1985:21, Table 10) and an even larger proportion of the softwood lumber production (u.s. International Trade Commission (usitc) 1985:91, Table 16) Third, it is noteworthy that for both wood and pulp and paper products, the Canadian industries must rely primarily on export markets, whereas the demands of the u.s. domestic market exceed the production of the u.s. industry. Fourth, Canadian producers rely heavily on the u.s. market for the sale of their products. About two-thirds of Canadian production of softwood lumber is exported to the United States. Over half of Canadian production of pulp and paper products is also exported to the u.s. Fifth, Canadian exports of forest products to the United States consist primarily of commodities for which the value added by processing is low. Lumber accounts for about 80 per cent of the value of wood exports to the u.s. Newsprint and pulp account for about 85 per cent of the value of pulp and paper exports to that country.

The dependence of Canadian producers on the u.s. market combined with the fact that the United States has a very large domestic forest products industry are the basis for forest product trade conflicts between the two countries. On the Canadian side there is a strong incentive to capture as large a share of the u.s. market as possible. U.S. producers are motivated to limit imports as much as possible so as to keep prices up and, to the extent that they have the plant capacity, to supply as large a share of the domestic market as possible. The clash resulting from these two motivations becomes most pronounced when the market is depressed or when one side or the other has a production cost advantage because of the application of a superior technology, supply availability, or government policies that have the effect of reducing the production costs of firms.

ECONOMIC INFLUENCES ON THE PATTERN OF TRADE

Supply Outlook

The two countries compete with one another largely in products made from coniferous softwood. The U.S. has a large hardwood industry, which utilizes species that, at best, can only be produced in small volumes in Canada. There are quantitative estimates of long-term supplies in both countries, but these are a subject of debate because of differing assumptions made by analysts. Zivnuska (1967:14,42) estimated Canadian softwood lumber production capability to be only slightly less than that of the U.S. Since this estimate was made, plantation forestry in the southern United States is reported as showing considerable promise (Sedjo 1987:6). The inventories of old-growth forests appear to be larger in Canada than in the United States.

Quantities that will be economically harvestable could be significantly lower than the physically sustainable yield. Williams and Gasson (1986) point out that estimates of available supplies must take into account wood prices and production costs in order to be realistic. In their study of the coastal region of British Columbia, they found that only 26 per cent of the inventory of timber would be economical to harvest at current production costs and log prices. On the other hand, as prices increase or as technologies which reduce production costs are applied, the quantities that can be economically harvested rapidly increase. The adoption of technologies currently being developed which permits the use of kinds of wood not currently considered usable for most commercial purposes, serves, in effect, to expand the resource base. Sedjo (1987:7,8) stresses the importance of new technologies in meeting future resource needs. Thus, the supply will depend in large part, as with most commodities, on production technologies and market prices.

The foregoing factors, as well the limitations of inventory techniques, the difficulty of predicting future price levels, and the possibility that environmental considerations may reduce the rate and area of harvest (see discussion below), make it impossible to predict with confidence how the economically harvestable supplies in the two countries will compare during the coming decade.[1] For purposes of this analysis the important point is that: 'Both countries have sufficient forest resources to support for some time into the future large forest product industries of much the same size as at present. However, there is considerable uncertainty about whether one of the countries will have a comparative advantage over the other in supplying a portion of future markets.'

Market Outlook

The market outlook is probably more uncertain than the supply. Sedjo (1987:11) has observed that, with regard to pulp and paper, 'the final market will continue to expand into the indefinite future.' At the same time, he foresees that technological advances will result in greater use of hardwoods as well as reduce the wood requirement per unit of output.[2] The optimistic outlook for pulp and paper has led to large investments around the world in productive capacity. One analyst forecasts 'a gradual softening of pulp markets in 1991 and 1992 as North American capacity increases continue' (*Globe and Mail* 21 Dec. 1988).

The demand for softwood lumber is closely related to housing construction, repair, and remodelling. New residential construction accounted for 39 per cent of softwood lumber consumption in 1984 and housing repair and remodelling accounted for 24 per cent (USITC 1985:118). After reviewing in detail the factors that influence the level of housing construction, Clawson (1985:183) concluded that 'the uncertainty about the future is so great that no great confidence can be placed in any forecast.' At the same time, he offers the judgement 'that decade average rates of building [in the u.s.] are likely to average not above 1.5 million units.' There were 1.7 million new housing starts in the u.s. in 1984 (USITC 1985:104) and there were 1.8 million in 1986 (COFI 1987:10). Sedjo (1987:8) states that 'most observers now anticipate that homebuilding will be modest through the 1990s.' On the other hand, Smyth (1986) of the UWA concludes that the 1990s should see a sustained revival of the u.s. housebuilding industry and the demand for softwood lumber.

Clawson (1985:77) points out that the general business cycle and the house building cycle 'are rather closely correlated in timing of rise and fall and peaking dates.' In light of the foregoing analyses, one is led to the conclusion that the demand for softwood lumber in the u.s. during the 1990s will depend in large part on the business cycle. There is little evidence of either a strong upturn or downturn in demand that might be attributed to other factors.

With regard to the future market outlook for Canada-u.s. trade in softwood lumber, it is appropriate to consider that: 'The demand for softwood lumber is likely to fluctuate around recent levels, and the amount of the fluctuation will depend upon economic conditions in North America, and particularly in the United States. The demand for pulp and paper, which is rising, could soften as new capacity catches up with growing demand.'

Comparative Efficiency of Processing Enterprises

In its report on the softwood lumber countervail action in 1985 and in a follow-up study in 1986, the u.s. International Trade Commission (USITC 1985:80-120; 1986:4) made detailed comparisons of production costs for softwood lumber in the United States and Canada, including the cost of milling. It found that Canada had lower labour costs per unit of output than did the u.s., in spite of higher wages in Canada. This was attributed to greater efficiency in Canadian milling operations. In its first report, the USITC estimated that Canadian mills produced 60 per cent more board feet of softwood lumber per employee than did u.s. mills, and in a second report this estimate was reduced to 26 per cent. A study by the International Woodworkers of America estimates that in 1984 the number of board feet of lumber produced per hour worked by a Canadian employee was 66 per cent greater than that of a u.s. employee (IWA 1985:31, Table 9). The Canadian industry, in general, has, during recent years, been more efficient than the u.s. industry because of greater investment in labour saving equipment by Canadian firms.[3] The greater efficiency of the Canadian industry has certainly given it an advantage in selling on the u.s. market, but, since firms in both countries have equal access to labour saving technologies, u.s. firms should be able to catch up.[4]

Other than softwood lumber production, no information has been found that suggests that there are significant differences in production efficiency for wood products in the two countries nor has comparative efficiency been an issue for the pulp and paper industry. If the softwood lumber industry in the u.s. continues to be protected by trade barriers, it is conceivable that u.s. firms will not be motivated to invest in labour saving technologies to the same extent as are Canadian firms, but this prospect is uncertain. This examination leads to the following conclusion: 'The comparative efficiency of forest product mills in the two countries could be an important economic determinant of the division of market shares between them, but in general relative efficiency is likely to converge. However, the outlook with regard to lumber production is uncertain because of the possible negative influence of trade barriers on investment in labour saving technologies in the u.s.'

Exchange Rates

It is generally accepted that the lower nominal value of the Canadian dollar relative to the u.s. dollar has provided Canada with considerable advantage in competing for market shares in the United States. However, the real exchange rate differs from the nominal exchange rate. Because the rate of inflation in Canada has been higher than that in the United States, the advantage to Canada has been less than the differences in the nominal rate would imply. In its consideration of the effect of the exchange rate on softwood lumber imports from Canada into the United States, the usitc (1985:125) concluded that whereas the nominal value of the Canadian dollar declined by 21.9 per cent between the first quarter of 1977 and the fourth quarter of 1984, the decline in real terms, when the higher rate of inflation in Canada is taken into account, was only 11.3 per cent.[5]

Over the last year the nominal exchange rate of the Canadian dollar has increased significantly, and the exchange rate for u.s. funds has declined substantially, relative to other major currencies. Over the long term the exchange rate for u.s. funds could continue to decline relative to other currencies. If this occurs, the advantage that the Canadian industry has experienced will diminish substantially. Thus, it is reasonable to conclude that: 'Although the exchange rate in recent years has provided an advantage to the Canadian forest products industry in competing in the u.s. market, that advantage is diminishing and could disappear.'

Competition from Off-Shore Supplies

Imports by the United States from countries other than Canada could become significant during the coming decade, but these prospects are uncertain. Sedjo (1987:6) foresees the 'emerging regions of (largely) the Southern Hemisphere' as becoming a major source of future wood supplies. These include Brazil, Chile, Venezuela, South Africa, and Australia as well as Spain and Portugal in the Northern Hemisphere. Sedjo comments that: 'The unusually good growing conditions of certain locations in the Southern Hemisphere, the var-

ious forms of governmental subsidies and assistance to forest plantation establishment, together with the already very significant activities of some markets, suggest that these countries are likely to be
very real competitors in the foreseeable future' (Sedjo 1987:6).

Should competition from off-shore sources become significant in
North American markets, Canada and the United States would be
precluded from imposing tariff barriers to limit imports from these
sources. An article of the General Agreement on Tariffs and Trade
(GATT) provides that where a free trade area is established, tariffs on
a product imported from GATT members who are outside of the free
trade area must not exceed the average of the tariffs imposed on that
product by members of the free trade area immediately prior to the
establishment of the free trade area. Since Canadian and U.S. tariff
barriers on forest products which existed immediately prior to the
execution of the free trade agreement were nil or very low (except for
plywood), other countries will have approximately the same access
to the North American market as do Canada and the United States.

UNCERTAINTIES AND ISSUES ARISING FROM CURRENT AND POTENTIAL PUBLIC POLICIES

In Canada, approximately 90 per cent of the commercial forest land is
owned by the provincial governments, and in the United States over
half of the current inventory of commercial timber is in the National
Forests. Therefore, government policies relating to the use of commercial forests in both countries can have important implications for
trade in forest products between the two countries. Government tax
policies and subsidies may influence the costs to firms of producing
forest products and thus influence their ability to compete in international markets. In addition, governments may impose tariffs and
other barriers to imports, which may limit the ability of foreign producers to compete in domestic markets.

Policies for the Management and Use of Publicly Owned Forest Land

Government policies on the use and management of publicly owned
forests can have a major influence on the wood supply available to
the North American market. With regard to the U.S. National Forests, Clawson (1975:99) has commented: 'If the Forest Service were
to offer substantially more or substantially less stumpage for sale,
this would affect the price of all lumber and all stumpage.' This comment applies equally to Canada.

Public policies can influence supplies in two ways. One way is by reducing the area of public land on which timber harvesting is permitted by designating forested lands as parks or other reserves that are not open to timber harvesting. The other way is through regulation of the rate of harvest permitted on public lands available for timber production.

With the growing concern about the environment manifest in Canada and the United States, there are mounting public pressures to allocate more publicly owned forest lands to reserves. In British Columbia, South Moresby in the Queen Charlotte Islands, which has a large stand of old-growth timber, is now a national park reserve. In addition, a number of environmental groups in Canada have called for a major increase in the area of publicly owned lands devoted to parks (see, for example, Valhalla Society 1988).

With regard to lands used for timber production, three influences could significantly reduce the amount of timber produced and marketed during the coming decade. One of these is the growing public pressure in both countries to give greater emphasis to non-timber values in forest management. In a large area in the Pacific Northwest of the United States, timber production has been halted to protect the habitat of the spotted owl. In both countries, there has been strong objection to clear-cutting for aesthetic reasons. In some parts of the United States, there is an interest in designing forest management practices to enhance water supplies. The growth of the tourist industry in Canada has increased pressures to manage forest land to serve outdoor recreation demands and to preserve wildlife populations. Some of the uses may be compatible with high levels of timber production, but in most cases the amount of timber harvested will be reduced. At this juncture it is not clear what the effect of serving these non-timber uses to a greater degree than in the past will be.

A second influence is a mounting public concern,[6] shared by some members of the science community,[7] that public forests are not being managed on a sustainable basis. The scientific literature that is beginning to appear concludes that existing forest practices threaten species and genetic diversity and, thus, the sustainability of the forests. This literature proposes major changes in forestry practices which, if implemented, would undoubtedly influence the supply of timber available over the next decade.

A third influence that could disrupt supplies available for processing and export is the settlement of aboriginal claims in Canada. It now seems likely that some of the major claims will be settled during the coming decade, and such settlements could transfer large forested areas to the control of aboriginal people. If this occurs, the aboriginal owners could decide to continue the harvesting of timber in accord with present practices or, alternatively, they might place greater emphasis upon uses of the forests dictated by their culture (such as hunting and trapping) and reduce timber harvesting.

The foregoing potential influences on timber supply in North America cannot be dismissed lightly. The public concerns about the environment and the sustainability of resources has become a powerful political force in both the United States and Canada, and the response could well be a reduction in the quantity of timber available for harvesting from publicly owned lands. Aboriginal claims in Canada are approaching settlement, albeit slowly, and the consequences of the settlements that are reached cannot be forecast with any degree of confidence.

Government Policies and Higher Value-Added Exports

In recent years, two categories of forest products have been subject to tariff barriers imposed by Canada and the United States, namely, plywood and most paper other than newsprint. The FTA provides for the gradual elimination of the tariffs on plywood,[8] and recent actions through the GATT had virtually eliminated the tariff on paper products prior to the FTA. The elimination of these duties could alter the pattern of trade for plywood and fine paper, which have higher value-added components than do lumber, pulp, and newsprint.

In commenting on this situation, Uhler (1987a) states that:

> This tariff [on plywood] has clearly restricted the development of an export oriented plywood sector in Canada for had U.S. plywood tariffs been nil, there is no reason to think that this sector of the industry would not have developed on a parallel course with softwood lumber and made significant inroads into U.S. plywood markets. Since the manufacture of plywood is a high value added activity compared with lumber production, an enlarged plywood industry could be of considerable economic significance to Canada.

In commenting on the virtual elimination of the tariff on fine paper, Uhler et al. (1987:8) state: 'it is probably because of U.S. tariffs on paper products, other than newsprint and market pulp, that these segments of the Canadian industry failed to develop beyond simply supplying the domestic market. And probably they developed to this extent only because this segment of the Canadian industry was protected from foreign competition by Canadian tariffs.'

The results (suggested by Uhler) of tariff reductions on plywood and paper would, of course, be a benefit to the Canadian economy. With regard to wood products, it is uncertain that increased production of higher value-added products is to be expected. This uncertainty is heightened by the high degree of corporate concentration in the Canadian forest industry.

The corporate concentration issue has received more attention in British Columbia than elsewhere in Canada. For example, the BC Royal Commission on Forest Resources of 1976 (Vol.2:B-8) found that in 1974 about 59 per cent of the harvesting rights in British Columbia was controlled by ten companies. More recently, a study concluded that 'there are only four major interlinked groups of companies controlling 93.2 per cent of the allocated public forest cut and 84.1 per cent of overall provincial timber cut in British Columbia' (Wagner 1987). Since the industry has a high degree of integration, manufacturing by the industry is also highly concentrated. Although specific studies of concentration in other provinces are not available, it appears that most of the industry in Canada is dominated by a few large corporations. The u.s. industry is reported to be less highly concentrated in a few large firms than is the Canadian industry (USITC 1986:1).

Associated with this high degree of concentration has been the development of large sawmilling operations. For example, 60 per cent of the Canadian mills had production capability in excess of 25 million board feet per year, whereas only 20 per cent of the u.s. mills had such capability. Also, the Canadian mills have a more narrow product line (largely dimension lumber) whereas u.s. mills have a more varied product (USITC 1986:1).

The development of large specialized mills has undoubtedly made the Canadian industry more efficient than the u.s. industry in producing large quantities of standard items such as softwood lumber. However, this practice may reduce the motivation of the Canadian industry to diversify into secondary manufacturing, which increases the value-added component of the product. In a study of vertical integration and diversification in the forest industry in Canada, Schwindt (1985:71) concluded that

> it is highly likely that Canadian forest products enterprises will remain committed to a strategy of low cost production of commodity or near-commodity products. It is what these companies do best, and it is a strategy which has served them reasonably well in the past. Moreover, the production of basic, standardized products is the only activity capable of absorbing the volumes of timber being cut, and predicted to be cut in the future.

For a number of years, there has been a call for the forest industry to diversify into secondary manufacturing (see, for example,

Woodbridge-Reid 1984). If Schwindt's analysis is correct, such a
change may be slow in coming about. Although the FTA improves
the access to the U.S. market of secondary products, Canadian exports may continue to be dominated by products having a low value-
added component.

A more speculative issue relates to whether the industry in both
countries will become dominated by a small group of large corporations, each of which has operations in both countries. Numerous
mergers and take-overs are now occurring, and the possibility exists
that the rate of concentration will accelerate across the international
boundary because the FTA (Chapter 16) increases the ease with
which transboundary mergers and take-overs can be undertaken.
Therefore, it may not be far-fetched for the industry in both countries to become dominated by the same few firms.

Should this transboundary concentration occur, it might, for example, be profitable for the industry generally to lobby for low
stumpage fees in Canada and to undertake the secondary manufacturing of wood products in the U.S. This would permit the industry
to continue investment in Canada in large, efficient mills producing
standard products and would provide it with a share of the rent from
forest land. It would also permit manufacturing to occur close to
markets with a labour force that currently, at least, is less expensive
than is Canadian labour. An important effect would be to remove the
basis for the Canada/U.S. conflict over forest trade, which gave rise
to the softwood lumber dispute.[9]

At this stage, one should not lose sight of the fact that the trend towards greater concentration in the forest industry increases uncertainty with regard to the future prospects of forest trade. The scenario hypothesized above would help ensure that the flow of forest
products across the border would not be hindered by non-tariff barriers. The flow from Canada to the United States would consist
largely of products that have not gone beyond the stage of primary
manufacturing, and secondary manufacturing would occur largely
in the U.S. While some of the available information supports this
scenario, it is unfortunate that recent trends in forest industry concentration and their likely consequences have not been subjected to
more intensive study.

Potential U.S. Actions to Limit Imports of Canadian Forest Products

As long as the economy of the U.S. remains relatively prosperous, it
seems unlikely that any significant change in U.S. policies will occur. On the other hand, if there is a significant downturn, an effort to

limit imports of Canadian forest products is very likely. In spite of u.s. obligations under GATT and the existence of the FTA, there remain a number of ways in which the u.s. can limit imports of Canadian forest products. In considering these possibilities it should be kept in mind that the FTA made little change in the ability of each country to impose non-tariff barriers. The legislation of the two countries governing the use of such restraints is quite similar.

One type of non-tariff barrier that can be imposed is referred to as a Safeguard Action. (In the u.s. the term used is an 'escape clause' action.) This legislation is designed to provide relief to a domestic industry threatened with serious injury from imported commodities by imposing a surtax upon such imports. In the United States (Stowell 1985: sections 2,251-53), the president makes the decision on the basis of recommendations of the International Trade Commission (ITC), an independent, quasi-judicial agency. However, he can reduce the amount of relief recommended or grant no relief whatsoever. The Shakes and Shingles Case, in which the president imposed a duty of 35 per cent on imports from Canada, was based on this legislation.[10] In both countries, it is the intent of safeguard legislation to give a domestic industry an opportunity to adjust to import competition. Thus, relief is provided only for a temporary period.

The u.s. could decide to make its safeguard (escape clause) legislation more effective. As previously noted, the president has discretion to decide whether to accept or to reject the recommendations of the ITC in such cases, and, if he does accept its recommendation, he can lower the amount of the duty imposed. Goldstein's analysis (1986:170-3) indicates that presidential actions have greatly impaired the ability of industries to gain relief through an escape clause action. In the period from 1958 through 1981, a total of 140 petitions were filed with the ITC. The ITC approved fifty-seven of these, but the president accepted only twenty-six for some relief. Only seven of these received the full amount of the relief recommended by the ITC. If the escape clause is to be a more effective trade barrier, the policies that presidents have pursued would have to be changed. One way of doing this would be through legislation to remove the discretion of the president to reject or modify the recommendations of the ITC.[11] It is conceivable that the same result might be achieved through an unwritten understanding between the Congress and the president that the president will abide by ITC recommendations.

A second way that the u.s. could limit imports of Canadian forest products would be to impose countervail duties on products other than softwood lumber, which is now subject to a 15 per cent export tax or higher stumpage fees to replace the tax.[12] Countervailing duties can be applied to imported commodities, the production of which is supported by subsidies in the exporting country. The Softwood Lumber Dispute of 1986 stemmed from a countervailing duty petition.[13]

In both countries, action is initiated by the affected industry. In the United States, the ITC determines whether domestic industries are suffering injury, and the International Trade Administration (ITA) of the Department of Commerce determines the amount of the subsidy. If injury exists or is threatened, a duty is levied that is equal to the amount of the subsidy. The president cannot over-rule the decision of the ITA. (Stowell 1985: sections 1,671-6).

By applying the same rationale as that employed in the softwood lumber case of 1986 – namely, that stumpage fees are being subsidized – the U.S. might claim that all products made from wood are subsidized.[14] With the Memorandum of Understanding relating to softwood lumber still in force, a countervail action would not be applied to softwood lumber, and BC, which has raised its stumpage fees, would probably be exempt from the action. Quebec might receive a partial exemption because it is subject to reduced export taxes on softwood lumber in recognition of the increase it has made in stumpage fees.

A third way that the U.S. might endeavour to limit forest product imports is for the Congress to enact legislation to define a subsidy so that it would be easier for an industry to secure relief through a countervail action. HR3 (a bill approved by the House of Representatives in 1987) is probably a good indication of the kind of changes in countervail legislation that could occur. With regard to forest products, its provisions would alter the way in which a determination would be made as to whether stumpage fees constitute a subsidy. Where stumpage fees are administratively determined, the effect of the proposed legislation would provide that

the first benchmark which Commerce should consider is freely available, market-determined domestic rates for such or similar items. If the administering authority determines that an appropriate internal commercial benchmark is not available, it shall look to appropriate external rates for such or similar goods. Among the external benchmarks which the administering authority should consider are freely available, market-determined export prices for such or similar goods by the government; the world market rate, if any, for such or similar goods; or the freely available, market-determined rate for such or similar goods or services in another country if Commerce finds that such external market resembles the market in question. (Committee on Ways and Means, House of Representatives 1987:125)

Although the report indicates that the proposed legislation recognizes that no external benchmarks may be appropriate, enactment of this legislation could result in the ITA determining that an unsubsidized rate for stumpage in Canada would be the competitively determined stumpage fees in the u.s. Since, for a variety of reasons, these rates are much higher than Canadian rates, Canadian exporters of forest products could be faced with countervail duties on their products destined for u.s. markets that could be higher than the 15 per cent arrived at in the preliminary determination of the ITA in the Softwood Lumber Case of 1985-6.

It is reasonable to anticipate that the u.s. may impose countervailing duties on forest products other than softwood lumber, or even that the basis for applying a countervailing duty could be defined in law so as to make it easier for countervail petitions to succeed. The structure of political relationships within which the u.s. federal government operates is such that a well organized, regionally concentrated industry adversely affected by imports can usually muster the strong support of senators and congressmen from the affected region. These delegations are in a position to bargain with other senators and congressmen for their support. The bargaining power of the delegations is enhanced if they include the chairman or members of the key committees of the House and Senate on trade matters. In the absence of significant concern in other regions of the country, a minority of the Congress representing a minority of the population can succeed in determining Congressional policy. The president may intervene with members of his party to influence a proposed Congressional action, but party discipline is not strong, so that even when the president intervenes, the aims of the regional delegation may prevail: Where such a result is in prospect, the president may find it desirable to act in accord with the objectives of the regional delegation or face the possibility of losing his bargaining power with the Congress on other matters of major importance.[15]

It is noteworthy that under the final settlement of the Softwood Lumber Dispute, the u.s., in responding, on the one hand, to domestic, regional political pressures and, on the other hand, responding to its foreign policy need to maintain good relations with Canada, agreed to a solution that had a sizeable negative effect on the u.s. economy (see Boyd and Krutilla 1987, 1988; and Kalt 1987).

Needless to say, it is not practicable to predict the course the u.s. might pursue. Yet, if economic conditions are depressed in the United States, the possibility of some kind of action to restrict imports of Canadian forest products cannot be dismissed. This assessment is based on the premise that the structure of the forest industry would remain much as it was during the Softwood Lumber Dispute.

If further concentration of the forest industry results in an identical group of firms producing a large proportion of the forest products in both Canada and the United States, protectionist pressures in the u.s. to limit imports of Canadian forest products could diminish and, possibly, disappear.

Potential Canadian Actions to Counteract u.s. Trade Barriers

Should the United States alter the implementation of its safeguard legislation to be more effective in restricting imports of Canadian products, there is relatively little that Canada can do to counteract such measures except to retaliate by taking safeguard action against imports of u.s. products, as it did in the Shakes and Shingles Case (Wilson 1986). However, the Memorandum of Understanding, which concluded the Softwood Lumber Dispute and possible increased resort to countervailing duties, poses more complex issues.

The 15 per cent export tax (or replacement measures in the form of higher stumpage fees) as provided for in the Memorandum of Understanding confronts the provinces and the Canadian forest industry with a major problem. The export tax when initially imposed did not appreciably reduce exports, although it undoubtedly reduced the profits of the industry. Should the demand for lumber and prices decline because of a softening of the u.s. economy, the export tax (or the stumpage fee replacement measures in the case of British Columbia and Quebec) could make it difficult for the Canadian industry to compete in the u.s. market. This situation may be aggravated if the exchange rate changes to approach parity of the Canadian and United States currencies.

Industry representatives in Canada have already called upon the federal government to negotiate elimination of the requirement in the Memorandum of Understanding for a 15 per cent export tax or equivalent replacement measures (*Globe and Mail* 1988b). Securing u.s. acceptance of such a change appears very unlikely, unless Canada adopts a stumpage fee system which results in charges for publicly owned timber that can be demonstrated to be at least equal to prices that would be established through a competitive market.[16] If this is not done, what rationale or inducement can Canada use to convince the u.s. government and the u.s. lumber industry that the 15 per cent export tax should be eliminated?

The same issue arises with regard to the possibility that the u.s. might apply countervailing duties to forest products other than softwood lumber, to which the export tax does not now apply. This issue will also confront Canadian producers if u.s. legislation is enacted that makes it easier for u.s. industries to have countervailing duties applied (see discussion above).

Throughout the debate over countervailing duties, the position of the u.s. government, including Congressional committees, has been that the prices charged for inputs to the production of a commodity should be equivalent to competitively determined prices. Canadian stumpage fee practices are vulnerable to non-tariff barriers applied by the United States because fees are administratively determined. The basic question that needs to be addressed is how stumpage fee systems can be designed and implemented by Canadian provinces so as to eliminate this vulnerability. Some may feel that the negotiation over a period of three to five years of a definition of a subsidy, as called for by the FTA, may resolve this problem.[17]

A careful and systematic study of this issue in light of current policies in each of the provinces would make an important contribution to such negotiations. The study should proceed on the premise that stumpage fees will be vulnerable unless it can be unequivocally demonstrated that timber prices are not below those that would be established by a competitive market. It is unrealistic to expect the u.s. to agree that any other standard would be acceptable. Some years ago, Anthony Scott (1976) proposed for British Columbia that a portion of the timber harvest (e.g., 20 per cent) be sold on the basis of competitive bids. The portion sold in this manner would need to be representative of timber values in various parts of the province. The prices established by competitive bidding for each representative area would determine the stumpage prices to be charged for timber in comparable areas. This suggestion appears to have considerable merit and may be applicable to other provinces as well as to BC.[18]

It must be recognized, however, that the degree of corporate concentration in the forest industry together with the existing tenure system may make it impracticable to establish a fully competitive market for even a fraction of the supply of timber in some provinces, including BC. A competitive market in timber would reduce the security of supply that much of the industry now enjoys, and the forest industry is a potent political force in the provinces which produce most of the output of Canadian forest products. Nevertheless, the study should be undertaken because the stumpage fee issue continues to pose a major threat to the orderly and economically efficient flow of forest products between Canada and the United States.

SUMMARY AND CONCLUSIONS

The outlook for trade in forest products between Canada and the United States is clouded by a number of uncertainties that cannot be completely dispelled through policy changes or policy research, although some of the uncertainties could be defined more precisely through further study. These include:

(1) The implications of technological advance for the future supply of forest products;
(2) The effect of public pressure on timber supplies in both countries to increase the proportion of publicly owned forest land in reserves not subject to timber harvesting;
(3) The effect of aboriginal claims settlement in Canada on the supply of forest products available for export;
(4) The effects on forest product markets of North American and world economic conditions;
(5) The effects of exchange rate changes on the comparative advantage of the two countries;
(6) The effects on the North American market of imports from other parts of the world;
(7) The possibility that the u.s. will increase its use of safeguard actions to restrict imports of Canadian forest products.

There are other uncertainties that might be resolved through public policy changes based on knowledge that could be gained through research. Three of these are inter-related. One is the likelihood that the u.s. will not agree to eliminate the 15 per cent export tax on softwood lumber, which could have serious implications for the Canadian forest industry, especially if economic conditions decline in the United States. A second is the possibility that the u.s. will impose countervailing duty charges on Canadian forest products other than softwood lumber on the grounds that such products are subsidized through low stumpage fees. The third is the possibility that the u.s. will enact legislation that will make it easier for industries to succeed with petitions to impose countervailing duties on imported products. The only way to ensure that these conditions will not arise is for the Canadian provinces to adopt stumpage fee systems which can be unequivocally demonstrated to be at least equal to stumpage prices established by a competitive market.

In view of the importance of this issue to the economies of a number of provinces, it behooves Canada to thoroughly investigate possible ways of designing stumpage fee policies that meet this test. Yet, it should be anticipated that in view of the high degree of corporate concentration in the Canadian forest industry, it may be difficult to arrive at stumpage prices that faithfully reflect the results of competitive conditions.

It is also essential to thoroughly investigate current forest management practices because of the widespread concern that forests are not being managed on a sustainable basis and that adequate consideration is not being given to non-timber values. Until this issue is resolved to the satisfaction of the general public through sound research, there are the twin dangers that the forests will not be properly managed and that policies will be pursued on the basis of misguided public perceptions which fail to deal effectively with management issues and which are damaging to the economies that depend to a large extent on forest based industries.

Finally, Canada has an important interest in understanding why its output of higher value-added products is so low. Is this situation attributable to tariff barriers that are now being eliminated; to the factors that Schwindt has identified; or to other factors now imperfectly understood? Imaginative research on this issue could lay the foundation for policies that would foster the production and sale of higher value-added forest products, which, in turn, would provide much needed stimulation to the economies of forest product based communities in Canada.

NOTES

1 Beyond the 1990s, climate change could greatly alter supply conditions because of the higher incidence of drought, pest infestations, and fire (Pollard 1989:58).

2 The term 'hardwoods' includes the poplars that have been usable to only a limited extent up to now in pulp and paper manufacture. Both countries have large supplies of this category of wood.

3 For a detailed discussion of this issue, see Percy and Yoder 1987:38-42.

4 See Webb and Zacher (1985:96-8) for a discussion of 'convergence' of technologies in industrial countries.

5 A paper by Adams et al. (1986) on 'The Role of Exchange Rates in Canadian-u.s. Lumber Trade,' which employed an econometric model of the North American lumber market, concluded (p. 20) that 'increases in the Canadian-u.s. exchange rate have played a definite role in the expansion of the Canadian share of u.s. markets over the past decade but appear to account for only part of the market share trend.'

6 In Canada, a recent poll sponsored by Forestry Canada indicated that about three-fifths of the public feel that forests are being over-harvested and about three-fourths believe that the environment is being threatened by the forest industry (Environics Research Group Ltd. 1989). In the United States, some environmental groups are calling for changes in

the management of the National Forests (see, for example, Wilderness Society (1988) and undated).

7 For reports by scientists that reflect this perception, see Harris (1984) and Maser (1988).

8 The U.S. tariff on plywood has been 20 per cent and the Canadian tariff has been 8 per cent.

9 It is significant that two multinational corporations (Boise Cascade and Weyerhauser) that operate in both Canada and the U.S. did not support the 1985-6 countervail petition of the U.S. forest industry relating to softwood lumber.

10 For a detailed examination of this case, see North (1988).

11 The Shakes and Shingles Case was among the relatively few instances in which the president granted the full amount of the relief recommended by the ITC. It seems likely that the president and his advisors concluded that acceptance of the ITC recommendation would help strengthen the president's hand in dealing with Congress on trade legislation that it was then considering.

12 The Memorandum of Understanding, which settled the Softwood Lumber Dispute (see Percy and Yoder (1987): Appendix B), provided that Canada would impose an export tax of 15 per cent on softwood lumber in lieu of the imposition of a countervail duty of the same amount by the U.S. Individual provinces could increase stumpage fees to replace the export tax completely or in part. British Columbia has increased stumpage fees that are regarded as a full replacement, and an increase in stumpage fees by Quebec replaces seven per cent of the export tax.

13 For a detailed analysis of this dispute, see Percy and Yoder (1987).

14 U.S. domestic politics relating to the pulp and paper industry may differ from those relating to softwood lumber. Since the politics of pulp and paper has not been investigated, no estimate can be made of the likelihood that this course of action might be pursued with regard to these commodities.

15 For an analysis of both Canadian and U.S. politics of Canada-U.S. trade in forest politics, see Fox (1989).

16 The procedures for calculating stumpage charges followed by British Columbia prior to settlement of the Softwood Lumber Dispute were designed to arrive at charges that approximate competitively determined prices. However, these procedures failed to convince U.S. interests, and some in Canada, that this was in fact the case (see, for example, Haley 1980).

17 The FTA envisages the negotiation of a subsidy definition within three years but provides for an extension to five years if additional time is required to reach agreement.

18 The policy proposed by Scott would also assure the public that an appropriate return is being received from publicly owned land.

CHAPTER TWELVE

The Economic Impact on British Columbia of Removing Log Export Restrictions

Michael Margolick and Russell S. Uhler

INTRODUCTION

The province of British Columbia restricts the export of raw logs, with the net effect that the sawlog market in coastal British Columbia is separated and isolated from the major international sawlog market on the Pacific Rim. This market consists of Japan, China, and Korea as principal buyers and the United States and the Soviet Union as principal suppliers. As a direct result of this market separation, in recent years prices in coastal British Columbia have been substantially below those in the Pacific Rim market. In 1983, for example, grades of Douglas-fir sawlogs that sold for $114 per cubic metre in the Pacific Rim market sold for only $82 per cubic metre in the Vancouver log market.

These restrictions impose a cost on the logging sector of the British Columbia forest products industry in that logs must be sold at a price below what it would otherwise receive. On the other hand, the processing sector of the industry derives a benefit since it can buy logs at prices below what it would otherwise have to pay. It is the recognition of these costs and benefits in the forest industry as a whole that has sparked interest in examining whether British Columbia would be better off if log export restrictions were removed or, at least, modified. The purpose of this study is to examine the economic impact on British Columbia of one scenario for modifying these restrictions; removing completely restrictions on the quantity of logs that are exported.

It is commonly believed that sawlogs could be exported from coastal British Columbia in substantial amounts without having a noticeable effect on Pacific Rim prices. If so, it would mean that mills in British Columbia would be faced with log prices that were roughly at the level of those in the Pacific Rim sawlog market. This does not appear to be the case. It will later be shown that coastal British Columbia production of 'structural' sawlogs relative to the volumes traded in the Pacific Rim market is large enough that a complete integration of the two markets could be expected to result in a significant decline in Pacific Rim prices. This decline is expected to be in the range of 20 to 25 per cent, depending upon the assumptions used. Likewise, coastal British Columbia prices could be expected to rise in the order of 20 per cent. But even with such price changes, the results of the computer model used in this study show that it may still be a net economic benefit to British Columbia to remove these restrictions completely.

This paper describes the methodology used to: (1) determine the new market price and quantity equilibrium after the complete integration of these two markets, and (2) calculate net economic benefits to British Columbia from such integration in both the short and long run, and it discusses the concept of a 'sawlog aggregate.' The data used to determine the parameters of market equilibrium and the net economic benefits of market integration are also discussed, as is the impact of market integration on sawlog prices, on exports from British Columbia, and on net economic benefits to the province.

METHODOLOGY

A variety of species and log grades, each having different prices, are traded in the Pacific Rim and British Columbia coastal log markets, which indicates that logs traded in these markets are a highly heterogeneous commodity. For example, top grade Douglas-fir logs can sell for up to five times the price of lower grade logs of the same species. There is an even greater price variation across species. Thus, it is clear that when reference is made to the price of logs in either of these two markets without indicating a particular species or grade that price must be some average price of several species and grades. This study examines that portion of each of these markets that deals in 'structural' species and grades. That is, the species and grades listed in the first column of Table 1, which are sawlogs used primarily to produce high strength lumber for the structure of buildings.

Even though it would have been preferable to carry out the analysis of the integration of the two major markets in terms of the different species and grades, adequate data were, unfortunately, not available for this task. Instead, the analysis was conducted in terms of a particular log 'aggregate' made up of structural logs, where the price for this log aggregate is calculated as a volume weighted aver-

TABLE 1

Log prices and quantities: VLM, U.S. exports, BC exports, 1983[1]

Species[2]	Grade	VLM quantity	VLM price	VLM share	U.S. export quantity[3]	U.S. export price	U.S. export share	BC export quantity	BC export share
BA1	C,D	51.6	60.09	0.02	10.0	97.90	0.01	97.7	0.06
BA2	H,I,J	341.2	38.24	0.11	66.3	75.09	0.05	225.7	0.14
DF1	A,B,C,D	125.1	81.66	0.04	59.2	113.59	0.05	169.1	0.10
DF2	H,I,J	360.4	44.40	0.12	404.9	76.47	0.33	392.2	0.24
CE1	D,F	129.1	91.43	0.04	5.8	133.90	0.01	3.6	-.-
CE2	H,I,J	671.8	68.89	0.22	50.8	88.73	0.04	36.6	0.02
CE3	K,L,M	418.3	49.46	0.14	15.9	92.81	0.01	6.0	-.-
HE1	D	31.3	65.12	0.01	17.0	95.13	0.01	41.5	0.03
HE2	H,I,J	774.3	39.75	0.25	565.4	62.80	0.46	480.6	0.29
SP1	C	7.9	68.70	-.-	-.-	-.-	-.-	13.5	0.01
SP2	D,E,F,G	36.1	142.47	0.01	0.6	175.93	-.-	34.4	0.02
SP3	H,I,J	87.9	55.66	0.03	23.4	71.59	0.02	143.6	0.09
PI1	D,H,I,J	9.9	22.45	-.-	0.4	116.38	-.-	0.8	-.-
Total		3,044.9	54.11	1.0	1,220.0	73.26	1.0	1,645.3	1.0

NOTES: [1] Quantities = thousands of cubic metres; prices = $Can. per cubic metre
 [2] BA - Balsam, DF - Douglas Fir, CE - Cedar, HE - Hemlock, SP - Spruce, PI- Pine
 [3] Sample of U.S. log exports

age price of these structural logs. Further details of the calculation of this average price are given in the next section.

In order to determine the net benefits to the British Columbia economy of removing log export restrictions, it is first necessary to estimate the impact of the removal of these restrictions on the quantity of logs demanded by the processing sector and the quantity that the logging sector could supply at the new average price as a result of market integration. The determination of this price and the related quantities supplied and demanded by the two sectors is conducted using a standard market model. In Figure 1, the market is modelled using ordinary demand and supply analysis prior to and subsequent to the removal of export restrictions. The British Columbia demand and supply curves are shown in the right portion of the diagram and are labelled D_d and S_d. The intersection of these two curves results in a market clearing price of P_d. In 1983, this average price for structural grade logs was estimated to be about $45 per cubic metre.

The Pacific Rim demand and supply curves are shown in the left portion of the diagram, where quantities increase from right to left and the curves are labelled D_i and S_i. The intersection of these curves results in a market clearing price of P_i. In 1983 this average price for the same mix of structural logs was estimated to be about $73 per cubic metre. The prices in the two markets can only remain different so long as they are effectively separated by export quantity or export tax restrictions. Currently, both types of restrictions exist but by far the

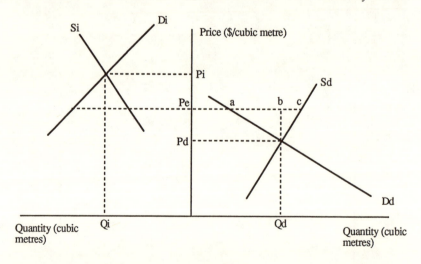

FIGURE 1
Demand and supply analysis of the Pacific Rim and BC log markets

most important is the quantity restriction that the British Columbia government places on log exports. However, there is also a log export tax in British Columbia, which is known as the 'log export levy' and which varies with the species exported. For those species that made up the 1983 Pacific Rim supply, the tax averaged about $1.20 per cubic metre.

If these restrictions are completely removed, then the markets will become a single integrated market with a single price given at the point where the excess supply in British Columbia equals the excess demand in the Pacific Rim market. In terms of Figure 1, this occurs at the price P_e. At this price, British Columbia exports are indicated by the distance between points labelled a and c in the diagram and come about from two sources: (1) the reduced quantity bought by the British Columbia processing sector as a result of the higher price – the distance a b – and (2) the increase in the quantity supplied by the logging sector as a result of the higher price – the distance b c. It is apparent from this diagram that most of the increase in exports comes from a reduction in the quantity demanded by the British Columbia processing sector rather than from a rise in the quantity supplied by the logging sector, but this result is entirely dependent upon the slopes of the D_d and S_d curves. In other words, it depends upon the magnitude of the response of both the quantity demanded and the quantity supplied to a change in the price of logs or the elasticity of demand and supply.

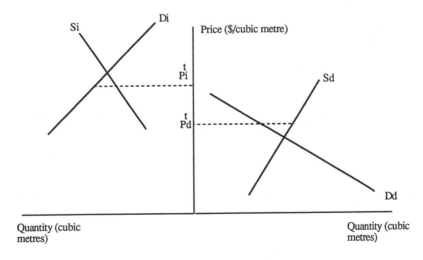

FIGURE 2
Effect of a tax on exported logs

The market model illustrated in Figure 2 can be used to illustrate the effect of a tax on exported logs. Such a tax drives a wedge between British Columbia and Pacific Rim prices. For example, if the tax is set at some amount t, then, in the absence of quantity restrictions, the Pacific Rim price would become P_i^t and the British Columbia price would become P_d^t. These are the prices that set coastal British Columbia excess supply equal to Pacific Rim excess demand given the level of the tax, which is equal to the difference between these two prices. The tax reduces the incentive to export and could be set to eliminate the incentive altogether. Therefore, it is of interest to know how such a tax used as a policy tool affects the level of overall benefits once quantity restrictions are removed. It is for this reason that the tax is made explicit in the computer model.

The government receives revenues not only from the log export levy but also, and primarily, from stumpage fees. In this market model stumpage fees are calculated on the basis of the Rothery formula, subject to a minimum stumpage of eight per cent of coastal British Columbia log prices.[1]

The price and quantity changes resulting from the integration of the British Columbia and Pacific Rim markets can be determined given sufficient knowledge of the demand and supply relationships in the two markets. An estimate of the net benefits to the British Columbia economy of market integration can then be derived from these changes. Net short run benefits to the British Columbia economy are measured in money terms and are defined as the net increase in revenues from log sales (the change in revenue from Pacific Rim sales plus the change in revenue from British Columbia sales) less the increase in logging expenditures, less the net revenue reductions as a result of lower British Columbia lumber and chip production. In the long run, net revenue reduction in the processing sector would not be included in the calculation of net benefits, because factors of production which are fixed in the short run are assumed to be able to shift to other economic activities.

It is useful to summarize in more detail how changes in net benefits are distributed between the sectors of the British Columbia forest products industry as a result of the complete removal of restrictions on the quantity of log exports. The changes in the variables that affect the change in the net benefits in each sector are as follows:

Logging sector:
(1) log export revenues
(2) revenues from British Columbia log sales
(3) log export levy payments

(4) stumpage fees

(5) expenditures on logging operations

Processing sector:

(1) lumber and chip revenues

(2) operating expenditures (excluding logs)

(3) expenditures on logs.

Provincial government sector:

(1) log export levy revenues

(2) stumpage revenues.[2]

As noted earlier, the sum of the net benefits in each of these sectors yields the total short run net benefits to the British Columbia economy as a whole. In the long run, the net revenue losses in the processing sector would not be included in the measurement of net benefits, since factors of production in this sector are assumed to be reallocated to other areas of economic activity and, thus, are a benefit in the sense that these factors generate production elsewhere.

In order to measure the net benefits to the British Columbia economy of removing log export restrictions and to measure the effects on a variety of other associated variables a computer model was constructed. The computer model consists of two main parts: the market model and the net benefits model. Given the information about the demand and supply relationships in the two markets prior to integration, the model solves for the integrated market clearing price and for changes in the quantities supplied, demanded, and exported and then uses this information, along with other data, to determine the net benefits as outlined earlier.

It should be emphasized that the benefits and costs to the different sectors of the forest industry are measured in financial terms and do not take account of the other costs of reallocation of economic activity. Whole communities may be adversely affected, and the personal and psychological costs of such upheaval are not taken into account in this analysis.

DATA

The Product and Its Price

To avoid having to study separately the markets for a large number of species and grades, this study uses the concept of a quantity aggregate of 'structural' species and grades selling at an average price. The British Columbia quantity supplied and demanded at the weighted average price, P_d, is an aggregate quantity of wood consisting of several species and grades (see Figure 1). Likewise, P_i should be the weighted average Pacific Rim price of a quantity aggregated from the same combination of species and grades, since integration of the two markets requires the same product in each market.

Table 1 compares quantities, prices, and quantity shares traded in the Vancouver log market,[3] a sample of the United States portion of the Pacific Rim market,[4] and the British Columbia portion of the Pacific Rim market in 1983.[5] In 1983, Douglas-fir and hemlock constituted about 85 per cent of United States exports and cedar constituted about 6 per cent, whereas Douglas-fir and hemlock accounted for about 42 per cent and cedar accounted for about 40 per cent of the Vancouver log market total. The British Columbia export shares of Douglas-fir, hemlock, and cedar are much closer to the United States export shares of these species than they are to the percentages actually traded in the Vancouver log market. In any case, the species mix in the two markets is different enough to cause concern about representing the integrated market situation by the summation of aggregate demand and supply curves in the two markets when these curves are located by the volume weighted average prices in each market.

One solution is to simply use the same weights when calculating the weighted average price in each market. For example, the United States export proportions could be used as weights when computing the average Vancouver log market price, or the Vancouver log market proportions could be used as weights in computing the United States export price. Since United States exports make up the major portion of North American exports to the Pacific Rim market for purposes of this study, it was decided to use the United States export proportions as weights, but calculation of average prices using the different weighting systems are shown in Table 2. Thus, the 1983 market clearing price in the British Columbia market is estimated to be $45.70 per cubic metre, and, in the Pacific Rim market, it is estimated to be $73.26 per cubic metre. Using the United States export proportions as weights to determine the average Vancouver log market price of course produces a lower price than does using Vancouver log market proportions because of the high share of cedar in the Vancouver log market. However, the lower price may, in fact, be more representative of the entire British Columbia log market, because a higher proportion of cedar is traded in the Vancouver log market than in British Columbia as a whole. For example, in 1983, western red cedar accounted for only 25 per cent of the Coast timber harvest, but it accounted for 40 per cent of Vancouver log market sales.

TABLE 2
Weighted average log prices[1]

U.S. export prices with U.S. weights	73.26
VLM prices with U.S. weights	45.70
U.S. export prices with VLM weights	83.49
VLM prices with VLM weights	54.11

NOTES: [1] $Can. per cubic metre

Some observers may object to the inclusion of red cedar as a structural species in the Pacific Rim market, because it is currently not heavily traded in that market and because of the uses to which it is traditionally put in North America. For this reason, it was decided to run the computer model under scenarios which both included and excluded red cedar.

Locating the Demand and Supply Curves

The market clearing quantities of logs must be determined in order to locate the points of intersection of the supply and demand curves in each market. The quantity of structural logs traded in the Pacific Rim market in 1983 was estimated to be a little over 20 million cubic metres. This is the sum of United States structural (or building grade) exports, British Columbia exports, and exports from the Soviet Union. Soviet exports consist largely of spruce and larch, but the prices of these species indicate that they are substitutes for the structural species from North America. Exports from Chile and New Zealand consist mainly of radiata pine, which in 1983 was not considered to be a structural grade.

In 1983, the output of structural grade sawlogs from coastal British Columbia was estimated to be about 19 million cubic metres, which is only about 1 million cubic metres less than that supplied to the Pacific Rim market in the same year. Since most coastal British Columbia logs are transferred directly to mills from logging operations without actually being traded in a log market, the quantity of sawlogs produced in the region in 1983 is based on a coastal lumber output of 9.8 million cubic metres and an average lumber recovery factor of 0.54.

These quantities, and the average prices, permit the location of one point on the supply and demand curves in each market. In terms of Figure 1, the intersection of the British Columbia demand and supply curves in 1983 occurred at a price of $45.70 per cubic metre (which is indicated by P_d) and a quantity of 19.20 million cubic metres (which is indicated by Q_d). In the international market, the price and quantity was estimated to be $73.26 per cubic metre and 20.5 million cubic metres, respectively. These amounts are labelled P_i and Q_i in Figure 1.

If the market clearing price and quantity in the integrated market is to be determined, then it is necessary to find more than one point on the supply and demand curves in the two markets. If the functional form of the curves is simple enough, one point per curve and the slopes of the curves is sufficient to locate the entire curve in the price-quantity plane. In this study, the supply and demand curves are all assumed to be linear in the logarithm of the variables, so that the logarithmic slopes are constant at each point, independent of the location of the curve. In other words, we have assumed constant 'own price elasticities.' The elasticities of each of the curves that were chosen for the base case analysis are as follows:

(1) Price elasticity of British Columbia demand: -1.53
(2) Price elasticity of British Columbia supply: 0.30
(3) Price elasticity of Pacific Rim demand: -0.24
(4) Price elasticity of Pacific Rim supply: 0.75

These elasticities have been estimated by Constantino (1986) and Flora and Vlosky (1984) in the course of carrying out other studies but represent the best guess of the magnitude of the response to price changes in the two markets. The sensitivity of the integrated market clearing price and the net benefits to the British Columbia economy to these elasticities will be examined by varying them over an appropriate range of values.

The determination of the base case elasticities deserves some additional comment. Of particular interest is the price elasticity of coastal British Columbia supply, since this elasticity determines how the logging industry in the region responds to price increases in the short run. The magnitude of this elasticity indicates that the short run response will be small. In other words, large price increases are required to bring about any substantial increase in the quantity supplied. One explanation for this small response is that to supply more logs to the market the industry must push into higher and higher cost stands of timber and hence must receive a higher and higher price. But this explanation fails to distinguish between the short run and the long run. Over time, the short run supply curve shifts to the left in response to higher costs, but this happens slowly over time, since in each year only a small portion of the timber inventory is harvested.[6] The estimated inelasticity of the short run supply is thus explained mainly by the Annual Allowable Cut constraint, since one would expect that in the absence of this constraint the quantity of logs supplied would respond strongly to increases in log prices. Hence, the effectiveness of this constraint can be measured by varying the magnitude of the supply elasticity.

The base case supply relationship in the international market also warrants some additional comment. It is assumed to have a constant elasticity but there is reason to believe that the curve may become more elastic as the price declines. The reason is that at lower prices United States suppliers would find domestic markets more attractive and thus might substantially reduce the quantity supplied to the Pacific Rim market. This behaviour can be approximated by increasing the elasticity of supply in the Pacific Rim market and then examining the impact of this change in elasticity on the integrated market price and the net benefits to the British Columbia economy.

Other Data Requirements

In this section the remaining data requirements for estimating the net economic benefits to British Columbia are considered, including those required to measure the employment effects in each of the logging, processing, and government sectors of the British Columbia forest industry.

Logging Sector

The net benefits from the removal of log export restrictions consist of the change in net logging revenues that are made up of revenues from exports and sales in British Columbia less the change in timber export taxes, less the change in stumpage fees, less the change in logging expenditures. All of these quantities, except for the change in logging expenditures, can be determined from the previous data. In this study, a logging cost estimate of $44 per cubic metre is used to determine the change in logging expenditures, and it is based on evidence from: (1) a large sample of cutting permit appraisals for cut blocks in the Vancouver forest region in the years 1983 and 1984,[7] (2) Statistics Canada data,[8] and (3) a sample of 1983 costs reported by 23 logging operations to the Council of Forest Industries.[9]

The removal of log export restrictions causes the price of logs in coastal British Columbia and the quantity supplied by the logging sector to rise, thus increasing the demand for labour in this sector. The employment effects are estimated by assuming that employment in the logging sector is proportional to the production of logs. Thus, the percentage change in direct employment in this sector is equal to the percentage change in log production. In addition to direct employment in the logging sector, a rise in log production will also produce indirect employment in those businesses that service this sector. It is estimated that for each direct job created in the logging sector 1.4 jobs are created in related parts of the British Columbia economy.[10]

Processing Sector

The short run change in net benefits to the processing sector from the removal of export restrictions consists of a change in lumber and chip revenues less the change in operating expenditures, less the change in log expenditures. The change in lumber revenues is determined as the product of the average lumber price in 1983 of $144.11 per cubic metre and the change in lumber output. The change in lumber output is determined as the product of the cross price elasticity, which is the percentage change in lumber output for each percentage change in the price of logs, estimated by Constantino (1985) to be -1.31, the percentage change in the price of logs, and the base lumber output. This estimate of the change in lumber output does not assume that lumber output is proportional to log input, otherwise the cross price elasticity would be the same as the price elasticity of demand for logs, which was estimated to be -1.53. The smaller cross price elasticity implies that a decrease in log input decreases lumber output – but not proportionally. This result suggests that as the price of logs rises the processing sector becomes more efficient in their use.

The change in operating expenditures other than on logs and labour is the sum of energy, materials and supplies, and maintenance and repair expenditures per unit of lumber times the change in lumber production. These expenditures are estimated to be $18.23 per cubic metre of lumber in 1983, based on 1982 data from Statistics Canada that has been adjusted by appropriate price indexes.[11]

The change in expenditures on labour in the processing sector due to the decline in the quantity of labour demanded is given by the product of the cross price elasticity of labour demand with respect to log price, the proportional change in log price, and the base total wage expenditures. The cross price elasticity is estimated by Constantino (1985) to be -1.59, and total base wage expenditures are estimated as the product of wages per cubic metre of lumber (in 1983 about $50 per cubic metre), and base lumber production in 1983 is estimated at 9.77 million cubic metres. Direct employment effects in this sector can also be estimated from this cross price elasticity. Indirect employment effects in this sector are estimated to be 1.2 jobs for each direct job.[12]

It is estimated that pulp chips constitute 41 per cent of the difference between log consumption and lumber output (See Larsen, Gee, and Bearden 1983). The change in pulp chip revenue is estimated as the difference of the change in log consumption and lumber output times the base price of chips. The assumption that the price of chips will remain unchanged is probably unrealistic, since British Columbia pulp- and papermills rely heavily on chips. In the short run these mills cannot easily substitute for other sources of pulpwood, so the price of chips would be expected to rise. This would moderate the reduction in chip revenues predicted by this model. However, chip revenues are only about five per cent of lumber revenues, so the assumption of a fixed price of chips is not expected to significantly affect the results.

IMPACT OF MARKET INTEGRATION

In this section the results of the computer model which determines market clearing price and quantity in the integrated market and the net benefits of this integration for the British Columbia economy are presented for different measurements of demand and supply elasticities. The results of the model for the base case in which the elasticities and other data are all taken to be the values given in the previous sections are shown in Table 3. It cannot be overemphasized that these numbers are completely dependent upon the market model that has been used to generate them and the methods that have been chosen to determine net economic benefits to the province. That they are reported to two decimal places of accuracy should not be misinterpreted as an indication of the ability of the model to predict with this degree of precision the actual outcome of the removal of log export restrictions. They are only meant to provide an indication of the magnitude of the changes in the variables of interest.

With these reminders, the model indicates that under the base case data assumptions the integrated market price of logs falls by about 25 per cent from an initial value of about $73 per cubic metre. To many observers, a decline in price of this magnitude will seem too large, but it must be remembered that the supply in each of these markets is similar in size, so the integrated market price can be expected to be roughly the average of the prices in the two markets. It should be pointed out that this result is also very robust with respect

TABLE 3

Impact of market integration: base case (red cedar included as structural log)

Variables	Before market integration	After market integration	Change	Per cent change
Pacific rim log price[1]	73.26	55.34	−17.92	−25
BC log price	45.70	54.13	8.43	18
BC log demand[2]	17.55	13.55	−4.00	−23
BC log supply	19.20	20.19	0.99	5
BC log exports	1.65	6.65	5.00	303
Stumpage revenue[3]			18.79	
Log export levy revenue			2.14	
Net benefits[3]				
Logging net benefits			118.58	
Processing net benefits			−97.80	
Gov. net benefits			20.93	
Total short-run net benefits			41.72	
Total long-run net benefits			139.51	
Logging employment[4]			0.56	
Processing employment			−3.20	

NOTES: [1] 1983 dollars per cubic metre
[2] Millions of cubic metres; log export levy of $1.21 per cubic metre is based on 1983 mix of species and grades in the market
[3] Millions of dollars
[4] Thousands of jobs

to a wide range of specifications of the supply and demand elasticities. It will be noted that the lower British Columbia log price is due to the log export levy, which in the base case is $1.21 per cubic metre. This is the levy that is estimated to result from the 1983 mix of species and grades in the Pacific Rim market and not the average levy that applied to actual exports from British Columbia in 1983.

Table 3 also reports the impact of the removal of log export restrictions on the quantities of logs demanded and supplied in coastal British Columbia. The model predicts that the quantity of logs demanded by British Columbia processors will decline by about 23 per cent, the quantity supplied by the coastal logging sector will rise by about 5 per cent, and that log exports rise by about 300 per cent from a small initial amount of only 1.65 million cubic metres. As is evident from the table, most of the increase in British Columbia exports is offset by a decline in sales to British Columbia processors, but these exports receive a substantially higher price.

The relatively small rise in logging output is due to the small elasticity of supply which arises primarily from current Annual Allowable Cut (AAC) restrictions. However, since more stands of timber in the province would become 'economic' as a result of higher log prices the actual harvest might be increased, which would have the effect of increasing the quantity response to the higher price; that is, it would increase the elasticity of supply. To account for this possibility, when the supply elasticity is doubled to 0.60 from the base case of 0.30, price drops by an additional 1 per cent and exports rise by an additional 0.25 million cubic metres. On the other hand, if the supply elasticity is even smaller than it is in the base case because of even tighter AAC restrictions, say, 0.10, then the price drops by less and log exports increase by less than they do in the base case. Other results of these alternative specifications are shown in Tables A.1 and A.2 in the Appendix.

Referring again to the base case results in Table 3, short run net benefits to the logging sector rise but are largely offset by a decline in net benefits to the processing sector. However, when government net benefits that arise from higher stumpage and log export revenues are included, total short run net benefits rise by about $40 million per year. These net benefits are flows that are sustained on a yearly basis as long as conditions remain unchanged.

Long run net benefits are calculated at nearly $140 million per year. In calculating these benefits, the negative net benefits to the processing sector are removed on the assumption that in the long run unemployed factors of production in this sector would be employed elsewhere in the economy and would thus be contributing to aggregate economic activity in another capacity.

In the base case, results of the model show that direct employment positions in the logging sector increase by about 560, again due mainly to the small elasticity of log supply, and employment falls about 3,200 in the processing sector. Indirect employment changes can be estimated from the factors relating changes in indirect jobs to changes in direct jobs in each sector.

Alternative Specifications of the Model

It was mentioned earlier that a possible objection exists to the inclusion of red cedar as a structural species. For this reason we have examined a situation where this species is excluded from the data. The effect of this change is evident from the first column in Table 4, where log quantities prior to market integration have been scaled downward to reflect the removal of red cedar which makes up about 25 per cent of the total. The Pacific Rim market quantity was also scaled downward, although red cedar made up only a very small fraction in this market. Prices were kept unchanged, since they were not expected to be affected significantly. As shown in Table 4, the impact of market integration on the Pacific Rim log price is reduced, but it is still a substantial 22 per cent decline. Short run net benefits are increased greatly because the cost to the processing section is reduced, as all cedar is still processed in British Columbia. Changes in employment in the two sectors is also reduced.

It has been suggested that if the current Pacific Rim price for structural logs was to decline by the amounts suggested above, United States suppliers would substantially reduce supply to this market, as they would have alternative opportunities in the Pacific Northwest log markets. To examine this possibility we have run the computer model with the supply elasticity in the Pacific Rim market doubled from 0.75, in the base case, to a value of 1.50. These results are presented in Table A.3 in the Appendix. In this case, the Pacific Rim log price falls by 20 per cent, instead of 25 per cent, as in the base case, and British Columbia exports increase substantially over the base case results. Both the British Columbia logging and government sectors benefit more while the processing sector suffers more in this case than in the base case.

It is also of interest to examine the case wherein the elasticity of demand for logs by British Columbia mills is -1.00 rather than -1.53. It is evident from Table A.4 that short run net benefits are very sensitive to this change. The logging and government sectors benefit substantially, but this is more than offset by the costs to the processing sector, so that total short run net benefits of the removal of the log export restrictions are negative. Long run net benefits are, of course, still quite large.

Impact of the Log Export Levy

It was suggested earlier that there are two common ways to separate markets. The first is to simply place quantity restrictions on the ex-

TABLE 4

Impact of market integration: base case (red cedar excluded as structural log)

Variables	Before market integration	After market integration	Change	Per cent change
Pacific Rim log price[1]	73.26	56.88	−16.38	−22
BC log price	45.70	55.65	9.95	22
BC log demand[2]	13.34	9.87	−3.47	−26
BC log supply	14.94	15.85	0.91	6
BC log exports	1.60	5.98	4.38	274
Stumpage revenue[3]			17.26	
Log export levy revenue			1.32	
Net benefits[3]				
Logging net benefits			103.10	
Processing net benefits			−32.85	
Gov. net benefits			18.58	
Total short-run net benefits			88.83	
Total long-run net benefits			121.68	
Logging employment[4]			0.49	
Processing employment			−2.83	

NOTES: [1] 1983 dollars per cubic metre
[2] Millions of cubic metres; log export levy of $1.21 per cubic metre is based on 1983 mix of species and grades in the market
[3] Millions of dollars per year
[4] Thousands of jobs

port or import of the product and the second is to impose an export or import tax. The log export levy is an export tax and, therefore, could be used as a policy instrument to control the degree of integration of the two markets while at the same time raising revenues for the British Columbia government by taxing away some of the differ-

ence between the Pacific Rim and British Columbia prices. It is for
this reason that we are interested in the results from the computer
model under different assumptions about the magnitude of the log
export levy. The effect of varying the levy on certain key variables of
interest are shown in Figures (3), (4), and (5). Figure 3 shows that as
the levy increases, the difference between the Pacific Rim and coastal British Columbia log prices also increases as this tax drives a
wedge between them. Of greater interest is the effect of the levy on
short run and long run net benefits. Long run net benefits decline
slowly over most of the range of the tax and then drop off sharply as
the tax becomes very high. On the other hand, short run net benefits
grow to a point at which the tax is about $15.00 per cubic metre and
then decline, thus suggesting that from a short run perspective the
tax is optimal at about $15.00 per cubic metre. It should be pointed
out, however, that these results are for the base case specification of
the model and would change for other specifications.

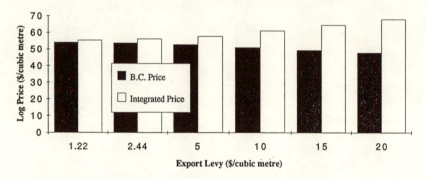

FIGURE 3
Effect of an export levy on log prices

Figure 5 shows the increase in government revenues from the log
export levy and stumpage as the levy increases. As the tax increases,
additions to revenues from this levy grow until the tax reaches
somewhere between $15.00 and $20.00 per cubic metre, after which
these increases in revenues begin to decline. Additions to stumpage
revenues decrease as the tax increases, but these declines are more
than offset by the increases in revenues from the export tax.

CONCLUSIONS

This study shows that the coastal British Columbia sawlog market is
large enough so that the complete removal of log export restrictions,

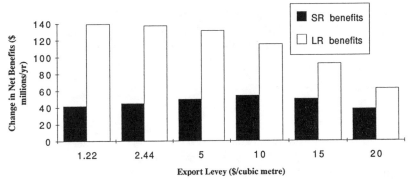

FIGURE 4
Effect of an export levy on short-run and long-run benefits

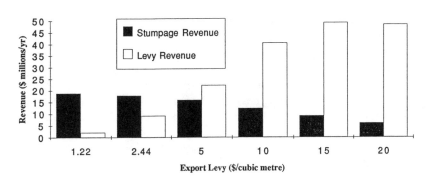

FIGURE 5
Effect of an export levy on government revenues

resulting in a total integration of the current Pacific Rim log market and the coastal British Columbia log market, would result in a substantial decline in current Pacific Rim log prices. This decline would be in the order of 20 per cent to 25 per cent, depending upon demand and supply elasticities in the two markets. Likewise, the price of logs in coastal British Columbia would be expected to rise by about 20 per cent. The study also shows that under most of the specifications of the demand and supply elasticities in the two markets, the removal of log export restrictions results in higher short run net benefits to the British Columbia economy and always results in a gain in long run net benefits.

Instead of using quantity restrictions to separate the two markets, the use of the log export levy for this purpose was also examined. It was found that for the conditions that existed in 1983, a levy in the order of $15 per cubic metre would maximize short run net benefits to the British Columbia economy but, of course, these net benefits are received largely by the provincial government. Any increase in this tax always results in a lower level of long run net benefits to the economy.

NOTES

1 This formula is given by max(0.08Pd; Pd/(1 + r) - logging costs) where r is the average BC coast profit and risk allowance of 0.20.
2 Changes in the corporate income tax and the special tax on logging profits are not incorporated into this study.
3 About 20 per cent of the annual cut enters the Vancouver log market.
4 The sample constitutes about 10 per cent of Pacific Northwest log exports in 1983 and appears to be a representative sample of total Pacific Northwest exports.
5 In order to develop this table, it was necessary to determine the equivalence between United States and Vancouver log market grades. For this purpose the BC Council of Forest Industries (COFI) (1982) was used.
6 In the very long run, when reforestation programs begin to have their effect, one might expect the supply curve to begin to shift downward.
7 The data set was made available to the Forest Economics and Policy Analysis project at the University of British Columbia.
8 Statistics Canada Catalogue 25-201 - Annual.
9 B. McCloy, COFI, personal communication.
10 H. Singh, Central Statistic Bureau, Ministry of Industry and Small Business, personal communication.
11 Statistic Canada, Catalog 35-204, 1982.
12 H. Singh, Central Statistic Bureau, Ministry of Industry and Small Business, personal communication.

TABLE A.1

Impact of market integration: BC supply elasticity $= 0.10$[1]

Variables	Before market integration	After market integration	Change	Per cent change
Pacific Rim log price[2]	73.26	56.29	−16.97	−23
BC log price	45.70	55.07	9.37	21
BC log demand[3]	17.55	13.19	−4.36	−25
BC log supply	19.20	19.55	0.35	2
BC log exports	1.65	6.36	4.71	285
Stumpage revenue[4]			17.48	
Log export levy revenue			1.79	
Net benefits[4]				
Logging net benefits			131.30	
Processing net benefits			−109.03	
Gov. net benefits			19.27	
Total short-run net benefits			41.54	
Total long-run net benefits			150.57	
Logging employment[5]			0.20	
Processing employment			−3.55	

NOTES: [1] Red cedar is included as a structural log
[2] 1983 dollars per cubic metre
[3] Millions of cubic metres; log export levy of $1.21 per cubic metre is based on 1983 mix of species and grades in the market
[4] Millions of dollars
[5] Thousands of jobs

Impact of market integration: BC supply elasticity = 0.60[1]

Variables	Before market integration	After market integration	Change	Per cent change
Pacific Rim log price[2]	73.26	54.22	−19.04	−26
BC log price	45.70	53.00	7.30	16
BC log demand[3]	17.55	13.99	−3.56	−20
BC log supply	19.20	20.98	1.78	9
BC log exports	1.65	6.99	5.34	324
Stumpage revenue[4]			20.34	
Log export levy revenue			2.55	
Net benefits[4]				
Logging net benefits			102.12	
Processing net benefits			−84.48	
Gov. net benefits			22.89	
Total short-run net benefits			45.86	
Total long-run net benefits			125.01	
Logging employment[5]			1.00	
Processing employment			−2.77	

NOTES: [1] Red cedar is included as a structural log
[2] 1983 dollars per cubic metre
[3] Millions of cubic metres; log export levy of $1.21 per cubic metre is based on 1983 mix of species and grades in the market
[4] Millions of dollars
[5] Thousands of jobs

Impact of market integration: Pacific Rim supply elasticity = 1.5^1

Variables	Before market integration	After market integration	Change	Per cent change
Pacific Rim log price[2]	73.26	58.58	−14.68	−20
BC log price	45.70	57.35	11.65	25
BC log demand[3]	17.55	12.40	−5.15	−29
BC log supply	19.20	20.55	1.35	7
BC log exports	1.65	8.15	6.50	394
Stumpage revenue[4]			29.05	
Log export levy revenue			3.97	
Net benefits[4]				
Logging net benefits			178.58	
Processing net benefits			−136.36	
Gov. net benefits			33.02	
Total short-run net benefits			45.86	
Total long-run net benefits			211.60	
Logging employment[5]			0.75	
Processing employment			−4.42	

NOTES: [1] Red cedar is included as a structural log
[2] 1983 dollars per cubic metre
[3] Millions of cubic metres; log export levy of $1.21 per cubic metre is based on 1983 mix of species and grades in the market
[4] Millions of dollars
[5] Thousands of jobs

Impact of market integration: BC demand elasticity $= -1.0$[1]

Variables	Before market integration	After market integration	Change	Per cent change
Pacific Rim log price[2]	73.26	57.23	−16.03	−22
BC log price	45.70	56.01	10.31	23
BC log demand[3]	17.55	14.32	−3.23	−18
BC log supply	19.20	20.40	1.20	6
BC log exports	1.65	6.08	4.43	268
Stumpage revenue[4]			22.71	
Log export levy revenue			1.45	
Net benefits[4]				
Logging net benefits			155.43	
Processing net benefits			−190.47	
Gov. net benefits			24.16	
Total short-run net benefits			−10.88	
Total long-run net benefits			179.59	
Logging employment[5]			0.67	
Processing employment			−3.91	

NOTES: [1] Red cedar is included as a structural log
[2] 1983 dollars per cubic metre
[3] Millions of cubic metres; log export levy of $1.21 per cubic metre is based on 1983 mix of species and grades in the market
[4] Millions of dollars
[5] Thousands of jobs

CHAPTER THIRTEEN

Distributive Issues in Forest Policy

David N. Wear and William F. Hyde

INTRODUCTION

Resource allocations can be evaluated on both efficiency and equity grounds. While those in the private sector may focus exclusively on the former, equity or distributional questions have come to dominate the field of public forest management and policy. The profession's current approach to forestry policy issues focuses, however, on efficiency issues and generally fails to sufficiently address distributional consequences. The purpose of this paper is to identify the critical distributional issues currently faced by public forestry and to discuss directions for research into this area.

In the sections which follow, we examine two types of issues which, by their nature, are focused in the two major forest production regions of the United States: the Pacific Northwest and the South (both represent about one third of domestic production). First, we address public forestry management issues which are necessarily focused on the National Forests in the western United States. The primary focus of our discussion is on the 'community stability' issues regarding the influence of public forestry on local economies and employment. Second, we examine issues regarding forestry policies aimed at the private sector, namely, special tax treatments for timber growing and programs designed to promote timber supply through subsidies for the planting of trees. Private timber growing activities are concentrated in the South, where concerns are focused on the interface between forestry and the other major rural land-using sector in the region: agriculture. Shifts between agriculture and forestry, especially through massive programs such as the Conservation Reserve Program, may have dramatic influences on the landscape and, therefore, on the structure of rural economies, especially upon rural employment. We close with a summary of important distributive issues in forest policy.

PUBLIC FORESTRY AND COMMUNITY STABILITY

'Community stability' is often used to describe the influence of public forestry on local economies. It encapsulates distributional issues in forest management and serves as our starting point for discussing emerging distributional issues in public forestry. We start by defining the current approach to community stability within the organizational context of the u.s. Department of Agriculture (USDA) Forest Service. This approach to community stability which, put succinctly, aims to support employment in timber-based sectors through public timber harvesting, is much too narrow to capture the full spectrum of the distributional effects of public forestry. The paper goes on to question this relationship between harvesting and jobs as an exclusive distributional focus and suggests a broader view of the role of public forestry in the composition and stability of local economies. Actual recent changes in the way which the Forest Service views its relationships with local communities suggests that broader, distributive concerns are indeed emerging issues in forest policy.

Community stability is a 'policy capsule' for the distributional side of public forestry. Its history is as old as the practice of public forestry in the United States and its roots go back, even further, to the European practice. Its definition and application have changed over time and Schallou and Alston (1987) provide a comprehensive treatise on this evolution of community stability policy in the u.s. We direct the interested reader there for historical context. After reviewing u.s. public land laws, Schallou and Alston find little in the way of a legislative precedent for current community stability policies and adopt Marquis'(1947) view of community stability as forestry folklore. Its persistence and the seemingly deep conviction with which it is still held suggests, however, that it is more than a vestigial tradition. It is perhaps instructive to view community stability as an ideology, rooted in the self perceptions and values of the forestry profession, especially among those in the public sector.

Downs (1967), in his study of the development and behaviour of government agencies, defines a bureaucratic ideology as a simple statement of policy which comes to encapsulate a complex and perhaps inconsistent set of issues and professional views and which provides 'a verbal image of that portion of the good society relevant to the functions of the particular bureau concerned, plus the chief means of constructing that portion.' Within an agency it puts an intractable and complex political/professional issue into a simple package, rationalizes the inherent ambiguities of necessarily situational policies and directives, and communicates 'images of relevant portions of the good society' to the public. The ideology also promotes cohesion within the agency. Once established, these ideologies are slow to change. The policy capsule called community stability translates timber harvesting into social benefits in the form of jobs and is an example of an ideology held by public foresters in the United States – an ideology which is changing only slowly.

Community stability arguments have typically been invoked only to address stability in local timber markets. The basic rationale is that a stable long-term supply of materials 'allows firms and communities to undertake substantial investment projects without fear of a loss of a source of raw material' (Schallou and Alston 1987). Timber supply policy has also been applied in attempts to counteract the effects of business cycles on the wood products industries and the detrimental consequences these cycles have on local economies. In recent years, community stability has been used to explain below-cost timber sales on the National Forests – sales where timber receipts do not cover the costs of development, sale preparation, and administration.[1] In a memo discussing timber sale policies on the National Forests, the former chief of the Forest Service, Max Peterson (1985), clearly states this rationale:

> As a general rule, the timber sale program on a National Forest should be managed so that total benefits equal or exceed the costs over time. Exceptions may be appropriate where there are overriding considerations such as the need to control insect and disease outbreaks or maintain the stability of dependent communities. For example, the livelihood of a dependent community should not be threatened by a short-term downturn in the timber market which adversely affects the short-term economics of the timber sale program.

It is unclear that such a factor supply policy can substantially influence production through a recession. Daniels et al. (1991) show that if such a policy were effective, it would, at best, be costly and would skew benefits towards owners of capital rather than towards local labour.

Even if a timber supply policy could effect stable production, production stability does not necessarily imply income and employment stability. Technological change in the wood products industries has improved labour efficiency since the early 1950s (Stier 1980;

Wear 1989), and employment per unit of output has dropped accordingly. Stabilizing local employment with timber harvests during this period would have actually required steadily increasing harvest levels.[2]

Changes in labour demand have been especially dramatic during the 1980s. Employment per unit of output and wood-based income in the western states of Oregon, Washington, Montana, and Idaho fell precipitously between the years 1979 and 1985 (Keegan and Polzin 1987). This period spanned a deep wood products recession, and these observations suggest that the recovered industry is a different one. Wear (1989) tested whether these shifts in labour demand could be explained by the steady rates of technological progress experienced in the sixties and seventies and by changes in relative wage rates. The hypothesis was rejected, indicating that the industry had experienced an employment-reducing structural change during the period. Accordingly, the relationship between harvests and employment shifted.

These types of changes influence the community stability issue in two ways. First, they make local concerns for wood-based employment, and, therefore, public timber harvesting, more urgent. Second, the employment effects of public timber harvests are reduced. Furthermore, the distributive winners in a capital intensive wood products industry become, increasingly, the owners of mill capital. To the extent that mill capital is held by corporations from outside the local area, the distributive argument for harvesting extramarginal public timber is further weakened.

Community stability policies which seek to support local wood-based employment do so at a cost to other forest uses. While public forests may provide a critical share of the timber input to local wood products industries, harvesting is not the exclusive link between forestry and local economies. The other goods and services which flow from public lands also have an important bearing on the character of local economies. Forest-based recreation, which has become increasingly important to Western economies over the last three decades, is both consumed and packaged for tourism by local communities. National projections suggest that both the scarcity of undeveloped land and the demand for wildland services will continue to increase and will contribute to rising opportunity costs for timber harvesting. That is, current timber supply policy will have a long run bearing on the comparative advantage to regions of producing other products, such as outdoor recreation.

Shifts between sectors, especially shifts between manufacturing and service sectors, have implications for wages which raise additional distributional concerns. For example, relatively high-paying jobs in a wood products industry may be replaced by lower-paying jobs in a service-oriented recreation sector. This is an important issue, which is compounded further by the direct income which is derived from public forests. The connections between timber harvesting, lumber production, employment, and income, though complex, seem clear enough. They do not, however, capture the effects of a community's environmental setting on the quality of life of its residents. Environmental amenities, including the services of public lands, translate directly into compensation for local residents. Power (1980) argues that while these services may seem intangible, their effects are clearly seen in the income differences between urban workers and their counterparts in the 'hinterlands.' If workers are fully mobile in the long run, then a persistent wage-differential can only be explained by differences in the cost of living and in the value of these environmental services. This relationship 'between income and nonmonetary determinants of utility' (Obermiller 1982) suggests that, to the extent that forest management influences the environmental setting of a community, it has an indirect bearing on the 'real' income of a group of local people much broader than that of the workforce employed by the wood products sector.[3]

Effects on an even broader group are often the focus of debate over use of the National Forests. Local communities are not the only consumers of forest outputs. A critical distributional issue faced by National Forest managers in the United States is how to reconcile the demands of local and national constituency groups in natural resource policy. This conflict is embodied in the two major resource planning laws which direct the management of the National Forests. The Resource Planning Act of 1974 (RPA) defines a process for developing national resource management strategies and is a top-down process which focuses on national concerns. The National Forest Management Act of 1976 (NFMA, which amended the RPA) directs the planning of individual forests and places a great deal of emphasis on local public involvement. Wilkinson and Anderson (1987) have observed that the law does not define how this bottom-up process meshes with top-down national planning. However, this meshing clearly involves trade-offs between local and national demands; that is, it involves redistributions between regions.

In sum, community stability has been used as a policy capsule for the local impacts of public forestry and has focused exclusively on the relationship between timber harvesting and employment in the wood products industries. This focus excludes the contributions of other non-timber products from the distributive analysis of forest management and weights emphasis towards wood-products concerns. As demands for other non-priced uses of public forests increase in the future, their importance, both in terms of local consumption and regional recreation sectors, will expand. At the same time, the relationship between harvest policy and local production and between local production and local employment is dynamic. Little empirical evidence supports the argument that even-flow policies actually stabilize local communities, and the income which wood products industries have actually contributed to local economies has declined over the sixties and seventies and has dropped precipitously in the early eighties. These observations offer strong support for re-examining this distributive view of public forestry.

DIRECTIONS FOR DISTRIBUTIVE POLICIES AND ANALYSIS IN PUBLIC FORESTRY

The distributive issues of public forestry have expanded from community stability to address the broader web of interactions between resource production, environmental quality, and human welfare. Driven by growing populations, changing incomes and preferences, and increasing resource scarcity, these changes are at the very heart of recent introspective debates within the forestry profession.[4] They are also reflected in recent efforts by the u.s. Forest Service to define its social role in terms of rural development (USDA Forest Service 1990a,b). This broadens considerably the agency's vision of its interactions with social systems. This section first discusses the definition of distributive policies in this broader context and then the process of implementing them through natural resource planning. It begins by examining u.s. legislative support for a redistributive role in the National Forest planning process and considers the analytical tools presently used in that process. The section closes with proposals for addressing broader distributive issues and with suggestions for future research.

Is there, in fact, a legitimate distributive role for public forestry in the United States? Schallou and Alston (1987) find no specific legislative support for a community stability policy in particular, but they agree with Wilkinson and Anderson (1987) that its pervasiveness throughout the history of the u.s. Forest Service establishes it as a legitimate concern. Krutilla and Haigh (1978) examine the NFMA for evidence of the economist's standard rationales for public intervention in market economies. Of the three, allocative efficiency, redistribution, and stability, they find the Act generally consistent with an efficiency rationale tied particularly to the provision of non-market goods. They dismiss the possibility of a redistributive or stabilizing role for the agency. However, they note two possible exceptions to the efficiency model. One is the definition of timber harvest rules which are tied to physical or volumetric criteria. The other is the emphasis the Act places on local public participation in planning. Krutilla and Haigh suggest that this kind of input might be consistent with their allocative efficiency standard but only if the public participation were used to solicit information on the willingness-to-pay for certain non-priced forest outputs. In this regard, the local public would act as a sample of the relevant consumers of these nonmarket goods. It is difficult, however, to define where the local public is the only relevant consumer of the resource. To the extent that the local willingness-to-pay for various forest outputs differs from a national norm – if for no other reason, due to regional differences in the distribution of income – the NFMA places a disproportionate weight on the local impacts of forest management. This supports a redistributional role for the agency but on a geographic rather than on an income-class scale. Because it focuses on location, rather than income, this kind of redistributive view is consistent with the agency's emerging rural development model of forest-human interactions.

The shift from a community stability to a rural development model of forest-human interactions seems to recognize the increasing complexity of trade-offs between forest-using publics which are separated in several dimensions. Successful policies for managing public forests will need to address these differences between regions (rural and urban), between sectors, (commodity and non-commodity), and between income classes. A first step in building a planning approach which successfully addresses distributional concerns is to define how they can be incorporated within a planning process strongly grounded in efficiency principles. This requires shifting attention away from what should be done to stabilize communities (or 'that portion of the good society' provided by public forestry) to a focus on providing a clear definition of the distributional consequences of management actions (in all the dimensions listed above). With this kind of information, public forestry decisions can address efficient resource allocation with careful consideration of who loses and who wins in the process. In a practical sense, public decisions based on efficiency criteria are always tempered by these distributive considerations, and political/public participation processes ultimately provide the judgement on equity weights. The challenge for economists and planners is to provide the appropriate economic information for these kinds of decisions.

Numerous economists have pointed out that, except under very restrictive conditions, the methodology of economics does not provide a formula for trading distributive impacts against the efficiency of resource allocations. Accordingly, no single analysis can provide an operational criterion for decisionmaking in public forest management. Not surprisingly, the u.s. Forest Service conducts resource planning at a number of spatial levels using a variety of approaches. However, the greatest emphasis is placed at the national (RPA) and the national forest levels. While in both cases, economic models are used to gauge efficiency and distributive effects, we will focus our attention on planning at the National Forest level. National Forest planning uses an optimization model (FORPLAN) to formulate and evaluate the allocative efficiency of various management alternatives. Distributive issues are then examined in two ways. First, the production levels for alternatives are used in an input/output model (IMPLAN), which calculates employment and income impacts. Second, and perhaps most importantly, the optimization model is often constrained to schedule a minimum level of timber harvesting in the first period of the plan in order to address community stability. This constraint, combined with the nondeclining-even-flow harvest rule, can radically alter resource production from efficient levels for the entire planning period and often defines a costly (in efficiency terms) remedy for employment concerns.

The current approach was built on the community stability model and focuses exclusively on the relationships between timber harvesting and jobs. Broader distributive issues have yet to be addressed with this structure, and it is not at all clear that these models can provide the needed information. To model the connections between resource management and all relevant sectors will require some fundamentally different approaches to analysis. In particular, models will need to be extended to address the dynamics of resource production and related factor markets, the interaction between resource quality and human benefits, and the variety of scales associated with different resource issues. These areas are discussed, in turn, below.

Input-output models in general and IMPLAN in particular are static models based on snap-shot views of an economy. While appropriate for short run analyses of changes at the margin, they provide biased views of structural changes in production. Forest planning, however, necessarily takes a long run view, and public discourse over public lands suggests that structural change in the production from the National Forests should be expected in the future. These kinds of changes are also anticipated by recent national plans (u.s. Forest

Service 1990b). Measuring the distributive impacts of changes in resource production will require a dynamic analysis which captures
the significant adjustment costs in the short to medium run as well
as in the long run consequences of management plans. For example,
reducing timber production implies a set of social costs, especially
in the short run, as communities adjust. An accounting of these
costs should be a part of planning how to implement any kind of reduction in production. We presently do not have tools for measuring
these costs.

Distributional effects of public forest management also need to be
addressed at appropriate spatial scales. Understanding the connections between forest management and employment requires analysis at a regional or labour market scale.[5] The present forest-by-forest
approach to management planning likely misstates their accumulated effects on communities which are influenced by several forests
(see Sullivan and Gilless 1989). In most cases, National Forest
boundaries are essentially arbitrary in relation to the human communities which they influence. Matching forest areas up with their
spheres of human influence will be essential for measuring short
run and long run connections between local labour and capital and
resource supply, production relations between all sectors of local
economies, and the interacting effects of public and private land
management on communities. Of course, this criticism can be extended to other dimensions of resource planning as well. The appropriate scale for managing wildlife populations, for example, is much
smaller than the National Forest. These differences in scale support
the notion that planning needs to be conducted at a variety of spatial
levels, though it should be noted that meaningful co-ordination between scales is a non-trivial problem.

In addition, we are concerned about the ability to account for important resource production relationships in the current planning
models. While production quantity has been the focus, the influence
of resource quality on value (especially recreation values) can be significant (e.g., Duffield). Measuring quality often requires an accounting for spatial processes at a landscape scale. In many cases,
this may exceed the limits of present knowledge. In many instances
the biophysical production relationships are simply unknown.

Another area which deserves attention, as we shift focus from the
forest to its connections with broader social systems, is the potential
interactions between public and private land management. This requires assessing the market power of National Forests in resource
markets. The efficiency and impact analyses in the current planning
approach imply conflicting views of this market power. The effi-

ciency analysis conducted with FORPLAN treats all prices as exogenously determined values, and views forests as typical market players – that is, they have no market power. The impact analysis conducted with IMPLAN, however, assumes that increments in USFS
harvest plans translate directly into increments in total harvesting –
that is, they do have power to determine total local production. Actual market power in most areas of the U.S. West is likely somewhere
between these two extremes, suggesting important interactions between public and private production plans. Most importantly, market power of this sort would suggest that a National Forest plan
would produce an impact on resource supplies from private lands.
Accordingly, the accumulation of National Forest plans would have
a critical influence on regional economies, which could not be captured in the current forest-by-forest approach.

The preceding discussion has focused attention on several areas
which require additional research. We summarize three here. First,
the temporal and spatial scales of distributive impacts needs to be
defined and incorporated in resource planning analysis. In particular, the time path of impacts and associated adjustment costs should
be considered in the design of production plans and policies. Total
impacts can only be measured when labour and other affected factor
markets are considered at the appropriate market scale. Otherwise,
important feedbacks and distortions cannot be accounted for. Second, a lack of information on biophysical production relations suggests some obvious research work, especially for defining the connections between management activities and resource quality, and
between resource quality and human benefits. In the area of policy
analysis, this suggests a research focus on the effects of uncertainty
in the resource planning process. Third, the actual mechanisms
through which public forestry impacts resource markets is poorly
understood. To the extent that National Forests are not typical market players, their market power may indirectly influence private production as well.

FORESTRY POLICIES AND PRIVATE LAND MANAGEMENT

Previous sections have addressed direct forest market interventions
through public forest management. Policy measures may also be indirect, influencing private land management through incentives
such as cost-sharing for forest regeneration, technical assistance,
and preferential tax treatments. These policies define two important
sets of distributional questions. First, there is the question of redis-

tributive goals for forestry programs directed at private lands. These programs are a part of a much larger rural development agenda, which intends to redistribute income from urban to rural or from higher- to lower-income households. Can forestry be an effective part of such an agenda? Second, even when policies have little specific redistributive intention, their distributive consequences are an essential part of program evaluation. Policy analysts should ask whether programs redistribute in progressive, neutral, or regressive fashion. This section considers distributional issues and policies which address forest management on private lands and focuses on one of several such programs: the Forestry Incentives Program.

There are several forestry assistance programs in place in the United States, including the Conservation Reserve Program (CRP) enabled by the Farm Bill of 1985, the Agricultural Conservation Program (ACP) enabled by the Soil Conservation and Domestic Allotment Act of 1936, and the Forestry Incentive Program (FIP) enabled by the Agriculture and Consumer Protection Act of 1973. While each of these programs has an important bearing on forest management, FIP is a good focus for the discussions which follow, because it has been studied extensively and has a legislative history which can be separated from the massive farm bill in which it was introduced. It is also an example of the most pervasive policy instrument applied to forestry: tree-planting through cost-sharing between government and land owner. The Forestry Incentives Program is intended to 'encourage the development, management, and protection of nonindustrial private lands' in order to 'provide for production of timber and related benefits' (U.S. Congress 1973a:245). Incentives are restricted to those lands which are 'capable of producing crops of industrial wood' and are limited to small non-industrial landowners.[6] While the non-timber benefits of forests are also listed as returns to tree-planting, it is clear that the primary intention of the program is to promote timber production on small, privately held tracts of land.[7]

In general, this focus on timber production in forestry policies has been justified by perceived failures in private timber markets. Proponents argue that because timber has a long production period relative to the planning horizon of wood products industries, future returns to timber production have been discounted too heavily and underproduction has resulted. That is, futures markets have failed to provide for optimal intertemporal allocation of timber resources. A resulting timber famine has long been pervasive in the psyche of forest policy. Modern concerns regarding timber shortage have perhaps been focused by the study of Barnett and Morse (1963), which found that while, in general, mineral resources had become less scarce, forestry had experienced persistently increasing scarcity in the industrial age.

The notion of timber, a renewable resource, becoming increasingly scarce (as measured by increasing prices) seems disturbing. However, empirical evidence has not supported an impending timber famine. The investigations of Johnson and Libecap (1978) and of Berk (1978) suggest that the wood products industries have discounted the future at a socially acceptable rate. In addition, Lyon (1981) finds that rising timber prices have been consistent with a transition period between the mining of an economically nonrenewable endowment of old-growth forests and the establishment of an agricultural forestry enterprise. In addition, unlike oil and other subterranean natural resources, timber producers and timber prices have not benefited from discoveries of new reserves – in essence, there exists close to perfect information regarding current timber stocks and potential.

Justification for forestry programs for non-industrial private landowners rests more specifically on perceived market failures at an individual producer level. Small landowners control an extensive share of potentially productive timberlands in the u.s., with most of this area concentrated in the South. Studies of investment potential in this region have suggested that these landowners fail to realize the full potential returns from timber management on their lands (USDA Forest Service 1987). This perceived underinvestment in forestry is explained by either a lack of technical information or constraints on the capital available for timberland investments. To the extent that they reduce the costs of these investments, cost-sharing programs for afforestation address this latter issue. While these local market failures are quite plausible, their national consequences are not necessarily severe. Because timber market failure has been rejected in the broader studies described above, the influence of underinvestment on non-industrial lands can be questioned.

An evaluation of FIP must start with its primary motivation. Does the program increase timber supplies from private lands? While several researchers have examined the efficiency of FIP and other programs, methodologies have varied greatly. This body of literature is not surveyed here. Instead, we focus our discussion on the results presented by Boyd and Hyde (1989) for the FIP program in North Carolina. This is the only work which examines equity as well as efficiency aspects of the policy.[8] The authors show that FIP's influence on timber supply in North Carolina is minimal; they cannot reject the hypothesis that the program has no influence at all on timber supply. Their results show that because of the real-income effects on households and because input subsidies are by nature distortionary, the clear effect that a subsidy has on tree-planting does not necessarily carry through to timber supply.[9] Therefore, they find no significant impact of the policy instrument on the primary policy goal in North Carolina.

However, FIP also has a distributional focus, both on the small landowners who cannot afford forestry investments and on enhancing the economies of rural America. This distributional focus is described by Robert Sikes, congressman from Florida, in remarks accompanying the introduction of the House version of the Forestry Incentives Program of 1973:

> The average owner is 55 years of age and has the equivalent of a junior high education. Two-thirds of all owners live on their property and one-third of the tracts of land has been in the owner's family for more than one generation. One-fourth of the owners have sold timber to meet some pressing financial need. Now let me make this point – the incentives bill will help the little people of the land the ones who need it most. That is why we are limiting the application of the bill to owners of less than 500 acres and payments to not more that $2,500 per year. (U.S. Congress 1973b:4-5)

Size of land holding is viewed as a proxy for landowner income, and at least the author of the bill suggests that the program should redistribute to lower-income owners.

Boyd and Hyde (1989), using results from a study by Royer (1981), provide insight into the actual distribution of benefits from FIP across income groups in North Carolina. They compare the income distribution of those receiving program benefits with the income distribution of the nation as a whole. In general, the income distribution of non-industrial forest landowners is above the national distribution. Furthermore, most acres treated under the FIP program are held by the most affluent of these landowners. While only 7.3 per cent of U.S. households had incomes in excess of $45,000 (1982 income in 1980 dollars), 55 per cent of the acres treated under FIP during that year in North Carolina were held by households in this group. Seventy-two per cent of the acres treated were held by households with incomes of $35,000 or more. While economists are reluctant to recommend income redistribution beyond obvious Pareto improvements, these regressive results are neither consistent with the redistributive intentions stated above nor with any egalitarian standard.

Congress has also clearly pursued a program of rural development through a multitude of programs such as rural housing loans, rural community fire protection grants, rural housing for domestic farm labour, and business and industrial development grants. The intent of these programs is 'to see that rural areas of the country receive treatment from the Federal Government similar and also equal to that received by urban areas' (u.s. Congress 1975:46). These programs have sought either to provide direct benefits to lower-income groups in rural areas or to diversify rural economies. Wood production has been viewed as a way of diversifying economies dominated by agriculture and providing manufacturing jobs in these rural areas. This development role for forestry, and for FIP in particular, is described by John C. Stennis, Senator from Mississippi, as follows: 'This program helps relieve unemployment without any requirement for extensive training. In the future there will be more and larger job increases, from the harvesting, transporting, and processing of timber. All of this contributes toward the revitalization of rural areas, so important throughout the country' (u.s. Congress 1972:7). A wood products industry is an attractive way to diversify rural economies because it is a land-based endeavour. In addition, wood products are processed in close proximity to raw material supplies, and their manufacture does not require a highly skilled work force – a requirement which might favour an urban location. Production and employment may also be less seasonal than they are for agriculture. This rural development argument for private forestry programs is essentially the same as the community stability justification for public timber harvests, and the issues raised earlier apply here as well. That is, what influence can a factor-supply policy have on regional production, and would an industry require a perpetual subsidy?

While forestry programs such as FIP have been driven primarily by concerns for timber production and rural development, they also provide the non-timber benefits of forests. The multiple-use language of FIP and other tree-planting programs indicates that a set of non-market benefits from tree-planting is anticipated. However, it is clear that these benefits are only ancillary to the timber production objectives of the program. If we cannot support the program on efficiency and equity grounds, it is conceivable that the non-market returns to wildlife habitat, outdoor recreation, and water course protection might justify program expenditures. However, it is unlikely that a program designed to promote intensive management for softwood timber would be the optimal instrument for providing these non-timber services.

DIRECTIONS FOR DISTRIBUTIVE ANALYSIS OF FOREST POLICIES

The preceding discussion of policies directed at forest management on private lands has considered only one of several important programs. The Forestry Incentives Program is a good focus for these discussions, because it clearly emphasizes timber production and, therefore, public intervention in a well-defined private market. It has also been a long-standing and well-funded program. FIP intends to increase timber supplies from non-industrial private lands through cost-sharing for forest management, primarily regeneration, activities. In addition, equity considerations may provide a secondary justification for FIP both through redistribution to lower-income households and as a part of a federal rural development and diversification agenda. Results of previous research question the efficacy of cost-sharing for afforestation to promote timber supply. They indicate that while this type of subsidy has a definite effect on tree-planting, it may not carry through to timber supply. Previous research also questions the distributional effects of the policy. Boyd and Hyde's study of FIP in North Carolina suggests, first, that households in the non-industrial ownership are generally more affluent than is the nation as a whole and, second, that the majority of FIP benefits go to the most affluent owners in that group. While their study is limited to North Carolina, and they note that results would differ between regions, these results suggest a serious flaw in the policy design. Acreage class is not a good proxy for income class.

The use of private forestry assistance to develop rural economies should be questioned on the same grounds as should the use of 'community stability' arguments for public timber harvesting. The only difference is that the policy instrument is much less direct. Analysts should question how a forest regeneration policy carries through to a timber supply effect and then how the effect can influence a region's industry. Two more important questions concern the appropriate duration of the program and whether or not the supported industry would require a perpetual subsidy. Analysts should also examine the distributional consequences of dedicating large areas of land to timber production and supplanting other agricultural endeavours. Shifts between these two land-using sectors hold implications for regional employment, income, and infrastructure.

These observations on FIP suggest the following issues for policymakers: First, there is the need for a clear definition of program goals. Mills (1975) points out that few federal programs are ever evaluated in terms of their intended effects. The first step in such an evaluation is to define the intentions of the program. The somewhat anecdotal evidence found in Congressional testimony suggests that many of these goals, especially distributive goals, are vague. The development of a metric or a set of metrics for measuring the extent of rural development would provide a first step towards adequate program evaluation. Analysis tools which provide information on the return to a region's basic resource and land factors of production would provide useful information in this regard. Second, while discussion here has focused on one policy intended to promote timber supplies, there are many other programs motivated by timber production concerns or by other non-market benefits. These and other agriculture programs have a critical bearing on land-use choices on private lands. Their accumulated effects, interactions, and contradictions provide a challenge for researchers and policy analysts. Rural development in general has been a piecemeal endeavour undertaken by several government agencies. A recent USDA report on the topic finds 'no single rural policy for the United States,' and that 'rural development programs operate without clearly stated and understood goals' (USDA 1989:3). Forestry programs are only a small part of the total effort in this area, and their influence can only be examined in the context of other sectors and rural development policies.

CONCLUSIONS

This paper has discussed distributional issues in forest policy in reference to two types of programs. One is the management of public forests where scheduling timber harvests and allocating land to various uses are motivated in part by concerns about local income and employment. The other is a somewhat less direct approach, aimed at influencing land-use and forest management on private lands through inducements such as tree-planting subsidies. Both types of policy intend to address regional, especially rural, economies primarily by encouraging wood production.

There are common themes in these two discussions. First, there is the need for clear statements of distributional or rural development roles for forestry programs. A part of defining these roles is an understanding and acceptance of the real limitations these policies may have in influencing rural development and income. Second, there is removing the vague normative focus of community stability and rural development policies and focusing instead on measuring the distributional consequences of management actions at the level of regional labour markets in terms of specific goals.

Research is needed in several areas. One area consists of defining the linkages between public production and subsidies and regional timber supplies. Especially important is the connection between public production and policies and the production from both industrial and non-industrial private lands. Another area is the increasingly important role of recreation and other non-timber benefits from forests in rural economies. How can forestry programs help rural areas capitalize on their comparative advantage in providing these services? In addition, the non-monetary benefits which rural residents derive from these services is an important aspect of the distributional effects of forestry programs. To the extent that public forest management and policies influence this rural quality of life, they also influence rural labour supply and income.

Two critical issues for program design are their spatial and temporal breadth. The diverse character of the national landscape and large regional differences in rural incomes suggest that certain areas would benefit more than would others from these programs. Targeting forestry program dollars in these areas would likely improve their effectiveness. In addition, program duration is a critical part of program design. Rural development programs, typically, intend to install community infrastructure or to develop human capital. Once these goals are achieved, communities and individuals are relieved of undesired isolation and may enter the economic mainstream. Other programs may be used to ease communities through transitions which necessarily alter infrastructure and population. In both cases, the objectives suggest programs with finite duration and that the optimal policy design includes policy termination.

NOTES

1 Schallau and Alston distinguish between (1) these timber suitability issues which are dominant in the Rocky Mountain States and (2) their definition of community stability, which addresses long run sustained yield harvests and focuses more on the Pacific Northwest. Because the U.S. Forest Service uses distributional criteria to schedule extramarginal timberland for harvesting (see, for example, USDA Forest Service 1987b:32), we find suitability to be an important part of the broader community stability issue.

2 Schallau and Alston discuss this issue and cite the original Douglas Fir Timber Supply Study in Oregon, which noted that communities in Oregon would lose population even with even-flows of timber.

3 Obermiller (1982) discusses equity-efficiency trade-offs in the context of

public grazing lands, the Taylor Grazing Act, and the 'Sagebrush Rebellion.' Because of geographic proximity to these 'free public goods,' local residents bear the greatest consequences of changes in public land management.

4 These issues have been discussed under the broad banners of new forestry and new perspectives in forestry. For a survey of viewpoints, scan the 1990 and 1991 issues of the Journal of Forestry. For a good general discussion see Salwasser (1990).

5 The NFMA anticipates the need to co-ordinate planning between National Forests. Analysis of regional effects might fall under section 219.8, which outlines regional guides.

6 The law initially limited the program to landowners with tracts no larger than 500 acres but gave the secretary of agriculture discretion to change the limit. In the intervening years this cap has risen to 1,000 acres.

7 While introducing the Forestry Incentives Act of 1973 to the Agriculture Committee of the U.S. House of Representatives, its author, Robert Sikes of Florida, described timber scarcity and attendant price increases as 'the principal reason for this bill' (U.S. Congress 1973:13).

8 For a survey of this literature, we refer the interested reader to a paper by Lee, Alig, and Moulton (1990).

9 Boyd and Hyde also investigate the effectiveness of technical assistance programs and suggest that these programs, aimed at disseminating information, have greater potential for influencing timber supply.

CHAPTER FOURTEEN

Instability in Forestry and Forestry Communities

Peter Berck, Diana Burton, George Goldman, and Jacqueline Geoghegan

Employment and output stability in timber industries has always been an objective of the National Forest System. It appears in the Organic Administration Act of 1897, which established the National Forest System (Waggener 1977:710). The Pinchot Letter of 1905, written by the first chief of the Forest Service, Gifford Pinchot, sets forth a priority of consideration for the local dominant industry (Schallau and Alston 1987). The Sustained-Yield Forest Management Act of 1944 clearly states forest policy objectives by beginning: 'In order to promote the stability of forest industries, of employment, of communities, and of taxable forest wealth, through continuous supplies of timber ...' (Waggener 1977:711). This stability objective is reflected in the sustained yield mandate of the Multiple-Use Sustained Yield Act of 1960, the long-range planning and non-declining flow provisions of the forest, the Rangeland Renewable Resources Planning Act of 1974, and the National Forest Management Act of 1976, respectively. These laws and their surrounding administrative policies reflect the extreme dependence of communities on the timber industry (Belzer and Kroll 1986:18).[1]

Given the attention to instability of forest dependent communities, it is natural to ask what is special about these communities. The second section of this paper examines the meaning of instability. It distinguishes growth or decline from economic fluctuation. The third section presents measures of instability for many industries in Oregon, a state heavily dependent upon the timber industry. From these estimates one can judge whether the timber industry really has less employment stability than do other industries. This is a different question from why the community has more or less employment instability than do other types of communities.

Studies in the literature concerning the problem of employment and community stability have been largely concerned with economic multiplier models or economic base models. In such models, a change in the timber industry employment affects total community employment directly and also through its impact on the employment in supporting industries (Kroll 1984; Perloff, et al. 1960; Perloff and Wingo 1961). Economic multipliers can be calculated from structural equations (e.g., Connaughton and McKillop 1979). For instance, input-output models have been used to construct multipliers resulting from shifts in demand for timber products (Connaughton and McKillop 1979) and from shifts in the supply of timber (Schallau and Maki 1983). They have also been used to assess the impact of different types of pulpmills on a community (Carroll and Milne 1982). The Forest Service has conducted extensive research to assess the economic efficiency and to determine the impact of cut decisions (e.g., Schallau and Polzin 1983; Forest Service 1982). A recent study by Connaughton, Polzin, and Schallau (1985) demonstrates that the traditional unidirectional approach of most input-output and economic base models misses important feedback from other sectors to the timber sector. Enlarging an input-output study to include such feedbacks creates a social accounting matrix (SAM), which is the approach taken in the third section of this paper. From a SAM one can determine how variance in the demand for a particular economic activity leads to variance in the level of overall output. We use the SAM framework to make estimates of how variable output would be in Humboldt County, California (a very timber dependent community) if it were dependent upon auto production or a diversified basket of the gross national product rather than upon timber. The model allows us to separate the effects of being a small, isolated county with an open economy from the effects of being dependent upon timber per se.

STABILITY

For community stability to make sense as a concept, it must be separated from community economic development. Consider the case of the United States, whose gross national product (GNP) growth rate is about 3 per cent. If GNP grew at exactly 3 per cent every year, it would not be described as unstable. Yet, a series with a 3 per cent growth rate for twenty years has a coefficient of variation (CV) (standard deviation divided by mean) of almost 20 per cent – quite a large value. The instability is the 'cycles' and fluctuations around these growth rates. By the same token, there is just as little sense in describing a sector whose employment shrinks at a constant 0.1 per cent per year as an unstable sector. These are not matters of stability; these are, logically, matters of growth or development or the lack of it.

Income and employment in forestry dependent communities depend upon both demand conditions and the resource base. Demand for wood products varies across the business cycle, giving rise to instability in income. In the Pacific Northwest, including northern California, the resource base is declining: the region is shifting from an old-growth to a second-growth economy. This secular trend, reinforced by technical progress, leads to the decline of some forest dependent communities. To those living in a forest dependent community, it matters quite a bit whether the mill closes because there is not any more timber or there is not any more demand. Downturns in demand are usually reversed: they are transitory and not permanent. Depletion of the resource base, or technical progress in milling, is more permanent. More generally, changes that are expected to last are, logically, matters of growth or development or the lack of it. Changes that are not expected to last are the problem of stability. While there are many possible definitions of stability, each of them separates the growth (or decay) process from some fluctuation around it.

There are three major ways of examining stability. The first concerns structural equations. Output (or employment) is modelled as depending upon a set of variables, some of which are random and some of which have trends. This gives a decomposition of changes in output and divides them into those attributable to permanent factors and those attributable to transitory factors. Structural equations do not explain the trends or cycles in the underlying variables, so the other two methods are then relied upon. The second method concerns regression (or smoothing) on time – output (or employment) is simply regressed (or smoothed) on time. The residuals are an estimate of what is transitory. The third method concerns the removal of the stochastic trend. It is the method of Beveridge and Nelson (1981) and is a logical extension of the second method to the case where trend is taken to be a random walk. We now discuss each method in turn.

The structural method requires an econometric model of the sector under consideration. For the old-growth redwood stumpage sector of the Northern California coast, Berck and Bentley (1989) estimated a reduced form model that would serve that purpose. They found that the redwood stumpage inventory elasticity of harvest was 0.5. Thus the rapid depletion of the old-growth resource causes a similarly rapid deterioration in output and, for that matter, employment. This process has some variation to it, mostly as a result of the establishment of new parks, but most of the variability in output is accounted for by a different set of variables. In the same study, the housing start elasticity of output was 0.3 and the addition and maintenance elasticity of output was 0.4. Thus a general 1 per cent increase in the level of housing activity results in a 0.7 per cent increase in redwood output. Housing activity varies between 1 million and 2 million starts within a couple of years, so this is truly a great source of variation in output.

While this structural description is useful in understanding why one should see both trend and cycle in forest related employment and output, it does not solve the problem of trend and cycle. It merely pushes it back to the problem of what is trend and what is cycle in forest inventory and housing. It still leaves the problem of what can reasonably be expected to persist, called trend, and what should wash out in the long run, called cycle.

The simplest way to separate trend from what is transitory (cycle and noise) is to regress the series on a function of time. This is a deterministic trend model. The residuals from the regression are taken as the transitory component – they comprise the cycle and they also comprise any random variation about the cycle. The logic is that the trend tracks the long-term processes while the residuals track the short-term fluctuations. The residuals represent changes in economic activity that are not expected to persist, so they are a measure of the stability of the economic activity. The cv is the summary statistic we use to measure stability.

In this study we used both simple regression on time and time squared and Lowess (Cleveland 1979)(a consistent form of nonparametric regression) for estimating the trend. The more flexible the regression surface, the smaller the apparent transitory elements, which is to say the smaller the instability.

The last method is that of Beveridge and Nelson (1981), which has the advantage of a firm logical base if not uniqueness. These authors reason that the level of activity can be decomposed into a permanent component and a transitory component. The permanent component consists of the current level of the variable, $z(t)$, plus a cyclic component $c(t)$. Assume the process z naturally grows at a deterministic rate, m, plus some stochastic rate. Define c as the forecast k period, hence $z(t+k \mid t)$ less $z(t)$ less the deterministic growth, $k\,m$, for suitably large k. The cycle is constituted by how much the series will rise or fall because of past stochastic events; it indicates how much the series would change if there were no further growth of either the stochastic or the deterministic kind. While this is an appealing definition of cycle, devoid of the rank empiricism of regression on time, it

depends upon a particular decomposition of the underlying time series. Since there are many such decompositions, it is not the only
way to get a stochastic trend model.

To examine the stability of the forestry sector, we will take recent
employment data for the state of Oregon. We have used total annual
forestry employment for the state of Oregon for 1947 to 1987 to estimate the cyclical component. Actual employment was on the order of
70-90 thousand employees. Figure 1 is both the actual and Lowess
predicted plot of employment on time.

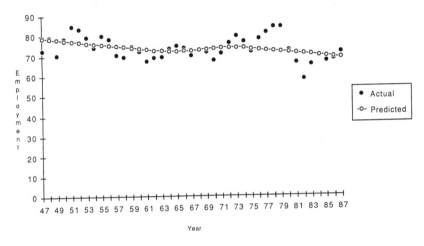

FIGURE 1
Oregon forestry employment (thousands)

The residuals of this regression are indicated by the solid dots in
Figure 2. On this basis, the difference between the top and bottom of
the cycle can be close to 20 per cent of employment. These are not
trivial fluctuations. For comparison, the residual standard error
from regression on a constant was 5.8, on a time trend it was 5.6, and
the residual standard error from Lowess was 5.3. Using the more
complicated technique reduces the estimate of instability by 10 per
cent.

The Beveridge and Nelson method is much more difficult to accomplish. The series is first fit to an ARIMA (autoregressive integrated moving average) model. A single differencing reduced the
log of series to stationarity. ARIMA (2,1,2) with a constant was selected based upon the autocorrelations and partial autocorrelations.
None of the residual autocorrelations approached two standard errors in size, and the Box-Pierce-Ljung portmanteau test statistics at

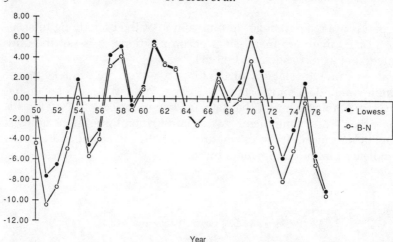

FIGURE 2
Cyclical portion of forestry employment (thousands)

12 lags and 24 lags were satisfactory (P = 0.7 and 0.9). The additional coefficients were not significant in either a (3,1,2) or (2,1,3) model. Thus the model seemed adequate. The coefficient estimates and their standard errors are presented in Table 1. The open dots in Figure 2 are the Beveridge and Nelson method estimates of the cyclical component of employment. They are remarkably similar to the Lowess residuals.

In summary, both the Beveridge and Nelson and the deterministic trend models provide plausible models of cyclic behavior. In both definitions, stability refers to only part of the variation in the series; the other part is attributed to trend. In the case examined, the answers from these two models are not much different. For the remainder of the paper we will stick with the simpler definition of

TABLE 1
ARIMA estimates

	Parameter estimates	STD error	T-statistic
AR(1)	−0.134	0.164	−0.82
AR(2)	0.316	0.164	1.925
MA(1)	−0.019	0.05	−0.377
MA(2)	0.95	0.044	21.39
Constant	−0.002	0.002	−0.93

transitory – the residuals from a regression – and quantify instability as the cv of these residuals.

COMPARING THE STABILITY OF SECTORS:
THE OREGON CASE

Oregon is generally regarded as a state in which forestry and forest products constitute a relatively large and important part of the economy. In addition to government employment in the national forests, roughly 38 per cent of private employment in Oregon is in the lumber, wood products, and paper sectors, with several counties more than 70 per cent dependent on lumber (Lettman 1988). The national forests cover 47 per cent of the commercial timberland in Oregon (Brodie, McMahon, and Gavelis 1978), and the users of timber got about 43 per cent of their logs from national forests in 1987 (Nokes 1987).

Monthly and annual data on those non-public sector jobs covered by state unemployment insurance (i.e., covered employment) were analyzed for the years 1947 through 1987. The data were detailed at the two digit Standard Industrial Classification (SIC) code level, allowing the forestry and wood products industries to be analyzed separately. The database covers all but a small number of those employed in Oregon; the notable exclusions from these counts are government employment and self-employed entrepreneurs.

Statistics on the raw monthly data for selected groups of SIC codes are presented in Table 2. The third column of Table 2 displays the coefficient of variation for each employment category, which measures the amount of variation, or stability, in the series. The highest coefficient by far is for agriculture and fisheries, where the standard deviation of the series is about 1.5 times the mean. These are highly seasonal industries. The smallest variation is in textiles and apparel manufacturing, suggesting relatively stable employment over the period of study. Overall, forestry has a surprisingly low coefficient of variation for an industry which is generally thought to have large variations in employment.

The consideration of the employment stability of an industry, over such a long time, should take into account long-term trends which may affect employment due to long-term changes in demand, technology, or resource availability. Therefore, each series was detrended and deseasonalized using a regression on a constant, eleven monthly dummys, a time trend, and a squared time trend. The R-squared indicates the amount of variability in each series explained by the constant, dummys, and trends. The regression re-

TABLE 2
Summary statistics for Oregon employment

Industry	Mean (000)	Standard deviation mean (000)	Standard deviation
Forestry	73.1	7.8	0.106
Forests	1.3	1.1	0.897
Lumber	72.4	8.0	0.110
Manufacturing	95.8	31.8	0.332
Equip. instrs.	28.5	17.2	0.604
Food	21.6	5.3	0.243
Metals	14.1	5.5	0.387
Paper	8.1	1.6	0.203
Printing	7.1	2.4	0.333
Petroleum, chemicals	2.3	0.5	0.201
Textiles, apparel	5.1	0.5	0.099
Other	6.0	2.4	0.393
Non-manufacturing	360.1	165.7	0.460
Services	89.9	63.1	0.702
Finance	32.2	16.4	0.511
Retail	118.8	48.8	0.410
Wholesale	42.5	16.0	0.376
Transportation & utilities	39.2	8.6	0.220
Construction	30.4	8.8	0.290
Mining	1.5	0.4	0.241
Agriculture & fisheries	5.6	8.3	1.469
Non-forestry (manufacturing plus non-manufacturing)	455.9	196.4	0.431
Total covered employment	529.5	195.7	0.369

sults, for some main aggregates, are presented in Table 3. For all of the main aggregates, except forestry, most of the variation is explained by these variables. The Durbin-Watson statistics show that all of these regressions have highly autocorrelated residuals. It is the autocorrelation of these residuals that give the residual series its cyclic shape. From the regression coefficients and t-statistics, one can see that the dummy variables for month are important and, for all but forestry, so are the time variables (either time or time squared or both). Forestry is the exceptional case, most particularly, the lumber sector.

Overall, variation in forestry employment is not very well explained by a constant and trends. However, the two components of this category have very different results for this regression. Covered private employment of foresters is largely explained by a constant, a negative trend, and a positive trend-squared. These coefficients are all highly significant. A negative trend for the overall forestry category was expected in view of technology changes and the depletion of private forestlands over the years. On the other hand, lumber employment is not well explained by the trends, though the constant is highly significant.

The detrending process has decreased the variation in all of the series, but a good amount of variation still remains in construction, mining, and agriculture and fisheries, which are typically seasonal industries. Compared to other categories, forestry is not markedly more variable.

The residuals of the data series are then composed of detrended, deseasonalized values, which represent the remaining variability of the employment. It is the stability of these numbers that can be appropriately discussed in terms of the stability which can be addressed by relatively short-term public policy. The statistics for these data are presented in Table 4. The means of the detrended, deseasonalized series are zero, and a residual variation coefficient (standard deviation of the residuals divided by the original mean) is employed.

Table 4 shows that there is nothing very special about employment in forestry. The cv for forestry is not meaningfully above that of manufacturing as a whole. The extractive sector (forests), which is small compared to the lumber sector, has a cv which is half of agriculture and fisheries but which is higher than any other sector in our study. The combined cv of the lumber and forests sectors, however, ranks in the middle of the sectors studied. Construction, mining, agriculture, metals, and equipment all have a much higher cv. The proper conclusion is that there is nothing very different about the

TABLE 3
Regression of employment (monthly data)

Variable	Coef. forestry	T-stat	Coef. manu-facturing	T-stat	Coef. non-manu-facturing	T-stat
Constant	70.33	51.87	37.01	21.52	147.44	25.54
Trend	-0.01	-1.09	0.20	18.13	0.11	3.08
Trend SQ	-8.38E-06	-0.52	3.04E-05	1.49	1.95E-03	28.47
Dec	3.29	2.32	1.97	1.09	13.71	2.27
Nov	6.03	4.24	5.04	2.79	14.23	2.35
Oct	8.40	5.91	9.30	5.16	18.40	3.04
Sep	11.28	7.94	14.06	7.80	25.97	4.29
Aug	11.93	8.40	14.42	8.00	26.27	4.34
Jul	10.90	7.67	8.89	4.93	25.16	4.16
Jun	10.55	7.42	6.98	3.88	23.03	3.81
May	7.56	5.32	1.47	0.82	12.46	2.06
Apr	5.07	3.57	0.69	0.38	8.19	1.35
Mar	2.32	1.64	0.37	0.21	3.07	0.51
Feb	0.71	0.50	0.00	0.00	-1.48	-0.24
R-square		0.33		0.94		0.97
Durbin-Watson		0.13		0.04		0.02

TABLE 4
Coefficient of variation by industry

Industry	Coefficient of variation	R-squared	Residual coefficient of variation
Forestry	0.106	0.334	0.086
Forests	0.897	0.885	0.304
Lumber	0.110	0.389	0.086
Manufacturing	0.332	0.936	0.084
Equip. instrs.	0.604	0.939	0.149
Food	0.243	0.921	0.068
Metals	0.387	0.877	0.136
Paper	0.203	0.989	0.068
Printing	0.333	0.720	0.036
Petroleum, chemicals	0.201	0.720	0.106
Textiles, apparel	0.099	0.365	0.079
Other	0.393	0.951	0.087
Non-manufacturing	0.460	0.973	0.075
Services	0.702	0.984	0.090
Finance	0.511	0.973	0.084
Retail	0.410	0.974	0.066
Wholesale	0.376	0.966	0.070
Transportation & utilities	0.220	0.960	0.044
Construction	0.290	0.635	0.175
Mining	0.241	0.558	0.160
Agriculture & fisheries	1.469	0.806	0.647
Non-forestry (manufacturing plus non-manufacturing)	0.431	0.970	0.074
Total covered employment	0.369	0.963	0.071

occupation of forestry. It is not more plagued by economic fluctuations than are other sectors in the economy. What is different about forestry is the extreme reliance of communities upon the forest industry (Belzer and Kroll 1984). The next section uses a SAM to examine that reliance.

COMMUNITY INSTABILITY: A SOCIAL ACCOUNTING
MATRIX ANALYSIS

To compare forestry with other (hypothetical) dominant sectors in a 'one industry' area, we examine the case of Humboldt county. We have taken an extended input-output (I-O) model for Humboldt County (Dean et. al. 1973) and recast it in the SAM framework. This SAM expresses the economic activity of 1969 as a function of exogenous demand for the county products. We use the model to find the implied instability in the county's value added and production as a function of the instability in the demand for its products. Also, we compare the existing instability with the instability that would result from several hypothetical alternatives.

A SAM (Pyatt and Round 1985; Pyatt and Thorbecke 1976) has all the elements for a small, linear, fixed price, general equilibrium model of a very open economy. The entries in Table 5 are all the production, transfer, and consumption flows, in thousands of dollars, for Humboldt County in 1969. The entry in the ith row and jth column is a sale or transfer from sector (or institution) i to sector (or institution) j. Equally, it is a purchase by j from i. The upper left hand corner (twenty-eight columns by twenty-eight rows) of the SAM is the transactions table, an unnormalized Leontief I-O model. For sector purchases, read down each column, and for sector sales, read across each row. For instance, forestry (the first column) purchases $23,000 from the logging sector and sells $31,357,000 to the sawmill sector. Below the I-O are rows representing the factors of production, labour and capital, institutions, households, government, and corporations; numbers in these rows represent payments to these agents.

For instance, forestry pays $5,377,000 to labour. To the right of the I-O matrix are the added columns representing factors of production and institutions, so that numbers in these columns represent the flow of goods and services to these sectors. For instance, labour pays households $247,751,000. In turn, households purchase goods from most other sectors (including $2,916,000 of other wood products). The penultimate column of the SAM is sales to the rest of the world – the county's net exports. These exports, also called final demand (FD), are taken as exogenous to the county and are determined mostly by macroeconomic conditions. In the experiments below, we simply replace FD with the value that exports would have in various years and under various circumstances, and we recalculate the table.

These experiments were carried out on a multiplier version of the SAM, which is explicitly written as an equilibrium system. To get this representation of our model required several steps. First, consider the first thirty-three columns and rows of Table 5, which are the whole of the SAM excluding the rest of the world and row and column totals. Divide each of these elements by its respective column total and call the result A. It is a matrix whose i,j^{th} element gives the percent of the jth sectors payments made to the ith sector. Let TP be the (33) vector of the total payments, TS be the (33) vector of total sales, and FD be the (33) vector of the final demands (labelled rest of world). Then

$$A \cdot TP + FD = TS.$$

Since total sales and payments are the same,

$$A \cdot TP + FD = TP$$

which can be solved in terms of the multiplier matrix, $(I-A)^{-1}$, for the multiplier equation:

$$TP = (I-A)^{-1} \cdot FD.$$

This equation gives the total payments vector as a function of the final demands. Our concern is with the payments to institutions within the county, most particularly to households. We have made the assumption that corporate profits are all taken out of the county, which is equivalent to saying that ownership of the timber companies is mostly from outside the county (which is true). Thus, we are interested in the 32nd element of TP, payments to households. Let e be a vector with zeros everywhere except the 32nd element, which is one. Local income in year t, L_t, is then a function of demand in year t given by

$$L_t = e' \cdot TP = e' \cdot (I-A)^{-1} \cdot FD_t$$

By collecting a series of observations on FD_t, it is a simple matter to construct a series of local payments L_t and calculate their CV or display their histograms. The major sectors in this economy are the forestry sectors, and we constructed FD_t for these sectors as follows: We collected time series data (1959-85) on county forestry employment and assumed that the variance in demand and employment were nearly the same. Sullivan (1988:43) shows, for the state of California, that the relation between sales and employment is more like 0.9, which seems close enough for our purposes. We scaled the employment series so that its mean was the same as forestry sales in 1969.

TABLE 5
Social accounting matrix

EXPENDITURES	Forest Products						Agriculture					
RECEIPTS	Forestry	Logging	Sawmills	Veneer-plywood	Pulpmills	Other wood	Field crops	Dairies	Other ag. items	Meat processing	Dairy process.	Other food proc.
Forest Products												
Forestry	770	33	31,357	6,564		275						
Logging	23		16,644	3,375		141						
Sawmills			186		13,034	1,155						
Veneer-plywood				594		409						
Pulpmills												
Other wood prod.						242			39			3
Agriculture												
Field crops						6	28		44			71
Dairies								267			7,000	
Other ag. items	516								99	19		27
Meat processing												7
Dairy processing												73
Other food proc.												117
Fishing and mining												
Seafood process.												
Mining												
Fisheries												

Other industry												
Construction						17						15
Boat-building						14						
Other local manf.		550	397			192	57	98	78			42
Transportation												
Water						30						12
Other	426	900	1,528		9,122	323		104		25		171
Trade												
Comm. & util.	76	57	1,386	126	3,047	145	23	93	113	10		70
Wholesale & retail	86	263	5,659	677	2,454	297	26	463	134	4	136	179
Finance & insur.	34	198	1,327	16	149	42	9	95	235	2		23
Real estate						131					107	46
Services												
Lodging												
Select. services	63	356	556	92	707	24	12	43	26	2	19	34
Entertainment												
Med., legal, etc.	23	116	522		142	36	3	143	79	1		29
Factors of production												
Labour	5,377	14,964	39,587	12,805	14,807	2,965	794	3,500	2,194	202	1,508	1,663
Capital	27,548	630	6,334	1,440	3,027	463	4	118	47	18	92	238
Institutions												
Corporations												
Households												
Local gov't	2,039	58	1,784	406	3,629	242	86	435	480	5	83	148
Rest of world	2,115	2,210	16,922	2,153	9,243	2,405	178	2,712	463	493	5,398	2,837
Totals	39,096	20,335	124,189	28,248	59,361	9,540	1,234	8,071	4,031	781	14,343	5,805

(continued next page)

TABLE 5 (*continued*)

EXPENDITURES	Fishing and mining			Other industry			Transportation		Trade			
	Seafood proc.	Mining	Fisheries	Construction	Boat-building	Other local manf.	Water	Other	Comm. & utils.	Whole & retail	Finance & insur.	Real estate
RECEIPTS												
Forest Products												
Forestry										50		
Logging												
Sawmills				539		967			3	6		
Veneer-plywood				333		213						
Pulpmills												
Other wood prod.				192		195			67	39		
Agriculture												
Field crops								7				
Dairies												
Other ag. items				8					2			
Meat processing						2				2		
Dairy processing						36				58		
Other food proc.								2		35		
Fishing and mining												
Seafood process.												
Mining	7,316			157								
Fisheries								8		8		

Other industry												
Construction	139	5	481		1	18	28	432	256	135	62	83
Boat-building							3		2			
Other local manf.	99		44				4	22	26	154	134	18
Transportation												
Water							409	11		13		
Other		9	105	343	2	12	37	908	92	308	25	18
Trade												
Comm. & util.	107	17	68	131	3	235	33	166	1,450	1,030	701	32
Wholesale & retail	57	7	397	1,341	1	226	22	265	34	56	171	31
Finance & insur.	68	29		94	2	109	47	124	133	452	2,345	33
Real estate							36	281	33	591	906	62
Services												
Lodging												
Select. services	15	9	33	67	1	70	8	26	98	311	189	25
Entertainment										26	87	
Med., legal, etc.	34	135		22	1	191	20	97	256	630	746	40
Factors of production												
Labour	3,053	1,420	5,288	4,987	320	10,862	2,448	11,194	12,020	50,264	10,920	2,744
Capital	438	372	61	927	4	177	0	800	6,887	1,605	1,903	72
Institutions												
Corporations												
Households	133	72	56	404	12	506	90	440	650	1,101	566	91
Local gov't												
Rest of world	623	763	805	8,252	140	6,110	333	2,823	3,850	7,371	3,471	317
Totals	12,082	2,838	7,338	17,797	487	19,929	3,518	17,606	25,859	64,245	22,226	3,566

(continued next page)

TABLE 5 (continued)

EXPENDITURES	Services				Factors of production		Corps.	Institutions		Rest of world	Totals
	Lodging	Select. services	Entertainment	Med., leg., etc.	Labour	Capital		Households	Local gov't		
RECEIPTS											
Forest Products											
Forestry							0			47	39,096
Logging										152	20,335
Sawmills					0					108,260	124,189
Veneer-plywood						0				26,699	28,248
Pulpmills										59,361	59,361
Other wood prod.								2,916		5,886	9,540
Agriculture											
Field crops								817			1,234
Dairies			7				0			1,071	8,071
Other ag. items					0	0	0	3,353			4,031
Meat processing				2				768			781
Dairy processing				28				5,715		8,433	14,343
Other food proc.				14				5,637			5,805
Fishing and mining											
Seafood process.					0	0	0	1,361		10,721	12,082
Mining		3								2,667	2,838
Fisheries										11	7,338

	Lodging	Select. services	Entertainment	Med., legal, etc.	Labour	Capital	Corporations	Households	Local gov't	Rest of world	Totals
Other industry											
Construction		5	25	106	0	0	0	5,745	2,732	7,980	17,797
Boat-building					0	0	0				487
Other local manf.		22	43	149	0	0	0	1,322		16,478	19,929
Transportation											
Water					0	0	0			3,043	3,518
Other		12	10	28	0	0	0	347	347	2,751	17,606
Trade											
Comm. & util.	241	1,229	99	471	0	0	0	13,303	738	591	25,859
Wholesale & retail	11	72	87	205	0	0	0	47,635	1,044	2,670	64,245
Finance & insur.	4	59	39	142	0	0	0	10,860	470	4,582	22,226
Real estate		61	494	225	0	0	0		14	686	3,566
Services											
Lodging					0	0	0		344	4,100	4,444
Select. services	56	257	25	78	0	0	0	2,496	84	7,182	12,964
Entertainment		106	106		0	0	0	3,499		1,235	4,953
Med., legal, etc.	11	172	236	748	0	0	0	21,034	1,878	1,161	28,506
Factors of production											
Labour	3,463	5,603	1,163	21,636	0	0	0	0	0	28,607	276,358
Capital	8	235	1,791	0	0	0	0	0	0		55,239
Institutions											
Corporations					28,607	55,179	0	0	0	0	83,786
Households	328	4,904	124	725	247,751	0	83,786	46,731	29,503	36,206	360,191
Local gov't		330			0	60	0	14,981	0	12,793	42,797
Rest of world	322	704	704	3,949	0	0	0	172,018	5,643	0	353,373
Totals	4,444	12,964	4,953	28,506	276,358	55,239	83,786	360,191	42,797	353,373	1,735,136

Then we smoothed the series and saved the residuals from the smooth. These residuals, our estimate of the variation in (the six) total forestry demands, were added to the 1969 value of forestry demand to produce the section of the time series FD_t relating to the forestry sectors. Manufacturing was treated similarly. For agriculture and fisheries, actual output figures were used and the same procedure was followed. This procedure yielded L_t, and from there it was a simple matter to compute its cv. By construction, its mean was exactly its 1969 value. Another way to reach the same result is to take the variance of the expression for household income. Let v be the variance operator, so $v(FD)$ is the variance covariance matrix of final demands, then

$$V(L_t) = e' \cdot (I\text{-}A)^{-1} \cdot V(FD_t) \cdot (I\text{-}A)^{-1'} \cdot e.$$

The formula shows that the variance in household incomes depends upon the covariances of the various final demands. Thus, adding an activity to Humboldt County that is well correlated with forestry will do little to reduce the cv of activity. This way of thinking about the problem is akin to portfolio theory, although previous practitioners do not recognize the role of the SAM multiplier. We shall not follow this approach further here.

We compare the instability in household payments caused by the actual instability, mostly caused in the forestry sectors, to several hypothetical cases. Our first counterfactual is that Humboldt County is dependent upon a (properly scaled) automobile sector rather than on forestry. That is, we replace the stochastic elements in FD_t with elements that mirror the smoothed residuals of automobile production in the United States rather than with forestry in Humboldt County. For the second case, we examine a dominant industry with the same stochastic element as one-half of the forestry section and one-half of the automobile section. It gives an example of the power of diversification. Finally, we consider the maximum diversification possible – an export sector which mirrors the national GNP in stability characteristics. To preserve the covariance structure of $v(FD)$, twenty-seven years worth of data from Humboldt County containing the fish, dairy, and 'other industries' sectors are contained in all the counterfactuals.

The coefficient of variation in the forestry case (.056) is less than the coefficient of variation in the auto case (.080), less than the coefficient of variation in the one-half autos and one-half forestry case (.065), and slightly more than the coefficient of variation (.047) in the GNP-like industry case. Thus, the forestry case has less instability than the automobile case and the one-half auto, one-half forestry case and only slightly more instability than the GNP-like case.

Should a local industry which is one-half forestry and one-half autos reduce the variability of total payments of the local economy? If the two industries were counter-cyclical, then this kind of diversification should produce a smoother economy with less instability. As it happens, we can see from the results that the one-half forestry and the one-half auto economy lie in between the auto economy and the forestry economy, as might be expected if the correlation between them is small.

An economy based on forestry has the hazard of being based on one industry but, in terms of the stability in total payments based on the business cycle, may be no worse off than other communities based on one industry. Certainly, the forestry industry has been in decline since the 1960s, and this decline has had disastrous consequences for communities. However, as mentioned above, that is not the issue we are looking at here.

As might be expected, the GNP-like economy has the lowest instability of any of the experiments. This is not very surprising. The somewhat surprising result is that the forestry-based local economy is not that much worse off than is the GNP-like economy insofar as the instability in total payments is concerned. Having demand follow the stochastic elements of GNP rather than forestry reduces cv by only 16 per cent. This is partially because export sectors (such as forestry) with high leakage to the outside world are insulated by this leakage from the full effects of the instability of the outside world. This has very interesting and ironic implications as far as community development and local economic development strategy is concerned. For some time, rural communities in decline have been told to look for import substitution and/or low leakage activities for economic development purposes. Our GNP-based experiment is an extreme example of such a policy. However, this experiment does not capture the full consequences of diversification. An import substitution policy necessarily has lower leakages to the rest of the economy. Lower leakages mean higher multipliers, and stability varies as the square of the multiplier. Thus, our estimate that cv can be reduced by 16 per cent by full diversification is certainly an upper bound of what can be accomplished by full diversification.

The other strategy for rural development has been diversification (Belzer and Kroll 1986). As we have seen with our one-half forestry and one-half auto economy experiment, this strategy does not necessarily lead to less instability than exists in the forestry economy. If the 'diversified' new activities respond to movements in the national GNP in the same way as do the forestry sectors, or if they are simply highly variable in and of themselves, this diversification may actually increase the instability problem.

CONCLUSION

Humboldt County and other forestry dependent communities do indeed suffer from considerably more variation in employment than do urban areas. Humboldt has two and one-half times the employment coefficient of variation (cv) of the state of California as a whole. The causes and cures for this large variation in employment, however, are not necessarily to be found in forest policy.

In the West, forest employment is declining because of the change from an old-growth to a young-growth economy and the attendant technological progress. Superimposed upon this decline is a variation in employment caused by the business cycle. The variation caused by the business cycle is what we call instability.

The instability in forestry, as an industry, can be measured many different ways. Deviation from trend or stochastic trend both give the same answers in this case. The instability in forestry as an industry is about the same as that in other manufacturing and a good deal less than that in agriculture. We performed the experiment of constructing a 'Humboldt' dependent upon automobiles rather than on forests. The results are striking. Taken from the position of employment cv, Humboldt would have an even higher cv of employment if its one major export industry were automobiles rather than trees.

One line of argument is that the workings of monetary policy are responsible for the instability across the business cycle: the Federal Reserve is responsible for employment instability in Humboldt County and, therefore, someone in Washington should fix it. This paper has shown that instability in forestry is basically no different from instability in many other industries. Therefore, if Washington should fix the forestry problem, it should also fix the problems in all other cyclical industries. Special national level counter-cyclical policy for forestry does not seem justified.

Although forestry does not have a different cv from much of the rest of manufacturing, forestry is usually practised in a far more isolated locale than is manufacturing. Big expanses of big trees simply do not exist in large, economically diversified places. This isolation, true more for California forestry than for California agriculture, leads to areas (such as Humboldt County) having very little economic diversification. Clearly, the lack of diversification costs Humboldt a higher cv of employment. However, this does not mean that there are any feasible policies to reduce the cv.

We performed the experiment of constructing a 'Humboldt' with the forest industry replaced by an industry with the instability characteristics of the u.s. gnp. This is surely the limit of feasible diversification. In this case the cv decreases from .056 to .047, which is a 16 per cent decrease. It is hard to see what industries Humboldt could attract to achieve even this limited benefit. A single manufacturing plant, such as the Hewlett Packard plants in Corvallis or Roseville, is not beyond the realm of imagination. Ten such plants in different industries would be impossible, as the infrastructure or the pool of skilled labour does not exist. Thus, diversification as great as the economy as a whole is surely not possible.

All the experiments that we have performed keep intact the basic structure of Humboldt County: the strong interaction among the industries (dictated by remote location), the farm economy, and so on. Since changing the major industry for a diversified portfolio of industries only reduces the cv by 16 per cent, and Humboldt has 250 per cent of the cv of California as a whole, it must be the special structure of Humboldt that causes the variation. We believe that this special structure is constituted by the strong linkage of activities caused by the remote location and high transportation costs. This, we believe, is inherent in the remote nature of Western timber producing regions.

Two types of policies could reduce the employment cv in forest-dependent communities. The national government could intentionally stabilize housing starts. While this would certainly be appreciated in Humboldt county, the same argument could be made with greater force for those Midwest communities dependent upon agriculture and for just about any community dependent upon a single manufacturing industry. This lack of truly special status, combined with a desire to use monetary policy to meet other macro goals, makes this type of national policy very unlikely. The second type of policies is constituted by those that diversify industry locally. The remote nature of the Humboldt economy and its small size both argue for a rather limited amount of possible diversification. Without changing the nature of the economy by turning it into a major metropolitan area, the limit to diversification seems to be a 16 per cent reduction in employment cv.

ACKNOWLEDGMENTS

We would like to thank H. Alan Love and Vijay Pradhan for comments; all remaining errors are our responsibility. This is Department of Agricultural and Resource Economics Working Paper No. 512.

NOTES

1 Other relevant literature includes a study concluding that employment in a timber-dependent town is more unstable than it is in a large diversified town both relatively and in absolute numbers (Byron 1979). Stevens (1979) claims that a better understanding of the nature of wood products employment is needed to account for those peripheral workers who also work in other industries. Rufolo, Strathman, and Bronfman (1988); Stere, Hopps, and Lettman (1980); Schallau, Olson, and Maki (1988); Olson and Schallau (1988) all have analyzed community stability with respect to timber-dependent regions, and most recommend consideration of policy actions to alleviate the changes in employment which are observed or modelled.

2 In macroeconomics the same dichotomy is often made, but see James Stock and Mark Watson (1988) for a more modern view that emphasizes the interaction of trend and cycle.

CHAPTER FIFTEEN

Global Markets in Forest Products: Sociological Impacts on Kyoto Prefecture and British Columbia Interior Forest Regions

M. Patricia Marchak

The development of global markets in forestry, as in other industries, has impacts on local communities. The growth of the paper and paperboard industry in Osaka and other industrial cities of Japan, for example, has affected several communities in British Columbia, where large pulpmills have been constructed or enlarged to serve that market. The sale of logs and lumber by BC companies to Japanese buyers, as another example, has affected small, rural communities in the Kyoto Prefecture where the imports have displaced domestic supplies. This article is concerned with these local effects of global change in the forest industry.

My purposes are to investigate the social and environmental impacts of markets that link regions in Japan and British Columbia together; to introduce a comparative perspective into the study of BC's forest industry; and to suggest that the cost of economic transactions is not fully estimated unless the social and environmental impacts are included in the accounting.

Data sources include both documents and fieldnotes obtained in interviews during the summers of 1988 and 1989. Interviews were conducted in the mountain villages of the Kyoto Prefecture of Japan and in towns located in the Fraser Fort-George and Cariboo regional districts of British Columbia. In Japan, research was directed to the impacts of the changing log market. In the BC interior regions, research was directed to the social context in which both logs and raw pulp are exported to Japan.

OVERVIEW

British Columbians think of BC as one of the world's great suppliers of forest products, and they think of Japan as a minor player in this

TABLE 1
Selected BC exports, forest products

		Total	% to Japan
Logs exported			
(thousand cubic metres)	1979	776.3	100
	1987	3,394.9	73
	1988	2,831.1	66
Lumber shipments			
(million board feet)	1979	12,743.0	12.6
	1987	16,790.8	12.6
	1988	17,089.0	11.7
Market pulp shipments			
(thousand metric tonnes)	1979	3,095.0	19.4
	1987	4,238.0	20.0
	1988	4,141.0	21.2
Woodchips export			
(thousand metric tonnes)	1979	887.0	38.4
	1987	775.0	67.3
	1988	1,416.0	42.6

SOURCE: Council of Forest Industries, British Columbia Forest Industry Statistical Tables, compiled from Statistics Canada data, Ministry of Labour data, and other sources. Market pulp data from COFI library, based on Canadian Pulp and Paper Association data

particular industry. As data presented in Table 2 indicate, Japan has less acreage, fewer trees, and its sawmills are many but small; nonetheless, with imported wood, chips, and pulp supplies, Japan actually produces lumber equivalent in quantity to about 85 per cent of BC's total, and Japan is the world's second largest producer of paper and paperboard (the United States is the largest). The implication is evident: BC produces more raw material, while Japan produces much more of the finished product.

Forestry in Japan is not conducted by integrated corporations. Families own private woodlots; co-operatives of owning families and communities manage forest lands; sawmills are independent and, often, co-operatively owned by communities. Pulpmills, located outside the forest regions (except on the northern island of Hokkaido), purchase logs and woodchips on both domestic and foreign markets and use recycled paper as part of their resource input. Table 2 provides a profile of the differences between the Japanese and BC organization and production.

TABLE 2

Comparisons, selected features of forestry in Japan and British Columbia

Feature		Japan	BC
Forest area			
(million hectares)		25.2	51.1[1]
ownership			
(as % of total forest land)		private: 56[2]	crown: 95
		national: 31	companies: 5
		community: 13	
organization, woodlands		co-operatives	companies
linkages between sectors		limited	integrated
log production			
(ooo cubic metres)	1979	33,270	76,194[3]
	1985	32,944	76,868
Sawmills			
(# establishments)	1979	22,541	350
	1985	18,834	349
Lumber production			
(ooo cubic metres)	1979	39,586	30,359
	1985	28,403	33,044
Sawmills			
(# employees)	1979	197,570	51,369
	1985	139,475	39,044
Pulp production			
(ooo metric tonnes)	1979	9,065	5,523
	1985	8,417	6,175
Paper, paper-board production			
(ooo metric tonnes)	1979	16,156	2,154
	1985	18,569	2,753

SOURCES: Japan: R. Handa (ed.) (1987), *Forest Policy in Japan*, appendices; BC: Statistics Canada (various years), *Canadian Forestry Statistics*, cats. 25-202, 36-204, and compilations provided by COFI

NOTES: [1] CFS 1986; however, BC Min. Forests 1987-8 lists 45.9 million ha. Total and 26.6 million ha. stocked with mature timber

[2] 89% of private owners are households

[3] for BC, 90,591 in 1987 and 86,807 in 1988

Since the opening of the Japanese log market to imports, the rural villages dependent on log and lumber production have suffered economic decline and depopulation. Japanese forest economists and many villagers in the Kyoto Prefecture believe that log imports are largely responsible for these developments. They also believe that North Americans insufficiently restock trees and inadequately practise forest management and that the cheapness of imported logs is due to these inadequacies. Widely shared beliefs, or perceptions of events, are important features of social life, and they are among both the impacts and the causes of social change. The nature of these beliefs is examined, together with their context. It is suggested that the perceptions have some basis in fact. The log market contributes to, but it does not in itself cause, economic decline and depopulation; and the cheapness of North American logs may be due to various factors, including the relatively low cost of the resource to North American harvesters.

The export of logs to Japan is also controversial in BC, where opponents of the practice argue that jobs in secondary industry are thereby foregone. However, there is not similar debate about the export of woodchips and pulp, which embed labour inputs. These exports are perceived to sustain employment and to stabilize forest towns. This perception is also examined. Profits and production levels in BC have increased in response to Japanese market demand, but employment in the forest industries has steadily declined and dependent towns are far from stable. As well, the capacity of mills in BC exceeds the sustainable resource base.

Of particular note for comparisons of the Kyoto Prefecture and the interior regions of British Columbia is the difference in the nature of communities. The prefecture's communities are organized first on a basis of kinship and ancient mutual obligations and then through numerous co-operatives. Governments at the national, prefectural, and municipal levels are understood to be supportive allies for co-operative and village enterprises. Negotiations between government agencies and local leaders are normal and frequent occurrences. There are neither unions nor any other institutionalized form of opposition to co-operatives and private forest owners. By contrast, British Columbia's communities are organized on a basis of individual employment in large corporations or businesses serving these corporations; conflict is institutionalized via company/union and company/contractor negotiations; there are numerous oppositional interest groups, including aboriginal peoples and environmentalists; and government is not viewed as an ally so much as an umpire (and, for some, as an enemy). Because of these differences in culture and social organization, the impact of declining employment in the Kyoto Prefecture is expressed not only in individual terms but also in terms of the community. In British Columbia, unemployment tends to be an individual experience even when unions or other associations decry it.

Another difference is in community attitudes towards forests and wood. Culture, as much as economics, influences forest practices in the prefecture, and the aesthetic value of wood is crucial to rural Japanese culture. There is no evidence that a similar value orientation is prevalent in British Columbia.

In examining the impacts of the log and lumber markets in the prefecture and the expansion of pulp production in the BC interior regions, I note developments that undermine the economic and social viability of rural communities and contribute to the depletion of softwood forests. It is not, however, my objective to argue that international markets are, in some absolute sense, 'bad.' Rather, my intention is to show cause for taking such social and environmental impacts into account and for including them in our evaluations of economic transactions.

FORESTRY IN JAPAN

Since the re-opening of the Japanese log market to imports in 1959, hemlock and other softwood species from Canada and the United States have provided raw material for Japanese sawmills and pulpmills. Domestic timber constituted some 70 per cent of total fibre supplies in Japan in 1965 but only 50 per cent in 1969 and 44 per cent in 1985 (Handa 1988:23, Appendix Tables 6-2).[1] Japanese forest economists conducted fieldwork in the northwestern United States in 1987 and argued, on the basis of their data, that u.s. log sales were causing economic decline and out-migration in Japanese rural forest regions and unemployment in corresponding regions of the United States. They did not investigate the situation in British Columbia as rigorously but suggested that the same effects pertained in Canadian regions (Iwai 1989). The Canadian component of the International Woodworkers of America and others independently argued a similar case. The Japanese economists also argued that American log exports in the early 1980s created a shortage and escalation of prices on the domestic American market, thus creating a niche for relatively less expensive Canadian lumber imports. They suggested that the countervailing duty imposed on Canadian imported lumber was an outcome of the high price of American wood (Iwai 1989). Exports of logs from BC to Japan increased markedly after the imposition of the duty.

At the time of the Japanese study in 1987, up to 25 per cent of all privately-owned timber cut in the Pacific Northwestern states was exported as logs (Iwai 1989). In British Columbia, the export limit of 2.6 per cent in the 1970s was modified after 1982 and up to 4 per cent of the total harvest was exported, most of it to Japan, by 1987. With marginally improved lumber prices in 1988, the proportion exported declined slightly, and in March, 1989, the BC government imposed a higher fee-in-lieu of manufacturing for sawlogs to reduce their export. However, in May of that year, when I conducted field research in Japan, the Kyoto log market was heavily stocked with imported sawlogs from both the United States and Canada.

Some portion of these logs consists of Douglas-fir and other high-quality species and grades, for which there is no competitive domestic source in Japan, and the Japanese foresters were not arguing against their importation. Logs imported by pulpmills in the coastal regions of Japan were also not the source of anxiety, since there is insufficient local supply. Rather, their concern was with hemlock, cedar, and other species and/or grades which compete with locally produced *sugi* (Japanese cedar) and *hinoki* (a yellow cypress) for use in general construction.

Imported lumber was not yet recognized as an issue of the same order as imported logs by the economists or forest owners in the Kyoto Prefecture, whom I interviewed in 1989. This may be because relatively small quantities reach the rural region, their sawmills have decreasing shares of the national market in any event, and imported lumber is thus less easily identified as a local problem. However, Japan is now, by far, the largest single market for lumber exported from North America (The United States remains Canada's largest market), and, with declining timber supplies in North America, more lumber is likely to be shipped to Japan in place of logs (Hay-Roe's PaperTree Letter, 1 Oct. 1989).

Imported logs in Japan were cheaper than were domestic logs throughout the 1980s. The low price must reflect, in some part, at least, the exchange rate on the dollar and the escalating value of land in Japan. However, Japanese forest owners interviewed during my study attributed this largely to conditions in North America; specifically, the low stumpage value of publicly owned timber, a lack of reforestation, and insufficient silviculture. They argued that because Canadians and Americans undervalue the resource and do not adequately nurture or replenish it, the companies can log and ship it to Japan at a total cost well below the costs of production within Japan.

Japanese forestry is labour-intensive. Average wage rates for silvicultural workers rose steadily between 1961 and 1985 (estimates provided in interviews varied from between five to fourteen times), while the average stumpage price of (privately owned) sugi rose by only 67 per cent (Kumazaki 1988:12). Wage rates were cited as a cause of the price differential but always in the context of the low labour input to reforestation and silviculture in North America.

The Japanese economists argued, further, that millworkers in North America, whose wages were also rising, were disemployed by forest companies when the decline in prices for dimensional lumber in the early 1980s reduced company profits and companies chose to export logs instead of manufacturing lumber. Such a disregard for the rights of workers would be unusual in Japan, where most employees have lifetime security.

Forestry in Japan has evolved as a non-integrated industry, with the woodlands operations organized largely around co-operative village enterprise and with a strong emphasis on afforestation, silviculture, and good resource management. Some reference to this history will contextualise the issues perceived by Japanese forest owners and economists.

Organization and History of Forestry in Japan

Forest land in most of Japan (excluding Hokkaido) is largely owned by private families, and most holdings are less than five hectares, though there are occasional large holdings. In addition, there are National Forests under central government control and community forests under municipal control. Some private holdings date back to the late Tokugawa period, from 1590 to 1868, when some hamlets divided forest land amongst residents (Totham 1986; Funakoshi 1988). Shogunate lands were similarly distributed in the subsequent Meiji era, from 1868 to 1912, with the larger part divided amongst ex-samurais and other high-ranking persons. The landowning class was further enlarged under the terms of the National Forest Law (1899) and other legislation, but, throughout this history, hamlets or municipalities retained control of some forest land to be cultivated as a commons, and a National Forest reserve was established and maintained. A Forest Service was established in 1879, and its management role was enhanced through subsequent legislation. Both reforestation and afforestation were undertaken, with planting in both private and public sectors reaching a peak around 1910 (Totham 1985; Kumazaki 1988).

The formation of forest owners' co-operatives took place after a 1907 amendment of the Forest Law, allowing owners to form a co-operative when two-thirds of their number in a region, owning in total two-thirds of the forested area, agreed to do so; once formed, all owners in the municipality were obliged to join (Funakoshi 1988:20). Subsequent legislation imposed obligations on forest co-operatives to carry out National Forest policies. The co-operatives, thus, became the basic management units, with the Forest Service providing the professional expertise and maintaining the National Forests. In 1939, the forest co-operatives were obliged by new legislation to draw up silvicultural plans for all members and to engage in afforestation. Subsidies were provided for planting.

During the Second World War, overcutting depleted forests and further depletion occurred during the following decade of high wood demand (Kumazaki 1988:12). There were few construction alternatives to wood and no imported competitive timber. Domestic lumber enjoyed high prices. The central government actively encouraged afforestation, and new sugi and hinoki forests were planted during this time in order to reach commercial size by the turn of the century. A new Forest Law, enacted in 1951, charged the prefectural governments with drawing up regional forest plans in non-governmental forests. Private owners had to cut or plant in accordance with government plans, and prohibitions on cutting trees under the standard rotation age (about thirty-five to forty-five years) were imposed. At the same time, subsidies for new plantations were provided and low interest loans were given to forest owners (Handa 1988b:22-4).

Another law of 1958 introduced the share renting system in afforestation. Forest owners, capital suppliers, and groups in charge of afforestation could opt to join forces under contract to divide the revenue from harvests. The central government's intention was to induce pulpmill companies to provide capital for afforestation. Pulpmills located in coastal cities had, up to that time, gradually enlarged their paper and paperboard production, but they obtained much of their fibre off-shore. They were disinclined to integrate backwards within Japan, except in Hokkaido and northern Honshu, where traditional practices were less firmly embedded. The central government finally provided the capital.

The removal of the quota system of foreign exchange for timber imports in 1959 was occasioned by a domestic supply shortage. This continued through the early 1960s, despite increased production in national and private forests. The banning of (oak-based) charcoal burning intensified the dependence of forest owners on softwood markets. Thus, the two market forces were developing, simultaneously, an increased reliance on imported wood and an increasing participation in the market by domestic suppliers.

Government policies since the 1960s have aimed at increasing the self-sufficiency of small forest owners while retaining restrictions on silviculture and planting on larger holdings. Small woodlot owners have been encouraged to draft their own management plans, and they receive income tax incentives for cutting according to approved plans. Hamlets have been encouraged to divide community forests amongst residents and to rent portions of the national forests. Many of the community forests, amounting to about 10 per cent of the total forest land base, have been reorganized as forest producers' co-operatives – a uniquely Japanese form of private/community ownership. In 1974, further amendments to the forest management plan system encouraged owners to form blocks comprising between 30 and 50 hectares and to develop regional plans for these rather than for private holdings. Government subsidies have been provided throughout the years since 1964 for forest roads, silviculture and logging equipment, and for start-up costs to build co-operatively owned sawmills (Handa 1988b). In numerous other ways, government policies have supported the development of co-operatives.

The high market demand for general construction lumber continued until about 1973, though by that time ferral cement, metal, and other wood substitutes had come into general use. Since that date, the demand for both lumber and logs has declined. Yet the potential domestic supply has steadily increased. Human-made forest stands of fifteen to thirty years now account for half of all stands and will reach commercial age by the turn of the century. Thus, the problem in the forest regions is the result of several conditions: a declining demand, a highly competitive external supply, and a domestic supply that is now approaching maturity. The external supply, essential in earlier conditions, is now perceived by forest owners and workers to be an impediment to the economic survival of domestic suppliers.

As demand shifts downward, further afforestation and previous regional plans are put in doubt. Even the National Forests, which had provided the leading role in control of the domestic timber market during the 1960s, have, since the mid-1970s, accumulated a deficit. The central government has revised its harvesting plans and reduced its employment. [2]

Opinion polls in Japan indicate strong support for reforestation irrespective of commercial values, and members of hamlet co-operatives and private owners alike appear to hold forests in high regard for immaterial reasons (Handa 1988b; Ishii 1985; Mitsuda and Geisler 1988 and fieldnotes); nonetheless, forestry regions are caught in an economic bind. For economic purposes, it is hardly worthwhile thinning and selectively harvesting trees; even the forest owners seek work in urban centres, with their forest lands becoming more like hobby farms than central work locations. A gradual out-migration from the more remote towns, and growth of commuter work patterns in regions closer to industrial centres, are predominant trends in the 1980s; rural Japan is disappearing just as the new forests reach maturity.

Kyoto Prefecture

Since my research task was to understand the local impacts and local interpretations of these events, I conducted fieldwork in the Tanba Highlands of the Kyoto Prefecture in May 1989. Also, since the identified issue there was the log market, I concentrated on it. What follows are brief summaries based on fieldnotes in three municipalities (cho, translated somewhat misleadingly as towns), each with populations of under 8,000. Prior to the building of roads in the 1920s and 1930s, these towns produced rice, matsutake and shiitake mushrooms, charcoal (from oak), and some construction timber, but they were quite isolated from the cash economy. They were more or less self-sufficient in food production. Following transportation improvements, and subsequent legislation outlawing charcoal, logs and lumber became major products and remain so today.

Private forest holdings in these towns are small, with between 65 and 71 per cent of all holdings under five hectares (varying by town).[3] Community and temple forests are managed by community organizations and local forest owners, with residents providing free labour or the town contracting work by local loggers and silviculturalists. Proceeds from community forests are used for local projects.

Two of the three towns, located furthest from Kyoto, have suffered extreme depopulation. In one, the population has declined from over 10,000 in 1960 to just under 6,000 and, of those remaining, 30 per cent are over sixty years of age; the other town is similar. Ninety-five per cent of high school graduates left one town for city employment in the 1980s. A town councillor and leader of the forest owners addresses the problem. He grew up in the town, and stayed on, as was always the custom, because he was the eldest son. His son attends high school in Kyoto, because his chances of gaining entry to a good university are thereby much improved. The son should, like his father before him, inherit the forest land and return there to live, but the father is unsure that the inheritance is sufficiently attractive under current economic conditions. The forests are not capable of providing a livelihood at the present time, and local owners, who earlier anticipated increasing returns on their investments in replanted forests as they reach maturity, now recognize the distinct possibility that the region's economy is no longer viable.

In both towns, local forest owners together with other town leaders have formed co-operatives to mill local wood and, in one case, to chip it for the pulpmill markets in Osaka. Their logs, produced primarily from thinning of immature forests, are small in diametre and command low prices on external markets. Their costs, nonetheless, are high, because the forests require silvicultural and other labour-intensive management. Under Japanese law, a replacement tree must be planted within seven years of cutting, and reforestation is expensive. These owners and town councillors, while recognizing that their trees are not yet of the highest quality, hold the opinion that the low prices for them are the result of imported competitive logs. They believe that their small industries would be capable of sustaining communities and stemming the out-migration if their wood did not have to compete with imports.

Five private, family-owned, long established sawmills in the region, none owning timber, used to purchase logs from local owners. Three of the mills now cut only imported logs. Total production of lumber in all five mills, as in the prefecture more generally, has decreased markedly since the early 1970s. The owners of the two mills using domestic wood are of the opinion that Japanese wood is superior in quality, though its greater cost is a disincentive to its use. One, the owner of a ninety year old family firm, believes the present economic difficulties will dissolve as more local wood reaches maturity, because Japanese consumers, now becoming more affluent, will prefer it. He suggests that the greater problem for rural forestry communities is the lack of training given their populations for dealing with urban construction companies.

To entice young people to stay in, or to return to, one of these towns, the municipal government joined together with the prefecture government and an organization of local business people to purchase land from a forest owner, then sold this to the Panasonic company at 80 per cent of cost to create a factory. The town built a new city hall, using laminated local cedar. They have also expanded the mushroom industry, but there are biological limits to its expansion even with a high-demand market. The community is sponsoring English language classes and trying to develop marketing skills. One town official noted: 'We live in a small local region, but the world operates with a global market. We can't compete with the sogo shosha and other big companies.'

This theme runs through many interviews. Forest owners say of themselves that they are not good capitalists and that they lack entrepreneurial skills. They inherited forests that were traditionally maintained for aesthetic, more than for economic, reasons, and their culture demands that they act as wise stewards of the land irrespective of its economic value. They feel that they are vulnerable in the markets beyond their region because they lack business training. While trying to gain entrepreneurial skills, they also hold negative views of the external marketplace. In particular, they distrust the large merchandising houses (the sogo shosha) and large Japanese corporations on the coast. At the same time, when discussing the impact of imported logs on rural communities, town officers give a carefully weighted answer: for the sake of Japan as a whole, the opening of markets is essential. It just happens that they are the losers, while the big companies, especially the big pulpmill and construction companies elsewhere, are the beneficiaries.

In the third town, closest to Kyoto and blessed with a river route for transportation of logs, the forest industry is in healthier condition. Its forests are closer to maturity, and larger harvests are now possible. It is more dependent on decorative poles, which are not yet strongly affected by imports. These poles have ceremonial positions in traditional Japanese houses and shrines, and, with the growing affluence of the urban population, the poles are in demand for new houses, restaurants, and various public and private buildings. Here, about 40 per cent of silviculture work and 25 per cent of logging are carried out by co-operatives on contract to private owners and forestry owner co-operatives; the remainder is contracted individually. These proportions are lower than they are in neighbouring towns, hinting at an important trend. The closer the rural region is to industrial Japan, the less it resembles traditional forest regions. Co-operatives are still vital organizational forms, and only they can obtain government subsidies where they propose an enterprise likely to employ local residents, but there is also more individual activity in this district; more of the entrepreneurship that everyone seems to applaud.

The wages in this third town are somewhat higher than in neighbouring regions, but they are not competitive with wages in the labour-short markets of Kyoto and Osaka, to which many residents commute on a daily basis. The forest co-operatives employ loggers and silviculturalists for life (as do many employers in Japan), but they cannot provide the fringe benefits, especially medical insurance and pension funds, of urban employers. A visit to the forest underlines the problem: the loggers were all over fifty years of age, and the main feller was a healthy sixty-five years old.[4]

A development company has contracted with one forest owner to purchase just under a hectare of land to build summer cottages for Osaka residents; the owner will harvest the trees somewhat before maturity, but his profits will be on the land and his share of the lumber will be used in construction. The community must have agreed to this: a landowner does not simply sell to outsiders without the agreement of others, though there is no actual law prohibiting external ownership. I asked whether developers might take over more land and whether forest owners might see this as a way out of their dilemma. The answer was a strong and collective 'no.' Informants were certain that the communities would never agree to widescale 'foreign' (their phraseology for external) ownership of land. That may be the case, but there is evidently an increasing market demand for summer cottages.

A forest co-operative for polished poles seems to be thriving. It purchases trees from forest owners who comprise its sixty-six members, puts on tick binding to ripple the poles in various exotic ways, cuts the trees in due course (hiring a co-operative logging crew), barks and polishes the wood, and sells the poles at auction to wholesalers. In the off-season, its four employees purchase materials and distribute them to members, package and truck purchased poles to buyers, and help owners to gain new information. Owner-members may have their own trees cut or may purchase trees from neighbours or on the local market; they rarely have enough of their own trees to satisfy the demand for 1,500 poles per year. The market has steadily grown over the past quarter century.

The pole business has become a substantial entrepreneurial enterprise, but it is still conducted in the traditional Japanese fashion – through community co-operatives. More individualistic enterprises, though still uncommon, are becoming evident. For example, one forest owner also engages in real estate and construction and has built up a considerable enterprise on the original basis of an inherited logging business. He did not inherit land, but he has used opportunities to market land to affluent city-dwellers wanting summer resorts and to tourist businesses. His building company uses a high proportion of imported logs and lumber.

An especially unusual individual is the owner of a prefabricated housing company. Not being a member of a co-operative, he could obtain no subsidies to start up a business, and he had not inherited land. However, he taught himself how to make prefabricated log houses by reading North American brochures, obtained bank loans, and started a family business. He now has orders far into the future. He imports lumber and cedar shakes from Canada and the United States. In his opinion, North American kiln-dried lumber has less variability and lower water content than does the domestic variety. He emphasizes quality, which he can obtain in imported wood, and he can produce houses at lower cost than he could with domestic timber.

While the town closest to Kyoto has more profitable enterprises, it also has a large commuter population. Forest owners, as well as workers and students, travel daily to urban jobs and schools. Villagers say that most people cannot make a living from the forest enterprises and must supplement their family incomes by employment elsewhere. Imported logs are perceived to be the primary cause of this economic decline. Immature timber, the relatively low quality of some domestic sugi, and the lack of entrepreneurial skill are viewed as secondary contributors. There is widespread suspicion here that North Americans do not invest in silviculture or reforestation and, thus, incur fewer costs of forest reproduction; also, there is suspicion that the North American resource is given away to big companies which mass produce lumber and freely export timber. They point out that even with the cost differential on transportation, North American logs are cheaper than domestic logs.[5] One or two informants mention the lesser influence on Japanese policy of the Ministry of Agriculture, Forestry, and Fisheries relative to the Ministry of International Trade and Industry (MITI), but, if my understanding is correct, the structure of the central Japanese government and the dominant role of MITI are somewhat foreign topics in these rural regions. In any event, the considerable subsidies provided by government to rural regions in Japan do not substantiate the view that they are neglected.

The log market, these interpretations notwithstanding, will not in itself explain the exodus of young people. They move to cities to obtain education, access to universities, and employment. They express in their moves a preference for office jobs over the manual work in forestry. Occasional informants, after much discussion, offered yet another reason for the exodus: young people may not want to maintain shrines and temples and give ten to twenty days free each year to silviculture and other community service. They are much less interested in their place in the community than are their parents. These insights considerably modify the more public stance that links out-migration to the log market.

Older residents are reluctant to discuss the role of women in Japan, but it is germane to the depopulation of rural regions. Japanese women, especially in these traditional rural regions, are subject to patriarchal controls not experienced by women in most industrial countries today. They do not inherit land and are not forest owners. If a male forest owner has only daughters, one must marry a local boy willing to take on the forest owner's family name. The adopted son-in-law then becomes the heir. Young women, now well educated and having access to the mass media, may well conclude that they have greater probability of living less servile lives in cities.

It would be inaccurate, then, to blame imported logs and lumber for depopulation; other market and social forces are at work. However, the log market is a significant factor in the total societal change. Without competition from imports, the rural communities would, at least, have an economic future based on their maturing forests. The opening of the log market undoubtedly was essential. Japan was under severe pressure to reduce protection of domestic producers across the industrial spectrum. As the informants noted, free trade might have been beneficial for the urban, industrial regions; it was not, however, beneficial to them. For the remaining, elderly population of these rural towns, this may be the last generation to fully honour the range of mutual obligations that constituted the communities of both rich and poor, landowners and landless. For them, the welfare of the community is a measure of the worthiness of the élite, and there are still numerous checks on the élite's power. Property and inheritance taxes are high, and members of owning families may divide property in order to reduce their tax burden, but the family, even so, must perform community services and provide political and social leadership. In their homes and public buildings, aesthetic sensitivities are nurtured, ancient rituals are practised, and peace and harmony are prized. Wood, in the forms of polished centre poles, floor and wall panels, and furniture, is central to the aesthetic harmony. Such communities may seem stifling and static to young Japanese today, but however else one may characterize them, they do provide a conservationist and environmentally sensitive context for forests.

FORESTRY IN BRITISH COLUMBIA

The upshot of the competition from Canadian lumber in u.s. markets was the imposition of a countervailing duty in 1986, later transferred to an export tax on lumber, and finally embedded in a higher stumpage fee in British Columbia. As this process developed, the off-shore export restrictions from Canada were modified, and, as noted above, substantially larger quantities of logs made their way to Japan from BC.

The larger part of trade in forest products between Japan and Canada, however, does not consist of logs. It consists of pulp, woodchips, and, to a lesser extent, lumber. Pulpmills located in coastal Japanese cities obtain half their fibre sources from recycled newsprint and, of the remainder, 40 per cent is sourced off-shore (Kawake 1988:20).[6] They purchase nearly a fifth of BC's annual pulp production, and they constitute the second largest single market for BC mills, which themselves produce very little of the finished paper products (see Table 1).

To serve this market, Daishowa, a major Japanese pulp company, has constructed two large pulpmills in Quesnel, and other companies have enlarged their production facilities and taken on marketing contracts with Japanese buyers. In addition to pulp and wood-chip markets, BC companies have gradually developed lumber markets in Japan, either through the aid of the BC Council of Forest Industries or in direct contact with the sogo shosha. While the lumber exports are still relatively small, they are important for BC sawmill companies.

Although the major forest union in BC, the International Woodworkers of America (IWA), objected to the export of logs, it has not objected to the export of lumber; neither have the pulp workers' unions mounted objections to the export of pulp.[7] These exports are viewed as beneficial, since both embody BC labour inputs. As well, the provincial government has welcomed foreign investment and hailed the expansion of pulp markets. In the long run, however, one might well question this conventional wisdom; the export of logs deprives millworkers of jobs, but the excessive exploitation of forests to maintain the large pulp- and sawmills may ultimately have greater and more widely detrimental impacts. Further, though employment is generated by mills serving these markets, the mills constructed or modernized for this purpose are not labour-intensive. Overall employment in BC's forest industries in 1986 was, in fact, only 76 per cent of the 1979 level, while production in all sectors had increased.[8]

The argument mounted in favour of log exports, prior to new legislation in March of 1989, was that the over-mature stands must be cut anyway, lumber prices were low, and sales to the United States would be reduced by the new resource costs. As one analyst observed, an even more salient argument was that the companies were suffering a cash-flow problem in a general recession (Widman 1984). The new legislation imposed higher penalties for exporting logs in lieu of manufactured products. The reduced sales had as much to do with high interest rates and consequent low construction activity in the United States and Canada as with stumpage rates. The social context in which these arguments and this logic justified the sale of logs also provides the rationale for ever greater allocation of harvesting rights to supply pulp and lumber mills.

TABLE 3

Number of employees, annual averages for BC forest industry,
1979-86

Year	Logging	Wood Ind.	Pulp & paper	Total
1979	24,474	51,369	20,998	96,841
1980	24,270	49,708	21,540	95,518
1981	19,561	46,627	20,660	86,848
1982	16,371	40,309	18,458	75,138
1983	19,906	40,392	17,390	77,688
1984	20,586	38,901	17,433	76,920
1985	19,468	39,603	16,850	75,921
1986	19,848	37,204	17,254	74,306

SOURCE: Statistics Canada (1986), *Canadian Forest Statistics*, catalogue number 25-202

History and Organization of the Industry in BC

A major and obvious difference between the Kyoto Prefecture and British Columbia is the size of operations. Allotted harvesting areas for BC producers are enormous by Japanese standards (by world standards, in fact), as are the capacities of sawmills. Forests are under provincial jurisdiction, and the provincial government in British Columbia has chosen to grant lengthy harvesting tenures to selected companies while retaining Crown rights to 95 per cent of the land. Since the 1950s, the stated policy has been to bestow these cutting rights on large, integrated companies, irrespective of national origins of parent companies. The rationale for this, expressed by the minister of forests in 1978, IWA spokesmen, and government policy papers in the late 1970s, was that large companies bring capital to the region, and they will build mills only if they have secure timber supplies; and they are more reliable employers and resource conservers than are small companies or families because they have long horizons (Marchak 1983: Ch. 3).

The integrated companies, or sawmill companies linked via marketing agreements to pulpmills, have harvesting rights that in numerous respects are tantamount to ownership. For example, though they cannot sell Crown land, they can sell their operations, and these have value only if the allotted timber supplies are transferred too; only once has the BC government threatened to remove licenses – in the case of Canadian Pacific's bid (subsequently withdrawn) to increase its control of MacMillan Bloedel. There are allotted annual cuts (AAC's) established by the government, but these are extensive and flexible, and provide upper limits to harvesting more than carefully monitored management plans.

Despite the faith in the long horizons of large companies, six foreign-owned companies left British Columbia between the mid-1970s and mid-1980s.[9] Though cash-flow problems were the immediate causes, there were other reasons as well. In particular, new species were being planted in warm climates, new pulping technologies for pines, hardwoods, and eucalypts were coming on stream, and new market conditions were imminent. Companies presumably weighed the various investment opportunities, and some concluded that BC's remaining timber, and the century or more required to regenerate a softwood forest, offered unattractive conditions for further investment. They were burdened with obsolete mills in a quickening race to use computer technology. Their capacity to retool woodland operations and mills might have been restricted by existing obligations to a strongly unionized labour force. Since their exit, the industry has become even more concentrated, both within BC and on a world scale.

These large companies are now required by law to contract out half of all logging, and, in fact, most logging is done by contractors. The companies have phased out many of their logging employees. There are no lifetime guarantees and no long-term security of tenure for contractors or their employees. The Canadian IWA is a very much smaller (and no longer international) union.

The present (1978) provincial Forest Act makes no provision for public hearings or community controls on resource management. The recently established Permanent Forest Resources Commission (named 29 June 1989) is charged with the responsibility for suggesting means of involving the public and 'may hold public meetings.' The commission was appointed following loud and frequently hostile public objections to proposed tree farm licences, especially on Vancouver Island and in the Mackenzie region north-east of Prince George. Public information sessions were held in the spring of 1989 to deal with these objections, and it became clear that they could not be easily dealt with or ignored. Pending changes that the commission may introduce or recommend, communities still have little recourse if they disagree with logging plans other than to barricade roads or to take more destructive action. Over the past half-dozen years, such actions have become frequent on the Coast, where old-growth forests are now rare; and, more recently, in the Interior, where bands of aboriginal peoples are contesting land ownership rights.

The demand for BC pulp and newsprint began to decline again in late 1989, and industry analysts anticipate a continuing decline as new mills come on stream in countries that now import from Canada. Many of the investors in these new mills and plantations are the same as, or are allied to, companies in BC. For example, Fletcher Challenge of New Zealand now controls 20 per cent of the newsprint capacity of the Pacific Rim and has forestry complexes in BC, Chile, and Australia; Abitibi and Bowater have acquired properties and are building a mill in Venezuela; Noranda is still planning a joint-venture with North Broken Hill of Tasmania. Daishowa has recently bought into mills in Washington State and into another in Alberta. At present growth rates, the world pulp industry will again have over-capacity within the next few years, and older mills using a depleted softwood forest base are unlikely to be competitive.

Forest policies have been somewhat modified since the 1978 Forest Act. With revisions in 1987 to Section 88, companies are required to provide more of the forest management tasks and are expected to accept greater costs for infrastructure and reforestation. At the same time, the Forest Service has lost more of its already limited capacities to regulate the yield. The 1989 increase in fees-in-lieu of manufacturing decreases the incentive to export logs. A small business enterprise program has been introduced, whereby independent logging companies can bid on timber-cutting rights over small territories carved out through a general 5 per cent reduction of harvesting rights granted to large companies. However, as field notes discussed below indicate, these modifications are not serious impediments to continuation of traditional practices and may, indeed, positively enhance the capacity of large corporations to cut forests at excessive rates.

The Cariboo Region

There are two very large pulpmills in Quesnel, a city of 8,000 in the Cariboo region. One of these is half owned by Daishowa and Marubini of Japan and half owned by Weldwood (itself owned by Champion International). This mill was built in 1971 and has since been fully modernized. The other, built in 1981, is half owned by Daishowa and half owned by West Fraser (controlled by the Ketchum family of the U.S. but now with a majority of Canadian shareholders). Both Weldwood and West Fraser had extensive harvesting licences and numerous sawmills in the region before Daishowa came in but neither had pulpmills. Daishowa had ready cash for investment and building and, in 1981, with BC's forest economy in a deep slump, it was well situated to establish the second alliance. Half of the output from these mills goes to the Japanese market; the remainder is shipped to Europe and other off-shore markets.

Weldwood and West Fraser sell much of their chip supply to the pulpmills, but they also have other alliances in this and neighbouring forest regions and other sawmills and woodland divisions outside the Quesnel area. Their wood supplies are thus essential to the Quesnel mills, and Daishowa's marketing expertise and the Japanese guaranteed market are vital to their well-being, but they are not wholly dependent on the Daishowa linkage.

Other and independent sawmills in Quesnel are in several cases more dependent on the pulpmills for chip sales. With increased stumpage costs, high labour costs, declining u.s. lumber markets, and stiff competition for off-shore markets, these mills are more vulnerable than either West Fraser or Weldwood. They are scrambling to obtain (and in at least one case, retain) a small share of the Japanese lumber market.

The forest industry in this region used to depend on varied softwood species; now it is largely dependent on small-diametre lodgepole pine that would have been left as junkwood only a decade ago. The forest used to be close to the mills in town; now it is ever more distant. In this context, the major topic in Quesnel is the mountain pine bark beetle. Because of an infestation, a five-year incremental increase of 40 per cent in allowable cuts over the basic 2.3 million cubic metres was introduced. The five years ended in 1989, but the pulp- and sawmill capacity have been geared to the high volume inputs. The town's population is fully aware of the implications of reduced volume: lay-offs, unemployment, and a general downturn in the economy are reluctantly anticipated. Once that additional supply is exhausted, there will be a scramble over the remaining and more remote forests. Already there are mounting arguments that the allowable cut should be increased to fit economic, and not just biological, parameters and further arguments that what is left is overmature anyway so, as one person put it, 'why waste it?' In none of these arguments are forests valued for non-economic reasons.

Unemployment rates are expected to rise because of diminishing resource supplies and also because of technological upgrading in the mills. Sawmills are now leaner, here as elsewhere, with the labour-intensive greenchain and lumber handling fully computerized. In the past, when sawmills were more labour-intensive, their managers sought out immigrant sources in the (correct) expectation that immigrants were less likely to mount grievances and support militant labour action. Punjabi Indian labour was preferred. Now the same mills are automated, and these workers have seniority, but the new jobs require proficiency in the English language, education levels, and general knowledge of machinery that the immigrants lack. The immigrants are the ones most obviously affected by the changes – in one mill, upward of 75 per cent of the workforce; but Canadian-born workers with low education and skill levels also suffer from lack of technological upgrading. This is a rural town that did not send many of its young to university in the distant city of Vancouver until very recently; there are many inhabitants who are dropping out of the industrial system. Aboriginal peoples have long fallen outside the system, and few have jobs in Quesnel mills though many reside in the region.

Fewer than 100 hourly workers are employed in the modern thermo-mechanical and chemi-thermo-mechanical mills, about 30 per cent being tradesworkers and most of the remainder being technicians; about half of management staff are professional foresters. In pulping, just as in modern sawmills, there are declining jobs for unskilled labour and the process is more capital-intensive. There is vague talk about the new employment that will come about when the forests are more human-made. With the new demands on forest companies, there are a few new jobs in silviculture and forest management. Nevertheless, there has been no significant expansion in these directions.

A 1987 community study and questionnaire survey was conducted by a group of residents concerned about the state of regional forests. They concluded that about 400 direct jobs had been lost since 1979 in the processing sectors, even though, with the incremental supplies moving through the system, production was at an all-time peak. They argued that the capacity of mills exceeded the AAC. This means that the mills would necessarily operate at reduced output once the beetle infestation was dealt with; and with diminishing wood supplies, the town would have to anticipate a decline in their forest industry. On a positive note, they determined that 40 per cent of Quesnel's present population had lived in the region for over twenty years. They discussed the possibility of creating new jobs in intensive silvicultural work, fisheries enhancement, tourism expansion, and potential manufacturing industries (NCCF Report 1987). At the time of the study, the official unemployment rate was 10 per cent.

Optimism about alternatives may be in order, but, for the moment, the major industry appears to be depleting the forest base in its scramble to serve the Japanese market. Young people are migrating out of Quesnel; there are few jobs, and upward mobility lies in

advanced education elsewhere. Thus, the same malady that affects
the rural Japanese towns turns up in Quesnel, despite its temporary
boom conditions. In the Kyoto Prefecture, imported logs are
blamed; in Quesnel, there is no blame for Japanese investors and
buyers – quite the contrary; but there is puzzlement about community decline. While many long-time residents express concern (as
shown in the NCCF study), other residents, more tied to the industry
than to the town, are indifferent. Said one: 'Who cares about this
place? It's not worth saving, and the kids will have a better life in the
big world beyond it.'

Fraser-Fort George Forestry District

The Japanese connection is less obvious in the neighbouring district
of Fraser-Fort George. There, two pulpmills are owned by New
Zealand's Fletcher Challenge, two by Noranda, and one by Canadian Forest Products. A growing proportion of the product from
these, and from associated and independent sawmills, however, is
destined for Japan, and all producers in the region are eagerly seeking expansion of Japanese markets. It is in the context of this market
competition, together with the dramatic changes in the global context of pulp and paper markets, that the communities of this district
are situated. Like the mills in the Cariboo region, the mills of Fraser-
Fort George are no longer located close to the resource. Their transportation costs have increased, and their resource supplies are well
below the total mill capacities of the district, even though the district
contains nearly a quarter of all forest land in British Columbia.

The pulpmills own sawmills throughout this and adjacent regions
and have contracts for chip supplies with independent sawmills.
There are 127 sawmills in the district altogether; nine large-sized independent sawmills with harvesting rights, some of which, still
reeling from the increased stumpage, are having difficulties surviv-
ing. Their estimates of increased costs, however, suggest how low
the base stumpage was: one estimate was an increase of 600 to 800
per cent. One major Prince George sawmill has recently been sold to
a pulpmill company; as lumber prices decline, the linkage provides a
guaranteed market for woodchips. A sawmill company with a history going back to the 1880s in the United States has five times exhausted a resource base on which it fed and then moved on to
greener forests, including its present location. There are no parallels
to these events in the Kyoto Prefecture.

All large sawmill and pulpmill companies throughout the region
are arguing – both in direct contacts with the provincial govern-

ments and in public fora – that they need an increased timber supply to sustain their present operations (see, especially, the BCFP/FFI TFL proposal 1988). The problem is that cutting has diminished supplies closer to mills, and where replanting has taken place, new forests are far from maturity. A spruce bark beetle infestation provided some participants with less costly logging sites for the past three years, but they are now obliged, like others, to move farther from their mills for new resources.

The unstated problem is that the mill capacities were not designed for harvesting at a sustainable yield level; they were designed for massive and rapid cutting of first-growth forests. Not only is each sawmill capacity enormous (reportedly among the largest in North America and far larger than any found elsewhere in the world), but there are more mills (even if fewer corporate owners altogether) than the region can comfortably sustain on present forest resources. To these are added the pulpmills. And to these already existing massive mills there is anticipated increased consumption from new plants planned or already underway in this and neighbouring regions.[10]

The companies' argument in favour of both more timber supplies and more secure tenures, apart from provision of employment, is that if they choose to invest in the region they should be guaranteed all future benefits from the investments. Investments in this sense include replanting and silviculture; past harvesting profits notwithstanding. Indeed, spokespeople for some companies say that it is unfair and unreasonable to expect them to plant trees without assurances for the future. If there are no assurances, the planting will likely be a minimal effort only, and silviculture will not be seriously undertaken. Anger is expressed against the government: in the view of large company managements, the companies paid for reforestation under Section 88 of the old Forest Act, but the government spent the funds on other things; thus, the NSR (not sufficiently restocked) lands for which industry is unfairly blamed.

Smaller companies and individuals opposed to the massive cutting argue that, on the contrary, it is unfair and unreasonable for companies not to plant trees in place of those they have cut; and that a company benefiting for years from a natural resource has an accumulated responsibility to replant and nurture the forest. In addition, there are numerous other arguments about the ecosystems of old-growth forests, already destroyed in much of the province; the importance of forests for the Earth's atmosphere; aesthetic values; and concerns about the more general irresponsibility inherent in a system of huge, highly concentrated extraction companies.

There is further conflict over the small business program and the contracting system. This results in a continuing undercurrent of resentment, cynicism, and anger about a perceived unfairness in the rules of a game that leaves some small businesses bereft of contracts while others, allegedly more amenable to corporate controls, obtain the lion's share. I will not document these complaints in this paper; my point in mentioning them is to underline the numerous fronts of conflict in forestry towns of BC. Prince George and its smaller neighbouring towns are communities more in the sense of aggregations of individuals and companies than in the Japanese sense of people with shared cultures. Profits are paramount, divisions between interest groups are pervasive, and it is difficult to discern any consensus about the general welfare.

One of the small towns in the region, Mackenzie, was established in the mid-1960s around two pulpmills and several sawmills. The smaller of the pulpmills has been part-owned by Jujo of Japan throughout its history, but the dominant partner since the late 1970s was BC Forest Products, the owner of the other and larger mill complex. Since then, both pulpmills, together with a large harvesting tenure area throughout north-eastern BC on either side of Williston Lake, have been taken over by Fletcher Challenge. That company had investment capital just as the industry in British Columbia was in the depth of the depression in the early 1980s. It purchased forest lands from Crown Zellerbach first, later purchased the assets of BC Forest Products, and throughout the 1980s has invested as well in plantations and mills elsewhere. It was Fletcher Challenge (via its component companies, BC Forest Products and Finlay Forest Industries) that proposed a controversial tree farm licence (TFL) for its northern operations in 1988.

The town's population, entirely dependent on a single employer either as millworkers or as loggers on contract, does not constitute a community in the sense used to describe the Japanese towns of similar size. The turnover rates, extremely high in the 1970s (Marchak 1987: Ch. 11), are reportedly lower in the tighter employment market of the 1980s, and there are more single family dwellings in place of trailer camps, but the essential ingredients of communities are missing. There is no public involvement in policy decisions, the population has no shared history, there is still no independent business community to speak of, and internal divisions between strata of workers are endemic. These characteristics reflect the short lifespan of the town and, even more, the view held by residents that it is a temporary residence. Managers for the controlling company might come and go, moving in accordance with their career objectives and company interests; millworkers take for granted the possibility that they will be displaced by new technologies, or that mills will be phased out if the company so chooses; loggers on contract never know how secure their employment will be a year into the future. This is the nature of the instant resource town, and Mackenzie is not alone in its situation. The TFL proposal underlined the general insecurity, bluntly stating that a mill would be closed and other mills downsized if the government failed to accept the bid (BCFP/FFI Proposal 1988). According to the proposal, the mill owners believe they have insufficient resource supplies for their operations.

The McLeod Lake Tsekani (also spelled Sekani) Aboriginal band, consisting of about 600 individuals, resides partially on a small reserve thirty miles south of Mackenzie and partially wherever else in the region members can find temporary employment. Elderly members recall being forced to flee their traplands when Williston Lake, a vast hydroelectric reservoir, was created by flooding their territory in 1967. They have endured impoverished circumstances ever since, neither covered by treaty nor with access to industrial employment. About a decade ago, they began negotiations for inclusion under Treaty Eight,[11] but proceedings stalled in the mid-1980s and the band had no funds. The band's objective now, in instituting legal proceedings for inclusion under the Treaty and recognition of land claims, is to prevent corporate logging on 55,000 hectares of claimed lands and to develop their own expertise and skills to mount logging operations as both contractors and small business owners.[12] Band leaders emphasize the need for intensive silviculture and present a version of their people as conservationists. That claim is contested by others, but in both cases the version is hypothetical, since aboriginal peoples have not had the opportunity to demonstrate their conservationist capacities in this region. Opposition to aboriginal land claims is strong, as companies (with already excessive milling capacity for the resource base) and contractors compete for timber cutting rights and employees strive to maintain employment in a labour market that has diminishing demand.

Summary: BC Interior

The expansion of the Japanese market demand for logs, lumber, and pulp since the mid-1970s has enabled BC interior towns to maintain their forest industry despite the imposition of greater stumpage fees and the slight decline in American markets. The growth of the industry has involved a considerable expansion in cutting rates, in pulpmill capacities, and in production. However, these have been accompanied by a decline in employment. In the Cariboo region, the employment rate is expected to decline sharply again when the incremental cut, allowed because of a pest infestation, is stopped.

The declining employment is not due, nor do local residents attribute it, to Japanese market demand. It is due, rather, to technological changes in lumber and pulp production methods. Further, it is obviously true that without the Japanese market, Daishowa-Marubeni would not have invested in pulpmills in the region nor would local sawmills employ as many workers as they do. But the short-term profits for the industry as it is presently organized are, even so, not sustainable at an annual cut consistent with forest capacities, and the increasing distance between mills and remaining timber supplies constitutes a serious problem for continuing operations.

There is nothing to prevent internationalized companies from moving elsewhere. Since they have relatively little stake in the communities where their plants are located, and since alternative fibre sources are elsewhere, it might well be in their interests to cut BC's forests at a rapid pace while there remain markets for logs and pulp rather than to conserve trees that will have less economic value in the future or to manufacture lumber at low market prices. Economic value, in this context, refers to the market value of the resource as it is presently produced; that is, in either raw form or as a mass-produced standardized product. The value of BC trees could increase substantially in a market for speciality products but that would require selective logging, more intensive silviculture and thinning, and re-designed manufacturing plants.

If the objective of forest policy and the development of a forest industry is to provide stable employment conditions for regional populations, the present operation of the BC forest industry in these interior regions appears to have serious flaws. Neither stable employment conditions nor cohesive communities are generated by industrial policies designed primarily to serve export markets for pulp and lumber.

CONCLUSION

It is a truism of sociology that human interpretations of events are as important as the events themselves for determining responses. In rural Japan, one of the social impacts of the changing log market is the belief that North American forestry practices cause economic decline and village depopulation. In the interior towns of British Columbia, the prior belief in the benefits to be derived from exports has been crucial to the receptivity towards expanded Japanese demand for pulp. In both cases, we can point to contrary evidence, but local responses to market conditions are filtered through belief systems and values, and are not simple reactions to objective conditions.

While Japanese forest owners are struggling with declining fortunes, there is not yet an indifference to the immaterial values of forests, and the noted lack of entrepreneurial aptitude of rural farmers becomes a protection for the environment. The costs exceed profits in the Kyoto Prefecture both because imported logs undercut their domestic markets, and because their costs include intensive silviculture and reforestation. Without the imports, the rural communities might be better able to increase the wages of forest workers and to continue to nurture and replant their forests. That they have so far continued to invest in the forests is due to cultural, not economic, incentives. Their demonstrated concern with wood quality, a precise grain, the matching of woods, and the infinite care they take in growing, thinning, then fashioning and manufacturing wood products attest to this.

The fate of the rural communities is not the fate of industrial Japan. The other side of the equation is the growth of the pulpmill industry in coastal regions and its dependence on imported fibre. As well, the construction industry flourishes with cheap imported wood, and without imports it might well prefer wood substitutes to more expensive domestic materials. The rural industry could not supply the whole of current market demands in any case, and industrial Japan cannot, in the current political and economic context, choose to be partial about its acceptance of free market forces.

By contrast with the rural regions of Japan, the resource regions of British Columbia are fully industrialized and have been so throughout most of their existence, even though they have few secondary industries beyond sawmills and pulpmills, and their pulpmill industry produces more pulp for Japanese manufacturers than finished paper of its own. Non-urban areas are hosts to large industrial companies engaged in extracting and exporting the resource. The class structure and local culture are contemporary outcomes of the way industry is organized.

The BC forest industry is geared to mass production; the infinite beauty of a single tree is lost in the process of clearcutting. The difference in attitudes between BC and Japan in this respect may be due more to rural, kinship-based social organization than to nationality. The attitude of the rural Japanese is mirrored in many of the stated beliefs of BC's aboriginal peoples.

With the growth of new plantations elsewhere, BC communities will be affected by fibre supply competition and changes in locations by multinationals. If priority continues to be given to short-term profits, it is improbable that much more than minimal attention will be given to growing a new forest that would not reach maturity for at least a century. Communities dependent on the resource industry could not depend on their employers to save them when the resource is depleted or when technological changes reduce labour demands.

Some companies in BC blame the government and 'common property rights' for deforestation. It is true that too little public money, some of it gleaned through stumpage in the prolonged boom period of the 1950s to 1970s, was allotted to tree-planting, so the blame is not entirely misplaced. But this interpretation ignores more fundamental issues. If the BC government is to be blamed, the focus might be better placed on its allocation of harvesting rights in excess of sustainable yields; on its excessive reliance on huge, integrated forestry companies for economic survival; and low stumpage during the boom years. There are no common property rights in this business: the Crown has formal ownership, the companies have control, and the public has virtually no input into management decisions.

The issues raised here are global. Industrial societies and free market forces do not protect, and in BC's case, have not given rise to cohesive, family-oriented communities; neither do they protect forests and aesthetic values. In both Japan and North America, rural regions and their values are anachronisms. Yet in the context of an environmental crisis finally recognized, and with greater awareness of the considerable costs of fully industrial social organizations to human beings and other species, we may wish to consider alternatives.

The Kyoto Prefecture provides an instance of alternative organization: private ownership on a very small scale, extensive use of cooperatives with government support, and explicit requirements for reforestation and good management. Instead of big companies arguing that they must have greater resource guarantees to keep huge mills in operation, the prefecture has small community-owned mills built around a sustainable resource and appropriate to its capacities. Instead of companies threatening to walk away from reforestation if not given more trees to cut now, there are community companies creating a business out of reforestation. Even the Japanese pulpmill regions provide an alternative: the recycling of waste-paper is a major source of fibre for paper production.

There are obvious objections to an argument in favour of adopting the prefecture's model. BC has no historical experience with cooperatives, and its culture is not an outgrowth of a system based on kinship and village networks. Private ownership would quickly become, again, corporate ownership, since families are not the core organizational unit of this society. Communities grow, they are not artificially created; and few BC communities have the cohesion required to maintain small forest industries over several generations. Social organizations are not successfully grafted onto alien cultural infrastructures.

At a political and legal level, the Canada-U.S. Free Trade Agreement would prohibit the development of co-operatives under a government aegis, government participation in economic development, or subsidies of any kind. There can be little doubt that from the American perspective, this Japanese behaviour constitutes non-tariff barriers to liberalized trade, and, while Japan may so behave in non-competitive rural industries, Canada would be threatened with countervailing duties and free trade appeals were it to introduce a similar system in forestry.

In any event, one might point to the failure of the policies to stimulate industry in the prefecture. There, the costs exceed profits, and the villages are being depopulated. Within another generation, much of what I saw during this fieldwork will be gone. Moreover, the urban populations of Japan are no more likely to grieve over their loss than urban Canadians have grieved over the passing of the rural communities established in Canada before the 1920s.

The prefecture's organization, then, is not a viable alternative, but it does suggest other ways of valuing forests. If forests matter, reforestation in Japan (or elsewhere) has to be connected to reforestation and higher valuation of trees in British Columbia. The practices in one place affect practices in others. Japanese paper industries are already learning this from their neighbours, whose hardwood forests they have long exploited and who are belatedly attempting to restrict exports. Perhaps for BC that lesson will become clear only when the lodgepole pines go the way of the Douglas-fir.

What would be the consequences of a re-valuation of trees at the real costs of reforestation, including wages for silviculturalists and the full costs of intensive forest management? If prices did reflect these real costs, there would be a general decline in lumber and pulp production both in North America and in Japan. Pulp manufacturing would use more recycled paper and other fibre sources. Lumber would be displaced by substitutes and wood would become a luxury item. Direct employment in production would decline. But there might also be an increase in investment in tree-planting, as each tree provided higher returns while mass production provided less. There would be improved utilization of trees and a sustainable base for small communities in rural regions. Japanese rural villages might not be renewed, but they might be able, at least, to economically sustain their forests.

It is possible, in the new context of environmental concerns within BC, that there will be changes in evaluation of forests, communities, and markets. The enthusiasm for growth that has dominated the region throughout its history might diminish, and the industry might be obliged to downscale its assault on the forest. Such a change does not appear to be imminent, but we can never discount the impact of changes in perceptions.

ACKNOWLEDGMENTS

I am indebted to Professors Manabu Morita, Ryoichi Handa, Yoshiya Iwai, and Hiroshi Matsuda for their great kindness in facilitating my visit to the Kyoto Prefecture. I also wish to thank my able research assistant, Jacqueline Tracey, who gathered data on the BC forest industry during the summer of 1989.

NOTES

1 Tariffs on imported wood were relaxed after the Kanto earthquake in 1923, when demand for construction lumber escalated beyond the capacities of domestic producers. However, with falling prices for domestic wood, producers prevailed in lobbying for re-introduction of import duties in 1933. By the 1950s domestic supplies could not meet the demand, and the quota system on foreign exchange for timber imports was abolished. It should be noted that tariffs on spruce-pine-fir lumber were retained and only gradually relaxed over the 1980s.

2 Employment was about 70,000 in 1964 and about 43,000 in 1987 (with another 20,000 scheduled for reduction by 1997) (Handa 1988b:31).

3 Between 1 and 2 per cent of owners (thirteen to sixteen separate households) own over 100 ha. (Miyamacho nd:3; Woody Life-Keihoku nd:3; and fieldnotes).

4 That said, however, during a visit to a logging site, I watched a crew of four fall mature cedars at the rate of one per three minutes; they felled, debranched, cut into six metre lengths, and yarded the trees at the rate of one per ten minutes.

5 Iwai, in private correspondence, estimates a transportation cost from

Vancouver to Tokyo at Y5,000 per cubic metre; from Miyama to Osaka at Y1,000-2,000 per cubic metre.

6 Hardwoods from South East Asia and softwoods from the USSR are also pulpmill fibre sources. That portion of fibre sourced in Japan comes primarily from the northern island of Hokkaido and northern Honshu Island, and there is some integration there between the pulping and logging sectors.

7 However, the IWA has, in numerous publications and public fora, argued in favour of better forest management practices.

8 In the interior regions, there was a 23 per cent drop in employment in lumber production between 1979 and 1986 (Statistics Canada 1986). The volume of timber cut in that time increased nearly 32 per cent in the Cariboo region and 13 per cent in the Fraser-Fort George region (BC Ministry of Forestry, Annual Reports).

9 These included: Columbia Cellulose; Rayonier (ITT); Crown Zellerbach (in stages); Canadian International Paper; Mead and Scott (respective holdings in BC Forest Products).

10 A Report issued in 1987 on the Prince George Timber Supply Area (Woodland Resource Services; also known as 'the Ewing Report,' p. 2) stated the problem in another way: 'the time is fast approaching when readily accessible timber will no longer be available to all traditional licensees. This phenomenon has been hastened in the Prince George TSA primarily because of the large concentration of licensees, the volumes harvested annually, and the natural disasters which have forced increased harvesting in the southeast prime area of the unit.'

11 Treaty 8 was established in 1922 with territorial boundaries that stretched from northern Alberta into northern BC and include the McLeod Lake area. The Treaty states that it covers 'the Cree, Beaver, Chipewyan and other Indians, inhabitants of the territory' so described. However, BC aboriginal peoples were never legally included in the Treaty and, at the time of signing, they did not participate. Reserves in BC, such as that at McLeod Lake, were not established by treaty.

12 As this was written, the neighbouring Sekani bands of Ingenika and Mesalinka reached agreement on monetary compensation for their lost hunting grounds in the same flooding of Williston Lake; other claims are still pending (Struek, 5 Aug. 1989 newspaper report on the settlement).

CHAPTER SIXTEEN

Multiple-Use Forestry: Management of a California National Forest Watershed for Augmented Water Yields

Michael D. Bowes, John V. Krutilla, and Thomas B. Stockton

INTRODUCTION

Among the federal lands managed by the U.S. Forest Service, the National Forests have perhaps the broadest directives for multiple-use management. Multiple use was fully incorporated into the enabling legislation for the National Forests only with the enactment of the Multiple-Use Sustained-Yield Act in 1960. Nevertheless, de facto management for multiple use has existed for the National Forests since their inception. Indeed, an explicit directive to manage National Forests for 'securing favourable conditions of water flows' and, equally, for timber was included in the Organic Administration Act of 1897, legislation to which the Forest Service traces its origin.

Scientific research in forest hydrology, related in part to the effects of vegetative manipulation upon soil erosion and water yield augmentation, has long been part of the U.S. Forest Service research tradition. However, forest hydrology tends to deal with that segment of the hydrologic cycle that is bounded by precipitation at the one end and by 'water available for streamflow' at the other. Thus, there has been little significant work on the uses of streamflow itself and on the valuation of the increment or decrement of flow affected by vegetative manipulation. The value of the augmented yield is derived from what uses can be made of increased volume and the more favourable timing of releases from the water resource systems.

The relative lack of attention to the valuation of water flows from the National Forests is, unfortunately, typical of the manner in which the non-timber services of the forests were dealt with in the recent multiple-use planning effort mandated by the National Forest Management Act of 1976 (NFMA). Few people, for example, spent much effort in estimating the value of the recreational services of their forest lands in this recent round of forest plans. The reasons for this lack of attention are varied, but in most cases the National Forests were simply not staffed with the individuals who could have performed such valuation exercises.

The Forest Service is now facing rising pressures to provide high levels of both timber and non-timber services. The planning effort, however, despite its great expense, has proved inadequate to convince the public of either the good faith or the expertise of the Forest Service. The planning exercise was at such a level of abstraction as to provide little real management guidance or justification for management action. It is our belief that if the future role of the Forest Service is to accomplish something more than bowing to the most vocal claimants, they must undertake the difficult task of providing convincing economic analyses of management actions for specific forest units. With this in mind, we describe one illustrative example of the type of analysis that might be required. Although this is a study of a very specific area, we present it as typical in its requirement for combining the skills of various disciplines.

This paper represents an effort to incorporate the value of these non-priced services of water flow into a more complete economic treatment of multiple-use public land management. In an earlier study (Bowes, Krutilla, and Sherman 1984) we investigated the relation between forest management practices and the associated increment in water yields in the subalpine forests of the Central Colorado Rockies. The location and circumstances for that study were recognized to be particularly favourable. The precipitation on the west slope in the higher elevations is fairly substantial, providing at least the potential for significant augmentation in streamflow. Additionally, the Upper Colorado River Basin system has a great deal of over-the-year storage capacity that would permit the effective utilization of any such increased flow. Finally, there had been a significant amount of relevant research conducted on the subalpine Fraser Experimental Forest in determining the augmented water yield from managed forests.

By the same token, the conditions that made the earlier study area favourable also suggested that the results might not be generalized to areas outside the Upper Colorado River Basin region. Consequently, it was deemed desirable to review other situations. The Northern Sierra Nevada forests, in California, afforded a combination of circumstances that appeared to be potentially promising for water yield augmentation but with circumstances that differed significantly from those of the subalpine forests of the Central Rockies.

Augmentation of water yield through explicit practices tends, up to a point, to be positively associated with the amount of precipitation. In this respect, the Northern Sierra west slope appears to have promise, since it receives from two to three times as much precipitation as do the subalpine forests of the Colorado River Basin. There are other pronounced differences in the basic hydrology of these two regions. In the subalpine forests of the Colorado Basin, precipitation falls predominantly as snow, with runoff primarily associated with the snowmelt. In the higher elevations of the Northern Sierra forests, while much of the precipitation does fall as snow, the snow is often wet, and there is some rain, often falling on wet snow. With wet snow, less of the canopy interception is lost in sublimation than is true of the Central Rockies subalpine forests. Moreover, with the winter rain and a later release of water in the period of snowmelt, a bimodal distribution of runoff occurs.

A more significant difference between the two regions is in the limited storage of many of the reservoirs of the hydropower system of the Northern Sierras. On the South Fork of the Feather River, the drainage we have selected for our analysis, there is only seasonal storage. Finally, the availability of research results for the Northern Sierra forests which is of relevance to our problem is not as substantial as it was for the Colorado forests of our previous investigation. The sparse research results for the Northern Sierra forests should perhaps be addressed briefly at this point.

What research results are applicable to the Northern Sierra Nevada mountains might at first seem to indicate a limited economic potential for augmenting yield through watershed treatment practices. For example, in a paper by Kattelmann and co-authors (1983:400), we find an estimate of only a 0.5 per cent to 2.0 per cent increase in potential water yield through watershed treatments. At the same time a hydrograph is shown for Berry Creek (Kattelmann et al. 1983:398) that seems to belie that limited estimate of potential yield. Upon examination it is seen that there are two quite different questions. The modest estimate of 0.5 per cent to 2.0 per cent relates to an average over a substantial land area where the actual area treated (accommodating numerous constraints and mixed land ownership) is somewhat limited. The more directly relevant Berry Creek example relates to the water yield response to timber removal from a small primary watershed where the areas of treatment and monitored water yield response are contiguous.

The relevant magnitude for our purposes is not the percentage increase in overall water yield that can be achieved with some kind of incremental water augmentation practices for the forests as a whole.

Rather, our concern is with the water yield from individual treated watersheds – and with the net economic value (positive or negative) of both timber and water that becomes available upon harvesting. These are the specific questions that need to be addressed when preparing projects to implement multiple-use forest management.

In this paper, we will investigate the opportunities for augmenting water yield from a single drainage on the west slope of the Sierras of Northern California within the Plumas National Forest. This potential management area is the drainage above Little Grass Valley Reservoir on the upper reaches of the South Fork of the Feather River. Here the elevation ranges from about 5,000 feet upward to 7,500 at the top of the western slope. Soil depths are largely between twenty-two inches and forty inches. Across the drainage, annual average precipitation ranges from seventy inches to eighty inches, with the average throughout the drainage at about seventy-five inches. The area is representative of the mixed conifer/red-fir snow zone.

The total area of the Little Grass Valley drainage is 16,512 acres, but of this area only about 7,500 acres are considered for treatment. Of the remainder about 4,000 acres are in private ownership and are not subject to management for water augmentation purposes. About 2,700 acres of the watershed is land in a management compartment of the Plumas National Forest, which otherwise lies outside the South Fork drainage and for which appropriate data were not available. The rest was unsuited for management either because of insufficient canopy density, excessively steep slopes, or the existence of water surface areas.

On the South Fork of the Feather River, below our multiple-use management area, there currently exists a hydropower system of the Oroville-Wyandotte Irrigation District (OWID). This is a relatively small system in that the volume of water is not large, but there is a very considerable developed head (3,225 feet) over which this water falls. Figure 1 provides a schematic of the OWID hydropower system. The system contains two primary storage reservoirs, the Little Grass Valley Reservoir at the 5,000 foot elevation mark on the South Fork of the Feather River, with a catchment area of 16,512 acres above the dam (the forest management area), and the Sly Creek Reservoir at about the 3,500 foot elevation mark that receives water from the Lost Creek and Sly Creek drainages, along with regulated diversion inflow through tunnels from the South Fork and Slate Creek. The Little Grass Valley Reservoir on the South Fork has 94,700 acre feet of storage capacity while the Sly Creek Reservoir has 65,650 acre feet. This storage capacity is virtually fully used for seasonal streamflow regu-

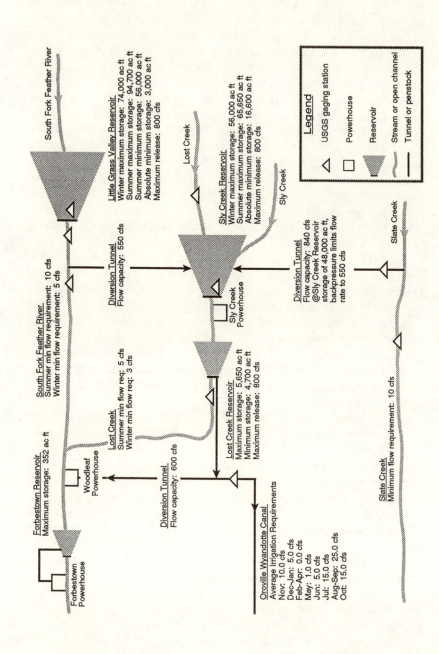

FIGURE 1

Schematic diagram of diversions and storage in South
Fork Feather River Basin

lation with no over-the-year storage capacity. The small Lost Creek Reservoir below the Sly Creek Reservoir and the small Forbestown Reservoir below the Woodleaf Powerhouse serve, largely, pondage functions. There is the question, then, whether the hydropower system on the South Fork, with only seasonal storage, can be managed so as to utilize any increment in flow, given its timing, from water yield augmentation practices in the primary watersheds draining into the Little Grass Valley Reservoir in the headwaters of the system. This is the question we are going to investigate below.

The paper is organized as follows: First, we take a brief look at the potential to produce water and timber from the Little Grass Valley drainage and decide the determinants of water yield augmentation as well as our procedures for modelling forest management. Forest management options are modelled through the use of a linear program that incorporates our estimates of the water yield associated with harvesting practices. Second, we develop the procedures used for valuing augmented water flow into the hydropower system. The existing stochastic seasonal pattern of streamflow is modelled and optimal system operating practices of the full hydropower system are determined. With this model of the reservoir system, we determine the expected value of increments to the South Fork streamflow. Finally, we provide a discussion and economic analysis of various watershed management options.

MULTIPLE-USE FOREST PRODUCTION MODEL

For the purpose of developing options for a water augmentation program in the South Fork drainage above the Little Grass Valley Reservoir, we use the microcomputer version of FORPLAN developed by Norman Johnson (Department of Forest Management, Oregon State University). This is a smaller version of the FORPLAN linear program development tool (Johnson et al. 1986) used by the U.S. Forest Service in its land management planning exercises directed by the NFMA. We use FORPLAN essentially as a simulation tool, a convenient accounting device to track the overall costs and the timber and water outputs resulting from specific land management programs.

First the forest planning area is divided into a set of homogeneous analysis areas. The South Fork drainage was classified into fifty-four distinct analysis areas, with the groupings based on approximate homogeneity with respect to slope, soil depth, forest cover type, and stocking conditions. Data on production and costs were then entered into the FORPLAN data base. Our data on existing timber conditions, on timber volumes and prices, and on management costs (including costs of sales, regeneration, stand improvement, and roads) were those used by the Plumas National Forest in its development of forest plans. Management costs and received timber prices are dependent upon characteristics of the analysis area and on the type of harvest practice. Timber harvest volumes depend upon existing stocking conditions, the inherent productivity of an analysis area, intensity of stand management, and the age at harvest.

FORPLAN is designed to be a multiple-use management tool, tracking the flow of both timber and non-timber outputs from forest lands. We have concerned ourselves only with the production of timber harvests and water. Incremental water yields are included as a time sequence of flows that are triggered by timber harvesting. Our estimates of these water flows were developed from hydrology information provided by the Plumas National Forest and incorporated into the FORPLAN data. We turn now to a description of the forest hydrology.

Determinants of Water Yield

The increment in water yield achievable by vegetation removal is a function of several variables. First, in this snow zone, the density of cover on lands surrounding cleared areas needs to be adequate for shading and for managing snow redistribution (Kattelmann et al. 1983:399). Given the forest density, then precipitation, soil depth, and elevation are instrumental in determining the increase in water yield resulting from vegetation removal. In reality these variables represent surrogates for a more detailed set of factors that can be more or less adequately subsumed under the surrogates noted. For example, species composition, particularly with reference to rooting depths, is picked up to a greater or lesser degree by the combination of precipitation and elevation along with soil depth.

Our estimates of water yield are derived from Plumas National Forest documents.[1] In Figure 2, water yield is shown as dependent upon precipitation, soil depth, and elevation. Water yield here represents the increase (in inches) in annual water flow from one acre in the year immediately following timber removal. Dashed lines mark the yields for our three different soil depth classes at an elevation of 5,500 feet and at a precipitation level of seventy-five inches per annum.

The increment in water yield that follows vegetation removal begins to tail off as the area from which the timber has been removed

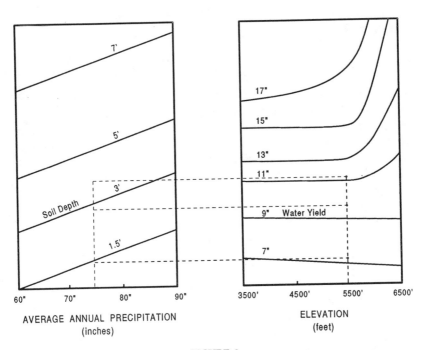

FIGURE 2
Increment in annual water yield (inches/acre) immediately following
harvest in the Plumas National Forest (west side)

recovers with colonizing vegetation. The harvesting regime, whether selective harvesting or clearcutting, and the clearing width will determine whether the rooting structure of the residual stand invades the clearing or whether the evapotranspiration recovery occurs only by revegetation. In the case of clearcuts or larger patch cuts, reasonable choices for timber or water yield management, the bulk of the increment in runoff is dissipated by revegetation over the course of about twenty years. The annual water yield in each year following harvest was estimated by Plumas National Forest staff to decline to about 90 per cent of that in the previous year (Bennoit and Schultz c. 1979). Annual increments to water yield following harvest were converted to equivalent decadal flow to allow incorporation into the FORPLAN data set.

Increments to water yield were taken to continue for two decades after any harvest. The amount of incremental yield was made dependent upon the soil depth in each analysis area, with greater flow from harvest on lands with the deeper soils. With the hydrology of the forest modelled, we can proceed with the development of the multiple-use production model for the forest drainage.

The Multiple-Use Management Options

The FORPLAN program provides a convenient mechanism for developing a large set of harvest scheduling prescriptions for analysis areas. Each such prescription represents a particular time stream of management actions and the associated flow of outputs and costs. The array of prescriptions for each analysis area or, more specifically, the possible combinations of these prescriptions across analysis areas make up a multiple-use production possibility set for the forest management area. A linear program is used to choose between these production possibilities, selecting that combination of prescriptions that best meets a specified objective function while also meeting any constraints imposed upon the use of resources or the levels of output.

In our analysis, we use FORPLAN and the linear program not so much as an optimizing tool but more to build tightly limited options that represent the range of management choices for the watershed. In all options it was felt prudent, in the interest of forest aesthetics, that we limit overall harvest from the drainage to no more than a quarter of the area in each decade. Further, in all options, the linear program is allowed to freely select a date for the cutting of existing mature timber stands. However, the allowed rotation periods for the subsequent regeneration harvests are of predetermined length, depending on the objectives of management. If merchantable timber is the primary requirement, the harvests are restricted to what might be considered ideal timber rotation periods. In the event that vegetation removal is undertaken predominantly to minimize uneconomic transpiration losses, the cycle of vegetation removal is much shorter than is required to provide for timber to reach merchantable size. Similarly, the efforts taken to ensure regeneration and stand growth are restricted within the model, as appropriate to the management goals. For example, with augmented water yield as a primary management purpose, actions taken to ensure prompt stand regeneration are reduced. These are the aspects of the management regime we shall be exploring.

The six initial options to be analyzed range from a water management option that is consistent with providing high net present value from water yield with little continuing timber production to an option that gives high net present value of timber production with no explicit attention to water. The linear programs for each management option were run with a time horizon of 180 years. The net present value of timber production was maximized in each case. In all cases, present values are calculated at a 4 per cent rate of discount, the rate used in Forest Service planning. Each of the linear programming runs results in a unique stream of incremental water flow, the value of which must be assessed. Before we can provide an analysis of the economic feasibility of an explicit watershed yield augmentation program, it is necessary to determine the value of increments in water from the drainage. Once an estimate of such a value is available, we can, as a final management option, run the FORPLAN model, permitting the full choice of management intensity and the harvest cycles so as to optimize the combined multiple-use value from the South Fork drainage. We now describe the hydrologic modelling of the South Fork reservoir system.

MODELLING THE SOUTH FORK RESERVOIR SYSTEM

An important consideration when evaluating management explicitly for capturing water value, as well as timber, is the use of an increment in flow. The Oroville-Wyandotte Irrigation District (OWID) hydropower system on the South Fork of the Feather River has little excess storage capacity. There is the question, then, as to whether this system can be managed so as to utilize any increment in flow from water yield augmentation practices in the watersheds above the Little Grass Valley Reservoir.

To determine whether the increment in flow that could be teased out of the upstream watersheds above Little Grass Valley Reservoir will be usable, we need to understand how the water management facilities are utilized to take economic advantage of streamflow. Water in higher runoff periods is impounded in the Little Grass Valley Reservoir. As needed, water is then diverted by means of the South Fork Diversion Tunnel through the neighbouring ridge into the Sly Creek Reservoir in the adjacent drainage (see Figure 1).

There are no power generating facilities between the Little Grass Valley Dam and the diversion tunnel. The water that is captured from the drainage above Little Grass Valley Reservoir must pass through the turbines immediately below Sly Creek Reservoir at the Sly Creek Powerhouse. Thus, an integral component in determining the usability of augmented streamflow in the Little Grass Valley watershed is the available storage in Sly Creek Reservoir. Sly Creek Reservoir has two other major sources of inflow – Lost Creek and the Slate Creek Diversion Tunnel. Flows through the two diversion tunnels can be regulated but is limited by tunnel capacity, by the flows within the streams, and by the requirement that a certain minimum streamflow be maintained below the diversions.

Downstream, below the Lost Creek Reservoir, water is diverted back into the South Fork drainage, by tunnel, for use in the Woodleaf and Forbestown power plants. A small amount of water is withdrawn below the Lost Creek Reservoir for irrigation use. Below the Forbestown Power Plant, there are limited water withdrawals for municipal and irrigation use and also for the Kelley Ridge Power Plant (not shown in Figure 1). The remaining South Fork flow goes into the large Oroville Reservoir. For the present, we consider the value of increments to water flow only up to the point of entry into the Oroville Reservoir.

Overview of The Modelling Exercise

Before we get into a technical treatment, a general overview of the reservoir system modelling effort may be useful. There are about twenty years of daily records of streamflow. From these records, a synthetic trace of hydrology of longer duration must be generated, with characteristics corresponding to those of the observed streamflow into the two storage reservoirs. The streamflow generator will need to mimic the actual record insofar as mean flow, variance, and perhaps other moments of the distribution that define the generator are concerned.

In addition, we must develop a model to simulate the operation of the reservoir system as a whole. This requires detailing of the various capacity constraints for the reservoirs and diversion tunnels, information on power plant output, and a set of rules describing the operation of the reservoirs and tunnels. A synthetic streamflow can then be routed through the reservoir system, allowing us to determine an expected value from the power production under current conditions.

Once that is accomplished, the estimated augmented yield from a vegetation manipulation option is added to the synthetic streamflow, and the incremental value resulting from this augmented yield is evaluated in economic terms. An augmented streamflow is derived from results of the FORPLAN models of the management zone. For each different watershed augmentation alternative, the model provides 180-year sequences of decadal values for the increments to flow. We must convert this incremental flow into an equivalent annual flow and, finally, into a weekly flow that can be fed into the reservoir system model.

There is yet one more aspect to the analysis that needs mentioning. It was not possible to determine with precision the current reservoir operating policy of the owid hydrosystem. Therefore, we have found it necessary to determine the optimal operating policies. Apart from this, even if we had determined existing policies, it would perhaps be desirable to develop an optimization model for use in evaluating system output so that our results would conservatively measure improvements in system output due to the added increment of streamflow. In the absence of this step, we might attribute the improvements in system output from more efficient use of the reservoirs to the improvement in system output due to augmented flow.

With that as background we are ready to begin discussing the problem in its more technical dimensions. The task at hand is to develop the synthetic streamflow, the reservoir model, the optimal operating rules for Little Grass Valley and Sly Creek reservoirs, and the derivation of the augmented streamflow. Once this is accomplished, the marginal benefit of incremental yield from various timber management practices can be analyzed.

Stochastic Streamflow Generation

The u.s. Geological Survey (usgs) maintains several stream gaging stations in the South Fork drainage basin (see Figure 1). Gaging station data typically consist of stage height measurements taken at fixed intervals over a day. Streamflow is estimated from these stage height measurements through a rating curve and is published in daily averages. To provide a manageable time frame for the analysis and subsequent management decisions, the twenty-two years of daily streamflow series from each of the gaging stations were aggregated into a weekly series. From these weekly streamflow series, statistical streamflow generating models were developed for: (1) net inflow into Little Grass Valley Reservoir; (2) Lost Creek flow into Sly Creek Reservoir; (3) Slate Creek flow at the diversion tunnel to Sly Creek Reservoir; (4) runoff into the South Fork between Little Grass Valley Dam and the diversion tunnel; (5) other flow into Sly Creek Reservoir; and (6) runoff below Sly Creek Dam into the Lost Creek Reservoir drainage.

Streamflow tends to follow an underlying annual cycle, with random variation around this cycle observed within any particular time period. We model the deviations of streamflow around this mean periodic behaviour. Before we describe the generating models let us define some notation. Subscript t is used for counting time. The subscript s (running from one to fifty-two) is used to refer to the week within the annual cycle of the water year in which a particular time t occurs. Streamflow at time t is represented by q_t; μ_s is the mean of the log of observed streamflow in a week s of the water year; and $z_t = \ln(q_t) - \mu_s$ is the deviation of the log of streamflow in time t from its corresponding mean in the annual cycle. We will also use $\bar{q}_s$ to represent the mean value of observed streamflow in week s.

The three primary instances of streamflow (the inflow to Little Grass Valley, the Lost Creek flow into Sly Creek Reservoir, and the Slate Creek flow) are considered first. For each of these, we take streamflow as being generated by separate first-order autoregressive models (AR[1]) of the form:

$$z_t = \rho z_{t-1} + \xi_{st} \tag{1}$$

where ρ is an estimated parameter and ξ_{st} is a random normal variable with a mean of zero and an estimated standard deviation of σ_s. We allow for the possibility of seasonal heteroskedasticity in the random error term of the flow-generating equations (1). Note also, again, that it is the deviations around the periodic annual cycle that are taken to be autocorrelated. The annual periodicity in each of the three log series is removed prior to estimation of the AR[1] coefficients.

The model is based on our assumption that the streamflow series q_t is lognormally distributed. As is typical for streamflow data, the actual streamflow series were found to be skewed in a manner that suggested that such a log transformation would normalize the series. The choice of an AR[1] process, rather than alternative ARIMA (antiregresser integrative moving average) models, was based on Box-Jenkins (Box and Jenkins 1970) identification procedure. Each AR[1] coefficient and the weekly variances r_s were estimated using an iterative generalized least squares regression procedure.

Once the parameters of equations (1) are estimated, unbiased synthetic streamflow is generated through the following sequence of steps:

(a) Begin with values for z_0 based on the last period of observed data,
(b) With z_{t-1} and a draw of the random variable ξ_{st}, generate z_t using equation (1),
(c) Determine the flow in time t from the equation:
$$q_t = \bar{q}_s \exp(z_t - \omega_s^2/2) \tag{2}$$
where
$$\omega_s^2 = \sigma_s^2 + \rho^2\sigma_{s-1}^2 + \rho^4\sigma_{s-2}^2 + \ldots \tag{3}$$

(d)   Repeat steps 2 and 3 until a full sequence of weekly flow is produced.

The term ω_s^2 in equation (3) gives the overall variance in the process generating z_t. We estimate ω_s^2 from (3), incorporating terms for five previous weeks.

The derivation of equation (2) require some explanation. Transform the definition of z_t back into terms of the original flow to find:

$$q_t = \exp(\mu_s + z_t). \tag{2a}$$

Rather than using (2a) directly to generate flow, we form an equivalent expression for q_t:

$$q_t = \exp(\mu_s + \omega_s^2/2) \exp(z_t - \omega_s^2/2)$$

and then, based on features of the lognormal distribution, find:[2]

$$q_t = E(q_t) \exp(z_t - \omega_s^2/2) \tag{2b}$$

Finally, replacing the expected value $E(q_t)$ in equation (2b) with the estimated means $\bar{q}_s$ gives us our flow generation equation (2).

Weekly flow sequences were generated for each of the three primary sources of inflow previously described. Since existing flows in these streams were found to be highly correlated (the correlation coefficient for Slate Creek and inflow to Little Grass Valley Reservoir was estimated as 0.95), the assumption was made that all flows were perfectly cross-correlated, thereby greatly simplifying the flow generation procedure. Streamflows were generated for 180-year sequences, corresponding in length to the planning horizons used in the Plumas FORPLAN studies, in order that the effects on power outputs could be evaluated using a comparable time-horizon.

The three instances of secondary inflow are estimated from the projections for the instances of primary streamflow. The runoff into the South Fork between the dam and the diversion tunnel is derived from the inflow into Little Grass Valley Reservoir. This is based on a regression fit of historical inflow below the dam to that above. Total inflow to Sly Creek Reservoir was determined by scaling up the predicted Lost Creek flow (1.56 x Lost Creek flow) to account for the relative land area that drains into Sly Creek Reservoir through drainages other than Lost Creek. The runoff that enters Lost Creek Reservoir below Sly Creek Dam is similarly predicted to be a fraction (0.42) of our generated flow in Lost Creek.[3]

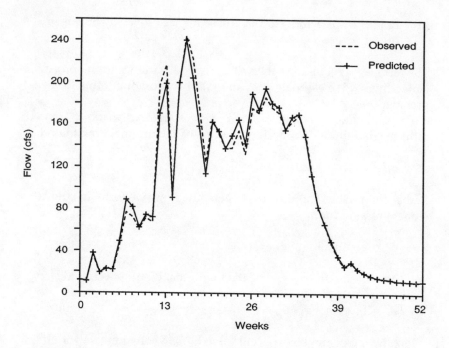

FIGURE 3
Comparison of predicted versus observed mean annual inflows,
Sly Creek Reservoir

The accuracy of our analysis will depend largely on the fidelity of the stochastic streamflow prediction model. Figure 3 compares the annual mean cycle of one sequence of predicted flow into Sly Creek Reservoir superimposed on the mean flow from the twenty-two years of record. We can see from Figure 3 that the streamflow generator closely mimics the actual hydrograph. More complete comparisons of the generated and actual flow can be found in Krutilla, Bowes, and Stockton (1989).

Hydrologic Simulation Model

Synthetic inflow was generated for weekly time intervals and routed into the stream system. Reservoir releases for each interval are determined as a function of reservoir storage, the simulated reservoir inflow, and water demand (minimum flow requirements, hydropower demand, irrigation demand, etc.). Reservoir release rules are subject to the set of 'hard' constraints that result from the physical limitations of the reservoir's storage capacities, release structures' capacities, and the diversion tunnels' flow capacities. These constraints cannot be violated. Releases are also subject to a set of 'soft' constraints or targets that include minimum instream flow requirements, irrigation requirements, and recreational storage requirements. The hydroelectric production is a function of the productive releases (spills are non-productive) and the operating head.

Simulation of the hydrologic systems relies mostly upon the modelling of reservoir release policies. Reservoir storage is characterized by the continuity equations:

$$S_t = S_{t-1} + Q_t - R_t \qquad (4)$$

where S_t is reservoir storage at the beginning of time t, Q_t is total inflow to the reservoir at time t, and R_t is quantity of reservoir release during a period of one week at time t.

Our procedure is to first develop a target release. Seasonally varying operating rules for Little Grass Valley and Sly Creek reservoirs were modelled, with target releases depending upon current storage, inflow, and downstream demands. If the target release is found to be feasible, with the resulting reservoir storage violating neither the minimum storage requirements nor the maximum storage capacity of the reservoir, then this planned release is accepted.

If the target release leads to the violation of the maximum storage capacity constraint, then any excess is spilled. If the target release would drive storage below minimum requirements, the planned release is reduced. In this latter case, the actual release will be the amount that would leave storage at the minimum storage requirement. There is a policy of meeting minimum storage levels needed for summer recreational purposes in the Little Grass Valley Reservoir. This latter storage requirement may be violated only in order to meet instream flow and irrigation commitments.

Releases are routed through downstream reservoirs and diversion tunnels to powerhouses where electricity is generated as a function of head and regulated flow. Tunnel diversions are reasonably assumed to operate as close to capacity as is feasible, given streamflow and instream flow requirements. The limited diversions to irrigation and municipal water systems are contractual obligations that are met to the extent possible. These obligations are fulfilled unless minimum instream flow would be violated.

The release function describing the target release $\tilde{R}_t$ from Sly Creek Reservoir has the form:

$$\tilde{R}_t = \alpha_s + \beta_s W_t^2 \qquad (5)$$

where $W_t = (S_{t-1} - \text{Min}_s + Q_t)/(\text{Max}_s - \text{Min}_s + E(Q_t))$, with Max_s and Min_s the maximum and minimum reservoir storage requirements in week s, and $E(Q_t)$ the expected total inflow to Sly Creek Reservoir from streams and diversions. With this policy, target release is an increasing function of current storage relative to capacity and of current inflow relative to expectations for inflow. The release coefficients α_s and β_s are parameters that vary seasonally and were determined to maximize power production, as will be described shortly.

The release function for Little Grass Valley (LGV) Reservoir takes a more complex form. It incorporates a dependence on the current storage available downstream in Sly Creek Reservoir and a look-ahead projection for inflow. The target release is given by the expression:

$$\tilde{R}_t = \alpha_s + \beta_s X_t^2(1-W_t) + \gamma_s X_t(1-W_t)^2 + \delta_s Z_t \tag{6}$$

where X is formed in the same manner as W in the Sly Creek release rule, making the planned releases dependent upon relative storage and inflow into LGV reservoir; term (1-W) makes releases dependent upon the availability of storage in Sly Creek; and Z is the ratio of the sum of projected inflow over the next four weeks to the expected inflow to the reservoir over the same four weeks. The term Z is intended to reflect the role of snowmelt forecasts. Snowmelt forecasts give the manager considerable information on future inflow for the more important periods of high flow.

Reservoir Operating Rules Optimization

Several algorithms have been developed in the water resources literature to derive optimal reservoir operating rules (Yeh 1985). Our analysis employed a modification of the approach proposed by Simonovic (1987). The algorithm incorporates the synthetic streamflow simulation in an iterative procedure to optimize the parameters of a set of reservoir release rules of predetermined form.

The reservoir management policies are chosen to maximize the average annual energy produced by the hydroelectric facilities – with penalties for not meeting instream minimum flow or irrigation requirements and for violating minimum storage requirements during the summer recreational season. The problem is to search for the seasonal release coefficients of reservoir release functions (see equations (5) and (6)) so as to maximize this objective function.

As formulated, the optimization problem is multivariable and unconstrained with respect to decision variables – the seasonal release coefficients. Nine distinct seasons were considered for the release coefficients. These seasons were chosen primarily to allow for the policy differences that must result from the seasonal changes in the reservoir minimum and maximum storage limits. One four-week interval was used as a shutdown period, with the powerplants considered down for maintenance. Additional seasons were then added to allow the release policy to adapt better to the pattern of streamflow over the year.

A modified conjugate gradient method was employed to optimize iteratively the objective function. Occasional non-gradient steps were taken to ensure that the search did not get stuck. The solution provides the set of seasonal release coefficients that maximizes power production while reasonably meeting the constraints of the reservoir system. Penalties on violation of the soft constraints on minimum instream flow and recreational storage were chosen to yield reservoir operations that approximate current operating policy.

Since the stochastic streamflow generator will yield variations in flow, the optimal coefficients may be dependent upon the particular generated sequence of flow. To deal with this potential problem, the final choice for the coefficients of the reservoir release rules was obtained in the following way. The hydrosystem output was maximized for three different 180-year hydrologic traces, giving three different sets of reservoir operating coefficients. These sets of coefficients were then tried out on five other streamflow sequences. The one set of coefficients that performed best on average across these five streamflow sequences was then chosen for use. Once operating rules have been developed based on the existing hydrologic system and expected inflow variability, incremental yield from timber management can be routed through the optimization model and analyzed for increases in power production.

Relating Augmented Water Flow to Predicted Streamflow

An expected value, by decade, for augmented water yield corresponding to each different watershed management regime was derived from our FORPLAN linear programming model of the management zone. This FORPLAN model, described earlier, incorporates results from the Plumas hydrologic model, allowing us to relate water yield to vegetation removal in the drainage above the Little Grass Valley Reservoir. The decadal flow from the FORPLAN model runs was converted back into equivalent sequences of expected annual increments to streamflow. The actual predictions for augmented runoff from the management zone are formed as random variations around these expected values for the increments to annual flow. The variation in the augmented flow will depend upon the level of base streamflow.

It is reasonable to assume that the increments to annual runoff fluctuate in much the same manner as do base levels of streamflow, with fluctuations in both the incremental runoff and the base level of streamflow presumably dependent upon the same underlying pattern of precipitation. As a simple hypothesis, the incremental runoff coming from our management zone might be expected to be in the same proportion to its expected value as is the simulated annual base streamflow into Little Grass Valley Reservoir to its mean value. However, hydrologists suggest that the fluctuations in increments to runoff resulting from vegetation management are likely to be more exaggerated than are those for the base streamflow.[4] We have tried to take a conservative approach in estimating the amount of incremental water available. In particular, in wet years with high streamflow, we assume that increments to flow exceed the expected value in the same proportion as does base streamflow. In dry years we assume a somewhat more than proportionate decline in incremental flow.

Ultimately, it is necessary that we find the weekly increments in water flow from the management zone corresponding to our predicted annual increases. There is little solid evidence as to how augmented water flow will be distributed throughout the year. Depending upon soils, slopes, and local vegetation cover, the pattern to the annual cycle of flow increments arising from our management zone may lead or lag the cycle in base streamflow. We consider various possibilities.

As the first case, we take the weekly increment in flow to be in the same ratio to the annual increment as is the predicted weekly streamflow to the predicted annual streamflow, with:

$$i_t = Ib_t/B$$

where i_t is the predicted increment in flow from the managed drainage in week t, b_t is the predicted flow into LGV reservoir in the same week, I is predicted annual augmented flow from the management zone, and B is the predicted annual base inflow into LGV reservoir.

We also consider the possibility that increments to weekly flow might lead or lag the cycle of predicted weekly streamflow. For example, with:

$$i_t = Ib_{t-2}/B$$

the annual cycle of increments to weekly flow lags two weeks behind the annual cycle of primary streamflow.

Procedures for Valuing Augmented Water Flow

We get the increment in water value for any given watershed management regime by first estimating the total power and water value resulting from the increased streamflow from a specified water yield augmentation regime. From these, we subtract the corresponding values of the outputs resulting from a base level streamflow sequence, exclusive of any yield augmentation practices. Because of the stochastic nature of streamflow, the incremental value from watershed management is itself stochastic. Means and standard deviations for the increment in water value were based on thirty-six different runs of 180-year flow sequences for the with and without management alternatives.

The data in Table 1 show: (1) the results of the base system without explicit water augmentation; (2) the results of a polar case with management for water without regard to timber; and (3) the net output and value due to the incremental flow. In these summary tables we present for each output the mean (MN), the standard deviation (SD), and the minimum (MIN) and maximum (MAX) value for average annual output derived from thirty-six independent runs of 180 years each. Annual hydroelectric power is measured in gigawatt hours (gwh). Water routed to irrigation (IRGN) or to municipal and industrial (M&I) use is measured in thousand acre feet (maf). Also included within each table are the annual streamflow (maf) into the full system and the average present value of power (thousands of dollars) produced over the full 180-year time horizons. A discount rate of 4 per cent is used in computing present values.

Below each sub-table, we present the average value of an acre foot of water flow. For example, with base-level streamflow, in an average year $58.04 of power value is produced from each acre foot that flows into the full system. With the augmented streamflow, $58.03 of power value is produced per acre foot of overall flow into the system. Of more relevance to us is the value of increments to flow resulting from watershed management. The produced increments to flow provide only $54.82 of power per acre foot. These values are based on power sold at $32,400/gwh. The overall value for water given (at $63.69/af for incremental water) reflects, in addition to power value, irrigation water sold at $16/af and municipal water supplied at $260/af.

It is necessary here to make a potentially important point. When

TABLE 1
Incremental yields from maximum water augmentation option (WT40)

Yields with base flow				
	Mean	SD	Min	Max
Annual power (gwh)	673.48	11.36	647.56	695.36
Annual IRGN (maf)	20.17	0.17	19.78	20.53
Annual M&I (maf)	30.26	0.20	29.81	30.70
Annual inflow (maf)	375.96	11.01	344.22	399.78
PV of power (M$)	568,332.28	23,131.34	522,387.79	612,753.37

Power value per acre foot: $58.04
Overall value per acre foot: $79.83

Yields with augmented flow				
	Mean	SD	Min	Max
Annual power (gwh)	675.50	11.38	649.58	697.41
Annual IRGN (maf)	20.19	0.17	19.80	20.55
Annual M&I (maf)	30.30	0.20	29.85	30.73
Annual inflow (maf)	377.15	11.04	345.34	401.04
PV of power (M$)*	569,950.99	23,131.45	523,943.75	614,293.15

Power value per acre foot: $58.03
Overall value per acre foot: $79.78

Net gains from incremental flow				
	Mean	SD	Max	Min
Annual power (gwh)	2.02	0.07	1.83	2.20
Annual IRGN (maf)	0.03	0.00	0.02	0.04
Annual M&I (maf)	0.04	0.01	0.02	0.06
Annual inflow (maf)	1.19	0.03	1.13	1.26
PV of power (M$)*	1,618.71	94.83	1,382.28	1,901.68

Power value per acre foot: $54.82
Overall value per acre foot: $63.69

NOTE: Present values calculated over a 180-year planning horizon at a 4 per cent discount rate we look at a single South Fork watershed amenable to water augmentation treatment, the increment in yield is somewhat sporadic over time and not significant in relation to the total volume of water stored in the Oroville project on the main stem downstream. As a result, the water that is added to the contents of the storage reservoir from a single watershed yield augmentation program will not alter the amount of water that can be reliably supplied from the Oroville storage project. Accordingly, it must be treated as non-firm water eligible for sale only on an 'if and when available' basis. Spot transactions for such water run at prices within the range of $3.00 to $5.00 per acre foot. It is important to realize that these transactions involve only a single season's supply, not a water right in perpetuity. However, we can conceptualize a multiple National Forest watershed yield augmentation program from which the increments in yield would be aggregated. We cannot say, a priori, that the aggregate increment in yield would not be sufficient to reduce the length of the critical period. If this would in fact occur, then the conditions would exist for an increase in volume of firm water contracts written on the augmented yields that would command a price of around $160 per acre foot. This value is very large in relation to the values that we have estimated for the increment in yield becoming available as firm water.

Some Observations on the Hydrologic Model Results

Some preliminary observations might be noted. In Table 1 we show an increment in annual streamflow of 1,190 acre feet, which represents only a 0.3 per cent increment to the base level mean annual flow. This, of course, is a comparison of the increment in flow generated in the upper South Fork watershed with the mean annual flow into the total South Fork drainage. More meaningful is a comparison of the increment with the mean inflow to Little Grass Valley reservoir. Here we find that the augmented flow represents about 1.4 per cent of the spatially more similar baseline flow originating in the drainage above Little Grass Valley Reservoir. Even so, this is not a very large amount. The relatively minor amount is accounted for partly because the water augmentation regime was assumed applicable only to federal land holdings in the watershed suitable for yield augmentation treatment, a little less than one-half of the land in the drainage. So, to estimate the full potential for augmented streamflow from the drainage, we might get, as a first approximation, somewhat more than two times our earlier estimate of 1.4 per cent or, roughly, 3 per cent of the present drainage runoff.

A second factor that merits discussion relates to the timing of the increment of water in relation to the base flow. There is a paucity of experimental data that would fix with precision the timing of the augmented runoff in relation to the base flow. Kattelmann and associates (1983:400) comment that regarding snowmelt delay, small openings are an improvement over large clearcuts. With respect to the uncut forest, small openings are not likely to delay the snowmelt but, owing to snow redistribution as well as to reduced evapotranspiration, a greater amount of runoff will be available. Quoting Kattelmann and associates:

> Anderson (1956) found more than 50 cm snow water equivalent was present in narrow strips at the time of snow disappearance in large open areas. The strips became bare about two weeks later. Where silvicultural conditions and logging costs permit, modifying timber harvests to delay snowmelt appear to have a significant potential for increasing the utility of streamflow from the forest snow zone. Again, the question of treatable area looms large in assessing downstream effects.

We have already accounted for the factor regarding land suitable for treatment. We have based our estimates in Table 1 on yield from just the area that appears suitable for appropriate water augmentation treatment. The estimates given correspond to one scenario, that is, snowmelt timing not differing from that of the general watershed area. Although the increment in runoff might not be advanced over that from the forest as a whole, it may be useful to estimate the results when the augmented flow would precede the base flow, as it might under conditions where the augmented flow would correspond to large clearcut harvest regimes.

In Table 2A we present the results for augmented flow leading the flow from the general forest by two weeks. We see that a cycle of runoff generated ahead of the hydrograph for base flow results in lower system output as compared with augmented flow coincident with runoff from an uncut forest (Table 2B). To follow through, we also present, in Table 2C, the results of simulated system performance when the augmented flow lags two weeks relative to the uncut forest. We have mentioned the paucity of experimental data on augmented yields and their timing with the result that our analysis is more illustrative than it is based on scientifically determined yield and lead/lag relationships. It is noteworthy, however, that, given the configuration of hydrosystem components and their capacities, generally speaking the longer the augmented yield is delayed within the four-week period, the greater the system output. For example, if

TABLE 2

Effects of timing in the release of augmented flow

A. Net gains - incremental flow leading uncut forest flow by 2 weeks

	Mean	SD	Max	Min
Annual power (gwh)	2.01	0.07	1.81	2.18
Annual IRGN (maf)	0.03	0.00	0.02	0.04
Annual M&I (maf)	0.04	0.01	0.02	0.06
Annual inflow (maf)	1.19	0.03	1.13	1.26
PV of power (M$)*	1,606.47	96.22	1,368.04	1,895.33

B. Net gains - incremental flow coincident with uncut forest flow

	Mean	SD	Max	Min
Annual power (gwh)	2.02	0.07	1.83	2.20
Annual IRGN (maf)	0.03	0.00	0.02	0.04
Annual M&I (maf)	0.04	0.01	0.02	0.06
Annual inflow (maf)	1.19	0.03	1.13	1.26
PV of power (M$)*	1,618.71	94.83	1,382.28	1,901.68

C. Net gains - incremental flow lagging uncut forest flow by 2 weeks

	Mean	SD	Max	Min
Annual power (gwh)	2.06	0.07	1.88	2.23
Annual IRGN (maf)	0.03	0.00	0.02	0.04
Annual M&I (maf)	0.04	0.01	0.03	0.06
Annual inflow (maf)	1.19	0.03	1.13	0.04
PV of power (M$)*	1,653.75	90.79	1,435.59	1,924.08

NOTE: Present values calculated over a 180-year planning horizon at a 4 per cent discount rate

large clearcuts tend to experience snowmelt early by as much as two weeks compared with an uncut forest, the present value of the extra power produced from augmented flow over the 180-year management horizon is on the order of $12,240 less, expressed as a present value, than the value of power produced by an augmented flow whose timing coincides with snowmelt from an uncut forest. By the same token, if experimental results would establish that the augmented yield could be delayed by as much as two weeks, the present value of the increased power produced would be about $35,000 more, expressed as a present value.

All of the lead/lag analysis was performed using the augmentation of yields appropriate to a maximum water yield watershed management regime. Also, a comparable set of lead/lag relationships
were simulated for the case in which the identical area was managed
for high timber value without regard to effect on water yield. The results are quite similar.

It should be noted that although there appears to be a significant
difference in system performance depending on whether the augmented flow leads or lags the flow coming from an uncut forest, the
amount expressed in monetary terms is not great. It seems insufficient to justify any great amount of research directed towards finding means by which to delay the runoff from treated areas. This observation relates to the particular water and hydropower system on
the South Fork drainage that establishes what gains can be achieved
from delaying runoff. It is conceivable that the difference in gains
from lags that would occur for larger systems would warrant a
greater effort. In any event it needs to be understood that here we
have been evaluating the incremental yields as a function of the timing, and not the difference, of the waterflow with (as compared to
without) an augmentation program.

Finally, there is another factor that will affect the hydrosystem
output. It involves a restriction on drawing down the Little Grass
Valley Reservoir during the summer recreation season. There currently exists an informal understanding between Watershed Management on the Plumas National Forest and OWID, with the objective
of limiting the Little Grass Valley Reservoir drawdown to 56,000 acre
feet during the summer season. We have simulated the hydrosystem performance under several different drawdown policies to estimate how much power, if any, is lost as a result of summer drawdown restrictions of different degrees of severity.

We have optimized reservoir operations under four alternative
levels of the penalty that limits summer drawdown. These penalties
range from prohibitively high, enforcing rigid adherence to summer
recreation storage needs, through two penalty levels of lesser severity and, finally, to no penalty. It should be noted that, even in this
last case, the system model has built-in limitations on summer reservoir operations. In all cases, if the recreation storage requirement
is unfulfilled, no releases are allowed except as needed to meet minimum instream flow requirements.

We show in Figure 4 the difference in the contents of Little Grass
Valley Reservoir as a function of severity in penalties for violating
the recreation drawdown restrictions. Reservoir contents over the

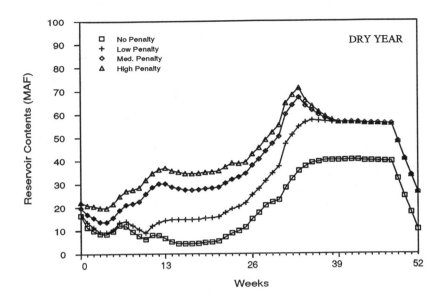

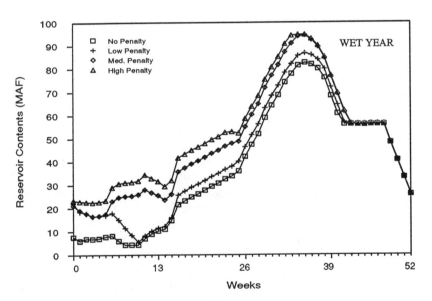

FIGURE 4
Effect of recreation penalty on Little Grass Valley storage

TABLE 3
Effect of variation in LGV reservoir recreation penalty

	Penalty severity			
	High	Moderate	Low	None
Annual power (gwh)	668.7	671.8	676.6	678.6
Annual IRGN (maf)	20.3	20.4	20.4	20.3
Annual M&I (maf)	30.7	30.7	30.6	30.
Annual inflow (maf)	381.1	381.1	381.1	381.1
PV of power ($M)*	568,666.4	572,696.2	578,650.8	580,516.7

NOTE: Present values calculated over a 180-year planning horizon at a 4 per cent dis count rate

year for a typical dry year (top figure) and wet year are illustrated. Enforcing the recreation storage requirements prevents the aggressive early drawdown of reservoir contents that is necessary to accommodate the peak inflow. Table 3 provides a summary of the output that results under the various penalty levels.

How is the value of the power generated affected by the severity of the penalty? We note that the value of power generated, assuming no penalty and only minimal restrictions on the operation of the reservoir, will be in the vicinity of $11.8 million greater, expressed in present value terms, than operations subject to high penalties for violating the limit. If a moderate penalty is in force (perhaps most like the actual operation of the reservoir by OWID), then we find a loss in the present value of power of about $7.8 million relative to operations under no penalty. Now the recreational receipts at the developed areas on the reservoir came to roughly $45,000 for the 1987 recreational season, with a modest annual increase being experienced. The present value of receipts, assuming modest growth, would be in the neighbourhood of from $1.25 million to $1.50 million. We note that this is considerably short of the lost power value, and it raises interesting issues.

Perhaps the first issue is that the National Forest System has a legislative charge to provide outdoor recreation and has no similar directive under its legislation to provide hydroelectricity. We do not know what conditions attach to OWID's permit to develop a federally owned site, but almost surely some restrictions apply. Secondly, there is an important distributional question pitting the users of the federal lands for recreation against the gains to the customers of the Pacific Gas and Electric Company. This is not an issue we elect to settle, since it is not within the competence of economics to settle equity issues. It is nonetheless important to take note of the issue.

ECONOMIC ANALYSIS OF VARIOUS WATERSHED MANAGEMENT OPTIONS

In the hydrologic section we have illustrated the effect on hydrosystem performance of a maximum water yield augmentation policy. We have conducted a sensitivity analysis to illustrate the difference that would occur if the snowmelt could be advanced or delayed by two weeks. We have also considered the difference that modifying the penalty for violating summer drawdown restrictions on Little Grass Valley would have on hydrologic system outputs. All of this was done exclusively in a hydrologic analytical framework. But in order to get an economic measure of performance we need to take into account the management costs and the differences in output and value of both timber and water as different watershed management options are played out. This we will do next.

To analyze the economic feasibility of a water augmentation program in the drainage above Little Grass Valley Reservoir, we simulated the multiple-use forest using a linear programming model. The necessary data on land characteristics, stocks, yields, and management costs were provided by the Plumas National Forest. We consider six initial watershed management options, with these options ranging from one that seeks to provide high present values from water yield with little attention to timber to one that seeks high value from timber production without explicit attention to water.

In all cases, the initial forest stands are harvested over a four-decade period. This rate of harvesting reflects our constraint that no more than one quarter of the forest area be harvested in any decade. The differences between the options arises with respect to the management of the regenerated stands. The maximum water augmentation option (WT40) involves no effort to ensure regeneration into productive timber stands and the clearing of vegetation each forty years to reduce depletion of runoff by reason of evapotranspiration from colonizing vegetation. The high timber production option (TM60) calls for intensive efforts at stand regeneration and improvement, more costly roading effort, and a harvest of regenerated stands every sixty years. Other options reflect various combinations of the harvest cycle and management effort. In each of the six initial management options, rotation age and management intensities are imposed upon the model solution. As our seventh management option (MAX), we allow the linear programming model to freely select the management and harvest date for each analysis area so as to maximize the combined net value from timber and water output. In all cases, it is assumed that water value, timber price, and management costs are not systematically changing over time.

The results for each management option are summarized in Table 4. In the table we present the average annual increment in water flow provided by each option, the average annual value from each incremental acre foot of water, the present value from the services of the incremental water within the hydropower system, and the total present net value from the combined production of timber and water (at a 4 per cent discount rate). Two immediate observations can be made. First, there is an overall similarity in the present value of all options. This should not be surprising since, in each option, the revenues and water flow that result from the harvesting of existing forest stands will dominate the present value. Second, we should note that the present value from water is small relative to the overall present value. There might then be a presumption that timber management concerns should dominate.

Look first at the results of our high timber yield option (TB60). For this option it is assumed that we have a sixty-year rotation with immediate artificial rotation and other prescribed practices for fully managed stands, as called for within the Plumas forest plan. The sixty-year rotation period is perhaps a little shorter than is typical, but it is very close to the economically optimal rotation period were we managing for timber value alone. In comparison to other options, management for timber provides only modest increments to waterflow because of the relatively infrequent harvest entries.

To get some insight into how a shorter rotation period might improve the balance of timber and water production, we play out a short rotation consisting of a combined timber and water management option (TB40). In this option, timber harvests on the regenerated stands occur on a forty-year rotation cycle. As before, stands are promptly regenerated by artificial means and fully managed to promote timber yields. We can see that a shorter rotation period, although yielding a 50 per cent increase in average annual increment to water flow, results in a large overall reduction of $1.264 million in net present value. The extension of the rotation period from forty to sixty years more than compensates for itself, because timber values increase more than the loss of water value decreases, due to the longer harvest cycle. This might seem to suggest that management to improve water yield is not economically desirable.

However, look now at the results of our high water yield option (WT40). The results here were arrived at without regard to the continuing production of timber value. This is not to say that timber does not contribute significantly to the outcome. Looking behind the summary value we would find that the revenues from the harvest of the original stock of timber represents the substantial part of the total net present worth, as it does in all the options. However, timber considerations after the first entry harvests figure here only through their absence. With no effort taken to ensure regeneration or improvement of the cleared stands, and with the short entry cycle, no significant timber volume is produced from the second growth stands. But along with the absence of timber value from otherwise regenerated stock is the absence of regeneration cost and a reduction in other costs associated with continuing timber management. To get an insight into how timber value and management cost for the second growth vegetation play out, compare the results of the water management option (WT40) to the similarly short rotation option (TB40) that includes timber considerations along with a heavy water augmentation regime.

There are a couple of inferences to draw from the results of Table 4. It will be noted that the mean annual increment of water and water values for TB40 are, for all intents and purposes, equivalent to those shown for the high water yield option (WT40). This is not surprising, because the periodic rate of removal of existing vegetation in the two options is the same. However, the net present value of all output is substantially reduced in option TB40. The revenues from timber harvests upon first entry will be the same, and that provides the bulk of the overall net present value. What enters as a difference in the net present value is the reduction in the complex of management and transportation cost balanced against the modest discounted value of revenue from future timber harvests. From the summary data, it is clear that in foregoing continued timber production, the present value of costs is reduced by almost $2.5 million more than is the present value of foregone timber harvests. Overall, the water management option (WT40) provides greater net value than does either of the two managed timber options. This reflects the fact that continued intensive timber management is unprofitable because of the high costs of regeneration. This being the case, it is useful to address the question as to whether regeneration costs can be reduced in the timber options.

What we have done is to accept a presumption that by avoiding artificial regeneration cost after the first entry harvests, we will be able to reduce the net negatives. In Table 4, we present the results of two timber management options that rely upon natural regeneration to a great extent, using supplemental artificial regeneration only to im-

TABLE 4

Summary results for watershed management option

	Management option							
	WT40	TB40	TB60	LF60	LR60	LF80	Max
Water increase (AF)	1,119	1,119	800	800	800	660	920
Water value/AF ($)	63.69	63.69	63.76	63.76	63.76	63.35	63.70
PNV water (M$)*	1,618.7	1,618.9	1,412.5	1,377.2	1,377.2	1,337.1	1,432
Total PNV (M$)*	50,000	47,679	48,943	49,470	49,618	49,826	50,289

NOTES: Present values calculated over a 180-year planning horizon at a 4 per cent discount rate

WT40 = High water yield option

TB40 = Combined water and timber management option (with forty-year rotation cycle)

TB60 = High timber yield option

LF60 = Timber management option with natural regeneration for first twenty years and sixty-year harvest cycle

LR60 = Natural regeneration only and sixty-year harvest cycle

LF80 = Timber management option with natural regeneration for first twenty years and eighty-year harvest cycle

Max = Optimal solution

prove the stocking after twenty years of natural regeneration. In option LF60, harvesting occurs on a sixty-year cycle, with harvest volume (reflecting the twenty-year lag in regrowth) equivalent to that expected from the fully managed forest at age forty. In option LF80, harvests occur on an eighty-year cycle, providing a yield equivalent to that from a fully managed sixty-year old stand.

It may be the case that these options are too artificial, and we are not prepared to argue that they are fully consistent with the forest ecology in the region. In the absence of the sort of input from Forest Service personnel that would permit a more carefully contrived option, we present the analysis to illustrate a significant question. Is it not possible to rely on natural regeneration to offset some of the cost of immediate artificial regeneration to provide a better overall economic result than that given by the intensive management options TB40 and TB60? Our illustration suggests that the elimination of the costs postulated in the amended options (LF60 and LF80) significantly reduces the difference in net present value between the water management option (WT40) and the timber management option (TB40). We find that if the bulk of the regeneration can be accomplished by natural means (with selected artificial regeneration of only the remaining poorly stocked sites) in order to achieve a fully stocked condition, then the net present value will be increased more than it would be through immediate artificial regeneration.

This raises an ancillary question. If an increase in net present value is achieved by delaying artificial regeneration and reducing it to only supplementary regeneration, can a further improvement be achieved by eliminating artificial regeneration altogether? We have played this option through in the case of the sixty-year harvest cycle (LR60) and show the results in Table 4. The results for option LR60 must be interpreted differently from those for other options. Having no information on the harvestable volume that might be available with fully natural regeneration, the sacrifice in volume was preselected (e.g., a 30 per cent reduction) to provide for an overall net present value as close as practicable to that from option LF60. Accordingly, all we can say is that if natural regeneration on any given site would provide up to 70 per cent of the volume expected from the fully stocked stand, one should be at the margin of indifference between delayed artificial regeneration and fully natural regeneration.

We have presented six options, ranging from a water maximization option without regard to timber consideration to full timber emphasis without regard to water yield consideration. We can observe that two extreme options (WT40 and LF80) result in overall net present values of roughly equivalent amounts. That does not mean that the two management programs reflecting the options are roughly similar. The water option WT40 will provide roughly 80 per cent more annual incremental waterflow and $380 thousand dollars greater present value from water. Conversely, the best timber management option LF80 (a low management intensity option), while producing less in water value will produce equivalently greater timber value. Does this mean that there is little to choose between the two? Not quite.

The timber option, all things considered, will be more capital-intensive. Higher costs will be incurred for regeneration and other timber management costs. If there is no capital or budget constraint, then only the net present values are relevant for choice. If there are binding constraints on the forest's budget, then it may be that the lower expenditure program is the one to choose. This is an issue we do not elect to address in detail. It is enough to note that, overall, the rate of return to investment for the primarily water option will be greater, albeit not much greater, than that for the timber management options. In fact, both options prove to have their role to play in the full multiple-use management scheme.

As our final management regime (MAX), we have run the FORPLAN model permitting the choices of management prescriptions and harvest cycles to be selected optimally. The summary results are presented in Table 4. The land allocation solution turns out to combine elements of both the water management regime and the lagged regeneration alternatives. The most productive timber lands are put into continued timber production, with low intensity management. The remainder of the land area is assigned to the water management option, with this assignment reflecting the poor economics of restoring these lands to productive timber as much as showing the inherent value of water management. It is interesting to note that in the MAX solution, the overall production of water yields and value is not greatly higher than results from the sixty-year timber management rotation option TB60. This reflects the rough split of the forest area between the short forty-year water management cycle and the long eighty-year cycle for option LF80. Overall present value, however, is greatly improved over the sixty-year timber rotation choice.

CONCLUSIONS: AN INTERPRETIVE SYNTHESIS

This study was motivated by an interest in learning whether management of watersheds explicitly for joint water augmentation and timber yields might provide an economic justification for managing land in cases where management for timber alone might not. The

Northern Sierra Nevada appeared to be a good region in which to examine this question, because the precipitation there provides more than 50 per cent of the non-saline water that occurs in California. And there is a large and growing demand for water in the California economy. While Pacific slope forests are productive timber growers in the mid and lower elevations, they are not equally productive at all elevations. Managing these upper elevation lands may require a conscious effort to produce both water and timber as explicit joint products.

In assessing the land in the South Fork drainage suitable for watershed augmentation treatment we confirmed what Kattelmann and associates (1983:399) developed at some length. Not all of the land in the South Fork drainage which we examined for our study is in federal ownership, and, even on that which is, insufficient cover density and perhaps other factors reduce the amount suitable for yield augmentation treatment. Even so, with only about a half of the South Fork drainage available for water yield augmentation, we obtain an increment in flow amounting to roughly 1½ per cent of the total flow from the drainage at the point of entry to the Little Grass Valley Reservoir. This suggests that for a drainage which is wholly within federal ownership (National Forests), yet with the distribution of cover density, land use, and other factors similar to the South Fork drainage, we could expect an increment in streamflow in excess of 3 per cent. These data are not inconsistent with the estimates of Kattelmann and associates.

It is generally believed that the timing of increments to streamflow is an important factor in determining how effectively they can be used in productive applications (Kattelmann et al. 1983:400). Our test of the difference in the increment in yield due to time of snowmelt in our particular case, which incorporates the waterflow and hydropower structures downstream from the Little Grass Valley Reservoir on the South Fork, is generally consistent with the existing hydrologic research done on northern Sierra forests. Delaying the snowmelt, under circumstances represented by the development on the South Fork, will yield increased economic value. But the amount of the increase that is related solely to the delay in snowmelt is somewhat marginal. It is conceivable that a different configuration of conditions on the land from those encountered in the South Fork drainage, along with a different set of water resource structures, would increase the relative magnitude of the differences due to the timing of snowmelt, but there may be room for skepticism here. The only way to come to any unambiguous conclusions would be to undertake additional intensive hydrologic analyses of the type we have done in the current study for the different configurations of factors that exist in other drainages.

We have looked at another factor that will affect the hydrosystem performance. This has to do with the summer recreational constraints on the drawdown of Little Grass Valley Reservoir. We began with a condition in which no penalty was incurred for drawing down the reservoir. This would provide an increment in the value of power of some $11 million, expressed as a present value, as compared with a condition that would impose a high penalty for violating drawdown restrictions. The results of such a policy, however, would doubtless often violate the low flow restrictions for the South Fork as well as recreational drawdown constraints on the Little Grass Valley Reservoir. Holding OWID liable to the extent of moderate penalties for violating the drawdown restrictions consistent with minimum streamflow requirements below Little Grass Valley Reservoir would reduce the power losses to $7.8 million, expressed as a present value, as compared with high penalties for violating drawdown restrictions.

When this value is related to a relatively small geographic area, it looms as potentially significant. It must be noted, however, that the production of hydroelectricity is not within the scope of the Multiple-Use Sustained-Yield Act; nor is it required by the NFMA. On the other hand, there is a mandate to provide recreational services in both legislative acts. It is questionable, then, whether concern for the improved efficiency of hydroelectric power production is within the Forest Service's legal authority.

When we leave the factors which dominate the hydrologic analysis to address the issues that arise primarily in the context of economic analysis of alternative watershed treatment regimes, we first need to say the following: We have taken all of the timber yield, timber management cost, and prices available from the Plumas National Forest's FORPLAN data base. We have to acknowledge some skepticism concerning, among other things, the prices for timber used in the Plumas FORPLAN analysis. Be that as it may, we have presented eight variants of watershed management regimes for comparative purposes. It is of interest to note that the variants that either eliminate artificial regeneration entirely, or delay incurring artificial regeneration costs as long as possible, appear to be superior to those which proceed immediately with artificial regeneration. Even accepting the high prices imputed to timber, the variant that does not provide for continuing timber harvests compares more than favourably with a typical timber management regime. This variant benefits from the harvest of the initial stock but avoids all explicit timber management cost thereafter. If there are grounds for questioning the realism of the imputed timber value, then the water value maximizing variant is clearly the most economic.

The reason for the dominance of the non-timber regime relates primarily to the cost of artificial regeneration. With no artificial regeneration the total net multiple-use present value of forest management is greater than it is for any variant which involves artificial regeneration in its timber management program. An important corollary here is that the value of the 'second generation' timber for which artificial regeneration is undertaken has a lesser present value than does the present cost of establishing timber management. Put another way, the reason for positive net present worth of timber management regimes is solely related to the value of the initial harvest.

This brings us to the question concerning the transportability of our analytic models to other Northern Sierra forests. We need to make a distinction here between the method and the calibrated models. So far as the streamflow generator and the system optimization models are concerned, the methods developed are perfectly general – they can be applied to any drainage and water resource system. But, insofar as the calibration is concerned, it depends exclusively on the hydrologic data in the South Fork drainage, on the particular configuration of the projects existing on the river, and on the legal and administrative constraints (e.g., minimum flow requirements and pattern of contractual obligations) that govern OWID's operations.

Two points might be made here. Our stochastic streamflow generator incorporates a wrinkle that provides for superior fidelity in mimicking the actual flow and may be of note for avoiding problems of non-correspondence between predicted and actual hydrographs encountered with the standard methods of developing streamflow generators. Secondly, the hydrosystem optimization model provides for convenient optimization for a system which has more than one storage reservoir. This, too, is an advance over standard models.

ACKNOWLEDGMENTS

We are indebted to the following for assistance given in the preparation of this study: Robert Schultz, Hydrologist, Plumas National Forest; Stephen C. Onken, Superintendent, Power Division, Oroville-Wyandotte Irrigation District; and Rhey Solomon, Water Resources Program Manager, USDA Forest Service. We are especially indebted to Lewis Manhart, USDA Forest Service, Policy Analysis Staff, for his help in facilitating the conduct of this work under contract. We alone are responsible for any errors of interpretation or analysis.

NOTES

1 Our estimates of water yield are drawn from unpublished documents provided by Robert Schultz, Hydrologist, Plumas National Forest (c. 1979).
2 If q is lognormally distributed, so that ln(q) is distributed normally with mean and standard deviation, then the expected value of q is given by $E(q) = \exp(\mu + \omega^2/2)$.
3 The land area calculations were provided by Robert Schultz of the Plumas National Forest (private correspondence 1988).
4 This assertion is based on conversations with Dr. Rhey Solomon, Water Resources Program Manager, USDA Forest Service.

CHAPTER SEVENTEEN

Policies for the Management of Temperate Mountain Forests: A Comparison from Switzerland and Colorado

Martin F. Price

Sustained-yield forestry is a persistent concept in forest management in both Europe and North America.[1] Although the concept is centuries old, it was first formalized as the basis of scientific forestry in early nineteenth century Germany (Clawson and Sedjo 1984). While the concept was mainly developed for lowland forests, a primary impetus behind the formulation of national level forestry policies in many European and North American countries came from perceptions and studies of the conditions of mountain forests in these countries. This paper traces the antecedents, evolution, and effects of policies for the management of the forests of the Swiss Alps and Colorado Rocky Mountains over the past two centuries, identifies common and divergent themes, and assesses whether the traditional concept of sustained-yield forestry is appropriate for these regions.

NINETEENTH CENTURY

Switzerland

For centuries, the forests of the Swiss Alps have provided the region's inhabitants with wood for fuel, construction, and agriculture as well as with protection from natural hazards such as avalanches, floods, and landslides. These forests were, and still are, mainly owned by adjacent civil communes.[2] From since at least the thirteenth century, to ensure the continued provision of the forests' benefits, communes promulgated policies limiting certain or all uses of the forests and their products. These policies were not wholly successful. By the early nineteenth century, the treeline had been lowered by 200-300 m (Langenegger 1984), supplies of wood had become inadequate, especially as demand increased as a consequence of industrialization and the spread of railroads, and natural disasters, including floods, landslides, and avalanches, were growing in number and severity (Tromp 1980). Recognition of these problems (due in part to the efforts of the first Swiss foresters, mainly trained in Germany (Schuler 1984)), led to the passage of cantonal forestry legislation and other policies in the century's first decades (Price 1988)[3] and, in 1858, to federal sponsorship of a study of the Alpine forests.

The resulting report was published in 1861. It described the conditions outlined above, emphasizing that annual utilization was, on average, 32 per cent greater than increment, and that regeneration was insufficient, especially because of excessive grazing by livestock. The report proposed that scientific forest management, based on the sustained-yield concept, was essential for the economic survival of communities and industries in the region (Schoeffel 1978). In 1868, severe floods caused substantial damage and loss of life in the Alps. This provided further impetus for the Swiss Forestry Association (SFA) to propose an amendment to the constitution, establishing federal superintendence over the forests of the 'high mountains.'

The amendment was passed in 1874, enabling passage of the Forest Police Law in 1876 (Bloetzer 1978). The law was intended to create a healthy, resilient, and, as far as possible, continuous Alpine forest in order to prevent damage from avalanches; to protect settlements, transport routes, and cultivated land from rockfall and landslides; to avoid soil erosion; and to regulate water flows. The law mandated surveys as the basis for management planning for sustained-yield forestry but largely left the initiation, implementation, and funding of forestry policies and activities to the cantons, although it provided for federal reimbursement for some activities.

In 1886, a second survey of the Alpine forests was conducted. This concluded that existing policies were having few positive effects on the condition of the forests (Bloetzer 1978), although surveys had been made in some areas, providing the basis for sustained-yield prescriptions in management plans (Price 1990). Hence, stimulated again by the activities of the SFA, a new constitutional amendment was introduced in 1892 to establish federal superintendence over all Swiss forests. This passed in 1897 and was followed in 1902 by enactment of a revised Forest Police Law, which decreased cantonal autonomy with respect to forestry and provided substantial financial support from the federal government (Bloetzer 1978).

Colorado

Colorado was organized as a territory in 1861, soon after the first gold rush began, and became a state in 1876. During this period, and until the end of the century, Colorado's economy depended primarily on mining, which went through a number of booms and busts. Wood was essential for fuel, construction, mining, and railroads both in the mountains and in the expanding settlements along their edge. While, in the early 1860s, 'the mountain-sides were covered with thick forests,' by 1870, it was estimated that 'certainly one-third, possibly one-half [of the forests] in all the settled portions [of Colorado were] dead – killed by fire ... Some of this destruction [was] fairly attributable to accident, more of it to culpable carelessness, and yet more to criminal design' (Hough 1878:588).

These conditions, which persisted and intensified until the century's end, derived from the interaction of a number of factors. First, large areas of forest were felled, with much timber left unused. In the slash that remained, fires were easily started by discarded cigarettes, lightning, or sparks from sawmills and railroads (Wilson 1876; Ensign 1888a). Second, miners started fires to expose the rock beneath.[4] Finally, the federal Free Timber Act, passed in 1878 with strong support from Colorado's congressional delegation, allowed local residents to remove dead timber, but not green trees, from public lands.[5] Surreptitiously started fires were an easy way to circumvent the law by providing dead trees that could be used to meet growing demands for timber (Ise 1920).

In spite of widespread recognition of these problems, the actions of the Colorado legislature with regard to forest management were limited. An 1885 law created the post of forest commissioner and designated existing officials as forest officers (Ensign 1885). However, no funds were provided for these officials' activities until 1887, and in 1890 the Commissioner resigned, frustrated by lack of response to his proposals for legislation, forest management, and policing (Ensign 1888a). Since 1877, agents of the federal General Land Office had attempted policing of the forests, but they had little success, having little power and being spread very thinly (Fernow 1888). A federal Division of Forestry had also existed since 1881, but was limited to an advisory capacity, with no jurisdiction over forests on public land. Many of the division's reports during the 1880s, especially one on the forests of the Rocky Mountains (Ensign 1888b), emphasized the need for a coherent national forest policy. By 1890, President Harrison had also been persuaded of this, and he submit-

ted memorials proposing such legislation to Congress. These led to
the passage of the Creative Act in 1891, allowing presidential reservation of public forest lands. Of the sixteen reserves set aside nationwide by Harrison by the end of 1893, five were in Colorado
(Wengert et al. 1979).

Public and political opposition to neither the Creative Act nor the
reserves was very great. The law had little effect on logging or burning in the reserves since it said nothing about forest policing or
management. Primarily for this reason, Harrison did not set aside
any reserves after 1893. From 1892 to 1897, twenty-seven bills to protect and administer the reserves were introduced in Congress. The
Colorado delegation supported those bills that emphasized free use
of timber for local benefit (Ise 1920); one of these eventually passed
as the 1897 Organic Act. The Act's primary purposes were to allow
free use of timber, prospecting, and mining by local people; and to
protect and improve forests in order to provide reliable supplies of
water and timber. From 1898 onwards, appropriations for these purposes were included in federal legislation (Cameron 1928), and officers were appointed to police Colorado's reserves (Shoemaker 1958).

Comparative Analysis

The constellations of conditions leading to the development of nineteenth century policies for the forests of the two regions appear to
have been rather similar, in spite of significant differences in patterns of forest ownership and exploitation and in natural conditions
of climate and ecosystem development (Price 1990). Three interacting factors contributed to early policy formulation: increasing imbalances between demand for, and supplies of, wood; fears, sometimes realized, that continued loss of forest cover would lead to natural disasters of increasing number and severity; and the efforts of
early foresters, principally trained in the German tradition, to establish coherent national policies for forest management.

In both regions, early regional- and national-level policies were
ineffective, because governments committed insufficient resources
and because the policies ran counter to the beliefs of local people that
nearby forests were primarily for their own benefit. However, by the
turn of the century, local opposition to federal jurisdiction over the
forests of both regions had generally been overcome, and federal
legislation, including financial commitments, existed to protect and
to manage these forests. A primary aim of this legislation was to ensure reliable supplies of wood and water. In the Swiss Alps, strong
emphasis was also placed on the forests' protective functions; a cru-

cial difference deriving from the much higher density of settlement and transportation networks in this region. As discussed below, these early pieces of legislation officially guided forestry in both regions for much of this century.

Switzerland

Although it derives from conditions in an era which was very different from today, the 1902 Forest Police Law remains the basis for the management of the forests of the Swiss Alps. However, the law has been modified by subsequent legislation, and the management of forests in each canton is further directed by federal and cantonal regulations and cantonal forestry legislation. The 1902 law mandated the passage of such legislation, which is subject to approval by the federal government. To trace the evolution of policies for forest management during this century, both federal policies and the policies of the three largest cantons in the Swiss Alps – Berne, Grisons, and Valais – are discussed below.

The partial revisions of the 1902 federal law and other federal laws which affect mountain forestry (Price 1988) changed federal policy in two main directions. First, additional financial support was provided for various activities intended to improve the management of the forests through rationalization of ownership, increased access, protection against natural hazards, and the exclusion of damaging animals (both livestock and game) and diseases. Second, particularly in revisions passed since 1950, the cantons were given greater responsibility for both policy implementation and financial support. However, the ratio of federal to cantonal funding for forestry projects varies between cantons, depending on both the financial resources of the canton and the viability of its forestry programs.

The evolution of federal policy is shown particularly well by changes in the regulations pursuant to the 1902 law. The first regulations were passed in 1903; the most recent major revision was in 1965. The regulations have three main components: means for implementing the law's general requirements, regulation of specific activities, and legal definitions. One of the most important of the latter defines protective forests, which include all of the Alpine forests. In the 1965 regulations, these are defined as 'of importance for the gathering and supply of water, the cleansing of air, the recreation and health of the population, and landscape protection.' This definition reflects substantial changes in attitudes to these forests since they were defined more narrowly in the 1902 law: 'forests located in the catchments of mountain streams, as well as those which through their location can provide protection against damaging climatic influences, avalanches, rock- and ice-fall, landslides, and extreme water levels.'

The pace of development of cantonal legislation has varied greatly. For instance, while Berne passed an overall forestry law in 1905, and Valais passed one in 1910, Grisons did not have a forestry law until 1963. In the meantime, forestry in Grisons was guided by a series of regulations passed from 1877 through 1942 (Rageth 1983). The most recent forestry law for Berne dates from 1973; Valais passed a new law in 1985. While the current cantonal forestry laws all include the preservation of the forests and the improvement of protective functions as primary objectives, there is a marked diversity in the additional primary objectives. For instance, the Grisons law further stresses that, within the restrictions of the primary objectives, the forests must be managed so that yields increase. In contrast, the later laws specify the encouragement of good management and the improvement of 'welfare functions' as additional primary objectives. Welfare functions relate to values of the forests such as the conservation of ecosystems and the importance of forests as part of a landscape also used for tourism and agriculture. The Valais law has a much wider range of primary objectives than do the others, including both 'increasing the potential yield of the forests' and the 'maintenance and preservation of the cultural landscape and a healthy environment.' To a certain extent, the diversity of objectives reflects the federal nature of Swiss government. However, they may also be viewed as responses to changing economic conditions and attitudes towards forests in recent years.

Until the 1950s, most Alpine communities were essentially self-sufficient, with adjacent forests important for providing income and employment, raw materials, and fuel. During this period, forests were the main source of income for many Alpine communes (Leibundgut 1956), and wood harvests from the Alpine forests grew steadily, with a growing emphasis on wood for sale rather than local use (Auer 1956). The end of the Second World War represented a turning point in the development of the Alpine forests, resulting from the coincidence of management-ecological and socioeconomic trends. The forests began to experience decreasing levels of maintenance[6] and harvesting; levels which were insufficient for the optimal growth of their trees, most which had begun life near the turn of the century when substantial regeneration began as a result of the implementation of the directives of the Forest Police Law. The symptoms were many even-aged stands of trees that were relatively thin for their age and site conditions and a relatively low level of regeneration (Ott 1972). These characteristics are linked to decreases in the forests' productivity and ability to fulfil protective and recreational functions (Combe and Frei 1986).

These functions, however, have grown ever more important with the increasing integration of Alpine communities into national and international economies. In particular, tourism, made possible by the greater mobility and financial resources of people throughout the Western world, has become the economic backbone of most communities rather than of just the few where tourism had been important since the late nineteenth century (Bridel 1984). Thus, the forests have grown more important both as components of the landscape and for recreation and the protection of facilities, which have been increasingly constructed in locations with considerable danger from natural hazards (Kienholz 1984).

Post-war relationships between tourism and forestry in the Swiss Alps have been discussed by Price (1987), who concludes that the former has generally developed at the expense of the latter. Critical, interacting factors in the decline of forestry include low access levels; the financial insecurity of forestry enterprises; a workforce of inadequate numbers and training; and a lack of management planning which reflects the current values of the forests. Many of these factors have economic bases; in general, the dominant impacts of tourism on forestry are economic. One important impact relates to employment: tourism provides better-paid, easier, and safer jobs than does forestry. A second is that investment in, and the maintenance of, facilities for tourism leads to a lack of resources for forestry. Yet, as noted above, the long-term survival of tourism depends on the protective and recreational functions provided by the forests. Consequently, the tourist industry should support forestry, both through the provision of winter employment for forestry personnel and by direct involvement, including financial support, in forestry planning, production, and maintenance.

The principal need of forestry, throughout the Swiss Alps, is to increase levels of maintenance and timber extraction. This is necessary to improve forest structure, that is, to provide a more even distribution of trees of different ages, with increased regeneration, less dense stands, and lower reserves. The purpose of these changes is to maximize the ability of the forests to withstand natural and anthropogenic stresses and to provide a high-quality environment for recreation along with high quality timber. At present, much extraction is compulsory, as a result of physical and/or biological damage, and is limited by access (Affolter 1985; Ott 1984). Consequently, areas and volumes of extraction usually bear little relationship to the prescriptions in management plans.

In spite of the increasing tendency for both federal and cantonal policies to consider the non-market values of the Alpine forests, this trend is appearing very slowly in operational management planning. Most existing plans are based firmly on the sustained-yield concept, primarily considering timber harvesting, and were written without input from individuals in other sectors of the mountain economy. Also, some plans are so old as to have no current relevance (Price 1990). However, forest stability assessments (Langenegger 1979; Ott and Schönbachler 1986) are now being introduced into the planning process, and flexible planning methods are now being developed at the Federal Technical Polytechnic in Zürich (e.g., Gordon 1985) and by the Forest Service of Valais. In contrast to existing plans, which prescribe activities for historically demarcated areas of little functional relevance, these methods emphasize functional zoning of forests, divided into rational management districts, as a basis for planning.

As noted above, a crucial need for Swiss Alpine forestry is to increase levels of timber extraction so that the forestry industry can eventually become self-sufficient. To some extent, this may be encouraged by actions in the forestry, wood products, tourism, and other industries at the local or regional level. Yet a critical problem is that Swiss timber is highly uncompetitive in the European market, and possibilities of improving the internal Swiss market through import tariffs are generally precluded by the General Agreement on Tariffs and Trade (GATT). An inescapable conclusion, therefore, is that, in spite of considerable increases in the level of support and activities covered in recent years (Wandeler 1985), further changes in cantonal and federal policies are necessary.

The critical lack in existing policies is that they do not prescribe the minimum management levels vital to ensure that the forests provide their functions in the long-term. Thus, Forest Service officials cannot persuade forest owners to do anything in their forests, unless it can be shown that their protective function is directly endangered.[7] Since most forestry operations result in deficits, forest owners will not cut trees if the only apparent beneficiary is a nebulous 'public.' Similarly, they will not invest in new roads, plant trees, or undertake any maintenance if returns on these investments, or rises in wood prices, appear unlikely in the near future.

In response to these concerns, a new forest law was proposed by the federal government in 1988 (Anon 1989). Its primary goals are to assure the minimum forest management levels described above and to provide assistance so that forest owners do not suffer financially in undertaking activities in the common interest. The law's objectives are to preserve the forest in its area and spatial distribution; to encourage its natural vitality and its diverse functions – protection, welfare, and wood production – including support for the forestry industry and owners; and to support measures to protect living space from natural hazards. This law, which should be enacted in the early 1990s, will provide the first step towards management of all Swiss forests, with funding prioritized according to the importance of actions in the public interest. The law's effectiveness will require acceptance of its goals – and the policy, planning, and economic changes they demand – by many parties, especially cantonal governments, the forestry profession, forest owners, and the tourism, forestry, and wood-products industries.

Colorado

By the end of 1907, well over half of the land in Colorado's mountains had been designated as National Forests (Shoemaker 1944). These lands were managed by the federal Forest Service, founded in 1905 when the Transfer Act gave the Department of Agriculture jurisdiction over the forests (Steen 1976). Until 1960, the primary policies guiding the management of the National Forests were the Organic Act and a letter sent by the secretary of agriculture to Gifford Pinchot, the chief of the Forest Service, on the day the Transfer Act was signed. The letter, drafted by its recipient, stated that 'all land [in the National Forests] is to be devoted to its most productive use for the permanent good of the whole people ... where conflicting interests must be reconciled the question will always be decided from the greatest good of the greatest number in the long run.' The letter had three major themes: a sound technical basis for conserving and using National Forests; decentralized administration, with discretion exercised locally to fit local conditions; and a commitment to the economic stability of communities in and near these forests (Dana and Fairfax 1980).

The letter's first theme, in particular, reflected Pinchot's training in forestry in France and Germany. The National Forests were to be managed according to the sustained-yield concept, using detailed resource inventories as the basis for planning to produce the desired outputs (Wilkinson and Anderson 1987). Yet, at the same time, the primary duty of Forest Service officers was fire prevention (U.S. Forest Service 1907); a management activity that, unlike harvesting and reforestation, was not specifically considered in Pinchot's planning process. As Pyne (1982:101, 231-2) has commented, 'the fire scenes of western America and western Europe were irreconcilably different ... Forestry as an intellectual discipline could only lend theoretical support to the generally accepted proposition that wildfires ought to be controlled.'

The belief that European principles of forestry were relevant throughout North America applied not only to the officials at Forest Service headquarters but also to the graduates of the fast-growing number of forestry schools (Clepper 1971). Yet, as late as 1917, written plans for Colorado's forests, based on detailed inventories and estimates of demand, were the exception rather than the rule (Lowell 1917). Timber management plans were prepared for most forests in the 1920s and 1930s, though they were often based on inventories of questionable validity. Even where plans existed, their prescriptions were of little practical importance. During this period, there was generally little active management (e.g., thinning, reforestation); harvesting depended mainly on local demands, tied closely to the fortunes of rail and mining companies, and was spatially limited because of highly variable access (Price 1990).

Thus, for the first half of this century, the main emphasis of forest management in Colorado was not on the wood production foreseen by Pinchot but on fire prevention. This emphasis existed at least as early as 1909 (Riley 1909). A significant stimulus to this activity was the loss of two million ha of National Forest and 85 lives, mainly in Idaho and Montana, to fires in the summer of 1910 (Pyne 1982). Though these losses did not occur in Colorado, they strongly affected management policies and activities there. During the next decade, Forest Service personnel considerably extended the road and trail network in Colorado's National Forests, built lookout towers, and began a widespread public education program. Yet, as late as 1927, there were no written fire plans for these forests (Waha 1927).

A review of the success of fire prevention programs in Colorado up to 1942 (Brown 1942) concluded that they had primarily been successful in persuading the public that '[p]reventing fires was a good thing.' However, the emphasis on fire prevention had made Forest Service personnel bored and had limited resources for other activities. In addition, the number of fires was increasing, mainly started by campers and smokers. Just as the rangers were losing their enthusiasm for the crusade, the forests were being increasingly used for recreation by people who were unindoctrinated or who were forgetful about the importance of fire prevention.

Recreation was not mentioned as a forest output in the Organic

Act or in the 'Pinchot letter' and was mentioned only in passing in other early official Forest Service documents. Though at least one early official in the Washington headquarters (Cleveland 1910) recognized recreation as a growing, legitimate use of the National Forests, this view was rare. However, recreational use was mentioned in national annual reports from 1912; and in 1915 Congress passed a law authorizing the Forest Service to grant permits for the private construction of summer homes, stores, and hotels in National Forests. Around the same time, three factors began to stimulate the Forest Service to consider planning for recreation: the formation of the National Park Service in 1916; the arrival of automobiles as a reliable and affordable form of transport; and federal highway building programs (Cate 1963).

A report to the chief of the Forest Service by Waugh (1918) noted that recreation was a paramount, if not exclusive, use in some National Forests, and that clear planning and policies were vital. These conclusions, among others, led the chief to formally recognize, in 1919, that management planning should consider recreation and, in 1921, to declare that recreation was a major use of the National Forests (Wilkinson and Anderson 1987). However, this use was not legitimized until 1960, and Congress and many secretaries of agriculture and foresters continued to regard it as unsuitable and in conflict with the ethos of forestry. Thus, in general, adequate funds were not available, and personnel were unwilling to spend their time to plan and to develop recreational facilities to manage rapidly-increasing levels of recreational use (Maughan 1932; Gilligan 1953; Cate 1963).

Waugh's (1918) conclusions were not surprising to Forest Service personnel in Colorado. Even before their legal designation, some of Colorado's National Forests had received considerable recreational use from both local residents and tourists. In 1909, 100,000 people visited the Pike National Forest; this rate was increasing at 10 per cent a year. In 1916, 400,000 people visited the forest, accounting for 60 per cent of the total use in Region Two of the National Forest system, which includes Colorado[8] (Price, 1990).

Faced with these statistics, Region Two's regional forester became a prime mover in developing a national recreation policy (Cate 1963). He was faced with a dilemma. The Forest Service's primary responsibility was fire prevention, which required the construction of roads and trails. Yet increased access resulted in increased visitation, especially as automobile ownership grew. In addition, it was Forest Service policy to provide maps identifying camping and fishing sites and scenic areas. All of these factors not only encouraged recreational use but also led to the growing risk and frequency of fire

(Price 1990). One result of these interactions was that Region Two led the nation in planning for recreation; a full-time recreation specialist was appointed in 1917, two years before one was appointed in Washington (Cate 1963). Regional documents identified recreation as a major forest output by 1919 and noted that careful planning, development, and promotion of facilities were needed (Price 1990). By 1928, recreation was classified as a formal output to be considered within Pinchot's policy-setting framework (u.s. Forest Service 1919; 1928).

In 1930, Colorado's National Forests received 2.34 million visits (Johnson 1930), and the supervisor of the Pike Forest, which received a third of this use, foresaw that recreation would become the dominant use of most of these forests (Spencer 1930). However, most forest supervisors did not share this view, describing watershed protection, timber production, and grazing as the most important current and future forest outputs (Maughan 1932). One likely reason, apart from the widespread antipathy of foresters to recreation and the lack of funds for developing facilities, is that recreational use in most of Colorado's forests was not increasing as rapidly as it was in the Pike Forest, which was close to the rail-served cities of Denver and Colorado Springs. The trend of increasing recreational use slowed, and then decreased, in the Depression of the 1930s.

After the Second World War, recreational use of Colorado's forests again rose rapidly in summer and in winter (nearly all potential skiing sites were in the National Forests). This rapid growth occurred both because Colorado's population was growing rapidly, and because improved transportation networks allowed easier access to the mountains from both Colorado and other parts of the nation. Urban growth also led to increased demand for water, further underlining the importance of watershed protection. The improved transportation networks also made cost-effective the import of wood and wood products from elsewhere, so that local wood production had become even less important than it had been before the Second World War. Finally, demands for wood for agricultural uses and fuel declined. These interacting trends led Forest Service employees to realize that overall forest planning would have to balance the supply of all forest outputs, including recreation, timber production, watershed protection, and livestock grazing (Spencer 1946).

As described above, the concept of multiple-use planning had been recognized in Region Two's policies since the late 1920s. Again, Colorado had led the nation; the concept was only defined at the national level in 1933 and was better received outside the Forest

Service than within (Steen 1976). However, after the Second World War, nationwide demand for many forest outputs, many of which were not legislatively recognized, grew quickly: 'There was no longer sufficient land to accommodate all uses without conflict' (Dana and Fairfax 1980:205). In spite of the lack of legal mandate, both multiple-use and recreation plans have been prepared for Colorado forests since the early 1950s.

The first bill recognizing the concept of multiple use was introduced in the u.s. Senate in 1956 but did not pass. By 1960, supporters of the concept had persuaded recalcitrant Forest Service officials and members of opposed interest groups and Congress of its public benefit (Cate 1963). The 1960 Multiple-Use Sustained-Yield (musy) Act provided recognition that 'the national forests are established and shall be administered for outdoor recreation, range, timber, watershed, and wildlife and fish purposes.' This very broad legal definition of multiple-use, while explicitly stating that the National Forests were to be managed to produce diverse outputs, provided the Forest Service with little direction for managing forests in such a way as to fulfil the law's objectives (Nelson 1985). However, the enactment of the musy Act led to a major and continuing emphasis on planning within the Forest Service. This planning has been undertaken in a milieu of increasing complexity.[9] The recent evolution of federal forestry legislation and policies has been considered in detail by many authors (Dana and Fairfax 1980; Hewett and Hamilton 1982; LeMaster 1984; Wilkinson and Anderson 1987) and is discussed below with reference to Colorado.

In spite of the imprecision of the goals of the musy Act, two types of legally-sanctioned, multiple-use planning began soon after its passage. The first was the preparation of regional planning guides, used as the basis for land management plans (lmps) for ranger districts, the smallest subdivision of the National Forest system. The second was the preparation of plans for each resource in individual National Forests. All of these plans were completed for Colorado's National Forests during the 1960s. The lmps tended to be descriptive rather than prescriptive. In contrast, even in areas where wood production was of little economic importance, timber management plans defined silvicultural practices in considerable detail, according to the sustained-yield concept (Price 1990).

After the musy Act, the next law of major significance to National Forest planning and management was the 1964 Wilderness Act. This gave statutory recognition to the concept of wilderness, established a National Wilderness System, and provided means for expanding it. Previously, wilderness had been administratively designated as a land use since 1924 and was mentioned as a forest output in the MUSY Act. Wilderness areas had been designated in Colorado since 1926 (Gilligan 1953). They now account for 25 per cent of the Forest Service lands in the state (U.S. Forest Service 1983b).

In 1969, the National Environmental Policy Act (NEPA) was passed. Unlike the legislation discussed previously, NEPA applies to all federal agencies. It affects the planning and management of the National Forests in two main ways. First, an Environmental Impact Statement (EIS) must be filed for every proposed federal action 'significantly affecting the quality of the human environment.' Second, other government agencies and the public are to participate in the development and review of each EIS. One result is that Forest Service policies and plans can be challenged in court; the agency lost its almost total immunity from judicial oversight (Wilkinson and Anderson 1987). To bring Forest Service planning into line with NEPA's requirements, a new approach was established in 1973. The chief developed broad policies, which were interpreted in planning area guides in each region. These gave direction for individual National Forests' land use plans which, in turn, guided the preparation of unit plans for areas within the forest. In Colorado, these areas were, typically, smaller than a ranger district. Work began on plans in the mid-1970s.

Almost as soon as the requirements resulting from NEPA had been incorporated into the planning process, new legislation led to another redirection of National Forest management policies. As LeMaster (1984:175) has commented, the 'statutory authority for the [Forest Service] was effectively rewritten.' The process began with the passage of the 1974 Forest and Rangeland Resources Renewable Resources Planning Act (RPA). Its main effect was to emphasize national-level planning, subject to Congressional review, on a five-year time-scale. These plans are to be based on a comprehensive assessment, prepared every ten years, of 'present and anticipated uses, demand for, and supply of renewable natural resources ... through analysis of environmental and economic impacts, coordination of multiple use and sustained yield opportunities ... , and public participation.' RPA specifies the provision, management, or improvement of not only the 'renewable' resources specified in the MUSY Act but also wilderness, and water, air, and aesthetic quality. RPA emphasizes cost-benefit analyses of investment alternatives in order to maximize economic efficiency in the allocation of resources. This was a new approach to planning for the Forest Service, and it assumed that values can be obtained and compared for all forest outputs in 'an overwhelming expression of faith in the utility of accumulating and analyzing data' (Dana and Fairfax 1980:325).

Two years after RPA was passed, and before it was implemented in any more than a rudimentary fashion, it was amended by the National Forest Management Act (NFMA). The main changes that NFMA made to RPA concern timber management, a reflection of NFMA's history (LeMaster 1984). It also introduced the concepts of ecosystem and genetic diversity as forest outputs. NFMA further changed the Forest Service's approach to planning and management in two significant ways. First, a committee of independent scientists was to develop regulations, subject to public comment, to guide the Act's implementation. These were published in 1979 and revised substantially in 1982. Second, interdisciplinary teams were to prepare plans for each National Forest, assessing the potential for change in all forest outputs.

The first significant policy document produced in Colorado as a result of these new laws and policies was the regional guide (U.S. Forest Service 1983b). This guided the preparation of land and resource management plans for each National Forest. All of these have been completed, but some are still under administrative or judicial review. These documents all illustrate the tension between the approaches to planning mandated in RPA and NFMA. The RPA emphasizes the setting of national targets for the production of the resources it mentions. These targets are then divided up between regions and National Forests. In contrast, NFMA emphasizes planning at the regional and, particularly, National Forest levels. As Wilkinson and Anderson (1987) have noted, the result is an 'uneasy compromise,' which has resulted in 'confusion and dissension' in the Forest Service. For this reason, and also because many dominant forest outputs, such as recreation, are not adequately considered in a planning process that stresses economic criteria and goals and remains implicitly oriented to wood production through sustained-yield forestry, there is increasing discussion of the need for another major redirection of Forest Service policy at the national level (e.g., O'Toole 1988).

In Colorado, there is an additional reason to consider substantial policy changes. While most of Colorado's forests are fire ecosystems (Peet 1981), this primary successional agent has been excluded throughout this century in the interests of sustained-yield forestry. As a result, large areas of Colorado's forests are composed of trees that are increasingly susceptible to disease and fire; a paradox of policy. According to the traditional sustained-yield concept, which dominates in forest management planning, these trees should be removed by logging. However, this is a highly uneconomic proposition under conditions of limited access and demand for wood; for years, most timber sales in Colorado have lost money (Wilderness Society 1988). An alternative approach is to remove such trees by prescribed burning.

Prescribed burning has been successfully used in other parts of the United States to increase the diversity of fuel stands and decrease fuel loads (Pyne 1982; Lotan et al. 1983). While it is increasingly being used in Colorado on a site-by-site basis (Colorado State Forest Service 1988), in spite of a number of constraints to its use (Price 1991), it has been given little consideration in the development of official long-term policies for managing even those of Colorado's forests where constraints are few. Yet, since the dominant outputs of these forests are now, and are likely to remain, recreation and watershed protection, the optimum mix of methods of providing these outputs should be used. This is not only a policy issue to be resolved in Colorado. The catastrophic fires which occurred throughout the western states in 1988, particularly in Yellowstone, may either help or hinder in the development of such policy changes (e.g., U.S. Forest Service 1989). At present, the likely directions of change are unclear; it is to be hoped that future policies will consider both the ecology of the forests and the benefits that society demands from them.

Comparative Analysis

This century's policies for the management of the forests of the Swiss Alps and Colorado Rocky Mountains show substantial changes in emphasis, driven both by national-level political pressures and by economic and environmental conditions within these regions. A key factor in both regions has been tourism's rapid rise to economic dominance since the 1950s. Policies for the forests of both regions have undergone a philosophical evolution, with increasing consideration of outputs additional to those defined in the long-lived federal legislation enacted at the turn of the century. To date, this evolution has gone further at the national level within the United States, where the 1897 Organic Act placed greater stress on timber production than did the 1901 Swiss Forest Police Law, and the laws of the 1960s and 1970s now essentially consider all actual and potential forest outputs, including those with option or existence value (Krutilla and Fisher 1985) such as ecosystem and genetic diversity. In both Switzerland and the United States, this evolution proceeded more rapidly in the mountain regions discussed in this paper than it did at the federal level.

Colorado's foresters have long recognized that their forests are more important for protecting watersheds than for producing timber. Through the 1950s, management was principally custodial, emphasizing the suppression of forest fires and the provision of wood for local use. In general, forest management plans, based on the sustained-yield concept, were only prepared when guaranteed markets were available. In contrast, as mandated by legislation, comparable plans have been in existence for most of the forests of the Swiss Alps throughout this century. Yet, as in Colorado, the patterns and volumes of timber harvests have depended more on access to the forests, local demands, and opportunities for wood sales than on the prescriptions in these plans.

In addition to watershed protection and limited wood production, the other forest output that gained early recognition in Colorado was recreation. Both watershed protection and recreation were outputs which, in various ways, Colorado foresters were forced to consider because of public pressure. The growth in recreation was initially a trend to be coped with rather than planned for, but planning and management to provide this output were in existence well before it was formally recognized in national-level policies and, especially, in legislation. In comparison, recreation has not been a significant concern of Swiss forestry until recently. This was primarily because the civil communes which own most of the Alpine forests are not responsible for the development and maintenance of recreational facilities. However, this tendency is changing as tourism has become dominant in the Alpine economy and important for the economy of Switzerland as a whole.

A principal difference between the two regions is that the main locus of planning has remained with local foresters in Switzerland, while Colorado's foresters have lost much of their autonomy since about 1960. This has resulted largely from the enactment of legislation which mandated regional planning and introduced nationally-set targets for the production of forest outputs. These laws also mandated public participation and planning based primarily on economic efficiency analyses. The net result has been that an increasing number of Forest Service employees and other resources are utilized in fulfilling the requirements of these laws and other policies rather than on managing the forests for the outputs these policies are meant to ensure.

The public participation process in Colorado also provides a contrast to the Swiss Alps, where local people, even if they are forest owners, have little influence on policymaking. However, Swiss forest owners do influence policy implementation through decisions, based mainly on economic grounds, as to whether specific activities should be undertaken. Again, in contrast to Colorado, these economic criteria relate mainly to local conditions (although the availability of cantonal or federal subsidies is often critical) rather than to analyses from economic models or to national or regional targets for the production of specific outputs. Economic criteria still tend to dominate planning and management decisions in Colorado. A general conclusion is that in both regions, both past and existing policies have been, and are, generally inadequate to ensure that the forests are managed to provide the intended outputs in the long-term. However, Switzerland's new Forest Law has the potential for solving many of these inadequacies.

CONCLUSION: SUSTAINED YIELDS FROM MOUNTAIN FORESTS

For nearly a century, the policies that have guided the management of the forests of the Swiss Alps and the Colorado Rocky Mountains have, either explicitly or implicitly, been guided by the concept of sustained-yield forestry. The objective of the seminal legislation enacted around the turn of the century for both regions was to ensure reliable supplies of both wood and water; in Switzerland, an additional primary objective was to maintain the forests' function of protection against natural hazards. Policies for both regions implicitly assumed that these objectives could be met by the regular harvesting of trees from all parts of the forests. Yet the social, economic, and environmental conditions influencing the forests of these regions in the past and present are very different to those existing when the sustained-yield concept was formalized.

This conclusion discusses the relevance of the sustained-yield concept for managing these temperate mountain forests in light of the concept's history. Three of the conditions existing in early nineteenth century Germany are crucial: (1) that all areas of forest could be managed; (2) that a demand for wood existed; and (3) that there would be an adequate workforce to supply this demand. A fourth, implicit, assumption was that the optimal method of regenerating the forests was to cut trees.

The first of these conditions has never applied in either the Swiss Alps or the Colorado Rocky Mountains, since access to many parts of each is limited. As a result, a significant part of the forests of both regions has not been subject to human influence in the past century. Two caveats should be made here. First, under the traditional pattern of logging in the Alps, winter was the primary logging season rather than, as at present, summer.[10] Consequently, greater areas were available for harvesting, since the location of roads was not a major constraint. Second, anthropogenic fires have influenced many otherwise inaccessible sites in the Rocky Mountains.

The second condition was valid in the wood-based economy that existed in both regions into this century. An additional demand was for railroad ties. Before the First World War, these had to be replaced at least every seven years in the United States (Olson 1971). Subsequently, new methods of cutting, preserving, and installing ties led to considerably lower demands. Other demands for local wood in both regions were decreased or removed by other types of technological change; only a few primary ones are mentioned here. First, the introduction of more efficient transportation systems meant that, even when wood was needed in mountain areas (especially for construction), it could be supplied more cheaply from areas where trees grew faster and could be extracted at lower cost. Second, harvesting costs in mountain areas have been affected by mechanization to a far lesser extent than they have been in less steep areas, further decreasing the competitiveness of mountain wood. Third, the introduction of new fuel sources, such as fuel oil and electricity, minimized the demand for fuelwood. And, fourth, the intensification of agriculture, in both lowland and mountain areas, substantially decreased demands for wood products.

The third condition is linked to the second to the extent that if there is a high enough demand for wood, prices will be high enough to pay people to harvest it. Conversely, when demand is low, the cost of employing contractors may be excessive in relation to the small or non-existent potential for profits, so that harvests to provide wood for sale will decrease. This was the case in Switzerland from the 1950s onwards, when, as described above, demand for wood decreased and tourism came to dominate the Alpine economy, providing new employment opportunities for local people. In Switzerland as a whole, forestry wage levels have risen far faster than have wood prices since 1950; and prices have decreased in the 1980s (Affolter 1985). In addition, forestry is not perceived as a particularly desirable profession: wages are relatively low, accident rates are high, and many positions are part-time; and the number of full-time jobs decreased about 40 per cent from the 1950s to the 1980s (Butora 1984; Schwingruber 1985). The number of Forest Service employees in Colorado has generally increased since 1960. Yet, in general, very few of these additional employees have been used in forest management; recreation and planning have tended to be the areas of greatest growth. Logging contractors do not have a secure existence, in spite of the Forest Service's concern for community stability (Schallau and Alston 1987); their employees are generally seasonal.

The fourth assumption (i.e., that the optimal method of regeneration is through cutting) holds true in the Swiss Alps, where the processes that would lead to regeneration under natural conditions have been successfully mimicked by local people for centuries, permitting the supply of both wood, usually on a reliable long-term basis, and protection from natural hazards. However, in Colorado, where fire is the primary natural agent of succession, prescribed burning would often be a more efficient means of ensuring regeneration, especially when the costs of logging (including road construction) are higher than those of burning, and both are greater than the price for which wood could be sold. These costs are not only short-term and purely monetary in nature; road construction, particularly on the thin, friable soils characteristic of much of the region, often has long-term costs, such as increased erosion and lowered water quality.

In sum, many of the conditions assumed for forestry based on the production of sustained yields of wood no longer exist in the two regions – if they ever existed.[11] Thus, the policies based on this traditional sustained-yield concept, which have officially guided the management of the forests of these regions for most of this century, have been and continue to be inappropriate. Furthermore, the prescriptions contained in management plans based on the concept were rarely implemented to any great extent except, perhaps, in the few easily-accessible parts of the forests of each region able to provide wood for which demands existed. A primary consequence is that the current structure of the forests is neither what was intended by the policies nor is it particularly suitable for fulfilling their objectives (Price 1990).

Recent policies for both regions realize, to a greater or lesser extent, that a new concept of sustained-yield forestry is necessary for managing mountain forests where the provision of public goods, such as recreation and protection (from natural hazards and of watersheds), is a primary objective. This philosophical change has been proposed by Wiebecke and Peters (1984), who suggest that the concept should be redefined as having the objective of ensuring the provision of all outputs desired by present and future generations. Thus, it should explicitly consider long-term, often unquantifiable values of the forests as well as economic criteria and need not necessarily be based on wood extraction as the primary means of producing these outputs. For instance, in Colorado, prescribed burning could be used as a management tool where appropriate. Similarly, in both regions, some areas of forest could be effectively ignored in terms of active management; an approach foreshadowed by the concept of wilderness in Colorado but also applicable in parts of the Swiss Alps. The 1985 Valais Forestry Law and the proposed Swiss Forest Law implicitly approach forest management from this new philosophical perspective; it is to be hoped that future policies for the management of Colorado's forests will also do so.

Finally, one should discuss the possible wider implications of the findings of this study. It considered a rather limited sample of sub-regions within two mountain chains whose ecological, political, economic, and social systems have evolved in very diverse ways. Nevertheless, the study indicated some strong parallels between the Swiss Alps and the Colorado Rocky Mountains, which suggests that there may be parallels both within the two mountain chains as a whole and also to other temperate mountain regions. In particular, the concept of sustained-yield forestry has been, and continues to be, widely applied both in such regions and in other mountain regions with rather different climates, none of which can be characterized by their similarity to early nineteenth century Germany. A further reason for considering that the lessons of this study may have a broader applicability is that the values provided to human populations by all mountain forests are broadly similar, even though the relative importance of different values varies greatly both between and within regions.

Mountain forests, by virtue of their location in the upper reaches of watersheds, are important to downstream communities, because they influence the rates at which water reaches, flows over, and infiltrates the ground surface. At the local scale, they also influence patterns of avalanches, rockfalls, landslides, and other geomorphic processes which can endanger settlements, transport infrastructure, agricultural land, and animal and human life. These values, which may broadly be subsumed under the heading of 'protection,' have been recognized by people in mountain areas from time immemorial. A further long-recognized value of mountain forests has been as a source of wood. Yet, many of these forests are now recognized – though not always in forestry policies and even less frequently in their implementation – as the source of many other values, including recreation, landscape, wilderness, and genetic and ecosystem diversity. In the Swiss Alps and the Colorado Rocky Mountains as well as in other mountain regions, some of these values are at least as important as are the long-recognized values – if not more so. Consequently, conclusions drawn from the study of these two sub-regions may well be relevant to other mountain regions. This suggests, in particular, that there may be a need to redefine the concept of sustained-yield forestry so that policies for mountain forests in general consider their full range of values over the long-term and accept that a wide range of methods of management may be applicable. In a period of rapid change in economic and political systems, and with the prospect of anthropogenic climate change within the next few decades, it seems appropriate to consider that flexibility should be a key characteristic of all forest management policies and their means of implementation.

ACKNOWLEDGMENTS

This research was supported in part by the Swiss Man and the Biosphere program, the U.S. National Science Foundation, the University of Colorado, and the Colorado Mountain Club Foundation.

NOTES

1 As Wiebecke and Peters (1984) and other authors (see Steen 1984) have noted, there is no clear definition of sustained-yield forestry. Clawson and Sedjo (1984:4) describe it as a timber supply theory, in which '[t]rees [are] grown on a regular rotation or cycle with a steady and constant annual or other periodic harvest.' An early (1818) Swiss definition described sustained-yield management as 'felling not more per annum, but also not less, than nature produced annually' (Schuler 1984).

2 There is a critical distinction between civil communes (Burgergemeinden) and political communes (Bürgergemeinden) which have identical names and boundaries. The members of the former are from families with centuries-old rights to the forests, who may not even live in the area. The political commune includes all Swiss citizens who live in the area and is responsible for local taxation, regulation, and the maintenance of community facilities, including hiking trails. In general, taxes and other income collected by the political commune are not invested in forest management, since the political commune's members derive no direct benefit from the forests unless they are members of the civil commune.

3 From 1803 to 1874, the cantons had superintendence over the forests.

4 This practice has been known since Roman times (Pyne 1982).

5 Nearly all of Colorado's mountain forests were (and are) on public land administered by the federal government.

6 Planting, thinning, and the control of game, pests, diseases, and livestock.

7 For example, because a widespread epidemic of bark beetles is likely, or because trees have been damaged or killed by avalanches, windstorms, or other causes.

8 The other states in Region Two are Wyoming, Nebraska, Kansas, and South Dakota. However, the majority of recreational use in the region has always been in Colorado.

9 One measure of this complexity is that, while seventy-one Acts of Congress relating to National Forest management were passed from 1872 to 1959, seventy-six were passed in the following twenty-three years (U.S. Forest Service 1983a).

10 Two major reasons for this change are that much logging is still undertaken by farmers, who now often work in the tourist industry in the winter, and that logging would interfere with skiing, which is a major basis of the economy in many Alpine communities.

11 Schuler (1984) notes that Kasthofer, an early Swiss forester, recognized that sustained-yield forestry was inapplicable for the management of mountain forests in the first decades of the nineteenth century.

CHAPTER EIGHTEEN

Social Forestry: A Working Definition and 21 Testable Hypotheses

William F. Hyde

Forestry for economic development traditionally suggests large-scale timber and fibre operations. More recently, we have come to understand that another variety of forestry, the local use of trees and forests for domestic consumption, or, more briefly, 'social forestry,' contributes substantially to economic well-being for some of the world's poorest populations. This paper is about this social forestry.

Social forestry is an exciting topic, dealing with both intellectual inquiry and public action and is of interest to both foresters and to those with more general interests in rural development. The poor, often subsistence, economies associated with forests attract our sensitivities for rural poverty and for social welfare in general. The marginal, often fragile, physical environments associated with forests attract our concern for resource conservation. Furthermore, the attraction of the topic is greater because social forestry extends beyond national, and even continental, boundaries. It includes local, indigenous initiative as well as activities sponsored by external development agencies, domestic forestry agencies, rural development agencies, and international donor agencies. The term 'social forestry' is closely associated with the experience of the Indian subcontinent, but its recent use has expanded. Today's discussions of social forestry, typically feature the developing countries of Africa and Asia, but the better forested areas of Latin America and even some farm forestry applications in the developed countries of North America and Northern Europe also find their way into the social forestry literature.

Traditional forestry focuses on commercial production of timber and fibre. Traditional training in forestry features either forest production or protection for these two outputs. Commercial production and traditional training may complement, but often compete with, a great variety of the products of social forestry: fuelwood, fodder, forage, and other domestic consumption of tree and interplanted non-wood crops.

This diversity of possible products is one indication of both the range of interests that now comprises social forestry and the multiplicity of possible forestry-related responses to local community demands. The diversity of human institutions, particularly the many customs and conventions for property rights in trees and in forestland, is another. Such diversity is an indication of the intellectual richness and the economic development potential of the topic. (It is also an indication of the potential error inherent in comprehensive cross-cultural proscriptions for forestry and rural development.)

The many products of social forestry have always been important to indigenous human populations. Nevertheless, the importance of social forestry has only been a topic of serious inquiry by foresters and rural developers for, perhaps, the last twenty years. It is still in its earliest and most formative years. The term 'social forestry' first appeared in Gujarat in the mid-1960s. Jack Westoby gave the term broader recognition in his address to the Ninth Commonwealth Forestry Conference in 1968. In the early 1970s, the Ford Foundation, with the special insights of Jeff Romm, Marshall Robinson, and their Asian colleagues, provided further discussion and organized financial support. Other individual observers and other development agencies have extended these Gujarat, Westoby, and Ford observations, and there is now a broad literature composed of many casual observations and a few informal hypotheses.[1] The next steps in the intellectual development of the topic require data analysis and the rigorous empirical and quantitative examinations of formally-stated hypotheses. The objective of this paper is to introduce some of the formal hypotheses.

Our approach is through several classes of hypotheses which, together, encourage inquiry across a wide spectrum of regional and conceptual problem characteristics. It is initially apparent that these hypotheses must consider: (1) the broad and general importance of local forest consumption for poor rural communities, (2) the more precise impacts of forest consumption on social welfare and its potential as a contributor to economic growth, and (3) the demographic and social characteristics that explain local acceptance of social forestry activities.

The responses to these hypotheses would be an incomplete set of information, however, for any socially responsive activity. Knowledge of the extent of forestry's impact, its efficiency and social welfare effects, and the criteria for local acceptance are necessary, but not sufficient, conditions for understanding forestry's potential role in rural development. Social forestry activities designed with the most complete knowledge of these items can still fail unless they include a clear understanding of both (4) the local institutional framework in which forestry and rural development must operate and (5) the influence of external policy variables on social forestry. A fourth class of hypotheses inquires about institutional issues, such as property rights, that help identify good locations and project orientations for social forestry activities. The final class of hypotheses reminds us not to overlook exogenous factors such as macroeconomic policy variables (e.g., general taxes and tariffs) or agricultural regulations, subsidies, and price supports that have unintended but substantial negative impacts on the forest resource. The paper finishes with three summary hypotheses and an appeal to the many researchers interested in social forestry to begin rigorous empirical examinations of this topic and, thus, to replace unsubstantiated and often unreliable opinion with organized scientific inquiry.

DEFINITION

This first section of the paper builds a working definition for general social science use of the term 'social forestry.' There are numerous terms associated with forestry for local use in rural development. There are also numerous definitions associated with each of these terms.[2] The terms include 'social forestry,' 'community forestry,' and 'agroforestry.' Their definitions must be diverse and inclusive in order to satisfy the multiple purposes of the many individual users. Argument about them is pointless. Perhaps we can best satisfy our purposes, and those of most practitioners, with a comprehensive definition which features the exclusions. That is, forestry for local use in rural community development, which we abbreviate as 'social forestry,' is any forestry (except large scale commercial plantation and industrial forestry) so long as it emphasizes the responses of local consumers to forest-produced goods and services: usually fuelwood, fodder, forage, sometimes water, soil protection, and other tree and inter-planted non-wood crops.

Consider carefully what this definition permits – it permits domestic consumption of household-produced forest products, and it permits market exchange. It incorporates the original concept of social forestry as well as the concepts of community forestry and agroforestry. Social forestry has always referred to local use and rural development, but it also has a strong, and sometimes restrictive, association with South Asia. Community forestry usually refers to commonly owned or controlled forests, and agroforestry refers to the techniques of either growing trees as a crop or of growing trees and agricultural crops intermixed. 'Social forestry' is probably the best brief descriptor for 'forestry for local use in rural development.' In the context of this paper, however, and from the perspective of opportunities to contribute to economic development, the term social forestry extends past the Indian subcontinent to include, for example, the rural migration and new upland settlement and land tenure issues common to Thailand and the Philippines.[3]

Moreover, this variety of forestry need not be restricted to either subsistence economies or to communal activities. Market exchange of the products of social forestry does not hinder the definition. Production for household consumption is a fact, but very few, if any, poor farm families exist solely on their own domestic production. Most households offer some labour or agricultural products in the local market, receive some currency in exchange, and purchase some share of their total consumption. Therefore, some fuelwood and fodder production from social forestry activities may be consumed by producer families, but we should not be surprised, and we should not alter the definition of social forestry, if some is also exchanged for currency in local markets.[4]

Furthermore, local institutional distinctions and the distinctions between community forestry and agroforestry do not alter our definition of social forestry. Expanding social forestry production and local economic development together suggest both increasing market diversity and shifting incentives for resource management. New incentive structures, in turn, suggest changing institutions, particularly the institutions explaining local property right arrangements for the relevant resources: trees, land, fodder, and forage. Therefore, shifts from established common ownership and management arrangements to more individual and private property arrangements often accompany economic development. The task of designing successful social forestry activities assumes new difficulties as a result of this dynamic situation. There are important opportunities for both community forestry and agroforestry, but successful community forestry activities are more difficult to design than are successful agroforestry activities because agroforestry most often involves small private landholdings where the incentives are clearer. Moreover, we might anticipate that the ambitious subset of all landowners who willingly accept the risks and who can afford the costs associated with initiating new forestry investments is more promptly market responsive than are communal decisionmakers. Altogether, this suggests integral roles for property rights and common access in any assessment of social forestry. It also suggests the categorization of both community forestry and agroforestry as special applications of social forestry.

OBJECTIVES OF SOCIAL FORESTRY

If responsiveness to local consumers largely defines the limits of social forestry, then we can probably say that the primary objective of social forestry is to use forest resources to assist local community development. The communities in question tend to be rural and poor. Therefore, helping the rural poor is a complementary objective of many social forestry projects. The first objective is concerned with efficiency and the second objective is concerned with income distribution.

We might examine these standard efficiency and distributive objectives more carefully. They are important because it is against measures of success in achieving these objectives that we judge the quality of any social forestry activity. Empirical inquiry must provide insight as to how we might design and where we might anticipate the location of those social forestry activities which best satisfy these two basic objectives.

Efficiency implies a concern with economic growth with, in this case, social forestry as the means. It means that acceptable social forestry activities promote economic growth. That is, their social marginal benefits exceed their social marginal costs. For example, public participation and improved seedlings are useful inputs and halting deforestation and controlling erosion are useful outputs only if, in the final social account, the marginal costs associated with these and other inputs are less than the marginal benefits associated with the resulting outputs. Furthermore, the net benefits resulting from these social forestry investments must equal or exceed the net benefits resulting from an identical level of investment effort in agriculture, water, or other alternative development activity. Efficiency means that neither the inputs and outputs of social forestry nor of any other physical resource project are justified without satisfying these rigorous tests. Successful locally initiated social forestry activities necessarily pass this test, or the local actors would not permit them to continue. The test must be more formal for the resource management ministries and international donor agencies.

The distributive objective invites more extensive discussion, beginning with two questions and continuing with some thought about the diffusion of new ideas among poor populations. The first question: Do we care whether the benefits of social forestry activities reach all the poor or is it acceptable if they reach only some groups of the poor? Must some benefits accrue to the poorest of the poor? Second: Do we care whether beneficial activities help the not-so-poor so long as they also help the poor? What if the not-so-poor gain more than the poor but the poor gain nonetheless?

Distributive questions like these are one entry point for the important discussions about women's roles in forestry. We can just as easily substitute 'women' for 'poor' and ask the same questions. Indeed, women often are the poorest of the poor – although it clearly would be a mistake to use the terms 'women' and 'poor' interchangeably.

The answers to these distributive questions are subjective. They may vary with one's personal perspective and they certainly vary with the geographic and demographic boundaries of inquiry. They are important because rarely does any activity, social forestry or otherwise, benefit all of any target population, and rarely is any target group of benefactors universally poor. Indeed, all too often the greatest benefactors are not the truly poor, despite the stated program objective. Social forestry activities, for example, may intend to benefit the very poor, but they often have their initial and most obvious impacts on aggressive and receptive larger landowners. Is this a bad outcome if even the (recipient) largest landowners are poor from a policymaker's or a donor agency's perspective and if small (unaffected) landowners and the landless are poorer yet? Is it a bad outcome if large landowners benefit first, but small landowners and the landless obtain subsequent benefits?

Clearly, the assertion that a program intends distributive gains is insufficient. Thoughtful analysis is a requirement for understanding whether the target population is a realistic benefactor of the action in question and, if realistic, whether this population is truly deserving of redistributive gain.[5]

Household Budgets and Consumption Elasticities

These distributive issues cause us to ponder whether there are any generalizable expectations which might guide programs and policies designed with distributive objectives. Perhaps there are two: search for goods and services which require large household budget shares (where 'budget' implies 'all household consumption,' market and non-market) and which show large income elastic-ities and small price elasticities of demand among the targeted poor population.

The advantage of household budget share as a decision criterion should be obvious. If the budget share is small, then the distributive impact of the best-conceived program may be desirable but it can only be small. The likelihood of a significant impact is greater if the budget share is greater.

The concept of consumption elasticities refers to the increase in consumption of the good or service in question relative to increases in income and price over some income and price ranges. A large in-come elasticity implies that the distributive objective probably re-mains valid even as the region begins economic development and the target population's income and wealth begin to rise. It also im-plies that the distributive objective may be satisfied even if analysts slightly mis-assess either the initial target population or its initial income level. A small price elasticity implies that consumption lev-els change little relative to changes in the price of a good or service. Inelastic prices also imply that the distributive objective remains valid over a wide range of relative prices, regardless of whether or not these prices are slightly mis-assessed.

It is unclear what budget shares the rural poor spend on the prod-ucts of social forestry. Indeed, this is an important empirical ques-tion and the answer probably varies widely across regions and cul-tures. Nevertheless, it is a widely held (if implicit), and probably ac-curate, expectation that the expenditures for fuelwood, fodder, and forage are large. For example, most poor people burn wood for both heat and cooking. Those who are too poor to afford fuelwood may still prefer it to the alternatives of dung or other agricultural resi-dues. Fuel is a primary consumption good in the poorest house-holds. Therefore, it probably exhausts a large share of the budget in the poorest households, and this first generalizable expectation probably encourages social forestry activities.

Diffusion

Our knowledge of diffusion patterns for new ideas in other popu-lations and for advanced agricultural opportunities in rural poor populations suggests a second generalizable expectation. The ag-gressive, educated, and wealthier members of any society in transi-tion are the first to accept new ideas and to adopt new techniques (Feder, Just, and Zilberman 1985; Rogers 1983; Ruttan 1977; Schultz 1964). Certainly it would be unusual for the poorest members, who have the least amount of risk capital (discretionary land, labour, or financial capital), to be the first to try a new idea – including improved seedlings, new planting or management arrangements, new marketing opportunities, or anything else having to do with introducing advanced social forestry techniques.

One implication of this observation is that well-designed new social forestry activities should probably include local demonstrations in order to achieve a satisfactory rate of acceptance. Furthermore, we must probably accept that the initial local respondents to any new technique will be among the wealthier community members who, perhaps, are not among the target population for the eventual distribution of benefits. These wealthier respondents bear the initial risks, and their successes demonstrate the merit of new techniques to those poorer households (who may be the real target population). Poor households often cannot afford the risk of failure of even a single crop on a single small garden plot. They cannot afford either the technical risks or the personal and subjective uncertainty accompanying innovation. They may rapidly adopt proven techniques, however, after their wealthier neighbours demonstrate initial success. (Of course, not all households ever adopt any particular technique because no technique can be universally relevant – even for a small population.)

This observation on diffusion justifies the hypothesis that successful local adoption of new social forestry activities depends on the important local economic and political leaders. This hypothesis has the potential to be misunderstood as a 'trickle down' justification for what is actually redistribution to the wealthy. We must carefully guard against this. Our interests are in the improved well-being of the rural poor. Legitimate diffusion arguments favour that sub-set of all policies that might have favourable initial effects on those who are better off but that have clear and substantial positive secondary impacts on their poorer neighbours.

Fortunately, policymakers and project planners can restrict perverse redistributive policies by ensuring that they couple an understanding of diffusion with the prior selection criterion for outputs associated with large household budget shares, high income elasticities, and inelastic prices for the target population. This coupling restricts us from, for example, any interest in those plantation and industrial forestry projects that probably bring greater benefit to wealthier capital owners. It encourages activities favouring important products for low income households even though these products or technologies might first be tested and accepted by the relatively better off members of the comparable local population before their less prosperous neighbours subsequently adopt them and before the policy or practice encouraging this production achieves its full desired impact.

Some Initial Hypotheses

This discussion of objectives raises at least seven questions regarding the general merits of social forestry. They might be restated as hypotheses. (1) Does social forestry have a large net economic effect on local rural populations? The related hypothesis A is: social forestry accounts for large budget shares for poor rural households. (How large? Perhaps larger than the share for any single agricultural staple?) Hypothesis B: the budget share for fuelwood is greater than the share for forage or fodder. If we do not reject hypothesis B, then, in a general way, fuelwood must be the most important product of social forestry. (2) Are the distributive effects of social forestry activities as enlightened as we prefer to believe? Hypothesis: social forestry activities, where otherwise justified by the efficiency criterion, yield greatest benefit to low income, generally rural, households. (3) What is the income elasticity of demand for the products of social forestry? Hypothesis A: the income elasticity for fuelwood is (a) large (but less than one) and (b) increases with moderate increases in income for the poorest rural households. Hypothesis B: the income elasticity for fuelwood remains large throughout all income groups in many poor rural communities. Hypothesis C: the income elasticity for forage and fodder is initially low (the very poor have no livestock) and then increases. (Does it decrease again for even higher levels of rural income?) (4) What is the demand price elasticity for the products of social forestry? Hypothesis A: fuelwood is price inelastic (a) over the ranges of price and income common to most developing countries and (b) particularly for the rural poor of these countries. Hypothesis B: forage and fodder are price inelastic, yet not so inelastic as fuelwood.

A good understanding of the local household production and consumption relationships must underlie the accurate appraisal of these hypotheses. These household functions will also show the relationships between forestry and other, primarily agricultural, activities. For example, household labour is an input to both forestry and agricultural activities. Limits on available labour mean that labour used to collect fuelwood or the other products of social forestry is unavailable for agricultural production. This can mean that the efficiency gains from some social forestry activities are best measured by the resulting labour transfer and expansion of agricultural production.

Savings of labour and other agricultural inputs are all the more important where the agricultural products are even more income elastic and price inelastic than are the alternative forestry products. The common expectation is that agricultural products are among the most income elastic and demand price inelastic, particularly for low income populations.

The household production and consumption functions may also show us further distributive justifications for social forestry activities. For example, wood gathering may be mainly a women's and children's activity. Where there are cultural restrictions on substituting women's and children's labour for adult male labour, then scarcer forest inventories mean fuelwood collection requires more women's and children's labour, less women's and children's labour is available for their specialized agricultural and food preparation activities, and there is a wedge between the marginal products of female and male labour in agriculture. Furthermore, decreasing women's time available for food preparation probably means decreasing nutrition for all. Decreasing nutrition implies decreasing productivity for both sexes in all activities. Ever scarcer forest inventories only make the situation worse.

This competition between forestry and other activities for scarce household labour inputs suggests two more questions and their related hypotheses: (5) What are the relative efficiencies of household labour in social forestry activities and in agricultural activities? Hypothesis: The marginal value product of labour in agriculture is in excess of one, and there are social gains from forestry activities that release labour for use in agriculture. (6) Are there cultural constraints on male-female labour substitution and resulting social inefficiencies? Hypothesis A: many forestry activities are women's and children's activities. Hypothesis B: women's labour has a marginal value product greater than one in select agricultural activities and in select household chores. Hypothesis C: there are disproportionate social gains from the release of women's labour from activities like fuelwood and fodder collecting and permit their transfer to other productive activities.

We also inquired about the introduction of new technologies into rural communities. (7) Assuming the demonstrable local efficiency of a new social forestry technique, then what is the best way to introduce it into a new community? What are the best communities in which to begin a new program? Hypothesis A: homogeneous communities with strong, receptive leaders most readily and completely accept new ideas from outside. Hypothesis B: economic factors outweigh cultural and political factors in explaining both initial acceptance and the continuing rate of acceptance. Hypothesis c: households with risk capital, (perhaps larger landholdings, greater wealth, or better education) most readily accept new ideas from outside.

These are all important questions. We should conduct empirical studies which provide insight into them – and which provide either supporting or contrasting evidence for the associated hypotheses.

FURTHER IMPLICATIONS FOR PUBLICLY SUPPORTED ACTIVITIES

The previous discussion is relevant to indigenous social forestry activities and also to public policies and public investments in social forestry. Social forestry is not always associated with public projects or programs – but a large share of current interest in social forestry features public agency activities. Therefore, public projects and programs are an appropriate interest for us.

Public investments are implemented as activities of large development institutions, sometimes domestic government resource management agencies, but, often, international donor or lending agencies. These institutions often apply two additional criteria – sustainability and public participation – to social forestry projects. These criteria are not objectives of social forestry – and they are reasonable as criteria only in certain special situations. We might reflect upon them.

Sustainability

Sustainable resource management is not a reasonable development criterion where it conflicts with long-run social well-being; that is, where resource extraction and depletion yield greater social well-being. The socially responsible objective is sustained social well-being not sustained resource management. The two conflict, for example, in many acceptable cases of mineral development. They can conflict in socially acceptable cases of forest extraction and land conversion to more productive agricultural uses. Nepal's tarai is an outstanding example. Removing the forest cover may provide only temporary, non-sustainable financial gains from timber harvests, but it also permits development of Nepal's most productive agricultural region.

Nevertheless, while we can have no objection to unsustainable development activity if it improves long-run social well-being, unsustainable forestry activities are probably the greater responsibility of agricultural, industrial, and other development experts. They are seldom the responsibility of foresters and they are not the interest of this paper. Forestry's – and our – professional interests are in continuing forestry activities. These are often new and almost always longlasting and potentially sustainable – depending on conditions of demand and supply for forest products and competing demands on forestland.

In the sustainable case, three easily recognizable situations respond to the efficiency and distributive criteria, each in a manner that justifies public investments in social forestry (whether from external donors or from local government agencies): First, where the distributive objective dominates and the final exchangeable benefits of a justifiable public investment in social forestry do not exceed its costs, then only long-term and continuing external support can sustain the project.[6] Second, where the efficiency objective is sufficiently important but non-market values are such a large share of total benefits that financial benefits still do not exceed costs, then, too, only continuing external support may be able to sustain the project. Neither of these situations is a good candidate either for loans or for eventual conversion to local public agency support. Expected project benefits cannot fully repay loans, and project conversion to local support, in these cases, can occur only in conjunction with an expanding local public sector.[7]

Expanding local public sectors are difficult to justify in cash-poor developing countries. Only development agencies that are willing to provide indefinite support should accept social forestry projects that fit either of these descriptions. Projects like these may be of great social merit but they are unsustainable without external financing. Donor expectations to the contrary can only create false hopes and future financial burdens for either the donor or the recipient community. Of course, the transitory nature of donor interests makes the recipient community the more likely supporter in the long run when donors eventually withdraw. This makes a sham out of any public spirited justification for economic development. Because of the distributive objective and the rural poor orientation of many social forestry projects, there are numerous examples of considerable social merit that must fail for lack of continuing capital inputs when the donor withdraws.

In a third situation, justifiable public investment in social forestry projects may occur where investment bottlenecks and thresholds restrict the eventual realization of benefits. In this situation, external financial assistance can provide the initial input from which sustainable benefits follow. Bridges break bottlenecks and dams can

provide new thresholds of agricultural opportunity. Education, research, extension, and demonstration activities all provide new
knowledge which can become permanently endowed in the local
population. Therefore, projects featuring these activities can create
permanent contributions and can create potentially sustainable benefits. Similarly, permanent institutional changes, such as securing
land tenure, permit new and sustainable management incentives.
Many social forestry projects feature education, extension, and
demonstration components. Others feature permanent changes in
land tenure or institutional modifications within local public agencies.

The options are numerous. Social forestry projects clearly have the
potential to respond to the different requirements of both loans and
grants and they have the opportunity to provide sustainable local
development. Just as clearly, social forestry projects must be well-
designed so that their outputs satisfy local objectives as well as donor requirements.

These summary comments on sustainability can be restated as
two hypotheses. Hypothesis 1: social forestry activities that are sustainable with only local resources may satisfy distributive objectives. They always satisfy strict local market efficiency criteria. This
is true for (1) indigenously originating activities, and for (2) externally assisted activities that continue after the external institution
and its funds depart from the local area. Hypothesis 2: social forestry
activities collapse and an adjustment period follows, which includes
some local economic hardship when donor agencies withdraw their
grants and loans from unsustainable activities.

Public Participation

Like sustainability, public participation is often a design requirement for community-oriented development projects. This requirement, however, is often poorly defined and its usefulness in any
particular social forestry project is often poorly understood.

Public participation is always an important guide that can save
sponsoring agencies from projects that are ill-designed to satisfy the
target population. Its intention is to learn what will permit the sponsoring agency to participate usefully in the life of the rural community – not the opposite. The problem is that the public participants
for any given project are likely to be either the organized or the out-
spoken and dissatisfied among the local population. They may not
even be an important segment of the target population. For example,
they may be male village elders rather than the much more reticent,

the landless and the women, who occupy the least-advantaged positions in many rural economies and who may gain most from the increased availability of fuelwood, fodder, and forage.

There is no easy solution to this problem. The concept of public participation is easy to support but its formal organization and application is often casual, void of useful information, or even misleading. For example, where efficiency is the key objective and markets do exist, then demand and supply analyses provide most of the necessary information. The public participates; that is, it reveals its preferences through the market. The opinions of aggressive local leaders who can venture risk capital and, thereby, invest and demonstrate the merits of new techniques provide the remaining information. In this case, formal and comprehensive political measures of public participation (e.g., surveys which suggest equal weights for each citizen's observations) are worse than expensive and unnecessary. They are probably misleading as well.

In the more common case for social forestry, where the distributive objective is also important and where market information is poor, public participation can assume a more positive role – but only if the project's special information requirements guide both this role and the design of the formal public participation activities that seek this information. General political measures of preference are still unsatisfactory. Project designers and managers must listen to those among the local leaders who can provide the initial risk capital, but they must be particularly inquisitive of the budget shares and income and price elasticities of demand for the true affected population. We previously discussed how a general understanding of these facts is essential to project design, yet project designers can only learn about them through the most precise and organized interactions with the target population. This kind of public participation is essential but choice of the correct public and the correct form for its participation is crucial, as is the correct assessment of the information gathered from public participation. Surveys, particularly those which intend to provide information on income or wealth levels, are always difficult to design. Their results are questionable.

Questions about diffusion and the long-term impacts of new technologies can provide another justification for organized public participation in social forestry. Comparative analyses that search for additional demographic characteristics can help explain public acceptance of social forestry projects. The importance of better information, yet the difficulties in obtaining it, remain key issues in these, as in other, surveys of community opinion.

These comments on the general importance of public participation might be restated as hypotheses. Hypothesis 1: where there is an adequate market (or other means of exchange) for the products of social forestry, formal public participation procedures only provide extraneous – and potentially confusing – information about either the efficiency or distributive objectives of public forestry investments. Hypothesis 2: formal public participation works best when designed to provide a proxy for unavailable market information. Carefully designed case studies may provide insight into the reliability of these two hypotheses.

SECURE RESOURCE TENURE

The previous discussion prepares the way for many quantitative and empirical inquiries. Our comments at the beginning of this paper also refer to the importance of institutional change in general and changes in property rights, secure resource tenure, and common resource management in particular. We should develop this institutional change issue more completely.

Open access resources are resources, like many forests and grasslands, which no one owns. Therefore, no one can anticipate a secure claim on future production from the resource and no one has the incentive to invest in or to manage the resource for its future outputs. Open access resources either tend to be of very low value, or, if of higher value, they tend to be depleted rapidly as nearby citizens each rush to claim a share of the resources for themselves. Observations of real resource values increasing over time are likely to be an indication of open access and associated resource depletion. Increasing prices provide increasing incentives to reforest but open access restricts the private opportunity to capture the financial incentive.

Sometimes, however, institutional changes occur in the access rights and act as a brake on depletion. That is, as the region develops and the resource becomes more valuable, local custom or convention tends to establish more permanent rights to the future management and use of the resource in question. Better understanding and expanding concerns for forestry today are creating just the necessary sensitivities for such changes in the customary rights to many local forest resources. Indeed, increasing forest values cause local citizens in many places to assert property rights for previously open access forest resources. Regardless of the process, newly established rights provide the incentive for sustainable management, because those with the management rights are also those who obtain the future gains from current management.[8]

This sequence bears more careful consideration. During the initial change from open access, either custom or convention may justify common resource management and use by some well-identified local population. As development proceeds, the pressures of changing tastes, technology, and population levels render some customs and conventions no longer effective in maintaining all the old resource use rights. The rights establishing common management of any resource may be subject to greater pressure than the rights establishing private management, because organized group dynamics may be less flexible and less responsive to external change than are the preferences of single economic actors. Therefore, as development proceeds, well-managed commons may have some tendency either to break down and to become open access resources or to become the property of smaller, more responsive, economic entities. For example, community forests may become the property of a few private landowners who are able to fence or otherwise to establish and to maintain claim to the previously commonly managed resource.

This sequence from open access to well-managed commons to private property rights is important because much forestland in lesser developed areas today is still either an open access or common property resource. Forests may be legally managed by the national government, but this management is often ineffective at the local level and either open access or management-in-common may be an operative fact. If the forests remain an open access resource, then the accompanying potential for depletion raises concerns with deforestation, soil erosion, and so on. If commonly managed forest resources become private, then their management incentives remain effective, but the new distribution of property rights may justify our concern.[9] Commons are often the domain of poorer population groups. If the new private managers are wealthier landowners, then the poor who previously occupied the commons may be even more justifiable targets for development assistance. In this case, the same land or forest resource is a less obvious choice for public social forestry projects, however, because the new landowners are less reasonable targets for development assistance.

Finally, policy and project designers must ask whether successful development assistance will convert a poor community's common resources into likely candidates for privatization and, if so, who are the likely benefactors? Can the policy or project design ensure that the target group of original common owners is the greatest benefactor?[10] Clearly, an understanding of local institutions is important to all involved in economic development. The customs and conventions explaining local property rights are especially important to a resource-based development like social forestry. Indeed, altering or strengthening property rights can be a substantial social forestry contribution to economic development.

On the other hand, without careful empirical examination, it is easy to claim too much for differences in resource tenure and property rights. Nepal's forest nationalization and more recent community forestry program may be an example of misplaced hypotheses which empirical analysis could correct. Nepal nationalized its forests in 1957 under the Private Forests Nationalization Act. Most forests were previously the property of large (birta) grantholders but were managed in common by local user groups.

Arguably, nationalization is one source of Nepal's severe deforestation problem. The national government is not strong enough to securely enforce its own property rights. Therefore, since 1957, the local population treats Nepal's forest as an open access resource. Local households extract the forest's bounty while it is available and before someone else can extract it. The forest deteriorates and the land erodes as a result. The solution is to return some forest management responsibilities and some benefits from them to the panchayats (local communities). The government of Nepal and several donor agencies accept this solution. Five current projects are investing at least u.s. $69 million in it.[11]

This argument is logically sound. It errs, however, in overlooking another, more basic, argument that the national government never had any impact beyond a few miles from the capital city of Kathmandu. Nepal has few roads and little other rapid communication even today. Therefore, nationalization may have been a meaningless act in this context. It was an act that caused no change in most panchayats. Therefore, forests have always been, and remain, commonly managed resources. If this second argument is correct, then the community forestry/panchayat forestry solution creates no change in local action.. Whatever deforestation has occurred cannot be due to the de jure jurisdiction of Kathmandu.[12]

Nepal's community forestry program is more complex than this brief comment suggests. We cannot deny that it is certainly more sophisticated than the many programs in many countries that plant trees without regard for property rights. Nevertheless, it should be clear that property rights are important and also that rigorous empirical examination is advisable before sponsoring agencies to invest scarce resources in social forestry projects based on apparently thoughtful impressions rather than on empirical facts.

This discussion raises at least five general questions about secure tenure and its management implications. These questions can be re-stated as hypotheses and examined empirically: (1) are forest resources and resource services with insecure tenure causally linked with increasing relative prices for these resources and resource services? An affirmative answer means that alternative tenurial arrangements can be the solution to increasing fuelwood scarcity and forest depletion. Hypothesis A: relative prices are increasing over time where tenure is insecure. Hypothesis B: tenure is insecure where relative prices are increasing. (2) Do proposals to implement more secure tenure satisfy efficiency criteria? Hypothesis: the net value of increased output resulting from the more secure resource rights exceeds the increased costs of establishing and enforcing the more secure rights. (3) Does more secure tenure create undesirable distributive losses? Hypothesis: securing resource tenure only causes transfer of the resource from poor current users like squatters or shifting cultivators to wealthier holders of the new rights. Acceptance of this hypothesis raises questions about what happens to the poor current users. (4) Does privatization create distributive losses? Hypothesis A: privatizing commonly managed resources generally precedes loss of access for the former managers of the commons. Hypothesis B: the previous managers-in-common are worse off as a result. (5) Are the poor the most frequent users of common property resources? Hypothesis: the poor receive net benefits from commonly managed resources which are disproportionate to either (a) their proportion of the local population, (b) their contribution to common resource management, or (c) their share of benefits from the sum of all local resources.

These are all empirical questions the answers for which may change from case to case. The empirical answers are generally unknown, although there is no shortage of professional opinion (see, for example, Panel on Common Property Resource Management 1986).

PERVERSE EXOGENOUS POLICIES

To this point, we have examined the direct effects of policies and programs designed for their impacts on forestry and rural communities. In most policy analysis, we expect direct policy impacts to be most important. We might, however, also inquire about the secondary impacts on social forestry of policies external to the social forestry sector. There is some recent argument (Binswanger 1989; Hyde 1988) that such 'ex-sector' policies can have substantial detrimental, although unintended, impacts away from their target sectors and on forestry and rural communities. Several possible examples come to mind: (1) Capital inducements (subsidies, tax concessions, specialized trade advantages) drive marginal labour from the commercial, industrial, and advanced agricultural sectors. Some of this labour migrates to rural areas, thereby increasing settlement on marginal lands and increasing pressure on the forest. (2) An effective minimum wage can have the same displacement effect on marginal labour, therefore the same effect on rural settlement, marginal lands, and the forest. (3) Macroeconomic policies causing high rates of inflation encourage asset holding in durable resources like land. Therefore, they induce a bidding-up of land values, extension of the margin of developed land, and inefficient conversion of forestland. (4) Agricultural price supports encourage excess conversion of forests and grassland for agriculture. (5) Energy policies induce fuel substitution. Those that induce substitution away from woodfuels also remove incentives to reforest. (This is a problem of income and price effects. In any particular case, it is unclear which dominates.) (6) Finally, second country policies can also have detrimental effects. For example, several western European countries are discussing import taxes on tropical timber as a response to tropical deforestation and associated environmental concerns. Import taxes may decrease harvests, but they also reduce the incentive to reforest. The net effect on tropical deforestation is unclear.

In each of the foregoing examples, the inefficient use of trees and forests can be an unintended policy impact. Furthermore, in all, except perhaps the last two, examples of the largest policy benefits tend to accrue to wealthier citizens not to the rural poor. Not all of these ex-sector policies occur in any one country or affect any one rural community. Moreover, they are of uncertain importance where they do occur. Nevertheless, singly or as a group, ex-sector policies conceivably have large impacts on social forestry. Their impacts are conceivably greater than, and opposite to, the intended direct impacts of specifically designed social forestry policies. Where this is the case, the best social forestry advice may be to change the relevant ex-sector policy to make it neutral with respect to forestry.

The important question is which ex-sector policies are important and what are the magnitudes of their efficiency and distributive effects on social forestry? This question can be restated as multiple similar hypotheses, one for each potentially detrimental policy. Hypothesis 1: the policy has measurable, significant, and detrimental secondary impacts on the forest resource and on rural community welfare. Policies with unsatisfying secondary effects, nevertheless, may have net positive social efficiency or distributive effects because of the strength of their socially satisfying effects on target sectors. These policies need to be identified and redesigned to maintain their target sector effects while reducing their negative effects on social forestry. They can be identified as policies which reject neither Hypothesis 1 nor a new hypothesis, Hypothesis 2: the policy has positive efficiency or distributive effects in its target sector. Of course, we anticipate that many ex-sector policies that disturb social foresters (they cannot reject Hypothesis 1), similarly cannot withstand the test of Hypothesis 2. These hypotheses require empirical tests based on multi-sector models. Support or rejection of the hypotheses will vary across rural areas, countries, and policies.

THREE SUMMARY HYPOTHESES AND AN APPEAL

Previous discussions of social forestry respond to a broad spectrum of specialized topics. The review in this paper touches on some of these topics. No doubt all previous discussions have their important features but not all address the significant impacts of social forestry on the welfare of affected populations. That is our focus.

There are numerous thoughtful opinions, but little of the evidence concerning social forestry and rural community welfare has been subject to analytical rigour. That is the justification for suggesting the eighteen testable hypotheses in the body of this introductory paper. Anticipating the results of the appropriate tests brings us to three, more general, hypotheses: (1) Hypothesis A: successful opportunities for social forestry are dependent upon secure tenure for the land owner or manager, whether the managing institution is private, common, or public. Hypothesis B: improving on-site tenurial security permits operational incentives for long-term management. Long-term management includes productivity increasing conservation practices, and more secure tenure generally improves environmental quality. (2) Hypothesis: where secure resource tenure does exist, then social forestry activities are most likely to be successful where: (a) the net gains from growing and harvesting are (i) positive, and (ii) greater than other, non-social forestry activities on the land in question; and (b) consumers' (i) budget shares for the products of social forestry are large, and (ii) income elasticities are high and price elasticities are low. (3) Hypothesis: in some countries, ex-sector policies can have substantial detrimental effects on forestry and local communities. Revising the important ex-sector policies can improve the environment for social forestry and rural communities. Revision can also improve the aggregate domestic economy and, in some cases, it can even improve conditions in the target sector.

These three, more general, hypotheses obviously build on knowledge of the previous eighteen. Understanding the answers to tests of these three will save the policymakers of the world a large number of forestry errors. Of course, even discovering the answers, let alone understanding them, is a tall order. We should begin now. Previous discussions of social forestry tend to emphasize casual and qualitative personal experience. They are seldom rigorous, analytical, and quantitative. The topic of social forestry has achieved a high level of international importance – it is entitled to the respect of scientific inquiry. Its potential human impact demands greater intellectual care. The hypotheses in this paper are a place to begin more scientific inquiry. I appeal to others to test these and other hypotheses and generally to raise the quality of discourse about social forestry to its next level.

ACKNOWLEDGMENTS

This paper benefits from N. Ginsburg's, D. Griffin's, L. Hamilton's, G. Taylor's, and N. Byron's insistence on sharp statements, precise definitions, and clear understanding of the previous literature. The first three scholars made their comments as part of the East-West Center's generous support and hospitality in August 1987. Winrock International and the East-West Center funded this inquiry.

NOTES

1 The introduction of social forestry as a topic of inquiry and the re-evaluation of plantation forestry as a tool for economic development coincides with the broader re-evaluation, in the early 1970s, of the Great Development Decade of the 1960s and the change in the general thrust of economic development from industrial processes to 'poverty focused rural development.' Chenery et al. (1974) highlight this re-evaluation. N. Byron (personal communication) clarified this point.

2 One publication devoted to collecting the definitions of terms like these found twenty-seven definitions for the one term 'social forestry' (Anonymous 1985).

3 The new settlement issue is well known as a component of 'transmigration' in Indonesia. It is also well known, albeit in the lowlands not the uplands, in Nepal's tarai. L. Hamilton (personal communication) re-

minded me of the frequent distinction between social forestry for stable populations in South Asia and for new immigrant populations in Southeast Asia.

4 Indeed, the initial conceptualizers of the dual economy understood this point well. See Boeke (1948, 1953) and Furnival (1939, 1948) or see Ginsburg (1973) for a review. Beoke's and Furnival's dual economies did *not* feature populations, or even households, which were totally subsistence oriented and which did not participate in market exchange. Rather, the population in one sector of their dual economies was predominantly subsistence oriented and its market participation was occasional. N. Ginsburg (personal communication) clarified this point and referred me to this literature.

5 These are empirical questions which are all too easily assumed away. For example, a large number of forest policies are justified, at least partially, on distributive grounds. Yet in the only wide-ranging assessment of the distributive impacts of forest policies known to me, Boyd and Hyde (1989) find that eight of nine u.s. forest policies redistribute from poorer in the direction of wealthier benefactors. Even their one counterexample redistributes from wealthier owners of integrated forest products firms to not-so-wealthy timber landowners. These landowners' wealth is, nevertheless, considerably above the u.s. median and further yet above any measure of poverty which normally attracts our distributive concerns. This Boyd-Hyde set of examples points to the need for thoughtful assessment before casually accepting assertions regarding distributive wealth.

6 Exchangeable benefits, in this context, include benefits from goods that exchange for currency and from those which exchange directly for other goods and services. Both are 'marketed.'

7 This discussion implicitly refers to 'hard' loans and makes no allowance for 'soft' loans. The soft share of a loan is the same as a grant. As such, it might reasonably support distributive objectives and non-market values that are not otherwise matched by sustainable net market benefits.

8 The topic of property rights begs inquiry into the implicit thresholds associated with changes in the institutions of tenure. For example, how can we predict the cost levels that must be overcome in order to break down a well-managed traditional commons arrangement. Or, how great must the private benefits be in order to sustain a new assertion of individual claims where there were no prior private claims. There has been no rigorous inquiry into these thresholds, costs, or benefits.

9 There can be social losses even if members of the same population group maintain control as individual private owners of the former commons. For example, the commons can provide a form of insurance available to, but rarely used by, any participant in the commons who is struck by personal disaster. Dividing the commons among the population removes

its potential to serve as a pooled insurance policy. D. Griffin (personal communication) provided this insight from his personal observations in Nepal.

10 Or can project design at least minimize loss to the target population? For example, preferences of the local poor for social forestry projects that emphasize more immediate fodder and fuelwood returns may be an attempt to provide more certain gain for those (the local poor) who have current access to the resource. The timber production alternative takes longer to develop and those of the rural poor with current access are less certain of their access to the common forest resource in the more distant future. This point is also D. Griffin's (personal communication).

11 This investment is equivalent to 3 per cent of Nepal's 1986 gross domestic product. In addition, twenty more international donor activities (by 1989) are involved in related forestry, watershed, forestry training, and national park projects (Carter 1987). The World Bank alone planned another U.S.$ 80 million project beginning in 1988.

12 Mahat et al. (1986 a,b) explain more fully the sequence of events having to do with Nepal's forest nationalization and its impacts.

CHAPTER NINETEEN

Property Rights as Authority Systems: The Role of Rules in Resource Management

Daniel W. Bromley

Concern for disappearing hardwoods, global warming, and droughts in sub-Saharan Africa give special urgency to the improved management of the world's tropical forests. I want to address here one particular aspect of that concern – one that underlies any effort at improved forest management. I have in mind the property regimes that define the structure of rights and duties that inhere in a stock (and flow) of a valuable natural resource such as a forest. I will discuss the essential characteristics of different types of property regimes. More fundamentally, however, I will emphasize the point that any property regime over natural resources must first be understood as an authority system. I will then discuss the extent to which we might expect success from efforts to re-establish property regimes as authority systems in tropical forests.

THE DECLINE OF AUTHORITY SYSTEMS: AN HISTORICAL OVERVIEW

Much of early human history was characterized by self-conscious natural resource use, in which people would move or would take extreme actions (infanticide, gericide, imposed 'family planning') to control their total demands on the natural resources on which they depended. The first major break in this pattern of indigenous (and clearly self-conscious) resource management appeared with the gradual breakdown of internalized social mechanisms for controlling resource demands – a process that was greatly abetted by the rise of powerful leaders presiding over large territories that transcended traditional 'villages.' Natural resources came to be regarded as sources of revenue instead of merely as sources of sustenance for the local population. Many such rulers sought to create quasi-military states, an exercise that required the generation of considerable revenue. These accumulators of wealth relied on two general sources for their income – the agricultural produce of their subjects and the export of whatever natural resources were available. And this brings us to the second phase of breaking with the past.

Colonial powers were interested in the tropics for the timber and minerals found there and considered it expedient to undermine local-level administrative structures. It was necessary for alien sources of power and authority to undermine and destroy local systems of power and authority; otherwise, the legitimacy and authority of the alien power would be compromised and challenged. These changes – territorial governments replacing local-level administration and, in its turn, colonialism, largely destroyed any vestiges of real authority residing at the local (or village) level.

My point here is that villages have, over time, lost their ability to be the locus of control and authority over the actions of their residents with respect to natural resource use and management. As the village became more atomized – more individualized – it became increasingly difficult to take the necessary, and customary, collective actions to address natural resource shortages. As populations grew, aided by new medical technologies that reduced infant mortality, many collectively managed 'village' lands were invaded and illegally appropriated by families – a process that was facilitated by the powerlessness of the village management regime to prevent such incursions. The poorest segments of the village, afraid or unable to privately appropriate the village 'commons,' were left behind and forced to rely, increasingly, on the poorest lands that remained in the shrinking commons. With the collective area shrinking because of illegal 'privatization,' a rapidly increasing population was forced to rely on an ever-smaller area. Small wonder that deforestation and resource degradation resulted.

The effectiveness of the village as an authority system was dependent upon the exercise of influence and control over actions of individual members of the community. Prior to colonialism, ruling monarchs/leaders exercised control over the political and economic life of villages. The villages were not only suppliers of necessities for such leaders but local outposts of control and authority over scattered peoples in the hinterland. The political legitimacy of the ruling entity was secured through the extension of representatives down through the political structure of regional town to, ultimately, rural village.

In India, the disintegration of the important role played by villages can be traced to the introduction of new land laws, the related intrusion of urban interests into the rural village, the opening up to external trade and markets, and the centralization of revenue and judicial administration, leaving the village councils with little or no formal role. With the full spread of colonialism, much of this political and economic structure – already under stress – was finally destroyed. The essence of colonial administration was to harness the political power of the villages to secure legitimacy for the alien power. It became necessary to undermine existing authority systems responsive to the pre-colonial rulers and to supplant them with authority systems that would be responsive to the interests and imperatives of the colonial administration.

The individualization of village life, fostered by the privatization of the better village lands, left the peasant increasingly dependent on the market and on the moneylender. It would not be correct to assume that all of these forces leading to the disintegration of the village were the result of colonial rule; many changes were underway prior to colonial administration. But, of course, the subsequent introduction of new land laws and the civil courts sealed the fate of the villages as a locus of administration.

The story of colonial administration of village political and economic life consisted of imposing European institutional arrangements so as to: (1) encourage the cultivation of those crops of interest to the colonial administration; (2) generate tax revenues to support that same administration; and (3) undermine indigenous political structures and processes to further strengthen the position of that colonial administration. These transformations essentially destroyed the village as an autonomous decisionmaking unit, which was, of course, the very reason for those imposed institutional changes.

Once colonialism gave way to national independence (largely in the two decades following the Second World War) prevailing systems of authority at the village level were once again in need of modification and realignment with the new imperatives and interests of a national government. The disruptions destroyed, yet again, evolved relationships of power, influence, and authority. During these eras of creation and modification of local-level systems of authority and control over daily life, populations were expanding rapidly and technology was altering the way in which people used, and interacted with, their environment. At the very time when the ability to control individual behaviour at the village level was at its lowest, populations were expanding and the pressure on the natural resource base was accelerating. Degradation of forested areas was the predictable outcome.

The new independent nation-states that arose following the Second World War have shown little interest in revitalizing local-level systems of authority. As with previous rulers and colonial administrators, the governments of these nation-states do not relish the thought of local political forces that might challenge the legitimacy and authority of the national government. This means that many forested areas have become the 'property' of the national government – an act of expropriation when viewed from the perspective of the residents of millions of villages. This expropriation is all the more damaging when the national governments lack the rudiments of a management capability. These new governments are struggling with the problems of governance, economic development, self-sufficiency, and political stability. In this setting, we see forest destruction continuing, and even accelerating, with only a very indirect causal link to population growth.

PROPERTY RIGHTS AS SYSTEMS OF AUTHORITY

I am concerned with authority systems precisely because a natural resource regime is an explicit (or implicit) structure of rights and duties characterizing the relationship of individuals to one another with respect to that particular resource (Bromley 1991). New institutional arrangements are continually established to define the property regime over land and related natural resources – whether that regime be one we would call state property, private (individual) property, or common property. These institutional arrangements define (or locate) one individual vis-à-vis others both within the group (if there is one) and with individuals outside of the group. By thus defining one individual's choice domain vis-à-vis that of others, property rights indicate who has the legitimate authority to act in a predetermined manner. This authority, coming, as it does, through officially recognized property relations, carries the implicit backing of the state. Officially sanctioned property rights mean, at bottom, the willingness of the state to step in to protect the interests of those holding the property rights under discussion. Without effective (or credible) enforcement one has anarchy; small wonder that the relentless theme of the propertied classes down through history has been to insist that the primary function of the state is to protect private property. One can search in vain for the dispossessed making a similar argument.

We can define property relations between two or more individuals (or groups) by stating that one party has an interest that is protected by a right only when all others have a duty. It is essential to understand that property is not an object such as land but is, rather, a right to a benefit stream that is only as secure as the duty of all others to respect the conditions that protect that stream. When one has a right, one has the expectation in both law and in practice that one's claims will be respected by those whose duty it is to do so. For most purposes it is sufficient to consider four possible resource regimes: (1) state property regimes; (2) private property regimes; (3) common property regimes; and (4) non-property regimes (open access). These are ideal types, and we should understand that the real world will be somewhat more complex than is depicted by these four classes.

State Property Regimes

In a state property regime, ownership and control over use rests in the hands of the state. Individuals and groups may be able to make use of the resources but only at the forbearance of the state. National (or state) forests, national (or state) parks, and military reservations are examples of state property regimes. Shifts from state property to other types, or vice versa, are possible. For instance, the 1957 nationalization of Nepal's village forests by the government converted a common property regime at the village level into a state property regime.[1] The state may either directly manage the use of state-owned natural resources through government agencies, or it may lease them to groups or individuals who are thus given usufruct rights over such resources for a specified period of time. As an example, we can consider the 'tree growing associations' created experimentally in West Bengal (and elsewhere in India). These associations consist of groups of landless or marginal farmers who are given a block of marginal public (state owned) land for tree planting. The members are not granted land titles, but the group is given usufruct rights on the land and ownership rights of its produce (Cernea 1985).

Private Property Regimes

The most familiar property regime is that of private property. While most think of private property as individual property, note that all corporate property is private property, yet it is administered by a group. Also, recall the pervasive duties that attend the private control of land and related resources; few 'owners' are entirely free to do as they wish with such assets.

Private property is the legally and socially sanctioned ability to exclude others. Private property regimes entail the socially sanctioned capacity of an owner to force others to go elsewhere. Those who see ultimate wisdom in private property must answer for several phenomena. First, much of the world's landlessness is not attributable to an absolute physical scarcity of land but rather to its ownership being concentrated in the hands of a few powerful families. This is especially prevalent in large parts of Latin America. Second, we are often told that private property leads to the 'highest and best use of land.' With large segments of Latin America's best agricultural land devoted to cattle ranching while hungry peasants attempt to grow their corn and squash on steep hillsides, skeptics may be excused if they challenge the universality of that particular allegation. Private property is not necessarily, as Proudhon put it, 'theft,' but a good deal of theft has ended up as private property – especially in the Western world, where European colonizers appropriated vast terrain inhabited by tribal peoples.

The best land in most settings has already been privatized and the worst has been left in the 'public domain' – either as state property, as common property (res communes), or as open access (res nullius). It is not legitimate to ask of common property regimes to manage highly variable and low-productivity resources and also to adapt and to adjust to severe internal and external pressures when conditions beyond the bounds of that common property regime preclude adaptation to those pressures. That is, the 'internal pressure' of population growth may be impossible to resolve if traditional adaptation mechanisms (hiving off, for instance) are now precluded by increased population growth beyond the confines of the common property regime under study. Likewise, if private property and associated fences prevent the traditional movements of a people and their livestock, it is hardly legitimate to blame them and their property regime. Private property regimes appear to be stable and adaptive because they have the social and legal sanction to exclude excess population and effectively to resist – through the power of the state – unwanted intrusions. These powers have been eroded for common property regimes. To see the exclusionary aspect of private property, recall the effects of primogeniture in many societies. The dispossession of younger sons (to say nothing of all daughters) is regarded as a costless social process, and, therefore, it looks as though private property is robust and adaptable; it 'works.' Private property in such a setting may 'work' for the oldest son; but those with no rights in the estate may be harder to convince.

Common property is private property for the group and, in that sense, it is a group decision regarding who shall be excluded. But when options for gainful and promising exclusion of excess population have been destroyed by surrounding political and economic events, then those engaged in the joint use of a resource are left with no option but to eat into their capital. However, to blame this situation on their failure to create private property is misplaced. Common property is not the free-for-all of open access resources. Individuals have rights and obligations in common property situations just as in private property situations. The difference between private and common property is not to be found in the nature of the rights and duties as much as it is to be found in the number of people to which inclusion or exclusion applies. The difference is also in the unwillingness of the group to evict redundant individuals when that eviction will almost certainly relegate the evicted to starvation. In a sense, the group agrees to lower its own standard of living rather than to single out particular members for disinheritance.

It will be said that we must 'privatize' such lands in order to save them. Since there is no clear evidence that privatization reduces land exploitation when other economic incentives are left unaltered, this simplistic tenurial explanation of economic behaviour must be challenged. Moreover, since privatization will simply mean exclusion and the shifting of population elsewhere (to city slums or to other common property areas), the appeal of privatization as a 'solution' is suspect.

Common Property Regimes

The third regime is the common property regime (res communes). First, note that common property represents private property for the group (since all others are excluded from use and decisionmaking) and that individuals have rights (and duties) in a common property regime (Ciriacy-Wantrup and Bishop 1975). This capacity to exclude – a trait shared with private property regimes and with state property regimes – stands as the sine qua non of common property as distinguished from open access. This fundamental point is missed by all of those who confuse open access resources with common property resources. Common property is corporate group property. The property-owning groups vary in nature, size, and internal structure across a broad spectrum, but they are social units with definite membership and boundaries, with certain shared interests, with at least some interaction between members, with common cultural norms, and, often, with their own endogenous authority systems. Tribal groups or subgroups, villages or subvillages, neighbourhoods, transhumant groups, kin systems or extended families are all examples. These groupings hold customary ownership of certain natural resources such as farm land, grazing land, and water sources.

Corporate group property regimes are not incompatible with private, individual use of one or another segment of the resources held under common property. For instance, the ownership of certain farmland may be vested in a group, and the group's leaders may then allocate portions of the land to various individuals or families. As long as those individuals cultivate 'their' plot no other person has the right to use it or to benefit from its produce. But notice that the cultivator holds use rights only (usufruct) and is unable to alienate or to transfer either the ownership or the use of that land to another individual. Once the current user ceases to put it to good use, the land reverts to the jurisdiction of the corporate ownership of the group. The common belief that there is no land tenure in Africa because one does not observe fee simple ownership of a sort we recognize is simply false.

Note that common property of this kind is fundamentally different from the land-based property regimes in collective farms or agricultural co-operatives in the centrally planned socialist economies of Eastern Europe and the Soviet Union. Land in these entities does not belong to the members of the collective as common property. Rather, the land belongs to the state. The profound restructuring now going on within eastern European (and Soviet) agriculture, similar in several respects to what is happening in China, reveals the impasse of state property and its effects on management patterns for natural resources that are *not* common (or group) property.

Contrary to such state ownership regimes, the customary common property regimes in the developing world are characterized by group/corporate ownership, with management authority vested in the respective group or its leaders. In many developing countries, some of the resources in the public domain (that is, non-private land) are managed as common property, some are managed by the public sector as state property, and some are not managed at all but are, instead, open access. It is well to apprehend the differences between these regimes and to formulate programs accordingly.

Several recent events, including new findings from socioeconomic research in various developing countries, give cause for optimism in the efficacy of common property regimes under well-defined circumstances. The u.s. National Academy of Sciences has produced an impressive volume reporting many instances of successful common property regimes in a variety of countries. The volume also documents the ways in which various pressures have caused the dissolution of particular resource management regimes

(National Academy of Sciences 1986). The results of this research hold promise for a clearer design and implementation strategy for agricultural projects that deal with such natural resources. Another book, *Village Republics*, documents the successful collective management of common property in a number of South Indian villages (Wade 1986). A recent volume, *The Question of the Commons*, provides additional evidence of the confusion sown by the fallacy of 'inevitable' degradation of collectively managed resources (McCay and Acheson 1988). The authors of this latter volume make clear that common property regimes survive and thrive. Finally, a recently published anthology, *Whose Trees?: Proprietary Dimensions of Forestry*, documents the property rights issues pertinent to successful reforestation efforts in the developing countries (Fortmann and Bruce 1988). These books, plus a sense that the development community is increasingly open to innovative ideas about resource management regimes, are cause for being optimistic that the simplistic answers of the recent past – when the general policy 'solution' to resource management problems was privatization (individual property) or nationalization (state property) – are now being reconsidered.

It seems important to discuss, if only briefly, the incentives that exist in a common property regime. This is important in view of the fact that received doctrine would have us believe that the only incentive is to pillage and plunder natural resources managed collectively. To the contrary, a common property regime is defined by group ownership, in which the behaviour of all members of the group is open for all to see. In the developing countries, it is not stretching the truth to say that, at the local level, conformity with group norms is an important sanction against antisocial behavior. An effective common property regime thus has a built-in incentive structure that encourages compliance with existing conventions and institutions. Unfortunately, in many settings, those sanctions and incentives have become inoperative – or dysfunctional – largely because of pressures and forces beyond the control of the group. But that does not undermine the essential point that in a social setting in which individual conformity to group norms is the dominant ethic, common property regimes offer precisely the incentive compatibility that is vital for effective performance.

The essence of any property regime is an authority system that can assure that the expectations of rights holders are met. The presence of compliance through the expedient of an authority system is a necessary condition for the viability of any property regime. Private property would be nothing without the requisite authority system that makes certain that rights and duties are adhered to. This same situation exists for common property. When the authority system breaks down, for whatever reason, then common property (res communes) degenerates into open access (res nullius). It is not the property regime that explains compliance and 'wise' natural resource use. It is, instead, the authority system. In private property regimes the owner can always call on the coercive power of the state to assure compliance and to prevent intrusion by non-owners.

In common property regimes two problems may arise. The first is that a breakdown in compliance by co-owners may be difficult to prevent because of the loss of opportunity arising from changes elsewhere in the economy. If spreading privatization precludes seasonal adaptation to fluctuating resource conditions, then overuse of a local resource by members of the group may be necessary. Second, if the state holds common property in low esteem – that is, if the state disregards the interests of those segments of the population totally dependent upon common property resources – then external threats to common property will not receive the same governmental response as would a threat to private property. The willingness of the state to legitimize and protect different property regimes is partly explained by the state's perception of the importance of the citizens holding different types of property rights. If pastoralists are regarded as politically marginal (a reality in many parts of the world), then the property regimes central to pastoralism will be only indifferently protected against threat from others. If those threatening pastoralist property regimes (sedentary agriculturalists, for example) happen to have more favour from the state, then protection of common property will be haphazard at best.

Open Access Regimes

Finally, we have the open access situation in which there is no property (res nullius). Because there are no property rights in an open access situation, it is logically inconsistent to assert, as many often do, that 'everybody's property is nobody's property.' It can only be said that 'everybody's access is nobody's property.' Whether it is a lake fishery, grazing forage, or fuelwood, a resource under an open access regime will belong to the party to first exercise control over it. The investment in (or improvement of) open access regimes must first focus on this institutional dimension. If property and management arrangements are not determined, and if the investment is in the form of a capital asset such as improved tree species or range revegetation, then the institutional vacuum of open access ensures that use rates will eventually deplete the asset.

Open access results from the absence, or the breakdown, of an authority system whose very purpose was to assure compliance with a set of behavioural conditions with respect to the natural resource. Valuable natural resources that are available to the first party to effect capture have become open access resources through a series of institutional failures that have undermined former collective management regimes. There is no authority in an open-access regime. Governments who have appropriated forests from local-level management bodies (primarily villages) and have then failed to manage them in an effective manner have created de jure state property but de facto open access; the absence of effective management and enforcement has simply turned the forest into a resource that can be exploited on a first-come-first-served basis.

CAN AUTHORITY AND MANAGEMENT REGIMES BE RESTORED?

The dismal record of forest management in many developing countries leads to the obvious question as to whether or not there are alternative institutional arrangements that offer some promise. That is, the widespread nationalization of forested areas has exceeded the capacity of many governments to implement effective managerial systems, and so forests are often 'national' in name only. As an alternative to this system of indifferent management, I suggest that the misunderstood common property regime may actually offer some promise for enhanced forest management. Such common property regimes would entail enfranchising local groups (villages, perhaps) to undertake forest management. Skeptics will respond that it is, after all, local people who engage in practices that often result in overgrazing and the excessive harvest of small timber and fuelwood. Isn't this sufficient evidence that local people are indeed the enemies of the forest? My earlier arguments have suggested that local people who rely on the forest for their sustenance are often the victims of policies and forces beyond their control. If there were less interest by governments in commercial timber would there be more land available for fuelwood? If forest departments were less interested in creating European-like forests would there be more scope for people-oriented forests? If agricultural policy had to take account of millions of people pushed onto forested areas would the directions of that policy change? My tentative answer to all three questions is in the affirmative.

Assuming that progress might occur on these three fronts, the pertinent question still remains: how would villagers behave with respect to a local forest? Could they be 'trusted'? One can only offer tentative answers to such questions, but even speculation is useful if we are serious about a reform of land-use policies in the developing countries that will redound to the benefit of their forests. Fortunately, we need not resort to idle speculation; recent research is suggestive of behavioural intentions in the middle hills of Nepal.

My interest here is in the 'nationalization' of all forest lands in Nepal. This action, taken in 1957, upset centuries of traditional forest control by village governance structures; the existing political structure, with its attendant rights and duties, was pushed aside in favour of 'national forests.' Prior to the Private Forest Nationalization Act, villagers made use of contiguous forest lands for a variety of products. Although there was no binding legal claim attached to the lands, they were usually considered to be the 'private' domain of the nearby village.

The government was moved to nationalize forest lands for several reasons. First, medical technology had reduced infant mortality and so Nepal's population was suddenly increasing quite rapidly – putting more pressure on local resources. Second, malaria-control programs had made the terai lands (the lower hills and plains) inhabitable, and so relatively pristine areas were being cleared for agriculture. And third, there was a new conviction that ultimate resource control should rest with the state rather than with a large number of isolated villagers. As might be expected, nationalization in such a setting was destined to fail for two very obvious reasons: (1) villagers were left with no alternative source of supply for the many products formerly collected on such lands; and (2) the clear inability of the national government to enforce the new institutional arrangement. The new resource management regime was also undermined by the realization on the part of the villagers that local timber was to serve as a revenue source for the state. As mentioned previously, the Nationalization Act increased the rate of forest destruction as villagers hurried to convert affected lands into agricultural uses so as to exempt them from the transfer.

Nationalization shifted the locus of resource concern and management from the village to the national government. When responsibility for control was taken away, the village lost something in terms of its own sense of responsibility towards the forest. It is this perception on the part of villagers that was of interest in our research. While we were not able to examine the impact of nationalization on the attitudes of villagers, we did investigate attitudes regarding forest use. To this end, a number of interviews were conducted among households in a Nepal village. The intent was to learn about intended resource use patterns and how the expectations of what other villagers would do might influence those use patterns.

Our experimental work follows in the tradition of Marwell and Ames (1981). We asked the heads of 140 households in Belkot Panchayat, Nepal, about their intentions with respect to a willingness to contribute towards the enhancement of a village asset (the forest). It should be clear that we were attempting to measure their behavioural intentions rather than their actual behaviour. Each respondent was presented with a hypothetical situation in which they were told that they would receive an amount roughly equivalent to the current average annual tax burden. At the time of our survey (April 1983) this was Rs.100. Each respondent was asked to allocate that windfall between a private use (one that would benefit only the household) and a public use (one that would benefit the collectively used village forest or a community irrigation ditch). Both investment alternatives were said to return 10 per cent per year. In addition, the public investment allocation from households would be exactly matched by the national government. It was stressed that all villagers would continue to benefit from the collective resource whether or not they agreed to contribute anything.

The mean investment in the collective good from the Rs.100 windfall was Rs.49.29, with the remainder going to private investments (Rs.50.71). That is, the 140 households split the windfall almost evenly between the collective good and their own private investment. Fifty-one households (36 per cent) donated the full amount of the windfall to the collective good, and an additional thirty households (21 per cent) donated Rs.50. Combined, eighty-one households (57 per cent) contributed at least one-half of the windfall to the collective good. Only forty-eight households (34 per cent) refused to contribute anything to the collective good.[2]

We asked all 140 respondents to indicate how much of the windfall would constitute a 'fair' contribution to the collective good. While one-quarter of the respondents had no opinion on this, the mean of those who responded (105) was Rs.61.5. This estimate of a fair contribution exceeds by 25 per cent the mean contribution of all 140 households (Rs.49.29). Approximately 70 per cent of the responding households considered it 'fair' to contribute at least Rs.50 to the collective good. Two-fifths of the respondents (forty-four) considered it 'fair' to donate the entire windfall of Rs.100 to the collective good. Only one respondent considered it 'fair' to donate nothing to the collective good.[3]

When concerned with renewable natural resources, it is possible to contribute to their sustainable yield by refraining from use – or using the resource less intensively than one might otherwise consider. We were concerned about this aspect of 'contribution' to the collective asset. This forbearance may also represent a more reasonable hypothetical situation than did our first group of experiments, where we offered an imaginary windfall and asked the respondents to allocate it between their private investment and a collective investment. Respondents were asked to imagine that a nearby forested area had been opened up to the village for the collection of firewood, and that thirty bundles of firewood per year per household could be harvested by villagers on a sustained-yield basis; this quantity of firewood is slightly less than one-third of the annual firewood consumption by village households. The mean quantity of firewood that respondents said they would harvest was twenty-four, with nearly 60 per cent of the respondents (eighty-two) indicating that they would harvest less than the sustainable yield of thirty bundles per household. An additional 30 per cent of the households (forty-eight) said that they would take exactly thirty bundles; only 10 per cent of the respondents indicated that they would take more than thirty. Ninety per cent of the households considered it 'fair' to harvest at or below the sustainable yield. This intended cutting behaviour was unaffected by another question included in the interview, which asked how their behaviour would change if they knew that a privileged group in the village was taking more than the sustainable yield.

CAN VILLAGERS BE TRUSTED IN THE FOREST?

The question requiring an answer is: Can effective village-level structures and procedures be counted upon to restore a sense of management responsibility to local forests and grazing areas in the tropics? For national and regional administrative agencies to relinquish managerial control, it will be necessary to have some assurance that natural resources will not be squandered more seriously than they are at present. Of course, one study of intended behaviour in a Nepal village will not satisfy everyone; but it may be suggestive. The ultimate question will come down to one of compliance by members of a village with the evolved rules and conventions. That is, will some villagers 'free ride' on the good behaviour of others? The idea that free-riding is a dominant strategy among people is a venerable one in economics literature. Would Nepal villagers free ride? Even recognizing the limitations of our survey, I am not persuaded that they would. The matter of how much influence the likely actions of others will have on an individual's response is also of interest in a policy sense. We asked the 140 respondents whether or not the likely behaviour of others influenced what they would do with respect to their natural resource use and, in each of the experiments, approximately 60 per cent said that it would not. Thirty-five per cent of the households said that they would be influenced by the amount of contribution made by other households in the case of the Rs.100 windfall; but when it came to cattle grazing, only 19 per cent of the respondents said that they cared what others would do. I stress that this independent behaviour exists regardless of whether the respondent intends to free ride or to be 'a good citizen.'

A very frequent response for why the villager intended to act independently of what others would do was that the respondent 'could not read others' minds.' Many respondents also indicated a strong desire to 'make their own decisions.' It seems safe to conclude that we found a substantial interest on the part of our respondents to contribute to a collective village asset and to refrain from exploitive behaviour with respect to such an asset. At the same time, a majority indicated that their behaviour was not much affected by the likely behaviour of others. A clear majority do not free ride – nor would they if they thought that others would. Village resource use behaviour seems to be very much influenced by a sense of the collective well-being. This does not mean that some would not overuse collective resources – especially in the case of grazing. But the magnitude of that overuse is not considered to be large.

The model that guided this investigation links one individual's contribution to a collective good to the anticipated actions of others in the same social unit. Across all of our experiments, we found that approximately one-third of the respondents considered the likely actions of others to be decisive in their own resource-use decisions. At the same time we found that a majority of the respondents said they would make contributions to the collective good. Hence, while the villagers seem to imply that they do not much care about what others intend to do, we believe it is reasonable to assume that the villagers know what is expected of them and that others know likewise. Hence, while claiming that the actions of others are not generally of concern to them, they may be secure in the knowledge that the resource-use decisions of others will not be greatly out of line with some accepted norm.[4]

We hypothesize the presence of a 'background ethic' or norm that influences collective resource use decisions. This norm has evolved over time as the members of a village struggle with the daily task of making a living. The majority care about the collective welfare, a minority will take more than is 'safe or fair,' and both will do so irrespective of what they think others will do. This is not striking unless one believes that all individuals are greedy free riders. But working against this background ethic are two serious threats – one coming from the villagers themselves, the other from the state. The first is population pressure. The second is the kind of resource policy formulation discussed at the outset; government passing laws and formulating administrative policies that threaten the existence of individual households. Such external influences are critical in the process of pitting villagers against themselves and of ultimately shifting resource stewardship away from the village. When resource responsibility is taken away from the village so is the concern for the viability of the resource. It is the 'patron syndrome' turned on its head; villagers do not care much for things that the state gives to them, and the same thing would seem to apply to the things that the state takes away. We should not be surprised.

The research seems to suggest a residue of concern for collective management of natural resources in a country that has been characterized as one of the most seriously exploited and where the state has usurped local resource management in name but not in deed. The lessons for the formulation of resource policy would seem to be several. First, the state must not decree what it cannot enforce; to nationalize the forest in name, yet to leave it unmanaged and unadministered, is probably worse than having done nothing. Second, supply-side policies that restrict local resource access must be matched by innovative policy on both the supply side (in the form of providing alternative supplies) and on the demand side (in the form of helping to develop techniques and institutions that will dampen the need for the threatened resource).

CONCLUSIONS

I have argued that property rights must be understood as authority systems in which individual participants have rather clear notions of acceptable behaviour. Private-property regimes give the impression of 'working,' because the state stands behind such regimes as the source of authority and enforcement. State-property regimes, along with common-property regimes, will likewise 'work' if there is an effective structure of institutional arrangements to give rise to a meaningful authority system. One might offer the observation that the nominal property structure (where by 'nominal' I mean whether something is held as private property, as state property, or as common property) is less important for managerial performance than is the effectiveness of the authority system (the rights and duties) that accompanies a particular property regime. These institutional arrangements represent the 'real structure.'

Much effort is expended arguing over which particular property regime is most conducive to improved forest management in the developing countries. If some small fraction of that effort were, instead, devoted to a careful consideration of the institutional arrangements that give meaning to each property regime, forest management would be much improved. A national forest (an example of state property) can be as degraded as a village forest (an example of common-property) if there are no institutional arrangements and associated organizational mechanisms to prevent wanton cutting of trees on either. Regardless of the nominal de jure property regime, both are de facto open-access situations. Forest management will be enhanced in the developing countries when this critical distinction is grasped.

For most of the past thirty years, newly independent nation-states have viewed forests as preserves to be taken away from the people. In the absence of adequate administrative capacity to enforce this expropriation, and with no alternatives open to the dispossessed, much forest policy in the tropics is counter-productive to the long run maintenance of forest cover. It will remain this way unless, and until, governments realize that rural people in the developing countries are essential ingredients in the forest ecosystem. There are not enough forest guards in Africa and Asia to prevent indigenous people from making use of the forest – and it is a good thing too. What is needed is a new vision of forest management in which people and their animals are understood to be vital ingredients in the sustained management of forested areas. This will require that governments cease to regard forests as a source of foreign exchange and begin to see them as important ingredients in a comprehensive strategy of sustained development. Once indigenous people realize that they can trust their government, then governments will be able to trust people in the forest. It is time to replace state property regimes with common property regimes.

NOTES

1 However, in the absence of effective enforcement of the new property regime, coupled with the villagers' perception that 'their' forests had been expropriated by the government, the resource became, for all practical purposes, an open-access resource which villagers felt free to squander.

2 We found an interesting relationship between the size of the contribution to the collective good and the caste of the household; since caste is also highly correlated with the size of private land holdings, the contribution to the collective good increased with the size of private holdings.

Specifically, low-caste households with less than one-half hectare contributed, on average, Rs.31.25 as opposed to Rs.68.75 for high-caste
households owning more than three hectares.

3 In a slight variation on the above experiment, we attempted to determine
how the household heads would respond to a situation of unequal wind-
falls. Specifically, we told thirty-six respondents that they would be
given Rs.200 (rather than the original Rs.100) and that the other 104
households would be given Rs.66. The mean contribution of both
groups to the collective good remained almost the same – at slightly under 50 per cent of their windfall; a finding consistent with that of Marwell
and Ames. Interestingly, the proportion of free riders increased to 40 per
cent (from 34 per cent) among households receiving the small windfall
(Rs.66) when compared to a uniform windfall of Rs.100 for all households. For the larger windfall (Rs.200), free riding went from 34 per cent
of the households down to 25 per cent.

4 The way the problem is framed will often influence the likelihood of cooperation. When the choice problem is framed as a decision on how
much to take from the collective, research has shown that individuals
tend to follow the lead of others in the group (i.e., they would take more
if others do; take less if others do). When it is framed as a decision about
how much to give to the collective, individuals tend to choose contrary to
the lead of others (i.e., they would give more if total contributions are
small; give less if they are large); that is, they free ride if there is a ride
available (Brewer and Kramer 1986; Fleishman 1988).

CHAPTER TWENTY

Property and Forestry

John W. Bruce and Louise Fortmann

INTRODUCTION

To an extent rarely recognized by professional foresters, the practice of forestry and the fate of the forests are governed by property relationships. This is not to say that foresters never think about property. To the contrary, three conventional wisdoms about forestry and property are readily identified:

(1) People only plant trees on land with secure property rights.
(2) Forests and trees held in common will inevitably be degraded/deforested.[1]
(3) The best way to protect forests is exclusion managed and enforced by the state.

In this article we explore in detail the relationship between afforestation/deforestation and property rights in the three tenurial situations paralleling the three conventional wisdoms: the agricultural holding, the commons, and the state forest reservation. We consider more briefly some emerging issues in property rights in forestry.

We begin with a few definitions. We include under the rubric of forestry not only commercial timber and fibre production and conservation forestry practised by professional foresters but also subsistence production of so-called minor forest products (fodder, fuelwood, medicine, etc.) by rural residents. Nor do we limit our purview to the 'forest.' The 'agrification' of forestry, as noted by Romm (1989), has meant not only the encroachment of agriculture into the forest in the form, for example, of grazing and *taungya* but also the incorporation of forestry into the farmstead. Rural residents make decisions about trees in terms of their overall access to tree products whether on or off an agricultural holding. While a farmer may have the most extensive rights over the agricultural holding, he/she may also have use rights in a communal forest as a member of the community and may hold a license (for instance, for gathering dead wood) in a state forest. Landless rural residents may have rights only on the latter two areas. Options concerning trees in any one of these tenure situations cannot be defined in isolation from the options in the other situations.

THE AGRICULTURAL HOLDING

The majority of farming units in most countries consist of individual or household farming operations. These range from the households of subsistence cultivators in many developing countries to the heavily capitalized and incorporated American family farm. Tree-planting as part of the farming system on these holdings takes a variety of forms, for example, commercial monocropping of trees, alley-cropping, or windbreaks. In developing countries, planners and donors tend to think of tree-planting as a result of 'projects,' but rural people around the world have long planted trees on their holdings. For example, planting of trees by individual farmers for fuelwood occurs on a large scale in Kenya, where a high percentage of farm families collect and replant with seedlings on their holdings (Kenya Woodfuels Survey 1984:10). But in other cases either few trees are planted or not enough are being planted to meet future needs (Fleuret and Fleuret 1978). What determines the extent of tree-planting on the holding? Does tenure have an effect? The 'security of tenure' model widely used in analysis of land tenure on the agricultural holding suggests that it does.

The notion that security of tenure affects agricultural production is relatively recent. Redistributive land reforms in the classical and medieval periods aimed at equity and new political equilibria. France's eighteenth century philosophes, however, saw pre-revolutionary tenure patterns as stifling agricultural improvement, and, in 1776, Adam Smith argued, in *The Wealth of Nations*, that large-scale holdings and servile tenures discouraged progress.

There is, in fact, a folk consciousness of tree/tenure interactions rooted in early English tenure history. Denman (1969:1) quotes an old English epigram, 'Oaks scorn to grow except on free land.' Before the abolition of copyhold tenure, he notes, oaks belonged not to the copyholder, but to 'the lord who held the manor in fee. Copyholders would not plant oaks to enhance a bounty which was not their own. Freeholders in contrast owned what grew on their land.'

By 1870, when John Stewart Mill urged productivity as well as equity considerations in establishing the Land Tenure Reform Association, the idea of 'development' had entered popular thought. A variety of development-oriented arguments for reform of land distribution and land tenure rules have since been articulated. The most influential, and the one of particular interest to us here, is the argument that a landholder's incentive to invest in the landholding increases with security of tenure (the sense that one is safe from ouster from the holding).

The literature on land tenure in developing countries is replete with references to the relationship between land tenure and investment in the land. The simplest relationship, and the one most often noted, is that insecure tenure discourages investment, because the farmer cannot be confident of the opportunity to reap the returns from investment. While the planting of a new annual crop is an investment in the land, it is usually excluded from such analysis. Most crops only take a few months to mature, and, after all, a farmer must plant crops even in the face of some insecurity if the household is to survive. Where the right to the land is lost, the loser may still have the right to reap crops in the ground so that there is no risk in planting them (Bruce and Noronha 1987).

The investments which concern us, however, are the planting and conservation of trees. Trees are so slow-maturing that they must be treated differently from annual crops. Seedling costs may represent a substantial investment, especially where fruit or other economic trees are planted. When trees take up land that would have been used for other crops, there are considerable opportunity costs involved – costs which will only be recouped in the long run. At least in terms of the relationship of land tenure to investment in the holding, most tree-planting resembles more closely a permanent improvement, such as the digging of a well or the construction of a fence, than the planting of annual crops (Bruce 1986:28,87; Brokensha and Castro 1984).

Authors directly concerned with encouraging tree-planting on farmers' holdings in developing countries, such as Nigeria, Haiti, and Jamaica, have stressed the importance of clear tenure rules, assuring the farmer that the trees planted on the holding will belong to the farmer (Adeyoju 1976; Murray 1982; Blaut 1973:63). The sources of insecurity are varied. A traditional tenure system involving annual redistribution of parcels, such as that reported by Uzozie

(1979:344) among the Ibo of Nigeria, clearly poses problems for on-farm forestry. Uncertainties about rules of inheritance may also present difficulties. In West Java, there has been conflict between three very different sets of rules (Roman-Dutch, Islamic, and customary), which might govern the inheritance of trees (Bompard et al. 1980). Where the state has legislated state ownership of trees on the holding and cutting permit requirements to protect such trees, as under forestry codes in the Sahel, the principal consequence has been a loss of incentives to plant trees on the part of the landholder (Thomson 1982; Lai and Khan 1986; Elbow and Rochegude 1989; see also Sitaraman and Sarin 1980 for Indian examples).

Perhaps the most straightforward evidence of the impact of tenure on tree-planting is provided by studies of farmers who have access to a number of parcels of land under different tenures. The cash crops of farmers in Tucurrique, Costa Rica, include coffee and peach palm, and their tenure arrangements include ownership, relatively secure use rights, tenancy, land-borrowing, and squatting. Survey research found that farmers were growing trees on land held in more secure tenure and annual food crops on less secure landholdings (Sellers 1977). In St. Lucia, tenure considerations explain why trees are planted on soils and in ecological niches for which they are not best suited, with farmers utilizing individually titled valley land for trees and hillside land, under the somewhat ambiguous 'family land tenure' regime, for food crops (White 1986:83).

Given the relationship between trees and tenure, it follows that state action or inaction with respect to tenure systems can encourage or discourage tree-planting and commercialization of tree crops. Tenure reform may, then, be a part of the answer to the question of how we can create adequate incentive packages for farmers to plant more trees. There are few relevant studies, but Burley's comparative examination of India and Kenya concludes that tree-planting responds to tenure reform (Burley 1982). In a more localized study from Kenya, Brokensha and Riley examine 'forest, foraging, fences, and fuel' among the Mbere of Embu District in the late 1970s, during Kenya's major program of tenure individualization and land registration. They conclude that tenure change has had a positive impact on tree-planting, but they make an important point: tenure reform may be a necessary, but is almost never a sufficient, condition for adequate fuelwood production – markets must also offer adequate incentives (Brokensha and Riley 1978).

The model presented above, in which insecurity of tenure dilutes farmer incentives for tree-planting and in which those incentives can therefore be increased by providing greater security of tenure, appears fundamentally sound. It is increasingly apparent, however, that it has some important limitations. Empirical research has thrown up several insights which suggest that its indiscriminate use can be misleading.

Tree Tenure

People who have been exposed only to the more familiar forms of Western property law often assume that trees are part and parcel of the land on which they grow. They are 'fixtures,' and, like buildings, are assumed to be owned by whoever holds the land. Indeed, this is an unstated assumption of the model outlined above. But, in fact, trees can, like minerals and water, be an object of property rights separable from the land on which they are located – a concept obvious to anyone who has witnessed the Japanese transplanting a twenty-foot tree carefully wrapped in rice straw or the wholesale movement of twenty-five foot palm trees from a nursery to a California subdivision. These are rights in trees which have been severed from the land, but many tenure systems confer property rights in standing trees quite distinct from the land on which they stand and may confer those rights on someone other than the landholder.

A tree tenure regime can be complicated, drawing important distinctions on several bases (Fortmann 1985). It may distinguish between planted trees and wild trees (Duncan 1960; Obi 1963:89-94). Even where the ownership of land is one determinant of ownership of the tree, the species of tree may be subject to particular tree tenure rules which affect the outcome. Among the Naga tribe in India, bamboo was the property of the planter irrespective of the ownership of the land. Unless a landowner had forbidden the planting in advance, the owner could not uproot the new plants on land near the village and was responsible for clearing a fireline around them to protect them when burning the land for shifting cultivation. However, if the land were far from the village, the landowner could uproot and discard the bamboo (Hutton 1921:68). The Ibo law of property in Nigeria reflects similar principles (Obi 1963:89-94). Rights to use trees' products may also depend upon the nature of the use, for instance, whether the produce is taken for personal or commercial use (Brokensha and Riley 1978; Mukwaya 1953). It may also reflect the user: in Kenya and Sri Lanka children have special rights to the produce of certain trees, and fruit-stealing by children enjoys a customary tolerance in southern California and elsewhere (Fortmann and Bruce 1988:14; Aschmann 1963).

Rights in a tree may be distributed between several individuals, often according to provision of labour and other productive factors. In the riverain Sudan, a particularly complex system of rights to date palms and their produce is linked to provision of the seedling, land, labour, and water. Each may be provided by a different individual (Leach 1919). The practice continues today. In parts of Portugal, the division of the fig and olive crops between the farmer and the land-owner similarly depended on the division of labour and costs. The valuable prunings were the property of whoever paid for the work (Stanislawski 1963:21, 204). In both the Sudanese and Portuguese cases, subdivision on succession led to trees with numerous co-owners; in the case of Sudan, it led to a multitude of co-owners. Not only does Elwin (1950:55) describe a similar system of heirs sharing the produce of sago plants in the Bondo highlands of India, but the same system has been utilized by heirs of a large California timber-land estate (Don Beattie, personal communication).

In short, tree tenure is a system of property rights every bit as variable as land tenure, mineral rights, or water rights. Tree tenure is not some bizarre phenomenon found in out-of-the-way places, and it should no longer be treated as an exception. Rather, as a mat-ter of course, the following question should be asked: What rights exist in trees, and what factors, possibly land rights among them, determine the distribution of those rights? We are only beginning to understand the potential of such rights in trees as development tools. They were critical in the commercialization of cocoa on cus-tomary tenure holdings in West Africa, allowing trees to serve as se-curity for loans when farmers could not legally mortgage their communally-owned land (Adegboye 1969; Berry 1975; Hill 1963). Where there are few individual rights in land, whether because shifting cultivation is still practised or for other reasons, tree tenure may provide the requisite security of expectation of continued use and control of trees and their products. Similarly, where some class of individuals is disadvantaged in terms of land rights (for example, women in Africa, who often hold land only as their husbands' wives), tree tenure for that class may provide the necessary incen-tives for tree-planting or for conservation through security in the trees themselves. And in states where nationalization of land may have diluted farmers' incentives to plant trees, perhaps tree tenure can provide the needed security and incentives. If we focus on tree tenure rather than simply on land tenure, we will be more likely to discern such potentials and, eventually, to better gauge their effec-tiveness. Tree tenure has been ignored too long, then treated as an exception, simply because it is a complication. The security of tenure model must be applied to trees themselves and not to land with trees as fixtures.

Trees May Secure Tenure in Land

The 'security of tenure' model we have reviewed assumes that without tenure security in land, tree-planting on the holding will be discouraged. One flaw in this line of reasoning has already been discussed: tenure in trees may be secure even if tenure in land is not. But there is also evidence that in certain circumstances tree-planting can increase security of tenure in land.

In some cases, this is simply a consequence of tree tenure and the fact that control of trees often confers (for most practical purposes) control of land on which they stand – at least if they are thickly planted. A farmer may thus obtain, de facto if not de jure, long-term control over land by planting trees. But tree-planting may actually give rise to land rights under customary tenure systems, because the planting of trees is seen as tantamount to ownership – proof of an intention to assert a right which, if unchallenged, ripens into conclusive proof of right. For example, palm planting is proof of ownership of land under several customary laws in Tanzania (James and Fimbo 1973:301, 353). It is in these circumstances that landowning groups may resist attempts by members to plant trees (a phenomenon noted in Tanzania (Brain 1980; Ng'andwe 1976)), or permission from a chief may be necessary (as in Lesotho (Duncan 1960:95)). The problem of community opposition was more recently encountered by alley-cropping trials in south-eastern Nigeria, where tree-planting would have disrupted a community-managed system of rotation (Francis 1987).

There is a more complicated relationship between trees and tenure where the farmer enjoys only derivative, temporary rights to land, such as leasehold. Sellers (1977), writing of Costa Rica, notes that where tenure rights are ambiguous, trees can provide a means of prolonging the farmer's possession of a parcel. Landowners often react against this possibility by refusing to allow tenants to plant trees, regarding this as an attempt on the part of the tenant to tie down the land indefinitely. In Africa, the planting of trees by someone other than the owner of the land is commonly seen as a claim to ownership of the land (Elias 1963; Ng'andwe 1976; Tanner 1960; James 1971:264). In the developing world, tenancy arrangements are usually not arm's-length bargains freely negotiated by the parties but instead institutionalized conquest, with those whose ancestors owned the land now working it as tenants for the victorious tribe or clan. Tree-planting may be a way for a subject group to reassert claims to land. A well documented case concerns Giriama tenants and squatters and Arab landlords on the Malindi Coast of Kenya. The Arabs established themselves on the Coast in the eighteenth century, during slave-raiding times. Giriama cultivators, as early as 1937, began to plant cashewnut trees on Arab-owned land, thereby claiming long-term rights to land use and generating disputes that troubled both the colonial administration and, later, the government of independent Kenya (Shambi, c.1955).

A somewhat different dynamic operates in cases where the modern state is the owner of the land in which tenure is to be secured by planting trees. Here one is commonly dealing with tenure systems in which land is subject to allocation by the state to others if 'unused,' in which case tree-planting can be motivated by a desire to incontestably establish use. Cocoa and coffee planting in an area development project in Liberia in the early 1980s was apparently driven by such a dynamic (Harbeson et al. 1984:6). Equally, tenure systems which authorize grants of more secure rights based on demonstrated use can encourage tree-planting as an unambiguous demonstration of use. This dynamic has been cited as central to the Ivory Coast's impressive record in expansion of smallholder cocoa having led both to clearing of virgin forest and planting of tree crops (Hecht 1983:33). On the other hand, it has been suggested that natural forest has been destroyed on a more extensive scale than would otherwise have been economical, because more extensive land rights were thereby established (Rassam 1990). Serious tensions exist between forest conservation and tree commercialization objectives under such systems.

The practical implications of tree-planting securing land rights are clearer in some respects than in others. If tree-planting is, in certain circumstances, a response to land tenure insecurity, measures to increase land tenure security will not have the positive impact on tree-planting which might be anticipated under the classic security of tenure model. It could conceivably slow tree-planting, though no one would seriously contemplate insecurity of land tenure as a means of encouraging tree-planting; security of tenure has many values beyond its impact on tree-growing. On the other hand, when tenure is weak or ambiguous and tree-planting is, in any case, economically sound, to tie creation or upgrading of land tenure to tree-planting could be a useful strategy. It would need to be used with caution, however, and targeted on already deforested areas. Otherwise it could, potentially, speed up destruction of natural forests in the rush to claim land by planting commercial tree crops.

The Gender Issue: Whose Security, Exactly?

Those who use the security of tenure model tend to assume that the household's holding is under a single management, and that the security of tenure of the household head is the only relevant security of tenure for the household. This cannot be assumed to be the case, especially in many developing country situations. There, the household's landholding, even if 'owned' by a male head of household, may consist of several plots, each held and managed fairly independently by a wife. Insofar as the wife makes the management decisions, whose security of tenure matters, hers or her husband's? If she is the one who must make the decisions concerning trees and bear the cost of planting trees, certainly her own security of tenure is critical. This is cause for concern, because, in African societies, whether inheritance is patrilineal or matrilineal, most women do not inherit land. If they do inherit it, they tend to inherit it in lesser amounts. Except for a very few transactions, they have access to it by virtue of their rights to use of a part of their husband's land (Fortmann 1986; Cloud and Knowles 1988; Davison 1988). A wife's security of tenure may depend in part upon her husband's security of tenure but be subject to additional limitations; a husband may be entitled to shift his plots between wives as he chooses. Recent land tenure research in Senegal's Peanut Basin has provided a framework for analysis of security of tenure on a field manager (rather than on a parcel 'owner') basis. Within a single compound, the land of which is owned by the head of the compound, perceived security of tenure varied dramatically between field managers such as wives, brothers, and sons of the owner, with wives feeling the least secure (Hardy 1989).

Since the specific rights which women may enjoy will differ significantly from one society to another, in order to understand the likely effect of gender, in a specific situation, on planting and conservation of trees, a series of questions may be useful: What are women's use rights? Can women use the full range of tree species that grow locally or are they prohibited from using certain kinds of trees that might be useful in fulfilling their responsibilities? Do women have access to all trees on the holding or are they restricted to certain niches, such as the garden-plot near the house?

Women may want to increase the security or convenience of ac-

cess by planting their own trees. This raises additional practical
questions. Will they be allowed to plant trees at all? Chavangi et al.
(n.d.) describe cultural restrictions on women's tree-planting in Kenya and means for circumventing them. They demonstrate the need
for understanding trees as social as well as biological constructs.
Will women be allowed to plant the species they want? Will they
control the trees they plant? Does this depend on where they plant
them? Rocheleau (1987) points out that farms and other land used by
women comprehend several socio-ecological niches, in some of
which (such as the garden plot near the homestead) women are better positioned tenurially than in others. Not only the tenure niche (a
category of land to be used by certain groups in the society and for
particular purposes) but species considerations affect women's
rights to plant trees. The full array of rights of women in trees and
land rights relevant to tree-planting can be elaborate, as among the
Ibo in Nigeria (Obi 1963:89). Land tenure and tree tenure jointly determine women's security of access and rights in trees.

Insecurity of access for women can also result from life cycle
changes (marriage, childbirth, divorce, widowhood), changes in national policies such as land registration (Rocheleau 1987), in technology, and in the value of tree products. Widowhood is probably the
most significant life cycle event in terms of security of property
rights. A widow may retain certain of her husband's land and tree
rights (Chubb 1961; Hoben 1973:146-8; Obi 1963:89-94), or she may
lose them altogether, as in the case of a Peruvian co-operative (Skar
et al. 1982). Upon divorce, women in Cameroon lost all rights to personal possessions, food supplies, and unharvested crops – hardly a
property system conducive to tree-planting by women (Brain
1972:162). Even during her husband's lifetime, a woman cannot necessarily depend on him to protect her property rights. Women in the
Dominican Republic who used trees controlled by men for hog food
lost their supply of palm fibres for handicrafts when, after a swine
fever epidemic, the men cut down the trees (Fortmann and
Rocheleau 1985).

There is a paucity of literature on the questions we have raised
here and a need for considerable further research. Still, it is clear that
people who do not consult or consider women cut themselves off
from women's specialized knowledge and skills, ignore the poorest
section of the community, and may harm the on-going activities of
women (Fortmann 1986; Hoskins 1979, 1980, 1983). Many social forestry and agroforestry projects address women's problems (e.g., the
scarcity of fuelwood and fodder), but, because of the distribution of
property rights, they do not necessarily benefit women. A first step

is to begin to adjust our tenure analysis to treat the rights of women managers and users of land and trees as a discrete and explicit category. While the degree of independence of plot management by women landholders will differ substantially from case to case, it is no longer tenable simply to assume that security of tenure for a male head of household translates into incentives for women in the household to plant trees.

THE COMMONS

Any discussion of the commons must consider Garrett Hardin's (1968) theory of the 'tragedy of the commons.' Briefly, Hardin held that resources held in common would inevitably be degraded due to the tendency to maximize individual benefits. Under this theory, we would expect high rates of deforestation in common forests. Hardin's thesis has been criticized by scholars using contrary empirical evidence and/or theoretical critiques of his assumptions as well as by Olson's (1971) more sophisticated articulation of the theory of free-riding (Ciriacy-Wantrup and Bishop 1975; Gilles and Jamtgaard 1981; Runge 1981; McCay and Acheson 1987). However, as Bonnie McCay (personal communication 1989) has pointed out, Hardin's model is perhaps best used as a Weberian ideal type against which is posed the question: What factors facilitate successful management of the commons?

A basic starting point is the understanding that common property forest (as opposed to open access) involves a community (the proprietor of the communal forest), whose members are the only persons entitled to use of the commons. There are a number of advantages to such community control of forest resources. First, the resource can be managed as a whole, eliminating the unanticipated cumulative effects of myriad individual management strategies. For example, Hosmer (1922) and Netting (1981:67) note that communal management has maintained Alpine woodlands intact in order to prevent avalanche damage. Second, use can be spread over a wide area rather than be concentrated in a single spot. Third, forest products can be distributed more equitably across the community. Fourth, the community can use the forest as an asset to meet community needs, as in the case of a Yoruba community described by Lloyd (1962), which harvested oil palms communally, sometimes using them to pay debts incurred by the village as a whole. Finally, the combined social and physical force of a community may be better able than are single individuals to protect a resource against incursions by outsiders. Community property provides the basis for management of use and the possibility of control and restraint in the common interest. This management may, however, be unambitious and ineffective. Whatever the right or the aspiration, effective control is often difficult.

We explore two tenurial issues relating to forest commons. First, a series of problems arise out of the state's frequent failure to recognize the commons. Often the state advances the claim that it owns all uncultivated land, frequently in concert with the principle that individuals can establish their claims to land by clearing it (the legal term is 'assartment'). This latter idea is partially responsible for the drive by peasants and others into the world's natural forests. They are, as it were, 'privatizing' state forests. Second, we consider the dynamic aspect of property relations – factors affecting the emergence and success of institutions for community management of common forests and trees.

When the State Will Not Recognize Commons

Deforestation has been promoted by laws or customs that fail to recognize rights in the commons and instead confer land rights on the person who first 'clears' the land. This is still the legal situation in many developing countries today. The legal concept of assartment, developed in a less crowded world, appears across centuries and in cultural situations as diverse as seventeenth century England, where John Locke saw the origin of property in the mixing of labour with the soil, and seventh century Arabia, where the Koran enunciated the concept of *ihya al-mawat*, which grants title to vacant land to the one who clears it and places it under cultivation (Schacht 1964:141).

The process of deforestation now underway in the Third World took place centuries ago in Europe. This history of the clearing of the woodland in Europe makes clear the importance of assartment in the destruction of European forests both in post-Doomsday Britain and on the continent (Darby 1956:191-5). The process has gone on into relatively recent times in some parts of Europe (e.g., Ireland) (Regan 1982). Forest regeneration has proved, and continues to be, difficult in particular situations all over the globe and is currently a matter of popular concern. Griffin (1971) discusses problems encountered in trying to regenerate oaks in California, and Farnsworth and Golley (1974:31) discuss tropical forest regeneration.

Throughout South and Central America today, in Honduras (Jones 1982), Mexico (Nations and Nigh 1978), Panama (Bishop et al. 1981), and Brazil (Mauer 1979; Mahar 1989), a land-hungry peasantry, drawn by the promise of land and tenure, clear forests and initiate cultivation. But titling proves an onerous and prolonged process, and often soils are of poor quality and will not sustain agriculture under available and affordable technologies. Export-oriented cattle ranching operations push smallholders out or simply move in behind them as they move on to clear more land. Vast areas are titled to these large-scale operations. Not only forests are destroyed but cultures and peoples as well – witness the Amazon (Mauer 1979; Grasmick 1979). Denevan (1982) examines tenure as a factor in this process and notes that while landless peasants may be the immediate agents of deforestation, the local cattle industry and multinationals are the sponsors and ultimate beneficiaries of the land policies concerned. Binswanger (1988) has recently drawn attention to the role in environmental destruction in Brazil of artificial incentives created by the public policy for the opening of new lands.

These policies are seductive, with deforestation presented as development. The Ivory Coast has a land tenure regime which recognizes land rights created by demonstrated use and development, a policy blamed for deforestation on the one hand (Rassam 1990) and credited with the Ivoirien economic 'miracle' in smallholder cocoa production on the other (Hecht 1983:33). In 1963, the Ivoirien Parliament voted in a law providing for comprehensive recording of land rights acquired by development. The prospect of a once-and-for-all adjudication of land rights apparently galvanized farmers. The story is told of the president being awakened in the middle of the night with the news that forests throughout the country were in flames, farmers having set fire to clear them as a prelude to making land claims. The president suppressed the law, returning it to Parliament – where it still languishes – for further consideration (Rassam 1988:30).

The inability or unwillingness of the state to perceive or acknowledge local property claims and management practices lies at the root of the problem. The alternative 'free land' policies constitute the squandering of a resource, and these policies, together with other subsidies to forest clearing, drive deforestation quite as much as does the land hunger of peasants. A fundamental reconsideration of such policies is required.

Managing Trees as Common Property

The difficulty of management of trees as common property differs from case to case. Both the scale of the resource and the concentration of management decisionmaking are factors. Just as there is a clear contrast in the management challenges posed by a large communal forest and a village woodlot, so there is a definite distinction between management in which there are many decisionmakers, as in communal use, and in the case of a commercial community forest in which the management is concentrated. But in no case is communal management a simple matter.

Unfortunately, much that has been learned during centuries of communal forestry management is not readily accessible, since the agendas and preconceived notions of outside observers have often kept community forestry invisible. For example, the Chinese have been concerned with forests and the effects of deforestation for centuries. But historically, both Chinese and European observers provided only the most fragmentary information on forest practices of local communities, requiring a heroic effort to piece together even a minimal view of community control (Menzies 1988:51). The China case is part of a broader pattern of the state sometimes purposefully ignoring community control, as Fortmann and Bruce (1988:107) point out: 'For their part, state and national governments have no particular reason to acknowledge the rights or competence of community foresters since historically central governments have competed with local communities and local people for control of forest land. All over the world, for centuries, peasants and the state have been slugging it out in the forest.'

Despite the ambitions and the power of the state, local communities continue to play an important role in the use and management of forests and trees. However, in recent decades, the nature of community involvement has often been recast in terms of development projects. The dismal history of these efforts, particularly in the form of village woodlot projects, has driven development planners back to common property theory to understand why their efforts went so badly awry (Bruce and Noronha 1987:136-9). In the process, some scholars have concluded that collective village management is simply not feasible. Thomson (1982), writing of the Sahel, examines what he refers to as the 'village woodlot fallacy,' and urges clearer definition and privatization of rights in trees. He concludes that the institutional and managerial problems of afforestation on community land are so serious that a stronger emphasis on tree-planting on individual or family holdings is required, and that tenure must evolve in a manner supportive of tree-planting on those holdings. Similarly, development agencies have generally come to regard community-based forestry initiatives with great skepticism. While traditional resource management systems may be impressive, the argument goes, development project planners have not proved at all adept at reproducing them in the context of their projects. Opinion has swung heavily in favour of 'farm-forestry.'

Nonetheless, there have been some very effective community afforestation programs. The 'New Community Movement' in South Korea involves community initiatives, supported by national law, which have compelled individual landowners to contribute their lands for reforestation. If the landowners concerned fail to reforest, the Village Forestry Association undertakes the reforestation on a cost-sharing basis. Contracts set production shares for the owners and the VFA. The program has been highly successful (Gregersen 1982). Compulsion, of course, has often failed, as in the compulsory tree-planting program in post-Mao China (Ross 1983).

The question, then, is what leads to successes. Ostrum (1986) has suggested that groups emerge to manage common property when the user population lives close to the resource and is relatively small and when supply is moderately scarce compared to demand and is subject to multiple uses requiring management and co-ordination. Groups seem to survive if they have clear-cut rules that are enforced by both users and officials, internally adaptive institutional arrangements, the ability to nest into external organizations for dealing with the external environment, and different decision rules for different purposes. And their chances are better if they are subject to slow exogenous change. More recently, in an echo of Norman Uphoff's frequent call for 'diversity in the face of diversity,' Ostrum (1987) has further acknowledged that there are a wide variety of institutional arrangements that can result in successful management of common property. The remainder of this section explores the importance of two dimensions of diversity in the management of communal/community forests: the diversity of the community itself and the diversity of appropriate institutional arrangements.

Community Diversity

Afforestation or conservation efforts have often proceeded as if a village or a community were homogeneous, as if all members had an equally strong interest in the use and husbandry of tree resources. Far from being homogeneous, many communities are divided by class, caste, religion, ethnicity, gender, geographical origin, length of settlement, and even household cycle considerations. This diversity, combined with the multiple and sometimes mutually exclusive uses that can be made of trees (trees cut for timber cannot continue to be used for fodder or human food) complicates the equitable distribution of rights to access.

Land tenure systems offer a variety of alternative tenure 'niches.' Different strata of the community, different members of a household, and households in different stages of their life cycle differ in their needs and tend to concentrate their use of resources in different tenure niches or make different uses of the same niche. The poor in dry regions of India are more likely to use common pool resources, including village forest, for fuel and fodder while the rich use them as a supply of timber (Jodha 1986). Similarly, we have already noted that women's activities tend to be concentrated in specific niches, often common property. Thus, the selection of a particular area of land for tree-planting can, by virtue of the tenure niche in which the land falls, determine who in the community will benefit from the trees. Planting trees on the village commons, for instance, may permit the village landless to benefit from the project along with property owners (Mukhoti 1986). However, caution must be exercised lest the poor be displaced from other subsistence uses with detrimental results (Sarin 1980).

Although community management of resources is likely to reflect community struggles and cleavages, the myth of the homogeneous community may lead the unwary into simplistic plans that fail to take community diversity into account. It is of course possible to set aside particular parts of a forest resource for use by sub-sets of the community with consistent interests, though this rapidly becomes complicated. But careless exclusion has serious results. Molnar (1985:8) describes a Nepalese village in which the men decided to protect their village forest from degradation by closing the forest 'to all grazing and cutting, only allowing villagers a few days per year to enter the forest and cut small wood and leaf fodder.' The result was that the women, who had not been consulted in the decision, were forced to steal wood from the forest of the adjacent *panchayat*. The women of that *panchayat*, whose forest had been placed under a similar system, did the same in the forest of yet another *panchayat*. This domino-effect was a direct result of decisionmaking without consulting the full range of village users.

Institutional Diversity

The range of institutional forms of communal/community forest management and control is also diverse. A community does not have to own forest land in order to exercise de facto control over it (Moench 1988). Nor does community ownership of a resource automatically lead to community control over it. Community control requires the ability to control the behaviour of community members as well as the ability to exclude outsiders. Neither follows automatically from statutory or customary ownership. For example, Eastman and Gray (1987:57) report concern among local residents about overcutting on community lands in New Mexico. Similarly, a community organized during the sixties in California has been unable to persuade the membership to observe its own tree cutting ban (Don Flickinger 1987 personal communication). The question for those who want to institute or strengthen community management of resources is: What institutions are necessary and sufficient to initiate and sustain community control of the resource? Three options, not necessarily mutually exclusive, are explored here: control by a professional state forester, control by a private professional forester, and control by non-professional local institutions.

Experience with community woodlots in Lesotho highlights a continuing dilemma: should communities rely on professional state forestry personnel or on traditional chiefs to ensure the survival of newly planted seedlings? The former often have little local presence and less authority, while the latter may abuse their authority, cutting the trees for their own use. Only a small fraction of the trees planted in the Lesotho woodlot program have survived (Turner 1984:12). While combining the advantage of community control and professional expertise, control by a professional forester (or even a barefoot forester) on behalf of the community, as described by Hosmer (1922), requires that the value of the off-take be sufficient to pay a salary. Thus, control by professional foresters (whether state foresters or foresters hired by the community itself) may be more acceptable and more effective in conjunction with commercial community forestry than with subsistence use of a common property forest.

Another option is community control through indigenous institutions, which can take numerous forms. Willan (1967:5), for example, describes traditional forest management by the Sherpa of Nepal: 'Certain members of the community were designated ... whose function was to report any person who cut trees without permission having been obtained from the village council. Fines were imposed for wrong-doing and were paid in the form of beer.'

Traditional authorities have not been indifferent to the destruction of the resources upon whose continued productivity the livelihood of their subjects depend. While their efforts at conservation have most often been overwhelmed by the great weight of economic forces, it is important to note that they have sometimes used their powers as traditional land managers in attempts to conserve trees. These efforts have only rarely been recorded, but a few examples include legislation by Tswana chiefs in the interest of conservation of trees in early twentieth-century Botswana (Schapera 1943:416), similar restrictions on tree cutting in the Law of Lerotholi in Lesotho (Duncan 1960:95), and village regulation of the Japanese forested commons (McKean 1986). In some traditional systems, chiefs, or even, as in the case of the Kikuyu of Kenya, private landholders could establish tree reserves (Leakey 1977).

A notable advantage of control through indigenous institutions is that users and enforcers are in daily interaction. Such control takes a variety of forms. Successful indigenous systems of common forest management have been reported for Mali (Montagne 1985/86), India (Brara 1987), Switzerland (Netting 1981:189), and colonial New Hampshire (Pennsylvania Department of Forests and Waters 1932). Where such systems fail, it is often because government and/or new economic forces have undermined the authority of traditional managers. This has occurred in the Sudan's gum arabic producing region of Kordofan, where desertification has been initiated by fuelwood cutting. There, 1970 legislation claimed title to most rural land for the government, and the powers of the village *sheikhs* to control tree cutting went into decline. The breakdown of social control of land use was also a consequence of the replacement of traditional 'native authorities' with less effective 'people's councils' by the post-independence governments (El-Arifi 1978). In the face of a growing market for charcoal and a declining market for gum arabic, social control of tree cutting largely collapsed. Vast areas of gum trees were cut for fuelwood. Even where Acacia senegal survived, population pressure forced the telescoping of the traditional cultivation cycle from seventeen to nine years, resulting in declining fertility and increasing wind erosion (Digernes 1977:107). In a parallel case, when the Sherpa system described above was abolished with the nationalization of the forest in Nepal, deforestation of centuries-old village forests began. The new system was inconvenient for users and there was no local monitoring of use (Thompson and Warburton 1985a:122; 1985b:205-6).

These, then, are key insights into common property management. First, holding forests and trees as common property is a rational and sometimes necessary tenurial arrangement. Second, it must be recognized from the outset that, either in degree or in kind, there are differences in interests among members of the community. Policies and programs involving common property need to take into careful account the diversity of common property users, their needs, and the claims they press. Third, the creation or modification of management institutions should avoid cookie cutter approaches. Instead, both the diversity of possible institutional arrangements and the amount of time (generally more than is initially recognized) that is necessary for an institution to get up and running should be considered with care. For example, one approach might be to organize discrete units for more intensive management with narrower participation. In analyzing this option, one would consider that on the one hand, creation of new management institutions is extremely ambitious, while on the other, traditional institutions should not be overloaded with multiple tasks or over-idealized (many traditions, it should be remembered, have been invented). Their tasks were simpler when there was less pressure on resources, and a variety of factors saps their vitality and authority in our time. There is a need to take a leaf from recent thinking on non-forest commons and to consider how local institutions can participate in decisionmaking on commons management but also enjoy the services of technically competent staff and receive rule enforcement and other backstopping from government (Lawry 1987, 1988). These very basic considerations are frequently ignored in practice.

THE STATE AND FOREST RESERVES

There is a long tradition of conflict between the state and local communities over the control of forests. It was one of the matters at issue in the Magna Carta (Cox 1905:6,12; Hinde 1985:28), and one of Karl Marx's early writings concerned the struggle between national and local powers over the right to use forest land in the Rhineland (Linebaugh 1976). In the 1870s the Klamath Indians in northern California had to resort to various subterfuges in order to cut and sell timber that the courts held was under trust status and, therefore, property of the United States government (Stern 1965:62). Similar struggles continue to the present day (Fernandes and Kulkarni 1983; Fortmann 1988a) and leave their mark on forestry efforts.

A recurrent theme of colonial forestry, especially salient in the former British colonies in South Asia and Africa, is that forests must be shielded from growing use driven by demographic pressure. The major tenurial initiative of this period was the establishment of forest reserves. Private and communal tenure of forests were thought to pose a serious danger to preservation and sound exploitation, and it was considered that the state must take over control of the forests and carefully regulate their use. The forests became resources to be protected by the state against their former users. In India, this process has been chronicled by Kaul (1979) and Stabbing (1922). The process of reservation has taken place more recently in some Asian countries (in this generation, in Nepal). It has generated insecurity on the part of traditional users and, because the state has not been able to police reserves effectively, has led to increasingly abusive exploitation by users who no longer see themselves as having a long-term interest in the resource (Fleming 1983). The opposition and incendiarism which forest reservation provoked among peasants in Kumaun in the Central Himalaya at the turn of the century initiated a tradition of protest of exploitation of forests by outside agencies which endures today in the Chipko movement (Guha 1985). Fortmann and Fairfax (1987:7) have argued that American forestry professionals (and presumably those whom they train) bring to their work in the Third World a strong predilection for large-scale comprehensive government resource management – a progressive era tenet which perpetuates colonial forest policy legacy and is not necessarily appropriate to the conditions of some developing countries.

The state has appeared to win most of these arguments. But the state is sometimes an inefficient forest manager, and the 'soft states' of the Third World sometimes cannot manage to protect their forests. They may lack the will to do so, or their authority may simply collapse. When the Ugandan state collapsed, forest guards' salaries were no longer paid and the former guards were directly implicated in the encroachment on the reserves (Makerere Institute for Social Research and Land Tenure Center 1988). This section of the paper examines the tradition of state control, then explores alternatives, such as *taungya*, born out of that experience and asks whether it may not be more viable to create proprietary interests – rights to limited use of forests – which give local communities an interest in the preservation of the forests.

Alternatives: Taungya and Proprietary Solutions

Under a system developed in Asia and known as *taungya*, limited numbers of traditional cultivators were allocated areas to be reforested, where they could provide labour for tree-planting and at the same time cultivate their subsistence crops among the young trees. Once the canopy closed, they would move on to another area to be reforested (Goswami 1982). The term *taungya* is Burmese. The system is said to have originated in its present form in Burma in 1855 (Evans 1982) but undoubtedly has precedents elsewhere. The tenurial basis of *taungya* was a contract between the Forestry Department and the participant (King 1968). While *taungya* provided cultivators access to land scheduled for afforestation, the system provided only the most temporary tenure in a particular piece of land and provided access to land for only so long as there was land to be reforested. The current trend in Thailand is to provide cultivators with more secure tenure within the forests (Goswami 1982; Boonkird 1978; Boonkird et al. 1984). Where this is not the case, inefficiencies result. In Indonesia, there is a tendency for those employed in the *taungya* system to damage the young trees in order to prolong their access to the forest land for their crops (Soerianegara 1982).

As population pressure around forest reserves has increased, there has been a growing interest in ways to provide at least partial livelihoods for some citizens from the reserves that would be consistent with sound management. Since 1983, in the Guesselbodi Forest Reserve in Niger, a management plan has been in place whereby the Forestry Service licenses individual woodcutters from the area to cut wood in sustainable amounts to sell to a local marketing co-operative. All income from the sale of wood by the co-operative is distributed on an equal share basis among resident villages. The Forestry Service controls grazing and illegal harvesting. The Guesselbodi model appears to be working well and is promising because it casts local people and the state in a collaborative mode (Lawry 1989).

Reforestation of denuded 'forest reserves' can sometimes be accomplished through the introduction of agroforestry systems with appropriate incentives for individual households. At Betagi in Bangladesh, the local forest reserve had been completely deforested through encroachment and timber theft, sometimes with the collusion of officials of the Revenue Department and the Forestry Department. Landless labourers were later settled on a group leasehold basis and replanted the land. Now, after years of struggle against local élites who sought to take the land from them, the households have been given twenty-five year leaseholds. The level of conflict which has accompanied this process makes an important point: rights are easily lost and, in the words of Bangladeshi sociologist Zillur Rahman, 'must be reestablished every day' by their exercise (Fortmann and Bruce 1988:338-41).

In the case of natural forest reserves, which sometimes have limited commercial potential because of their mix of species, policies of exclusion of traditional users have been increasingly questioned. At certain population levels and ecologically sound use levels, these forests provided a livelihood or part of the livelihood for traditional cultivators and herders. Why can they not continue to do so? In this vein, Grandstaff (1980) examines the land tenure and land use practices of Thai and other ethnic swidden cultivators in northern Thailand, whose incursions into forested areas have been a source of growing concern to government and other observers. He makes an

important distinction between 'established' and 'pioneer' swid-
deners, in terms of their impact on the environment. He argues for
the establishment of systems of sustainable, integral swidden cultivation and for the granting of tenure over discrete territories, including forest to villages, as a key element in this process. The proposal
represents a new and attractive angle of approach, which argues not
for state protection but for providing local communities with secure
tenure in forest resources and, therefore, the incentive to manage
them soundly.

The advocates of such an approach sometimes characterize it as
'integral' (rather than 'partial') *taungya*, the former being described
by one author as 'a more complete and culturally integrated approach to rural development; not merely the temporary use of a piece
of land and a poverty level wage of labour, but a chance to participate
equitably in a diversified and sustainable agroforestry economy'
(Raintree 1987:54). The distinction was developed by Conklin
(1957). Nations and Nigh (1978) have argued for a Lacandon Maya alternative to current patterns of overexploitation in Central America.
For Borneo, Weinstock (1983) has stressed the need to maintain the
traditional use and tenure patterns and ecological balance in the rain
forest, and Dove (1986) has recently produced a searching analysis of
the misperception by development officials of the interests at stake
in traditional use systems in the Riam Kanan valley in South
Kalimantan. Fernandes and Kulkarni (1983) and Commander (1986)
have called for a new forestry policy for India based on a more integral approach to forestry planning.

The need for and viability of local control over resources is the central message of these authors. While traditional institutions may
sometimes provide the best basis for such control, non-traditional
institutions may also be successful. Protection restrictions have
been effective in the case of the Maria Tecum Forest in Guatemala
because it is the property of the local municipality, governed by a respected council of elders (Budowski 1982). In the Ikalahan area of
Luzon, the Philippine Bureau of Forest Development in 1974 'released' 14,730 hectares on a twenty-five-year lease to the Kalahan
Educational Foundation, to be managed under an agroforestry plan
for the watershed by a local board of trustees. An evaluation conducted in the seventh year of the project indicated substantial acceptance of some elements in the land use control plan and a marked decline in tenure insecurity (Aguilar 1982). Peluso and Poffenberger
(forthcoming) describe a process of diagnostic research through
which co-operation and collaboration between various actors (from
both universities and the Department of Forestry) in the forest sec-

tor was brought about in Indonesia. In addition to providing a model for action, the Indonesian case also illustrates that players outside the Department of Forestry and the village itself can make important contributions.

Here we have come full cycle, moving from the state protection of forest reserves to proposals for sustainable use of forests as common property. Such proposals will be less viable where the value of the forest is a source of genetic diversity. In these situations, protection by the state may have to be the central strategy for preservation, though tenure adjustments in surrounding areas may relieve pressure on the reserve. In the case of genetic resources to be protected by the state, the question becomes whether the state has any proprietary interest in those resources from which it can derive a return for the costs of protection.

FOREST PROPERTY RIGHTS IN TRANSITION

We have by no means provided the last word on proprietary dimensions of forestry. Like all forms of social relations, property rights are constantly evolving. Two emerging issues in forest property are especially worth noting. The first, most easily discerned in the United States, is the shift in the distribution of portions of the bundle of rights to forestland as the result of a variety of attempts to control or influence the use and management of forestland owned by others. This is particularly noticeable in the case of struggles over control of state-owned forests. Despite lack of formal recognition, rights over federal forests have been successfully exercised both by local communities and national environmental groups. Nelson (1986:364, 371-3) has observed that when the Reagan Administration attempted to sell public lands, it discovered that 'a wide array of public land users considered themselves as holders of vested rights to continue existing land uses.' He argues that 'the long-run trend of public land zoning is towards a system of collective private rights to use public lands,' asserting that the ability of various organized groups to control use through political power has made them 'partners with the government in owning wilderness areas' (Nelson 1986:371). Similarly, Fortmann (1988a) has documented the use of protest by local communities to protect the exercise of claimed customary usufructuary rights on national forest land. Likewise, individuals and small groups have succeeded in using protest as a sort of 'zoning equivalent of a citizen's arrest' in order to influence the use and management of private forest land (Fortmann 1988b).

On the international scene, a recent phenomenon which might be termed 'moral high ground property rights' has been associated with popular concern over deforestation and global warming and involves the attempt to control forestland owned by others across international boundaries. Adherents of this persuasion claim the necessity (and moral rectitude) of restricting local rights to forest use in the tropics in the name of the global environment, genetic diversity, and so on. The extent to which these assertions, with their disturbing neo-colonial overtones, will be acted on remains to be seen.

The second major trend in forest property rights has to do with the growing controversy over property rights in germplasm. Concerns that plant breeders in the North were freely using genetic materials from the South to develop commercial varieties that were then sold back to the South at a profit led, in 1983, to a Food and Agriculture Organization (FAO) International Undertaking on Plant Genetic Resources which stated that 'plant genetic resources are a heritage of mankind and consequently should be available without restriction' (Kloppenberg and Kleinman 1988:174). This undertaking, which includes 'elite and current breeders lines,' has, not surprisingly, been vigorously opposed by the private seed industry. While the controversy has been focused on food crops, it applies to the breeding of tree species as well. In an interesting twist, Sedjo (1988) has argued that granting property rights to natural species would provide financial incentives for the protection and maintenance of 'the natural habitat in which rare and as yet unknown species may reside.' This issue of who benefits from forest germplasm, and to what end, clearly will be a matter of major controversy for some time to come.

SUMMARY AND CONCLUSION

We have shown both that tenure affects incentives to plant and husband trees and that there are many more nuances in the relationship between tenure and trees than the three prevailing conventional wisdoms would suggest. Each conventional wisdom relates to a basic tenure type: the holding (conventional wisdom: the need for security of tenure), the commons (conventional wisdom: the 'tragedy of the commons'), and the reserve (conventional wisdom: the need to exclude local users).

The 'security of tenure' model has been used to explore tenure issues on the holding. The basic model is sound. A tree crop is a long-maturing investment and is not likely to be undertaken by a landholder who fears loss of the land and trees. But those familiar only with Western property law often misapply the model by assuming that security of tenure in trees is necessarily a function of tenure in the land on which the trees stand. Customary legal systems often confer tenure in trees independently of that in land. In addition, customary systems sometimes reward tree-planting with greater land rights. Within different legal frameworks, both cutting trees and planting trees can enhance tenure. The model is also misused when it is assumed that a household's holding is under a single management, and that the security of tenure of the household head is the only relevant security of tenure. In household farming systems in developing countries, it is common for a wife or wives to have their own plots which they manage with considerable autonomy, sometimes making the decision whether or not to plant trees. The forestry planner must get the facts and the local law straight before applying the model.

In the case of the commons, the conventional wisdom is 'the tragedy of the commons,' which suggests that resources held in common will inevitably be degraded due to the tendency to maximize individual benefits. But some forest commons do not involve open access. They are, instead, the common property of a community which, by virtue of its property right, can exclude outsiders and regulate use of the commons by its members. This said, it must be acknowledged that the creation of effective community forestry management is not easy. Sound planning for such management begins with a recognition of the diversity of interests within most communities. It should also involve careful consideration of the workings of customary resource management institutions. If customary or new local institutions are involved, however, they need not only autonomy but also the services of technically competent staff and backstopping (including rule enforcement) from government.

The forest reserve is the manifestation of a recurrent theme of colonial forest policy: private and communal tenure of forests pose a threat to their conservation. But the state is sometimes an inefficient forest manager and 'soft states' may utterly fail to protect forests. Policies of complete exclusion of local people are being re-examined. Experiments are underway with models which allow limited and sustainable use of forest products by local residents, creating an incentive in those residents to practise sustainable use and to protect the resource against others. Community management of resources, with ownership vested in communities or on contract from the state, can to some extent replace direct state management.

Foresters' failure to take property rights into account in planning afforestation and trying to prevent deforestation can have adverse results – such as burned forests and plantations (Guha 1985; Hoskins 1980) or acres of seedlings planted with their roots in the air

(Thomas 1964). In contrast, careful consideration of property rights can open up opportunities for diverse institutional solutions. We do not suggest that proprietary dimensions are necessarily the key constraint – the 'bottleneck.' The importance of tenure will vary dramatically from case to case, and elimination of tenure constraints will accomplish little if other incentive elements are not present. Tenure is not the 'silver bullet.' But because it is the factor most often neglected in addressing forestry issues, it requires immediate and careful attention in the development of forestry policy and programs.

ACKNOWLEDGMENTS

This paper was prepared for an American Association for the Advancement of Science Technical Session, 'Agroforestry: A Global Perspective on Potentials and Constraints,' San Francisco, 15 January 1989 and has appeared in an earlier version in Land Tenure Center Paper #135.

NOTES

1 This is a belief of long standing. In mid-nineteenth century Georgia, it was argued that lack of exclusive property rights was 'sad evidence of old fogyism, general ignorance, and backwardness of agriculture contributing to timber scarcity, inefficiency, and the proliferation of "useless scrubby stock"' (Hahn 1982:54).

CHAPTER TWENTY-ONE

Wood Energy Policy Development: Lessons from Kenya

Rutger J. Engelhard

INTRODUCTION

Domestic energy consumption is the major component of the energy economies of most African countries south of the Sahara. In Kenya and Zimbabwe, for example, it represents 52 per cent and 58 per cent of the total energy demands, respectively (O'Keefe et al. 1984; Hosier 1988). Under stagnating terms of trade between developed and developing countries, there is insufficient foreign capital to facilitate a shift to commercial, petroleum-based energy (such as liquefied petrolium gases (LPG) and kerosene). Moreover, the scope for other forms of renewable energy is limited without major technological breakthroughs. Woodfuel (fuelwood and charcoal) will therefore remain the most important source for domestic energy, and, because of a rising population, its demand will increase in absolute terms. Increasingly, however, the woodfuel supply is failing to meet the demand, and those most strongly affected are the poor in both urban and rural areas.

In the late 1970s, awareness was raised to the impending woodfuel crisis in Africa and to the likelihood that its potential impacts could be as severe as the recurrent food crises. Many governments and non-governmental organizations (NGO's) embarked on what appeared to be the most obvious remedy: to increase the numbers of community forestry projects, agroforestry programs, and fuelwood plantations. Although in some situations these projects have indeed contributed to increasing rural woodfuel supplies, in most cases their effects have been disappointing. To a certain extent this can be traced to the size of the projects, which are often too small to have a substantial impact. What may be more important, however, is that these projects focus only on the visible symptoms and usually fail to identify and tackle the deeper and less visible syndromes.

Woodfuel shortages are generally the spin-offs of other developments in society and are related to two shock waves that are currently hitting many African nations. First, the rapid increases in population that began thirty years ago and which are now having serious effects, such as the rapid expansion of agricultural frontiers, intensification of land use, and increased migration to urban centres and to marginal agricultural lands such as savannah rangelands. Second, many traditional subsistence agricultural and pastoral economies are becoming increasingly cash-based. In this process of 'modernization,' frictions are inevitably occurring between old and new socioeconomic value systems, particularly with regard to land tenure.

In this paper, two woodfuel projects in Kenya will be discussed to explore the intricacies of wood energy problems. The author will argue that foresters and wood energy planners should begin addressing the deeper and less visible syndromes of the impending wood energy crisis. Otherwise, development projects may result in some more trees being planted, but they will not help to avert the woodfuel crisis and the associated deforestation and degradation of the last remaining natural forest lands.

CASE STUDY 1: THE KENYA WOODFUEL DEVELOPMENT PROGRAM KAKAMEGA DISTRICT

Following a comprehensive energy planning study in 1980-2 (O'Keefe et al. 1984), the government of Kenya initiated the Kenya Woodfuel Development Programme (KWDP)[1] to go into areas identified as having a serious fuelwood problem and to develop and test remedial intervention approaches. Kakamega District, one such pressure area, contains the most densely populated lands of Kenya, if not of Africa, with over 900 people/km^2 and an average farm size of less than one hectare. It was anticipated that if farmers could be encouraged to plant trees on their farms, the woody biomass produced could fill the gap between the demand and the shortfalls in supply. It was thought that the principal problem to be solved lay in improving the distribution of tree seedlings from centralized government nurseries to farmers. The initial assignment of the KWDP in Kakamega was, therefore, to find ways of decentralizing seedling production by encouraging local church and women's groups to start group nurseries. It was assumed that the groups would also function as intermediate agents between the government extension services and the farming community to communicate technical information on tree-planting and management.

However, even a cursory tour of the district reveals an abundance of trees on private farms, with some areas closely resembling open woodland. Baffled by the sheer number and volume of trees that should produce enough wood on a sustainable basis to meet the district's domestic fuelwood requirements, the KWDP conducted a series of surveys to determine the origins of the trees, their uses, how they were generated and managed, and, ultimately, to verify that there was indeed a domestic fuelwood shortage in the district. The surveys did confirm an acute problem despite the fact that up to 25 per cent of farmland is covered by trees and shrubs, and they further provided an intricate picture of the underlying causes of this apparent paradox (Bradley 1988; Engelhard et al. 1986).

When, ten to fifteen years ago, the first generation of the population explosion came of age and needed their own farms, natural bush and forest land was progressively cleared and brought under cultivation. At the same time, all land was legally adjudicated into private farms, leading to a dramatic change in the cultural landscape. The change in land use depleted the standing stock of natural forest vegetation. Meanwhile, hedges and windbreaks were planted to demarcate farm boundaries, and permanent tree crops, such as Eucalyptus, were grown in woodlots on a short rotation basis to supply poles to a booming construction market in nearby urban centres. Thus, there was a rapid substitution of natural bush vegetation by deliberately planted trees, giving rise to the open woodland character of Kakamega we see today (Bradley et al. 1985).

In the past, all tree-planting and management activities were strictly confined to men; women were excluded, and this proscription still exists although its original reasons do not. These original reasons were associated with the traditional systems of land tenure that were followed before the land was adjudicated. Traditionally, land was collectively owned by the male members of a clan, who received rights to use parts of it for cultivation, for gathering forest fruits, and so on. Trees were deliberately planted to demarcate farm boundaries and, thus, to demonstrate the user's rights of an individual clan member. Women married 'into their husbands' clans,' in which they obtained a 'temporary' status. They could be sent back to their parents' homes if they did not satisfactorily carry out their five principal tasks: bearing children, growing food crops, fetching water, gathering fuelwood, and cooking the family's daily meals. Indeed, to marry and to cook is the same word in the tribal language of the people of Kakamega. Property rights over fixed assets, such as houses or users' rights on parcels of land, were considered to be incompatible with the 'temporary' status of women in their husbands' clans. Women could therefore not obtain such rights, and, hence, they were not allowed to plant trees (Chavangi et al. 1986).

This discrimination was and still is further sustained by a set of well manipulated social taboos that effectively eliminate the possibility of women's active participation in tree-planting. The strength of these taboos is such that if a woman is seen to break them, she is regarded as directly challenging her husband's authority (Chavangi 1985).

The process of land privatization and clearance has proceeded so rapidly that it has had dramatic effects on the traditional supplies of fuelwood. Yet the long-standing strict division of responsibilities between men and women still exists and women are expected to gather fuelwood from the natural forest vegetation that was abundant around their homesteads but has now been cleared. Meanwhile, only men retain the right to plant and harvest trees. The trees they plant are not used for fuelwood but are sold as cash crops. The need for cash is paramount and reflects the penetration of a cash-based economy. Fees for schools and medical treatment, for example, constitute a significant drain on the family's resources, particularly where it is normal to have six or more children, and men have come to use the trees as living bank accounts to meet such contingencies. In the men's opinion, women's needs for fuelwood pale into insignificance in comparison, and it is therefore no surprise to find that cash crop trees are kept off limits to the women. As a result, in the absence of any natural woody vegetation, they are forced to use poor-quality fuels (such as sugar cane stalks and other crop residues), and food requiring long preparation (such as cassava) is reportedly less frequently cooked, or, in some areas, the traditional hot meal at mid-day has been abandoned.

For both men and women, the deliberate production of fuelwood on private farms has so far not been considered as a way of alleviating the shortages. The rules that determine who has access to and control over wood produced on the farm, the division of responsibilities between men and women, and the recent occurrence of the shortage all inhibited men and women from jointly addressing the problem. The women's only alternative is to buy fuelwood on the market, thus draining the household's scarce cash resources and accelerating the depletion of natural wood stocks in other areas.

The Kakamega survey findings led to a realization that although a singular focus on enhanced tree-planting might have resulted in more trees on the farm, it would not necessarily have resolved the fuelwood crisis. The underlying problems are the men's lack of interest and probably awareness that their wives are experiencing a serious problem, and the prevailing socio-cultural value system that discourages women from raising the matter with their husbands or taking it into their own hands. An outside agency can only contribute to solving these problems in an indirect manner. The key rests in the hands of the local people themselves: only when they see the need to act can change be brought about.

It was only with a full understanding of the broader contexts of the domestic fuelwood problem that effective intervention strategies could be designed. In light of a wider range of considerations, the KWDP was able to reformulate the problems to be addressed. These included, besides those discussed above, the growing fuelwood market that is having adverse environmental impacts in other areas, the small farms that already possess a significant number of deliberately planted trees, the privatization of land to the exclusion of the commons, the traditional but strongly felt relationship between trees and land landownership, and the contrast between trees as a cash crop and fuelwood as a waste product. Rather than focusing on improving seedling distribution, the KWDP switched its attention to the task of finding means of promoting the idea that individual households could become self-sufficient in energy through deliberate on-farm wood production.

The KWDP successfully designed an intervention strategy that began with raising awareness of the predicament of traditional socio-cultural values, which – although they may have served the communities well in the past – are at present blocking self-reliant solutions to the acute domestic fuelwood shortages. This campaign, supported by films, comic strips, and discussion groups, exposed farm families to the dilemmas of a women's problem that only men can solve. Rather than presenting solutions, women and men were encouraged to discuss the problem among themselves, at home, during women's group meetings, and at village meetings. Technical information as to how to incorporate a new tree component in a small and apparently fully utilized farm was only provided during subsequent stages of the intervention. By transcending technical considerations and encompassing traditional value systems in its intervention strategy, the KWDP created an ambience in which change could take place and the domestic fuelwood problems could be solved.

CASE STUDY 2: THE BURA IRRIGATION AND SETTLEMENT SCHEME

The Kakamega case study illustrates the intricate socio-cultural factors that may underlie an observed fuelwood problem. The Bura Irrigation and Settlement Project (BISP) reveals other, not immediately visible, factors that must be taken into account when planning for remedial development action.

The BISP scheme is located in a semi-arid area on the Tana River and was established in the late 1970s to produce food and cash crops and to accommodate landless families from Kenya's agricultural heartland. In the original design of the scheme the fuelwood requirements of the new settlers were taken into account, and substantial blocks of land were earmarked for irrigated fuelwood plantations. It was anticipated that by establishing these fuelwood plantations within the scheme and by supplying the settlers with fuelwood at 'reasonable' prices, the unique, pristine ecosystem of the nearby riverine forest could be protected and conserved (Engelhard et al. 1987).

In the process of establishing the scheme, all woody vegetation was removed and was stockpiled around the new villages to provide fuelwood until the plantations would start producing and fuelwood could be harvested. However, the plantations were not established as quickly as expected, the stockpiled wood ran out, and the demand for fuelwood rose as the number of settlers increased. Meanwhile, the scheme was becoming the major economic force in the area and its surroundings were increasingly sucked into its socio-economic dynamics. In response to the settlers' rising demand, the local residents of the area began selling firewood from the deposits of dead wood that were abundant in the dry open forests and the riverine forest surrounding the scheme. Later, when they had depleted this stock, they began cutting down forest trees to keep up the supply of firewood to the scheme. A flourishing local fuelwood market soon developed, and, in spite of the fuelwood plantations, the destruction of the riverine forest had begun.

The Tana riverine forest is a strip of dense forest vegetation that extends about 2.5 km back from both sides of the river. It is only a pristine forest in the eyes of outsiders such as the planners and donors of the scheme. To the local resident population it is a resource which they have managed for generations in relative isolation: the river is unnavigable and the nearest urban markets are at more than 150 km distance without an adequate road or transport linkages. What has undermined their traditional and sustainable management system has been the arrival of the scheme and all the forces for change that it represents. Formerly, the forest was an integral part of a clearly defined traditional system of land ownership and user rights based on subsistence agriculture and the use of the forest as a source of wood products. The sudden imposition of a vast irrigation scheme with its attendant cash economy has, however, led to the mining of what is now a rapidly diminishing resource. The cash economy has inevitably penetrated the life of the local population: the need for cash for school fees, medical expenses, tools, fuel for diesel pumps, and so on is ever increasing. In the absence of easily accessible markets other than the scheme, the cutting and selling of wood from the forest is the only way for these people to raise cash and, probably, at present is their main source of income.

The current, very high fuelwood price inside the scheme is not a direct consequence of absolute scarcity. The fuelwood consumed within the scheme is of very high quality and the tenants refuse to buy lower-grade wood. They themselves have no time to collect fuelwood and, having been brought up in Kenya's agricultural heartland, are often afraid to go beyond the scheme boundaries where 'there is nothing else than bush.' Consequently, the locals could establish a monopoly in the fuelwood market, not least by reinforcing the settlers' fears of meeting lions, buffaloes, and elephants during firewood-collecting forays outside the scheme. They adapted quickly to the new opportunities and one of them obtained a credit to buy a lorry that he intends to use for the wholesale supply of fuelwood to the tenants of the scheme.

When the BISP starts selling fuelwood derived from its plantations for a 'reasonable' price, it will be competing with the local suppliers. It is more than likely that the scheme will lose, because the market is imperfect and not determined by costs and benefits of the operation but by the cash needs of the suppliers and the fact that alternative sources of income are limited. Consequently, it can be expected that any 'reasonable' price set by the scheme for the fuelwood from the plantations will be undercut by the local suppliers, who will compensate for any loss of income by increasing the rates of off-take. They will supply larger quantities of fuelwood at lower prices, and fuelwood will be abundantly available at low prices until the accelerated cutting of the riverine forest trees has destroyed the very resource that the scheme's plantations were intended to conserve.

Solutions to the combined problems of providing sustainable fuelwood supplies for the settlers and of protecting the riverine forest vegetation cannot be confined to a remedial intervention within the scheme alone but should include components that facilitate the full integration of the local residents in the economic dynamics of the scheme. A two-pronged strategy may be more successful: (1) to reduce the settlers' fuelwood demands (through encouraging energy conservation and domestic fuelwood production on a subsistence basis with respect to the way vegetables and food crops are produced); and, (2) to support the income-generating ability of the local population (e.g., by introducing viable income-generating activities and/or by introducing new techniques for managing the forest vegetation and harvesting its yield rather than its stock on a sustainable basis).

DISCUSSION

These two case studies illustrate the bewildering intricacies of the causes of the impending wood energy crisis in Africa. Upon reflection, trying to find a solution seems to be like running in a maze without an exit. In the two cases, largely similar patterns of intervention planning can be found. Initially, a superficial analysis of the problem led to a project design emphasizing a singular, technocratic (agro-)forestry approach. When results were disappointing, evaluations showed the analysis had been too abrupt and had been founded on an oversight of underlying causes. The woodfuel crisis in Kakamega, for example, is not, in fact, the result of an absolute shortage of trees but of socially and culturally bounded problems of access. The conservation of the Tana riverine forest vegetation will not be achieved by exclusion but through its co-ordinated integration into a wider set of economic opportunities.

The points at issue here include not only the substance but also the approach. Each of the outlined problems is complex and difficult to pin down, but over-simplification for the sake of expedient action is often counterproductive. An individual issue, such as woodfuel supply, is only part of a much wider system of resource management on the part of the actors, who have to make compromises in the face of conflicting interests such as the need to secure food and fuelwood supplies and the need to raise a cash income with a minimum of risks in order to survive and to maintain social standing within the community. These and other crucial questions need to be addressed when dealing with an issue as complex and wide-ranging as the wood energy problem in Kenya and many other African countries. One can only hope to break what so often looks like a vicious circle by approaching the wood energy crisis with people rather than with a singular, technocratic tree-planting approach.

NOTE

1 The Kenya Woodfuel Development Programme was a national Research and Development effort of the Ministry of Energy implemented by the Beijer Institute/Stockholm and supported by the Netherlands Government, SIDA, and Canadian International Develoment Agency (CIDA).

CHAPTER TWENTY-TWO

Can Tropical Forest Management Systems Be Economic?

Roger A. Sedjo

The conventional wisdom among foresters, and, indeed, perhaps among development economists, is that natural tropical forests do not generate sufficient economic returns to justify management activities (e.g., Richardson 1970; Spears 1979; Food and Agriculture Organization (FAO) 1983). For example, Leslie (1987:178) states that 'the magnitude of the factors needed to make natural management profitable is unrealistically great.'

Lacking acceptable economic returns to natural forest management, the emphasis has been to move towards the substitution of plantation forests, which are generally believed to have higher economic returns and to meet the bulk of industrial and fuelwood needs (e.g., Spears 1984). An inference sometimes drawn from this view is that economic considerations suggest that natural tropical forest systems should be replaced by plantation forests, to which the financial returns are more favourable.

This paper compares the financial returns to two hypothetical forest management regimes undertaken on the same site in the dipterocarp Asia-Pacific region. Financial returns differ from economic returns to the extent that the returns/costs are 'external' and, therefore, are not captured/borne by the investor. Since the 'external' outputs of the natural forest are believed to be generally greater than they are for plantations (i.e., both provide watershed protection, but natural forests almost always provide more wildlife and biodiversity), considerations of the values of external outputs would strengthen the arguments of this paper that tropical forest management is more favourable than is usually believed.

An area is assumed to have been recently harvested of all merchantable trees. One investment possibility is that of the establishment of a plantation forest using Albizza falcataria on a twenty-year

sawtimber rotation (Table 1). An alternative possibility is investment in natural tropical forest management in which a lightly managed stand receives only modest management, with enrichment
planting being undertaken where natural regeneration is insufficient. A rotation of sixty years is assumed (Table 2). The cost, price,
and growth data used are drawn largely from recent Indonesian experience (Sedjo 1988).

This paper finds that under the reasonable set of conditions presented, the financial returns to natural forest management systems
can be much more favourable than is commonly believed, and that
financial returns to natural forest management are comparable to
those likely to accrue to plantation forests in many situations that are
common in the Asia-Pacific region. In addressing these issues, this
paper (1) discusses some broad locational considerations that suggest a potential role for both plantation and natural tropical forest
management, (2) addresses the current condition and regeneration
potential of the tropical forest, (3) compares the economic returns to
plantations and natural forest management for a prototype situation
in the Asia-Pacific region, and, finally, (4) speculates as to why plantations appear to be preferred over natural tropical forest management.

FINANCIAL RETURNS AND LOCATIONAL CONSIDERATIONS

Forestry has often been viewed as the land use of last resort. The
nineteenth century German economist Von Thunen developed a
concentric-zone theory of land use occurring around a village centre.
In this view, there was a place for forests, agriculture, and urban
land uses. The forest was typically reserved for lands that are most
distant, with the more accessible lands available for cropping and
other agricultural uses. Forests could not compete with agriculture
in the area closest to the village. However, this view also implied
that agriculture would not compete with forests in the more distant
locations. Location was important and accessibility and nearness to
market were of differential importance for the various economic activities. To this perspective must be added further considerations
that affect land-use decisions, such as soil types, topography, and
so forth.

This simple view has much to commend it even today. It suggests
that location bestows a comparative advantage on activities that are
best suited to a location and that these activities will displace other,
less well-suited activities. In forestry and agriculture, locational

TABLE 1
Twenty-year plantation sawtimber rotation: Albizza Falcataria

Year	Harvest volume (m³ha)	Harvest cost ($/m³)	Establish costs ($/ha)	Harvest price ($/m³)	Total costs ($/ha)	Total revenues ($/ha)	Net revenues ($/ha)	DPV (6%)
0	—	—	350	—	350	0	-350	-350
1			11		11		- 11	- 11
2			48		48		- 48	- 43
3			28		28		- 28	- 23
.								
.								
10	Thin to waste						-100	- 56
.								
.								
15	Thinning (return = cost)						0	0
.								
.								
20	250*	20		25	5,000	6,250	1,250	390
20-60						DPV (20 years)		-93
						DPV (20 - 60)		-29
						Total DPV		-131

SOURCE: Sedjo (1988)
* Sawtimber volume

TABLE 2
Natural tropical forest management[1]

Year	Harvest volume (m³ha)	Harvest cost ($/m³)	Establish costs ($/ha)	Harvest price ($/m³)	Total costs ($/ha)	Total revenues ($/ha)	Net revenues ($/ha)	DPV (6%)
0			50		50	0	-50	-50
.								
.								
.								
60	60[2]	35		70	2,100	4,200	+2,100 DPV	+58 +8

NOTES: [1] Costs and revenues from Sedjo (1988)
[2] Incremental volume associated with silviculture and management

considerations must be integrated with concerns about soils and moisture. Three activities that often compete for a location are agricultural cropping, plantation forestry, and natural forest management. Forestry has traditionally been viewed as uneconomic when pitted against other land uses (Waggener 1985). On fertile lands, where agricultural cropping is viable, forestry is unlikely to be financially viable. Plantation forestry, which is really a form of agriculture that involves tree cropping, can flourish in advantageous locations (Sedjo 1983). However, although plantation forestry has demonstrated substantial returns under favourable conditions, such conditions are absent in many tropical locations, and plantations often generate low financial returns (Sedjo 1988). Requisite conditions include locations having low-cost access to major markets and a scale of operations that allows for complete utilization of all or most of the raw wood. To achieve this, it is often necessary for plantations to be situated with favourable access to a pulpmill.

There are large areas of the tropics that do not have the requisite conditions to allow either sustainable agriculture cropping or large-scale integrated forest plantations. It is in these areas that natural forest management – typically, extensive forestry with modest investments per unit of land area – is likely to generate the highest financial returns.

If this view is correct, however, why do we find plantation forests often displacing natural tropical forests in many situations where large-scale integrated operations are not feasible? The answer is found largely in the wide array of financial incentives provided to plantation forestry and agricultural cropping that are not available to natural forest management. A major problem with the economic evaluation of natural forestry projects is that often they do not compare favourably with the alternative activities because they are being compared on locations where other land-uses have an inherent advantage. In addition, there is a tendency for foresters to prefer to manage intensively, when financial considerations will allow only low-cost extensive management. Exacerbating this situation is the tendency of governments to directly and indirectly subsidize cropping and plantation activities while ignoring natural forest management. Hence, natural forests appear to be noncompetitive because often they are competing where they, in fact, have a disadvantage; or when they have an economic advantage, this advantage is negated by subsidies that shift the financial advantage to the cropping or forest plantation modes. Repetto and Gillis (1988), for example, have demonstrated that Third World countries have supported a host of policies which promote activities that are both ecologically destructive and economically undesirable.

Furthermore, in many instances forest plantations are not the viable financial investments they are commonly believed to be. Often, it is only the effects of direct and indirect subsidies that make the financial returns to plantations appealing. Furthermore, the prevalent view that sustainable tropical forestry is not economically or financially feasible, together with the unqualified view that plantation forests generally provide high economic returns, has been detrimental to both economic and environmental values. Such a view promotes acquiescence to the conversion of tropical forests to other uses, including agricultural cropping and plantation forestry, when, in fact, these uses may be ecologically destructive and financially and economically unjustified. Finally, since it is generally agreed that native forests provide a larger volume of environmental services and non-timber values than do plantation forests, natural forest management should be preferred when the financial returns are roughly similar.

FORESTS IN THE TROPICS

Timber interests are active in many areas of the globe, including West Africa, much of South America (including the Amazon) and, most importantly, the Asia-Pacific region, which includes Malaysia, Indonesia, the Philippines, and the island of New Guinea. About 80 per cent of the world supply of tropical timber exports comes from the Asia-Pacific region. Today, much of what is called tropical forestry is simply logging in the tropical forest. The economics of logging the tropical forests depend on the accessibility of the site and the availability of merchantable size and species of trees. It is this consideration that accounts for the dominance of the Asia-Pacific region as a supplier. The dipterocarp forests of the region provide a family of species that have wide commercial acceptance. By contrast, the tropical forests of the Amazon Basin exhibit a much greater degree of heterogeneity, with a much smaller fraction of the forest trees being species that are readily accepted by the markets. This feature has resulted in high costs and a relative lack of interest by major commercial logging interests in the Amazon forests as a source of industrial wood.

REGENERATION

Intensive high-cost forestry is generally not required to maintain tropical forest systems. If the land is not used for non-forested purposes, tropical forests usually regenerate in a short time. This is particularly true where the harvests have consisted of selective logging of desired species. For example, the forests of southeast Asia that were logged a few decades ago have been heavily reforested. Even where the disturbance was dramatic, or catastrophic, tropical forests have shown great ability to regenerate. An example of such regeneration is found in areas adjacent to the Panama Canal that were denuded in the early 1900s but now have regenerated naturally to a lush tropical forest.

Other evidence also indicates that the forest has substantial regenerative capacity if the land use is not permanently changed. Of the 2,345 million hectares of tropical forests that existed in 1980, the area of potentially productive secondary forest – area that had been disturbed and then reforested – was about 896 million ha. Some 280 million ha were non-productive because of poor growth or inoperable terrain, and another 455 million ha were non-productive because of legal constraints such as being declared a reservation (FAO 1983). The area of secondary forest is increasing the result of fellings in primary and old-growth forests that are producing new cutover lands. However, conversion to other uses had resulted in a small net reduction for the five years prior to 1980.

Two categories of secondary forest are distinguished in the FAO inventory. One is residual forest cutover in the past sixty to eighty years which has never been completely felled. These forests may rapidly recover their former physiognomy, systemic processes, tree species, and other organisms. The other category of secondary forest, termed 'fallow,' is volunteer forest that invades after periodic cultivation. This forest, typically, lacks both the structure and composition of the mature forest, being usually composed of a large number of species that decreases rapidly as the girth increases (Wadsworth 1982:5-6). The FAO estimates that about 55 per cent of the secondary forest is cutover and that 45 per cent is fallow. Wadsworth (70) states that the data 'suggest that the potential productivity of the present area of cutover secondary forest [without fallow forest] is, in the aggregate, more than adequate to meet the wood requirements anticipated for the year 2000 [for the tropical countries].'

Although much is made of the purported lack of regenerative capacity by the tropical forest, there is a host of evidence that regeneration is adequate in the highly valued dipterocarp forest of the Asia-Pacific for most low and medium elevation sites (e.g., Proceedings 1980; Weideit and Banaag 1982; Whitmore 1984; Wyatt-Smith 1987).

These forests, due to the relative homogeneity of the stands, offer the best prospects for sustainable timber production with acceptable financial returns.

ECONOMICS OF PLANTATION FORESTS

Over the past couple of decades, plantation forests have established themselves as a viable economic activity in some places and under some conditions. Perhaps the most active region of tree-growing worldwide is the u.s. South, where about 1 million hectares of forest plantations are planted annually. Although some subsidies do apply to some tree planters (e.g., an assistance program to non-industrial forest ownerships), a large portion of the plantations are established with minimal subsidies. The subsidies that do exist for industrial ownerships are almost entirely in the form of certain tax concessions which allow early deduction of planting costs (USDA FS 1988). Even in the u.s., tree-planting must compete for land with agriculture which, as in most countries of the world, receives special concessions and subsidies.

In much of the other areas of the world where tree-planting is common, various types of incentives and subsidies apply. This is true also for the tropics and the subtropics. The fiscal incentive program in Brazil is well known for its effect in providing incentives for Brazil's forest plantations. Chile also has an incentive program in which most of the costs of establishing the plantation forest are borne by the state. Similar incentives apply in Indonesia, Malaysia, and elsewhere.

However, studies have suggested that the underlying economics of plantation forestry can be favourable in many places. A recent study (Sedjo 1983) examined the comparative economics of plantation forests for twelve regions around the world. These included the Nordic region of Europe, the u.s. South and Pacific Northwest, the Amazon, central and southern regions of Brazil, Chile, New Zealand, Borneo, West Africa, South Africa, and Australia. This study suggested that for most of the regions examined, the economic and financial returns to plantation forestry could be favourable if the plantations could be efficiently established on accessible sites with relatively high growth rates in sufficient volumes to allow integrated wood processing activities to be undertaken, thereby making for the maximum utilization of the wood produced. Furthermore, the favourable returns required that the wood-processing activities (as distinguished from wood-growing) were economically efficient. Also, the mills needed to be well situated with respect to their cost of access to major wood-consuming markets. Finally, the alternative uses of the land had to generate less value than did the production of industrial wood. The absence of a single critical ingredient could compromise the economic viability of the entire activity.

In many regions in the tropics, forest plantations are being suggested to replace, either directly or indirectly, natural tropical forests. The rationale is often expressed in terms of wood volume rather than wood value. Often, however, the plantation holdings are fragmented, poorly located, and with no obvious accessible markets. Furthermore, there is no clear market for much or all of the wood, especially for the residuals from sawmilling operations. The financial returns to these types of operations are likely to be quite low (Sedjo 1988). Even well-run, private plantations in the tropics may generate only barely acceptable returns (Golokin and Cassels 1987). Governments sometimes will introduce subsidies to make such projects financially viable. In such circumstances, it is the policy of subsidization that makes the project financially viable. An unfortunate side-effect of a policy to subsidize the establishment of inherently uneconomic plantations is that natural forest management is often a casualty. Given the subsidies to plantations, even economically viable natural forest management might well be replaced by costly, inherently uneconomic plantation forestry.

ECONOMICS OF NATURAL TROPICAL FOREST MANAGEMENT SYSTEMS

The natural resilience of the tropical forests and their ability (at least under many conditions in the Asia-Pacific region) to achieve acceptable natural regeneration of the commercial dipterocarp species suggests that natural forest management regimes which are characterized as 'extensive management' should be predominant. The major objective of these regimes is to ensure that regeneration is adequate and to provide forest protection. Although the species mix is important, the ability of technology to systematically utilize more species over time suggests some long-term flexibility with regard to species.

The financial advantages of such management systems are that: (1) the initial costs are low, and (2) the tree species produced are typically of higher value than are those from plantation forests. In addition, the environmental services and non-market outputs of the forest are usually maintained under such a management regime. Native species are maintained and natural ecosystems are only minimally disturbed. Wildlife, water protection, erosion control, non-

forest products, and so forth are all maintained. A disadvantage of
the system is that the biological growth rate of commercial wood is
modest. Whereas foresters are often concerned about the effect of
discounting on forestry projects, the low investment costs favour
extensive natural management systems vis-à-vis high investment-
cost plantations.

COMPARISON OF THE FINANCIAL RETURNS

Tables 1 and 2 present the financial returns to two alternative forest
management systems. These prototypes represent conditions that
existed in Kalamantan, Indonesia, in the late 1980s. The analysis is
conducted for a representative site after an initial harvest of an old-
growth tropical forest. Table 1 presents the costs, volumes, and returns from a plantation system that introduced Albizza falcataria on
a twenty-year sawtimber rotation. The plantation forest required
some additional clearing costs and site preparation, planting, weeding for four years, thinning, and harvest of sawtimber at age twenty.
This cycle was repeated to year sixty. Given the absence of pulpmills
in the region, small stems, thinnings, and waste from the sawmill
had no value. In addition, the prices paid for the sawtimber are assumed to be low (at $25 per cubic metre), because plantation timbers
had to compete in the local market with timbers provided by the native forest. Such a situation with low local prices for the plantation
sawtimbers and little or no market for pulpwood is common in the
region. An evaluation of the financial returns to the forest plantation
regime using a 6 per cent discount rate gives a discounted present
value (DPV) per hectare of -$122. An alternative investment criterion,
the financial internal rate of return (IRR), is also calculated. The IRR
for the plantation regime is calculated to be about 4 per cent.

Table 2 presents the costs, volumes, and returns to a hypothetical
lightly managed natural forest that relies to a high degree on natural
regeneration. Using experience from Indonesia (Sedjo 1988), the
natural tropical forest management system requires no additional
investment inputs beyond the first year, after the initial logging. Although natural regeneration is usually very adequate, initial management costs of $50 per hectare are assumed to enhance natural re-
generation. Although some harvesting systems in this region aim
towards a thirty-five-year selective harvest cycle, this analysis uses
a sixty-year period of growth since the large- and medium-sized
trees were logged in the initial harvest. The annual growth of commercial species in an unmanaged stand is assumed to be only 1.0 cubic metre per hectare per year. However, modest management and

silviculture are estimated to increase the growth of commercial species in that stand to 2.0 cubic metres per year (FAO 1980). At recent prices, this approach generates additional net revenues of $2,100 per hectare. Applying a 6 per cent discount rate over the sixty-year project gives a DPV of $58 to additional net revenues in the initial year. When the initial costs of $50 are subtracted, the DPV of the investment is $8. Using a financial IRR on natural tropical forest management yields an inflation-free IRR of 6.2 per cent or about two percentage points better than a plantation forest on the same site.

It is well known that different assumptions can yield different results using these two standard investment criteria. The purpose of this comparison is not to provide definitive estimates but, rather, to demonstrate that under reasonable assumptions the returns on natural tropical forest management can be as good as or better than the returns to plantation forests that are in some cases replacing the native forest.

WHY ISN'T NATURAL FORESTRY PRACTISED MORE OFTEN?

The above suggests that in many places in the tropics natural forestry management is preferable to plantation forestry. If this is correct, why isn't more natural tropical forestry management practised? One reason is that even poor investments may generate substantial future economic activity and, therefore, receive major government subsidies – perhaps under the guise of regional development. In the example above, the total revenues per land unit generated by an extensive natural forest management system are far less than those generated by intensively managed forest plantations. In addition, the plantation will require considerably larger investments, larger start-up costs, more employees, and so forth. Although this may appear to be desirable from the point of view of the regional economy, the greater economic activity generated by the inefficient plantations is unsustainable in the absence of large external subsidies, in addition to being a drain on the financial resources of struggling Third World countries.

By contrast, the natural forest regime generates far less revenues and employment. However, given a sufficiently higher rate of return, the private sector might undertake the activity without a subsidy and, even if a subsidy is required, the total expenditure will be far less. In addition, such activity is consistent with the continued production of a higher level of environmental and non-market goods and services.

It has also been well documented that governments frequently undertake inappropriate policies related to their natural resources, often, in effect, promoting economically and ecologically inferior projects (Repetto and Gillis 1988). These policies fail to properly value the timber resource as well as the environmental and other nontimber benefits provided by the forest. The policy followed by some countries, of fully subsidizing the costs of establishing a plantation forest in an effort to avoid deforestation, has had the reverse effect of inducing the conversion of natural forests to plantations, even when the underlying economics of natural management are superior to those of plantation forestry.

Furthermore, with institutional arrangements whereby firms are granted rights to harvest timber, concession agreements typically are provided for too short a period of time to provide the firms with incentives to take a long-term view towards the management and sustainability of the resource. In many tropical countries, for example, much of the natural tropical hardwood forest is currently being harvested on a selective cutting regime that anticipates a periodic and sustained year harvesting cycle. However, under the current concession system, loggers are limited in their harvesting rights to periods that are shorter than the harvesting cycle. In such a system, firms have no expectation of harvest beyond the initial logging and, therefore, no incentive to undertake natural forest management practices aimed at long-term forest improvements or sustainability which extend beyond the period of their harvesting rights.

A final speculation as to the apparent preference of non-economic plantation forestry over natural tropical forest management is the well-known preference of the large international development banks for large over smaller projects. Planting trees is considered desirable almost in itself, and large forest plantation projects require rather large amounts of financing. By contrast, extensive natural forest management is, as we have seen, an inherently modest operation. There is very little in such projects that would require the types of financing that the development banks find interesting.

CONCLUSIONS

The foregoing proposal argues that forestry projects, as with other investments, may generate competitive returns under some conditions but not under others. The specifics of the project become very important and locational considerations play an important role in determining the financial viability of forestry projects.

This paper suggests that in many places in the tropics, and particularly in the dipterocarpus forests of the Asia-Pacific region, the financial returns to natural tropical forest management are much better than is generally recognized. This challenges the conventional wisdom that natural tropical forest management is inherently financially inferior to forest plantations. The study further suggests that plantation forestry can generate low economic returns in the absence of a set of favourable conditions, and that these favourable conditions are often not present in real world projects. In many cases, plantation forestry is undertaken only because of subsidies to plantation management built into the system as the result of public policies. Finally, the paper demonstrates that under reasonable assumptions, the financial returns to natural forest management are often comparable or superior to the returns to plantation forests.

Comprehensive Bibliography

Adams, D.M. and R.W. Haynes (1980). 'The 1980 Softwood Timber Assessment Market Model: Structure, Projections and Policy Simulations.' *Forest Science* 26(3), Monograph 22

— (1983). 'The Distributional Impacts of Departures: Groups and Regions.' In Le Master, D.C., D.M. Baumgartner, and D. Adams (eds.), *Sustained Yield: Proceedings of a Symposium*. Washington State University, Coop. Ext. Service, Pullman, WA

— (1989). 'Changing Timber Policies May Bring Other Changes: The Impact of Potential Changes in National Forest Timber Supply.' *Journal of Forestry* 87(4):24-7, 30-1

Adams, D.M., B.A. McCarl, and L. Homayounfarrokh (1986). *The Role of Exchange Rates in Canadian-U.S. Lumber Trade*. Working Paper 8, CINTRAFOR, Seattle: University of Washington

Adegboye, R.O. (1969). 'Procuring Loan Through Pledging of Cocoa Trees.' *Journal of the Geographical Journal of Nigeria* 12(½):63-76

Adeyoju, S.K. (1976). 'Land Use and Tenure in the Tropics: Where Conventional Concepts Do Not Apply.' *Unasylva* 28:26-47

Affolter, E. (1985). 'Zunehmende Zwangsnutzungen: Holzmarkt und Holzverwendung aus der Sicht der Waldwirtschaft.' *Schweizerische Zeitschrift für Forstwesen* 136:805-18

Aguilar, F.V. (1982). *The Kalahan Educational Foundation: A Case Study of Social Forestry in the Upland Philippines*. Quezon City: Institute of Philippine Culture, Ateneo de Manila University

Allen, Leon H., Robert M. Peart, James W. Jones, R. Bruce Curry, and Kenneth J. Boote (1989). 'Likely Effects of Climate Change Scenarios on Agriculture in the USA.' In *Proceedings, Second North American Conference on Preparing for Climate Change*, The Climate Institute, Washington, DC 186-91

American Paper Institute (various issues). *The Statistics of Paper and Paperboard*

Anderson, H.W. (1956). 'Forest Cover Effects on Snow Pack Accumulation and Melt, Central Sierra Snow Laboratory.' *Transactions of the American Geophysical Union* 37(3):307-12

Anonymous (1985). 'Some Definitions of Social Forestry and Related Concepts.' Los Banos, P.I.: University of the Philippines Department of Social Forestry Occasional Paper (1)

— (1986). 'What's Happening in Europe: And its Influence on North America's Panel-Making Technology.' *Wood Based Panels North America*. (Mar.) 18-23

— (1989). 'Neues Waldgesetz in Griffnähe.' *Wald und Holz* 70:384-93

Apps, Michael J. and Werner A. Kurz (forthcoming). 'Assessing the Role of Canadian Forests and Forest Sector Activities in the Global Carbon Balance.' *World Resources Review*

Aschmann, Homer (1963). 'Proprietary Rights to Fruit on Trees Growing on Residential Property.' *Man* 63:74-6

Atkinson, William A. (1986). 'Zeroing in on Zoned Management.' *Journal of Forestry* 84(1):27-8

Auer, C. (1956). 'Die volkswirtschaftliche Bedeutung des Gebirgswaldes.' *Schweizerische Zeitschrift für Forstwesen* 107:319-26

Bach, W. (1988). 'Development of Climatic Scenarios: A. From General Circulation Models.' In M.L. Parry, T.R. Carter, and N.T. Konijn (eds.), *The Impact of Climatic Variations on Agriculture 1: Assessments in Cool Temperate and Cold Regions.* Kluwer Academic Publishers, Dordrecht, 125-57

Balassa, B. (1977). 'A "Stages Approach" to Comparative Advantage.' World Bank Reprint Series No. 136

Baldwin, Robert E. (1985). *The Political Economy of U.S. Import Policy*. Cambridge: MIT Press

Ballard, C.L. and D. Fullerton, J.B. Shoven, and J. Whalley (1985). *A General Equilibrium Model for Tax Policy Evaluation*. Chicago: The University of Chicago Press

Banfield, A.W.F. (1974). *The Mammals of Canada.* Published for the National Museum of Natural Sciences, National Museums of Canada, by University of Toronto Press

Barnett, Harold J. and C. Morse (1963). *Scarcity and Growth: The Economics of Natural Resource Availability*. Baltimore: Johns Hopkins University Press

BC Council of Forest Industries (COFI) (1982). 'Scribner/BC Log Grading Comparison Study: System Design, Implementation, and Testing.' Dec.

BC Forest Resources Commission (1991). *The Future of Our Forests*. Victoria, BC

BC Ministry of Energy, Mines and Petroleum Resources (1990). *Carbon Dioxide Inventory for British Columbia*. Prepared by B.H. Levelton & Associates and Western Ecological Services. File 439-1068. Victoria, BC

BC Ministry of Forests (1980). *Forest and Range Resource Analysis Technical Report*. Victoria: Queen's Printer

— (1984). *Forest and Range Resource Analysis, Summary*. Victoria: Queen's Printer

— (1984a). *Forest and Range Resource Analysis 1984*. Victoria: Queen's Printer

— (1984b). *Five-Year Plan: Steady State*. Victoria: Silviculture Branch

— (1986). *Annual Report 1985/86*. Victoria: Queen's Printer

— (1987). *Annual Report 1986/87*. Victoria: Queen's Printer

— (1987-9). Official news releases re Forest Act amendments, log export policies

— (1988). *The Small Business Forest Enterprise Program*. Information paper, Jul.

— (1988). *1988 Summary of Backlog Not Satisfactorily Restocked Forest Land*. Victoria: Queen's Printer

— (1988a). *Annual Report 1987/88*. Victoria: Queen's Printer

— (1988b). Unpublished data

— (1989). *Five Year Forest and Range Resource Program 1989-1994*. Victoria: Queen's Printer

— (1990). *1990 Summary of Backlog Not Satisfactorily Restocked Forest Land*. Victoria: Queen's Printer

Bee, Ooi Jin (1987). *Depletion of the Forest Resources in the Philippines*. ASEAN Economic Research Unit, Institute of Southeast Asian Studies, Field Report Series No. 18, Singapore

Belzer, Dean and Cynthia Kroll (1986). *New Jobs for the Timber Region: Economic Diversification for Northern California*. Institute of Government Studies, University of California at Berkeley

Bengston, D.N. (1985). 'Diffusion of Innovations in Forestry and Forest Products: Review of the Literature.' In C.D. Risbrudt and P.J. Jakes (compilers), *Forestry Research Evaluation: Current Progress, Future Directions*. General Technical Report NC-104, St. Paul, MN: USDA Forest Service, North Central Forest Experiment Station, 69-77

— and A. Strees (1986). 'Intermediate Inputs and the Estimation of Technical Change: The Lumber and Wood Products Industry.' *Forest Science* 32(4):1,078-85

— and H.M. Gregersen (1988). 'Income Redistribution Impacts of Technical Change: A Framework for Assessment and Empirical Evidence.' In Tarek M. Khalil et al. (eds.), *Technology Management I*, Technology Management Publication TM 1, Special publication of the *International Journal of Technology Management*, Geneva, Switzerland: Inderscience Enterprises, 680-9

— and P.J. Jakes (1988). 'The Impact of Technical Change on the Timber Market.' In *Minnesota's Timber Supply: Perspectives and Analysis*, Proceedings of a Conference, Staff Paper Series Report No. 64, Department of Forest

Resources, University of Minnesota, St. Paul, MN, 196-202

—, H.M. Gregersen, and John Haygreen (1988). 'Seesawing Across the Forty-ninth Parallel: The International Diffusion of a Wood-Based Technology.' *Journal of Forest History* 32(2):82-8

Bennoit, Terry and Robert Schultz (undated, c. 1979). 'Plumas National Forest Water Yield Model.' USDA Forest Service

Bentley, W.R. (1970). *Technological Change in the Forest Industries: A Problem Analysis*. Forestry Research Notes No. 151, Department of Forestry, University of Wisconsin, Madison, WI

Berck, Peter (1978). 'The Economics of Timber.' *Bell Journal of Economics* 9(2):147-62

Berck, Peter and William R. Bentley (1989). 'Hotelling's Theory, Enhancement, and the Taking of the Redwood National Park.' University of California at Berkeley, Department of Agricultural and Resource Economics, Working Paper No. 456

Berry, Sara S. (1975). *Cocoa, Custom and Socio-Economic Change in Rural Western Nigeria*. Oxford: Clarendon Press

Beveridge, Stephen and Charles Nelson (1981). 'A New Approach to Decomposition of Economic Time Series into Permanent and Transitory Components with Particular Attention to the Measurement of the "Business Cycle."' *Journal of Monetary Economics* 7(2)

Binswanger, Hans P. (1988). 'Fiscal and Legal Incentives with Environmental Effects on the Brazilian Amazon.' Washington, DC: World Bank, Discussion Paper (ARU 69)

— (1989). 'Brazilian Policies that Encourage Deforestation in the Amazon.' Washington: The World Bank Environment Department Working Paper No. 16

Bishop, John, Robert Hudgens, and David Gow (1981). *Dynamics of Shifting Cultivation, Rural Poor, Cattle Complex in a Humid Tropical Forest Life Zone*. Research Note No. 2, Washington, DC: Development Alternatives

Blair, Harry (ed.) (1982). *Report on Community Forestry Workshop*. Washington, DC: USAID

Blake, Donald R. and F. Sherwood Rowland (1988). 'Continuing Worldwide Increase in Tropospheric Methane, 1978 to 1987.' *Science* 239:1129-31

Blaut, James M, et al. (1973). 'A Study of Cultural Determinants of Soil Erosion and Conservation in the Blue Mountains of Jamaica.' In Lambros Comitas and David Lowenthal (eds.), *Work and Family Life: West Indian Perspectives*. New York: Doubleday Anchor, 39-65

Bloetzer, G. (1978). *Die Oberaufsicht über die Forstpolizei nach schweizerischem Bundesstaatsrecht*. Zürich: Schulthess Polygraphischer Verlag

BLS (1984). *Technological Change and its Labor Impact in Four Industries*. Bulletin 2182, U.S. Department of Labor, Bureau of Labor Statistics

— (1985). *The Impact of Technology on Labor in Four Industries*. Bulletin 2228,

U.S. Department of Labor, Bureau of Labor Statistics

— (1986). *Technology and its Impact on Labor in Four Industries*. Bulletin 2263, U.S. Department of Labor, Bureau of Labor Statistics

Boeke, J. (1948). *The Interests of the Voiceless Far East*. Leiden: Universitare Pers

— (1953). *Economics and Economic Policy of Dual Societies*. New York: Institute of Pacific Relations

Bompard, Jean, Catherine Ducatillion, and Philippe Heckseteweiler (1980). *A Traditional Agricultural System: Village-Forest-Gardens in West Java*. Montpelier: Academie de Montpelier, Universite des Sciences et Techniques du Languedoc

Boonkird, Sa-Ard (1978). 'Taungya System: Its Applications, Ways and Means of Improvements in Thailand.' In *Proceedings, VII World Forestry Congress*, Jakarta: IUFRO

Boonkird, S.A., E.C.M. Fernandes, and P.K.R. Nair (1984). 'Forest Villages: An Agro-Forestry Approach to Rehabilitating Forest Land Degraded by Shifting Cultivation in Thailand.' *Agroforestry Systems* 2:87-102

Bowes, Michael D., John V. Krutilla, and Paul Sherman (1984). 'Forest Management for Increased Timber and Water Yields.' *Water Resources Research* 20(6):655-63

Bowyer, J.L., S. Suo, K. Skog, and V.L. Morton (1987). *Predicting the Rate of Timber Utilization Innovations*. Final Report USFS-FPL/University of Minnesota, Cooperative Research Project, Contract USDA-FP-85-0748

Box, George E.P. and Gwilym M. Jenkins (1970). *Time Series Analysis: Forecasting and Control*. San Francisco: Holden-Day

Boyd, Roy G. (1988). *The Direct and Indirect Effects of Tax Reform on Agriculture*. Technical Bulletin No. 1743, Economic Research Service, U.S. Department of Agriculture, Washington, DC

— and Kerry Krutilla (1987). 'The Welfare Impacts of U.S. Trade Restrictions against the Canadian Softwood Lumber Industry: A Spatial Equilibrium Analysis.' *Canadian Journal of Economics*, 20(1):17-35

— (1988). 'The Politics and Consequences of Protectionism: A Case Study in the North American Lumber Market.' *Journal of Policy Modeling* 10(3):601-9

Boyd, Roy G. and William F. Hyde (1989). *Forestry Sector Intervention: The Impacts of Public Regulation on Social Welfare*. Ames, Iowa: Iowa State University Press

Bradley, P.N. (1985). 'Development Research and Energy Planning in Kenya.' *Ambio* 14(4-5):228-36

— (1988). 'Survey of Woody Biomass on Farms in Western Kenya.' *Ambio* 17(1):40-8

Brain, James (1980). 'The Uluguru Land Usage Scheme: Success and Failure.' *Journal of Developing Areas* 14:175-90

Brain, Robert (1972). *Bangwa Kinship and Marriage*. Cambridge: Cambridge University Press

Brara, Rita (1987). 'Shifting Sands: A Study of Customary Rights in Grazing.' Mimeo, Jaipur, India: Institute of Development Studies

Brewer, Marilynn B. and Roderick M. Kramer (1986). 'Choice Behavior in Social Dilemmas: Effects of Social Identity, Group Size, and Decision Framing.' *Journal of Personality and Social Psychology* 50(3):543-9

Bridel, L. (1984). 'Formes et Tendances de l'Évolution Touristique.' In E. Brugger et al. (eds.), *Umbruch im Berggebiet*, Bern: Haupt, 203-40

Brinkman, Dirk (1989). 'Economics of the Treeplanting Industry.' WSCA *Newsletter*, Fall, 4-8

British Columbia (1986). *Regional Index*

British Columbia, Special Log Export Policy Committee (1983). *Report on Legislation, Policies and Procedures on Log Exports from British Columbia*, Jul.

British Columbia Forest Products and Finlay Forest Industries (1988). Mackenzie Tree Farm License Application, 5 Aug.

Brodie, J. Douglas, Robert O. McMahon, and William H. Gavelis (1978). *Oregon's Forest Resources: Their Contribution to the State's Economy*. Research Bulletin 23, Forest Research Lab, Oregon State University, School of Forestry, Sep.

Brokensha, David and E.H.N. Njeru (1977). 'Some Consequences of Land Adjudication in Mbere Division.' Working Paper (320) Nairobi: University of Nairobi

Brokensha, David and Bernard Riley (1978). 'Forest, Foraging, Fences and Fuel in a Marginal Area of Kenya.' Paper prepared for a USAID Africa Bureau Workshop, Washington, DC: USAID

Brokensha, David and Alfonso Peter Castro (1984). 'Fuelwood, Agroforestry and Natural Resource Management: The Development Significance of Land Tenure and Other Resource/Management/Utilization Systems.' Paper prepared for USAID

Bromley, Daniel W. (1985). 'Resources and Economic Development: An Institutionalist Perspective.' *Journal of Economic Issues* 19:779-96

— (1989). *Economic Interests and Institutions: The Conceptual Foundations of Public Policy*. Oxford: Basil Blackwell

— (1991). *Environment and Economy: Property Rights and Public Policy*. Oxford: Basil Blackwell

Bromley, Daniel W. and Devendra Chapagain (1984). 'The Village Against the Center: Resource Depletion in South Asia.' *American Journal of Agricultural Economics* 66:868-73

Brown, A.A. (1942). 'Fire Prevention in the Western United States.' In *Proceedings, Priest River Fire Meeting*. Dec. 1941, U.S. Forest Service, 97-101

Brown, S. and A.E. Lugo (1982). 'The Storage and Production of Organic

Matter in Tropical Forests and their Role in the Global Carbon Cycle.' *Biotropica* 1:161-87

Bruce, John W. (1986). *Land Tenure Issues in Project Design and Strategies for Agricultural Development in Sub-Saharan Africa*. LTC Paper No. 128, Madison: Land Tenure Center, University of Wisconsin

— and Raymond Noronha (1985). 'Land Tenure Issues in the Forestry and Agroforestry Project Contexts.' Prepared for International Workshop on Tenure Issues in Agroforestry, 26-30 May, 1985

— and Raymond Noronha (1987). 'Land Tenure Issues in the Forestry and Agroforestry Project Contexts.' In John Raintree (ed.), *Land, Trees and Tenure: Proceedings of an International Workshop on Tenure Issues in Agroforestry*. Madison and Nairobi: Land Tenure Center and ICRAF, 121-60

Bruenig, E.F. (1987). 'The Forest Ecosystem: Tropical and Boreal.' *Ambio* 16(2,3):68-79

Brumelle, S.L., J.S. Carley, I.B. Vertinsky, and D.A. Wehrung (1991). 'Evaluating Silvicultural Investments: A Review Based on the Canadian Context.' *Forestry Abstracts* 152(9):862

Bruner, W.E. and P.R. Hagenstein (1981). *Alternative Forest Policies for the Pacific Northwest: Study Module V. Forest Policy Project*. Pacific Northwest Regional Commission, Vancouver, WA

Budowski, Gerardo (1982). 'The Socio-Economic Effects of Forest Management on the Lives of People Living in the Area: The Case of Central America and Some Caribbean Countries.' In E.G. Hallsworth (ed.), *Socio-Economic Effects and Constraints in Tropical Forest Management*. Chichester:Wiley, 87-102

Bullard, S.H. and T.J. Straka (1986). 'Role of Company Sales in Funding Research and Development by Major U.S. Paper Companies.' *Forest Science* 32(4):936-43

Buongiorno, J. and R.A. Oliveira (1977). 'Growth of the Particleboard Share of Production of Wood-Based Panels in Industrialized Countries.' *Canadian Journal of Forest Research* 7(2):383-91

Burgess, D.F. (1981). 'The Social Discount Rate for Canada: Theory and Evidence.' *Canadian Public Policy* 7:383-94

Burley, Jeffrey (1982). *Obstacles to Tree Planting in Arid and Semi-Arid Lands: Comparative Case Studies from India and Kenya*. Tokyo: United Nations University

Butora, V. (1984). 'Programm zur Steigerung der Arbeitssicherheit in der schweizerischen Forstwirtschaft.' *Schweizerische Zeitschrift für Forstwesen* 135:785-92

Byron, R.N. (1979). 'Community Stability and Forest Policy in British Columbia.' *Canadian Journal of Forest Research* 8(1):61-6

Cameron, J. (1928). *The Development of Governmental Forest Control in the United States*. Baltimore: Johns Hopkins University Press

Canada - British Columbia (1985). *Forest Resource Development Agreement (1985-1990)*

Canada, External Affairs (1988). *Canada-United States Free Trade Agreement*. Department of External Affairs, Ottawa

Canadian Forest Industries Council (1986). *Canadian Forest Industries 1986: Data Book*

Canadian Government (1988). *The Canada-U.S. Free Trade Agreement and the Forest Products Sector: An Assessment*. Industry, Trade, and Technology Branch, Canadian Forestry Service, Ottawa

Canadian Pulp and Paper Association (1985). *1985 Reference Tables*. Montreal

Carroll, M.R. and G.R. Milne (1982). 'Evaluating Forest Industry Developments in Alberta Using Socioeconomic Impact Analysis.' *The Forestry Chronicle*. 58(6):268-74

Carter, J. (1987). 'Organizations Concerned with Forestry in Nepal.' Kathmandu: Forest Research and Information Center Occasional Paper 2/87

Cate, D. (1963). 'Recreation in the United States.' Unpublished doctoral dissertation, Stanford University

Caves, D.W., L.R. Christensen, M.W. Tretheway, and R.J. Windle (1987). 'An Assessment of the Efficiency Effects of U.S. Airline Deregulation via an International Comparison.' In E.E. Bailey (ed.), *Public Regulation: New Perspectives on Institutions and Policies*. Cambridge, MA: MIT Press

Cecelski, Elizabeth (1985). *The Rural Energy Crisis, Women's Work and Basic Needs: Perspectives and Approaches to Action*. Geneva: International Labour Office

Cernea, Michael M. (1985). 'Alternative Units of Social Organization Sustaining Afforestation Strategies.' In Michael M. Cernea (ed.), *Putting People First: Sociological Variables in Rural Development*. New York: Oxford University Press for the World Bank, 267-93

Chavangi, N.A. (1985). 'Cultural Aspects of Fuelwood Procurement in Kakamega District.' KWDP Working Paper No. 4, the Beijer Institute, Nairobi/Stockholm

Chavangi, N.A., R.J. Englehard, and V. Jones (1986). 'Culture as a Basis for Implementing Self-Sustaining Development Programmes.' Paper presented at the International Conference on Women and the 'Other Energy Crisis.' ILO, Geneva, Apr.

— (1983). *Culture as the Basis for Implementation of Self-Sustaining Woodfuel Development Programmes*. Kenya Woodfuel Development Programme, Nairobi: Beijer Institute

Chen, Martha Alter (1986). *A Quiet Revolution: Women in Transition in Rural Bangladesh*. Dhaka, BRAC: Prokashana

Chenery, H., M.S. Ahlunwalia, C.L.G. Bell, J.H. Dulog, and R. Jolly (1974). *Redistribution with Growth*. London: Oxford University Press for the World Bank

Christensen, L.R. and D.W. Jorgenson (1969). 'The Measurement of u.s. Real Capital Input, 1929-1967.' *Review of Income and Wealth*. Dec., 293-320

Chubb, L.T. (1961). *Ibo Land Tenure*. Ibadan: Ibadan University Press

Ciriacy-Wantrup, S.V. and Richard C. Bishop (1975). 'Common Property as a Concept in Natural Resource Policy.' *Natural Resources Journal* 15:713-27

Clawson, Marion (1975). *Forests for Whom and for What*. Baltimore: Johns Hopkins University Press

— (1979). 'Forests in the Long Sweep of American History.' *Science* 204(43,908):1168-74

— (1985). *Shelter in America: Costs, Supply Constraints, and the Role of Forests*. Discussion Paper Series No. RR85-04, Washington DC: Resources for the Future

Clawson Marion and Roger Sedjo (1984). 'History of Sustained-yield Concept and its Application to Developing Countries.' In H.K. Steen (ed.), *History of Sustained-yield Forestry*. Durham: Forest History Society, 3-15

Clepper, H. (1971). *Professional Forestry in the United States*. Washington DC: Johns Hopkins University Press/Resources for the Future

Cleveland, T. (1910). 'National Forests as Recreation Grounds.' *Annals of the American Academy of Political and Social Science* 35(2):241-7

Cleveland, W.S. (1979). 'Robust Locally Weighted Regression and Smoothing Scatterplots.' *Journal of the American Statistic Association* 74(368):829-36

Cliff, E.P. (1973). *Timber: The Renewable Material*. Prepared for the National Commission on Materials Policy, Aug., Washington, DC: u.s. Government Printing Office, 151 pp.

Cloud, Kathleen and Jane B. Knowles (1988). 'Where Can We Go From Here? Recommendations for Action.' In Jean Davison (ed.), *Agriculture, Women and Land: The African Experience*. Boulder: Westview Press, 250-64

Cohen, A.J. (1984). 'Technological Change as Historical Process: The Case of the u.s. Pulp and Paper Industry, 1915-1940.' *Journal of Economic History* 44:775-99

— (1987). 'Factor Substitution and Induced Innovation in North American Kraft Pulping: 1914-1940.' *Explorations in Economic History* 24:197-217

Colorado State Forest Service (1988). *Burning Issues*. 2(2)

Combe J. and C. Frei (1986). *Die Bewirtschaftung des Bergwaldes*. Schlussbericht zum schweizerischen MAB-Programm 22, Bern: Bundesamt für Umweltschutz

Commander, Simon (1986). 'Managing Indian Forests: A Case for the Reform of Property Rights.' Network Paper 3b, ODI Social Forestry Network, London: ODI

Connaughton, Kent P. and William McKillop (1979). 'Estimation of "Small

Area" Multipliers for the Wood Processing Sector: An Econometric Approach.' *Forest Science* 25(1):7-20

Connaughton, Kent P., Paul E. Polzin, and Con Schallau (1985). 'Tests of the Economic Base Model of Growth for a Timber Dependent Region.' *Forest Science.* 31(3):717-30

Conservation Reserve Program Working Group (1989). *Conservation Reserve Program Progress Report and Preliminary Evaluation of the First Two Years.* u.s. Department of Agriculture, Washington, DC

Constantino, L. (1986). 'Modelling Wood Quality, Productivity, Demands and Supplies in the Sawmilling Industry: British Columbia and Pacific Northwest Westside.' PH.D. Thesis, Faculty of Graduate Studies, University of British Columbia

Constantino, L.F. and D. Haley (1988). 'Wood Quality and the Input and Output Choices of Sawmilling Producers for the British Columbia Coast and the United States Pacific Northwest, West Side.' *Canadian Journal of Forestry Research* 18(2):202-8

Council of Forest Industries (COFI) of British Columbia (1987). *BC Forest Industry Fact Book, 1987.* Vancouver

— (various years). *British Columbia Forest Industry Statistical Tables.* Compiled from Statistics Canada, Ministry of Labour, and other sources

Council on Competitiveness (1991). *Gaining New Ground: Technological Priorities for America's Future.* Washington, DC

Cox, J. Charles (1905). *The Royal Forests of London.* London: Metheun and Co.

Crosson, P. (1985). 'The Impact of Erosion on Land Productivity in the United States.' In El-Swaify et al. (eds.), *Soil Erosion and Conservation.* Ankey, Iowa: Soil Conservation Society of America

Crowling, E.B. (1989). 'Recent Changes in Chemical Climate and Related Effects on Forests in North America and Europe.' *Ambio* 18(3):167-71

Crutzen, Paul J. and Meinrat O. Andreae (1990). 'Biomass Burning in the Tropics: Impact on Atmospheric Chemistry and Biogeochemical Cycles.' *Science* 250:1669-78

D'Arrigo, R.G.C. Jacoby, and I.Y. Fung (1987). 'Boreal Forests and Atmosphere-Biosphere Exchange of Carbon Dioxide.' *Nature* 329:321-3

Dana, S.T. and S.K. Fairfax (1980). *Forest and Range Policy.* New York: McGraw-Hill

Daniels, Steven E., William F. Hyde, and David N. Wear (1991). 'Distributive Effects of Forest Service Attempts to Maintain Community Stability.' *Forest Science* 37(1):245-60

Darby, H.C. (1956). 'The Clearing of the Woodland in Europe.' In William L. Thomas Jr. (ed.), *Man's Role in Changing the Face of the Earth.* Vol. 1, Chicago: University of Chicago Press, 183-216

Davison, Jean (1988). 'Land and Women's Agricultural Production: The

Context.' In Jean Davison (ed.), *Agriculture, Women and Land: The African Experience*. Boulder: Westview Press, 1-32

De Borger, B. and J. Buongiorno (1985). 'Productivity Growth in the Paper and Paperboard Industries: A Variable Cost Function Approach.' *Canadian Journal of Forest Research* 15(6):1013-20

Dean, Gerald W., Harold O. Carter, Eric A. Nickerson, and Richard M. Adams (1973). 'Structure and Projections of the Humbolt County Economy: Economic Growth Versus Environmental Quality.' Giannini Foundation Research Report No. 318, University of California at Berkeley

Deaton, A. and J. Muelbauer (1980). *Economics and Consumer Behavior*. Cambridge: Cambridge University Press

Denevan, William (1982). *Causes of Deforestation and Forest and Woodland Degradation in Tropical Latin America*. Report to the Office of Technology Assessment, Congress of the United States, 16 Jul. 1982, Assessment of 'Technologies to Sustain Tropical Forest and Woodland Resources.' 25-43

Denman, D.R. (1969). *Land Use and The Constitution of Property*. Cambridge: Cambridge University Press

Dertouzos, Michael L., Richard K. Lester, and Robert M. Solow (1989). *Made in America: Regaining the Productive Edge. MIT Commission on Industrial Productivity*. Cambridge MA: MIT Press

Digernes, Turi Hammer (1977). 'Wood for Fuel: Energy Crisis Implying Desertification: The Case of Bara, The Sudan.' Thesis in Geography for the Cand. Polit. degree, University of Bergen, Norway

Dove, Michael R. (1986). 'Peasant Versus Government Perception and Use of the Environment: A Case Study of Banjarese Ecology and River Basin Development in South Kalimantan.' *Journal of Southeast Asian Studies* 17:113-36

Dowd, Richard M. (1986). 'The Greenhouse Effect.' *Environmental Science and Technology* 20:1208-9

Downs, Anthony (1967). *Inside Bureaucracy*. Boston: Little, Brown and Company

Duerr, William A. (1986). Forestry's Upheaval.' *Journal of Forestry* 84(1):20-6

Duncan, Patrick (1960). *Sotho Laws and Customs*. Cape Town: Oxford University Press

Easterling, William E., Martin L. Parry, and Pierre R. Crosson (1989). 'Adapting Future Agriculture to Changes in Climate.' In Norman J. Rosenburg et al. (eds.), *Proceedings, Greenhouse Warming: Abatement and Adaptation*. Resources for the Future, Washington, DC, 91-104

Eastman, Clyde and James R. Gray (1987). *Community Grazing: Practice and Potential in New Mexico*. Albuquerque: University of New Mexico

Edwards, S. (1986). 'Are Devaluations Contractionary.' *Review of Economics and Statistics* 68(3):501-8

El-Arifi, Salih (1978). 'Some Aspects of Local Government and Environmental Management in the Sudan.' In J.A. Mabbutt (ed.), *Proceedings of the Khartoum Workshop on Arid Lands Management*. Tokyo: United Nations University

Elbow, Kent and Alain Rochegude (1989). 'An Introduction to the Forestry Codes of Three Sahelian Countries: Niger, Mali and Senegal.' Draft, Madison: Land Tenure Center

Elias, Taslim Olawale (1963). *The Nigerian Legal System*. 2nd ed. London: Routledge and Kegan Paul

Elwin, Verrier (1950). *Bondo Highlands*. Bombay: Oxford University Press

Ember, L.R., P.L. Layman, W. Lepkowski, and P.S. Zurer (1986). 'Tending the Global Commons.' *Chemical and Engineering News* 64(47):14-64

Emerson, Michael et al. (1988). *The Economics of 1992: An Assessment of the Potential Economic Effects of Completing the Internal Market of the European Community*. European Economy, Commission of the European Communities, Directorate-General for Economic and Financial Affairs, No. 35

Englehard, R.J. et al. (1986). 'The Paradox of Abundant On-Farm Woody Biomass yet Critical Fuelwood Shortages: A Case Study of Kakamega District.' Invited paper presented at the International Union of Forestry Research Institutes (IUFRO) Conference, Ljubljana, Yugoslavia, Sep.

— (1987). *Bura Fuelwood Plantation Project, Phase 2, an appraisal of BFPP's Plan of Operations and Recommendations for a Strategy Towards a Sustainable Fuelwood Supply in Bura Division*. A report for FINNIDA, the Beijer Institute, Nairobi/Stockholm

Ensign, E.T. (1885) *Report for the Year 1885 of the Forest Commissioner of the State of Colorado*. Denver: Collier and Cleveland

— (1888a) *Biennial Report of the Forest Commissioner of the State of Colorado*. Denver: Collier and Cleveland

— (1888b) *Report on the Forest Conditions of the Rocky Mountains*. Bulletin No. 2. Forestry Division, Department of Agriculture, Washington DC: Government Printing Office, 41-152

Environics Research Group, Limited (1989). 'Forestry Canada Public Opinion Survey.' Mimeo, Toronto, Feb.

Environment Canada (1980). *National Inventory of Natural Sources and Emissions of Sulphur Compounds*. Feb. Ottawa

— (1981a). *National Inventory of Natural Sources and Emissions of Nitrogen Compounds*. Jan.

— (1981b). *National Inventory of Natural Sources and Emissions of Organic Compounds*. Feb.

— (1981c). *National Inventory of Natural Sources and Emissions of Primary Particulates*. Nov.

— (1981d). *National Inventory of Natural Sources and Emissions of Mercury Compounds*. Jul.

— (1989). 'Exploring the Implications of Climatic Change for the Boreal Forest and Forestry Economics of Western Canada.' *Climate Change Digest*. CCD 89-02

— (1990). *National Inventory of Sources and Emissions of Carbon Dioxide*. Environmental Protection Series, Report EPS 5/AP/2, May

Evans, Julian (1982). *Plantation Forestry in the Tropics*. Oxford: Clarendon Press

Faustmann, Martin (1849) 'On the Determination of the Value Which Forestland and Immature Stands Possess for Forestry.' English translation edited by M. Gane, Oxford Institute Paper 42, 1968

Fearnside, P.M. (1988). 'Jari at Age 19: Lessons for Brazil's Silvicultural Plants at Carajas.' *Interciencia* 13(1):12-24

— (1990). 'Deforestation in Brazilian Amazonia.' In G.M. Woodwell (ed.), *Earth in Transition*. Cambridge University Press, 211-38

Feder, G., R.E. Just, and D. Zilberman (1985) 'Adoption of Agricultural Innovations in Developing Countries: A Survey.' *Economic Development and Cultural Change* 34(1):255-98

Federal/Provincial Research and Monitoring Coordinating Committee (RMCC) (1990). *The 1990 Canadian Long-Range Transport of Air Pollutants and Acid Deposition Assessment Report*. Part 3, Atmospheric Sciences, Ottawa

Fernandes, Walter and Sharad Kulkarni (eds.) (1983). *Towards a New Forest Policy: People's Rights and Environmental Needs*. New Delhi: Indian Social Institute

Fernow, B. (1888). 'Introductory.' In Bulletin No. 2. Forestry Division, Department of Agriculture. Washington DC: Government Printing Office, 7-16

Flavin, Christopher and Cynthia Pollock (1985). 'Harnessing Renewable Energy.' *State of the World 1985*. W.W. Norton, 189-96

Fleishman, John A. (1988). 'The Effects of Decision Framing and Others' Behavior on Cooperation in a Social Dilemma.' *Journal of Conflict Resolution* 32(1):162-80

Fleming, William A. (1983). 'Phewa Tal Catchment Management Program: Benefits and Costs of Forestry and Soil Conservation in Nepal.' In Lawrence S. Hamilton (ed.), *Forest and Watershed Development and Conservation in Asia and the Pacific*. Boulder, CO: Westview Press, 217-88

Fleuret, Ann and Patrick Fleuret (1978). 'Fuelwood Use in a Peasant Community: A Tanzanian Case Study.' *Journal of Developing Areas* 12:315-22

Flora, D. and R. Vlosky (1984). 'Potential Pacific Rim Demand for Alaska's Construction Grade Logs.' Review Draft, Foreign Trade Research, Pacific Northwest Forest and Range Experiment Station, Portland, Oregon

Folland C.K., T.R. Karl, K.Y.A. Vimikov (1990). 'Observed Climate Variations and Change.' In J.T. Houghton, G.J. Jenkins, and J.J. Ephramus (eds.), *Climate Change - The IPCC Assessment*. Cambridge University Press, 220-33

Food and Agriculture Organization of the United Nations (FAO) (1980). 'Tropical High Forest Growth.' FAO Consultancy Study

— (1983). 'Management of Tropical Mixed Forests: Preliminary Assessment of Present Status.' FO:MISC/83/17, Dec., Rome

Food and Agriculture Organization of the United Nations (FAO) (1988). *Yearbook, Forest Products, 1977-1988*. Rome

Forest Service, United States Department of Agriculture (1982). *An Analysis of the Timber Situation in the United States 1952-2030*. Forest Resource Report No. 23, Dec.

Forestry Canada (1990). *Selected Forestry Statistics, Canada 1990*. Information Report, Economics and Statistics Directorate, Ottawa

— (1991). *The State of Forestry in Canada.* 1990 Report to Parliament, Canada's Green Plan, Supply and Services Canada, Ottawa

Forsyth, D.J.C., N. McBain, and R. Solomon (1980). 'Technical Rigidity and Appropriate Technology in Less Developed Countries.' *World Development* 8:371-98

Fortmann, Louise (1985). 'The Tree Tenure Factor in Agroforestry with Particular Reference to Africa.' *Agroforestry Systems* 2:229-51

— (1986). 'Women's Role in Subsistence Forestry.' *Journal of Forestry* 84(7):39-42

— (1988a). 'Locality and Custom: Non-Aboriginal Claims to Customary Usufructuary Rights as a Source of Rural Protest.' University of California at Berkeley, Institute of Governmental Studies, Working Paper 88-27

— (1988b). 'Predicting Natural Resource Micro-Protest.' *Rural Sociology* 53(3):357-67

Fortmann, Louise and Dianne Rocheleau (1985). 'Women's Role in Agroforestry: Four Myths and Three Case Studies.' *Agroforestry Systems* 2:253-72

Fortmann, Louise and Sally K. Fairfax (1987). 'American Forestry Professionalism in the Third World: Some Preliminary Observations.' Berkeley

Fortmann, Louise and John W. Bruce (eds.) (1988). *Whose Trees? Proprietary Dimensions of Forestry*. Boulder: Westview Press

Fox, Irving K. (1991) 'The Politics of Canada-U.S. Trade in Forest Products.' Vancouver: UBC Press

Francis, Paul (1987). 'Land Tenure Systems and the Adoption of Alley Farming.' In *Land, Trees and Tenure: Proceedings of an International Workshop on Tenure Issues in Agroforestry, Nairobi, May 27-31, 1985*, Madison and Nairobi: International Council for Research in Agroforestry and the Land Tenure Center, 175-81

Frank, D.L., A. Ghebremichael, T.H. Oum, and M.W. Tretheway (1988). 'Economic Performance of the Canadian Pulp and Paper Industry: 1963-1982.' Working Paper 107, Forest Economics and Policy Analysis Research Unit, University of British Columbia, Vancouver, Feb.

Furnivall, J. (1939). *Netherlands India: A Study of Plural Economy*. Cambridge: Cambridge University Press

— (1948). *Colonial Policy and Practice: A Comparative Study of Burma and Netherlands India*. Cambridge: Cambridge University Press

Fyfe, W.S., B.I. Kronberg, O.H. Leonardos, and B.N. Olorunfemi (1983). 'Global Tectonics and Agriculture: A Geochemical Perspective.' *Agriculture, Ecosystems and Environment* 9:383-99

Galloway, J.N. (1989). 'Atmospheric Acidification: Projections for the Future.' *Ambio* 18(3):161-6

Gear Annabel J. and Brian Huntley (1991). 'Rapid Changes in the Range Limits of Scots Pine 4000 Years Ago' *Science* 251:544-7

Ghebremichael, A., D.B. Roberts, and M.W. Tretheway (1989). 'Productivity in the Canadian Lumber Industry: An Inter-Regional Comparison.' Economics Branch Working Paper, Ottawa: Forestry Canada

Gibbs, R.J. (1967). 'The Geochemistry of the Amazon River System: Part I. The Factors that Control the Salinity and the Composition and Concentration of Suspended Solids.' *Geological Society of America Bulletin* 79:1203-32

Gillen, D.W., T.H. Oum, and M.W. Tretheway (1985). *Airline Cost and Performance: Implications for Public and Industry Policies*. Centre for Transportation Studies, The University of British Columbia

Gilles, Jere L. and Keith Jamtgaard (1981). 'Overgrazing in Pastoral Areas: The Commons Reconsidered.' *Sociologia Ruralis* 21:129-41

Gilligan, J.P. (1953). 'The Development of Policy and Administration of Forest Service Primitive and Wilderness Areas in the Western United States.' Unpublished doctoral dissertation, University of Michigan

Ginsburg, N. (1973). 'From Colonialism to National Development: Geographical Perspectives on Patterns and Policies.' *Annals of the Association of American Geographers* 63(1):1-21

Globe and Mail (1988a). 'Alberta Energy to Build Pulp Mill.' 21 Dec.

— (1988b). 'Lumber Firms Hurt by Tax on Softwood.' 28 Dec.

Globerman, S. (1976). 'New Technology Adoption in the Canadian Paper Industry.' *Industrial Organization Review* 4(1):5-12

Gold, B., G. Rosegger, and M.G. Boylan (1980). *Evaluating Technological Innovations*. Lexington, MA: Lexington Books

Goldstein, Judith (1986). 'The Political Economy of Trade: Institutions of Protection.' *American Political Science Review* 80(1):161-84

Gollop, F.M. and D.W. Jorgenson (1980). 'United States Productivity Growth by Industry, 1947-1973.' In J.W. Kendrick and B.N. Vaccara (eds.), *New Developments in Productivity Measurement and Analysis*. Studies in Income and Wealth, National Bureau of Economic Research, Chicago: University of Chicago Press

Golokin, Stan L. and Patrick K. Cassels (1987). 'An Appraisal of Sabah Softwoods Sdn. Bhd. 12 Years After Establishment.' Presented to Seminar of the Future Role of Forest Plantations in the National Economy, Kota Kinibalu, Sabah, 30 Nov.-4 Dec.

Gordon, R. (1985). 'Ueberlegungen zur Forsteinrichtung im Gebirgswald, anhand des Beispiels der Gemeinde Tarasp.' Unpublished Diplomarbeit, Institut für Wald- und Holzforschung, ETH-Zürich

Gorman, E. (1989). 'Scientific Understanding of Ecosystem Acidification: A Historical Review.' *Ambio* 18(3):150-4

Goswami, P.C. (1982). 'Agro-Forestry: Practices and Prospects as a Combined Land Use System.' *The Indian Forester*. 108(6):385-96

Grandstaff, Terry B. (1980). *Shifting Cultivation in Northern Thailand: Possibilities for Development*. Resource Systems Theory and Methodology Series No. 3, Tokyo: The United Nations University

Grasmick, Joseph (1979). 'Land and the Forest Dwelling South American Indian.' *Buffalo Law Review* 27:759-800

Greber, B.J. and D.E. White (1982). 'Technical Change and Productivity Growth in the Lumber and Wood Products Industry.' *Forest Science* 28(1):135-47

Gregersen, H.M. (1982). 'Village Forestry Development in the Republic of Korea.' Document (FAO) GCP/INT/347/SWE, Rome: Food and Agriculture Organization

— (1985). 'The University of Minnesota Forestry Research Evaluation Program.' In C.D. Risbrudt and P.J. Jakes (eds.), *Forestry Research Evaluation: Current Progress, Future Directions*. General Technical Report NC-104, St. Paul, MN: USDA Forest Service, North Central Forest Experiment Station, 31-3

Gregersen, H., J. Haygreen, S. Sindelar, and Jakes (1988). 'U.S. Gains From Foreign Forestry Research.' *Journal of Forestry* 87(2):21-6

Gregersen, H.M., A.L. Lundgren, and D.N. Bengston (1990). 'Planning and Managing Forestry Research: Guidelines for Managers.' FAO Forestry Paper No. 96, Rome: Food and Agriculture Organization of the United Nations

Griffin, James R. (1971). 'Oak Regeneration in the Upper Carmel Valley, California' *Ecology* 52(5):862-8

Guha, Ramachandra (1985). 'Forestry and Social Protest in British Kumaun, c. 1893-1921.' In Ranajit Guha (ed.), *Subaltern Studies IV*. Delhi: Oxford University Press, 54-100

Gupta, Sulekh Chandra (1964). 'The Village Community and its Disintegration in Uttar Pradesh in the Early Nineteenth Century.' In B.N. Ganguli (ed.), *Readings in Indian Economic History*. London: Asia Publishing House, 102-13

Hahn, Steven (1982). 'Hunting, Fishing and Foraging: Common Rights and Class Relations in the Postbellum South.' *Radical History Review* 26:37-64

Hakanson, S. (1974). 'Special Presses in Paper-making.' In L. Nasbeth and G.F. Ray (eds.), *The Diffusion of New Industrial Processes*. London: Cambridge University Press, 58-104

Haley, David (1980). 'A Regional Comparison of Stumpage Values in BC and the U.S. Pacific NW.' *Forestry Chronicle*. Oct.

Haley, David and Martin K. Luckert (1990). *Forest Tenures in Canada: A Framework for Policy Analysis*. Forestry Canada, Economics Directorate, Information Report E-X-43, Ottawa

Handa, R. (ed.) (1988). *Forest Policy in Japan*. Tokyo: Nippon Ringyo Chosakai

Handa, R. (1988). 'Timber Economy and Forest Policy after World War II.' In Handa (ed.), *Forest Policy in Japan*. Tokyo: Nippon Ringyo Chosakai, 22-35

Hansing, J. (1989). *Ransonering av trafiberravara (Rationing of Wood Fibre)*. Swedish University of Agricultural Sciences, Department of Forest Economics, Report No. 87, Umea

Harberger, A.C. (1972). *Project Evaluation: Collected Essays*. Chicago: Markham

Harbeson, John W. et al. (1984). *Area Development in Liberia: Toward Integration and Participation*. AID Project Impact Evaluation(53) Washington, DC: USAID

Hardin, Garrett (1968). 'The Tragedy of the Commons.' *Science* 162:1,243-8

Hardy, Elise (1989). 'The Importance of Correctly Characterizing the Compound's Tenure Distribution in Formulating National Land Tenure Policy: The Case of Senegal.' Madison: Land Tenure Center, University of Wisconsin

Harmon, Mark E., William K. Ferrell, and Jerry F. Franklin (1990). 'Effects of Carbon Storage of Conversion of Old-Growth Forests to Young Forests.' *Science* 247:699-701

Harrington, J.B. (1988). 'Climatic Change: A Review of Causes.' *Canadian Journal of Forestry Research* 17:1313-39

Harris, Larry D. (1984). *The Fragmented Forest*. Chicago: The University of Chicago Press

Harris, R.G. (1984). 'Applied General Equilibrium Analysis of a Small Open Economy with Scale Economies and Imperfect Competition.' *American Economic Review* 74(5):1061-31

— (1988). 'A Guide to the GET Model.' Working Paper 88-10, Canadian Department of Finance, Ottawa

Hay-Roe (1989). *PaperTree Letter*. Vancouver, 1 Oct.

Haygreen, J. H. Gregersen, I. Holland, and R. Stone (1986). 'The Economic Impact of Timber Utilization Research.' *Forest Products Journal* 36(2):12-20

Haynes, R.W. and D.M. Adams (1985). *Simulations of the Effects of Alterna-*

tive Assumptions on Demand-Supply Determinants on the Timber Situation in the United States. USDA, Forest Service; Forest Resource Economics Research, 113 pp.

Hayter, R. (1988). *Technology and the Canadian Forest-Products Industries: A Policy Perspective*. Background Study 54, Science Council of Canada, Hull: Canadian Government Publishing Centre

Heaps, T. and B. Pratt (1989). *The Social Discount Rate for Silvicultural Investments*. FRDA Report 071, Victoria: Forestry Canada

Heaps, T.M. and W.A. White (1991). 'Economic Analysis of Forest Fertilization.' In J.D. Lousier, H. Brix, R. Brockley, R. Carter and V.G. Marshall, (eds.), *Improving Forest Fertilization Decision-Making in British Columbia*. Victoria: BC Ministry of Forests, 108-21

Hecht, Robert M. (1983). 'The Ivory Coast Economic "Miracle": What Benefits for Peasant Farmers.' *Journal of Modern African Studies* 21(1):25-53

Hecht, Susanna and Alexander Cockburn (1989). *The Fate of the Forest*. Verso

Helpman, E. and A. Razin (1981). 'Comparative Dynamics of Monetary Policy in Floating Exchange Rate Regimes.' Working Paper 9-81, Foerder Institute for Economic Research

Hertel, T.W. and M.E. Tsigas (1987). 'Tax Policy and U.S. Agriculture: A General Equilibrium Analysis.' Staff Paper No. 87-2, Department of Agriculture Economics, Purdue University, West Lafayette, IN

Hewett, C.E. and T.E. Hamilton (eds.) (1982). *Forests in Demand*. Boston: Auburn House

Hileman, B. (1989). 'Global Warming.' *Chemical and Engineering News* 67(11):25-44

Hill, Polly (1963). *Migrant Cocoa Farmers in Southern Ghana*. London: Cambridge University Press

Hinde, Thomas (1985). *Forests of Britain*. London: Victor Gollancz Ltd.

Hoben, Allen (1973). *Land Tenure Among the Amhara of Ethiopia*. Chicago: The University of Chicago Press

Hodges, Donald G., James L. Regens, and Frederick W. Cubbage (1988). 'Evaluating Potential Economic Impacts of Global Climate Change on Forestry in the Southern United States.' *Resource Management and Optimization* 6(3):235-51

Hosier, R.H. (1988). 'Energy for Rural Development in Zimbabwe.' *Energy, Environment and Development in Africa, Vol. 11*. The Beijer Institute, Stockholm

Hoskins, Marilyn (1979). 'Women in Forestry for Local Community Development: A Programming Guide.' Grant No. AID/otr-147-79-83, Washington, DC: Office of Women in Development, USAID

— (1980). 'Community Forestry Depends on Women.' *Unasylva* 32(130): 27-32

— (1982). 'Social Forestry in West Africa: Myths and Realities.' In *American*

Association for the Advancement of Science Annual Meeting. Washington, DC: AAAS

— (1983). 'Rural Women, Forest Outputs, and Forestry Projects.' FAO:Misc/83/3, Rome: FAO

Hosmer, Ralph S. (1922). *Impressions of European Forestry.* Chicago: The Lumber World Review

Hotelling, H. (1931). 'The Economics of Exhaustible Resources.' *Journal of Political Economy* 39:137-75

Hough, F.B. (1878). *Report upon Forestry.* Washington DC: Government Printing Office

Houghton, R.A., R.D. Boone, J.R. Fruci, J.E. Hobbie, J.M. Melillo, C.A. Palm, B.J. Peterson, G.R. Shaver, and G.M. Woodwell (1987). 'The Flux of Carbon from Terrestrial Ecosystems to the Atmosphere in 1980 Due to Changes in Land Use: Geographic Distribution of the Global Flux.' *Tellus, Series B: Chemical and Physical Meteorology* 39B(1-2):122-39

Houghton, Richard A. and George M. Woodwell (1989). 'Global Climate Change.' *Scientific American* 260(4):36-44

House of Commons Canada (1990). *Forests of Canada: The Federal Role.* Report of the Standing Committee on Forestry and Fisheries, Ottawa

Hufbauer, Gary Clyde, and Joanna Shelton Erb (1984). *Subsidies in International Trade.* Institute for International Economics. Cambridge, MA: MIT Press

Hutton, J.H. (1921). *The Sema Nagas.* London: MacMillan and Co. Ltd.

Hyde, W.F. (ed.) (1983). *Economic Evaluation of Investments in Forestry Research.* Durham, NC: Acorn Press

Hyde, W.F. (1988). 'General Public Policy Impacts on Upland Resources and the Environment in the Philippines.' Washington: The World Bank, Unpublished discussion paper prepared for the FFARM project

—, D.H. Newman, and B.J. Seldon (1989). 'Recent Experience in Forestry Research Productivity and Expectations for the 21st Century.' In *Forestry on the Frontier,* Proceedings of the Society of American Foresters 1989 National Convention, SAF Publication 89-02, Bethesda, MD: Society of American Foresters

International Woodworkers of America, Research Department (1985). *Productivity and Unit Production Costs in the Softwood Lumber Industries of the United States and Canada, 1977 to 1984.* Portland and Vancouver, Jul.

Ise, J. (1920). *The United States Forest Policy.* New Haven: Yale University Press

Ishii, Yutaka and Hotoshi Arai (1986). 'A Study on the Present State of Plantation Forestry in Hokkaido.' Paper presented to XVIII IUFRO, Division IV

IUFRO (annual) *The Current State of Japanese Forestry: Its Problems and Future.* Tokyo: The Japanese Forest Economic Society

Iwai, Y. (1989). 'The Movement of the Lumbering Industry in U.S.A. and its

Influence on Japanese Forest Industry.' IUFRO, *The Current State of Japanese Forestry*, Jun., Tokyo: The Japanese Forest Economic Society, 12-22

Jacques, R. and G.A. Fraser (1989). 'The Forest Sector's Contribution to the Canadian Economy.' *Forestry Chronicle* 65:93-6

Jakes, P.J. and C.D. Risbrudt (1988). 'Evaluating the Impacts of Forestry Research.' *Journal of Forestry* 86(3):36-9

James, R.W. (1971). *Land Tenure and Policy in Tanzania*. Dar es Salaam: East African Literature Bureau

— and G.M. Fimbo (1973). *Customary Land Law of Tanzania: A Source Book*. Nairobi: East Africa Literature Bureau

Jegr, Karel M. (1985). *Overview of the North American Pulp and Paper Industry*. Forest Economics and Policy Analysis Project, Information Report 85-6, University of British Columbia, Vancouver

Jenkins, G.P. (1973). 'The Measurement of Rates of Return and Taxation from Private Capital in Canada.' In W.A. Niskanen et al. (eds.), *Benefit-Cost and Policy Analysis in 1972*, Chicago: Aldine, 211-45

Jenkins, G.P. (1977). 'Capital in Canada: Its Social and Private Performance 1965-1974.' Economic Council of Canada Discussion Paper No. 98, Ottawa

Jenkinson, D.S. (1981). 'The Fate of Plant and Animal Residues in Soil.' In D.J. Greenland and M.H.B. Hayes (eds.), *The Chemistry of Soil Processes*. New York: John Wiley & Sons, 505-61

Jodha, N.S. (1986). 'Common Property Resources and Rural Poor in Dry Regions of India.' *Economic and Political Weekly* 21(27):1169-81

Johnson, F.R. (1930). 'Recreation Planning.' In *Report of Supervisors' Meeting*. Dec. 1930. On file in Federal Records Center, Denver, CO

Johnson, K. Norman, Thomas W. Stuart, and Sarah A. Crim (1986). *FORPLAN Version 2: An Overview*. Washington, DC: USDA Forest Service, Land Management Planning

Jordan, Carl F. (1985). *Nutrient Cycling in Tropical Forest Ecosystems*. New York: John Wiley and Sons

Jorgenson, D.W. (1984). 'Econometric Methods for Applied General Equilibrium Modeling.' In H.E. Scarf and J.B. Shoven (eds.), *Applied General Equilibrium Analysis*,. New York: Cambridge University Press

Joyce, Linda A., Michael A. Fosberg, and Joan M. Comanor (1990). 'Climate Change and America's Forests.' USDA *Forest Service General Technical Report RM-187*. Rocky Mountain Forest and Range Experiment Station, Fort Collins, CO

Kalt, Joseph P. (1987). *The Political Economy of Protectionism: Tariffs and Retaliation in the Timber Industry*. Cambridge: John F. Kennedy School of Government, Harvard University, Mar.

Kattelmann, Richard C., Neil H. Berg, and John Rector (1983). 'The Potential for Increasing Streamflow from Sierra Nevada Watersheds.' *Water Resources Bulletin* 19(3):395-402

Kaul, S.K. (1979). 'Human Aspects of Forest Development.' In Krishna Murti Gupta and Desh Bandu (eds.), *Man and Forest: A New Dimension in the Himalaya*. New Delhi: Today and Tomorrow Printers and Publishers, 152-70

Kauppi, P. and M. Posch (1988). 'A Case Study of the Effects of CO_2-Induced Climatic Warming on Forest Growth and the Forest Sector: A. Productivity Reactions of Northern Boreal Forests.' In M.L. Parry, T.R. Carter, and N.T. Konijn (eds.), *The Impact of Climatic Variations on Agriculture, Vol. 1: Assessments in Cool Temperate and Cold Regions*. Kluwer Publishers Dordrecht, 183-95

Kawake, Jiro (1988). 'Characteristics and Tasks of Japan's Pulp and Paper Industry.' In Gerard F. Schreuder (ed.), *Global Issues and Outlook in Pulp and Paper*. Seattle: University of Washington Press, 20-8

Keegan, Charles E. and Paul E. Polzin (1987). 'Trends in the Wood and Paper Products Industry: Their Impacts on the Pacific Northwest Economy.' *Journal of Forestry* 85(11):31-41

Keihakutown (n.d.). Information/statistics pamphlet distributed by the town administration

Keizai Koho Center (1991). *Japan 1991: An International Comparison*. Japan Institute for Social and Economic Affairs, Tokyo

Kenya Woodfuels Survey (1984). Nairobi: Beijer Institute

Kienholz, H. (1984). 'Natural Hazards: A Growing Menace?' In E. Brugger et al. (eds.), *The Transformation of Swiss Mountain Regions*. Bern: Haupt, 385-406

King, K.F.S. (1968). *Agrosilviculture (The Taungya System)*. Bulletin No. 1, Ibadan: Ibadan University Press

Kinkead, Gwen (1981). 'Trouble in D.K. Ludwig's Jungle.' *Fortune*. 20 Apr. 1981, 102-17

Kloppenberg, Jack and Daniel Lee Kleinman (1988). 'Seeds of Controversy: National Property versus Common Heritage.' In Jack Kloppenburg (ed). *Seeds and Sovereignty*. Durham and London: Duke University Press, 175-203

Kramer, P.J. (1981). 'Carbon Dioxide Concentration, Photosynthesis and Dry Matter Production.' *BioScience* 31:29-33

Krause, G.H.M., B. Prinz, and K.D. Jung (1983). 'Forest Effects in West Germany.' In *Air Pollution and Forest Productivity*. Proceedings of the Symposium, Washington, DC, 4-5 Oct., 297-332

Kroll, Cynthia (1984). 'Community Disruption.' In Peter Berck and Larry Dale (eds.), *Economics and Minerals Planning*. Division of Agricultural and Natural Resources, University of California

Kronberg, Barbara I. (in press). 'Responses of Major North American Ecosystems To Global Change.' In *Contrasts in Global Change Responses Between Northern and Southern Hemispheres*. Academic Press

—, W.S. Fyfe, O.H. Leonardos, and A.M. Santos (1979). 'The Chemistry of some Brasilian Soils: Element Mobility During Intense Weathering.' *Chemical Geology* 24:211-29

— and W.S. Fyfe (1983). 'Geochemical Controls in Amazonia on Weathering Rates.' *Mitt. Geol.-Palaont. Institute, Univ. Hamburg* 55:215-22

— and A.J. Melfi (1987). 'Geochemical Evolution of Lateritic Terrains.' *Zeit Geomorphologie* 64:25-32

— and W.S. Fyfe (1989). 'Tectonics, Weathering and Environment.' In Balasumbramaniam et al. (eds.), *Weathering: Its Products and Deposits, Vol. 1: Processes*. Theophrastus, Athens, 3-13

—, R.E. Benchimol, and M.I. Bird (1991). 'Geochemistry of Acre Basin Sediments: Window on Ice-Age Amazonia.' *Interciencia* 16(3):138-41

Krutilla, John V. and John A. Haigh (1978). 'An Integrated Approach to National Forest Management.' *Environmental Law* 8:373-415

Krutilla, John V. and A.C. Fisher (1985). *The Economics of Natural Environments*. Washington DC: Resources for the Future

Krutilla, John V., Michael D. Bowes, and Thomas B. Stockton (1989). Management of Watersheds for Augmented Water Yields–Plumas National Forest, Discussion Paper ENR89-02, Resources for the Future, Washington DC

Kumazaki, Minoru (1988). 'Japanese Economic Development and Forestry.' In R. Handa (ed.), *Forest Policy in Japan*. Tokyo: Nippon Ringyo Chosakai, 1-35

Kurz, Werner A. (1991). 'Atmospheric Carbon and Pacific Northwest Forests.' In G. Wall (ed.), *Proceedings of the United States/Canada Symposium on the Implications of Climate Change for Pacific Northwest Forest Management, Seattle, Washington, October 23-25*. Department of Geography Publication Series, Occasional Paper, University of Waterloo

Kuusela, K. (1987). 'Forest Products: World Situation.' *Ambio* 16(2-3):80-5

Kyoto Prefectural Government (1987). 'This is Kyoto Prefecture.' Population data, Section 14, 61-2

Lai, Chun K. and Asmeen Khan (1986). 'Mali as a Case Study of Forest Policy in the Sahel: Institutional Constraints on Social Forestry.' Social Forestry Network Paper(3e) London: Overseas Development Institute

Langbein, W.B. and S.A. Schumm (1958). 'Yield of Sediment in Relation to Mean Annual Precipitation.' *Transactions American Geophysical Union* 39:1076-84

Langenegger, H. (1979). 'Eine Checkliste für Waldstabilität im Gebirgswald.' *Schweizerische Zeitschrift für Forstwesen* 130:640-6

— (1984). 'Mountain Forests: Dynamics and Stability.' In Brugger, E. et al. (eds.), *The Transformation of Swiss Mountain Regions*. Berne, Haupt, 361-72

Larsen, D., L. Gee, and D. Bearden (1983). *1982 Washington Mill Survey, Wood Consumption and Mill Characteristics*. Washington Mill Survey Report No. 8, State of Washington, Department of Natural Resources

Lawlor, A. (1985). *Productivity Improvement Manual*. Gower Publishing Co., England

Lawry, Steven W. (1987). 'Communal Grazing and Range Management: The Case of Grazing Associations in Lesotho.' Addis Ababa: International Livestock Centre for Africa, ALPAN Network Paper No. 13

— (1988). 'Private Herds and Common Land: Issues in the Management of Communal Grazing Land in Lesotho, Southern Africa.' PH.D. dissertation (Land Resources), Madison: University of Wisconsin, 277-300

— (1989). 'Tenure Policy and Natural Resource Management in Sahelian West Africa.' Madison: Land Tenure Center, University of Wisconsin

Le Master, D.C. (1984). *Decade of Change*. Westport, Connecticut: Greenwood Press

— D.M. Baumgartner, and D. Adams (eds.) (1983). *Sustained Yield: Proceedings of A Symposium*. Washington State University, Coop. Ext. Service, Pullman, WA

— and J.H. Beuter (eds.) (1989). *Community Stability in Forest-Based Economies: Proceedings of a Conference*. Timber Press, Portland, OR

Leach, T.A. (1919). 'Date-Trees in Halfa Province.' *Sudan Notes and Records* 2:98-104

Leakey, L.S.B. (1977). *The Southern Kikuyu Before 1903, Vol. 1*. London: Academic Press

Leefers, L.A. (1981). 'Innovation and Product Diffusion in the Woodbased Panel Industry.' PH.D. thesis, Michigan State University

Leibundgut, H. (1956). 'Das Problem des Gebirgshilfe.' *Schweizerische Zeitschrift für Forstwesen* 107:297-310

Lenway, Stephanie Ann (1982). 'The Politics of Protection, Expansion and Escape: International Collaboration and Business Power in U.S. Foreign Trade Policy.' PH.D. Dissertation, Berkeley: University of California

Leslie, A.J. (1987). 'The Economic Feasibility of Natural Management of Tropical Forests.' In Francois Mergen and Jeffrey R. Vincent (eds.), *Natural Management of Tropical Moist Forests*. Yale School of Forestry, New Haven, 177-98

Lester, J. and T. Morehen (1988a). 'New Estimates of Canadian Tariff Rates by Industry and Commodity.' Working Paper No. 88-2, Canadian Department of Finance, Ottawa

— (1988b). 'Trade Barriers Between Canada and the United States.' Working Paper No. 88-3, Canadian Department of Finance, Ottawa

Lettman, Gary (1988). 'Employment in Oregon's Forest Industry.' Draft paper, Department of Forestry, Oregon State University

Libecap, Gary A. and Ronald N. Johnson (1978). 'Property Rights, Nineteenth Century Federal Timber Policy, and the Conservation Movement.' *Journal of Economic History* 39:129-42

Likens, G.E. (1989). 'Some Aspects of Air Pollutant Effects on Terrestrial

Ecosystems and Prospects for the Future.' *Ambio* 18(3):172-6

—, (ed.) (1985). *An Ecosystem Approach to Aquatic Ecology: Mirror Lake and its Environment*. New York: Springer-Verlag

Likens, G.E., F.H. Bormann, R.S. Pierce, and W.A. Reiners (1978). 'Recovery of a Deforested Ecosystem.' *Science* 199:492-6

Lind, Robert C. (1988). 'Reassessing the Government's Discount Rate Policy in Light of New Theory and Data In a World Economy With Integrated Capital Markets.' Delivered at American Economic Association Annual Meeting, NY, 28 Dec.

Linebaugh, Peter (1976). 'Karl Marx, The Theft of Wood and Working Class Composition: A Contribution to the Current Debate.' *Crime and Social Justice* 6:5-16

Lloyd, P.C. (1962). *Yoruba Land Law*. London: Oxford University Press

Loose, V. (1977). 'Guidelines for Benefit Cost Analysis.' Victoria, BC: Environment and Land Use Secretariat

Lotan, J.E. et al. (eds.) (1985). *Proceedings: Symposium and Workshop on Wilderness Fire*. U.S. Forest Service General Technical Report INT-812

Lowell, J.W. (1917). 'Preliminary Planning.' In *Minutes of Supervisors' Meeting, District Two*, Jan. On file in Denver Public Library

Lundgren, A.L. (1986). 'A Brief History of Forestry Research Evaluation in the United States.' In Denver Burns (compiler), *Evaluation and Planning of Forestry Research*, General Technical Report NE-GTR-111, Broomall, PA: USDA Forest Service, Northeastern Forest Experiment Station, 83-96

Lyon, Kenneth S. (1981). 'Mining of the Forest and the Time Path of the Price of Timber.' *Journal of Environmental Economics and Management* 8:330-44

MacDonald, Gordon J. (1988). 'Scientific Basis for the Greenhouse Effect.' *Journal of Policy Analysis and Management* 7(3):425-44

MacKenzie, J.J. and M.T. El-Ashry (1988). *Ill Winds: Airborne Pollution's Toll on Trees and Crops*. World Resources Institute

McCay, Bonnie and J.A. Acheson (1988). *The Question of the Commons*. Tucson: University of Arizona Press

— (1988). 'Human Ecology of the Commons.' In Bonnie McCay and James Acheson (eds.), *The Question of the Commons*. Tucson: University of Arizona Press, 1-34

McKean, Margaret (1986). 'Management of Traditional Common Lands (*Iriaichi*) in Japan.' In Panel on Common Property Resource Management, Board of Science and Technology for International Development, Office of International Affairs, National Research Council, *Proceedings of the Conference on Common Property Resource Management*. 21-6 Apr. 1985, Washington, DC: National Academy Press, 533-89

McLaren, C. (1990). 'Heartwood.' *Equinox* 53:43-55

McLauglin, S.B. (1985). 'Effects of Air Pollution on Forests: A Critical Review.' *Journal of the Air Pollution Control Association* 35(5):512-34

— (1987). 'Whole Tree Physiology and Air Pollution Effects on Forest Trees.'

In *Interrelationship between Above- and Below-Ground Influences of Air Pollutants on Forest Trees*. Proceedings of Workshop, Commission of European Communities, Gennep, The Netherlands, 15-17 Dec

—, D.J. Downing, T.J. Blasing, E.R. Cook, and H.S. Adams (1987). 'An Analysis of Climate and Competition as Contributors to Decline of Red Spruce in High Elevation Appalachian Forests of the Eastern United States.' *Oecologia* (Berlin) 72:487-501

Mahar, Dennis J. (1989). *Government Policies and Deforestation in Brazil's Amazon Region*. Washington, DC: World Bank

Mahat, T., D. Griffin, and K. Shepherd (1986). 'Human Impact on Some Forests of the Middle Hills of Nepal. Part 1. Forestry in the Context of the Traditional Resources of the State.' *Mountain Research and Development* 6(3):223-32

— (1986). 'Human Impact on Some Forests of the Middle Hills of Nepal. Part 2. Some Major Human Impacts Before 1950 on the Forests of Sindhu Palchok and Kabhre Palanchok.' *Mountain Research and Development* 6(4):325-34

Makerere Institute of Social Research Land Tenure Center (1988). *Settlement in Forest Reserves, Game Reserves and National Parks in Uganda: A Study of Social, Economic and Tenure Factors Affecting Land Use and Deforestation*. Kampala: Makerere Institute of Social Research, Makerere University, and Madison: Land Tenure Center, University of Wisconsin

Manabe, S. and R.T. Wetherald (1986). 'Reduction in Summer Soil Wetness Induced by an Increase in Atmospheric Carbon Dioxide.' *Science* 232:626-8

Mangold, Robert D. Robert J. Moulton, and Jeralyn D. Snellgrove (1991). 'Tree Planting in the United States.' *USDA Forest Service Report*, State and Private Forestry, Washington, DC

Manning, G.H. and G. Thornburn (1971). 'Capital Deepening and Technological Change: The Canadian Pulp and Paper Industry 1940-1960.' *Canadian Journal of Forest Research* 1:159-66

Mansfield, E. (1988). 'The Speed and Cost of Industrial Innovation in Japan and the United States: External vs. Internal Technology.' *Management Science* 34(10):1157-68

Manthy, R. (1978). *Natural Resource Commodities: A Century of Statistics*. Baltimore: Johns Hopkins Press

Marchak, Patricia (1983). *Green Gold. The Forest Industry in British Columbia*. Vancouver: UBC Press

Margl, R.A. and P.V. Ellefson (1987). 'Assigned Patents: Technology Trends in 15 U.S. Wood-based Companies.' *Forest Products Journal* 37(1):47-50

Marquis, Ralph (1947). 'Bromides and Folklore in Forest Economics.' In *Proceedings of the Society of American Foresters Meeting* 76

Marshall, Eliot (1989). 'EPA's Plan for Cooling the Global Greenhouse.' *Science* 243:1,544-5

Martin, F., N Swan, I. Banks, G. Barker, and R. Beaudry (1979a). 'The Case of Roof Trusses.' In *The Inter-Regional Diffusion of Innovations in Canada*. Economic Council of Canada Research Study, Catalogue No. EC 2264/1979, Ottawa: Ministry of Supply and Services, 63-81

— (1979b). 'The Newsprint Industry.' In *The Inter-Regional Diffusion of Innovations in Canada*. Economic Council of Canada Research Study, Catalogue No. EC 2264/1979, Ottawa: Ministry of Supply and Services, 99-113

Martinello, F. (1985). 'Factor Substitution, Technical Change, and Returns to Scale in Canadian Forest Industries.' *Canadian Journal of Forest Research* 15(6):1116-24

— (1987). 'Substitution, Technical Change and Returns to Scale in British Columbian Wood Products Industries.' *Applied Economics* 19:483-96

Marwell, Gerald and R. Ames (1981). 'Economists Free Ride, Does Anyone Else?: Experiments in the Provision of Public Goods IV.' *Journal of Public Economics* 15:295-310

Maser, Chris (1988). *The Redesigned Forest*. San Pedro, California: R.E. Miles

Matalas, N.C. (1967). 'Mathematical Assessment of Synthetic Hydrology.' *Water Resources Research* 3(4):937-46

Mathiesen, L. (1985). 'Computational Experience in Solving Equilibrium Models by a Sequence of Linear Complementarity Problems.' *Operations Research* 33:1,225-50

Matthews, E. and F. Fung (1987). 'Methane Emissions from Natural Wetlands: Global Distributions, Area and Environmental Characteristics of Sources.' *Global Biogeochemical Cycles* 1:61-86

Mauer, Harry (1979). 'The Amazon: Development or Destruction?' *NACLA Report*, May/Jun. 27-37

Maughan, K.O. (1932). *Recreational Development in the National Forests*. Technical Publication No. 45, Bulletin of the New York State College of Forestry at Syracuse University

McCully, Patrick (1991). 'Discord in the Greenhouse: How WRI is Attempting to Shift the Blame for Global Warming.' *Ecologist* 21(4):157-65

Meade, R.H., T. Dunne, J.E. Richey, U de M. Santos, and E. Salati (1979). 'Sediment Loads in the Amazon River.' *Nature* 299:161-3

Meil, J.K., B.K. Singh, and J.C. Nautiyal (1988). 'Short-Run Actual and Least-Cost Productivities of Variable Inputs for the British Columbia Interior Softwood Lumber Industry.' *Forest Science* 34(1):88-101

Meil, J.K. and J.C. Nautiyal (1988). 'An Intraregional Economic Analysis of Production Structure and Factor Demand in Major Canadian Softwood Lumber Producing Regions.' *Canadian Journal of Forest Research* 18:1036-48

Mellilo, J.M., T.V. Callaghan, F.I. Woodward, E. Salati, and S.K. Sinha (1990). 'Effect in Ecosystems.' In J.T. Houghton, G.J. Jenkins, and J.J. Ephramus (eds.), *Climate Change: The IPCC Assessment*. Cambridge University Press, 283-310

Menzies, Nicholas (1988). 'A Survey of Customary Law and Control Over Trees and Wildlands in China.' In Louise Fortmann and John Bruce (eds.), *Whose Trees? Proprietary Dimensions of Forestry*. Boulder, CO: Westview Press

Mergen, F., R.E. Evenson, M.A. Judd, and J. Putnam (1988). 'Forestry Research: A Provisional Global Inventory.' *Economic Development and Cultural Change* 37(1):149-71

Merrifield, D.B. (1987). Speech to The Conference Board, 3 March, quoted in *Research Management* 30(3):4

Mertz, W. (1981). 'The Essential Trace Elements.' *Science*. 213:1332-8

Michaels, Patrick J. (1989). 'The Greenhouse Effect: Chicken Little and Our Response to "Global Warming".' *Journal of Forestry* 87(6):35-9

Mitchell, J.F.B. and D.A. Warrilow (1987). 'Summer Dryness in Northern Mid-latitudes Due to Increased CO_2.' *Nature* 330:238-40

Mitsuda, Hisayoshi and Charles C. Geisler (1988). 'Environmentalism as if People Mattered: A Case Study of the Japanese National Trust Movement.' Paper presented at the Twelfth World Congress of Rural Sociology, Bologna, Italy, 26 Jun.- 1 Jul.

Mixon J.W. and N.D. Uri (1985). *Managerial Economics*. New York: Macmillan

Miyamacho (n.d.). Information/statistics pamphlet distributed by the town administration

Moench, Marcus (1988). '"Turf" and Forest Management in a Garhwal Hill Village.' In Louise Fortmann and John Bruce (eds.), *Whose Trees? Proprietary Dimensions of Forestry*. Boulder, CO: Westview Press

Mohnen, V.A. (1988). 'The Challenge of Acid Rain.' *Scientific American* 259(2):30-8

Molion, L.C.B. and J.J.U. Betancurt (1981). 'Land Use and Agrosystem Management in Humid Tropics.' In J.J. Talbot and W. Swanson (eds.), *Woodpower: New Perspectives on Forest Usage*. Pergamon Press, 119-28

Molion, L.C.B. (1990). 'Climate Variability and its Effects on Amazonian Hydrology.' *Interciencia* 15(6):367-72

Molnar, Augusta (1985). 'Social Forestry Experiences in India and Nepal.' Unpublished Preliminary Draft, Washington, DC: General, Agricultural Division (ASPAB), World Bank

Montagne, Pierre (1985-6). 'Contributions of Indigenous Silviculture to Forestry Development in Rural Areas: Examples from Niger and Mali.'

Montrey, H.M. and J.A. Johnson (1988). 'The Role of Technology in Improving the Competitive Position of the U.S. Forest Products Industry.' In Jay A. Johnson and W. Ramsay Smith (eds.), *Forest Products Trade: Market Trends and Technical Developments*. Seattle, WA: University of Washington Press, 119-22

Mooney, H.A., B.G. Drake, R.J. Luxmoore, W.C. Oechel, and L.F. Pitelka (1991). 'Predicting Ecosystem Responses to Elevated CO_2 Concentrations.' *BioScience* 41(2):96-104

Moore, B. and B. Bolin (1987). 'The Oceans, Carbon Dioxide and Global Climate Change.' *Oceanus* 29(4):9-15

Moore, N.L. and C.R. Fink (1984). 'Federal Laboratory Research Benefiting the Pulp and Paper Industry.' In *Proceedings of the Technical Association of the Pulp and Paper Industry, 1984 Research and Development Conference,* Tappi Press, 261-7

Moulton, Robert J. and Kenneth R. Richards (1990). 'Costs of Sequestering Carbon Through Tree Planting and Forest Management in the United States.' *USDA Forest Service General Technical Report WO-58,* Washington, DC

Mukhoti, Bela (1986). 'Forestry Projects and Landless Farmers: A View of Issues from Within a Donor Agency.' *Culture and Agriculture* 30:7-12

Mukwaya, A.B. (1953). *Land Tenure in Buganda.* Kampala: Eagle Press

Murray, Gerald F. (1982). 'Cash-Cropping Agro-Forestry: An Anthropological Approach to Agricultural Development in Rural Haiti.' In *Haiti: Present State and Future Prospects.* Racine, Wis.: Wingspread

National Academy of Sciences (1986). *Common Property Resource Management.* Washington, DC: National Academy Press

National Acid Precipitation Assessment Program (1987). *Interim Assessment, The Causes and Effects of Acidic Deposition, Volume I, Executive Summary.* Washington, DC: U.S. Government Printing Office

National Acid Precipitation Assessment Program (1987). *Interim Assessment, The Causes and Effects of Acidic Deposition IV. Effects of Acidic Deposition.* Washington DC: Government Printing Office, Ch. 7

National Acid Precipitation Assessment Program (NAPAP) (1990). *Annual Report, 1989 and Findings Update.* Washington, DC, June

National Science Foundation (1989). *National Patterns of R&D Resources: 1989.* Final Report NSF 89-308, Washington, DC: National Science Foundation

Nations, J.B. and R.B. Nigh (1978). 'Cattle, Cash, Food and Forest: The Destruction of the American Tropics and the Lacandon Maya Alternative.' *Culture and Agriculture* 6:1-5

Nawitka Resource Consultants (1987). *Impact of Intensive Forestry Practices on Net Stand Values in British Columbia.* FRDA Report 014, Victoria: Canadian Forestry Service

Nelson, R.H. (1986). 'Private Rights to Government Actions: How Modern Property Rights Evolve.' *University of Illinois Law Review* 361-86

Nelson, R.M. (1985). 'Mythology Instead of Analysis: The Story of Public Forest Management.' In R.T. Deacon and M.B. Johnson (eds.), *Forestlands: Public and Private.* Cambridge, Massachusetts: Ballinger, 23-76

Netting, Robert McC. (1981). *Balancing on an Alp: Ecological Change and Con-*

tinuity in a Swiss Mountain Community. Cambridge: Cambridge University Press

Newell, R.C. (1971). 'The Amazonas Forest and the Atmospheric General Circulation.' In W.H. Kellog and G.D. Robinson (eds.), *Man's Impact on Climate.* MIT Press, 457-9

Newman, D.H. (1986). 'An Econometric Analysis of Aggregate Gains from Technical Change in Southern Softwood Forestry.' PH.D. thesis, Duke University

Ng'andwe, C.O.M. (1976). 'African Traditional Land Tenure and Agricultural Development: Case Study of the Kunda People in Jumbe.' *African Social Research* 21:51-67

Nokes, Gregory (1987). 'Out of Time: Environmentalists, Loggers Battling Over Centuries-Old Northwest Trees.' *The Oregonian.* Sunday, 8 Nov.

Normile, M. and C. Goodloe (1988). 'U.S.-Canadian Agricultural Trade Issues: Implications for the Bilateral Trade Agreement.' Agriculture and Trade Analysis Division, United States Department of Agriculture

North Cariboo Community Futures Group (1987). *Report*

North, Jeffrey F. (1988). *Administered Trade Protection and the Case of Wood Shakes and Shingles.* Case Studies No.4. New York: Center for International Business Programs, Pace University

Nye, P.H. and D.J. Greenland (1960). *The Soil Under Shifting Cultivation.* Commonwealth Technical Bulletin No. 51, Commonwealth Bureau of Soils, Harpenden, England

O'Keefe, P. et al. (1984). 'Energy and Development in Kenya: Opportunities and Constraints.' *Energy, Environment and Development in Africa Vol. 1.* The Beijer Institute, Stockholm

O'Toole, R. (1988). *Reforming the Forest Service.* Washington DC: Island Press

Obermiller, Fredrich W. (1982). 'Economic Efficiency vs. Distributive Equity: The Sagebrush Rebellion.' *Western Journal of Agricultural Economics* 7(2):253-64

Obi, Chinwuba S.N. (1963). *The Ibo Law of Property.* London: Butterworths

Office of Technology Assessment (OTA) (1983). *Wood Uses: U.S. Competitiveness and Technology.* OTA-ITE-210, Washington, DC: U.S. Congress

— (1984). *Acid Rain and Transported Air Pollutants: Implications for Public Policy.* U.S. Congress, OTA-O-204

Olson, Douglas and Con H. Schallau (1988). 'Capital Investment Associated with the Forest Products of Industry of Oregon.' *Assessment of Oregon's Forests,* Oregon State Department of Forestry, Jul.

Olson, Mancur (1971). *The Logic of Collective Action.* Cambridge: Harvard University Press

Olson, S. (1971). *The Depletion Myth: A History of Railroad Use of Timber.* Cambridge, Massachusetts: Harvard University Press

Oregon Department of Human Resources, Employment Division (various years). Oregon Covered Employment and Payrolls, State of Oregon

Ostrum, Elinor (1986). 'Issues of Definition and Theory: Some Conclusions and Hypotheses.' In Panel on Common Property Resource Management, Board of Science and Technology for International Development, Office of International Affairs, National Research Council, *Proceedings of the Conference on Common Property Resource Management*, 21-6 Apr. 1985, Washington, DC: National Academy Press, 599-615

— (1987). 'Institutional Arrangements for Resolving the Commons Dilemma: Some Contending Approaches' In Bonnie J. McCay and James M. Acheson. (eds), *The Question of the Commons*. Tucson: University of Arizona Press, 250-65

Ott, E. (1972). 'Erhebungen über den gegenwärtigen Zustand des Schweizer Waldes als Grundlage waldbaulicher Zielsetzungen.' *Mitteilungen des EAFV* 48:1-93

— (1984). 'Forest Potential.' In E. Brugger et al. (eds.), *The Transformation of Swiss Mountain Regions*. Bern: Haupt, 157-66

— and D. Schönbachler (1986). 'Die Stabilitätsbeurteilung im Gebirgswald als Voraussetzung für die Schutzwald-Ueberwachung und -Pflege.' *Schweizerische Zeitschrift für Forstwesen* 137:725-38

Ovendene, L. (1989). 'Peatlands: A Leaky Sink in the Global Carbon Cycle.' *GEOS* 18(3):19-24

Painter, M.F. and Associates Ltd. (1984). 'Not Satisfactorily Restocked (NSR) Lands in British Columbia: An Analysis of the Current Situation.' Prepared for the Association of BC Professional Foresters, Vancouver

Panel on Common Property Resource Management, National Academy of Science (1985). *Proceedings of the Conference on Common Property Resource Management*. Washington DC, National Academy Press

Pastor, J. and W.M. Post (1988). 'Responses of Northern Forest to CO_2-Induced Climate Change.' *Nature* 334:55-7

Pearse, P.H., A.J. Lang, and K.L. Todd (1986a). 'The Backlog of Unstocked Forest Land in British Columbia and the Impact of Reforestation Programs.' *Forestry Chronicle* 62:514-21

— (1986b). 'Economic Priorities for Reforesting Unstocked Forest Land in British Columbia.' *Forestry Chronicle* 62:522-7

Pearson, Charles (1989). 'Innovative Approaches by MNC's to Sustainable Development.' Draft, Environment Directorate, OECD, Mar.

Peet, R.K. (1981). 'Forest Vegetation of the Colorado Front Range.' *Vegetatio* 45:3-75

Peluso, Nancy Lee and Mark Poffenberger (1989). 'Social Forestry in Java: Reorienting Management Systems.' *Human Organization* 48(4):333-44

Pennsylvania Department of Forests and Waters (1932). 'Interesting Forest Facts.' *Service Letter* 3(149):16

Percy, M.B. and Christian Yoder (1987). *The Softwood Lumber Dispute and*

Canada-U.S. Trade in Natural Resources. Halifax: Institute for Research on Public Policy

Perloff, Harvey S., Edgar S. Dunn, Eric E. Lampard, and Richard F. Muth (1960). *Regions, Resources, and Economic Growth.* Johns Hopkins Press for Resources for the Future, Baltimore, MD

Perloff, Harvey S. and Lowdon Wingo, Jr. (1961). 'Natural Resource Endowment and Regional Economic Growth.' In Joseph J. Spengler (ed.), *Natural Resources and Economic Growth.* Resources for the Future, Washington, DC

Perry, D.A., M.P. Amaranthus, J.G. Borchers, S.L. Borchers, and R.E. Brainerd (1989). 'Bootstrapping in Ecosystems.' *BioScience* 39:230-7

Persson, T. (1980). '*Structure and Function of Northern Coniferous Forests.*' Swedish Ecological Bulletin 32, Swedish Natural Science Research Council

Peterson, R. Max (1985). Letter from the Chief of the U.S. Forest Service to Regional Foresters (except R-10), File Designation: 2,430, Commercial Timber Sales, Dated 31 May, USDA Forest Service, Washington DC

Phelps, S.E., W.A. Thompson, T.M. Webb, P.J. McNamee, D. Tait, and C.J. Walters (1990). 'British Columbia Silviculture Planning Model: Structure and Design.' Unpublished report to BC Ministry of Forests

Porter, Michael E. (1990). *The Competitive Advantage of Nations.* New York: Free Press

— (1991). *Canada at the Crossroads: The Reality of a New Competitive Environment.* A study prepared for The Business Council on National Issues and the government of Canada, Minister of Supply and Services, Ottawa

Postel, Sandra (1988a). 'A Green Fix to the Global Warm-up.' *Worldwatch* 1(5):29-36

— (1988b). 'Global View of a Tropical Disaster.' *American Forests* 94(11/12):25-9

Power, Thomas M. (1980). *The Economic Value of the Quality of Life.* Boulder: Westview Press

Prance, Ghillean T. (1978). 'Origin and Evolution of the Amazon Flora.' *Interciencia* 3:207-22

Price, M.F. (1987). 'Tourism and Forestry in the Swiss Alps: Parasitism or Symbiosis?' *Mountain Research and Development* 7:1-12

— (1988). 'A Review of the Development of Legislation for Swiss Mountain Forests.' *Forstwissenschaftliche Beiträge des ETH-Zürich* 6:153-70

— (1990). *Mountain Forests as Common-Property Resources: Management Policies and their Outcomes in the Colorado Rockies and the Swiss Alps.* Forstwissenschaftliche Beiträge 9, ETH-Zürich

— (1991). 'An Assessment of Patterns of Use and Management of Mountain Forests in Colorado, U.S.A.; Implications for Future Policies.' *Mountain Research and Development* 11:57-64

Prinz, B. (1987). 'Causes of Forest Damage in Europe.' *Environment* 29(9):11

Proceedings of Seminar on Selective Cuts in Indonesia) (1980). Jogyakarta Faculty of Forestry, University of Gajah Mada, 23-14 Jul. As reported in 'Final Report: Wood Raw Material Supply.' P.T. Inproma Engineering, 1985, 62-5

Pyatt, Graham and Erik Thorbecke (1976). *Planning Techniques for a Better Future*. Geneva, International Labour Office

Pyatt, Graham, and Jeffrey Round (1985). *Social Accounting Matrices: A Basis for Planning*. Washington DC: World Bank

Pyne, S.J. (1982). *Fire in America*. Princeton: Princeton University Press

Rageth, B. (1983). 'Die Forstdienstorganisation im Kanton Graubünden.' *Schweizerische Fortschrift für Forstwesen* 134:509-15

Raintree, John (1987). 'Agroforestry, Tropical Land Use and Tenure.' In John Raintree (ed.), *Land, Trees and Tenure: Proceedings of an International Workshop on Tenure Issues in Agroforestry*. Madison and Nairobi: Land Tenure Center and ICRAF, 35-78

Ramanathan, V. (1988). 'The Greenhouse Theory of Climate Change: A Test by an Inadvertent Global Experiment.' *Science* 240:293-9

Rassam, Amal (1990). 'Land Tenure in the Ivory Coast.' Madison: Land Tenure Center

Regan, Colin (1982). 'Colonialism and Reforestation: A Case Study of Ireland.' Maynouth, Ireland: Department of Geography, St. Patrick's College

Regional District of Fraser-Fort George (1989). General Information and Statistics, Mar.

Reichle, D.E., B.E. Dinger, N.T. Edwards, W.F. Harris, and Sollins (1975). 'Carbon Flow and Storage in a Forest Ecosystem.' In *Carbon and the Biosphere, AEC Symposium Series*, No. 30, 281-302

Reiners, W.A. (1975). 'Terrestrial Detritus and the Carbon Cycle.' In *Carbon and the Biosphere. AEC Symposium Series*, No. 30, 303-27

Repetto, Robert (1988a). 'Needed: New Policy Goals.' *American Forests* 94(11/12):58, 82-6

— (1988b). *The Forest for the Trees? Government Policies and the Misuse of Forest Resources*. World Resources Institute. Washington, DC

— and Malcolm Gillis (1988). *Public Policies and the Misuse of Forest Resources*. Cambridge University Press, Cambridge

Ricardo, D. (1971). *Principles of Political Economy and Taxation*. London: Penguin

Richardson, S. Dennis (1970). 'The Future Availability of Tropical Hardwoods.' *Commonwealth Forestry Review* 49(1):24-9

Riley, S. (1909). 'Preservation and Utilization of the National Forests.' *Proceedings of the Colorado Scientific Society* 9:159-80

Risbrudt, C.D. (1979). 'Past and Future Technological Change in the U.S. Forest Industries.' Ph.D. thesis, Michigan State University

Roberts, L. (1989). 'How Fast Can Trees Migrate.' *Science* 243:735-7

Robinson, V.L. (1975). 'An Estimate of Technological Progress in the Lumber and Wood-Products Industry.' *Forest Science* 21(2):149-54

Robson, M., J. Townsend, and K. Pavitt (1988). 'Sectoral Patterns of Production and Use of Innovations in the UK: 1945-1983.' *Research Policy* 17(1): 1-14

Rocheleau, Dianne E. (1987). 'Women, Trees and Tenure: Implications for Agroforestry Research and Development.' In John Raintree (ed.), *Land, Trees and Tenure: Proceedings of an International Workshop on Tenure Issues in Agroforestry*. Madison and Nairobi: Land Tenure Center and ICRAF, 79-120

Rodhe, H. (1989). 'Acidification in a Global Perspective.' *Ambio* 18(3):155-60

Rogers, E.M. (1983). *Diffusion of Innovations*. New York: Free Press

Romm, Jeff (1989). 'Forestry for Development: Some Lessons from Asia' *Journal of World Forest Resource Management* 4:37-46

Rosenberg, N. (1973). 'Innovative Responses to Materials Shortages.' *American Economic Review* 63(2):111-18

— (1988). 'An Outsider's View of Technological Change in the Forest Products Industry.' Paper presented at the forty-second annual meeting of the Forest Products Research Society, 19-23 Jun., Quebec City, Canada

Ross, Lester (1983). 'Obligatory Tree Planting: How Great an Innovation in Implementation in Post-Mao China.' In *Joint Committee on Chinese Studies of the American Council of Learned Societies and the Social Science Research Council Workshop on Policy Implementation in the Post-Mao Era*. Ohio State University, Columbus, Ohio, 20-4 Jun. Purdue, Ind.: Purdue University Press

Royal Commission on Forest Resources (Peter H. Pearse, Commissioner) (1976). *Timber Rights and Forest Policy, Volume 2*. Victoria: Province of British Columbia

Royer, Jack P. (1981). 'North Carolina Nonindustrial Private Forest Landowners Survey.' Durham NC: Duke University School of Forestry and Environmental Studies

— Jack P. (1987). 'Determinants of Reforestation Behavior Among Southern Landowners.' *Forest Science* 33(3):654-67

Rufolo, Anthony M., James G. Strathman, and Lois Martin Bronfman (1988). *Employment Decline in Timber Dependent Regions*. Center for Urban Studies, School of Urban and Public Affairs, Portland State University, Dec.

Rugman, Alan M. and Joseph R. D'Cruz (1990). *New Visions for Canadian Business: Strategies for Competing in the Global Economy*. Kodak Canada, Toronto

— (1991). *Fast Forward: Improving Canada's International Competitiveness*. Kodak Canada, Toronto

Runge, Carlisle Ford (1981). 'Common Property Externalities: Isolation, Assurance and Resource Depletion in a Traditional Grazing Context.' *American Journal of Agricultural Economics* 63:595-606

— (1983). 'Balancing Public and Private Sector Forestry Research: Rationale and Plan of Study.' In W.F. Hyde (ed.), *Economic Evaluation of Investments in Forestry Research*. Durham, NC: Acorn Press, 68-85

— (1984). 'Institutions and the Free Rider: The Assurance Problem in Collective Action.' *The Journal of Politics* 46:154-79

Ruttan, V.W. (1977). 'The Green Revolution: Seven Generalizations.' *International Development Review* 19:16-23

— (1982). *Agricultural Research Policy*. Minneapolis, MN: University of Minnesota Press

Salati, Eneas and Peter B. Vose (1984). 'Amazon Basin: A System in Equilibrium.' *Science* 225:129-38

Sampson, R. Neil (1988). 'ReLeaf for Global Warming.' *American Forests* 94(11&12):9-14

— (1989). 'Greenhouse Fact and Fiction.' *American Forests* 95(7&8):6-8

Sarin, S. (1980). 'Experiences in Community Forestry: Madhya Pradesh' In R.N. Tewari and O.A. Mascarenhas (eds.), *Community Forestry Management for Rural Development*. Dehra Dun: Natraj Publishers, 62-90

Schacht, Joseph (1964). *An Introduction to Islamic Law*. London: Oxford University Press

Schallau, Con H. and Paul E. Polzin (1983). 'Considering Departures from Current Timber Harvesting Policies: Case Studies of Four Communities in the Pacific Northwest.' Research Paper PNW-306, Pacific Northwest Forest and Range Experiment Station, Forest Service, United States Department of Agriculture, Jul.

Schallau, Con H. and Wilbur R. Maki (1983). 'Interindustry Model for Analyzing the Regional Impacts of Forest Resource and Related Supply Constraints.' *Forest Science* 29(2):384-94

Schallau, Con H., Douglas Olson, and Wilbur Maki (1988). 'An Investigation of Long-Term Impacts on the Economy of Oregon of Alternative Timber Supply Forecasts.' *Assessment of Oregon's Forests*. Oregon State Department of Forestry, Jul.

Schallou, Con H. and Richard M. Alston (1987). 'The Commitment to Community Stability: A Policy or Shibboleth?' *Environmental Law* 17(3):429-82

Schapera, Isaac (1943). *Tribal Legislation Among the Tswana of the Bechuanaland Protectorate*. London School of Economics and Political Science, Monographs on Social Anthropology, No.9, London: Percy Lund, Humphries and Co

Scherer, F.M. (1982). 'Inter-Industry Technology Flows in the United States.' *Research Policy* 11:227-45

Schindler D.W., K.G. Beaty, E.J. Fee, D.R. Cruickshank, E.R. DeBruyn, D.L. Findlay, G.A. Linsey, J.A. Shearer, M.R. Stainton, and M.A. Turner (1990). 'Effects of Climatic Warming on Lakes of the Central Boreal Forest.' *Science* 250:967-70

Schmandt, J., J. Clarkson, and H. Roderick (1989). *Acid Rain and Friendly*

Neighbors: The Policy Dispute between Canada and the United States. Durham: Duke University Press

Schneider, Stephen H. and Norman J. Rosenburg (1989). 'The Greenhouse Effect: Its Causes, Possible Impacts, and Associated Uncertainties.' In N.J. Rosenburg et al. (eds.), *Proceedings, Greenhouse Warming: Abatement and Adaptation*. Resources for the Future, Washington, DC, 7-34

Schoeffel, P. (1978). 'Das eidgenössische Forstrecht und seine Entwicklung zu einem Element der Umweltschutzgesetzgebung.' Unpublished doctoral dissertation, University of Basel

Schotter, Andrew (1981). *The Economic Theory of Social Institutions*. Cambridge: Cambridge University Press

Schubart, H.O.R. (1977). 'Criterios Ecologicos Para o Desenvolvimento Agricola das Terras-Firmes da Amazonia.' *Acta Amazonica* 7(4):22-9

Schuler, A. (1984). 'Sustained-Yield Forestry and Forest Functions, as seen by Swiss Foresters in the Nineteenth Century.' In H.K. Steen (ed.), *History of Sustained-yield Forestry*. Durham: Forest History Society, 192-201

Schwindt, Richard W. (1985). *An Analysis of Vertical Integration and Diversification Strategies in the Canadian Forest Sector*. Information Report 85-5. Vancouver: Forest Economics and Policy Analysis Project, University of British Columbia

Schwingruber, C. (1985). 'Ergebnisse 1984 der Lohnerhebung in der Schweizerischen Forstwirtschaft.' *Wald und Holz* 66:811-19

Scott, Anthony (1976). 'The Cost of Compulsory Log Trading.' In William McKillop and Walter J. Mead, (eds.), *Timber Policy Issues in British Columbia*. Vancouver: UBC Press

Sedjo, Roger A. (1983). *The Comparative Economics of Plantation Forestry*. Resources for the Future, Washington, DC

— (1987). 'World Timber Resources Overview.' (Mimeo) Washington DC: Resource for the Future

— (1988). 'The Economics of Natural and Plantation Forestry in Indonesia.' Field Document No. 2, FAO Project INS/83/019, Assistance to Forest Sector Development Planning, Jan.

— (1988). 'Property Rights and the Protection of Plant Genetic Resources.' In Jack Kloppenburg (ed). *Seeds and Sovereignty*. Durham and London: Duke University Press, 293-314

— (1989). 'Forests to Offset the Greenhouse Effect.' *Journal of Forestry* 87(6):12-15

— and Allen M. Solomon (1989). 'Climate and Forests.' In N.J. Rosenburg et al. (eds.), *Proceedings, Greenhouse Warming: Abatement and Adaptation*. Resources for the Future, Washington, DC, 105-20

— and Kenneth Lyon (1989). *The Long Term Adequacy of World Timber Supply*. Washington, DC: Resources for the Future

Seldon, B.J. (1985). 'A Nonresidual Approach to the Measurement of Social

Returns to Research with Application to the Softwood Plywood Industry.' ph.d. thesis, Duke University

Sellers, S. (1977). 'The Relationship Between Land Tenure and Agricultural Production in Tucurrique, Costa Rica.' Turrialba: Centro Agronomico Tropical de Investigacion y Ense]anza

Sen, A.K. (1967). 'Isolation, Assurance, and the Social Rate of Discount.' *Quarterly Journal of Economics* 81:112-24

Shambi, M.M. (c. 1955) 'The Problem of Land Ownership and Cashewnut Claims in Malindi Coastal Belt.' Nairobi

Sherif, F. (1983). 'Derived Demand of Factors of Production in the Pulp and Paper Industry.' *Forest Products Journal* 33(1):45-9

Shimotori, S. and Y. Akibayashi (1989). 'The Structure of Forestry Employ-ment in Mountain Villages in a Period of Slow Economic Growth and Re-vitalization of the Village.' IUFRO, *The Current State of Japanese Forestry*, Jun. Tokyo: The Japanese Forest Economic Society, 76-87

Shoemaker, L. (1958). *Saga of a Forest Ranger*. Boulder: University of Colo-rado Press

Shoemaker, T. (1944). 'National Forests.' *Colorado Magazine* 21(5):182-4

Shoven, J.B. and J. Whalley (1984). 'Applied General Equilibrium Models of Taxation and International Trade: An Introduction and Survey.' *Journal of Economic Literature* 22:281-322

Shreve, R. Norris and Joseph A. Brink, Jr. (1977). *Chemical Process Industries*. 4th ed., New York: McGraw-Hill

Shukla, J., C. Nobre, and Sellers (1990). 'Amazon Deforestation and Climate Change.' *Science* 247:1,322-5

Simatupang, P., T. Hamauzu, B. Saragih, H. Yonekura, J. Situmorang, and S. Hirashima (1988). *Primary Commodity Issues in Indonesian Economy*. In-stitute of Developing Economies, Joint Research Programme Series No. 70, Tokyo

Simonovic, Slobodan (1987). 'The Implicit Stochastic Model for Reservoir Yield Optimization.' *Water Resources Research* 23(12):2,159-65

Sitaraman, S. and S. Sarin (1980). 'Experiences in Community Forestry Uttar Pradesh.' In R.N. Tewari and O.A. Mascarenhas (eds.), *Community For-estry Management for Rural Development*. Dehra Dun: Natraj Publishers, 91-112

Skar, Sara Lund, Nelida Arias, and Cotarma Saturno Garcia (1982). *Fuel Availability, Nutrition and Women's Work in Highland Peru: Three Case Stud-ies from Contrasting Andean Communities*. World Employment, Research WEP, 10/WP23, Geneva: ILO

Smith, Kirk Joel N. Swisher, Rebekah Kanter, and Dilip R. Ahuja (1991). *In-dices for a Greenhouse Gas Control Regime that Incorporates Both Efficiency and Equity Goals*. The World Bank, Environment Department, Divisional Working Paper No. 1191-22

Smith, S. (1989a). 'Input Data for the FEPA Long Range Planning Model.' Unpublished report to BC Ministry of Forests

— (1989b). *Operational Yields Resulting from Typical Silvicultural Treatments under FRDA.* FRDA Report 099, Victoria, BC: Forestry Canada

Smith, V.K. (1980). 'The Evaluation of Natural Resource Adequacy: Elusive Quest or Frontier of Economic Analysis.' *Land Economics* 56:257-98

Smyth, J. Douglas (1987). 'The Employment Impact of the Canadian Export Levy on Softwood Lumber Shipments in the United States.' (Mimeo) Vancouver: International Woodworkers of America

Soerianegara, Ishemat (1982). 'Socio-Economic Aspects of Forest Resource Management in Indonesia.' In E.G. Hallsworth (ed.), *Socio-Economic Effects and Constraints in Tropical Forest Management.* Chichester: Wiley, 73-86

Solow, R.M. (1957). 'Technological Change and the Aggregate Production Function.' *Review of Economics and Statistics* 39:312-20

Spall, H. (1971). 'Factors Influencing the Receptiveness of Homebuilders to Cost Reducing Innovations in Greater Lansing.' PH.D. thesis, Michigan State University

Spears, John S. (1979). 'Can Wet Tropical Forest Survive?' *Commonwealth Forestry Review* 58(3):165-80

— (1984). 'Role of Forestation as a Sustainable Land Use and Strategy Option for Tropical Forest Management and Conversion and as a Source of Supply for Developing Country Wood Needs.' In K.F. Wiesum (ed.), *Strategies and Designs for Afforestation, Reforestation and Tree Planting.* Pudoc Wageningen

Spelter, H. (1984). 'Price Elasticities for Softwood Plywood and Structural Particleboard in the United States.' *Canadian Journal of Forest Research* 14:528-35

Spencer, J.W. (1930). 'Recreation Development.' In *Report of Supervisors' Meeting.* Dec. On file in Federal Records Center, Denver

— (1946). 'Why Colorado Needs National Forests.' *Address at Meeting of Committee on Livestock and Agriculture, Denver Chamber of Commerce.* 25 Sept., On file in Federal Archives, Denver

Spiro, P.S. (1987). 'Public Utility Finance and the Cost of Capital: Comments on Jenkins.' *Canadian Journal of Economics* 20:164-71

Stabbing, E.P. (1922). 'The Forests of India and the Development of the Indian Forest Department.' *Indian Forester* 48(2):81-98

Stanislawski, Dan (1963). *Portugal's Other Kingdom: The Algarve.* Austin: University of Texas Press

Statistics Canada (1986a). *Export by Commodities.* Catalog 65-004, Dec.

— (1986b). *Imports by Commodities.* Catalog 65-007, Dec.

— (1989). *Selected Forestry Statistics Canada 1988.* Ottawa: Economics and Statistics Directorate, Forestry Canada

— (1990). *Industrial Research and Development Statistics 1988.* Services, Science, and Technology Division, Catalogue 88-202, Minister of Supply and Services, Ottawa

— (1990). *Livestock and Animal Products Statistics.* Catalogue 23-203, Ottawa

— (1991). *Canada Yearbook 1992.* Ottawa

—, Annual Reports (1979-86). *Canadian Forestry Statistics* (Cat 25-202)

Steen, H.K. (1976). *The Forest Service: A History.* Seattle: University of Washington Press

— (ed.) (1984). *History of Sustained-Yield Forestry.* Durham: Forest History Society

Stere, David H., Blair R. Hopps, and Gary Lettman (1980). *1980 Oregon Timber Assessment, Projections of Future Available Harvests.* Oregon State Forestry Department, Dec.

Sterling Wood Group Inc. (1988). *Analysis of Changes in Timber Values due to Silviculture Treatments under the Canada - British Columbia Forest Resource Development Agreement.* FRDA Report 041, Victoria: Canadian Forestry Service

— (1989). *Expected Delivered Log Costs for Areas Treated under the Canada - British Columbia Forest Resource Development Agreement.* FRDA Report 079, Victoria: Canadian Forestry Service

Stern, Theodore (1965). *The Klamath Tribe.* Seattle: University of Washington Press

Stevens, Joe B. (1979). 'Six Views About A Wood Products Labor Force, Most of Which May Be Wrong.' *Journal of Forestry* 77(11):717-20

Stier, J.C. (1980a). 'Estimating the Production Technology in the U.S. Forest Products Industries.' *Forest Science* 26(3):471-82

— (1980b). 'Technical Adaptation to Resource Scarcity in the U.S. Lumber Industry.' *Western Journal of Agricultural Economics* 5(2):165-75

— (1982). 'Changes in the Technology of Harvesting Timber in the United States: Some Implications for Labour.' *Agricultural Systems* 9:255-66

— (1983). 'Technological Substitution in the United States Pulp and Paper Industry: The Sulfate Pulping Process.' *Technological Forecasting and Social Change* 23(3):237-45

— (1985). 'Implications of Factor Substitution, Economies of Scale, and Technological Change for the Cost of Production in the United States Pulp and Paper Industry.' *Forest Science* 31(4):803-12

Stock, James and Mark Watson (1988). 'Variable Trends in Economic Time Series.' *Journal of Economic Perspectives* 2(3):147-74

Stowell, Alan M. (1985). *U.S. International Trade Laws: 1986 Edition.* Washington, DC: Bureau of National Affairs

Strassman, W.P. (1978). 'Assessing the Knowledge of Innovations in Neglected Sectors: The Case of Residential Construction.' In Kelly and M.

Kranzberg (eds.), *Technological Innovation: A Critical Review of Current Knowledge*. San Francisco, CA: San Francisco Press, 262-73

Strueck, Wendy (1989). 'Indians to get $2.75 Million.' *The Vancouver Sun*, 5 Aug. A1

Styan, G.E. (1980). 'Impact of North American Timber Supply on Innovations in Paper Technology.' *Paper Trade Journal* 164(10):25-9

Subak, Susan, Ralph J. Cicerone, David G. Victor, Kirk R. Smith, Allen L. Hammond, Eric Rodenburg, and William R. Moomau (Letters) (1991). 'The Greenhouse Index.' *Environment* 33(2):2-5, 42-4

Sullivan, Bradley J. (1988). 'Cumulative Economic Impacts of National Forest Timber Harvests in California.' PH.D. Dissertation, University of California, Berkeley

Sullivan, Jay and J. Keith Gilless (1989). 'Cumulative Employment Effects on Northern California's Wood Products Industries from National Forest Timber Harvests.' *Forest Science* 35(3):856-62

Summer, M.T. (1980a). 'Benefit-Cost Analysis in Canadian Practice.' *Canadian Public Policy* 6:389-93

— (1980b). 'Comments on the Public Discount Rate: Response to Jenkins.' *Canadian Public Policy* 6:648-50

Sweden (1989). *Skogsstatistick Arsbok (Statistical Yearbook of Forestry)*. Stockholm

Tang, Hon Tat (1987). 'Problems and Strategies for Regenerating Dipterocarp Forests in Malaysia.' In Francois Mergen and Jeffrey R. Vincent (eds.), *Natural Management of Tropical Moist Forests*. Yale School of Forestry, New Haven, 23-46

Tanner, R. (1960). 'Land Rights on the Tanganyika Coast.' *African Studies* 19:14-25

Tans, P.P., I.Y. Fung, and T. Takahashi (1990). 'Observation Constraints on the Global CO_2 Budget.' *Science* 247:1,431-8

Thailand Development Research Institute (1987). *Thailand Natural Resources Profile: Is the Resource Base for Thailand's Development Sustainable?* Center for Development Information & Evaluation, U.S. Agency for International Development, Washington, DC

Thirgood, J.V. (1981). *Man and the Mediterranean Forest: A History of Resource Depletion*. Academic Press, London

Thirtle, C.G. and V.W. Ruttan (1987). *The Role of Demand and Supply in the Generation and Diffusion of Technical Change*. London: Harwood Academic Publishers

Thomas, John Woodward (1964). 'Employment-Creating Public Works Programs: Observations on Political and Social Dimensions.' In E.O. Edwards (ed), *Employment in Developing Nations*. New York: Columbia University Press

—, E.D. Forsman, J.B. Lint, E.C. Meslow, B.R. Noon, and J. Verner (1990). *A Conservation Plan for the Northern Spotted Owl: Report of the Interagency Scientific Committee to Address the Conservation of the Northern Spotted Owl*. Portland, OR, U.S. Government Printing Office, Document No. 1990-791-171/20026, 427 pp.

Thompson, Michael and Michael Warburton (1985a). 'Uncertainty on a Himalayan Scale.' *Mountain Research and Development* 5(2):115-35

— (1985b). 'Knowing Where to Hit: A Conceptual Framework for the Sustainable Development of the Himalaya.' *Mountain Research and Development* 5(3):203-220

Thomson, James T. (1977). 'Ecological Deterioration: Local-Level Rule Making and Enforcement Problems in Niger.' In Glantz, M. (ed.), *Desertification: Environmental Degradation in and Around Arid Lands*. Boulder: Westview Press

— (1982). *Participation, Local Organization, Land and Tree Tenure: Future Directions for Sahelian Forestry*. Paris: Club du Sahel/OECD

Tombaugh, L.W. and B.G. Macdonald (1984). 'The Next Twenty Years: Where Will Technology Lead?' In *New Forests for a Changing World*. Proceedings of the 1983 Convention of the Society of American Foresters, SAF Publication 84-03, Bethesda, MD: Society of American Foresters, 579-86

Totham, Conrad (1985). *The Origins of Japan's Modern Forests: The Case of Akita*. Honolulu: Center for Asian and Pacific Studies, University of Hawaii, University of Hawaii Press

— (1986). 'Tokugawa Peasants: Win, Lose, or Draw?' *Monumenta Nipponica* 41(4):458-76

Tromp, H. (1980). 'Hundert Jahre forstliche Planung in der Schweiz.' *Mitteilungen der EAFV* 56:253-67

Turner, S.D. (1984). *Land and Trees in Lesotho*. Maseru, Lesotho: Institute of Southern African Studies

Uhler, Russell S. (1987). 'The Canadian Wood Products Industry.' Vancouver: Forest Economics and Policy Analysis Project, University of British Columbia

—, Gary M. Townsend, and Luis Constantino (1987). 'Canada-U.S. Trade and the Product Mix of the Canadian Pulp and Paper Industry.' Vancouver: Forest Economics and Policy Analysis Project, University of British Columbia

UNDP/World Bank (1987). *Kenya: Urban Woodfuel Development Program, Feasibility Report, Executive Summary*. Energy Sector Management Assistance Program

United Nations (1990). *Statistical Yearbook 1987*. New York

United Nations (1991). *1989 Energy Statistics Yearbook*. New York

United Nations Economic Commission for Europe, and Food and Agriculture Organization (1988). 'Profitability, Productivity and Relative Prices in Forest Industries in the ECE Region.' publication ECE/TIM/43, Geneva

United Nations Environment Program (UNEP) (1991). *Environmental Data Report*. 3rd ed., 1991/92. Oxford: Basil Blackwill

United Nations Industrial Development Organization (UNIDO) (1986). *International Comparative Advantage in Manufacturing: Changing Profiles of Resources and Trade*. Vienna

U.S. Bureau of Commerce (various issues). *Economic Indicators*

U.S. Bureau of the Census (various issues). *Census of Manufacturers*

U.S. Congress (1972). *Forestry Programs*. Hearing before the Subcommittee on Environment, Soil Conservation, and Forestry of the Committee on Agriculture and Forestry, U.S. Senate, Ninety-Second Congress, Rep. No. 77-093

— (1973a). *Agriculture and Consumer Protection Act*. P.L. 93-86, Title X, Sections 1009, 1010:245-6

— (1973b). *Forestry Incentives Act of 1973*. Hearings before the Subcommittee on Forests of the Committee on Agriculture, U.S. House of Representatives, Ninety-Third Congress, Rep. 93-364

— (1975). *Report on Agriculture and Related Agencies Appropriation Bill, 1976*. Ninety-fourth Congress, First Session, Rep. No. 94-346

U.S. Department of Agriculture (1989). *A Hard Look at USDA's Rural Development Programs*. The Report of the Rural Revitalization Task Force to the Secretary of Agriculture

U.S. Department of Commerce, International Trade Commission (ITA) (1986). *Preliminary Affirmative Countervailing Duty Determination: Certain Softwood Lumber Products from Canada*. Billing Code 3510-DS, Washington, DC, 16 Oct.

U.S. Department of Labour (various issues). *Wholesale Price Indices*

U.S. Forest Service (1907). *The Use Book*. Washington DC: Government Printing Office

— (1919). *Vacation Days in Colorado's National Forests*. Washington DC: Government Printing Office

— (1928). *National Forests of Colorado*. Washington DC: Government Printing Office

— (1958). *Timber Resources for America's Future*. Forest Resource Report No. 14, Washington, DC

— (1974). *The Outlook for Timber in the United States*. Forest Resource Report No. 20, Washington, DC

— (1982). *An Analysis of the Timber Situation in the United States: 1952-2030*. Forest Resource Report No. 23, Washington, DC

— (1983a). *The Principal Laws Relating to Forest Service Activities*. Washington DC: Government Printing Office

— (1983b) *Regional Guide for the Rocky Mountain Region*. Lakewood, Colorado

— (1988). *The South's Fourth Forest: Alternatives for the Future*. Forest Resource Report No. 24, Washington, DC

— (1989). *Report of the Task Force on Prescribed Management Criteria*. Washington DC: U.S. Forest Service

— (1990). *An Analysis of the Timber Situation in the United States: 1989-2040. A Technical Document Supporting the 1989 USDA Forest Service RPA Assessment.* Rocky Mtn, OR and Range Expt. Station, General Technical Report RM-199, Ft. Collins, CO

U.S. General Accounting Office (GAO) (1985). *Potential Impacts of Tighter Forest Service Log Export Restrictions.* GAO/RCED-85-17, Washington, DC

U.S. General Accounting Office (GAO) (1991). *Forest Service: Better Reporting Needed on Reforestation and Timber Stand Improvement,* GAO/RCED-91-71, Washington, DC

U.S. House of Representatives, Committee on Ways and Means (1987). *Report on H.R.3. Trade and International Economic Policy Act of 1987.* Report 100-40 Part 1, U.S. Government Printing Office, Washington, DC

U.S. International Trade Commission (USITC) (1985). *Conditions Relating to the Importation of Softwood Lumber into the United States.* USITC Publication 1765, Washington DC, Oct.

— (1986). 'Refined U.S. and Canadian Softwood Lumber Employment Data.' (Mimeo) Washington, DC

U.S. President's Advisory Panel on Timber and the Environment (1973). *Report.* Government Printing Office, Washington, DC

USDA Forest Service (1982). *An Analysis of the Timber Situation in the United States, 1952-2030.* Forest Resource Report No. 23, U.S. Government Printing Office, Washington, DC

— (1987a). *The South's Fourth Forest: Alternatives for the Future.* Forest Resource Report No. 24

— (1987b). *Record of Decision, Bitterroot National Forest Plan.* Unnumbered report, Region One, Missoula, Montana 40 pp.

— (1988). *An Analysis of the Timber Situation in the United States: 1989-2040, Part II: The Future Resource Situation.* Draft technical document supporting the 1989 RPA Assessment, Washington, DC: U.S. Government Printing Office

— (1988). *The South's Fourth Forest: Alternatives for the Future.* Forest Resource Report No. 24, Washington, DC, Jun.

— (1990a). *A Strategic Plan for the 90's: Working Together for Rural America.* Unnumbered report, Washington DC

— (1990b). *The Forest Service Program for Forest and Rangeland Resources: A Long Term Strategic Plan.* Recommended 1990 RPA Program, Unnumbered report, Washington DC

Uzozie, L.C. (1979). 'Tradition and Change in Igbo Food Production Systems: A Geographical Appraisal.' Ph.D. dissertation, University of London

Valhalla Society (1988). *British Columbia's Endangered Wilderness*. New Denver, BC

Ventre, F.T. (1979). 'Innovation in Residential Construction.' *Technology Review* 82(2):50-9

Vitousek, Peter M. and Pamela A. Matson (1984). 'Mechanisms of Nitrogen Retention in Forest Ecosystems: A Field Experiment.' *Science* 225:51-2

Wade, Robert (1988). *Village Republics*. Cambridge: Cambridge University Press

Wadsworth, Frank H. (1982). 'Secondary Forest Management and Plantation Forestry Technologies to Improve the Use of Converted Tropical Lands.' Unpublished draft, submitted to U.S. OTA

Waggener, Thomas R. (1977). 'Community Stability as a Forest Management Objective.' *Journal of Forestry* 75(11):710-14

— (1985). 'The Economics of Shifting Land Use Margins.' In R.A. Sedjo, (ed.), *Investments in Forestry*. Boulder: Westview Press

Wagner, Bill (1988). 'An Emerging Corporate Nobility? Industrial Concentration of Economic Power on Public Timber Tenures.' (Excerpts from a Master's Thesis prepared by Bill Wagner at University of Victoria), *Forest Planning Canada*. 4(2):14-19

Waha, A.O. (1927). 'Inspection, District Two.' Memo on file in Denver Public Library

Wandeler, H. (1985). 'Die Revision der eidgenössischen Forstgesetzgebung: Stand und Schwerpunkte.' *Schweizerische Zeitschrift für Forstwesen* 136:657-64

Ward, Frank A. (1985). 'Income Distribution Issues and Natural Resource Policy: Welfare Effects of Nonfederal Water Plans.' *Western Journal of Agricultural Economics* 10(2):187-91

Waugh, F.A. (1918). *Recreation Uses on the National Forests*. Washington DC: Government Printing Office

Wear, David N. (1989). 'Structural Change and Factor Demand in Montana's Solid Wood Products Industries.' *Canadian Journal of Forest Research* 19:645-50

—, William F. Hyde, and Steven E. Daniels (1989). 'Even-Flow Timber Harvests and Community Stability: An Analysis of Short-Run Timber Sale Policies.' *Journal of Forestry*. 87(9):24-8

Webb, Michael C. and Mark W. Zacher (1985). 'Canadian Export Trade in a Changing International Environment.' In D. Stairs and G. Winham (research co-ordinators), *Canada and the International Political/Economic Environment*. Toronto: University of Toronto Press

Weideit, Hans Joachim and Valeriano Banaag (1982). *Aspects of Management and Silviculture of Philippine Dipterocarp Forests*. German Agency for Technical Cooperation, Eschborn

Weinstock, Joseph A. (1983). 'Rattan: Ecological Balance in the Borneo Rainforest Swidden.' *Economic Botany* 37:58-68

Wengert, H., A.A. Dyer, and H.A. Deutsch (1979). *The 'Purposes' of the National Forests: A Historical Interpretation of Policy Development.* Fort Collins: Colorado State University

White, Marcia (1986). 'Limited Resource Countries and Economic Development: A Methodology Used for the Caribbean.' PH.D. dissertation, University of Illinois

Whitmore, T.C. (1984). *Tropical Rain Forest of the Far East.* Oxford

Whittaker R.H. and G.E. Likens (1975). 'The Biosphere and Man.' In H. Leith and R.H. Whittaker (eds.), *Primary Productivity of the Biosphere. Ecological Studies* 14:305-28

Widman Management Ltd. (1984). *British Columbia Log Exports. An Analysis of the Real Economic Issues.* Nov.

Wiebecke, C. and W. Peters (1984). 'Aspects of Sustained-Yield History: Forest Sustention as the Principle of Forestry – Idea and Reality.' In H.K. Steen (ed.), *History of Sustained-Yield Forestry.* Durham: Forest History Society, 176-82

Wigle, R. (1986). 'Trade Liberalization: Scale Economies in a Global Context.' Working paper 86,044, Centre for the Study of International Relations, University of Western Ontario

Wilderness Society (1988a). *Forests for the Future.* Washington DC: Wilderness Society

— (1988b). *The National Forests: Policies for the Future, Vol. 2, Protecting Biological Diversity.* Washington, DC

— (1989). *New Directions for the Forest Service.* Washington, DC

— (undated). *The Wasting of the Forest.* Washington DC

Wilkinson, Charles F. and H. Michael Anderson (1987). *Land and Resource Planning in the National Forests.* Washington DC: Island Press

Willan, R.G.M. (1967). 'Khumbu: Country of the Sherpas.' *Unasylva* 21(84):2-9

Williams, D.H. (ed.) (1987). *The Economic Stock of Timber in the Coastal Region of British Columbia: Technical Appendices.* Report 86-11 II, Vancouver: Forest Economics and Policy Analysis Research Unit, University of British Columbia

Williams, D.H. and R. Gasson (1986). *The Economic Stock of Timber in the Coastal Region of British Columbia.* Report 86-11 Vol. 1, Vancouver: Forest Economics and Policy Analysis Project, University of British Columbia, Jul.

— (1986). *The Economic Stock of Timber in the Coastal Region of British Columbia.* Report 86-11, Vol. 1, Vancouver: Forest Economics and Policy Analysis Research Unit, University of British Columbia

— (1987). 'The Economic Stock of Timber in the Interior Region of British Columbia.' Unpublished report

Wilson, Honourable Michael (1986). *Notes for a statement by the Honourable Michael Wilson, Minister of Finance, to the House of Commons*. 2 Jun., Ottawa: Department of Finance Canada

Wilson, J.C. (1876) *Memorial from the Constitutional Convention of Colorado*. Miscellaneous Document 146, House of Representatives, forty-fourth Congress, 1st Session

Woodbridge-Reed and Associates (1984). *British Columbia's Forest Products Industry, Constraints to Growth*. Commissioned by Government of Canada, Ministry of State for Economic and Regional Development, Vancouver

Woodland Resource Services Ltd. (1987). *A Report on the Prince George Timber Supply Area Public Inquiry for the Ministry of Forests and Lands* ('The Ewing Report'). Victoria, BC, Feb.

Woodwell, G.M. (1983). 'Biotic Effects on the Concentration of Atmospheric Carbon Dioxide: A Review and Projection.' In *Changing Climate*. National Research Council, Washington, DC, 216-41

— (1987). 'Forests and Climate: Surprises in Store.' *Oceanus* 29(4):71-5

— (1990). *The Earth in Transition*. Cambridge University Press

World Resources Institute (WRI) (1990). *World Resources 1990-91*. A Guide to the Global Environment. New York: Oxford University Press

Wyatt-Smith, John (1987). 'Problems and Prospects for Natural Management of Tropical Moist Forests.' In F. Mergen and J.R. Vincent (eds.), *Natural Management of Tropical Moist Forests*. Yale School of Forestry, New Haven, 2-22

Yeh, William W-G. (1985). 'Reservoir Management and Operation Models: A State-of-the-Art Review.' *Water Resources Research* 21(12):1,797-818

Young, John E. (1991). 'Discarding the Throwaway Society.' *Worldwatch Paper* 101

Zivnuska, John A. (1967). *U.S. Timber Resources in a World Economy*. Baltimore: Johns Hopkins University Press

Contributors

DARIUS M. ADAMS is a professor in the College of Forest Resources at the University of Washington.

DAVID N. BENGSTON is principal economist at the North Central Forest Experiment Station of the USDA Forest Service in St. Paul, MN.

PETER BERCK is a professor in the College of Natural Resources at the University of California (Berkeley).

CLARK S. BINKLEY is a professor of forestry and Dean of the Faculty of Forestry at the University of British Columbia.

MICHAEL D. BOWES is a research associate with Resources For the Future in Washington, DC.

ROY BOYD is a professor in the Department of Economics at Ohio University.

DANIEL W. BROMLEY is Anderson-Bascom Professor of resource economics in the Department of Agricultural Economics at the University of Wisconsin (Madison).

JOHN W. BRUCE is director of the Land Tenure Center at the University of Wisconsin (Madison).

DIANA BURTON is a graduate student in the College of Natural Resources at the University of California (Berkeley).

JUDITH CLARKSON is with the Lyndon B. Johnson School of Public Affairs at the University of Texas at Austin.

FREDERICK W. CUBBAGE is project leader at the Southeastern Forest Experiment Station of the USDA Forest Service in Research Triangle Park, NC.

RUTGER J. ENGELHARD is a consultant to Foster Parents Plan International in East Greenwich and former senior consultant at VHB Research and Consulting in Toronto.

LOUISE FORTMANN is a professor in the Department of Forestry and Resource Management at the University of California (Berkeley).

IRVING K. FOX is a professor emeritus of the School of Community and Regional Planning and former director of the Westwater Research Centre at the University of British Columbia.

W.S. FYFE is Dean of the Faculty of Sciences at the University of Western Ontario.

JACQUELINE GEOGHEGAN is a graduate student in the College of Natural Resources at the University of California (Berkeley).

GEORGE GOLDMAN is a graduate student in the College of Natural Resources at the University of California (Berkeley).

HANS M. GREGERSEN is a professor in the Department of Forest Resources and Department of Agricultural and Applied Economics at the University of Minnesota.

J. HANSING is a professor in the Department of Forest Economics at the Swedish University of Agricultural Sciences at Umea.

DONALD G. HODGES is a professor in the Department of Forest Resources at the University of New Hampshire.

WILLIAM F. HYDE is branch chief in the Economic Research Service of the United States Department of Agriculture, Washington, DC.

B.I. KRONBERG is an associate professor in the Department of Geology at Lakehead University, Thunder Bay, ON.

JOHN V. KRUTILLA is Senior Fellow at Resources For the Future in Washington, DC.

KERRY KRUTILLA is an assistant professor in the School of Public and Environmental Affairs at Indiana University.

KENNETH S. LYON is a professor in the Department of Economics at Utah State University.

M. PATRICIA MARCHAK is a professor of anthropology and sociology and Dean of the Faculty of Arts at the University of British Columbia.

MICHAEL MARGOLICK is a resource consultant in Vancouver and a former research associate with the Department of Economics at the University of British Columbia.

PETER N. NEMETZ is an associate professor in the Policy Analysis Division of the Faculty of Commerce and Business Administration at the University of British Columbia and editor of the *Journal of Business Administration*.

TAE HOON OUM is a professor and chairperson of the Division of Transportation, Logistics, and Public Utilities in the Faculty of Commerce and Business Administration at the University of British Columbia.

P.H. PEARSE is a professor of forest resources management at the University of British Columbia.

MARTIN F. PRICE is former director of the International Centre for Alpine Environments in Le Bourget-du-Lac, France.

JAMES L. REGENS is associate director of the Institute of Natural Resources at the University of Georgia.

JURGEN SCHMANDT is director and a professor of public affairs at the Center for Global Studies at the Houston Advanced Research Center.

ROGER A. SEDJO is Senior Fellow and director of the Forest Economics and Policy Program at Resources For the Future, Washington, DC.

THOMAS B. STOCKTON is a research associate with Resources For the Future in Washington, DC.

W.A. THOMPSON is a research associate with the Forest Economics and Policy Analysis Research Unit at the University of British Columbia.

MICHAEL W. TRETHEWAY is an associate professor in the Division of Transportation, Logistics, and Public Utilities in the Faculty of Commerce and Business Administration at the University of British Columbia.

RUSSELL S. UHLER is a professor in the Department of Economics at the University of British Columbia.

G.C. VAN KOOTEN is an associate professor in the Division of Transportation, Logistics, and Public Utilities in the Faculty of Commerce and Business Administration at the University of British Columbia.

I. VERTINSKY is a professor of resource ecology and commerce and business administration as well as director of the Forest Economics and Policy Analysis Research Unit at the University of British Columbia.

DAVID N. WEAR is a research forester/economist with the USDA Forest Service at Research Triangle Park, NC.

S. WIBE is a professor in the Department of Forest Economics at the Swedish University of Agricultural Sciences at Umea.

Index